FATHER O'HARA OF NOTRE DAME
THE CARDINAL-ARCHBISHOP
OF PHILADELPHIA

✝

FATHER O'HARA
OF
NOTRE DAME

✝

THE CARDINAL-ARCHBISHOP
OF PHILADELPHIA

✝

THOMAS T. McAVOY, C.S.C.

UNIVERSITY OF NOTRE DAME PRESS

NOTRE DAME   *   LONDON

Nihil Obstat: Charles J. Corcoran, C.S.C.
Censor Deputatus
Notre Dame, September 26, 1966

Imprimi Potest: Howard J. Kenna, C.S.C.
Provincial Superior
South Bend, October 7, 1966

Imprimatur: ✠ Leo A. Pursley, D.D.
Bishop of Fort Wayne-South Bend
Fort Wayne, October 7, 1966

UNIVERSITY OF NOTRE DAME PRESS

NOTRE DAME, INDIANA

Library of Congress Catalog Card Number 66-14627

Manufactured in the United States of America

Preface

In his homily at the beatification of John Neumann, His Holiness Pope Paul VI observed: "It might be said that no form of life is less suitable to inspire wonder than the pastoral ministry which is composed of ordinary actions."

It would not be difficult to establish similarities between Blessed Neumann, the fourth, and Cardinal O'Hara, the ninth, bishop of Philadelphia. Both were members of a religious community. Both had exercised their ministry in various apostolates in different areas before coming to Philadelphia. Both worked for the good of the diocese and showed a particular zeal for promoting devotion to the Eucharist and Catholic education. Both worked with the skill of a play director, planning and directing the action from beginning to end, staying out of sight of the viewers, and deflecting the applause towards others. Though separated by a century, both assumed charge of the diocese of Philadelphia in a year 52 and both died in a year 60.

The Holy Father referred to Blessed Neumann as "a promoter, a trainer, and educator"; as a personification of "the type of shepherd who makes his own the natural and Christian virtues of a nation" and so "becomes the most normal and most understandable of men, but at the same time the loftiest and most singular because he so lives and fills these virtues with Christian meaning and grace. . . ."

John O'Hara's virtues reflect the strong influences of the deep Catholic life of his family and of the disciplined tradition of the German pastors who served the parishes in the Midwestern states. These virtues, thoroughly Catholic, were developed in the atmosphere of the American ideal of success in all things, and they helped to form a strong character unafraid of hard work.

Blessed Neumann introduced the Forty-Hours Devotion in our country. Cardinal O'Hara with unrestrained fervor throughout his life promoted frequent and daily Communion as the wellspring of Catholic life and of good citizenship. Blessed Neumann laid a solid foundation for the Catholic school system. Cardinal O'Hara was relentless in his efforts to expand the Catholic school system to provide for every child from the first grade through high school.

The epitaph on Christopher Wren's tomb in St. Paul's Cathedral, "If you seek his monument, look around," suggests that men who deserve monuments do not need them. The trail of Cardinal O'Hara's pastoral ministry is studded with monuments, but most of them bear no label and only a few are readily identifiable. He seemed to live by the rule which a poet expressed in the lines:

> Who builds a church to God not to fame,
> Will never mark the marble with his name.
>
> (Pope, *Moral Essays*)

As a seminarian, I welcomed the influence of Father O'Hara by an avid reading of his *Religious Bulletin*. As a priest and bishop, I followed his work and words with interest and admiration. As heir to his office and records, I realized how little I knew about this person whom I had known for many years. The broad spectrum of his character, interest, and influence was unknown to me and to many with whom he had worked. Many who knew him personally—who had been recipients of his kind concern and attention—knew him only in the context of their own personal experience.

Because Cardinal O'Hara exercised his pastoral ministry in different apostolates and in different places, because his ministry was composed of so many ordinary actions, and because he tended to obscure the measure of his accomplishments by focusing attention on what remained to be done, there was a risk that the exemplary and inspiring values of his life might be lost.

Speaking of Blessed Neumann, Pope Paul said: "He was one of that wonderful chain of bishops who prepared the leaders of the Catholic hierarchy in the United States and imbued them with those virtues of dedication, zeal, practical efficiency and absolute faithfulness which still distinguish the venerable and exemplary American episcopate." Cardinal O'Hara's dedication was total and selfless. His zeal was all-consuming. His dependence upon God was complete. He said: "To be in any measure fitted for the work of the priesthood, a man must have a deep sense of his own unworthiness and his complete dependence upon God." The students at the University of Notre Dame recognized in young Father O'Hara a quality of absolute faithfulness, and named him "John Faithful." Cardinal O'Hara is an example of the totally dedicated priests and bishops who made the American Church a strong and healthy sector of the People of God.

The inspiration and example of Cardinal O'Hara's life and work had to be preserved—not for his sake, but for the sake of succeeding generations. He needs no monuments. We need the eloquent lessons which his life and work can teach. Such a need could be fulfilled only by a thoroughly documented biography.

The possibility of such a biography was discussed with His Eminence, Cardinal Spellman, a dear friend of Cardinal O'Hara. His Eminence's reaction was instantaneous, enthusiastic and as always most practical. Through his efforts Father Thomas T. McAvoy, C.S.C., was directed to write a biography of Cardinal O'Hara. Cardinal Spellman's generous and practical interest in the biography has been most gratifying.

The selection of Father McAvoy as the biographer of Cardinal O'Hara was providential. His reputation as a historian, his capacity for diligent research, his personal knowledge of the subject as a fellow native of Indiana, a fellow religious, and a contemporary on the faculty staff of the University, all qualify him eminently for the role of a biographer.

To produce an authentic image of the Cardinal, Father McAvoy obtained information from the O'Hara family. He fine-combed the records at Notre Dame, the Military Ordinariate, and the diocesan files at Buffalo and Philadelphia. Whenever it was indicated, he followed up all possible leads. His notes and documentation could fill three such volumes.

Father McAvoy avoids a mere chronological enumeration of events in the life of the Cardinal. By judicious selection and adroit arrangement of well-documented facts and events, Father McAvoy provides the reader with an interesting and authentic image of a great churchman of our generation. I am pleased to recommend this biography without any reservations and with the assurance that it will be a source of information and inspiration to the reader.

✝ JOHN J. KROL
Archbishop of Philadelphia

December 21, 1966

Acknowledgments

The preparation of this biography was first conceived by His Eminence, Cardinal Spellman, and His Excellency, Archbishop Krol. Cardinal Spellman then asked the superior general of the Congregation of Holy Cross, Father Christopher O'Toole, C.S.C, to recommend someone for its preparation. At the request of Father O'Toole, Father Theodore Mehling, C.S.C., then provincial of the Indiana Priests' Province of the Congregation of Holy Cross, suggested my participation. Cardinal Spellman and Archbishop Krol gave generous financial help and full cooperation in the collection of materials for the biography. I had the full cooperation also of the chancery offices of the Military Ordinariate, the Diocese of Buffalo, and the Archdiocese of Philadelphia, and of the provincial archivist of the Indiana Province, Father James Gibbons, C.S.C. Under these heads I wish to acknowledge the assistance given me by so many. Others to whom I am deeply indebted for assistance are Monsignor Joseph McGlinn of Philadelphia, Monsignor Robert Duggan of Buffalo, Monsignor John J. Noone of Philadelphia, Monsignor Joseph E. Marbach of the Military Ordinariate, Father Bartholomew Fair, and Mr. Daniel O'Neil of New York. In signaling out these men I do not wish to underestimate the aid I received from countless others, but to acknowledge aid far above what I had any right to expect from those mentioned. I wish to acknowledge also a debt to His Excellency, the late Bishop Leo V. Smith. The family of Cardinal O'Hara cooperated generously at all times.

February 2, 1966   T. T. McA.

Foreword

To receive formally a large hat which he could not and would not wear was the ultimate in ceremonies for this ascetic who believed in direct and simple action. Even though this was the red hat of a cardinal delivered by a Roman monsignor and papal court attendant, there was a broad smile on the face of the newly appointed Cardinal John F. O'Hara. The ceremony was held in the auditorium of the Roman College of the Congregation of Holy Cross just outside Rome. Around him, besides the members of his own curia and his immediate family, were a few members of the Congregation of Holy Cross. The cardinal leaned forward to accept the *galero* from the papal attendants. He was tall and thin, but looked stately in his red cardinalatial robes. The *zucchetto* covered the back of his head to show the bald front and the gray hair at the sides. At the temples of his rather small, round head purple marks of the veins were visible. Behind his silver-rimmed spectacles were eyes in which fire sparked as he spoke, and a kindly smile accompanied the ready quip as he greeted old friends. His chin was small, almost pointed, and his neck was also thin. He was ready as always as an obedient servant to accept the new assignment, but his preference for retirement was plainly visible as he accepted the cumbersome headgear and told his friends that the only purple he had ever wanted was the two-inch wide band of purple that he had worn as a confessor. This was John Francis Cardinal O'Hara, of the Congregation of Holy Cross, receiving the highest honors of the Church short of the papacy, but assuring his friends that he had never changed from Father

O'Hara of Notre Dame who had years ago been regular confessor to some of the Notre Dame alumni in the background.

The story of Cardinal O'Hara includes many of these apparent contradictions: of a noted Pan American planner turned humble confessor; of a spiritual advisor become an active administrator of a noted university; of a university president become again by episcopal consecration confessor to hundreds of thousands of soldiers and advisor of priest chaplains, and then bishop and archbishop of a large, complex diocese and archdiocese, and finally cardinal, but all the time waving aside any hint of personal glory. In his own great work as prefect of religion at Notre Dame he had been a spiritual director who brought young men to unusual achievements, yet antagonized others by the strictness of his application of the law; as bishop in the Military Ordinariate there were some who criticized his closeness to the needs of the soldier and others who were shocked by his carelessness about liturgical splendor; as bishop and archbishop there were those who marveled at the physical accomplishments in building schools and religious institutions, and others who thought he was a wasteful spender. Throughout all this he never worried about what was said against him or sought any word of praise from others for his accomplishments. To most Notre Dame men of his day this tall, thin bundle of energy and contradictions was a holy man, and they nicknamed him years ago "John Faithful" because he was always ready to hear a confession or to give Holy Communion at any hour of the day or night. Although made a cardinal by Pope John XXIII, he belonged not to the *aggiornamento* but to the best of the age of Pius X to Pius XII.

Contents

Preface   v

Acknowledgments   viii

Foreword   ix

1. Ipsam Sequens Non Devias   1

2. A Career Begins   52

3. Prefect of Religion   90

4. Entering Administration   124

5. President O'Hara of Notre Dame   157

6. The Military Ordinariate   196

7. Bishop of Buffalo   268

8. Archbishop of Philadelphia   335

9. Declining Health   417

10. The Cardinalate   459

   Footnotes   492

   Index   507

ONE

Ipsam Sequens Non Devias

THERE IS A TRADITION AMONG SUPERIORS of Roman Catholic seminaries that the education of a priest begins with his grandparents. In the preparation of John Cardinal O'Hara, C.S.C., this eases the task of the historian because the Cardinal could never trace his ancestry beyond his grandparents who left Ireland amidst the terrors of the famine. In County Clare on the west coast of Ireland whence James O'Hara and Catherine Galvin came to America in 1847 stand the harsh stone cliffs of Moher which thrust themselves almost perpendicularly straight off the ocean up four to six hundred feet. Standing on their grassy tops and looking out to sea one is conscious that beyond the great blue sea is America, but one is also startled by the suddenness of the drop off from cliff to sea. But this sheer break from cliff to sea is very symbolic of the break in the lives of James O'Hara, Catherine Galvin, Ellen Brown, and James Thornton, the grandparents of John O'Hara, and in the lives of many of their fellow emigrants brought about by the Great Irish Famine that drove them from the peasantry and oppression of Ireland to the abundance and liberty of America.

The Great Irish Famine of 1845 to 1847[1] is a story of how an already overpopulated people, dependent upon the potato for its food, suffered famine and deprivation by the repeated failure of the potato crop which was complicated by attendant fevers and even typhus and how the people fled the stricken countryside to the ports and thence to the New World. There are books that

1

describe the horrors of these few years, but words can hardly combine into a single story the effects of oppressive landlords, poverty, the loss of the main source of nourishment, and the ensuing poverty that eventually swept the whole country. The famed temperance priest, Father Theobald Mathew, wrote: "I beheld with sorrow one wide waste of putrefying vegetables. In many places the wretched people were seated on the fences of their decaying gardens, wringing their hands and wailing bitterly the destruction that had left them foodless." Another observer wrote of a Galway town: "Out of a population of 240 I found thirteen men already dead of want. The survivors were walking skeletons—with men and women in some of the cabins too weak to stand. When here before I had seen cows at almost every cabin, and here were besides many sheep and pigs owned in the village. But now all the sheep were gone—all the cows—all the poultry killed—only one pig was left—the very dogs which had barked at me before had disappeared; no potatoes—no oats." Those who could, made their way to the ports seeking passage to Liverpool and thence to America. Some came by boat from the Irish ports, others from Liverpool, chiefly as ballast in the empty ships that had brought from America produce to Europe. Most of these Irish refugees had little more than the clothes on their backs.

James O'Hara, the son of Michael and Nellie (Quinn) O'Hara, a native of County Clare, left neighboring Limerick on April 13, 1847 to make his way eventually to Boston and Worcester, where he met Catherine Galvin. Mary Catherine and Bridget Galvin, daughters of John and Nellie (Quinn) Galvin of Kilrush, County Clare, Ireland, made their way first to Canada and then came down to Boston and also to Worcester, where they joined a brother John and a sister Nora, Mrs. John Collins.[2] In St. John's Church in Worcester on August 6, 1849, James O'Hara and Catherine Galvin were united in marriage before Father John Boyce with John Helney and Catherine Fox as witnesses.[3] The name of the groom was registered as James Hara because he had been told by the immigration officials that no one used the O' in this country. Probably he could neither read nor write. He was twenty-two and Catherine was twenty-six. From Worcester they made their way down the Ohio to Cincinnati, then the metropolis of the West. After a short time in Cincinnati the couple moved to Connersville, Indiana. James worked first as a canal worker and later as a packer, saving his money to purchase a farm. It was at Connersville that John Walter O'Hara, the father of the future Cardinal, was born on September 22, 1853. When James O'Hara died on October 19, 1861, at the age of thirty-six, he left to his widow six of their seven children, the oldest just ten years of age, but he also left to his widow of forty the title to eighty acres of farm land in Cass County near the present town of Galveston.

The Cass County land was part of a joint project of several Irish immigrants, among them Sullivans, Joyces, and Lawlers. There seems to have been already a log cabin on the eighty acres purchased by James O'Hara. Along with the other Irish families Catherine O'Hara gathered her brood—James, John Walter, Mary, Elizabeth, Henry, and Thomas—together with whatever household goods they had acquired and drove overland to the new home in Cass County, about a hundred and twenty miles away.

Life on a central Indiana farm in 1870 could have been the idyllic existence about which some poems have been written—snowbound in the winter and abounding in fruits and flowers in summer—but for these Irish immigrants who tried to create a home on these farms there were winter colds and fevers, much chopping of wood, backbreaking weeding of cornfields in the spring, gathering in the hay, helping the threshers, picking fruit, feeding the stock, and many other chores from early morning until sundown. The family tradition tells of Catherine O'Hara in the first year taking the child, Thomas, with her in a blanket to the field while she drove the plow. The youngsters were quickly trained to do their share of the farm work. The loneliness of this farm life was broken by the fun of family games, visits to the neighbors, and attendance occasionally at the nearest Catholic services. Morning and night prayers with the rosary in the evening was the usual substitute for church services, except when the visiting priest said Mass in the James Thornton home in nearby Galveston.

James Thornton was in some respects the most prosperous of the Irish in the settlement. Born in County Louth in 1821 James had spent some of his youth at sea before coming to New Orleans in 1850. He worked on Mississippi river boats until 1853 when he worked for a while on a boat on the Wabash-Erie Canal. In 1855 he married Ellen Brown of County Kerry who had come with her father from Ireland in 1847 and had traveled from Montreal, their first home, to Indiana. James Thornton decided that Lewisburg near one of the canal locks would be a good place to open a store and set up a small store there. He later bought also a farm near Galveston. His store which he also moved to Galveston became a meeting place for the Irish of the vicinity just as his house furnished a room for Mass and other religious services

when the priest from Logansport visited the neighborhood. In the
Thornton home nine children survived the toils of life in the
Wabash Valley.

Of the six children the widow O'Hara brought to Cass County,
James died a few years later leaving John Walter the oldest. He
was athletically inclined and among his favorite stunts was that of
riding barefoot standing on one of the family horses. It is no
wonder that his mother worried lest he run away and join a circus, an idea that the youngster himself might have suggested. Just
how soon he went to the nearby country school is not clear, but
he could not have been very small—one account says he was
twelve years old—when an incident brought even this education
to an abrupt end. The teacher of this school engaged in constant
bantering of his Irish pupil, and on one occasion the banter so
antagonized young John Walter that he seized a stick from the
schoolhouse wood pile and hurled it at the head of the teacher.
Luckily his aim was bad or the agility of this teacher was good,
and the stick missed its target. Nevertheless John Walter no
longer had to bear the taunts of the teacher and the teacher lost
him as a pupil. Just how much he had progressed in learning is
not recorded, but he was sufficiently grown to obtain a job in the
employ of James Thornton, working on the farm.

When John Walter O'Hara went to work for James Thornton
he met for the first time, apparently, Ellen Thornton, the second
oldest child of the family, then a talented young lady of fifteen
years. John O'Hara was four years her senior but there seems to
have sprung up an instant friendship that later blossomed into
love. The first effect of this friendship was that Ellen persuaded
him that he should complete his education by attending night
school and later a school for teachers. So rapid was his progress and
so superior were his attainments that in 1874 he applied and obtained the position of schoolmaster in the district school. Later he
obtained a position of teacher in the Bunker Hill grade school.
Just how many teachers there were in the school is not recorded,
but he became the principal of the school in 1878 and continued
to teach there until 1883. Ellen's plans to attend the boarding
school conducted by the Sisters of Holy Cross in Logansport were
ended in 1872 by the death of her father. On January 15, 1878,
John Walter O'Hara and Ellen Thornton were married in Saint
Patrick's Church, Kokomo, the nearest parish church for the Catholics of Galveston. John was also elected at this time to the office
of Justice of the Peace in Bunker Hill.

Perhaps love of knowledge was part of the bond that united

John and Ellen O'Hara. A portion of his diary for the year 1879
tells of some of his experiences as the local school teacher, and
indicates that Ellen likewise was still teaching school after their
marriage.[4] Eventually, of course, the arrival of young O'Haras
interrupted her teaching, although she did teach again at times
and was always ready to substitute for any teacher who was unable
to meet her pupils. The young couple—happy and resourceful
according to the diary—is not described in any contemporary
account, but other records tell us that John was a strong man
about five feet eleven inches in height and weighed about a hundred and eighty pounds and had brown hair and blue eyes; Ellen
was always thin, wiry, and energetic: she had brown hair and
bright blue eyes and was about five feet five inches tall.

The O'Haras lived in the village of Bunker Hill, where John
W. had become the principal of the grade school. But during the
summer of 1880, enticed by a prospect of an insurance agency,
John took his family with him to Columbus, Indiana. The insurance business was unsuccessful, and depressed by the death of
their only daughter, May, the couple became lonesome and unhappy and returned to Bunker Hill. In 1883 John O'Hara bought
from O. A. Larimer, *The Bunker Hill Press,* a rather successful
paper. *The History of Miami County,* printed in 1887, said of
this weekly: "The *Press* is now a five-column quarto, independent in politics, but fearless in the discussion of all the leading
topics of the day. Its mechanical execution will compare favorably with that of any other paper in the county, and its circulation and advertizing patronage, already quite remunerative, is
constantly increasing. Mr. O'Hara is an able writer, and we
bespeak for the *Press* a prosperous future."[5] In another part of
the *History,* the writer says that because of his "party service" and
his "acknowledged qualifications" Mr. O'Hara was appointed
postmaster of Bunker Hill in September, 1885. The writer also
added "Mrs. O'Hara is a lady of superior intelligence, and, besides
being a ready writer in prose, has written much in verse, which
is said, by those best acquainted with her writings, to possess
much worth."[6] The political party in power was the Democratic
Party, which had won the election of 1884 under the conservative
financial promises of Grover Cleveland.

The 1880's were probably the heyday of the country weekly
newspaper in rural Indiana, and in view of the slow means of
communication, these newspapers were an essential part of community life. The costs of printing were not great, and there seems
to have been some profit. But John W. O'Hara was not content

to be a newspaper editor. In 1887, while the *Press* was apparently doing well, he sold the paper and with the funds thereby acquired decided to go to the University of Michigan at Ann Arbor to study law. There, on May 1, 1888, John O'Hara junior was born. The names given the child were not John Francis as he later became known, but John Dillon in honor of the Irish leader of that name; yet John junior dropped the Dillon for Francis at Confirmation in honor of Saint Francis De Sales. John senior finished his one year of study in June, 1888, and returned to Bunker Hill, where he set up his law office, later moving to Peru.

Of the law practice of John W. O'Hara in the succeeding years there is scarcely a mention in the contemporary accounts. In civic affairs he was recognized as a ready and capable speaker. He was ardent in his interest in the affairs of Ireland, probably because in Indiana of that day Ireland meant not only the Irish people but also the Catholic people of the English-speaking world. He always made a speech somewhere on Saint Patrick's Day, and in 1896 he was elected the state president of the Ancient Order of Hibernians, the chief rallying center of the American Irish. Later with Bishop James McFaul of Trenton, New Jersey, he was credited with playing an important part in bringing together the original Board of Erin with the American Board of the Hibernians in the American phase of the twentieth-century struggle for Irish independence.

The life in the O'Hara home, a large frame house at 376 West Main Street in Peru, was much like that of most large Irish Catholic families in the smaller towns of the Middle West. The father was away most of the day at business, and the home, dominated by the mother, was the center of family life. Since both father and mother in this family had been school teachers, school work was important. Daily prayers, morning, evening and at meals with the evening rosary were taken for granted. Modesty in behavior and language did not prevent games, much laughter, and quick speech. Archbishop O'Hara later recalled: "When my father and mother sent their eight children to the Catholic school they made known to us that if we were punished in school we would also be punished at home. They let us know also that if we complained that we were punished unjustly, our punishment at home would be doubled. We learned early in life that we deserved far more punishment for our derelictions than we received. Further we learned that if we were to come after Christ we would have to take our cross daily and follow Him. As we grew older we came to appreciate this method of teaching us reverence for God in the

person of our superiors and we came to thank God for the incul-
cation of the spirit of sacrifice." The influence of a strict parish
priest helped in creating these ideals. Also by the time the children were ready for school, the Sisters of Providence, from St.
Mary of the Woods, had opened a parish school next door to
St. Charles Church. The school offered reading, spelling, writing, arithmetic, geography, and history with a class in catechism
for each grade. John F. passed all eight grades with ease.

The pastor of Peru, Father Henry Meissner, belonged to those
zealous German priests of the Middle West "of the old school"
who insisted on a strong parish life, with parish societies, a parish
school, and other strict traditions of a Catholic parish. Photographs show him a heavy man of moderate height with a large
face and heavy jowls, but with keen eyes and a well formed but
austere mouth. Like so many of these German pastors of the
Diocese of Fort Wayne, he worked towards the ideal of the
Catholic parish he had known in Germany.

Only those who have lived in the congregations of these immigrant German priests of the Wabash Valley can understand the
way they impressed their ideals upon their congregations. Most
of these priests had come already trained from a turbulent Germany, although some made their final theological studies at St.
Francis Seminary in Milwaukee or, as in the case of Father Meissner, at St. Mary's in Baltimore. They had a liking for formal
learning and personally conducted the religious instruction of
the children of the parish. Father Meissner would interrupt the
regular program of the parish school when he came to conduct
his catechism class, which was not an ordinary question and
answer session, but an elaborate explanation of the truths and
rules of the Catholic religion. Even Sunday Mass included a long
diagramatically organized sermon. Years later Cardinal O'Hara
added that every Sunday until he was fourteen-years-old—when
Father Meissner died—he heard a sermon in German as well as
English. The Irish were expected to say their beads during the
German sermon. The parish schools of north central Indiana in
the diocese of Fort Wayne were permeated with the theological
ideals of their German pastors, even when, as in Peru, the Sisters
of the parish school belonged to a community of French origin.

At the turn of the century the system of Catholic elementary
schools in the Diocese of Fort Wayne was one of the best in the
country, and it was from Father Meissner and the German priests
of the neighborhood that Cardinal O'Hara acquired his staunch
devotion to the Catholic parish school. Actually at the time of

his boyhood in the Diocese of Fort Wayne for parents to send their children to a public school where a parish school was available was a sin reserved to the Bishop according to the diocesan statutes. These German pastors generally agreed on the ideals of Catholic conduct. The pastor supervised the teaching of religion; the age for First Holy Communion was usually after twelve years —for Father Meissner's parish fourteen years; and the catechism was a translation from the German, usually that of Deharbe. In the schools the boys and girls were kept apart in seating and in recreation. While all ten commandments were taught, three moral principles were especially stressed: there was but one Catholic religion that must never be compromised; to lie and to steal were always sinful; and in matters of sex there was no small matter and therefore all deliberate sins against the sixth commandment were mortal. Practicing Catholics lived a strict life and kept to themselves.

The Catholics of central Indiana were usually railway workers or German farmers, and both groups accepted the rules of conduct set down by their pastors. In matters of faith there could be only the true and the false, and no Catholic could ever attend a Protestant service; Catholics tended to avoid all social intermingling with non-Catholics, particularly among youngsters of marriageable ages. Since there was practically no Catholic literature in English available, the public library was not used by Catholic children, and the youngsters were encouraged to do their reading in approved classical authors. Their German pastors had a low opinion of American literature. Partially because of the separation of Catholics from non-Catholics in grade schools, and to a great extent because they were conscious of a distinctive moral approach to life, Catholics and non-Catholics in the community were aware of a difference when they associated together. This difference was increased when Catholics were encouraged to seek their recreations in the parish social or picnic and in membership in a parish society or in local branches of such organizations as the Catholic Benevolent Legion or the Ancient Order of Hibernians. In the case of young John O'Hara, there was a passage from this strict discipline to the thoroughly Catholic atmosphere of Latin America, in which his practice of these rules became confirmed.

The O'Haras, like most Irish Catholic families in central Indiana, moved into the town. Nevertheless, as the son of a professional man, John had a higher social status than the sons of railroad men or farmers. John O'Hara senior had achieved his success by his intelligence and by hard work, and he wanted his children to rise even higher in American life. Also by reason of his superior ability to write and to speak the senior O'Hara was respected in the community, although none of his sons chose to follow him in the legal profession.

Commenting on his early training, Archbishop O'Hara said of his Peru Catholicism:

We were a distinct minority in a town that had more than its share of bigots. And more than its share of members of the A.P.A. Most of us were descendants of German or Irish immigrants. There were several Catholic Indian families; their children came to the Catholic school only for the year in which they prepared for their first Holy Communion. There was one Negro Catholic family consisting of a mother and daughter. The daughter completed her education in the Catholic school and then went away to study opera.

As members of a minority group (Catholics and foreigners) we received our share of insults—and rocks—that were intended to keep us in our place. We knew better than to bring stories home. Our teaching at home was that we must give good example as Catholics, that if we failed to do this we were endangering our Faith as well as giving scandal to those not of our Faith. The wounds received, especially the wounds to our pride, helped to form our character. We seldom found bigotry among our immediate neighbors, gradually the children from the Catholic schools who remained at home won the respect of the community by their integrity and sound citizenship. We left that town more than fifty years ago, but we are delighted to find in our visits back there that many conversions have resulted from the good example of the Catholic citizens.[7]

Just when John W. O'Hara changed his politics from the Democratic to the Republican party is not certain. Family tradition says that he changed about 1892 because of the parties' stands on the tariff. As an active political worker John W. O'Hara did not change his position easily; after studying the problem he had decided that the low-tariff policies of the Democratic party were a threat to the welfare of the American worker, and so he argued with his friends. He insisted that the lowering of the tariff would bring in a flood of cheaper foreign manufactures to ruin American industry and put the American worker in competition with cheaper foreign labor. His Republicanism was strengthened by his opposition to William Jennings Bryan and Free Silver. Most of the Catholics of Peru remained Democratic. John O'Hara's change of party was a mark of distinction, one that caused his son, John junior, some embarrassments among his schoolmates who were mostly sons and daughters of traditional Democrats. In time his father earned a reputation as an important Republican in the community.

John W. O'Hara had made one trip into Mexico, and he thought of a consulship in a foreign country as a necessary means to enable him and his family to live abroad. He secured recommendations from his friends in Peru as a suitable Consul for Mexico, but before he had time to present these testimonials, his friend, Senator Albert Beveridge, had obtained for him the nomination by President Theodore Roosevelt on March 7, 1905, as American Consul at Montevideo, Uruguay. This important decision was also a decisive event in the life of impressionable seventeen-year-old John junior.

Although young John O'Hara attended the parochial school of St. Charles in Peru from the age of six to fourteen, no school records remain. His surviving classmates insist that he was always a bright youngster, a trait of all the O'Hara family. In a group photograph taken when he was in the primary grades, probably about ten years of age, he appeared as a neatly dressed boy in a buster-brown suit with a large white collar, with his hair parted on the left side. As he approached his twelfth year he joined the special class for first communicants taught an hour a day for two years by Father Meissner and made his First Communion in June, 1902. He was confirmed on May 17, 1903, at the age of fourteen. Just how much personal contact the thin, wiry youngster had with Father Meissner is not recorded, but he credited his early convictions to the instruction of this priest. Years later he wrote to his classmate, Fred Becker:

The older I get the more vivid become the memories of Peru, of Father Meissner, the Sisters of Providence and the classmates of St. Charles. Certainly my first thoughts of the priesthood awakened there, but it took a long time to find the place I most wanted to be.[8]

At an early time he thought of entering the Jesuit order and visited members of that community in St. Louis when he attended the St. Louis World's Fair in 1904, but the Jesuits did not think his health good enough at that time.

As an intelligent town boy, John O'Hara was ready and willing to work when his health and his schoolwork permitted. He later told a Buffalo publisher that as a boy he carried papers for seven years. "My companions were better than average boys, mentally, morally, and physically. No drone could hold a newspaper job. Newspapers were smaller in those days and a four mile route to cover one hundred and fifty subscribers was not uncommon. The carriers developed the physical stamina of farm boys, whose rugged physique we envied."[9]

The Peru Public High School to which John transferred after the eighth grade was much like other high schools in the Indiana towns of that day. Their program was modeled slightly after the old classical course, but Greek was no longer taught and Latin was having a difficult time in competition with the new, more practical courses.[10] The basic course was English, and the history offered was ancient history. For the first year he studied English, Latin, algebra, history, physical geography, and geology and earned a half-credit in debating. The second year included courses in history, zoology, and plane geometry as well as Latin and English. In the third year he advanced to a higher algebra class and physics besides Latin and English. But before the end of the second semester of the third year John O'Hara accompanied the family to South America.

Between the evening of March 6 when the nomination to the consulship was announced in the Peru *Journal* and the departure for New York on April 30 there was not much time for readjustments to new situations in the family. Just what John junior thought of the change is not recorded. He had manifested to his sister, Elizabeth, some years before when she was studying at St. Mary of the Woods his decision to become a priest, but outside of his visit to the Jesuits in St. Louis, he seems to have taken no steps to carry out his decision. As a youth he showed no inclination towards social activities that might lead to marriage, and he did seem to be especially serious in his efforts to master Latin. He had also acquired an ability to play the piano by private instructions. But living in a large family, John O'Hara had plenty of other matters to think about as the family took the train to New York and boarded the boat to South America. They sailed on May 3 on the Lamport ship *Byron* to Rio de Janeiro. From Rio they took the Royal Mail Line ship *Thames* to Montevideo, arriving May 26 with a circus—a pleasant reminder of Peru, which was known then as Circus City.

Montevideo was the capital of the Republica Oriental Del Uruguay on the eastern shore of the La Plata River. The estuary of the river at this point is about twenty-seven miles across, and while Buenos Aires was on the western shore and the winter home of wealthy people, the eastern shore around Montevideo was for them a summer home. It is true that not the whole population moved across the river in this way, but the contrast between the two ports of central South America was derived from the better

beaches and mild weather of Montevideo. Uruguay was about
ninety percent Spanish, had no Indians since 1853, and very few
Negroes. A casual description of Montevideo of that day would
seem to compare it with a Spanish city such as Madrid with its
broad streets, its central park, its many flower gardens, and its
grand Cathedral in the center. Writing in 1912 John F. O'Hara
said of the city: "Home life is the center of the Uruguayan's
interest, and the handsome residences that adorn the broad streets
of Montevideo proclaim this fact. Marble is found everywhere.
Handsomely designed marble balconies set off the stucco fronts
of the houses; marble passages lead into marble courts; marble
staircases, gorgeously carved and polished, lead up from the street.
. . . The summer homes of the Montevidians, the suburban
"quintas," are the finest in South America; their architecture is
simple and elegant; and surrounding them are acres of flowers and
rare shrubs." The Government offices and other public buildings
were built in the grand style of the French and Italian Renaissance architecture with baroque fronts, but most of the city
consisted of buildings of one story along the wide streets that
stretched out for miles from the harbor. The business of the city
concentrated near the long wharves because the chief industry of
the country was the exportation of hides and beef and mutton.
At one end of the bay stood the low mountain, an extinct volcano
called the Cerro, the sight of which by the first explorers is said
to have given the city its name. It was once strongly fortified and
defended. Montevideo consisted of a series of low hills and intervening valleys. Besides its baroque government buildings and its
religious institutions the city itself also had a theatre in the grand
style and a large public museum of science and art. The main
park, called the Prado, was remarkable for the variety of its vege-
tation. The climate was always mild, and the tempo of Montevideo notably calm.

In crossing the equator "down under" the O'Haras had entered
South America in its winter season. For the school-age children
this meant an immediate induction into school conducted in
Spanish. The girls entered a convent school, chiefly to study Spanish for a while. John Francis entered the Jesuit school Sagrado
Corazon, a *colegio* in the Latin sense of the word. One of his
schoolmates, the sculptor Zorrilla de San Martin, recalled him as
"a rather quiet fragile boy, who undertook with bravery the difficulties of studying in a foreign country with boys he had never
met before, and in Spanish."[11] This thin youth soon developed a
persistent nosebleed, which prompted Father Madden of the

Mercy Fathers in charge of the neighboring parish to suggest that he spend some time at a ranch near the Mercy Fathers School, San Patricio, near Mercedes, Argentina. Father Madden made the arrangements, and young John O'Hara spent a few weeks and then a second longer stay on Estancia El Carmen, managed by M. J. Moughty for Thomas J. Duggan, a wealthy landowner. Besides rebuilding his health in the good country air the young man acquired a permanent mastery of Spanish and a good understanding of the Latin American way of life.

When John F. returned to Montevideo, he also went back to the Jesuit Fathers at Sagrado Corazon. On his transcript of studies at Notre Dame he is listed as having taken philosophy courses, chemistry, physiology, and mineralogy for thirty-eight weeks, as well as having acquired a proficiency in the Spanish, French, Portuguese, Italian, and German languages. Yet in his free time he worked as a kind of secretary at the American Embassy for General Edward C. O'Brien, the American Minister to Uruguay. There was little of the unusual in quiet Montevideo to report in the next two years. The two eldest girls, Elizabeth and Eva, returned to Indiana in 1906 and went to Peru and then to Indianapolis to live.

In the summer of 1907 the senior O'Haras returned to the United States for a vacation but John, who was in school, and Jim, who was acting as vice-consul and taking care of his father's office, did not return with them. Writing on June 23, John F. gave his parents a good view of his school life in Montevideo.

We have been having all sorts of "fiestas" out at school lately. Of course June and July are the months for feasts with the Jesuits anyway. The biggest thing of all was the feast of St. Aloysius the other day. We had to be there at 7:00 A.M. They had the receptions of the new Congregants at 7:30 and at 8:00 Monseñor Soler said the Communion Mass. They gave us coffee afterwards, then we had "charla" until 10:00 then we all went to the High Mass sung by Monseñor Isasa. After that we were "allowed" to go home until we could get ready to come back again. There was a football game between our "Division" and "Primera" scheduled for 1:30 but the rain and the fog, which had been continuous since the night before, put an end to any such ambitious hopes. I went back at about 3:00 and after a half hour of the "Vela," started in to celebrate. We had a Fourth of July celebration for fair. We had about $6.00 worth of firecrackers, a lot of sky-rockets, and 24 balloons. They were all made by the Seminarians and some of them were really fine. One of them, in the shape of a fish, was really a work of art. However, the rain spoiled that part of the sport, so we put the most of them away until the 15th of August. At 4:30 we had a "manger" down below and besides had been treated to "masitas" by one of the Seminarians in honor of his entering the "Congregación." At 5:00 the Cinematograph performance commenced. (That reminds me, papa, if you have not sent to Edison's yet for those catalogues, please send right away, as Padre Carreras is anxious to get the machine as soon as possible.) They showed us views of the wedding of Alfonso XIII, the Atentado de la Calle Mayor, a Pilgrimage to Lourdes, a kid learning to smoke, a storm at sea, and a half dozen others. It was very good. We got out at 6:30 and received orders to be back at 7:30 sharp. Of course that left us very little time, so I scarcely had time for supper. I got back just in time and we heard a sermon that was as good as anything I ever heard either in English or Spanish. Yesterday then, as we were kept up late, we were given an extra hour to sleep it off. Tomorrow is St. John's Day, and although it is not a holiday, the P.Prefecto has decided to let us off all day long, as none of us has been able to pull ourselves [sic] together since the "affaire.". . .¹²

The remainder of the letter told how their friends had invited them out during their parents' absence, related the shows they had attended, and gave an appreciation of the actors, including Coquelin as Cyrano de Bergerac and Eleanor Duse.

In a letter of September 19 John told of the more serious part of his education.

Well, things have been going on in school in more or less the same old way. As I told you in another letter I got a first and two second prizes in the August "concertación," and it made some of the kids jealous, as they had worked hard for them during the past month, and they thought it unfair that an "inglés," a rank outsider, and something of an undesirable citizen, should beat them to it. Naturally it made me rather sore, as I do not want the prizes, and had not worked for a single one since the beginning of the year. Some of them expressed their feelings in no-unmistakable terms, so I made up my mind that I was going to work for some the next time. Unfortunately, I caught cold, and before it was cured, I stayed up to twelve o'clock studying Chemistry for the "concurso" of the following day, and it gave me the grip. Of course, that gave me quite a set-back, and I was not able to carry out my program, as I was hardly able to study for about two weeks, but with it all I came out yesterday with first in Mineralogy, and second in Philosophy and Chemistry. My concurso in Chemistry was very good, too, by the way, but one of the Seminarians went me one better, and I lowered my colors. Schroeder got three prizes and one second the first month. I hate to do it, and there never was anybody that I despised more than a fellow who worked for prizes in school, but as long as they want to get sore and make an international affair out of it, I will go in and uphold the honor of my country all right. . . .

He also told how the fellow students asked him if he could box and how he tried to avoid any demonstration until they tried to take advantage of him. On one or two occasions he did defend himself with success.

. . . However, it is a good thing that neither of them wanted, or could fight after I had hit them, as they are both much stronger than I am and could make short work of me. I was just simply lucky enough to hit them hard in the right place, at the right time and the one was enough for them. . . .[13]

Many years later Cardinal O'Hara related some of the reactions of his teachers to this blue-eyed, thin Yankee youth.

Some of the Jesuits in the college I attended in Montevideo in 1905 had serious misgivings about letting these Yankees into school. Padre Ramon, whose observatory had been wrecked by the Yankee soldiers, paid his negative respects to us from time to time in no uncertain terms. One day he interrupted the class, looked at me intently, pointed his forefinger at his brains as if he were going to shoot himself, and exclaimed: "O'Jara, that's an Irish name, isn't it? You could be a Catholic."[14]

Before John W. O'Hara and Ellen left the United States, they were informed by the State Department that he had been transferred to the consulate at Santos in Brazil, and they did not return to Montevideo. Jim remained for a while in Montevideo, working in the consulate, but John W. summoned John Francis to serve with him in Santos as secretary. Santos was a sultry seaport town not far from Sao Paulo—but on a lower level—through which most of Brazil's coffee was shipped to Europe and the United States. The climate and temperature of the port were unattractive compared to Montevideo, and the social compensations for the family were less. Writing from Santos on February 16, 1908, John F. included more than one passage about the lackluster of his life there.

. . . Santos, outside of office hours is the dullest place I have ever seen, Mercedes not excepted. We spend our extra time reading, and we get all the novels that are to be begged, borrowed, or stolen, anywhere along the beach. . . . The weather here has been hot enough here for the past five days although it was relieved by a shower yesterday. This is the longest stretch we have had without rain since the first of the year. There is a mountain here, about six hundred feet from the Consulate which everybody climbs, but you cannot climb it after rainy weather, because of the red clay which covers the entire summit, and the sides, for a distance of about 100 feet from the top and which get so bad in rainy weather that there is no footing in it. I guess that nobody can climb it in summer.[15]

John F. began to plan his return to the United States as soon as a new secretary would be appointed, but had to delay when the new secretary showed no inclination to work. Then he announced his departure for June 25, and he did finally get away on July 8 with his brothers Jim and Bob. Mrs. O'Hara, when her health continued to suffer from the climate of Santos, soon followed them. John W. continued a rather lonely existence complicated by ill-health. While returning from a visit to the United States a year later, 1909, John W. was thrown violently against a wall of the ship in a sudden lurch in rough seas. Three ribs were broken and the surrounding cartilage torn. The ship doctors, lacking modern X-ray equipment, misjudged the injury and treated him for a liver ailment that probably did not exist. The suffering from this injury, the loneliness, and damp climate of Santos led Mr. O'Hara to give up any plans he had of staying on in the consular service.

Three years in Latin America had left John F. O'Hara a young man of twenty years, without family riches, and without preparation for any career, except that he apparently continued to plan to become a priest. He could boast of an unusual education and a variety of experiences. He was better educated than most American high-school graduates, but he had no diploma or certificate which would admit him to college. He had a mastery of Spanish and to some extent of French, and the benefits of foreign travel and of working as a secretary in a foreign office. His health seemed good enough for college work, and while he was slender, like his mother, he was also wiry and strong. He was a stranger in Indianapolis.

Indianapolis of 1908 was a burgeoning Midwestern city. It was often characterized as an overgrown country town in which everything closed at nine o'clock in the evening except on Saturday night. Most of the white population was of Anglo-American origins and Protestant. Catholics, numbering about ten percent of the people, were usually railway workers of Irish birth or descent or Germans engaged in small businesses or recently moved in from some Indiana farming community. The Irish were neither the richest nor socially the most respected citizens of the metropolis, and John O'Hara was just another young Catholic man looking for a job. Naturally he sought a business in which he could best use his South American experience. Besides trying to use his Spanish, he tried to become an agent for the sale of coffee. His immediate purpose was to acquire funds to complete his education.

Just what turned John F. O'Hara's mind toward Notre Dame
is not certain. Undoubtedly he had heard of Notre Dame before
he went to Montevideo. The Peru pastor after Father Meissner,
Father John Guendling, was a friend of the Holy Cross Fathers,
who conducted the University of Notre Dame. In his boyhood
visits to his grandmother, Mrs. Ellen Thornton, who lived across
the street from St. Patrick's Church in Kokomo, John had met
young Charles L. O'Donnell, who was then studying at Washington and would be ordained a priest of Holy Cross for Notre Dame
in 1910. In their visits to Kokomo the girls of the family had become acquainted with another Kokomo youngster, Frank Maher,
who was also studying for the priesthood at Notre Dame. During
a visit to Grandmother Thornton in 1908 the girls had invited
Frank to visit them in Indianapolis during his summer vacation.
When he came to Indianapolis, Frank took the opportunity to
talk to the young John O'Hara, who had just returned from Brazil. Probably the sisters and Frank had already talked of John's
desire to finish his education. Frank Maher lived in Holy Cross
Seminary across the lake from the University of Notre Dame, but
in the small student body of those days he was well acquainted
with the youngsters who lived in St. Joseph Hall and worked their
way through the University and suggested a similar solution of
John's problems. John O'Hara told his father that his education
had to be derived from his mastery of Spanish, and as his plans
developed, he wrote to him on August 30:

I had been looking around here for a good permanent job, but as
the chances were pretty slim I thought it a good plan to make use of
my Spanish. I didn't want to go to a large city so I decided to see what
I could do by teaching Spanish. I wrote a letter to Father Cavanaugh,
but didn't like the sound of it, so I decided to go up there to see him.
On Wednesday morning I was ready to start out.

Jim decided to go along with me as far as Peru and then to go on to
Chicago. I, too, thought it would be a good plan to see the rest of the
folks and then settle down, so I arranged with Jim to meet me at La-
porte. I changed to the Vandalia at Plymouth, and got over to South
Bend at 1:30. I got out to the college at 2:20 and met a great friend of
yours, Prof. John Ewing. He wanted to know all about you and wanted
to be especially remembered to you. I told him that the only trouble
with South America was that they had no KC's down there.

I finally met Father Cavanaugh—he was very busy—there were about
400 priests from the Chicago diocese there in retreat, and he was very
much in demand, but he always seems to have time for the boys. He
is very jolly and we had a pleasant chat with him, but didn't get a
chance to strike him for a job—in fact I didn't need to because we hadn't

been talking for five minutes before he offered me the Spanish profes-
sorship for the next year to defray the expenses of board and tuition at
Notre Dame. Of course, I jumped at the offer, and in the meantime I
want to work at something here. I will have enough to take me through
one term on my own, and I prefer to make it the second semester of
the year.

After fixing up our business matters I went around with Frank
Maher of Kokomo and saw Notre Dame and St. Mary's. I was very
much pleased with the place.[16]

There is no other record of the agreement reached between John
O'Hara and Father John W. Cavanaugh, the president and
superior of Notre Dame.

When he returned to Indianapolis, John began again his search
for a job. Although he was asked to do a few translations for some
business firms, the best offer he received was a promise of a job
to sell Climax Roasted Coffee to the retail grocers. That job
lasted only two weeks in the hard times, yet he did spend money to
attend a Notre Dame-Indiana University football game in Indianapolis on November 7, yelling himself hoarse to aid Notre Dame
to win 11 to 0. A minor crisis in his plans arose when he learned
that his father was unable to get a secretary to assist him in Santos,
and he felt bound to return there. His application for the government job, however, was not accepted, and instead he wrote on
December 6 to Father Cavanaugh renewing his acceptance of the
offer of the previous summer.

The correspondence on what was to mean so much in the
young man's life showed that John O'Hara had pinned much on
the agreement. Father Cavanaugh wrote:

My Dear John:
In reply to your communication dated December 6th, I desire to
say that without completely arranging the details, I already consent to
receive you into the University January 5th, with the understanding
that you are to defray the expenses of board and tuition by teaching
either literary or office work. These details may be arranged later.

Would it be possible for you to arrange to pay for your room in
South Bend? We are crowded for private rooms and several of our
students have already engaged rooms in the city with our consent. If
you can manage to pay about two and a half dollars a week for the rent
of a private room it would be an easy settlement of what would otherwise be a grave difficulty.[17]

The answer dated December 13 was prompt:

Dear Father Cavanaugh:
If you could have seen me this morning when I read your letter of

the 11th, you would have appreciated more than I can tell you, my profound gratitude for your kind favor. I can never repay you for your kindness but hope I may be able, in some way, at some time, to show my appreciation.

I will be glad to take a room wherever you suggest. I can well afford to defray this expense since you have taken the heavier burden of board and tuition off my hands. I will, if nothing unforeseen happens, report for duty the morning of January 5th.

Again thanking you, in my parents' as well as my own name, for your kindness and wishing you the full enjoyment of God's blessings during the approaching festive season. . . .[18]

Since his return from South America John O'Hara had made another acquaintance that would have a great importance in his later life, the coadjutor bishop of Indianapolis, Joseph Chartrand. Shortly after the family returned to Indianapolis they moved into the Cathedral parish, where the Coadjutor Bishop as pastor made a business of getting acquainted with the young men who came to church there. Associates of the Bishop say that he always acted as a bishop in his own church; and there is another tradition that he anticipated by several years the decree of Pope Pius X on frequent and daily Communion. One of his penitents related how as an assistant and later as pastor of the Cathedral, Father Chartrand spent hours in the confessional. His favorite penitents were young men to whom he gave personal attention. He urged them to go to confession and to receive Holy Communion frequently. Interrupting his work in the confessional occasionally, he gave them Communion himself. When any young man whom he knew failed to show up for a while, Father, and later Bishop, Chartrand would send him a card asking about the absence and would give the youth some token of recognition when he returned. He made no change in this habit when he became coadjutor bishop in 1910 or when he became the bishop of Indianapolis in 1918. To young men who visited the Cathedral to pray he gave pamphlets on religious subjects, particularly a small purple paperbound prayer book containing daily prayers and prayers for before and after Communion which he had compiled himself. He frequently expressed a slighting opinion of the Boy Scouts, of which troops were then becoming quite numerous in Indiana communities; he saw a much better means for forming young men in the practice of frequent and daily Communion. John O'Hara had acquired the habit of frequent Communion before he left South America, and this fact quickly brought him to the attention of Bishop Chartrand. There is no evidence that he told the Bishop then of his ambition to be a priest or that the Bishop guided him in his decision to go to Notre Dame.

John left Indianapolis on January 2 for South Bend, visiting Grandmother Thornton in Kokomo on the way. His first letter was written from Corby Hall, Notre Dame, after he met his first classes:

I am sitting in my room, or rather in "Red" Johnston's room waiting till it is time to go to bed, so that I can turn in. "Red" is from Washington, and hasn't returned from Christmas yet, so I have his room until I can secure a place in town, or rather move, as I have already secured a room. My roommate is John Tully, of El Paso, Ill., a nice young fellow, and Fr. Cavanaugh's Secretary. We have a dandy room at Tong's, #207 S. Scott Street and we expect to take possession tomorrow. My mail should be sent there. The room will cost me $8 per mo.

I am getting into the swing of things a little here now, even though I am not sure what studies I am taking, or what hours they come. I have German, Latin, English, Greek, History and Elocution—Freshman college work.

My particular graft is Spanish. I have taken two of the Spanish classes, and held the first, the beginners, this afternoon. They do pretty well, and I—well didn't get stage-fright anyhow. I have to study the Spanish grammar, systematically, like it is set down. The kids seem pretty good, and one or two of them were good Spanish scholars.

Well, it's a whole lot nearer bed time than it was when I started, so I will close for this time. As soon as I get settled you can expect a long letter from me. Some of you be sure to write once in a while and send everything to 207 S. Scott St. O, yes, I forgot to tell you that I even had a cold. It's good and cold here, nevertheless.

Because he did not mail the letter until two days later he added a postscript:

I didn't get my letter sent you yet, so I am adding a few lines. I am located at Tong's and everything is lovely. Today, Thursday, is our free day, and I am spending the time in getting straightened out.

It is as cold as time here, but fortunately, I don't mind it a bit. The thermometer is hanging around zero, but the air is dry, even if windy.

I have been meeting old friends here in the last few days. First was Ernest Whitehill who is in High School here. Next was Will Donohue and his brother, Joe. Next came Dick Dinnen and his brother, George, and last night I discovered that the other roomer was none other than Carl Schieps of Peru.

I saw Clark Macy and Ed Bloom on the street, but did not speak to either of them. I will have to look up the rest of the Peruvians here when I have the time.

I have had some of the funniest experiences ever about my teaching Spanish. I have heard all kinds of funny remarks about the new Spanish teacher from fellows who have only been here a day or so, and don't know who I am. It sounded funny, too, to hear the kids that are in the class say, "Good morning, Professor" Prof! Tee-hee!

Well, I'll have to cease my ramblings and get down to real work. I will drop a line once or twice a week for the first few weeks, and less often after that.

Give my love to all.

John
Prof—tee-hee[19]

One of his students recalls seeing this thin young man standing as was the custom outside the door of his classroom, waiting for the bell for the class to begin. Some, impressed by his ability in Spanish, called him "a Dago with an Irish name."

The Notre Dame of which John O'Hara had become a part offered a complete education for boys from kindergarten to college degree. The grade school for youngsters under thirteen years of age was concentrated in St. Edward's Hall, a three-storied building slightly to the rear and east of the main college building. The sisters supervised the domestic life of the youngsters; the brothers, particularly Brother Cajetan, the discipline; and priests and brothers did the teaching. The high-school boys under seventeen years lived in the west wing of the Administration Building, called Carroll Hall. Those over seventeen lived with the college students in Brownson. The college students lived in Brownson or in the separate dormitories: Norman towered Sorin; unadorned Corby, west of the church; and St. Joseph for student employees, some two hundred yards to the southwest. But the center of Notre Dame was beneath the golden dome of the Administration, or Main, Building, above which stood a golden statue of Notre Dame. Built after the fire of 1879, the Main Building housed the offices of the University, most of its nontechnical classrooms, and the old fashioned dormitories and study halls, Brownson and Carroll halls. Already beyond Washington Hall (the auditorium and music hall), Science Hall, Technological Hall, and the rectangular engineering building marked the spread and growth of the university.

Notre Dame was owned and maintained by the Congregation of Holy Cross, whose provincial superior, Father Andrew Morrissey, lived in the Presbytery behind the gothic-spired Sacred Heart Church, but the heart of Notre Dame was its genial president, Father John W. Cavanaugh, C.S.C. Of his college faculty of forty-five, seventeen were Fathers of Holy Cross; and of his high-school faculty of twenty-seven, eight were priests. John O'Hara was a student in the college and a teacher in the high school. The lines separating the two institutions were not too carefully kept except in the organization of the classes. The proper work of a university in the United States had not yet been carefully defined, and Notre Dame's chief claim to the title, besides the charter from the State in 1844, was the variety of its programs with her colleges of science, law, and engineering as well as the traditional college of liberal arts. Notre Dame was in name and in fact a national Catholic institution and drew its student body from all sections of the country. These youngsters were mostly sons of immigrants without a long tradition of higher education. They were seeking higher education mostly with the hope of entering one of the professions or of achieving higher success in the business world.

In 1909 Father John Cavanaugh had been superior of the University as well as its president for four years and was really the active head of the Notre Dame family, quite well acquainted with its students. He was a tall, stately, yet friendly priest with light complexion, a round smiling face, and large blue eyes. He had a soft, full voice and a command of language that included more than one tinted adjective. All decisions not reserved to the provincial were made by him—a standing tradition about superiors at Notre Dame dating from Father Sorin, the founder. Once he made his decision the details would be carried out by some lesser person, such as the tall, erect Father Matthew Walsh, the vice-president, or by the secretary, ascetic-looking Brother Alban Faherty (in financial matters); or by the director of studies, another tall, gracious priest, Father Matthew Schumacher (in matters of classes); or by the prefect of discipline, at that time young, handsome Timothy Murphy (in matters of discipline or student welfare). Most of this official family lived together in the Main Building, took their meals and recreation together, and said their community prayers together in the basement of the church.

College life for John O'Hara began with the handicaps involved in his residing off the campus. But he seemed to be taking everything in stride when he wrote to his folks on January 15:

For exercise we have been walking the distance of 31 blocks every morning and evening. We have to get a rather early start as we have to be at the College at 7:15 for breakfast, but we can manage by getting up about six. It takes us about 34 minutes to make the walk. It certainly is doing us a lot of good. I know that I, personally, must have gained five pounds in my eleven days here, judging from the fullness of my cheeks, and I know that Tully has improved a lot.

It surely has been cold here, even though the weather has, on the whole, been delightful. We made the walk the other morning with the thermometer registering six below zero.

In class my work is going along fine. I have German, Latin, English, Greek History and Elocution to recite and two classes, one Spanish-English and the other English-Spanish, to teach. I am getting along very well with it all, and have the best classes you ever saw to teach. I give them plenty of work to do and introduce some novelty or other every few days to hold their attention a little more. They are like first grade kids for stories and will know as much about South America as they will about Spanish before I get through with them.

I have Freshman standing in the College, that is, I have entered with the graduating class of 1912. It was very good of them to put me that far along, I thought.[20]

John O'Hara's South American schooling did not fit directly into the Notre Dame program. Not having any Greek, he was automatically shifted from the Bachelor of Arts course to the program leading to a Bachelor of Philosophy in Economics and History. He was given credit for his unusual proficiency in languages, for his knowledge of Latin American history, and for the philosophy and science courses he had taken in Montevideo. To prepare for the degree in economics and history during his two-and-one-half years, he took courses in political science, public finance, and the history of economic thought. He took the regular courses in English and elocution. As was the custom, there is no record of the teachers of these classes either in the catalogue or on the student's record. But there is some evidence that he had direct experience with a distinguished visiting Professor of English, Father John Talbot Smith, whose lectures he summarized in the school paper, the *Scholastic,* and whom he quoted in his aspersions on modern American literature in later life.

Granting that his scholastic record was incomplete, John F. O'Hara seemed to have taken little Latin, although the only financial record for him at this time was a charge for a copy of Sallust. His credit for English history was obtained by special examination. Apparently the maturity of the young man was so evident to the Notre Dame faculty that they did not question the credits he earned in Latin America. More than that, the few letters that remain of his correspondence with Father Cavanaugh at this time indicate that the President treated him more as a young friend than as a pupil. Also, in addition to his teaching he prepared a Spanish translation of the University Catalogue for distribution in Latin lands.

Of one social affair that he did not enjoy, he wrote on February 15. He spoke of returning to the Tongs's after a play rehearsal.

I returned at about 9:30 and found a small crowd whom they had invited in. I'll be darned! I never did see such a stupid bunch! One was the most popular debutante of the season and another was last year's debutante, but they surely disgusted both John Tully and me. I was sorry to disappoint Miss Tong, who thought she was doing us a favor, but I was very frank when she accused me, and she said she wouldn't invite any one else in. They certainly do treat us fine though and so I knew that I would not offend them.[21]

Soon it was examination time, and on February 25 he predicted:

. . . We have examinations from now on. I give one in Spanish on Friday and one on Saturday. I don't want to flunk anybody, but I think I will have to flunk at least one member of the class. He seems to be a particular friend of mine, but that makes not any difference. The examination is going to be rather hard, but they are pretty well prepared for it.[22]

Among his close friends were, besides John Tully, Paul Rush, Leo Clary, and Earl Dickens. His letters scarcely mention his class work. The Tong family apparently took the youngsters into their own family circle, but most of their recreations were with the students. Through the politics of John Tully, John O'Hara was elected toastmaster for the freshman dinner to be held on St. Patrick's Day, and he told his family: "It kind of makes a fellow feel good to think that somebody else thinks enough of him to take some notice of him on such short order scarcely two months at the University."

Like most new students John awaited the results of his first examinations. He wrote:

We had our examinations last week, and even the shouting is over now. I got through everything, and in Latin, the only subject that I was afraid of, I got the second highest grade, 95. I haven't heard my grades in the other subjects yet. In my classes, the results were more than satisfactory. Out of thirty men, 6 got 100—4 in the American class, and 2 in the Mexican. . . .[23]

He also told the family that his "Argentine Story" had been recommended by Father Carrico, the editor of the *Scholastic*, for inclusion in that publication, and in the March 13 issue appeared a story by him entitled "The Firing of the Fort" with an Argentine setting. He told his father, "You know Father Carrico put a ban on love stories, so I had to change the second part." The father had returned from Brazil for a visit and took the opportunity to visit young John during the first week of April.

As the end of the year approached, John began to plan his summer and his future attendance at Notre Dame. On May 18 he wrote to his father of his plans:

Everything here is the same as ever. Father Cavanaugh called me in this morning and told me that he would give me a room here next year, and that he would make any kind of arrangement that I liked as to my classes, so I intend to take on three classes, and make $200 on the side to pay my extra expenses. I think that I will spend the summer in some kind of hard manual labor, as it is what I need more than anything else, and I will not be running up any expenses in that way. Father Cavanaugh told me a few days ago that he wanted to see me before I perfected my plans for the summer, and I think he may want me to teach up at the Summer School at San Jose lake, near Lawton, Michigan. There will be a splendid chance for plenty of outdoor exercise—boating, fishing, and the like—up there, and if the offer looks all right, I may accept it. . . .[24]

Apparently the proposed summer at San Jose Park was not offered. Instead John returned to the family home at 3156 North Illinois, Indianapolis, and a less romantic series of experiences.

In the remaining weeks of school John again made the pages of the *Scholastic* on May 22, this time with an essay entitled "Modern Spanish Literature," in which he included recognition of some writers of South America, especially Juan Zorilla de San Martin of Uruguay. The issue of May 29 contained an editorial by him on the lectures of Father John Talbot Smith, but a reader of this essay might wonder if Father Smith had moralized as much as the commentator. John wrote: "He warned his hearers against the critics and 'long-haired people,' he shattered popular idols, he opposed the shameless methods of publishers and press agencies and gave a clear exposition of the forces which have caused the latter-day decadence in literature. The thesis of the series was the struggle between Christian principles and Neo-Paganism in the field of letters. . . ." The conclusion of the essay was equally sombre. "A series of lectures such as this should be a great power for good. In this day of sordid subservience to the publisher and the critic, it is refreshing to hear a courageous defense of truth. . . ." The June 5 issue added the name of John F. O'Hara to the masthead of the editorial staff.

This new Notre Dame student and teacher spent the summer weeks at home doing an occasional bit of translating for business firms and newspapers and enjoying the companionship of his

father, whose ill-health had caused him to resign from his consulship and return to Indianapolis. John wrote frequently to the new
friends he had met at the college, including Father Cavanaugh.
He had so many commitments at the end of summer that he asked
Father Cavanaugh if he might delay his return from September
10, the opening of the high school, until September 12, the opening of the College. Although he returned as a sophomore, sometime during the fall he was advanced to the rank of junior. Since
he was registered as a candidate for the degree in economics and
history, his program was considerably different from that of a
seminarian, not only in the absence of Greek and Latin, but in
the inclusion of more courses in economics and political science.
Apparently he did not regard the classical program as in any way
essential to his priestly vocation, an opinion he retained as a
priest. He manifested a serious interest in literature and history
and in writing for publication. In this last trait he was following
in the footsteps of his parents both of whom wrote well. Of his
reading during this period we know little except that his comments on the lectures of Father Smith indicated that he was reading in the field of English literature.

In group photographs of the Knights of Columbus and of the
Indiana Club, John O'Hara was a rather tall, thin young man. He
wore a fashionable coat with pleats and an unusually high collar.
His face was a bit fuller than in later life, but he had prominent
cheek bones. His forehead was high, and his hair was parted on
the left. His ears seemed large and rather noticeable as he leaned
forward in the photographs as if to portray animation. His activities were those of a good healthy student and included interhall
track competition, oratory, debating, and writing for the *Scholastic*. He became the Notre Dame representative in the Inter-State
Oratory Association, representing the University at the state meeting in Indianapolis and later at the interstate meeting at Creighton University. He did not have the physique for football but
joined in the fervor of the student body in rooting for the team
and admitted years later of making his way to Ann Arbor that
famous day Notre Dame defeated Michigan, then called the
Champions of the West.

Probably the best indications of his intellectual development
were his contributions to the *Scholastic*. In the October 16 issue he
gave a soft defense of the *mañana* spirit of the lands of the South
under the title "Practical South America." He praised the local
governments of Latin America, preferring their commissioners to
American aldermen. He did not approve of racial equality as

attempted in Brazil. He wrote the year's article on the great football team and another article for the Christmas number entitled "Christmas under Southern Skies."

An article in the February 5 issue was a fair indication that he had been deeply impressed with South America during his year there. The article entitled "Enlightened South America" probably was a comparison between the state universities of Uruguay and the Jesuit schools. In the state university he found that "the classes in history, philosophy, literature, and political science are as a rule hotbeds of anarchy and immorality. . . ." In contrast he praised the schools conducted by religious. "They have labored under untold difficulties and have been hindered at every step. Their classical courses have always been in accordance with their lofty aesthetic ideals of culture, been standards of excellence, and what is more remarkable, their courses in mathematics and the sciences have been surprisingly good. . . ." In another article about an Irish leader in Argentina he gave a brief account of the Mission of St. Patrick at Mercedes, where he had lived for a short time. His other contributions were the usual efforts of an articulate young college student. He probably composed during the late spring an essay published in the August issue of the *Scholastic* on the lectures of Father John Talbot Smith in American literature. Evidently John O'Hara felt that American literature had not accomplished much, even in the writings of Ralph Waldo Emerson.

For John O'Hara the summer of 1910 seems to have been much like that of 1909 except for a trip undertaken at the request of Father Cavanaugh at the end of the summer to meet some prospective Notre Dame students from South America. He made some occasional contributions to Indianapolis newspapers and prepared some translations. For recreation he visited Peru and Kokomo to visit relatives and in June assisted at the First Solemn Mass of Father Charles O'Donnell, C.S.C, at Saint Patrick's Church in Kokomo. His return to Notre Dame in September was that of a confirmed Notre Dame man.

There were many reasons why Notre Dame in 1910 was one large family. Most of the priests came in frequent contact with the students. The students knew each other, and South Bend in the day of the horse and buggy and the Hill Street trolley was a good two miles away. Walking to town was then more of an accepted thing, and the University's published regulations called for actual permission to leave the campus. The common dining halls, the common recreation halls, interhall contests in football,

baseball, and track, and the frequent debates and dramatic productions took the place of more widespread recreations that were
later to take the students so frequently to South Bend. The
alumni say they did not have extra money to spend in South
Bend. Father John Cavanaugh, the president of the college, was
personally acquainted with many of the students and chatted with
them frequently in recreations. He was witty, cultivated, and
possessed dulcet tones and a flowery vocabulary. Notre Dame was
known throughout Catholic America as Father Cavanaugh's
Notre Dame. Morning prayer and night prayer in common were
required along with Saturday and Sunday Mass and even Sunday vespers. A very important item in the lecture series was the
illustrated travelogues of E. M. Newman about the various distant nations of the world. Thomas A. Daly and James J. Walsh
came regularly, as well as did Father John Talbot Smith.

One letter of John O'Hara to his friend and schoolmate of
Montevideo, Alexander Schroeder, on September 9, 1910, gives
some evidence of his thinking at that time. His opinion of the
medical profession seems to indicate his inclination towards the
priesthood.

Dear Alexander:
You already know that the streets of hell could be paved with my
good intentions, but finally I am going to write you so as to calm my
conscience. I received your last letter several months ago, but they have
been tremendous months. I am really working like a donkey, and am
not quiet even for a minute. By the postcards that you probably received I suppose you know that I don't stay in the same place for much
time either. I have so many letters to write, so much work and so many
classes that I don't find time for anything.

I wrote to Manuel some time ago. I believe I hadn't answered him
for over a year. Your letters require more time than the others and
for that reason they are less frequent. Today I'm in my dad's office
and, although I'm leaving for the University tomorrow, I can rest now
and take advantage of the time in order to write you. Yesterday I
returned from Canada, Notre Dame, Buffalo and New York, which I
had visited during the past two weeks. I'm tired from traveling so much
by train—some 4,000 kilometers—and I need to rest up a bit before
going back to Notre Dame. Classes start on the 12th and I'm going to
be there by Sunday the 11th. From the looks of things the University is
going to be larger than ever. I believe there are more South Americans
too, but so far I haven't seen any Uruguayan matriculated. It's a pity
that so many go to Europe and to other countries to study and none of
them come to the greatest Catholic university in all America. I was
hoping that you would come, but from what you tell me in your last

letter there is no hope. And you don't tell me when you are coming to visit me either. The other day I was in New York. I came across six priests with whom I had lived in Argentina—Fathers from the Church of Lourdes in Montevideo. Everywhere I see adopted Uruguayans, but up to now I haven't found any native son nor any of my classmates from the Seminary. You people shouldn't delay in coming, my friend, because the best time to take advantage of such a trip is when one is still young.

How are the priests from the Seminary? I have wanted to write them, but I have never found enough free time. Recently I visited three of our principal universities here. Last November I visited the University of Marquette in Milwaukee. In May I was in Omaha, state of Nebraska, and there I became acquainted with Creighton University, and recently I visited that of Fordham in New York. All are good schools and in all of them they received me very well when I told them that I had studied with the Jesuits in Montevideo and that I was now at Notre Dame. They have some twenty universities and several colleges in the United States.

How do you like the study of medicine? By this time you ought to know how you are going to like it. For my part, it's the most horrible study imaginable. But—speaking only in the physical sense—at the same time the doctor has more of an opportunity to help poor humanity than any one else. A doctor is well acquainted with human misery, he sees the effects of sin, and that it profits a man nothing if he gains the whole world and loses his soul.[25]

When John returned to Notre Dame in September, 1910, he was a senior. There is no indication in his records what teachers he had in his final year. Fathers Charles O'Donnell and Patrick Carroll were teaching English, Father Thomas Crumley—for the students the deepest thinker of them all—taught philosophy, and Father Matthew Walsh taught history. The *Scholastic* indicated that the program for the degree of economics and history was drawing a large number of students. Undoubtedly John's experience in the consul offices of Montevideo and Santos and the associations with his father gave him a background for the study of economics and political science. And the influence of Brother Cyprian O'Hara, C.S.C., in accounting may have had some influence in making him statistically minded in later life.

Again his work on the *Scholastic* was the chief index to his intellectual activities. His unsung attainments seem to have been chiefly those of the witty editor of the "Stub" and "The Safety Valve," although sometimes he signed his initials to light verses and sardonic remarks. His verses were correct in meter but not deeply emotional, except for a couple of quatrains. The short stories and even some of his verse were a bit sombre in tone, and romance was notably lacking. Probably he was drawn into historical essays in search of suitable subjects for writing. His bachelor thesis was the first manifestation of his deep interest in economic problems.

In his letter of January 19 he listed the usual midwinter illnesses and added his plans for the rest of the year.

But that's enough for colds and sicknesses. Everything here is the same as usual, and I have outlined my work for the rest of the year so that if any extra time remains I may use it to advantage. If I can spare the time I am going to teach an extra class for the rest of the year instead of taking up newspaper work. I like it much better and there is assurance in it that is not met with in newspaper work, for you don't have to be on the lookout for news, and knowing what time has to be given to the work each day, you can dispose of the rest of your time accordingly. I have four subjects to finish by June, and a thesis to write, and if I can arrange one of them on the side I will have time for an extra class. I am doing nothing on either the *Scholastic* or the *Dome,* and making all my study time count for something.[26]

Apparently the resolution about the *Scholastic* did not exclude contributions because his writings appeared regularly. There was an essay on "The Drama of Calderon," in which he quoted often in translation and once in Spanish, and a verse, "Abandonment," about Christ on the cross. One phrase in this, "sin-choked," indicated a bad reaching for words. In a sombre bit of verse in April entitled "Anchored" he spoke of youth being anchored in lust, although two other bits of verse "The Lily of the Valley" and "Children of the Stars" were sprightly and filled with shining imagery. Besides the formal photograph of the graduating seniors there was in the *Dome* an informal snapshot of young John O'Hara lying on top of a student bed in Sorin Hall with his head propped up and corncob pipe in his mouth. That the commencement exercises and the reception of the degree of Bachelor of Philosophy in Economics and History made any great impression on him there is no evidence. The family and friends have retained no letters from him at this time, and nothing that he did attracted any mention in the commencement *Scholastic.*

The question naturally arises at this stage about John F. O'Hara's plans for becoming a priest. He apparently had not changed his ultimate plans, but there are no letters indicating his immediate plans except that he had been invited back to Notre Dame to teach. Apparently there was little difference between this summer of 1911 and that of 1910. In his plans for returning there was some understanding whereby his brother Bob also would enter Notre Dame. If there was a written agreement between him and the University, it has not been preserved.

When he returned to Notre Dame in September, he was given a room in Old College, the old square brick building near the lake that had once been the first college building of Notre Dame. It had served many purposes, and this year was turned over to some lay professors. There, apparently for the first time, John met another resident of Indianapolis, short, sturdy, broad-shouldered, Thomas Steiner. His serious mien was set off by his blond hair, blue eyes, and soft smile. He was a Notre Dame alumnus who had received his degree in Civil Engineering in 1899 and had been working as a civil engineer on the Big Four Railroad. Tom Steiner had written to Father Cavanaugh in April, 1911, that after sixteen years as an engineer he had decided to enter a seminary but had found that he was deficient in knowledge of Latin. He asked to return to Notre Dame to take classes in Latin and English so that he could qualify for entrance into a seminary, probably St. Paul Seminary in Minnesota where he had been rejected because of his linguistic deficiencies. Father Cavanaugh had invited him back and had suggested that he teach some classes in mathematics on the side to pay his expenses. Tom was the assistant engineer on the Big Four and had difficulty obtaining his release just in time to start classes in September.[27]

Of the many traditions of the lay teachers in Old College, that about the association of these two future priests is the most frequently repeated. There are no actual records of the hours these two spent in conversation, but at this time neither seemed ready to join the Congregation of Holy Cross. Later, when John decided to enter the Novitiate of Holy Cross, he urged Tom to join him, but Tom was not ready to go. Yet he did follow him later to Holy Cross, to the novitiate, to Washington, and back to Notre Dame. Their great collaboration was to be as fellow priests and educators, and tireless promoters of frequent Holy Communion. They had come to the seminary as older and matured men; they were selfless and hard workers. But in Old College they were the envy of those students living in the ordinary dormitories. The hall was designated in the 1912 *Dome* as "The Palace of the Muckraker, the *Dome* and the periodical profs; answers to 3826 many times, when She's call He's."

John O'Hara's bachelor essay was published in the *Scholastic* that fall, but there was little else to indicate that the busy teacher was at Notre Dame until his father came to visit the University in the spring. On March 26 the senior O'Hara gave a talk in Washington Hall on "Our South American Relations," which the campus reporter said corrected many false impressions about the countries of which he spoke. The aftermath of that visit John described for the folks in Indianapolis.

Sister Gertrude made all her boys write a summary of Papa's lecture, and send it home to the folks. She said the boys did very well at it, too. I found out later that on the afternoon of the talk in Washington Hall the whole stage was filled with sisters, who heard the lecture behind the scenes. They all wanted to send their Easter greetings.

Bob and I are finding it just a little bit hard to live down our Father's reputation here. I asked them in History class what seemed to be the chief trouble with Cromwell's son, and somebody said that he was not the man that his father was; and all laughed as if they had something on me.[28]

John did not record his thinking about the community or his family during this year of teaching. He did join in an early Mass and Communion service in the Brownson Chapel. There also appeared over his name some verses in the March and September issues of *Rosary Magazine* and a long essay on South America under the title "South America—What Ails It?" At the end of the school year he apparently returned to Indianapolis to visit his folks and also Grandmother Thornton in Kokomo and other relatives in Indiana and Illinois before going to the novitiate. The official record in Saint Joseph Novitiate, across the lake from the University, said:

On August 15, 1912, the feast of the Assumption of the Blessed Virgin, the cassock was conferred on John O'Hara. The ceremony took place in the chapel of St. Joseph's novitiate, in the presence of the members, Rev. W. R. Connor, C.S.C., Master of Novices presiding.

Witnesses   (signed) Brother Joachim, C.S.C.
(Signed by) John O'Hara (signed) Reverend W. R. Connor, C.S.C.[29]

Of the other novices at that time, the novitiate record speaks of Mr. Christopher Brooks and five brothers receiving the habit on July 5, 1912. Presumably John O'Hara and Christopher Brooks were the only clerical novices of that year.

Of Brother Joachim Polman, the assistant master of novices, a tall, dark, thin man of small head and pointed chin and nose who spoke imperfect English, there are traditions of a man who was heroic in sanctity and humble piety. A native of the Netherlands, he had the patience and skill common to the European apprentice farmer. Of his farming skill in caring for the novitiate plot of

about ten acres there was good evidence in a novitiate table filled
with plenty of good food and some rarities such as honey, straw-
berries, melons, as well as most vegetables that could be grown
in northern Indiana.

But the great personality of the novitiate was the master of
novices, Father William R. Connor, called "Pop" with great
affection by all the priests who knew him. He was a kind of
plump, cherubic figure with puffed cheeks of ruddy hue, bright
and smiling eyes behind rimless glasses. He had few hairs, but
these were well combed across his head to give a semblance of
cover. He never seemed disturbed. Some knew him only as the
perennial master of ceremonies at the solemn and episcopal ceremonies in Sacred Heart Church. But he seemed to have just the
right kindly humor and moral strength to qualify him as the
custodian of the spirit of the Congregation of Holy Cross in the
United States, for as master of novices he was just that for over
twenty-five years. He had understanding but no tolerance for those
extremes of piety which embarrass the hard worker in the Lord's
vineyard, but he could insist on the clear and exact fulfillment
of the rule. His novices had to be correct and endowed with solid
virtue.

Under the direction of Father Connor, John O'Hara was to
spend a complete year in the novitiate in systematic practice of
the religious life, in self-analysis, and under instruction on the
vows of poverty, chastity, and obedience which he would take at
the end of his second year of training, although the second year
was to be spent in another house of the community, in this
instance, Holy Cross College, Washington. The novices supplied
the manual power for the farm and the maintenance of the house.

The novice's letters to his family were filled with pleasant
chatter about the insignificant things that make up a novice's
day, including comments about the absence of Father Connor for
a week, attendance at Mass on the occasion of the visit of the
Apostolic Delegate, Sebastian Martinelli—at which he carried
the Archbishop's mitre—his frequent visitors from the college and
his singing a solo at the *Credo* of the Christmas Mass. He also
told of novitiate baseball.

You can hardly imagine me suffering from baseball injuries, but such
is the case. Besides a painful lack of elasticity in the joints and splices,
I have had one or two less painful bumps. I was explaining in my usual
dialect to a friend of mine from over the water that the ball should
go over the plate between the knee and the shoulder, and he did it

when my back was turned, and I was standing directly over the plate. But pshaw, it is nothing, for I have not lost my appetite.[30]

His letters do not speak of his interior thoughts. He was older than most novices—May 1 was his twenty-fifth birthday—more experienced, and more set in his notions of religious service.

One incident of this quiet year was enough to shatter the recollection of months. The *South Bend Tribune* account was correct in most details:

The novitate at Notre Dame University burned to the ground Saturday evening entailing a loss of $50,000. The fire was discovered about 6:15 in the northeast corner of the roof. At this time the novitiates [*sic*] were at supper, and it is probably for that reason that the building had been burning for some time without having been discovered.

The South Bend fire department was called, the central ladder truck, the chemical, No. 7, and 3 hose companies with 25 firemen under the direction of Chief Grant fighting valiantly to save what they could. Before the arrival everything possible had been removed from the building by the students and priests. By stretching hose across the lake for a distance of 4,000 feet, a stream of water was directed on the northeast wing which had remained intact. . . . The origin of the fire is a mystery. It was discovered at 6:10 by one of the novices, John O'Hara. Warning the other novices who were at supper, he ran to the infirmary where the alarm was given. . . . The novices have been temporarily housed in an out standing building, Rev. Father Conner [*sic*], the Rector, having his quarters in the bee house. The kitchen and the dining room were saved and with these intact the young men will go ahead with their work without being interrupted by the disaster.

There are many traditions about the fire. Father Christopher Brooks recalled that the fire was discovered by John O'Hara at 5:45 and that the novices got no supper that night. Writing to his folks a week later, John gave a humorous account of the fire.

. . . It is sufficient to say that the only home I have had for the last week has been the long bee-house, and that the other novices are enjoying like camping quarters. The fire which started in the roof at six o'clock, had destroyed everything but the kitchen by nine, and left the walls standing as a perfect shell. You could hardly imagine anything neater. The ivy on part of the building was hardly scorched, and the yellow walls were blackened in only two or three places, and yet it was one of the hottest and fiercest fires they have ever seen hereabouts. We have established temporary quarters in the little buildings on the grounds, and we will probably put in the summer in the perfect enjoyment of this outdoor life. The lawns are not a bit soiled at all, and the garden is in perfect condition. We missed only one meal here and really things are going on about as usual, in spite of the fact that we have no home.

Did I lose anything? Really I had presence of mind to keep my clothes on, or probably would have lost them. If you have tears, prepare to shed them now. That beautiful handbag is no more. John Tully was on hand to weep over it that night. I lost my trunk and suitcase, and everything in them; and in spite of that I have saved quite enough to get along on. I miss my books as much as anything. I was sorry to lose all my Spanish books and my Economics library, and my Tom Daly, but I have laughed more than I have cried over it. . . .[31]

In speaking of the new house to be built he noted that he would not be around to enjoy it, for his year would be over. He added:

I am getting along very nicely and I don't need a thing. I have enough clothes to go downtown, and I braved a tag day to go down yesterday to get my glasses fixed. Yes, spectacles. I broke them the second day I had them, so I can't tell just how much relief they are going to give me from my standing headaches . . ."

By August 15 John had completed his year in the novitiate and was sent on to Holy Cross College in Washington to spend his second year of novitiate and to begin his theological studies. But before he went to Washington he enjoyed a brief vacation with his folks in Indianapolis, including a visit with his grandmother in Kokomo and other relatives in Tipton and Peru.

The Chronicles of Holy Cross College in the Brookland suburb of Washington, D.C., say that Mr. John F. O'Hara, C.S.C., arrived there September 13, 1913. Holy Cross College was a large Indiana-limestone building of classical Corinthian style, trimmed in Vermont granite and standing on a hill overlooking The Catholic University of America. There, John would change from the single-purposed existence of the novitiate to the more complex discipline and work of a theological seminary, although the general plan of life was to be much the same as in the novitiate, with a substitution of intellectual work for manual labor, and the study of theological science for the classes in the religious life.

Heading the faculty of Holy Cross College as superior and also as professor of moral theology was Father James A. Burns, then forty-six years old, a tall, thin, dark-haired scholar with a rather small head, with thin lips, a small pointed nose and small ears, who wore pince-nez glasses with a string attached. There seemed to be a knowing smile playing about his eyes. His voice was a bit nasal, but he was a past master at intimate conversation. Undoubtedly Father Burns was already well informed about the young novice arriving from Notre Dame. The friendship now formed between these two men was to become intimate and continuous until the death of Father Burns in 1941. Later John

O'Hara credited Father Burns with what he knew about education. Father Burns, the historian of Catholic education in the United States, was also learned in the techniques of higher education, and the quiet composure of this priest gave little warning of the keenness of mind and real zeal for progress that enabled him to be a force in the early National Catholic Education Association, a promoter of the central Catholic high school, and an advocate of reform of the old classical program in the Catholic college.

Father Burns was a good teacher, not given to flights of fancy, but one whose students received clear information on the subject of his lectures. He was very conscientious about the formation of these young theologians into priests. His discipline was rather strict, and his insistence on cleanliness and orderliness was unrelenting. He taught many subjects at times during his superiorship, and in 1913 he was teaching moral theology. In 1913 Father George Sauvage, C.S.C., a brilliant Frenchman, driven into exile by French laws against religious, was teaching dogmatic theology. He was a capable student of contemporary French philosophy, whose theology students felt the inspiration of his thoughts while suffering from his inability to place properly the accents of his English words. Young Father Louis Kelley, C.S.C., had returned from Rome to teach moral and later dogmatic theology when Father Sauvage joined the French Army in 1914. Father John M. Ryan, C.S.C, tried, with the usual lack of student cooperation, to teach church history. Brilliant young Father Eugene Burke, witty and literarily solvent, taught Holy Scripture at a time when modern exegesis was making its first mark at The Catholic University. Teaching canon law and liturgy was another French exile, the sparkling, almost ecstatic, Father John B. Delaunay, C.S.C. Father Delaunay had finished his theological studies at eighteen and finally, by dispensation, was ordained at twenty-two. He stuttered slightly, as if his many brilliant thoughts were too numerous to find expression. Together this was, indeed, a remarkable theological staff, scarcely equalled in any theological school in the country. Father John A. Zahm, C.S.C, the ex-provincial of the Indiana Province, lived across town at Dunbarton Academy, but he was in some respects a part of the faculty and on occasion an important inspiration to the young scholars. To John O'Hara Father Zahm was of added interest because of his travels to South America with ex-President Theodore Roosevelt and because of his books about his trips to the countries to the south.

John O'Hara now became for the first time just another seminarian in a house where no class marks were given out to prevent rivalries that might disturb the community spirit. His actual marks were high, but the records show very few low marks given to anyone. For the most part the lecture system was used in teaching, but when the teachers sought confirmation of facts from the students, Mr. O'Hara was usually ready with good answers. There were public disputations every few weeks and written examinations before Christmas, in March, and at the end of the year. John found the course of studies difficult at first and had to spend all his spare time at his books. There were compulsory recreation periods, and the students had to visit the public places of Washington at least once a week. John visited the Pan American Building once a week and there occasionally met persons he knew in South America. He also visited the Senate and House galleries, watched the Supreme Court, surveyed the museums and art galleries, and occasionally went to the offices of friends of his father in the legations.

He began to have new trouble with his eyes. Writing to the folks on December 21 he said, "My eyes are still very bad and I can't do much writing. I have new glasses but the exams were too much of a strain at the start I am afraid. An hour a day is as much as I should use my eyes right now." Later, on June 4, he noted: "My eyes are still pretty bad. If they hold out two weeks more I will be able to give them a good rest." The low level and damp climate of the District of Columbia apparently also revived trouble in his sinuses, with which he had been afflicted in South America.

The students of Holy Cross College had a traditional task of teaching Christian Doctrine to the Catholic boys in the National Training School just outside of Washington. John was assigned to the visiting group and wrote much of his experiences there to his folks.

I haven't been downtown this week, so I haven't seen either Moran or Haltigan. I called the mother of the boy and asked her to take up the matter of a pardon at once, and she promised to take care of it. My hands are pretty well tied by our position out there: if the management knew we were trying to steal their boys from them there might be an Irish row. But I think it is safe enough the way things are going, and as Haltigan is a great friend of the family he will do what he can, I am sure. Young Emmett Haltigan has been pushing the matter with the boy's family for some time. . . . I was cruel enough to give Bess's letter to McIntyre—after correcting it (merely changing a letter to make it read "now and then" instead of "now and them"—the first meaning was probably intended). His name is Walter. Bess always did like that name. He is doing as well as could be expected—which is pretty good for a convict.

Another interesting case showed up the other day. We have one wild man out there, about thirteen or fourteen, who is serving his second term (four years so far) for carrying concealed weapons, etc. He came around about six weeks ago with a request for prayers for conversion and wanted an extra prayer book "for a boy over in the family." The next Sunday he was raising cain because the "man over in the family" wouldn't letter [sic] the boy in the family come over. I sat all over him and told him that if he wanted to save the kid's soul he'd have to mend his own ways—that he'd be sending him to hell in the meantime by his example. He said he was saying three Hail Marys eight times or something to that effect, and then he said he was going to teach him Catechism out in the yard. Last Sunday he came around and said it was all right now; he got the boy to write home, and he now had a letter giving him permission to take instructions. Now that he had landed his man I suppose we will have to fire him to prevent his spoiling the neophyte by his heathenism.

A little fellow handed me an awful one last Sunday. He had run away the week before and I was kidding him about it. Then he changed the subject. He said: "Say: I got the funniest thing right inside of me heah. Ma hea't jes gives (rattle the bones please) like that then she stops and do' go no mah; then she gives a big jump an' a lot o' little jumps, jes like that." I leaned over as far as my knees and whispered into his ear. "Chile, you'se sure got tobacco hea't; yo' got to quit chewing" (age 9 years). He said: "Is that what does it?" I says: "It shore is." He says: "Did it ever get you'all that way."[32]

Grandmother Thornton died in Kokomo on March 15, 1914, at the age of seventy-seven, the last of the near relatives who had been born in Ireland. John was not permitted to attend the funeral, but he received promises of Masses for her from the superiors, including Father John Cavanaugh. Father Cavanaugh also sent him the *Scholastic* and the issue of the *Republic* that announced the awarding of the Laetare Medal of that year to Chief Justice Edward White. As June approached, John joined the seminarians in planning the summer vacation at camp.

As had been the custom at Holy Cross for several years, the students of the College set up their camp near Charles Town, West Virginia. They lived in a large tent, usually cut their hair short and let their beards grow, and, outside of essential religious duties and some study of languages, spent most of the time in physical exercise. Father Sauvage boasted that he had convinced Father Burns that this summer camp was essential for the intellectual as well as the physical welfare of the seminarians. The camp meals were "alfresco," and the chef was traditionally a Negro cook from a Washington restaurant. In a letter of July 16 John described the camp for his folks:

. . . We are well situated here on a flat shelf along the Shenandoah, with the Blue Ridge up behind us, and a sulphur spring on the grounds. I think the water has been a little too much for me. I got sick yesterday up in the mountains, but I am feeling much better today. We walked 25 miles yesterday. I don't intend to do it again.

The men are cleaning two 5 lb. carps for dinner today, and tomorrow (Friday) we will make away with a 14 lb. one. The fellows who like such sport are having pretty fair luck.[33]

The summer was rather uneventful. He did note that his eyes were better but that he was doing very little reading. The camp closed and the seminarians returned to Washington the first week of September.

By this time John O'Hara had more than completed his second year of the novitiate, and he made his profession of the simple vows of poverty, chastity, and obedience in the Holy Cross Chapel on September 14. The next day he acknowledged the congratulations of Father Cavanaugh on this accomplishment. Father Cavanaugh had also announced that he would give the sermon at the annual Pan American Mass at St. Patrick's Church in Washington at Thanksgiving.

Dear Father:
Your message brimful of your own affectionate self came to crown "the happiest day." Many thanks to all of you.

I didn't realize until it was all over what a difference it could make, and I suppose I haven't begun to fathom it yet. The "center plum" seems to have come in the first twenty four hours.

Classes began this morning, but they haven't proved to be any distraction yet: One of these days the world will start moving again, I suppose, but I will always have a wonderful sensation to look back to.

We will be marking time from now until Thanksgiving, and of course you realize that a good football season will speed the day wonderfully for us. You may not appreciate this way of leading up to a climax, but when a Notre Dame football team and a Pan-American sermon come together within our partisan perspective, all sense of proportion is destroyed.

I said goodbye to you just a year and seven days ago, so you can't blame me for being anxious to see you. Take good care of yourself now, because this will have to be the big triumph.[34]

Early in October John went to another oculist, who changed his glasses for some improvement in the condition of his eyes.

However, he had to continue going to the doctor because the eyes were still inflamed. On November 24 he reported: "About the eyes: I have had relief for the past few days—the first in practically a year. I had the glasses changed again and the doctor seems to have reached the astigmatism at least. I have been taking treatment for conjunctivitis right along, but it is of no use as long as the cause of the trouble remained. I am not going to use the eyes more than is necessary, and I am hoping for a permanent cure this time."

In his letters home he spoke of a friendship with a fellow theological student whose health was failing, Mr. Joseph Quinlan. John apparently spent much of his recreation time attending this young victim of tuberculosis. In a letter of October 25 he spoke of their conversations about Father Zahm's books that Quinlan had been reading. But there was a sad conclusion to this episode. John wrote on December 20:

We had a funeral Thursday, as you may have seen in the paper. The first one ever held in this house. Poor Joe Quinlan, Father Quinlan's brother and Sister Al's nephew, died here last Tuesday and was buried at Notre Dame Friday, the very day set for his ordination by Bishop Shahan. It was a pity to see the poor boy go, but he was so well prepared and so willing that I can't have any regrets. He was a very good friend of mine, and towards the end he wanted me to do for him everything that anyone had to do. I was writing letters for him getting ready for the ordination, and I stayed up with him all the last night before he died.[35]

Apparently the death just before the holidays put a damper on the Christmas festivities. Twice in his post-Christmas letter he said that their celebrations were quiet. Otherwise his letters spoke simply of his continued activities at the reform school and of his singing with the choir at St. Patrick's parish.

His letters home continued to manifest an interest in family affairs, but added that he had had a cold. He also continued to look up friends of his father in Washington. One enclosure of his letters was a letter from Father George Sauvage, who was acting as an interpreter for the English army, and another was a list of some youngsters in the reform school, although he implied that he no longer went there.

There seemed to be more to John's health problems than he admitted. At least when Father Cavanaugh came to Washington, he persuaded Father Burns to allow John to go with him by boat to New York to consult a specialist, Dr. Francis J. Quinlan. John mentioned the matter rather casually in a letter of May 11.

My time is very limited now until next time for news about the trip. The *raison d'etre* was that Father C. didn't like the looks of my eyes and wanted me to rest them on the ocean as his guest. In New York I saw Dr. Quinlan the great nose etc. specialist, and he told me that very likely the trouble was nasal—there was an enlargement of a couple of ridges in the nose causing too much pressure against the base of the brain. He advised an operation, and I will probably have it performed this week. It is a very simple thing; I will not even have to go to the hospital for it. The specialist here seems to agree with Dr. Quinlan that there is a 50% chance that it is this that is causing all the pain and that the eyes themselves are not bad at all.[36]

He added on May 20:

The operation is progressing well enough, I guess, but it seems to take a lot of time. It is a simple displacement of a catarrhal growth in the nose. It doesn't pain me any, so I shouldn't kick if it cures the eyes.

But he continued to have minor troubles, eye trouble, headaches, boils, or the like.

The doctor is through with his operating and has only one more treatment to give. He says that the thing came out very well, and I am willing to believe this, because I have had more relief since the latter part of the week than I have had in years before. I still have serious pains at times, but they are neither regular nor constant, and the doctor says they are to be expected for a while yet. I am convinced that he found the seat of the trouble, because I can now distinguish the eye pains from the others, and in themselves they are really not serious. It must have been a case like Papa's when he got relief from his catarrh in Arizona, his eyes got better, too.

I'm still taking care of my eyes, however. Classes will end about the last of next week, and after the exams, the first week following, I won't have any reading until the middle of September. If this doesn't fix them, they're incurable.[37]

However, in his letter of June 18 he was not so sure.

My head is not clearing up as fast as it should but the doctor seems satisfied, so I guess it's all right. He says that the relieving of the pressure may cause the angle of astigmatism to change, causing further eye trouble, but a new adjustment of glasses should fix that up all right.

And he added on June 26:

My nose has been better in the last week than for some time before. The doctor will not be able to give more than 2 or 3 more treatments before we go to camp, but with the 15 or 20 he has already, he should have been able to do something.

John's letters from camp that summer consisted mostly of chatter about the usual camp experiences and about the family. He
did say he kept busy and had to drive to Charles Town once or
twice a week. Swimming and horseback riding were his favorite
sports, and he expected the summer to be profitable. There was a
notable repeated reference in the letters to Bishop Chartrand, to
whom he asked the family to extend his greetings. He did remark
on July 4 that his eyes "have been much better lately and the
pains in my head have disappeared almost entirely. I hope the
cure is permanent." This was a vain hope because his sinus
trouble remained all his life.

The letters that have been preserved from John make only occasional references to his father's health before the end of 1915.
John W. O'Hara had recovered considerably from the general
poor health he had suffered during the first years after his shipboard accident of April, 1909, but the wrong diagnosis and
improper treatment that he had undergone until the real cause of
the trouble was determined left him in impaired health. His
resistance to disease had permanently been weakened, and in the
fall of 1915 there were evidences of dangerous illness. Without
creating any undue alarm, John endeavored, with the cooperation of Father Burns and Father John Cavanaugh, to obtain permission to spend the Christmas vacation at home in Indianapolis,
but because of the iron-bound Holy Cross tradition that there
were no vacations from Washington at Christmas except in the
case of student illness, the request was not readily welcomed. But
the matter was well weighed because of the high regard of his
superiors for both junior and senior John O'Hara. Of this refusal
John wrote to the family:

I had a telegram from Father Cavanaugh this morning with the
final word. He said he was letting you know so that relieved me of the
necessity of sending a telegram to spill your hopes.

Father Cavanaugh said that the Provincial wanted to establish a
precedent, and I guess it is the only safe thing for him to do, as he
gets a good many such requests. He said, however, that he would let me
go at another time, so I have written Father Cavanaugh to urge
the time. I will be needed here for camp, so it can't be in the summer
very well, and unless he lets me go next week, it will be during the
school year. If he decides to do that, I will ask him to make it as soon
as possible—taking into account, however, that Father Cavanaugh may
be down here the first week in January. I can't afford to miss him.

Father Burns has been very kind. He advised me to telegram Father
Cavanaugh yesterday when no word had come from Fr. Morrissey, and

even sent me to town yesterday afternoon, during the retreat, to cash a check for the money in case I was to go. I think I told you before that he is just like Fr. Cavanaugh in his ways of treating people, so that accounts for everything.

I don't mind at all missing the trip home at this time and only hope you weren't expecting me with too much confidence. We are looking forward to a good day tomorrow. I am through with my Christmas work, and expect to get a good sleep this afternoon in anticipation of the disturbed rest tonight. A year ago today I was down buying holly and trimmings and it was terribly cold. Today the weather is delightful—almost too good to sleep through.

I've had to stop this letter a long time to plug up a nose bleed—the sign of the end of a cold in the head—and I'll have to cut it short now or it will be in one again. I had a delightful accident. I was starting for town just when Dr. Dougherty, the Vice-Rector of the University, was going down, and he took me into his machine. We had hardly got past the University gate when a front wheel came off and we started plowing the street-car track with the hub. He apologized and said, "You'd have been in town by now if I hadn't stopped you." If he wasn't as kind as he is deaf he could have seen that the car I would have gone on was behind him, waiting for him to get his machine off the track.

Happy New Year, then, and many of them. My nose is starting again, so Goodbye, . . .[38]

Apparently special permission for the visit was granted after Christmas because John did visit the family in Indianapolis at New Year's. His father was not bedfast and attended a funeral in Peru early in January. Nevertheless it is apparent that the O'Hara family understood that his health was in precarious condition. Writing to Father Cavanaugh on February 5, from Washington, John said: "I am getting bad news from home lately. Father has a bad attack of grip and it left his stomach in bad condition. He has been living on malted milk for the past week or so, and will have to remain in bed for two or three weeks longer. The Doctor says, however, that his condition is not at all dangerous, and that there is no need to worry."

Father Cavanaugh wrote to John on February 6, expressing his doubt that Mr. O'Hara could be seriously ill. But the family soon learned the seriousness of the illness, and John wrote the news to Father Cavanaugh on the eleventh:

I am answering your kind letter in haste because I want you to keep on praying for father. Last night I received a telegram telling me to come home, as he was very low, but I waited for more word this morning, and about noon another telegram said not to come until further notice. This afternoon I had a letter explaining the progress of the disease up to what seems to have been the crisis last night. It is acute liver trouble—jaundice and I don't know what else. He received Holy Communion Tuesday morning and Wednesday morning he was anointed. I understand he suffers a great deal.

In spite of the serious state of affairs I am not really worried about the outcome. Since he got through last night safely I think I have reason to hope that he will continue to mend. It will be a long sickness, however, and if the end should come now, I think we can all bear it bravely enough, with God's help. He has been a good man, working hard all through his life and heroically devoted to his family, and doesn't seem afraid to die. I would like to have him live long enough for me to give him a priest's blessing though, and I know he would want it.[39]

A few days later, however, he obtained permission to go to his father's bedside. He sent Father Cavanaugh a card:

I came home this morning to find father very low. I have just had a talk with the doctor and he says there is no chance for him at all. He hasn't eaten for three weeks, and his vitality is gradually getting less. He is beautifully resigned. Please tell Fr. Morrissey I have to spend most of my time with father.[40]

The sixty-two-year old attorney died Tuesday evening, February 15, 1916.

Father John Cavanaugh was ill and could not attend the funeral, which was held in the Cathedral of Saints Peter and Paul on February 18. Father Charles O'Donnell came from Notre Dame and gave the funeral sermon. Bishop Joseph Chartrand was in the sanctuary, and John was permitted to act as subdeacon in the Mass. Father O'Donnell paid high tribute to Mr. O'Hara's strong character, saying that he always eyed the "issues of eternity." He devoted some words to the high esteem in which the deceased was held by non-Catholics.

To many honest outsiders, John O'Hara, the country school teacher, in the old days up in Miami County, stood as the example and the exponent of the Catholic faith. They knew little of Rome and cared less. But they knew a true man when they saw one, and they liked a good neighbor; when they saw this isolated Catholic, in all kinds of weather, going seven miles to church on Sunday, from Galveston to Kokomo, walking the railroad ties when means of conveyance could not be had, these fair-minded folk could not but think kindly of the Church which made John O'Hara what he was.[41]

After the funeral John returned without delay to his studies.

John O'Hara's close association with Father Cavanaugh involved more than just the usual friendship that Father Cavanaugh had for all the youngsters in the seminary. John had an

unusual background in his Latin American experiences and his
general maturity. Father Cavanaugh was already beginning to plan
on using him. Both Father Cavanaugh and Father Burns encouraged him to continue his interest in the countries to the South, and
his contacts with Father John A. Zahm furthered this development.
The question of ordaining him before the completion of his four
years of theology were completed was now broached.

A permission for such an early ordination was not unusual in
religious communities where there was a shortage of priests. John
O'Hara had raised the question, perhaps before his father's death
and in view of his father's failing health. There seems to have
been also some plan involved by which after ordination John
would take classes in Latin American studies at The Catholic
University during his fourth year. As a simple priest he could
say Mass and carry on most sacramental functions while completing his last year of theological studies. Apparently he had spoken
to the family of his plans before the death of his father. His
enthusiasm was apparent.

> Father O'Donnell wrote scolding me for sending him the offering.
> Father Morrissey gave him the option of sending it back, but he
> thought it best—and beautifully—to keep it and say twenty Masses for
> the repose of poor Papa's soul. I am going to write him this morning.
> It is too bad that Papa couldn't have lived for what I have in hand
> now. Father Zahm has promised me his whole South American library—
> the best in the country I guess—if Fr. Cavanaugh will let me start a
> course in So. A. history at Notre Dame. I think he will be only too
> glad to do it.
> Fr. Morrissey will be here probably this week, and I will see him
> about ordination. It doesn't look just now as if it would be an easy
> matter. I will let you know the result.[42]

In the meantime John acted as a kind of intermediary between
the family and the University in the disposal of his father's law
library. Mrs. O'Hara suggested the purchase price be credited
towards the education of Robert O'Hara, who would enter college
the next fall. The value placed on the books locally was $200,
but Father Cavanaugh allowed $700 for the collection. In writing
the widow about the arrangements he added:

> I had the happiness of attending a council in which the question of
> John's ordination was raised, as is usual in all such cases. I need not
> say that everybody was happy to give a favorable vote.
> My own personal relations with John have been so happy and affec-
> tionate that I feel quite like one of the family. I also felt close to John's

father and to all the children whom I know. Please give them my most
cordial good wishes and my best blessing for a happy Easter.[43]

Between Father Cavanaugh and John O'Hara correspondence
was frequent and involved not only the subject of Latin American
studies but also the Edward Lee Greene herbarium, which John
packed up and shipped to Notre Dame. The class in Latin American history had been promised to secure the 600 books in Father
Zahm's library, but the theological training of John O'Hara had
also to be considered.

Just when the possibility of early ordination for John was
broached to superiors is not clear, but since Bishop Chartrand
seems to have been a party to it, the suggestion for this may have
arisen when John was home for his father's funeral, or even earlier
on the occasion of his New Year's visit. At least there seemed to
have been an understanding that Bishop Chartrand was to perform the ceremony, but the decision of the provincial council was
that the ordination would not take place until after summer
camp. John had not yet received all the minor orders, and his
activity in Latin American studies was a bit unusual.

In some way John O'Hara had become acquainted with an
Argentine priest, Father Manuel Rua, and he wrote to Father
Cavanaugh suggesting Father Rua as a possible teacher and as
an agent to secure Argentine students for the University. He also
told Father Cavanaugh that Father Zahm had suggested that
Notre Dame should acquire the services of Dr. Vicente G.
Quesada, a noted South American historian. Father Cavanaugh,
who was well aware of the limited means of Notre Dame, said that
if Quesada had gone to Harvard, he was beyond their reach, but
he did manifest some interest in Father Rua. Father Rua, however, insisted on a better proposal from Notre Dame, and negotiations were broken off. Instead Father Cavanaugh wrote teasingly
to John O'Hara. "I hope to have here next year the best Spanish
teacher in the United States. I may inform you that his home is
in Indiana and he is to be ordained in September. His name is
Señor Juan O'Hara and he is an old friend of mine."[44] Father
Cavanaugh was premature about the teaching assignment but
correct about the ordination.

John now felt free to tell Father Cavanaugh of his plans, and
on April 19 he outlined his hopes.

... I knew it would be quite in conformity with your plans that I
should be ordained as soon as possible—or at least I guessed so—and
that I should take up the work at the University that you are so anxious

to have me do. Dr. Guilday has promised to take great interest in my work, which he thinks had best be confined to the seminar, and I think I could find no one better equipped to give me training in the historical method. We can take up the details later.

As to the ordination itself, you know that the plan is to have it in Indianapolis in September. Poor mother is really in poor shape, and this will be a kindness to her as well as a courtesy to our zealous friend, Bishop Chartrand. I think I know how big your heart is, and that you would want to preach for the First Mass if such a performance were physically possible. It seems to me, though, with all deference to your superior judgment, that you should not attempt anything of this kind, because every exception to your rule of rest and quiet is a dangerous tendency. I will not expect you, then, and—again saving your better judgment I would really prefer to have no sermon and no celebration at all—if such a condition is not contrary to the holy laws of God and man. Mother is not well, and I have few friends in Indianapolis, and I could fulfill my obligations in Peru and Kokomo by Masses and blessings there in the succeeding Sundays, so that personally there seems to be no reason for any display. But I don't want to let any personal wishes stand in the way of higher motives; and I will leave the final decision of the matter to you and Bishop Chartrand. I have spoken to Father Burns about it, and he is in sympathy with my view.[45]

But Father Cavanaugh answered promptly.

You are wrong on all counts as regards your ordination. First of all you must have a celebration and a sermon, and secondly I must preach the allocution. I would not resign the privilege in favor of anybody else, so there you are.

At the moment John O'Hara was not even a cleric, but the proper ordinations were soon arranged. On May 13 he received tonsure and minor orders; on May 15 he received the subdiaconate and on May 16 the diaconate at the Dominican House of Studies from Bishop Thomas Shahan of The Catholic University. He announced his progress to Father Cavanaugh on May 17.

Dominus Vobiscum! I can now give you the holy salutation of a full-fledged Deacon. The last several days have been given to the ceremonies of ordination, and Bishop Shahan has prepared me for the final function that admits me to the *Introibo.*

Your last letter brought me great pleasure and any amount of anxiety. Your loving finality in the matter of my ordination gave me joy as a testimonial of your big-hearted affection, but it raised doubts as to the inflexibility of your resolution to take care of yourself. I am going to send your letter home, so that the folks can appreciate and enjoy the honor you do them and our diocese, but I cannot thank you without protesting again that you must take better care of yourself, and avoid

any transgressions of your rule to refrain from preaching and all such
riotousness. I know that the good of souls will be furthered by your
[sic] eloquency of your speech and of your presence, but the good of
souls also demands that you take the ordinary precautions to reach a
graceful old age.

Your presence will demand a very holy deacon and subdeacon though
there is enough time for that. I don't want Father O'Donnell to have
any other engagement for that time, however, and if Father Carroll
or Schumacher or Father Carrico or Father Hagerty or any of the rest
of the friends can't come down, I think I can find someone else
nearer home.[46]

To his family he enclosed Father Cavanaugh's letter and added:

He insists on a celebration, but I think it can be a modest one and
still suit him. I have written to thank him for the honor he is doing
us. Don't tell the Bishop he is going to preach, as courtesy demands that
I ask the Bishop first. If the Bishop happens to want to know something
about the date, you might suggest September 10th as the date of the
first Mass, and the Friday or Saturday for the ordination. I haven't
arranged it with Father Morrissey yet, but that date would be most
convenient all around, I think, and will very probably be the one Fr.
M. will want.[47]

To Father Cavanaugh, to whom he wrote about Father Rua on
May 28, he added some details:

Your letter gave a great joy to the folks at home, as I knew it would,
and they are planning to disregard my interdict on celebrations for the
ordination and First Mass. It was very kind of you to offer to arrange
with Father Morrissey for the other man, but that as you say, can be
left till later. The only matter to be settled at all soon will be the date,
which will have to be determined largely by your convenience and the
Bishop's. Father Burns wants me to remain in camp until the end, and
then to have a few days recollection on my return here. The first open
Sunday after that would be September 10th, and that would be entirely
agreeable to me if it would not conflict with your opening of school.
The ordination would take place either on the 8th, the Feast of the
Nativity of the Blessed Virgin, or the 9th. I don't suppose there will
be much difficulty in securing the Bishop for a week-day, as he doesn't
travel much, except on Sundays. Father Morrissey said that if the date
was convenient he would attend as *Notarius*. That was certainly kind
of him. I expect to write Father Morrissey about the date soon. I am
bringing it up here so that you can consult your convenience.[48]

The question of a celebration was a family decision, and on May
28 he surrendered:

Eva says there will have to be some celebration, and between her and
Father Cavanaugh I resign the chair. You can do whatever you like

about the whole business. Father Morrissey also said that if the time was convenient he would be down for the ordination. I only hope that in making the plans you will be guided by the principles of economy and regard for a fellow's feelings that I laid down in the *Motu Proprio* of something like a month ago. I don't like invitations, and I simply can't take care of them in camp, but you can have them if you want to and are willing to do the work. I also don't like First Mass cards, and really think it inadvisable to get them, at least until after the ordination. If there seems to be a need for them then, I can have them printed in a short time. . . .[49]

When Bishop Chartrand asked for dates suitable for Father Cavanaugh, supposing that Father Cavanaugh would agree, John had picked the dates September 9 and 10. He had learned that Father Frank Maher was coming to Indiana from Portland for a vacation and hoped that he could be subdeacon at the Mass. Father Guendling should be assistant priest, but since he was old, John suggested that Father Robert Pratt, the Kokomo pastor, be invited. The official decision came from the Cathedral residence in Indianapolis.

In answer to your letter permit me to say:
1) The hour of the ordination will be eight A.M. in the Cathedral—Saturday, September 9.
2) The hour of the solemn First Mass at 10:30 in the Cathedral, Sunday, September 10.
3) After this, a dinner will be given in your honor for all the visiting priests in the Bishop's home.
4) I shall be in the sanctuary at your First Mass.
5) Fathers Smith and Fitzgerald will be Masters of Ceremonies.
6) As Father Cavanaugh will preach, I suggest that Fr. Morrissey be the Assistant priest at the First Mass.
7) I shall select the Deacon and Subdeacon and invite the priests, unless you have some preference in this matter. I told *Pat* he would have to wear a silk hat. I hope this will be satisfactory. Let me know. Our full male choir will be out in glory on that day.

God Bless you
✠ J.C.[50]

During the last week of camp John O'Hara cut his foot, and when it became inflamed he was sent back to Washington to have it treated. He did not return to camp. Despite a threatened rail strike he stayed in Washington until the last minute to "avoid the unnecessary distraction and inconvenience of being around home," and arrived in Indianapolis on Thursday morning, September 7. He did not record his happiness at ordination and First Mass or the pleasure of his mother on receiving his first blessing.

The best accounts were those in the newspapers.

The *Indiana Catholic and Record* told of the ceremonies in great detail.[51]

The Rt. Rev. Bishop was assisted in the solemn ceremony by The Rev. William Connor, C.S.C., master of novices of the Congregation of Holy Cross, Notre Dame, as Assistant priests, Rev. George Smith, Pastor of the Oratory of St. Philip Neri, Indianapolis as deacon, and The Rev. Lawrence Monahan of Peru as subdeacon. The Rev. Alphonse Smith of the Cathedral was master of ceremonies, and The Rev. David Fitzgerald of the Cathedral was assistant master of ceremonies. The Rev. Robert Pratt of Kokomo, The Rev. James Coulter of Indianapolis and The Rev. Victor Brucker of Indianapolis, occupied seats in the sanctuary. The acolytes were seminarians of the diocese of Indianapolis who have been spending their vacation in this city.

Of the First Mass the next day the paper said:

Sunday morning the altars of the Cathedral were beautifully decorated with white flowers and the high altar was ablaze with lighted candles. The white hangings of the Bishop's throne were symbolical of the joy of the occasion. The Solemn High Mass was celebrated in the presence of The Rt. Rev. Coadjutor Bishop and the sermon was preached by The Very Rev. Dr. John Cavanaugh, president of the University of Notre Dame.

Father O'Hara was assisted at the altar by The Rev. William Connor, C.S.C., as arch-priest, The Rev. George Smith as deacon and The Rev. Victor Brucker as subdeacon. The Rev. Alphonse Smith was master of ceremonies, while Rev. David Fitzgerald was assistant master of ceremonies. The Very Rev. Andrew Morrissey, C.S.C., provincial of the Congregation of Holy Cross was detained at Notre Dame, owing to the sudden death of The Rev. Father O'Keefe, as was The Rev. Charles O'Donnell, C.S.C., who was to have been deacon of the Mass. The Rev. Raymond Noll and The Rev. Dr. John Cavanaugh occupied seats in the sanctuary. Fifteen seminarians participated as acolytes.

Father Cavanaugh spoke with his usual flow of eloquence, praising the dignity of the priesthood and the honors of the young priest at the altar. He also made mention of the father who had missed by such a short time the joy of the occasion.

One loved figure is, indeed, wanting to the happiness and the glory of this day—the noble Christian father who had looked forward with proud expectation to the ordination of his son. He was the ideal head of a model Christian family. A scholarly Catholic Gentleman, he was idolized in his home, and admired and honored by the whole community. He did not live to witness the beginning of the miracle of Our Lord, even as Moses did not enter the Promised Land.

But who can doubt that from his place near Christ this day—even in paradise he feels the added happiness as he leans over the battlements of heaven to view the First Mass of his son.

To the newly ordained he suggested that he think of the dead and weigh well the final judgment of his work.

. . . Remember the beautiful promise of Our Lord that they who instruct others unto justice shall shine as stars in the Kingdom of Heaven. Go think of it in silence and alone and weigh against a grain of sand the glory of a throne.

Of the other celebration the paper added:

Following the Mass, the clergy and seminarians were entertained at dinner by the Rt. Rev. Silas Chatard and The Rt. Rev. Joseph Chartrand. . . . at the episcopal residence. In addition to the clergy who participated in the ceremonies in the morning, there were present at the dinner, the Revs. Marino Priori and Patrick Griffin.

From 3 until 6 o'clock Sunday afternoon a reception was held in honor of Father O'Hara at the home of his mother. This was largely attended and the young priest was heartily congratulated by his friends. The Rev. John Cavanaugh was also a guest of honor at the reception. John Tully of Chicago, a Notre Dame alumnus, who was Father O'Hara's roommate during their college days, and Earl Dickens, formerly private secretary to Dr. Cavanaugh and now of Chicago, were among the out of town guests. At noon, Wednesday, Father O'Hara was guest of honor at a luncheon given by the Notre Dame Club of Indianapolis at the Hotel English.

But the ceremonies were soon over, and Father O'Hara had to settle down to very earthly realities. He had yet a year of theological studies to complete, and he was to start also to prepare for his special work at Notre Dame.

A Career Begins

FATHER JOHN O'HARA HAD ACHIEVED HIS principal goal through ordination by Bishop Chartrand, and yet in another sense he had merely acquired a new status in which he was about to begin his life's work. Most graduates of Notre Dame who return to the campus as priests of Holy Cross see their future involved in service to the University. Some, of course, are actually destined for other priestly ministry in parishes or missions, and others find their field of service in other teaching institutions of Holy Cross. But there seems to have been no question in the fall of 1916 in either Father O'Hara's mind or in the minds of his superiors—Fathers Morrissey, Burns, and Cavanaugh—that Father John O'Hara would be assigned to Notre Dame. These immediate plans were shaped by his knowledge of the Spanish language and his Latin American experiences. Yet, however important was this Latin American interest, the over-all ambition of this twenty-eight-year-old priest was simply to serve Notre Dame.

Latin American history holds no great interest for the ordinary American student who has not traveled south of the Rio Grande. So, also, John O'Hara's Latin America was the contemporary world in which his father had been a consul and in which he had studied, made friends, and became associated with inter-American business enterprises. He studied Latin American history only as the background for understanding the Uruguay and Argentina he had come to know firsthand in his youth. In his youthful enthusiasm he saw Notre Dame becoming the northern terminus of a grand exchange of people and commerce between the two worlds of the Western Hemisphere. His plans were large, and they fitted in well with the spirit of expansion that seemed to be dominant in Notre Dame as it approached its diamond jubilee celebration in 1917.

The expansion of Notre Dame at this time does not seem to have any real connection with the American excitement over the European war that had begun in 1914 and was involving American interests by 1916. American public opinion was deeply affected by the war, and at the University the Irish and German elements in American Catholicism were mirrored by the sympathetic statements that sometimes escaped from otherwise neutral American Catholics. Basically, however, the University was permeated with the general American patriotic isolationism that believed that European wars were not for this country. In 1917 the expansionism in the University arose partly from the general prosperity of the country and partly from Notre Dame's own prosperity. Under the guidance of Father Schumacher the University was planning to establish a school of agriculture and a medical school and to increase its offerings in commerce and business administration. The agricultural school was a natural development for a Midwestern university with a strong science school; the medical school was a similar development from the premedical program and science departments that had existed at Notre Dame for generations. The Commerce Department combined the growing student interest in business and foreign commerce and the prospective addition of Father John O'Hara with his Latin American background.

Earlier that summer while he had waited at the summer camp for the day of his ordination, John O'Hara had written on July 2 of his plans to Father Cavanaugh.

I might add by way of postscript that I have talked over with Father Schumacher the prospect of endowments for the schools of Commerce and Agriculture. It seems to me that the School of Commerce should be called the Grace School of Commerce and that the W. R. Grace and Co. of New York should furnish the reason for the name. Father Zahm says that they are Catholics, and they certainly are the biggest American firm in South America. They have the lion's share of the trade to the West Coast, in the Grace steamships and mining interests. It was Count Fea, one of their men, who sent Carlos Gonzalez, of Peru, on to Notre Dame in 1910, when I went to arrange for the Rizo Patron boys.

The other school should be called the Thomas J. Duggan School of Agriculture in memory of the late Mr. Duggan, who made many mil-

lions in Argentina *estancias*. Mrs. Duggan is still living, and has a very
fine family of grown sons and daughters, who should take an interest
in this. They have many charities of their own, but the need to take
Agriculture (construe this as you wish)—should appeal to them. With
W. R. Grace and Co. we should control Chile and Peru, besides building up the best Commerce course in the country, and with Duggan's
we could do the same for the Argentine and our Department of
Agriculture.

These are things to trouble your dreams these hot nights. We can
talk them over when we get together in the fall.[1]

Father Cavanaugh was undoubtedly amazed at the proposals, but
he was willing to entertain the suggestions as he answered.

Your plans to get Mr. W. R. Grace interested in our School of Commerce are admirable. Who can better do this than yourself, from whose
lips the Castilian eloquence flows as from the pen of Cervantes or
Lope de Vega. Go to it, my boy, and may the Lord bless thee! That
goes for the suggestion about Thomas J. Duggan. Why not use these
dull sightless days to write letters for this purpose?[2]

The young man was not daunted by the apparent banter as he
answered:

I shall start feeling my way towards the endowments I suggested,
although camp offers few opportunities towards elegance of correspondence. I am full of plans for the working out of a course in Foreign
Trade, the details of which I will go over with you as soon as we meet.[3]

A Latin American orientation would give to the Commerce
Department a special purpose. Young Father O'Hara's dream
for this development has proved fifty years later to have been correct but at the time was classified rather as the exuberance of a
talented young man anxious to raise the University to new heights
in his own field of interest. Father Cavanaugh saw the possibilities
of these same talents, but he also understood better the limits of
Notre Dame's financial resources. Also, Father John A. Zahm, the
explorer and writer on South America, stood back of Father
O'Hara, promising guidance and a growing library of nearly six
hundred books on condition that Father O'Hara offer at Notre
Dame a course in Latin American studies.

When he visited Notre Dame after his First Mass, Father
O'Hara spoke to Father Morrissey and Father Cavanaugh of his
plans to begin his Latin American studies at The Catholic University while completing his theological studies at Holy Cross
College. There was no indication that Father Cavanaugh objected
to this, since the year of theological study could hardly be spent

at Notre Dame. Father Cavanaugh, however, did not seem to expect the young priest to stay in Washington to study for his doctorate. Nor was Father Morrissey too much interested in having him study under Doctor Peter Guilday, the professor of American Church history at The Catholic University. The intellectual guide in these matters was Father James Burns, his immediate superior. At his suggestion Father John enrolled in the seminar of Dr. Guilday, even though Dr. Guilday's special interest was not Spanish America. Father Burns did object to the proposal of Dr. Guilday that Father O'Hara teach a class in Spanish at the University while continuing his studies. Eventually the Provincial, Father Morrissey, obtained a special permission from the Holy Cross Superior General, Gilbert Francais, for Father O'Hara to enter Dr. Guilday's seminar while doing this final year of theological studies.

Actually Father O'Hara's interest in Latin American history was only accidental to his general interests. Yet because his knowledge of Spanish and Latin America was his chief instrument for serving Notre Dame, he did not hesitate to use it, although there was some question about combining Latin American studies with Dr. Guilday's seminar. The young priest's chief occupation under Dr. Guilday seems to have been the preparation of articles and commentaries on Latin American history for the newly established *Catholic Historical Review,* of which Dr. Guilday was the editor. More and more, judging from Father O'Hara's letters, his theological studies slipped into the background as he became more deeply engrossed in these new activities.

Writing to Father Cavanaugh in October, Father Burns added a postscript that with the Superior General's permission Father O'Hara was attending Dr. Guilday's seminar in preparation for "the Spanish classes next year for you."[4] But Father O'Hara wrote to his family in November that the engrossing Latin American affairs were becoming a hindrance to his theological studies. He also noted that he had learned that Carlos Duggan had arrived in New York, and he was trying to locate him in the east to interest him in seeing Notre Dame when he went to Chicago. Certainly his great interest at that time was the program in Latin America at Notre Dame. He wrote of that to the family.

I'm having a fairly serious time of it with my History. There is an immense field to cover, and I want to see as much of it as possible. It will not be so strenuous after the next couple of weeks. However, I can go over the whole field by that time and the special work will be much more mechanical. I want to get together a book of readings on

S. A. Church history—selections from contemporary documents, etc. It will probably take several years. All I can expect to do this year is to outline the work and translate some of the important papers. The Library of Congress has a great collection, and I have a free hand in its use![5]

But there was a conflict between a program that would make him a scholar in Latin American studies and perhaps have him teach during the process at The Catholic University and the young priest's desire to be back at Notre Dame. As Father Burns told Father Cavanaugh, Father John had the talents, but his likings were for a quick return to Notre Dame. Again he wrote on December 20:

. . . Dr. Guilday wants me to stay here and teach Spanish and work at S.A. History for his Historical Magazine. In other words, he wants the course here instead of at Notre Dame. I wrote Father Cavanaugh about his intentions, but he hasn't answered yet. Father Zahm says to go to N.D. without delay, and has promised to turn over his library at once. I'll go over with a dray and get it one of these days.[6]

Father Burns thought differently about the program, as he told Father Cavanaugh when sending feast day greetings on December 27:

I should like to see Father O'Hara stay here till he is able to get his Ph.D. degree. He has the elements of a real scholar in him and I would like to see him given plenty of time and opportunity for their development. I think he would have more of both time and opportunity here than at Notre Dame, and therefore I favor his being allowed to come back for two more years. I think it would take that length of time to get his degree. As to Dr. Guilday's proposition to him, of which he wrote you—I may say that does not appeal to me. Whether he would teach a class in Spanish or not, would be of no particular consequence, so far as I can see. If he should teach a class of Spanish, we would have to see that it would be no detriment to his research work. It might be made a help to a better acquaintance with Spanish literature. But the main point is, it seems to me, to afford him the best opportunity possible. I need not say that he will be a most valuable man for you.[7]

In the meantime Father John began an article for Dr. Guilday's *Catholic Historical Review*. As the article grew in length, he told his family that he thought he would extend it into a master's thesis so as to get his degree in June. This was apparently the article that appeared in the January, 1917, issue of the magazine, under the heading, "A Frank Word about South American History." In it Father O'Hara outlined the growth of a certain erroneous tradition in the English world about the Catholic Church in South America, particularly through the publication in English translation of a private complaint by Don Jorge Juan and Don Antonio de Ulloa, *Noticias de America*. He added to his exposition a plea for corrective studies by Catholic writers in the United States. Probably Dr. Guilday arranged that the article received more than local newspaper recognition. His letters home were filled with his enthusiasm for the propaganda value of his work.

The article in the *Review* has had quite a vogue. Its heading runs clear across the page in the *Freeman's Journal* this week, the front page that is. I think I told you how it happened. It was a class report for Dr. Guilday, and he found it so sensational that he wanted it written out for his magazine. This week I have been working on another thing that will cause a sensation in the Smithsonian Bureau of Ethnology. They printed a beautiful book last summer—a 1630 report on the Franciscans in New Mexico. It deals with the Pueblos Papa was so enthusiastic about. In the meantime, Dr. Guilday has secured a set of manuscripts from the Propaganda, in Rome, that reduces its value to about two cents. The big thing is the later report—1634—written by the same missionary, that shows that the first version—printed in Spain in 1630—is a badly garbled affair, of very little historical value. The first is a physical geography of New Mexico, and the second, the one I am working on, is a history of the Missions and the Indians there. The edition of last year has a lot of footnotes by Hodge and C. F. Lummis, that are perfectly beautiful, but must now be dismissed as bad guesses, since we now have the facts in the handwriting of the historian. When we print this new Ms. it is going to be more of a sensation than the last article, though of course, in a more limited way.

I have been working with Father Zahm every Wednesday lately, and have finished the inventory of his South American library. There are more than 500 books, many of them very rare old prints. If I were to stay in Washington, it would be all I would need, because I could fill out from the Library of Congress and the Pan American; but for Notre Dame I will have to buy a great many new books, and I intend to start bombarding Fr. Cavanaugh for the money right away! The first thing I want is a set that costs $135.00. I can imagine his gasp, but with my article staring him in the face from all the big Catholic papers, calling for a complete South American history course immediately, I think I can gain my point. He will be down here March 15th for the consecration of Bishop Russell, but I am going to get busy in the meantime. I am going to write to Spain this morning for quotations on some books I want.

I think Fr. Cavanaugh intends to announce the new Foreign Trade course soon. I have gone over the matter pretty carefully and I think that we can make a great success of the course. I am going to start right away to interest influential men in the course, with a view to recognition first and a subsidy later. The Head of the Bureau of Appointments at the State Department told me that he could place all the men that I could sent [*sic*] him for clerkships, if they had the training I propose for the course.[8]

The ambitious and confident way the young man approached these projects showed a deep awareness of the value of public relations and of modern business methods. But apparently he was not fully aware that he was talking of two kinds of activity: that of the scholar in producing information and that of the administrator. His desire to be a part of Notre Dame determined his choice of fields: he planned on being at Notre Dame the following year, still in the field of Latin American affairs, but as a promotor of commercial exchange, even though this would be in a classroom.

He told his family in a letter of February 17 that he had drawn up an announcement of the course he hoped to teach the next year at Notre Dame. He waited for Father Cavanaugh's visit for a decision. But on March 20 he told them a bit quietly that Father Cavanaugh "did not settle the matter of next year before leaving and very probably the matter will drag along until it can be seen where I can do the best work."[9] When a slighting reference appeared in *America* about the Washington Pan American Union, he sent the editor a letter of protest that the magazine published. In gratitude the Pan American Union promised him some maps and duplicates of their publications. There was even a slight indication for a while that he might be interested in staying in Washington for further study. Later, however, he said that he could have continued in Latin American history in Washington but that he had had no real desire for that kind of work. His recollections of Latin American history and his interest in Latin America remained active most of his life, but in 1917 Father Morrissey, the provincial, and Father Cavanaugh welcomed his desire to go to Notre Dame. Under the circumstances Father Burns seemed to agree with them, and the newly ordained priest began to prepare for teaching at Notre Dame the following September. He told his family on May 17:

Fr. Morrissey was here last week. He wants me to be at Notre Dame next year. W. R. Grace and Co. have offered me free entry to their offices in New York this summer, so I will spend a week or so there. I may also take a course at the Wharton School for a few weeks, if I am feeling well enough: at any rate, I don't expect to go West before late in August. I suppose I will have a short time at home before classes start.[10]

On April 6, 1917, the United States entered World War I, and Congress soon passed the Selective Service Act. The need for chaplains for the armed services became very great, but Father O'Hara did not feel any immediate desire to become a chaplain. As he wrote to the folks on April 9: "I will be perfectly willing to go as a chaplain, if I see that my services are needed. I am not as patriotic as I am interested in the spiritual welfare of the men." He was more concerned with his preparations to work at Notre Dame and asked permission of Father Morrissey to stop off in Philadelphia on his way to New York to visit the museum there so that he would know what to seek from the Graces for Notre Dame's museum. In the meanwhile he had completed his final year of theology and passed his examinations with high marks. He then made his annual retreat and went to New York for a visit with W. R. Grace and Company, living with Father John Talbot Smith at Dobbs Ferry. He returned to Philadelphia for the opening of the University of Pennsylvania summer school on July 9, and resided at St. Francis De Sales parish, doing some parish work in return for his living quarters. At the University he registered for courses in Latin American relations, Caribbean interests of the United States, and practical finance. He did not try for credit in these courses and did not attend class regularly. He noted to his family that he had attended only six classes in two weeks but that he was seeing what was going on, and that was his purpose in being there. After summer school Father O'Hara returned to Washington, where he received his formal notification that he was to teach and prefect at Notre Dame.[11]

From Philadelphia Father O'Hara went to his home in Indianapolis for a vacation. On August 1, the day after his arrival home, he wrote to Father Cavanaugh that he had just spent a strenuous week in Philadelphia. He seemed much disturbed that Notre Dame was not better known in that city. He felt that the people of Philadelphia thought of Notre Dame as just another Villanova or Mount Saint Mary's. At Villanova he had learned also that engineering students were being exempted from the draft, and he thought quick action at Notre Dame might bring similar results for Notre Dame engineers. Finally, he said that he had written to Father Morrissey to ask the date he was to return to Notre Dame.

There was no welcoming ceremony when he returned to the campus. Notre Dame was feeling the effects of the American entrance into the War, but the change had not been so important locally as the grand celebration of the diamond jubilee of the University on June 8–11 of that year. The celebration had been one of the most elaborate affairs of American Catholicism of that era, with Cardinal Gibbons, the Apostolic Delegate, Archbishop John Bonzano, Archbishop George Mundelein of Chicago, Archbishop Edward Hanna of San Francisco, and many bishops, priests, and distinguished laymen in attendance. Notable among the priests were Fathers John A. Ryan and John Talbot Smith, and among the laymen, Admiral William S. Benson, Bourke Cochran, and Joseph Scott.

By 1917 all the founders of Notre Dame—many of whom had been alive with Father Sorin at his golden jubilee of 1888—had died, and with them had passed the image of the small college on the frontier. While the sermons of the jubilee celebrated the past accomplishments, there was more than one note of future greatness, chiefly in the dedication of two new buildings, the Indiana limestone library building and the new chemistry hall of yellow brick. The chief personality of Notre Dame on this grand occasion was Father Cavanaugh. Attractive in countenance, rich in expression, and genial in his manner, he was a perfect gentleman, a flowering of Notre Dame's old liberal arts college. His liberal culture, crowned by an unquestioned Americanism that made him acceptable to persons of all creeds and businesses, symbolized that Notre Dame at that time was the best achievement of young American Catholicism. But in another sense the celebration also marked the end of a period, and this change was indicated not only in the two new buildings—places of advanced study—but also by the World War, whose threats were already bothering the students.

Father Cavanaugh had able assistants in Father Matthew Walsh, the vice-president; Father William A. Moloney; and the other priests, brothers, and laymen who lived in the halls, prefected the campus, or taught in the classrooms. In the centralized administration the most important man after the President was the director of studies, whose office was required by the *Rules* of the Congregation of Holy Cross. In 1917 that office was held by Father Matthew A. Schumacher, a tall, handsome priest of broad countenance, large blue eyes, wavy locks, and calm self-assured movements. After Father Cavanaugh and closely with him, Father Schumacher was the planner who had instituted the classes in commerce, approved the program for the school of agriculture, and formed the shortlived program for a school of medicine. Actually the division of the University into colleges and departments in the catalog existed little more than in name because Father Schumacher assigned the teachers to their classes and classrooms and determined what was to be taught. Even before Father O'Hara had begun to think of his work at Notre Dame, Father Schumacher had founded the Department of Commerce in 1914, and it was with him that Father O'Hara began to plan the developments of 1917–1918 depending upon the progress of the war and its effects on the University. To Father Schumacher, Father O'Hara was actually, despite his previous experience as a teacher, beginning at the bottom of the ladder with youthful ardour. The youth himself soon learned that his grandiose plans for a Department of Foreign Commerce were mostly dreams because the money needed to carry out those plans was wanting, and the local council that had to approve expenditures was not interested in such adventures.

Father O'Hara did not arrive on the campus unannounced because his brother Bob had predicted in the *Scholastic* of the previous April the offering of his new courses. At the beginning, however, he did not teach a foreign commerce class, although he quickly received from the student body the title of "Dean of the Commerce Department" and soon organized a chamber of commerce. To this chamber of commerce, to which all students in commerce were expected to come, Father O'Hara invited prominent businessmen from South Bend and eventually from Chicago to give lectures. His one class that first year was a class in Christian doctrine, in which he had forty-one pupils. To these he added two sections of the chamber of commerce and a biweekly meeting of the Eucharistic Union, with which he had become acquainted in 1911-1912 when he was a lay professor. He found that these tasks took most of his time and that his accomplishments as an historian were negligible.

To add to his complications, the January issue of the *Catholic Historical Review*, of which he was reading the proofs, gave an outline of his proposed book of readings. Dr. Guilday added the hope in print that Father O'Hara's lectures would not cause any delay in the publication of his book. Father O'Hara caught the meaning of Dr. Guilday's remark and expressed his own feelings to Dr. Guilday.

The outline of the phantom book looks very tempting in print and makes me feel like pushing ahead, but the dig at the bottom of the column is really needed. So far I have been left free from the lecture rooms, but there are a couple of professors of economics here who are gnashing their teeth at my free time, and the Director of Studies is beginning to investigate. I think, though, that if you can get from Dr. Pace a statement of work required for a doctorate and permission to do the work *in absentia,* I can hold off the threat against my time.

But he was more realistic in his letter to his family.

I am busy with book reviews that give me more books and more money to buy books, I am also busy with the Eucharistic Union and the Chamber of Commerce. I haven't advanced an inch on my historical work yet, except that I have my Aztec secretary preparing cards for a bibliography.

And on November 27 he admitted further:

I have just received another batch of books, photos, etc. from Fr. Zahm. I am also writing a couple of articles for the next number of the C.H.R. So far I have not done anything towards the Ph.D. They have given me another class to teach—in Ancient History. It is interesting but it takes time.

The effects of the war included his assignment in January to replace Father Matthew Walsh in a class in ancient history when Father Walsh became a chaplain in the army. Another was the eagerness of some of the commerce students to enlist. On June 16 at the close of the shool year he wrote:

This war has certainly upset things. I had one of the dandiest little Commerce classes in the world gathered here, and they are all rushing to enlist now. I had a card from one yesterday. He says the home town is lonesome without the fellows and he is going to join the Marines. They will drop off that way right and left this summer, in spite of the fact that we now have Ed Hurley of the Shipping Board for our dean. He accepted last Monday, when he spoke here. I have wanted him for a long time.[12]

Father O'Hara's other activity that he did not mention at first in his letter to his family was that of counseller. At that time at Notre Dame there was strict discipline, and on each floor of the residence halls a priest was placed as prefect. The hall itself was under the charge of a rector, and in Walsh Hall, where Father O'Hara lived, the rector was beloved Father John Farley, a jovial priest and onetime football player who all but joined in the activities of the students. The other prefects were Father Bernard Lange, a close friend, and Father Charles Doremus, a Frenchman exiled by his country's laws against religious orders.

Father O'Hara's room in Walsh became the mecca of Latin American students and those interested in commerce and business administration.

In October, 1917, Father O'Hara replaced Father Charles O'Donnell as the director of the Eucharistic Union. This Union had been formed by Father Cornelius Hagerty and other priests who were worried about the disciplinary problems of Carroll Hall. As an inducement to good behavior, the Union promoted daily Mass and Communion in the little chapel of the Main Building and frequent meetings to promote other wholesome activities. By 1917 the Union was noted for its noisy meetings as well as its religious program and for its collections of books and tobacco for the soldiers. When Father O'Donnell was permitted to apply for a chaplaincy in the army, Father Cavanaugh asked Father O'Hara also to take over Father O'Donnell's work as prefect of religion. As he noted to his family, he now had Bishop Chartrand's work: "hearing confessions every morning and forcing them to go to Communion."[13] On February 9 the new prefect of religion was the principal speaker at the annual dinner for the "Lifers," according to the *Scholastic* "made up of all that is left of the anarchistic Eucharistic League of Carroll, whence came the custom of daily Communion among students." There was little else to say about the change in prefects of religion, since the job consisted chiefly in arranging for the speakers for Sunday Mass and for confessors for first Friday devotions. To this Father O'Hara brought the technique he had learned from Bishop Chartrand.

The war had only a superficially disorganizing effect on the University as a whole, although it did directly influence many individual students and members of the faculty. Nevertheless, despite President Woodrow Wilson's plea that college men should stay in college until they were called, many students rushed to the colors after the Declaration of War on April 6, 1917, and many prospective students went instead into the Army and Navy. By September, 1917, the number of Notre Dame students known to be in the services numbered close to two hundred, and the total enrollment was down to one hundred forty-six, a decline of nearly the same number. Twenty-five Holy Cross priests had volunteered for chaplaincies in the services, and eight eventually obtained the permission from Father Morrissey to enlist. Notre Dame had had its cadet corps for years, and optional military training existed with military trainers on the campus. When the government first announced that certain colleges would be permitted to enroll their students in the services while they remained on the campuses, Notre Dame was not on the list of approved colleges. But protests from interested friends secured the approbation of Notre Dame as one of the colleges to have its Students' Army Training Corps, in which the members had to pass a physical test, be at least eighteen years of age, and be accepted as students in the college. They were taken into the army and their board, room, tuition, and equipment were paid for by the Government.

Wartime orators came to the campus, among them Secretary of the Navy Josephus Daniels to dedicate the little Shillington monument set up in memory of the Notre Dame men who served in the Spanish American War. Some lay members of the faculty participated in the various war drives to support the Red Cross or to sell war bonds. The *Scholastic* began to print letters from Notre Dame students in the service, and Father Cavanaugh's correspondence with the boys in the service became very heavy. Besides the large number of Notre Dame men in the service the honor roll listed fifty-two Notre Dame men who gave their life for their country. The campus participation in the war, the Students' Army Training Corps, was not taken very seriously by the students during its short existence from September to November, 1918. The student members of the Corps had to spend eleven hours in military drill each week and follow a rather rigid military day, but otherwise they attended regular classes, except for an interval of about two weeks in which an epidemic of Spanish influenza caused a prohibition of all public meetings and the suspension of classes. In that epidemic there were four Notre Dame deaths and about fifty campus cases of influenza, but this was mild in comparison to the ravages of the epidemic elsewhere in the country.

The best summary of the effect of the Students' Army Training Corps on Notre Dame was perhaps the editorial in the *Scholastic* on its termination, to the effect that army training and student life could not mix. Captain William P. Murray, the commandant of the Corps said in his departing letter, however, that the Notre Dame experiment had been one of the best in the nation.[14] Probably the Corps had not existed long enough for a good test, but the short-time experiment was not highly regarded by either the students or the faculty.

Some of the Corps members who did not really care for college life left the campus when the Armistice brought about the termination of the Corps. The University opened its employment office for those who wanted to remain but did not have sufficient funds. Meanwhile, as the students in the services were released, they came back to college, some in February for the second semester, others for the following September. Of the effects of the war on the faculty there is no basis for serious measurement. Certainly contact with other peoples, foreign travel, and exchanges with persons of other ideologies left many impressions that were not listed as effects of military service. One public effect noticeable after the war was that most of the chaplains from the campus traveling into other countries had learned to smoke cigarettes, and this had much influence in breaking down the prejudice against cigarette smoking that had existed at Notre Dame. The corporate handling of masses of young men seemed to have affected the thinking of the chaplains, two of whom, Fathers Matthew Walsh and Charles O'Donnell, later became presidents of the University, and two, Father O'Donnell and Father George Finnigan, later became provincial superiors. The large dining halls erected in 1926 were said to have been a result of the observation by the chaplains of similar services in the army camps.

About the only other effect of the war on Notre Dame was an increase in enrollment made possible by scholarships provided the returning servicemen by the Knights of Columbus. The old discipline of Notre Dame was re-established in the halls with morning and evening prayers in Walsh, Sorin, and Badin halls and hall Masses at 6:30 each morning, and with the resumption of other campus regulations about study periods and recreation. But the expansion of Notre Dame begun before the war and the relaxation of war time had modified the old rules. Also among the new spiritual forces affecting the students was the spread of the practice of frequent Communion because those who had made an early First Communion were now going to college.

Father O'Hara as the prefect of religion had tried to conform his religious services to the needs of the military, arranging for a Mass at 5:15 in the morning and making himself available in his room in Walsh for conferences and confessions. Nevertheless, at this time Father O'Hara's chief interest was still the development of an important Department of Commerce, especially foreign commerce, at Notre Dame. He wrote to his family on July 10:

> I went over to Chicago last week to see Hurley. Sam Murdock drove me over and told us, by the way, that Papa's interview with Hurley some years ago, in Indianapolis gave Hurley his best information on S.A.—and we had dinner at the summer home at Wheaton. I never saw anybody so enthusiastic about N. D. as Hurley. He wants me to go to S.A. right away for students. I don't know what will come of it.[15]

But the war was still on, and although Father O'Hara opened an office in the Auditorium Hotel in Chicago for a few days to interview prospective commerce students, there was no sudden growth in the department. When classes began again, moreover, he had to take over Father Walsh's class in American history. He also taught a class in American government and politics, an economics class, and a moral class in Christian doctrine.

That he found these manifold duties taxing was indicated in a letter written in the following May, in which he also complained about one teacher and asked Father Cavanaugh to hire three additional economic teachers. One man he wanted Notre Dame to hire was Professor James E. Hagerty of Ohio State. To his proposal to hire three professors Father Cavanaugh said that hiring Professor Hagerty was "out of the question, until we get some money to pay salaries"[16] and suggested that Father James Quinlan and Father Charles Miltner might be assigned to teach economics.

Father Cavanaugh suggested that his successor as president might be interested in Father O'Hara's proposals. And to a proposal that Father O'Hara attend a conference in Washington and visit New York in the interests of the commerce classes in the spring the President gave a negative. Father O'Hara mentioned incidentally that his entire evenings were given over to his work as prefect of religion. The young men with problems were beginning to make a path to the door of the zealous and inspiring priest.

A busy summer followed. Father O'Hara taught summer school classes in the history of South America. On July 22–24 he represented the University in the meetings at Notre Dame of the executive committee that was forming the new National Catholic Welfare Council. The retiring president, Father Cavanaugh, had gone away, and the new president of Notre Dame, Father Burns, had not formally taken over. There is no record of Father O'Hara's activity in the meetings. It was noticeable, however, that Father Burns permitted Father O'Hara to go to New York later in the summer.

This change in the presidency of Notre Dame brought about by the enforcement of the six-year time limit on local superiorships imposed by the new code of canon law gave to Notre Dame a new type of president, and one that had considerable influence on the young teacher of commerce. Father Cavanaugh had not been well, and the celebration of his silver jubilee as a priest on April 24 had been made an occasion to recognize publicly the long years of tiring service he had given to Notre Dame. Besides his ill-health, Father Cavanaugh felt heavily the financial prob-

lems of Notre Dame and was willing to give to another the tasks
of the postwar years. Although Father Cavanaugh had been
appointed to the presidency by Father John Zahm and represented
the golden years of Notre Dame as a small liberal arts college, he
had been hampered in his administration by the conservative
policies of Father Zahm's successor and opponent, Father Andrew
Morrissey. A series of events changed this picture. In a provincial
chapter held at Notre Dame in the summer of 1919 Father Cavanaugh, according to custom, nominated his vice-president, Father
Walsh, and also Father James Burns to the chapter as his successor, and the chapter elected Father Burns, who was finishing
his superiorship of Holy Cross College in Washington. Father
Burns expressed a preference to go to the foreign missions in
Bengal to join his friend, Father Timothy Crowley, but he
accepted his election by the chapter to the presidency of Notre
Dame. A year later in a general chapter of the Congregation of
Holy Cross, Father Morrissey was elected coadjutor superior general to assist the ailing Father Gilbert Francais, superior general
since 1893. Father Charles O'Donnell, a younger and more progressive man, was elected provincial in the place of Father Morrissey, who lived scarcely a year as coadjutor general. Thus Father
Burns, with the backing of Father Charles O'Donnell, was able
to put into effect improvements at Notre Dame that had been
needed for a long time. In time the changes in the administration
of the University were quite numerous.

Under the provincialship of Father Andrew Morrissey there
had gradually developed a governing religious body at Notre
Dame, called the Local Council, which was distinct from the
official four-member Provincial Council. Besides the members of
the Provincial Council there were in the Local Council the superiors of all the religious houses at or near Notre Dame. All matters involving an expenditure of more than one hundred dollars
had to be approved by this council, which usually followed the
conservative ideas of Father Morrissey. Among the problems discussed in this council were such varied items as the salary of lay
professors at Notre Dame, the painting of the walls of the Main
Building, the fumigating of St. Edward's Hall, and the digging of
a ditch on St. Joseph's farm.[17] Under the cautious Father Morrissey there were few imaginative decisions by this council, and
the community and the University lived in a financially limited
world. When he succeeded to the provincialship in 1906, Father
Morrissey had rejected the grand plans of Father Zahm because
he felt that the community could not afford them, and the fact

that usually the community and University were without actual financial resources by the end of the summer seemed painful proof that notable expansion was impossible. Even as late as the first years of Father Burns's administration the Provincial Council had ruled that the first money from student payments in September would go to pay for money borrowed the previous summer. Yet when an alumnus, James A. Hayden of Chicago, had suggested in 1916 that the University celebrate the diamond jubilee of 1917 with a drive for endowment, Father Cavanaugh bowed to the opinion of the fathers at the University and declined the suggestion. With Father Burns in the spring of 1917, however, he had visited the representatives of the Rockefeller and Carnegie foundations in New York in search of help.[18] He could offer no solution to the pressing financial problems of Notre Dame which were to face his successor, Father Burns.

When the students returned in September, 1919, to Notre Dame they were greeted in the opening sermon not with the honeyed eloquence of the beloved Father Cavanaugh but with the dry nasal sentences of his successor, Father Burns, who did, however, speak first with praise and affection about his predecessor. Even the contrast between the large, round, smiling face and full body of the pulpit orator, Father Cavanaugh, and the small face and thin form of his successor could hardly have indicated the changes that were to take place in the University in the next three years. But there were other changes in personnel. Father Matthew Schumacher, who as director of studies had been the chief formulator of programs and the director of class content, had been elected president of St. Edward's College in Texas by the provincial chapter, and he was succeeded by quiet, studious Father Thomas Irving. Father Eugene Burke, a social inspiration in the family of Notre Dame, had likewise been elected to the presidency of Columbia University in Portland, Oregon. Also, before the first quarter of the new year had passed, the reorganization of the University from nominal to actual colleges and departments was announced. The appointment of deans of the colleges of arts and letters, science, engineering, and law, and of heads of departments was eventually of great importance in the academic advance of the University. Father Burns formed an Academic Council of the University, which met for the first time on February 21, 1920. Father John O'Hara was named head of the Department of Commerce, and this, together with his appointment to the Provincial Committee on Studies and the permission given him to travel, indicated that in the new administration

Father O'Hara had become a person of increasing importance. Finally in May, 1920, a separate graduate faculty was established, to which Father O'Hara was named along with the more active teachers of advanced courses among the clergy and laymen.

The limiting factor in these changes was the lack of working endowment to support the increasing lay faculty and to add to the library and other equipment necessary for the advanced classes. Notre Dame like most Catholic colleges was dependent on the income from student fees plus what stipends the clergy could obtain from priestly ministrations and from the attending to mission stations within a short distance from the University. An historian of American education during World War I noted that other American private colleges were dependent on endowment for from 41 to 45 percent of their income.[19] It was the lack of this endowment that checked the expansion plans at Notre Dame, including, of course, Father O'Hara's plans for expanding the Commerce Department.

Father O'Hara's participation in these changes at Notre Dame was quite important because of his zealous activity and because his superiors valued his knowledge of the contemporary world. On his own part he tried to build up his position as an authority in the field of foreign trade and Latin American studies, particularly by giving public lectures and by his publications. In the August, 1919, issue of the *Hispanic American Review*[20] he joined with five other Latin American specialists in "A Symposium on the Teaching of History of Hispanic America in the Educational Institutions of the United States." And in the *Grail* of St. Meinrad's for November, 1919, he published a lecture on "The Church in Spanish America in the Sixteenth Century," a paper he had given before the Notre Dame summer school in 1918. In addition he continued compiling a large collection of original source materials on South American history and culture. While this was intended to be a textbook on the history of Latin America and at the same time a book of documents, there was some notion that the book would likewise be accepted as a doctoral dissertation at The Catholic University.

In the fall of 1919 he had taught courses in exporting and the history of Latin America in addition to his economics courses and increased his Chamber of Commerce to four sections, with which he met once a week. Through the *Scholastic* he invited students from other departments to attend these meetings of the chamber, which were held in the basement of the library after night prayers the first four days of the week. He continued to invite businessmen from Chicago, South Bend, and other cities to address the chamber.

Probably the one to whom Father O'Hara confided most among the visiting businessmen was Edward N. Hurley of Chicago. This friendship apparently had its beginning in an earlier acquaintance between Mr. Hurley and Father O'Hara's father. Although Joseph Grace of New York was an earlier participant in Father O'Hara's plans, Hurley in Chicago was nearer and showed a greater interest. To him Father O'Hara outlined his plans, on November 15, 1919, plans that were years ahead in vision.

Dear Mr. Hurley:

I had a few hours in Chicago recently, and I tried to reach you at the plant, but you had remained at Wheaton that day, and I did not want to disturb you by telephone call. I am loath to break in upon your deserved rest now, but I want to give you the report I promised last spring, on the progress of our work in Commerce.

The Department of Commerce now includes a four-year course in Domestic Commerce, a two-year course in Accountancy, a four-year matter to be covered in two years, a four-year course in Industrial Engineering, and a one-year course in Engineering Administration. This last course is a graduate program and follows a degree in Engineering. We also arrange for combination courses with the Departments of Chemistry and Agriculture.

So far this year two hundred and sixty students have registered in the various courses, fifty-seven of them electing Foreign Commerce. Four of these are Seniors, six are Juniors, twelve are Sophomores and thirty-five are Freshmen.

This year we have registered sixty-seven Latin American students, including eighteen from Peru, and ten each from Colombia and Mexico. The other countries represented are: Argentina, Brazil, Chile, Ecuador, Salvador, Honduras, Cuba, Porto Rico, Santo Domingo, and the Philippine Islands. I am teaching Latin-American History to a class of twenty-six Juniors and Seniors.

We are holding strictly to the ideals of cultural preparation for Foreign Trade, and I feel sure that when our graduates demonstrate its worth, other schools will be willing to modify their course to meet the demand we hope to create. I notice that Georgetown has introduced Rhetoric, Public Speaking, Diplomacy, and Moral Philosophy. The bulletin announcing these cultural subjects (August, 1919) also advertises the following technical branches suggested in my address of last April: Export Sales Practice, Document Technique of Export Trade, Money, Banking, Foreign Exchange, and Business Law.

I wish to bring to your attention the following needs of Notre Dame:

1. *A Commerce Building.* All available classroom space is now taken, and the divisions in some of the classes are too large for adequate treat-

ment. For instance, four hundred students are studying Spanish, and we have only six divisions in these classes. Thirty should be the maximum number of a language class. Besides the practical value of additional space, a separate building and the organization of the Department as a distinct college would have great advertising value. A substantial building could be constructed for one hundred and fifty thousand dollars.

2. *An Endowment for Professors.* Our tuition fee is one hundred and twenty dollars, and most of our professors are priests who receive no salary: consequently, we are able to meet present needs by strict economy. An enlargement of the faculty is imperative, however, and for this an initial endowment fund of one hundred thousand dollars is needed.

3. *Scholarships for American Boys.* Although the University gives employment to some two hundred boys each year, to defray all or part of their expenses, several hundred applications had to be rejected this year because of lack of employment. It is distressing to see our ambitious young Catholics thwarted in this way when the Church is in need of educated leaders. The Department of Agriculture has more than a hundred tuition scholarships, contributed by the Studebaker Corporation and other manufacturers, but the Department of Commerce has only a few scholarships in Foreign Commerce, donated by the Supreme Council of the Knights of Columbus to returned soldiers.

4. *Scholarships for Latin Americans.* While the students here already enjoy the advantage of associating with the representatives of a great many foreign countries, more of these could be assimilated: and while the ambition of the Latin-American for higher education is more generally placed with the means to this end, there are plenty of boys in the southern continent who deserve assistance and would profit by it. There are four such boys here now. I know that you realize fully how friendly political relations can be fostered by the extension of such courtesies. The Oliver Chilled Plow Company has donated Agriculture scholarships for each of the Latin-American countries.

These are the present needs of Notre Dame, placed as I see the order of their importance. The first two I consider urgent. The need of Catholic schools of Commerce and especially of the kind of training we give at Notre Dame is more widely felt than even we imagined. There are Commerce students here from nearly every state in the Union. The school will get beyond us unless we have the means to meet every situation that arises.

I place these needs before you for your information, and I want to ask your assistance in relieving them. The work of Catholic education is one of the noblest works that can engage a man's attention today. I know your interest in it, and I feel that you will be willing to do whatever lies in your power to contribute to its progress.

I have written at great length, but only because I realize that you want to be fully informed of the situation here. Please take your time in considering the matter presented. I shall be glad to hear from you

at any time and to meet you in Chicago or at Notre Dame for an interview whenever you suggest.

Please remember me very kindly to Mrs. Hurley and the children.[21]

Had Father O'Hara achieved the major part of these proposals
in 1919 he would have been far ahead of most universities that
later developed programs in the field of Latin America. Edward
Hurley was indeed an enthusiast for the program, and he was the
best friend that the University had in this field, but the financial
stringencies that struck the country at this time delayed for years
the carrying out of his proposal to furnish the Commerce Building and other elements in the O'Hara plan. Father O'Hara turned
likewise to his other great business friend, Joseph Grace. He
wrote to Hurley on April 17 of the results of that trip.

Dear Mr. Hurley:

The proposition I made to Joe Grace was this:

1. The interchange of scholarships between the schools of North and
South America will do a great deal to remove mutual prejudice.

2. A generous supply of scholarships by Americans would be sure to
provoke concessions on the part of South American schools for our students who might want to do graduate work in South America.

3. To the ten Studebaker scholarships we already have, I wanted to
add ten Grace scholarships of $250 each (covering tuition and lodging
for a year). A charge of $2500 a year to advertising would do this.

I told him when I saw him Wednesday that I did not want to discuss
the proposition; that I had stolen the idea from you, and you would
talk it over with him. I simply outlined the plan to him, as I had in my
letter. I sent him also a statement of the advantages of the University's
Foreign Commerce course, dealing especially with the large number of
Latin-Americans here—80 this year.

Possibly you could find some other manufacturer or exporter willing
to invest in such a proposition. I would like to have at least twenty-five
scholarships at my disposal.

The Peruvian Ambassador, Senor Pezet, has an interesting proposition. He tells me that he has already proposed to the President, the
Nuntio and the Archbishop, the establishment of a branch of Notre
Dame in Lima. I told him we were too short of priests to consider it,
and he offered as a substitute the sending here of a number of seminarians to be trained as a nucleus of a Peruvian branch of the Order.
He will give me letters to his three friends so that the matter can be
taken up formally.[22]

Hurley proposed to visit Notre Dame later in the spring when
he would have a question and answer session with the commerce
students on foreign trade, but plans for this visit were interrupted
by the decision of Father O'Hara to attend the Foreign Trade Con-

ference in San Francisco in May. Father O'Hara traveled to the conference in the company of James J. Farrell, the president of United States Steel, whom he had invited to speak to the commerce students on his way west.

This trip to the west coast interrupted for the remainder of the year Father O'Hara's other main activity as prefect of religion. Through the *Scholastic* and with the aid of the pen of his brother Bob he began to urge the practice of frequent Communion. With the cooperation of Brother Alphonsus Sweet, the genial rector of Brownson Hall, the Apostolate Library of that hall was enriched with new Catholic writings. Father O'Hara used various means of encouraging daily Communions, making known the availability of confessors, and advertising the large number of communicants during Lent. At the end of the penitential season he boasted that the average daily number of communicants during Lent was 558 out of a total enrollment of 1207, which included the non-Catholics and religious. With considerable pride he wrote an editorial on this accomplishment in the *Scholastic* of April 24, making some generalizations about this side of Catholic education.

. . . . They show very clearly the educational trend of the University. What the Church needs in this country, what this country needs now, is a strong body of Catholic laymen who have outspoken confidence in prayer and have the spirit of sacrifice that will venture something big for an ideal. The needs of the individual Catholic are the same as those of the Church and state. And no student who made the sacrifices of early and uncomfortable rising in order to dedicate the best part of the day to God and be united with him in Holy Communion, will ever have reason to regret his choice of a Lenten penance. If a student practices this devotion for only a week, he has gained a new experience; he has set a bright spot in his life which will stand out in holy and comforting recollection long after other memories of Notre Dame will have passed away.

Father O'Hara had emerged among the priest confessors as one most accessible and as one dedicated to the promotion of frequent Communion, but his major work was still that of building up the Department of Commerce and that took him to the Trade Conference at San Francisco.

By traveling with James J. Farrell, Father O'Hara not only took the opportunity to talk to him about his plans and about the needs of Notre Dame but through Farrell he made friendly contacts with many other Catholic corporation heads who were in attendance at the conference. But his activities at the conference were seriously handicapped when he caught a severe cold and had to spend most of the time in his hotel room. Nevertheless, Father O'Hara wrote confidently to Father Burns that he should call on Farrell when he went to New York because Farrell already seemed to have been informed by Hurley of the plans for the Commerce Department. He told Father Burns that two other business executives, J. Rogers Flannery of Pittsburgh and J. J. Donovan of Seattle, had manifested an interest in the Notre Dame plans.

After his return from San Francisco Father O'Hara set out on a tour of South America in the interest of his program. But on his way to New York he again became ill in Washington, and some of his New York plans had to be cancelled. His companion on the trip was Joseph Thompson, and to obtain proper recognition in the countries he would visit, Father O'Hara had Hurley write letters to Secretary of State Bainbridge Colby and to Ambassador Joseph H. Shea at Santiago. Hurley wrote his letters as the newly appointed honorary dean of the Notre Dame Foreign Commerce School and begged of these men a cordial reception for Father O'Hara.

Father O'Hara traveled on one of the Grace liners through the Caribbean and on to Lima by way of the Canal. He found the best prospects for students in Peru and arranged for three to come to Brownson Hall. He then went on to Chile, where he found only one prospective student, Julio Prat, already known to Father Burns. Also, because of the approaching Chilean elections he could not establish proper contacts. Through Ambassador Shea a lecture on North American universities, especially about Notre Dame, was arranged in the Miraflores Theatre, a talk that received friendly notices in the Santiago newspapers.

From Santiago Father O'Hara set out on July 3 for Buenos Aires. The trip over the Andes in the South American winter was very cold, and he arrived late at night without proper arrangements for lodging.[23] Finally, through the Passionists he obtained a room and began what was later a friendly visit in the area in which he had spent happy years as a youth. While visiting old acquaintances in Argentina, Uruguay, and Brazil, Father O'Hara lost no opportunity to announce the purpose of his trip, especially his desire to arrange an exchange of students between Notre Dame and South American universities. Among the friendly notices in the press was that of *El Bien* of Montevideo, which described the purpose of his trip and the fine impression he had left with his audiences, adding:

During his brief stay in Montevideo, Father O'Hara has established deep and lasting ties in the bosom of our society, which finds in him, enhanced by virtue and apostolic zeal, the beautiful qualities of a solicitious and observing soul, possessed entirely by love and truth and in which there reechoes the highest importunities of justice and good.

Our house was honored with the visit of the renowned professor of the University of Notre Dame, worthy envoy of North American culture, and in the few moments of conversation which we had with him we experienced the pleasant impression of knowing an exalted and noble spirit of priest and scholar in which shine forth the most beautiful attributes of the mind and the most generous gifts of the heart.

In our farewell to Father O'Hara we take pleasure in repeating to him our vows of boundless and sincere devotion to his exalted person.

As Father O'Hara approached New York, he wrote to Father Burns about his trip, noting that he had some confidential information that he would have to deliver in Washington. He spoke also of the many college students who were working on the boats on which he traveled. They seemed satisfied with their work. He had proposed some similar arrangements for Notre Dame students to the United Fruit Company, but the company had rejected the proposal. Since Notre Dame was dropping the first two years of the preparatory school to make more room for college students, he proposed to Father Burns that the University offer to prospective commerce students a year of graduate work in a South American university with a guarantee of a position after graduation and opportunities for foreign cruises during the summer months as stewards or seamen. He was enthusiastic about the results of his trip.

. . . The treatment I have met with has been wonderful, and I have been assured of hearty cooperation everywhere. A good advertising campaign this winter in the countries visited will send us a stream of visitors and students and entrench us absolutely in the southern countries. I have at least 12 students signed up for the next few years, and have 3 with me: Ed Sullivan from Buenos Aires, J. P. Scaron Pallares from Montevideo and Ivan Pra from Santiago, of whom I wrote you.

In advertising I think it advisable to stress the positions offered graduates. I have a great many standing requests. . . .[24]

In the first *Scholastic* (September 25, 1920) after his return there was a column entitled "Father O'Hara in South America," along with his photograph, showing a thin, young, spectacled priest with advancing forehead covered by a center shock of hair. The article called the trip "one of the most important missions ever undertaken in the interests of Notre Dame" and said, "He was everywhere received with great warmth, and gained the complete confidence of prominent educators, national executives and

business men." Noting that American graduates were much in
demand especially in Peru, the writer of the article added "Father
O'Hara's plan, which no other University has considered, is of
national importance for it will bring to South America a group
that will understand the country and create there an amicable
attitude towards the United States."

These statements were overwhelmingly optimistic, and had
there been the proper financial support, Father O'Hara's plans
might have borne great fruit.

On the other hand, Father O'Hara was quite practical when he
told Hurley of his trip:

Tom Casey has probably told you a great deal about my trip. It was
successful in every way, I believe, and I want to thank you very cordially for your part in making it so.

In the first place I told everybody that you were the originator of
the plan of exchange, and your name did as much as the merits of the
plan, to popularize it. I was very well received everywhere, and the
Catholic educators especially have shown the warmest spirit of cooperation, and have promised to use their influence to direct students to
Notre Dame.

I brought four boys back with me at their own expense. Two from
the Catholic University of Santiago, one from the University of Montevideo and one a graduate of an English High School in Buenos Aires—
Edward Sullivan, Jr., son of the Manager of the American Trading Co.
in Buenos Aires. I sent one of this year's graduates, John Balfe, to the
Mercantile Bank of the Americas in Buenos Aires, where he will have
an opportunity of attending the University. Another graduate, John
Powers, is working for the United States Steel Corporation, and will go
to Chile in February to continue his class work. James Dower, the third
member of the class is considering a proposition to engage in educational work in Peru for a couple of years.

Your letter to Ambassador Shea received a great welcome. I found
that he and father were old friends. We had dinner at the Embassy,
and attended the Fourth of July reception there, where he presented
me to a great many important people. He sent warmest greetings
back to you.

The letter you obtained from Secretary Colby was an important
help in securing the interest of officials of both our government and the
governments of the countries visited. I found the diplomatic and consular officers, with but one exception, extremely cordial and helpful.

I wish that you could report the one exception to the Department of
State. A Vice Consul in Montevideo, whose name is Jennison, refused
to take his superior's letters seriously, and went out of his way to insult
me. He asked for information on the alleged corruption of the Catholic
clergy in South America, and when I accepted his question in good

faith and discussed the matter with him, and refused to permit the wholesale denunciation of South American clergy, he asked me if I was "straight." In answer to my protest he explained that he meant to ask whether I belonged to the same church as the men he was denouncing.

Although I told him that I did not care to discuss religion with him, and that my mission in South America was not of a religious character he asked further for information on the matter of indulgences, and spoke very slightingly of the intelligence of the people who would believe such a doctrine. Upon that I took the liberty of telling him that he was an ass, and an unworthy representative of the government. During the remaining days of my stay in Montevideo, I was at particular pains to inquire about his antecedents, and learned that he spends a considerable portion of his time denouncing the Catholic Church. He has been in Montevideo for six years. It seems to me most unfortunate that such a man should be allowed to give a wrong impression of American fairness in a country whose good will we are at pains to cultivate.

I might add that while I found an anti-American feeling among a great many of the Catholics in other parts of South America, I found a most enthusiastic defender of American ideals in South America, in Dr. Juan Zorrilla de San Martin, the editor of the Catholic daily, "El Bien Publico," of Montevideo. Their Fourth of July edition of this year is the best thing I have seen. I understand that it was brought to the attention of the State Department by Minister Jeffrey.

I gathered a good bit of useful information for Admiral Benson, and had a good interview with him in Washington. I intend to send him a memorandum within the next day or two.[25]

When Father O'Hara returned to Notre Dame, he could not help applying his energy to the changes that were going on around him. Actually he participated in two of these changes as a leader, as head of the Commerce Department and later dean of the College of Commerce and as the prefect of religion. Of his conversations with Father Burns there are no records, but they were most of the time under the same roof and met each day. Father Burns was trying to make two adjustments in the University, both very closely related: he wanted to make the academic divisions of the university—the colleges and departments and their officers—actually function, and by this change he hoped to offer a better reason for the second move of begging financial aid from foundations and others who would give the support necessary for successful higher educational enterprise. While Father Burns was a master of fruitful conversation, he was not talented in public persuasion or oratory. Perhaps he was not the man for the job of president of an undergraduate college despite his knowledge of the problem. After his first day of shaking hands with old and new students on the opening day of the school year, he told his vice-president, Father Matthew Walsh, that he could not endure such work, and that he would not take a second term as president. Nevertheless in the internal development of the University he worked a veritable financial and organizational revolution. Father O'Hara's special part of these changes was in the Commerce Department.

In September, 1920, Father O'Hara introduced in the Commerce Department small quiz sections as a method of insuring that the students grasped matters handled in lectures to larger groups. He also added four new elective courses, bringing the total electives to nineteen, and appointed as new teachers Joseph Rafter to offer classes in business law and contract, David A. Weir to teach money and banking and public finance, and Eugene Payton to teach commercial geography, to be in charge of the workroom and travel library in the mezzanine of the library, and to direct the Chamber of Commerce. He also arranged for Manuel Vial of Santiago, whom he had brought from South America, to lecture on international law. He divided the Chamber of Commerce into six sections, each meeting on a different day of the week, and on the first Sunday in October he held a commerce "smoker" noted for "cigarettes and fun" according to the *Scholastic* of October 9. In February, 1921, when Joseph Rafter left for Villanova and the Pennsylvania bar examination, his place was taken by James E. McCarthy, whom Father O'Hara had met on his trip through South America. Mr. McCarthy, a handsome young man with closely trimmed moustache, neatly parted hair, and fashionable clothes, exemplified the successful business executive Father O'Hara hoped to create in his students. He was the Buenos Aires representative of the United States Transportation Company when Father O'Hara induced him to come to Notre Dame. A graduate of Columbia University, James McCarthy was competent in the ways of foreign trade, especially that with South America.

Father O'Hara himself taught two Spanish classes, directed a section of the Chamber of Commerce throughout the year, and during the first semester taught a class in exporting. His classbooks have plenty of grade marks for the students, showing that these were not merely lecture courses. He also continued his public relations work for the department, giving two talks to the South Bend Chamber of Commerce on his South American trip and the prospects for South American trade. At Father O'Hara's request the Academic Council had discontinued the two-year course in commerce at the University and on April 20 established, with him as the first dean, the separate College of Commerce and Business Administration, which would award one degree for all departments of the college, that of Bachelor of Commercial Science. On December 17, *El Bien Publico* of Montevideo published what it announced as the first of a series of studies by Father O'Hara on "Los Cambios con Norte America." In the article dated Notre Dame, November, 1920, Father O'Hara discussed the financial reasons for the decline in commercial exchanges between the United States and the La Plata countries. In the spring he attended the Foreign Trade Convention in Cleveland. He wrote his family that he was also participating in Father Burns's drive to raise an endowment of $1,000,000. But his other interest, that of prefect of religion, was beginning to take much of his time and attention.

The increase in daily and frequent Holy Communion at Notre Dame during these years can hardly be attributed to any one man. In the first place there was the change in attitude throughout American Catholicism whereby the youngsters in the parochial schools received their First Communion at the age of six or seven and were encouraged to form practices of frequent Communion. Daily Communion in the ordinary parish school was difficult to arrange. At Notre Dame compulsory attendance at daily Mass had been dropped, although Communion was available for several hours each morning in the basement chapel of the church and in the hall chapels at the Masses of the priest prefects. Father O'Hara, more than any other priest, brought to the campus the practice of Bishop Chartrand of giving Communion frequently each morning outside of Mass and of making himself available to the students morning and evening for confession. Also having a bent towards statistical analysis, Father O'Hara began early in his career as a priest confessor to make a statistical measure of the religious life of the students. From time to time as prefect of religion he published in the *Scholastic* the results of his surveys. Thus he announced that during the student retreat there were 5,285 Communions, of which he said 4,033 were college students, and that the peak reception was 748 on Saturday of the retreat. He drew attention to peak numbers on All Saints day and the low numbers on football trips and holidays. On May 14 there was posted in the rear of the basement chapel a graph showing the attendance at the Communion rail during the year. This graph had been made by Father Steiner. In March he distributed questionnaires to the students to get their reactions to frequent Communion and to obtain information on student attitudes toward

this practice. Later Father O'Hara analyzed these student questionnaires and published the result of his analyses more or less as
a defense of his promotion of frequent Communion among college men. On June 19 he prepared a more confidential report to
the President, Father Burns.[26]

He listed first the opportunities for confession because he
and Bishop Chartrand regarded that as the key to frequent
Communion.

These were multiplied this year. Two priests heard confessions in the
basement chapel every morning from 6:30 to 7:00 a.m. and from 6:15
to 7:00 p.m., and there was always one priest in attendance for confession and communion from six o'clock till eight every morning. Confessions were heard in the hall chapels every evening after night prayer.
Hall prefects were assigned to this work until the Religious Survey
showed that this system was unpopular, and shifts were made.

There were only two evenings during the whole school year when no
penitent presented himself for confession after supper in the basement,
and there were generally penitents for the hall chapel confessions after
night prayer. It should be noted, however, that this device did not increase the number of communions in the hall chapels; it had no direct
bearing on morning prayer.

Father O'Hara recognized the many priests who cooperated with
him in the movement.

Special mention should be made of certain priests who were extremely zealous in promoting religious work. The Very Reverend Father Provincial [Father Charles L. O'Donnell] showed an admirable
example by assisting with the work of confession in the basement chapel
whenever there was need of an extra confessor. Fathers Joseph Burke
and Doremus heard confessions regularly every morning for forty
minutes, and were always willing to do extra work when there was
need of their services. Father Steiner's work was heroic. He heard confessions every evening in the basement chapel for three quarters of an
hour, and then went to Sorin Hall, whether there were penitents or not,
to hear confessions after night prayer. He also took care of the late
distribution of Holy Communion on Thursday and Sunday mornings,
and took the place of the Prefect of Religion whenever he was absent
from the University. Father Steiner prepared the graphs representing
the daily fluctuations in the number of communicants, and in every
way showed zeal worthy of imitation.

Father Lahey heard confessions every evening in Walsh Hall, and
took care of the late distribution every morning from 7:00 to 7:15. He
was always on hand, too, for any extra work for which his services were
needed. Father Stack replaced Father Doremus as the regular nightly
confessor in Corby Hall, and was always willing to do extra work. Father Mendez [O.P.] said the second Mass in the basement chapel faithfully every morning, and heard the confessions of Spanish students. He

always showed himself anxious to help in other ways. Father Benedict, O.S.B., frequently asked for opportunities to exercise his zeal. He heard confessions regularly during the High Mass on Sunday, and both he and Father Ill helped occasionally with confession in the basement. Father Ill performed this and other supernumerary services with a willingness that should edify younger members of the community. Father Broughall had a regular confessional during the High Mass on Sundays and showed great eagerness to help in other ways. Father Remmes heard Confessions in Badin Hall until the Hall prefects were taken from the work, and did a great deal through personal appeal, to start daily Communion among the freshmen in Badin Hall last fall.

There is room for great improvement in the matter of personal appeal for daily Communion and the development of the spiritual life generally. Students expect priests to be priests first of all, and they have frequently remarked that they have never heard a word of religious counsel from some members of the Community. Human respect should never deter a priest from exercising his priestly function: the boys expect it of him. This sort of cooperation would greatly relieve the duties of the Prefect of Religion.

Father O'Hara reported to Father Burns also on the effects of the student retreat and of the practice of all-day adoration on First Friday which he had introduced with the permission of the Bishop. He added nine special observations on the religious situation at Notre Dame. Some of his observations were very enlightening on the religious life of the students of the day.

1. There is considerable discrepancy in the amount of previous religious instruction received by the students. This suggests that they be graded at entrance and their instruction varied accordingly. This presents practical difficulties.

. . . .

5. Greater freedom in relations with the students of St. Mary's College might reduce the number of those who correspond only with non-Catholic girls.

6. Catholic reading is woefully neglected. I would suggest talks on the matter in the English classes, with the occasional selections to show the value of Catholic books, and the establishment in each hall of a library such as Brother Alphonsus maintains in Brownson Hall. . . .

7. The High Mass seems rather unpopular, partly because the students do not find the music attractive, and partly because they know too little about the Mass. Last year an attempt was made to have a series of sermons on different points of the Mass, but the preachers failed to arouse enthusiasm, probably because the sermons were too abstract. . . . a series of lectures on the Mass was given in Sorin Hall on Sunday mornings. There was an average attendance of 30 students and two professors at these lectures.

Consideration might be given to have a High Mass for the students

only on the Third Sunday—a solemn Mass of Exposition at 8:15. On
other Sundays they could have a Low Mass at 7:30 with breakfast at
8:15. This would give them the edification of a General Communion
every Sunday.

In discussing the obstacles to the religious life of the students
Father O'Hara suggested that the President "in his opening talks
on the rules, might do well to stress the danger which lies in
dance halls, drink, and the so-called 'petting parties' or 'spooning
bees' which have come to be very dangerous concomitants of even
the 'best' dances. . . ." He thought the President should tell the
individual rectors to enforce the rule on early rising and added:
"If the law is not to be observed it should be abolished, because
contempt for one law leads to contempt for all law." He noticed
that this contempt existed towards the classes in Christian doctrine, saying that he knew of certain individuals who had not
attended the three years of obligatory religious classes who yet
obtained their degrees. He reprobated the failure to organize these
classes promptly at the beginning of the year, but he did not insist
that the classes receive credit or be raised to the university level.

To supplement his observations Father O'Hara quoted to the
President some apt comments of the students which he had culled
from the answers to his questionnaire. He used two headings,
"Discipline" and "Means for Increasing Daily Communion." But
the two topics were evidently closely related in his mind and in
the quotations.

One point was made repeatedly by the students. They felt that
a fuller religious life meant a freer life. Father O'Hara quoted the
complaint of an older student:

I find that when your work is done and there are no athletic contests
here that there is a great temptation especially to gamble here. In the
catalogue it says that frequent visits to town are not allowed because a
college man should dream, etc. Do you expect a person to dream forever? About all you have to look forward to around here is your
mail. . . . We are men now and almost ready to go out in the world
for ourself. This kindergarten treatment does not prepare us for the
world. It makes us dependent upon someone else. You can't expect a
young man to lop around in his room all day. He desires company with
the opposite sex. The school takes away to a large extent the very thing
for which our country fought for, namely, personal freedom in every
respect. The football team had a large part to play in my return this
year, and it will have a larger part if I return next. I feel that I am old
enough not to be treated as a mere child, and a good football team is
not going to change my mind about coming back if I once decide to go
elsewhere.

Some students insisted on the abolition of the required attendance at Sunday vespers. One said, "I think the way to increase daily communion is to put them on their honor and abolish morning prayer." Another answering the question about his reason for coming to Notre Dame said, "Of my own free choice, it is a fine old school. I like it better every day, but I believe the whole student body is back of me when I say that the enforcement of regulations is at present in the wrong hands." Father O'Hara always printed these representative criticisms but did not indicate what he thought of their validity.

While Father O'Hara's mornings and evenings were mainly spent in looking after the religious problems of Notre Dame, his daytimes were chiefly concerned with the College of Commerce. Here he faced the general financial problem of Notre Dame: to equip classrooms and to hire teachers. Father O'Hara first met this problem when he began to tell Father John Cavanaugh of his grand plans for commerce at Notre Dame, and Father Cavanaugh told him that the University did not have the funds to pay the salaries of the professors they already had. The commerce school, even more than the science college, required lay teachers—men who knew the ways of modern finance. But the whole University was in need of financial guides to aid the Holy Cross priests in collecting and handling the large sums necessary for a large American college. In this sense the financial revolution introduced by Father Burns was even more important than the change in teachers and administration. This revolution was precipitated by a regulation of the State of Indiana. That state regulation required that to offer an advanced degree the granting institution must have an endowment of at least $500,000. In accordance with state laws State Superintendent of Public Instruction L. N. Hines wrote to Father Burns on April 7, 1921, asking for a statement of Notre Dame's endowment. Two days later Father Burns sent Mr. Hines a brief summary listing the productive endowment at $2,012,684.39. He itemized the statement of endowment as follows:

Real Estate Mortgage Bonds	$ 114,619.67
Real Estate	600.00
Liberty Bonds	19,464.72
Railroad Bonds	2,000.00
Capital Services	1,876,000.00
Total	$2,012,684.39

Fixed Annual Income	
From Invested Endowment As Above	$ 9,235.00
From Contributed Services	93,800.00
Total	$ 103,035.00[27]

On reading these figures one might think that the financial condition of the University with an endowment of two million dollars was quite good unless he also read the letter of Father Burns to the State Superintendent of Instruction explaining the figures. In reality the total actual endowment was about $113,000.00 in invested securities. Father Burns explained:

Our main endowment is, however, "The Living Endowment," which is characteristic of Catholic institutions of higher education. This consists of the gratuitous life teaching services of the members of the Congregation of Holy Cross which conducts the University. The Congregation is a teaching organization. It trains its men for the work of teaching. They are under religious obligation to devote their lives to this work. In this gratuitously rendered teaching service the University, therefore, possesses an endowment which is more certain and reliable than bonds or other forms of endowment funds. The North Central Association recognized this "Living Endowment" as the equivalent of standard productive funds, as is shown by the fact that Notre Dame University has long been a member of the Association. The matter was brought up at the recent meeting of the Association in Chicago, in connection with the application for admission of a certain Catholic institution, and it was explicitly stated by the chairman that the Association recognized this form of endowment.

For the fiscal year of 1919–1920, there were forty-seven religious teachers engaged at the University. Thirty-four of these were teachers and thirteen occupied administrative positions. If salaries were to be assigned to these men according to the nature of their work and their ability—the salaries paid to lay teachers at Notre Dame being taken as standard—the total amount of the forty-seven salaries so assigned would be $93,800; and this at 5% represents a capital of $1,876,000.00. These men have all been especially trained for their work. Many of them hold the degree of Ph.D.

I enclose a list of the religious faculty members, showing the work they are doing and the salaries that would be assigned them on the basis of the salaries of our lay teachers.

The list enclosed by Father Burns contained the president, seven directors, six assistant directors, one director of studies, one registrar, one secretary, one burser, one prefect of discipline, twenty professors, four assistant professors, and four instructors. This report of Father Burns was accepted with praise by the State Superintendent of Instruction, although he urged Father Burns to seek more of the other endowment. Father O'Hara was among those living endowments, but he realized that other endowments were needed to have new faculty members or to build a new commerce building.

The "President's Report"[28] which Father Burns sent to some
of the newly chosen lay trustees in the spring of 1921 depicted
this financial crisis of Notre Dame. In the first place he noted that
the Notre Dame collegiate attendance had grown from 459 in
1910–1911 to 1147 in the year 1920–1921, an increase of 150 percent, or 15 percent a year. This student body came from nearly
every state, and included 73 students from Latin America, 10
from China, and some from Japan and other foreign countries.
To make room for the increased student body the first two years
of the preparatory school had been abandoned in 1920, the other
two years to be discontinued later. Despite this there were 350
students living off campus. There were 125 students working off
campus, and 186 were employed part time on campus. Despite
this situation many others had to be turned away for financial
reasons. That year the University had had to add two professors,
two assistant professors, seven instructors, and three laboratory
assistants. This with the general rise in salaries had increased the
salary budget by $40,000. He continued:

. . . More professors are needed and the salaries we pay are still very
much below what is paid at institutions of similar rank. It is true that
one-half of our teachers receive no compensation whatsoever, being
members of the Congregation of Holy Cross. Their services are entirely
gratuitous. Their number is increasing gradually from year to year;
but their number is not increasing in proportion to the growth of the
collegiate student body. The consequence is that we have to procure
more lay teachers. I have carefully estimated the needs of the various
departments in this way and I find that we ought to have twenty additional faculty members at the present time.

Father Burns then listed these desired additional men by title
and estimated that their salaries would amount to an additional
$40,000. Among the first needs of the University were two addi-
tional residence halls to bring the 350 students back to the campus. The University needed an engineering building that would
cost an estimated $300,000. For the development of commerce and
foreign trade another building was needed that would cost about
$200,000. A building was needed to house the art collection and
the historical museum then occupying space in the library building. Father Burns also listed the benefactions of the previous year.
The efforts to raise a permanent endowment had been checked
by the depression of the fall of 1920, but funds had been received
to the amount of $91,411.26, besides gifts of equipment, prizes,
and partial scholarships to bring the total number of scholarships
to 81 in all categories. But he added that much more money was

necessary if Notre Dame was to carry on its tasks. The University was about to make its first public appeal for funds.

The first endowment drive undoubtedly had many unknown roots. Probably the first was the visit of Fathers Cavanaugh and Burns to the Rockefeller and Carnegie foundations in March, 1917. Father Burns wrote to Father Morrissey subsequently that Father Cavanaugh had been very frank in telling the representatives of these foundations of Notre Dame's problems. Henry S. Pritchett of the Rockefeller General Board then agreed to visit the campus the following month, and there were other such visits. At least three important results came eventually from these conversations and visits. At the suggestion of the Rockefeller Foundation, Notre Dame set up a board of lay trustees in the fall of 1920 to handle its endowment; secondly, during the summer of 1921 the University hired experienced accountants, H. E. Dalton and N. R. Feltes from the Studebaker Corporation of South Bend, to reorganize the finances of Notre Dame. The president of Studebaker was Albert Erskine, by that time also president of the Board of Lay Trustees of the University. And thirdly, the General Education Board of the Rockefeller Foundation granted Notre Dame $250,000 on condition that the University raise an additional $750,000 to complete a million dollars for endowment. Later the Carnegie Foundation added to the Rockefeller gift an additional $75,000.00. How deeply Father O'Hara was involved in these negotiations is not of record, but since his commerce program was dependent on raising an endowment, and since he was close to Mr. Hurley, who was one of the most active trustees, it is evident that Father O'Hara was involved even before he joined in the public drive for funds.

The announcement of the grant from New York by the General Education Board forced the University to proceed. Father Burns was not ready then to announce his plans for raising the other $750,000. He did tell the public that President Wallace Buttrick of the Board had visited Notre Dame twice, and said, "They have examined Notre Dame University from every angle and the present gift may therefore be regarded as an emphatic expression of their satisfaction with what they found here." When the drive was formally opened on May 23, Father O'Hara joined Father Burns and Father John McGinn in addressing the South Bend leaders of the drive. In his speech he promised benefits to South Bend industry through planned exchanges between Notre Dame and South American universities and industries. He also arranged a college night at the South Bend Chamber of Commerce in which the University officials and Notre Dame students staged a social evening to promote better relations between the city and the University. Nevertheless Father O'Hara had to remain on the campus for summer school, in which he taught two classes: "The Organization of the Church in Latin America" and "Latin American Colonization."

Father O'Hara's dream of an important school of commerce and business administration probably received its first disappointment when Edward N. Hurley, the honorary dean, found himself unable to furnish the proposed commerce building or the funds for professorships or students because of his financial difficulties in the depression of 1920. Without that aid or the aid of other benefactors Father O'Hara had to build his School of Commerce on meagre resources. Nevertheless his plans for a college business education for Catholic young men were well balanced.

His first and basic problem was to make the new program participate in the liberal education to which it properly belonged, even though it was no longer in the College of Arts and Letters. Father O'Hara said in the catalogue:

. . . Special emphasis is placed in such cultural subjects as English, history, philosophy, and political science, because it is believed that these subjects constitute the essentials of a college education and train men for the most effective citizenship.

Just as the old science program at Notre Dame had aimed at a liberal education while substituting mathematics and science classes for the study of classical languages and literatures, so the new commerce program replaced the same classical languages with courses in business, trade, and transportation. So long as Father O'Hara had the final word about the commerce program, this cultural ideal was retained.

A second factor in the growth of the commerce program was the influx of many students desiring a practical program of studies that would enable them to get a better job, particularly in business. The increase in college enrollments during the war, and immediately after with the aid of scholarships granted to veterans, multiplied the number of young men and women at college portals who not only did not have any interest in a classical education but who would not have any use for it once it had been attained. The public high schools had been offering practical courses for more than a generation, and while the greater portion of these high-school products were not expected to go on to college, there was no law to prevent them from doing so. The same

was true to a lesser extent of Catholic high schools, which were
ceasing to be the private academies of another day and were simply Catholic programs to raise the level of Catholic parochial
education to the new level expected of the first-class citizen. Far
from trying to check this tendency, Father O'Hara planned with
his program to direct this floodtide to the most advantageous
results. The number of students registered in commerce swelled
from 6 in 1913 to 132 by 1918 and 587 by 1923. It was indeed a
floodtide that swept by poorly manned barriers, carrying with it
the well-meant efforts to improve the standards of teaching by
offering a partially cultural program. The needed commerce
building did not come, and the teaching staff assembled by Father
O'Hara was too small.

Father O'Hara had an even higher dream for the Notre Dame
School of Commerce, one that anticipated the programs instituted forty years later. He undoubtedly knew that he had to continue to accept the ordinary commerce student who wanted to
know about corporations, banking, insurance, and accounting, but
he dreamt of establishing a school of foreign commerce catering
to business with South America that would be heavily supported
by the businessmen engaged in this rich trade and that would
enable Catholic Notre Dame to exchange not only students but
cultural traditions with the universities of the southlands.

Father O'Hara's report to the President in 1921[29] listed the
practical problems he faced: the need of a considerably greater
expenditure of money for teachers, buildings, and scholarships.
There were actually several elements in his plans that never became real or came so late as to limit their value. In the first place,
despite the endowment drive there were no classroom buildings
erected at that time for these five hundred additional commerce
students. Some classrooms were created in the unused basements
of Walsh and Sorin halls, and all available space in other classroom buildings were filled with benches and lined with black-
boards. The Hurley commerce building which seemed so near a
reality in 1922 did not come until 1933. The scholarships that
would have enabled the registrar to sort out applications were
not established. The additional teachers not only for business
subjects but also for those other cultural courses that justified the
Notre Dame program were wanting. Father William Bolger,
C.S.C., was a capable lecturer, but he could not really teach the
hundred and fifty students in his classroom in the library basement. The experiment of quiz sections for these large classes, in
which Father O'Hara occasionally participated, lasted for only a

year. According to his classbook he conducted four of these one day a week during 1922–1923.

The peak of Father O'Hara's efforts for his commerce program came when he announced in March, 1922, that if fifteen students applied within a few days for graduate work in commerce for the next academic year, a graduate program would be established. There were not fifteen applications, apparently, and there was certainly no staff to teach the program or additional facilities for graduate work. Instead the aims of the program began gradually to level off to the means at hand. Spanish remained one of the favorite languages of the commerce students, but mastery never seemed to be their aim. The history of South America soon lost out in the rush for more practical courses. Father O'Hara was given secretarial help at registration and some additional teachers were hired, but he was also becoming more deeply involved in his work as prefect of religion. In September, 1923, James E. McCarthy, the head of the Department of Foreign Trade, was given the title of assistant dean of the college, and Father O'Hara taught the commerce students only in their religion classes. In September, 1924, Father O'Hara was replaced as dean by Professor McCarthy. Father O'Hara's interest in the School of Commerce had not dwindled. The means to carry out his program were simply not at hand. In the meantime his work as prefect of religion had increased into a full-time task.

THREE

Prefect of Religion

MOST YOUNG PRIESTS WHO HAVE LIVED with students during the first years after ordination and have been able to win their confidence feel an urge to devote themselves entirely to the care of these young men, and no one can win the confidence of these students so well as the younger priest who opens his door and his heart to them. Father O'Hara later found an expression of this in Cardinal Newman's "Second Spring." Newman had said: "How Beautiful is the human heart, when it puts forth its first leaves, and opens and rejoices in its spring-tide." And Father O'Hara commented: ". . . Everyone who comes in close contact with youth, who becomes in any way their confidant and adviser, must feel the quickening influence of their very presence. The priest, most especially, to whom it is given to know the secret depths of the young heart must humbly thank God for the very marvelous power he possesses."[1] Father O'Hara was neither the only nor the first priest at Notre Dame to welcome the students to his room, but he combined with his invitation a special kind of understanding of the problems of Catholic youth.

The attendance of youths like these at Catholic colleges in the United States was growing steadily in the 1920's, and many of the youngsters who came to Catholic colleges were not the academic equals of those who were being admitted to Harvard and Yale and the other older colleges of the country. The public high schools, from which about half came, were faced with students for whom attendance was compulsory, so that public schools had to water down their programs to embrace all. And Catholic high schools had little choice but to do likewise, although the perfunctory teaching of a classic discipline such as Latin persisted in them long after there was any real mastery of the language by the student. There was nothing surprising in the rush of these new high-school graduates to the new college business and commerce departments, where classical languages had been dropped and where training for business was explicit. Science and technical schools could hold the line against these poorly prepared students because technical skill and accuracy were necessary prerequisites for science and mathematics. But besides the explicit business or science students the traditional liberal arts program was soon swamped by hundreds of applicants with little or no definite training in the classics or in any other language. Instead they came with a conglomeration of credits in English, mathematics, history, and elementary sciences that meant nothing more than a high-school diploma. Because college training meant a better job, there was some reluctance by Catholic educators to turn away the good boy even when he was not prepared for college work. The result was a serious lowering of standards and a multiplication of students.

It is doubtful that twenty percent of the students who came to Notre Dame in the 1920's had parents who had finished high school. These boys could, for the most part, read and write a good page of correct English, and they had completed a high-school course of mathematics to which had been added the elements of chemistry and physics. Father Charles Miltner, the new dean of the College of Arts and Letters at Notre Dame, tried hard to have a student continue with Latin if he had studied it in high school, but in so doing he was thereby driving some of the youngsters to desperation or into the commerce program. Realistically, however, he reorganized in 1924 the whole arts program and gave the treasured bachelor of arts degree for all courses of the arts and letters program, whether the student majored in the classics, English, economics, history, journalism, or library science. Unrelenting defenders of the A.B. course were loud in denunciation of this betrayal of the traditional liberal arts program, but the college administration had little choice. Actually the handful of students who tried to follow the old liberal arts program in most Catholic colleges were leaning heavily on English translations. The students in these new college programs were not scholars in the strict sense. They were fresh, and one might say innocent, youngsters, willing to learn and wanting to get an education in a Catholic atmosphere. These were the youngsters who had by 1920 already become the great concern of Father John O'Hara, as they had been of the cathedral priest of Indianapolis, Bishop Chartrand.

Despite the large number of students residing off campus, Notre Dame was still a boarding college and permission was required for absences from the campus. At least in theory and where the prefect could enforce the regulations in the study halls and dormitories, the student was supposed to be at his desk or in his room after evening prayer. He was in class from eighteen to twenty hours a week and was supposed to receive enough outside work in those class hours to require him to study at least one half time more than he was in class. There was also at Notre Dame a good tradition of physical exercise, centered in interhall football, basketball, baseball, and track competitions, with swimming in the lake in spring and early fall, although all these sports were also carried on informally. The movie or dance had to wait until the weekend.

The religious tone of the regime at Notre Dame at the beginning of the 1920's was supported by the requirement of daily morning prayer and evening prayer, and attendance at Mass on Saturday as well as on Sundays. Father O'Hara's plea that the Notre Dame student go to Communion daily or at least nearly daily involved little hardship so long as there were opportunities for the student to go to confession when that was needed before receiving Communion. The theory of frequent or daily Communion as advanced by Bishop Chartrand and as he had taught it to Father O'Hara in Indianapolis implied that unless the young man was a daily communicant he was missing much of the richness of his Catholic faith.

Just as Father O'Hara had not been the first to urge the students to study business at Notre Dame, neither was he the first to urge the practice of daily and frequent Communion at Notre Dame. Even while he was a student and lay teacher at Notre Dame the Eucharistic Union had been formed among the high-school students in Carroll Hall by some priest prefects, especially Father Cornelius Hagerty.[2] Gradually many college students and some teachers, such as Mr. O'Hara, joined in these services. The center of this first movement was the daily Mass each morning in the chapel on the third floor of the Main Building, to which the singing of hymns had been added. There were no early or late Communions, for the priests in charge of this Union insisted that giving Communion outside of Mass was giving in to laziness and would lead to a lack of appreciation for the Mass, the central part of Christian worship.

The reasoning of Bishop Chartrand and Father O'Hara was a bit different. They had no fear that the daily communicant would have less respect for the Mass because he could also receive Communion outside of Mass itself. Father O'Hara did not see why those who accidentally slept in or had not risen at the proper time for some other reason, or had even risen earlier for some purpose, should be denied the benefits of Communion. He had two further reasons for his stand. The main one was that the essential effects of Communion on the receiver were *ex opere operato,* from the sacrament itself, and not *ex opere operantis,* that is, dependent on the fervor and zeal of the recipient, granting of course he was already in the state of grace. He was sure that there would be grace and merit for the communicant above whatever the youngster would earn by his own personal piety. The second and in time the chief argument for Holy Communion was that the student who could so live as to be able to receive Communion daily would live a Christian life and be so constantly in the state of grace that all the other problems of religious living would thereby be solved. It was over this last idea that there arose much of the conflict between the work of the prefect of religion and other officers of the University because Father O'Hara made efforts to eliminate from the lives of the students everything that might impede this sacramental life.

The picture of Father John F. O'Hara that graduates of the 1920's best remember is of a tall, thin man hurrying from Sorin Hall to Sacred Heart Church or to the dining hall with his rather small, quick steps, a smile on his face and a greeting, usually by name, for everyone and perhaps a wave of the hand. For the rest of the time the students saw him giving out row after row of Communions in church on Sunday or in Sorin Hall, or sitting placidly in the confessional or at his overloaded desk in Sorin Hall, or pacing around the room with the inevitable cigarette. Somehow those troublesome sinuses behind his pince-nez glasses never seemed to be able to cloud that smile or to check that quip, although he was probably never without some annoying catarrhal condition. His only cure for this was to lie in the sun on the pier of St. Joseph's Lake, wearing little more than a loin cloth, soaking in the sun's rays, and displaying a physique that earned for him from his good friend, Father Lange, the nickname "The Splinter." He and Father Lange were in the lake nearly every day despite the fact that a South Bend physician had warned them that the marl-touched water of the lake was bad for sinuses. Father O'Hara told his family that he would have to swim with his head out of the water, and Father Lange denied that Father O'Hara joined him when he broke the ice on the lake for a spring or fall swim.

For his campaign to make all the students frequent communicants Father O'Hara had untiring zeal and a statistical ability that enabled him to measure quite adequately the success and failure of his efforts. He probably did considerable reading at the start of this full-time career as prefect of religion, especially while he was still teaching, but gradually as more and more of his attention was given over to conferences and confessions there was little time left except to read the daily papers, an occasional magazine, and some "must" books that he felt he should discuss.

To discuss the relations of a successful confessor with his penitents is generally impossible because of the confidential nature of the matters that are exchanged. As this confessor listened to the stories and problems of these young men for hour after hour, he acquired an intimate understanding of their lives. Thousands of Notre Dame alumni and former students have recollections of the peace and quiet Father O'Hara brought to them in the confessional. The judgment of Father O'Hara as a great confessor and counselor must not be made on the matters told in the confessional but on the external works manifested. The first measure of his work was the great number of communicants during his years as prefect of religion, and the confessions that most often preceded them. For many alumni the story of Father O'Hara as prefect of religion is the account of the charitable deeds, visitations, kind words, and sound advice that he gave without stint, and the other tools he mastered to produce the religiously ideal Notre Dame student in the 1920's. Of his impact on Catholic education in the United States through the later publication of the *Religious Bulletins* and his *Surveys*,[3] and by the example of Notre Dame students, no one can give even a proximate measure.

Father O'Hara's first bit of printed propaganda was a pamphlet based on his first survey of the religious life of the campus and was entitled *Frequent Communion for College Men,* which he drew up in the spring of 1921. Notre Dame was beginning to be known as the home of physically strong youth through the victories of the football team, and it was important to discover that the Notre Dame students found peace and happiness in frequent and daily Communion. Father O'Hara also used this ideal to induce other students to join the practice. Then in July, 1921,

Father O'Hara published his analysis of the students' answers to his questionnaire that spring. In the preface he said that the questionnaire had already served its purpose on the campus by inspiring discussion and he hoped that its publication would "bring about more systematic cooperation between Catholic colleges and parishes."[4] The editor made comments on some of the answers: that attendance at a Catholic high school did not produce any greater devotion to frequent Communion, that the students followed the usual readings for college entrance and consequently did not read much Catholic literature, and that the good effects of daily and frequent Communion are proved in students' lives.

Father O'Hara's appeal was deliberately universal—if one does not object to calling a male world universal—to the type of rugged Notre Dame student that the American public liked to see. That this Notre Dame student was a bit less known as a scholar did not seem too important to Father O'Hara at that time, and in this he was in tune with the spirit of the American years before the Depression, during which colleges seemed best known for their athletic activities, before most American colleges had begun seriously to screen the youngsters coming to them. College life was considered generally as an experience for those young men who had the means, and some claimed that college was 98 percent association and 2 percent studies. That, of course, was not true of all collegiate institutions, but bookishness was not the notable quality of the American college student of the early 1920's.

Father O'Hara understood that the essential need of religious counseling was to bridge the gap between the student wandering around in the labyrinthine ways of adolescent thinking and experiences and the priest with the sacramental guidance and remedies. He became the student's friend. His friendliness was unlimited. In the course of his endless conversations he knew practically everything that went on that concerned the Notre Dame student, but this knowledge was used merely to help the students. Just as soon as a student slipped and became entangled with the disciplinary regulations of the University, he usually went at once to see Father O'Hara—later it was said he went to the "Pope" for a "dispensation." Father O'Hara never participated in the enforcement of the discipline, and any effort he made to see that the penalties were not enforced was done quietly and in a manner that was not known publicly. Yet he did use opportunities to clarify the thinking of the young delinquent and to get him straight before the Lord.

Dan O'Neil of the class of 1925 joined the followers of Father

O'Hara while he was a freshman in Carroll Hall and went to the basement chapel early each morning, where he served the Masses of Fathers O'Hara, Steiner, and Irving. He watched Father O'Hara in the basement chapel in the early hours and knew of his later work first in Walsh and later in Sorin Hall. He studied the technique of Father O'Hara. Some students Father O'Hara learned to know because like Dan they were regularly in the chapel, and his remarkable memory quickly remembered the face and soon found out the name and family background. But he did not wait to meet the students at the Communion rail. He got a list of the incoming freshmen and their hometowns and began trying to connect the faces with the names. He always acted as the regular confessor in the evening for the freshman hall, although he also heard confessions immediately after supper in the basement chapel. He told Dan O'Neil that he would notice the groupings on the campus and deduce those who came from the same hometown by their association. Gradually by these and other means he got to know most of the students, and when he failed to reach some, he sent for those he had not met.[5] He also tried to give all the Communions at the Sunday Masses, and since at that time students were not permitted to attend Sunday Mass in the hall chapels, he had a good opportunity to know all the regular communicants. Once a student who had been going to the basement chapel decided that he wanted to go to Dillon Hall to attend Mass and Communion, only to be accosted by Father O'Hara, who asked him why he had not been coming to Communion. Only when the student proved by the rector of Dillon Hall that the story was true would he accept the student's story—although years later as Bishop of Buffalo he recognized the same man and recalled the incident.

This combination of a remembrance of the names of the student and of his home town and his associates on the campus coupled with a readiness to talk with them made him the easy confidant of the troubled student. The untroubled student was usually a daily Communicant, and Father O'Hara got to know him by his presence at the altar rail and usually managed to broaden the contact. Some students entered the Church under his guidance; others conquered personal problems with the aid of this patient confessor. Ray Geiger's story is a sample of the way these friendships grew.

I first met John O'Hara when I arrived on the campus and I was alone without a friend in the world, had stood in line all day long to try to register and arrived at the window at 6 o'clock at night, and just as I was about to register the window slammed down and I was told to come back the following morning. I had no room on the campus and had to go to town to look for a room and I must have been a rather sorry sight as I started walking across the quadrangle to walk down into town. Perhaps at my sorriest some young priest put his arm around me and said "What's the matter, son?" and I guess half tearfully I told Father O'Hara, who it was, of my rather sad arrival on campus. He immediately brightened me up by telling me some of the wonders of Notre Dame and asked me to serve Mass for him the following morning. This was my true introduction to Notre Dame and he became and stayed one of my fast friends.[6]

There are a hundred similar stories of the accidents that enabled Father O'Hara to gather the earnest student into his friendship. He knew as well those who did not become regular communicants, and heard the stories of those who had serious spiritual problems. Once when a priest went to warn him that a certain student had been married before a justice of the peace, he found that Father O'Hara already knew about him and was letting the student wait until he knew what were the problems of a mixed marriage. He was in no haste to give him a binding marriage bond under the circumstances.

During the students' mission of October, 1921, occurred an event that had unexpected results. To solve the problem of getting all the students to confession Father O'Hara posted a mission bulletin that read as follows:

Three hundred students, college men, tried to go to confession this morning. Four priests were hearing confessions in the church, and one priest can hear, at most, 25 confessions in 30 minutes.
Figure it out for yourself.
To Repeat: Confessions are heard after supper every evening in the church and in the basement chapel. Six priests can hear 250 confessions in the hour after supper.

CAFETERIA
150 students left the church before the instruction this morning and continued their meditation before the closed door of the cafeteria. To Repeat: Breakfast will be delayed until 7:20 a.m. during the mission.

LATE SLEEPERS
80 campus students took a beauty sleep this morning after 6:30. They would perform an act of generosity and would save themselves some wrangling with prefects if they would trade rooms with the 80 off-campus students who came out from town for the mission this morning.

Oct. 24, 1921   Rev. John F. O'Hara, C.S.C.
Communions THIS MORNING: 812   Prefect of Religion

To understand the details of this picture, there were 1,203 Catho-

lic students at Notre Dame, and the cafeteria was in the basement
of Badin Hall across the campus, since the regular dining halls
were still in the Main Building. The mission was being preached
by Father Thomas Kearny, C.S.C., an eloquent preacher, and
attendance was obligatory for all Catholics. The residence halls
were Carroll, Brownson, Corby, Sorin, Walsh, and Badin, but
there was room for all in the church. It was a tradition in the
halls that the spiritual life of the hall would probably be good if
the members of the hall turned out well for the mission.

The next day there was another mission bulletin.

There was no congestion at Confessions in the confessional during
Mass this morning. Thank you!

To Repeat: Confessions are still heard by six priests in the Church
and in the basement after supper. The names of the priests appear on
the printed notice of the mission.

Cafeteria

The weatherman promises colder weather tomorrow. The twenty-
five students who spent thirty-five minutes each in front of the cafeteria
this morning would do well to wear overcoats tomorrow morning.

To Repeat! Breakfast at 7:20.

Off-Campus Students

Extra seats will be provided this evening. If you think it will do your
soul good to hear a sermon on Death this evening do not let your shy-
ness keep you away.

The *Bulletin* of the next day asked those who were not making
the mission to delay claiming their morning newspapers so that
the newsman could make the mission and also suggested that they
leave the Main Building not by the Brownson Hall entrance near
the church but through the Main entrance so as not to disturb
those who were making the mission. The *Bulletin* on the fourth
day summed up the figures on attendance at Communion to show
the great improvement over the previous year.

The bulletins were quite a success, and on November 10 Father
O'Hara got out another to announce the Mass for the war dead for
the next day, Armistice Day, and to congratulate the seventy-five
who had attended the five o'clock Mass that morning—apparently
headed for a day of recreation. He added some statistics on the
increase in attendance at the sacraments over the previous year.
Each student was averaging 3.5 Communions a week. On Armistice Day itself Father O'Hara issued another *Bulletin* announcing
a special High Mass and called attention to the incident of the
football team receiving Communion in a body at Albany on their
way to play the Army. He called it "an incident worthy of the

ages of faith." On November 12 there was another *Bulletin* to announce the death of Father John A. Zahm and Lawrence Stephen of Fort Wayne, a student. On November 16 there was a *Bulletin* on the current novena before the quarterly examinations. Father O'Hara noted that whereas in other novenas the number of communicants tended to decrease, in this novena the number increased as they approached the day for examinations. There was a *Bulletin* on November 23, and again on November 29. The latter asked that the critics of the *Bulletin* sign their name to their letters, and the next one on December 3 under the caption "adios" said: "On account of the increasing density of a portion of the population the comic supplement of the Bulletin will be discontinued." The next one, on December 14, besides statistics suggested some very Catholic reading including *The Mill Town Pastor* and *San Celestino*. That of December 20 suggested the reception of the sacraments before boarding the train for the vacation.

After Christmas the *Bulletin* began to appear with a certain regularity when Father O'Hara had some special message to convey or some special request for prayers for the sick or the dead. He constantly included answers to objections to frequent and daily Holy Communion, appeals for answers to the new religious survey, and pleas to students not to read improper books. The next fall the *Bulletin* appeared with the same infrequency until November 7. Then it began to be a daily *Bulletin*. By that time the religious Bulletin had become a Notre Dame institution, a running dialogue between a witty religious journalist and the students. Later it would be called "Notre Dame's only Daily." Sometimes it was read out of curiosity, sometimes with wrath, but no one ever questioned the ability of the editor. But the *Bulletin* that for more than a year was literally a piece of paper tacked to the bulletin boards of the student halls was a family argument. The first time it was copied in the Chicago Catholic newspaper the editor protested that the one who had published it had acted improperly.

Later when the *Bulletin* became a kind of daily newspaper and was distributed not only on campus but in hundreds of schools and to residing pastors throughout the country, it lost the element that had made it a symbol of special effort, the drive to bring all the Notre Dame young men to frequent, if not daily, Communion. That ideal had its limitations, and the *Bulletin* properly understood had the same limitations. The chief obstacles to daily Communion were bad books, current American novels especially, the town dance halls, and the sins of the flesh generally. The editor wanted to hold up the ideal of the real Notre Dame man—not a sissy by any means—who found clean living and happiness in his work because he lived so that he could receive Holy Communion every day. Incidentally there were many other items that got into the *Bulletin*. Father O'Hara, its author, became the chief moral force on the campus, and the students became accustomed to listen to him on all moral problems.

With so much activity as prefect of religion, Father O'Hara had to turn over his activities as dean of the College of Commerce to Mr. McCarthy, who soon succeeded him to the title. The summer of 1922, however, was spent in a parish in New York partly to get him away from his stiff schedule and partly because his health had suffered. He promised to spend much of his time on the beach for the second reason. While he was away, a provincial chapter met and released Father Burns from the presidency of Notre Dame and elected in his place Father Matthew Walsh, the vice-president. Father Burns, however, had succeeded in raising the million dollars of endowment, and while the sum was just attained by dint of hard effort, he announced a new drive for another million dollars for the much needed additional buildings. To direct this drive Father Burns accepted the title of president emeritus, although after a year he became again the superior of Holy Cross College in Washington. When the students returned in September, 1922, Father O'Hara was there to receive them and to begin anew his campaign to get them into the practice of frequent and daily Communion.

Father O'Hara's campaign for increasing communicants was made for the occasion, although the general argument was that of the Church. He had the advantage that Notre Dame was a Catholic college in which the ordinary student was expected to be a practicing Catholic and in which nothing detrimental to Catholic life would be permitted. To this he added ease of going to the sacraments. He himself heard confessions most of the day, and when not in the confessional or giving Communion he was available for conferences with young men who had problems of faith or practice. There were other confessors in the hall chapels morning and evening and in the church at all the Sunday Masses. Daily he posted his *Bulletins,* in which he assailed the chief obstacles to frequent Communion. The smartness with which he wrote, with brief paragraphs and a facetious tone, allowed the student to read it as he ran. To further stimulate interest he promoted rivalries among the students in the service of the Church. As Dan O'Neil recalls:

He carried on a mock warfare of sorts with the Engineers by means of slighting remarks and disparaging comments in the *Bulletin*. He really loved us but it made good copy. In our senior year he took over a Religion class a group of us were in. We had it in the Corby Chapel and he always entered from behind the altar. As an indication of how wary we were of him, one day he asked how many of us could recite the last Gospel. I could but didn't say so, not knowing what might come next. Probably others could, too, but no hand was raised.

His needling was most helpful to me when I became President of the Engineers' Club. It enabled me to prod the members into such feats as winning the Homecoming prize for the best decorated building, electing a Vice-President of the Senior Class, securing the Senior Ball Chairmanship and taking over one issue of the *Scholastic*. What made the latter noteworthy was it was the best issue of the year, Bert Confrey's teaching resultants. Father O'Hara enjoyed every bit of the reactions.

Other reactions that pleased Father O'Hara were the student objections when he drew harsh pictures of the girls in the dancing parlors of South Bend, or attacked some of the offerings of the theatres in South Bend. His criticisms were not particularly appreciated in two fields: that of modern American literature and the field of sociology. He had the *American Mercury* removed from the library after it published a startling article and would not permit the writings of Ernest Hemingway to go on the shelves. There were many other individual books to which he objected, some by writers who were Catholic. In the field of sociology he objected to the materialistic rationalizing that was common among many sociologists of the day and he sought to have their books removed from the shelves of the library. Some of the books he destroyed, and others he asked the librarian to keep under lock and key.[7]

Notre Dame at this time was not an institution of great scholarship, although there were scholars like Father Julius Nieuwland who did work on the campus. Under Nieuwland the Department of Chemistry had been built up to national acceptance, but most of the more active teachers at Notre Dame were men of fine oral expression who had little time for writing and research. Among these, alumni like to praise Fathers Thomas Crumley, Cornelius Hagerty, and Charles Miltner in philosophy, Father Leonard Carrico and Professor Charles Phillips in English, Professor Henry Froning in chemistry, Professor Regidius Kaszmarek in biology,

Professor John M. Cooney in journalism, and Father William
Bolger in economics and politics. These men were not molding
scholars but Catholic gentlemen who were in time planning on
professional careers or going into business. In such an atmosphere
the work of Father O'Hara fitted in remarkably well except for
the literary dilettanti who were beginning to multiply. His dis-
taste for the risque whether in the novel or in the sociological
study, in the theatre or in the comic magazine was evident in his
Religious Bulletin and in his advice. He opposed such things
not only because so many of them were occasions of sin but also
because they would not help in molding the fine Catholic gentlemen who he thought should represent Notre Dame. Regularly
he attacked the philosophy of "naturalism," which he felt justified the unnecessary intrusion of that kind of literature and art
that could only deaden the spiritual vigor and occasion other sins.

The question of the intellectual interests of these young men
was for him not an open one. Notre Dame, and Father O'Hara
as its spokesman, had no respect for that kind of freedom that
regarded neither the family nor the church as sacred. Although
he did not recognize any conflict between the highest science and
Catholic teaching, he did not recognize this condition in either
philosophy or literature. That there was at this time no great
philosophical thinking or large-scale literary production at Notre
Dame was explained as incidental to the youth of the institution
and its students. That authority at Notre Dame was anti-intellectual was denied. Error whether doctrinal or moral simply had
no rights, and the godlessness of the secular campus and the liber-
tinage that was fostered by modern American literature could be
banished from Notre Dame without any great loss. There were
some protests at this time, but for the most part the faculty and
student body of Notre Dame were happy with these spiritual
ideals of the University. The clear statement of these ideals was
expressed in the senior oration of 1923 by graduate Raymond
Gallagher, under the title "The Heritage of Notre Dame."

Notre Dame is not an intellectual bedlam with no fundamental motives for her work. She insists on certain definite ideals, which permeate
the curricula, determine the school activities, and force themselves into
the soul of the students. These ideals constitute the heritage of Notre
Dame.

The first which she insists on is the religious ideal. Throughout
America today the outstanding characteristic of higher education is
its godlessness. Numerous institutions seem to have forgotten that man
has a soul as well as an intellect and a body, that the spiritual is the

most important side, that it, too, must be trained, and that any educative process which ignores this element turns out a product less than a full man.

At Notre Dame, this religious ideal is impressed on the very buildings that shelter us, it permeates the curricula we study, and it shapes the activities we engage in. Our years here have imparted to us a deeper understanding of the things of the spirit and made more intimate our relations with our Creator.

The other ideals included in this heritage he found to be brotherhood, fraternity, and unselfishness, to which he added a spirit of democracy—since the students came from all parts of the country and from all strata of society—and loyalty to the nation.[8] Strangely Gallagher did not insist on any intellectual accomplishments.

Another alumnus of this same period commented on the fact that some of the alumni of that period were disturbed by the charge that they were not intellectual. He observed:

If Alumni are concerned because they are accused of not being intellectual, I suggest maybe it is because we aren't. In that respect we may not be greatly different from other alumni—it's a common charge against college graduates in this country. My experience with other institutions is on a graduate level. It seemed to me the intellectual atmosphere was more pervading at both of them. I wouldn't be sure that would be true among the undergraduates. My impression of the conversational tone in other countries I've visited—Canada—for a near-by example—is that it is higher in content and in range. Any remarks on this subject have to be opinions: I distrust my impressions because they can be affected by many things inside and outside me. They aren't worth anything as generalities.[9]

This observation from a sympathetic follower and disciple of Father O'Hara is not a mere generality. Father O'Hara received a similar criticism, when the first *Religious Survey* was published in 1921, from the pen of George Bernard in the *London Tablet*. Bernard said of the choice of readings of the students: ". . . Their choices tend to demonstrate an ignorance of the field of Catholic authorship by the elevation of obvious mediocrity to places of prominence. Only 250 students expressed a preference, which would appear to be further evidence of the same ignorance."[10] Father O'Hara was stung by this criticism and tried to get its point to the student, but he did not offer any list of Catholic intellectual readings, except Cardinal Newman.

Father O'Hara's use of statistics to impel greater effort found its best application in measuring religious support of the football

team. Most of the publicized Notre Dame athletes were practicing Catholics and this fact he used to increase attendance of students at prayer and the sacraments. As soon as classes began in
the fall, he insisted to the freshmen that it was a tradition that
Catholic students receive Holy Communion before a game. Later
he insisted that the student receive Communion for the team—
not to win, but that they might escape injury and for general
divine protection. He also constantly warned about the evils of
drink that accompanied major football contests and celebrations
after the game to prevent the students from receiving Holy
Communion the next day.

There continued to be critics of the *Bulletin,* and among other
lines in his own defense he wrote a statement of his purpose on
January 20, 1923.

1. The religious Bulletin is the only independent publication on the
campus. It has no advertisers.

2. It is issued for the glory of God and the personal joy of the editor.

3. It does not strive to please its readers. If any of them get any fun
out of it it is because they have inherited or acquired the faculty of
laughing at the misfortune of others.

4. To those of its readers who grieve over its low tone it recalls the
parable of the talents.

5. To those who gnash their teeth over its judicious choice of materials, it recommends the cancellation of their subscription.

6. To those who wish it in hades it whispers that seldom a day passes
without someone telling the editor that it saved him from hades.

7. Its scope and method it takes from the following sources:

    (A) Its scope is from the Prophet Isaias who exposed evil wher-
         ever he found it, in high places and low:

    (B) Its method is based on an incident in the Temple of Jeru-
         salem, when the money-changers were lashed with a scourge,
         and the lowly sellers of doves were gently told: "Take these
         things hence."

8. It reserves the right to follow Isaias in lamenting over Jerusalem
and of Jonas in leaving the Chosen People to preach to the pagans.

9. Its harp has two strings; its score has but two notes; its song has
but two chords: vice and virtue.

"A fool receiveth not the words of prudence: unless thou say those
things which are in thy heart."—Proverbs, 81:1.

In June, 1923, Father O'Hara sent to Father Walsh another of his
"reports" in which he summarized the statistics for the year and
made some observations. He noted that twenty members of the
senior class had been daily communicants throughout their four
years at Notre Dame. Of the *Bulletin* he thought it was a stabiliz-

ing influence. "It was read conscientiously by the majority of the students and since it took the liberty of covering a wide range of vices, virtues, motives, and appeals it probably saved some resolutions and engendered others."[11] In turn he made some suggestions, one of which was that there be a department of religion that should classify its students according to their previous instruction, and that some attention be paid to the comic magazine, *The Juggler*. The editors, he complained, were content to make it the cleanest of college comics, but not necessarily clean.

The next year Notre Dame continued to expand, adding a second frame temporary hall on the east campus and accepting 713 freshmen. Father O'Hara, while still the dean of the commerce college, gave up his work of administering that college, as he began through the *Bulletin* to work on the freshmen to have them adopt his ideal of daily or frequent Communion. He professed to have special affection for the well-living freshmen who went regularly to the sacraments and the sinner who was repentant. But he had only scorn for the indifferent who were in his opinion perpetual gripers. To those who seemed embarrassed by being seen at the Communion rail he noted sympathetically: "As soon as you receive Holy Communion twice on the same confession the old ladies (and the nuns) congratulate your mother on having a priest in the family." He did not hesitate to return regularly to the religious support of the football team during the fall season. But when some away from the campus read the published surveys and criticized the *Bulletin*, he defended himself by pointing out that the *Bulletin*, of which only twelve copies were posted each day under glass on bulletin boards, was a caricature of the real Notre Dame, that he was purposely exaggerating for effect, and that his statements should not be taken literally when read off the campus. In the *Bulletin* he likewise defended the Communion service for late risers that he conducted in the Walsh Hall chapel. Against the charge that it cheapened the Eucharist he said: "While part of the grace of Holy Communion depends upon the sacrifice made by the individual, the great grace of the sacrament comes from Our Lord Himself working in the soul."[12]

Occasionally Father O'Hara took harsh note of the popular literature of the day among the students. Thus he advised a student who asked about Percy Marx's *The Plastic Age*, a cynical book based, it was said, on the author's years at Amherst, to burn the book. Later he spoke of that kind of literature:

. . . The A.B.C.'s of the group are *The American Mercury, Vanity*

Fair, Smart Set, the American novels; the more advanced studies are the Russian novelists and certain American and English psychologists, the graduate work is done by the German and French psychologists, the French novelists, and the Hindu mystics. We have hardly passed the elementary stage at Notre Dame. Thanks be to God, and we can retrace our steps.[13]

The summer of 1924 was only mildly eventful for Father O'Hara. On June 1 he presented in the name of the University the Laetare Medal for 1924 to Charles D. Maginnis in Boston. But he was back for the annual retreat. In the summer school he taught one class in apologetics. The main subject of the class was the content of Archbishop Sheehan's book, but the manner of teaching was conversational. The rest of the day was divided between conversations on the pier at the lake and compiling the next *Religious Survey,* with a vacation at home after the session. When classes began in September, his headquarters were moved from Walsh Hall to the northeast corner of Sorin Hall and the adjoining chapel. He was also listed in the catalogue as the head of the Department of Religion, although the actual assigning of classes was done by the director of studies. This became a more difficult task because the enrollment was not checked until there were about 750 students residing off the campus, and the Department of Religion was not amply staffed. The *Bulletin,* as usual, concentrated on the freshmen, trying to make them believe that the real Notre Dame man was a daily communicant. Father O'Hara mentioned to his family that Bishop Chartrand had sent him 1060 of his little purple prayerbooks, just in the nick of time.

In the fall of 1924 Notre Dame was in the newspapers because of its football team, the team of the "Four Horsemen," and while the press devoted many lines to their football prowess, Father O'Hara promoted the basis of their success as clean living and faithfulness to the sacraments. For the most part the team fitted into the category of the kind of young men that could be held up as good examples on the campus as well as in the view of most Catholic youngsters. Victory for such a team was a heartening experience and a national championship something special. Even Father O'Hara could not help joining in the commemoration of the victories. Before the Army game he wrote in the *Bulletin:* "Nothing will cheer the team more during the next two games than the feeling that back home there are two thousand men believing in them to the extent of praying for them—getting down on their knees to pray God and His Blessed Mother, in whose honor they play, to bless and protect them."[14] In another

Bulletin[15] he wrote: "But bear this in mind: the game will be won or lost in the basement chapel, not at the grid-graph." Perhaps the theology of that would be a bit difficult to defend, but it seemed quite obvious that the prefect of religion was drilling the players to give good example and the student body to believe that they would let the team down if they did not follow that example. He added a plea that the students would not gamble on the game.

When the victory over Nebraska indicated that the team could claim a national championship, the Editor of the *Bulletin* let loose a bit of hurrah himself in the issue of November 17, 1924:

A clean-cut national championship is not hard to take, especially after a clean-cut team has been playing Notre Dame football together for three years. . . .

And the world is beginning to realize the source of Notre Dame's brand of sportsmanship. The teamwork of a Notre Dame eleven is not inspired by the philosophy of Nietzsche, it has none of the earmarks of Schopenhauer or Kant; it is neither bloodless pessimism, nor festering selfishness; it is neither cynical nor brutal; it is the red-blooded play of men full of life, full of hope, full of charity, of men who learn at the foot of the altar what it means to love one another, of men who believe that clean play can be offered as a prayer in honor of the Queen of Heaven, Notre Dame football is a new crusade: it kills prejudice and it stimulates faith.

Father O'Hara's associations with many individuals on the team had been rather close, and when according to a tradition, some priest was to be chosen to be chaplain to the team on its trip to California to play in the Tournament of Roses bowl game, the team asked that Father O'Hara be the chaplain. After some persuasion he accepted. After the victory of January 1 the team spent a few days rejoicing, and Father O'Hara received additional recognition when his intervention helped save the life of one of the stars of the team, Jimmie Crowley. Crowley had been overtaken by a sudden sickness, and the Chaplain revived him with mouth to mouth breathing. While denying the heroic in saving Jimmie, the Editor of the *Bulletin* later did say in defense of his trip that "It was a crusade for the spread of Holy Communion." Most of the players received Holy Communion every day en route to the game, with the exception of the day after Christmas, when a thirty-six-hour journey across Texas and Arizona made Mass impossible. In the 1925 *Religious Survey* Father O'Hara took considerable space to show how football was an aid to religion: by using up idle time and lessening physical temptations, by its discipline, and by its promotion of a host of natural virtues. Again the work of the championship team was called a "spiritual crusade."

With the excitement of the championship football team gone, the Editor had some difficulty getting attention for his crusade for frequent Communion. He did express his notion of Jazz music, which was beginning to attract the interest of the students. "The lay mind can understand better when you say that Jazz is the antithesis of everything that is holy in man, and the glorification of all that is animal. It works on the periphera of our sensitive life, and it changes nature."[16] And when he criticized the men of Badin Hall for their dry rot, in answer there appeared for a few issues the *Badin Hall Irreligious Bulletin*. He also attacked the comic campus magazine, *The Juggler,* which had been criticized by the Catholic press for its off-color humor. He demanded a change in its policy, suggesting that those who had a copy of *The Juggler* destroy it and offer a Communion of reparation. The rest of the year passed placidly, and the number of daily Holy Communions averaged 1,118, an increase of 134 over the previous year. Again he taught summer school and spent the rest of the time—when not conferring with students—working on his survey or basking in the lake-side sun.

That summer there was considerable talk about Notre Dame when George N. Shuster, an alumnus, and a departing teacher, published in the August 15, 1925, *America* an article, "Have We Any Scholars?" The implied negative answer caused some roughened feelings at Notre Dame as well as in other Catholic colleges, and the debate that followed in the magazine did little to pacify the feelings that had been aroused. In *Commonweal,* about the same time, appeared an editorial quoting a Canadian archbishop to the effect that the *Religious Survey* showed that the Notre Dame student was lacking in proper social and charitable interests. The editorial was answered by Professor Burton Confrey, a friend and ardent admirer of Father O'Hara. There were discussions, of the *Religious Survey* and the religious life of Notre Dame under Father O'Hara that summer in other periodicals. The efficacy of Father O'Hara's program was a matter of considerable debate among Catholic college administrators.

In 1926 Father O'Hara was completing his tenth year as a priest. There was in fact little change in his features, although some traces of youth that had appeared in the only photograph of him in the press—which was probably made the first year he was at Notre Dame—had disappeared. His hair was not yet gray, although a bit thinner. The pince-nez glasses had been replaced by the more orthodox spectacles. His complexion was a bit on the brown side, as one would expect from the daily swimmer and sunbather. There was no fat to be found on him. In speedy trips across the campus he had developed his peculiar fast walk with its small steps and erect figure. His hands were usually animated, and if he stopped to talk or sat down for a conference, a cigarette was soon produced. He was always pleasant, but the smile had a touch of seriousness about it, and there was usually a glint in his eye as if he were watching to see if he had scored his point or had made the student realize that he had not forgotten him. His quips were fast and to the point. He had a deep voice that was not harsh.

His day was not easy. Rising early he said Mass at 5:45 so that he could begin to hear confessions at 6:30. In the basement chapel he heard confessions and gave Communion at intervals until seven o'clock. Then he went to Sorin Hall to the corner room near the Church. He was either in the room talking to students, getting up the day's *Bulletin,* or in the chapel next door hearing confessions or distributing Communion until noon. After lunch, he soon developed the habit of getting in a nap, a swim, and a visit to the sick in varying order. He came back to the office for a few minutes before eating supper early, and after that he heard confessions, first in the basement chapel, and then in Freshman Hall so long as penitents came, then he hurried back to 141 Sorin. When he taught religion classes, he met them usually in the afternoon on Tuesdays and Thursdays. His evening conferences sometimes lasted until midnight. The year's first *Bulletin* on September 10, 1925, was intended to arouse the ones needing reform.

. . . The place is overrun with fellows who were not coming back this year—going to Dartmouth, and all that. And the bragging about football and swell times that has gone on all summer has now given way to the old-time knocking. A good all-day rain would put the gang in mid-season form.

The fall of 1925 was another football season, but defeat by the Army 27 to 0 and other losses took some of the glory out of the season. Lacking the incentive of a championship team, the Editor used the sickness of Jimmie Powers, a student, who fought a hopeless fight against injuries from an automobile accident, to arouse the students to new prayers and attendance at the sacraments. Perhaps the Editor was not thinking of scholastic problems when he said in the *Bulletin:* "All that Notre Dame has to offer over and above other schools in that is the religious sacrifice that goes into the teaching to give it punch."[17] There was a note of sameness in

the work of Father O'Hara. He was later to tell his successor that
he had not missed an evening in the confessional when the students were on the campus in seventeen years. Nevertheless, each
student received a very friendly welcome to the room in the Sorin
tower.

The *Bulletin* continued to fight the obstacles to frequent Communion. For some weeks the Editor discussed the "Modern Girl,"
and later in the spring he devoted some time to the discussion of
the "Modern Boy." Occasionally the *Bulletin* discussed Henry
Fairfield Osborne, Darwin, Huxley, and other agnostics. The
novena for purity, the novena for a happy marriage, and the special warnings to the young men who had not made their Easter
duty were other subjects of daily comment. When summer came,
he headed for California to find a drier climate for his sinuses
and time to compile his next *Religious Survey*.

After his summer in California and a brief vacation with the
family in Indianapolis Father O'Hara, apparently much refreshed,
returned to the campus to welcome the freshmen. His first *Bulletin* for 1926–27 was startling and probably amusing with his
advice to the newcomers. "Notre Dame is a funny place. You
can't believe half of what you see with your own eyes. But you
can trust the *Bulletin*. If the *Bulletin* says it is so, it is so." His
California-near-Hollywood summer seemed to be mirrored in this
Bulletin, which explained why Rudolph Valentino had a Catholic burial and much-divorced Mae Murray got a Catholic marriage, using Ben Turpin "of the divergent point of view" as
another example. He announced a new daily devotion, rosary and
Benediction of the Blessed Sacrament every evening at five o'clock
for the team. Somehow he always managed to have a sufficient
number at this religious exercise to justify its continuance. If the
student organist failed to show up, Father O'Hara played the
organ and asked another priest to give the Benediction. On Saturday the Benediction was moved up to the noon hour.

Football as usual was a dominant theme in most conversations
on the campus, and Father O'Hara used the team to promote his
own kind of activity. In the *Bulletin* he maintained that the team
supernaturalized natural virtues in their victories and at the same
time that they were helped in their team spirit by their common
partaking of Holy Communion. He went a bit farther in explaining the part of prayer in the victory over Army, including the
prayer of nuns and girls in convents and the prayers of the team
itself. Then he added:

Who won the game: We won't know till we get to heaven; but the fact remains that it did the Poor Souls a lot of good and converted a lot of sinners.—And don't forget to thank the Poor Souls this noon, by attending Benediction for them, when the bell rings.[18]

When this *Bulletin* was printed in the Chicago diocesan newspaper, Father O'Hara objected that the *Bulletin* was not intended to go off the campus. But he added an observation that showed a more balanced appreciation of the relations between prayer and victory, saying that he would now have to explain future defeats by the failure of the student to pray, since he had seemed to attribute the recent victory to that prayer. The appeal to prayers for the team was a serious point with him because while he used the team and the game to promote devotion and Communions, his real interest was not the game itself which he seldom attended, but the prayer and the sacraments and the good he achieved in the souls of those who read his *Bulletin* or listened to his words.

The *Football Review* for 1926 published at the end of the season carried an article on Father O'Hara and his relations with the team by Franklyn Doan. It was emotionalized prose, but it also expressed the highly emotionalized college sports and college life of the mid-nineteen-twenties.

. . . Only the silent night remains and every one has gone to his rest—except one.

He's Father O'Hara and even the silent night cannot entice him from his duties. On, on, and on he labors, nor does the stilly night detract him if duty calls.

. . . In one man, Notre Dame spirit is lifeblood. It flows throughout his system into remote corners of his body an urge of service. That man is Father O'Hara.

. . . .

Notre Dame wins her victories in the basement chapel. Down in the worn alcove of worship, they pray and intercede, not that their team will win but that it may fight like real Notre Dame men—and win if God so wills.

. . . .

It must be that Father O'Hara will ever work and pray and labor for that sacred ideal—Notre Dame and her men.[19]

Aside from the devotion to football implied in this bit of poetic prose, there was the recognition of two important characteristics of Father O'Hara's service. The first was his absolute fidelity to his service of the student, and the second was his singleness of purpose. And if some thought his ideals of student life very nar-

row and less than humanitarian, he felt justified by the high
spiritual hopes he had for the Notre Dame students.

Father O'Hara did not hesitate to criticize his student readers. Later when the *Bulletin* in mimeographed copies was sent
throughout the country, he had to print an occasional "campus
supplement" to tell the students what he thought of some of them,
but in the earlier days one must remember the *Bulletin* as a
family notice first appearing on the bulletin boards of the halls,
and later multiplied simply so all could get the message. He
would say saucy things, even irritating and insulting things, just
to get a retort as from the members of the family. And, under-
neath, some of his facetious quips were serious criticisms of the
Notre Dame student that were not planned to go beyond the
campus.

When the Villagers' Club asked him to publish their protest
against the conduct of some students in a South Bend theatre, he
wrote the protest but followed it on the next day with a criticism
that there were too many Notre Dame students at the show. His
discussion of the public dance halls usually drew student protests
because these dance halls were about the only places where students could go to dance. Later in one *Bulletin* he called some of
the girls in these dance halls "pigs," and he received strong protests against his language. He admitted that some of these girls
were there because they lacked other entertainment but suggested
that they would be better off dancing with some factory hands
who would be clean of heart even if rough in their speech. He
would not relent on the purpose of his criticism.

Father O'Hara was also aware that some of his critics, besides
not sharing his aversion to the modern American novel, also felt
that he did not stress enough serious intellectual reading. He
retorted that when he asked the students in the annual questionnaire to list some profitable reading they had done, not one of four
hundred and ten students listed anything. Yet he charged: "right
now there is more vicious reading and less useful reading going
on at the University than at any previous time this year." To the
charge that he was too narrow-minded, he answered under the
phrase *Claque Claque*.

A little noise has been made during the past week by some little intellectuals who would divorce life from literature, God from Art. It
seems strange that such a thing should happen in a school devoted and
dedicated to the Mother of God, but it has always been possible, and
has generally been so.[20]

But for the most part there remained a sameness in the constant dialogue between Father O'Hara and his student friends. Again the next summer he sought peace, this time in New Mexico, to study the results of his questionnaire and his experiences and to report them in his *Survey*.

There were significant changes in Notre Dame during the summer of 1927. One that was not perceived quickly had to do with the government of the Holy Cross community. Father Burns returned to Notre Dame not as president but as provincial and from his rooms in the Presbytery behind the Church became again a force at Notre Dame. On the campus itself there was a dramatic change in the opening of the new dining halls, which was symbolic of many changes. The small boarding school that ate together in the small dining rooms in the basement of the Main Building had become a large college with dining halls capable of holding over two thousand students. The new building had been erected where once had been a series of barns, and it was the new center of a group of new halls erected in the previous few years, Howard, Lyons, Morrissey, soon to be followed by Dillon and Alumni halls. It was notable that Father O'Hara began at once to plan a new center of his activity and that he proposed for a while to have a small chapel built for him just east of the new dining halls. But when the new halls, Dillon and Alumni, were erected a few years later, his center was planned in the chapel of the nearest dormitory, Dillon Hall.

Reading the national news weeklies of the country during the mid-nineteen-twenties, one does not find much about Catholic education, and even less about Notre Dame, except in football. Football was an acknowledged overgrowth of the academic body of most American colleges. Notre Dame's progress in football, while sometimes challenged on the grounds that its importance overshadowed the more important elements of a college, was noteworthy chiefly because of its success. Notre Dame still represented the legend of the small college of the lesser men that entered combat and conquered the giant, and this legend had a remarkable appeal to the American public. Outside of the crowds that traditionally went to see the older colleges of the east, the public liked best to see the upstart win—the Fighting Irish, for instance —who seemed to win against all odds. The coaching genius of Knute Rockne was undeniable, but he had, besides some very good players, an inspired group of young men. Although probably at no time was the Notre Dame team composed of all Catholics, the inspiration of the team was Catholic. In some manner the "Fighting Irish" who were neither all Irish nor all Catholics represented the effort of the predominantly immigrant and poor Catholic group in the country to get ahead. Of course, some Catholics had already won in politics, but football was considered something better than politics. Also, there was created the tradition of the clean-living Catholic youngster and of a smaller, brainier, faster team beating a stronger but less inspired opponent that grew from the circumstances aided by some willful sportswriters.

But above all this admixture of education and football was the religious spirit of Notre Dame, manipulated by Father John O'Hara. Any suggestion to the Notre Dame men of the nineteen-twenties that they were intellectually inferior to later graduates runs into the persisting conviction drilled into them by Father O'Hara, chiefly through his *Religious Bulletin,* that in place of any deficiency in reading or smartness, the Notre Dame man had something spiritual that was not only religiously superior but actually a superior substitute for that smartness that he might not have. Surely Mencken and Nathan and Brown and Linsday, or anyone else who happened to be filling the pages of the smart journals or writing the best sellers of that day were not only off the beam spiritually, they were selling a kind of wisdom that could do no good, the kind of wisdom that gamins and alley rats learned in the cities and towns back home. This theme was repeated in the *Religious Survey* in criticism of those artists and litterateurs who indulged in much undraped realism. To this continuous harping on goodness the editor of the *Bulletin* and *Survey* hoped to add the education for hardness of the well-trained football player and the spiritual exaltation of the daily Communicant.

These were large premises, but once these theses are sketched into the Notre Dame picture, there was little variation in the story of Father O'Hara and Notre Dame during the year 1927–28. He started the year by calling it "Be Yourself Year," but disclaimed in the same breath that he was supporting in any way a philosophy of naturalism. Neither did he say that frequent Communion was a sure recipe for academic success. He observed:

Not all the academic delinquents, of course, are spiritual laggards, but the proportion is high: and while some of the boys who knock down the *Magna cum laude* are incipient apostates, the proportion is low. (The *Bulletin* seldom concerns itself with this latter group—who wouldn't read it if it did; it has, however, wasted a lot of ammunition on the academic liabilities, many of whom read it as they would a funny paper, hoping some day to find something funny in it.)"[21]

In general the year was rather successful, the number of Communions reaching a new high of 1910 on the first Friday of March.

That summer Father O'Hara went to St. Edward's University in Austin, Texas, to work on his *Survey,* and from there he welcomed to the presidency of Notre Dame the former provincial of Holy Cross, Father Charles O'Donnell. Also in July he recorded a letter from Father Joseph Luther inviting him to send a representative from Notre Dame to participate in a Spiritual Leadership Convention at St. Louis University in August. Father Luther made his challenge very direct:

> . . . In the matter of the surveys, promoting frequent Communion and issuing snappy and challenging *Bulletins* I think you are ahead of us all. But I think in the several other fields of Mission work, catechetics, teaching, student lectures, promoting Catholic reading, interest in the liturgy, developing vocations, etc. there are individual schools that will be represented at the Convention which lead in that particular work and that you would derive inspiration and profit from their reports, as they would derive the same from yours.

Father Luther meant the invitation in a kindly spirit, but Father O'Hara, after counseling with the new president turned down the invitation.[22] His idea of Catholic student leadership was different from the concept of the Sodality man advocated in other Catholic colleges.

To Father O'Donnell he wrote at the beginning of the school year suggesting that the off-campus students be eliminated. His reasoning implied the high type of spiritual life he planned for the Notre Dame student.

> . . . The spiritual side, of course, is my concern. My judgment is that the off-campus residence of a large body of our students is detrimental not only to the off-campus students themselves, but to the student body as a whole. The infiltration of the spirit of the world in our students is one of the things our cloister is intended to combat; the problem is made much more difficult when so large a proportion of our students are in active contact with the world so much of their time, especially when it is comparatively easy for them to be in contact with the worst the world has to offer.[23]

He substantiated his theory with the fact of the inability of the off-campus prefect to look after the students and the large number of them who he maintained had failed to receive their Easter Communion last year. Nevertheless, since the off-campus students continued, he had to resume his previous efforts to bring them into the spirit of the campus residents. That year was not a good

year for football, but there was no decline in the spiritual life. In
May, 1929, at the suggestion of some of the students the practice
of "perpetual adoration" during the month of May was begun
after the students gave written assurance that there would be
enough adorers to care for the devotion. He told of this to his
mother: "We have the Blessed Sacrament exposed ten hours daily,
and the students were asked to furnish three adorers for each half
hour of the day during the month. They have generally given us
between six and twelve instead of the three asked for, and never
has the number been below three. . . ."[24] Another suggestion
came from the students: that there be singing at the Grotto of Our
Lady of Lourdes each evening during May. He reported that there
were a hundred the first evening after supper and the practice
continued.

During the summer of 1929 Father Charles O'Donnell, the
president, suggested after reading Father Maurice Sheehy's *Christ
and the Catholic College* that Father O'Hara prepare a statement
of his religious program for publication, asking him that the
report be as "frank and as full as possible."[25] *The Report of the
Prefect of Religion with Supplementary Documents,* however,
attracted little more attention than the regular survey. But there
was in the appendixes to the document some important information on the background and purposes of the religious program at
Notre Dame.[26] Appendix A outlined the history of religious
developments at Notre Dame, and Appendix B gave samples of
the student reaction to the practice of daily adoration. Appendix
C was a lengthy criticism of L. H. Hopkins's *Report on Personnel
Procedures in Education,* a foundation-supported examination of
counseling procedures in several universities. In general, Father
O'Hara argued that all the problems solved or attacked in these
personnel procedures were handled much better in the religious
program at Notre Dame. He accused the other universities of
neglecting the soul of the student.

As the new school year opened, he began again his drive to get
the freshmen to the Communion rail, and to keep the whole student body living in such a way that the high percentage of daily
attendance at Holy Communion would be maintained. There
were some other occasional targets of the *Bulletin*. He attacked
Dr. Will Durant, whom he called "the ex-seminarian" who had
lost his faith by reading books on the index of prohibited books.
On another occasion he recorded Henry Fairfield Osborne's retreat
from belief in the missing link. And in a *Bulletin* after Christmas
vacation he wrote approvingly of John T. McCutcheon's descrip-

tion of the departed 1920's as "The Dirty Decade." He also described certain products of French literature as the effect of the authors' "not going to confession but writing confessions in books."

When the school year 1930–31 opened, the president, Father Charles O'Donnell was making news with a description of Catholic education on the Catholic Hour. He described the purpose of Catholic education in a way that explained to some extent the religious character of the Notre Dame program at that time. Speaking of the two dimensions of life, the outward appearance and the inner meaning, he added:

The principal result, therefore, which education aims at is the intellectual power of appraisal and the moral power of selection, amid the chaos of ideas and the conflict of moral standards which life as it is actually lived presents.[27]

Father O'Donnell probably had in mind the intellectual aims of Notre Dame education at that period of the University's development, something quite difficult to explain in the light of the great emphasis placed on the all-conquering football team and the dominating influence of Father O'Hara. With the exception chiefly of Father Nieuwland in chemistry, the research element of intellectual endeavor found in the great American universities was lacking at Notre Dame. Yet, an intellectual quality was really dominant in the undergraduate training of the Notre Dame student. To those attending the classes of Fathers Thomas Crumley, William Bolger, Leonard Carrico, Cornelius Hagerty, Thomas Steiner, Charles Miltner and Peter Hebert and of such laymen as Charles Phillips, R. M. Kaczmarek, and John M. Cooney there was no lack of intellectual content in their studies. These students were, indeed, not preparing to be teachers or researchers, but they were preparing to be Catholic professional or business men. Probably they learned mostly a kind of Christian salesmanship, but those that followed Father O'Hara's guidance brought to that salesmanship a deep respect for Christian living.

Strangely the depression that was shaking the foundations of so many institutions of the country did not seem to affect Notre Dame very much. There were some empty rooms on campus. Yet the lay trustees could report that the meager endowment of the University, while yielding less income, was invested in safe stocks and bonds that did not greatly shrink in value. The new stadium seating 55,000 people that was opened that fall was not then to be filled to capacity, but the financing of it, as planned by the lay trustees and the administration, did not cause any financial woes. The gothic law building finely designed by Maginnis and Walsh of Boston had been occupied and awaited a formal dedication. The dining hall that had been erected the year before was operating at a profit. The building of two new residence halls and the promised engineering and commerce halls could be done at a minimum of cost during the straitened years when their construction was a service to the financially depressed population of South Bend. And as Father O'Hara noted from time to time, on the whole the sacramental life of the students reached even new heights. But there were dark elements in the picture.

In his November 5 *Bulletin* on the topic "All idols have feet of clay" Father O'Hara concluded: ". . . Every Notre Dame man has a special obligation to fulfill the expectations of those who know what the school stands for." Two days later the followers of Notre Dame were shocked to hear in the press that one of their football heroes, Joseph Savoldi, the fullback, had secretly been married before a justice of the peace the previous April and had now filed and withdrawn a suit for divorce. On Wednesday, November 11, Father O'Hara's comment was merely to refer to the *Bulletin* of November 5 and to insist that the last line "still holds good." Savoldi was dropped from the University without further explanation, and friends had to explain the cause of the disciplinary action was not marriage but an offense against marriage.

The better news came the next day when Father O'Hara could announce that an old tradition that no one ever gave a building to Notre Dame had magnificently been broken by Edward N. Hurley, who had given $200,000 for a commerce building. Father O'Hara had more than ordinary pride in this benefaction by a personal friend and insisted on a special novena by the students in thanksgiving.

In a series of the *Bulletin* against bad reading, that of March 25 gave this reason why some read books on the Index:

. . . Freshmen read dirty books for their literary style, sophomores, because the Best Smellers are not mentioned by name, juniors cultivate "art for art's sake," and seniors allege that "to the pure, all things are pure." Back-scratching critics and loose-minded professors recommend such books for their "stark power," their "grim facing of the realities of life."

On March 31 the *Bulletin* published a *Supplementary Bulletin* confirming the death of Knute Rockne in the crash of an airplane. Father O'Hara wrote "Knute Rockne has had a wider influence in developing the ideals of fair play than any other man of his generation; he did it under the banner of the Mother of God. We may feel that she took care of him in his hour of need." On April 25 he joyfully announced the gift of another building by an alumnus, a $300,000 engineering building by John F. Cushing. There was to be another novena of Communions, this time for Mr. Cushing's intentions. That summer he prepared a new *Survey,* this time based upon questionnaires submitted to the alumni. In answer to the suggestion of the alumni he published in the following months occasional *Bulletin* pages in the *Alumnus* magazine, but they lacked the zeal associated with the daily *Bulletin.*

The University continued to expand, and Alumni and Dillon Hall—a bit delayed—opened that fall. The general life of Notre Dame seemed unchanged, although the initial number of Communions received as well as the total number of students began to show some decline. When an Asheville, North Carolina, paper asked in what way Notre Dame was great as an educational institution, Father O'Hara answered in the *Bulletin* of November 24: "Notre Dame does not confuse instruction and education. Education she conceives as a well-rounded cultivation of all the faculties of a man, of a whole man, not a part of a man at the expense of the will for other parts. . . . She has no college board examination for entrance, it is true; she has her own standards of admission and her own standards of scholarship, and they are recognized by every university and by every standardizing agency in the country. . . ." But he did admit in another *Bulletin* that Notre Dame did not accept the lower third graduating from high school, adding: "We miss the lower third this year. We miss the noisy laughter of the squirrels—of the extrovert freshmen who finished in the lower third of their high school class. They were the academic hoodlums, but they lent color to the campus. . . ." The next *Survey* was prepared in the summer of 1932, again at St. Edward's University in Texas. After a general chapter of the Congregation that summer he was chosen to replace Father Charles O'Donnell as a member of the Provincial Council, the first time he had had any executive office in the Community.

Dillon Hall was now completed, and the office of the prefect of religion, which had been operating unofficially there, was now officially centered in the Dillon chapel with a two-room office across the corridor. There were bell buttons in the vestibule of the chapel to summon him from his office, one ring for confession and two for Communion. Besides the ordinary confessional in the back of the chapel there was a special confessional in the wall

near the side altar where the Blessed Sacrament was reserved for
Communion. When the confessor was in the confessional, the
light was green and became red when the penitent knelt for confession. Everything seemed ready for a long career for him as
prefect of religion, but his election to the Provincial Council
already marked the beginning of the end he did not desire. Perhaps Father O'Donnell in his opening sermon felt obligated to
strengthen the regime of Father O'Hara. He stressed the religious
character of Notre Dame.

. . . The whole point is missed if this idea is not grasped that the Faith
at Notre Dame is inclusive of the everyday human life we must all live,
of all human concerns and activities. Elsewhere it may be thought that
religion is for Sunday, that it is for mature persons and old people, that
it is for the times of sorrow and trial, that it has no connection with the
libraries and laboratories, with social relations, with sports. That simply
is not our understanding of religion.[28]

Over the years the stories of Father O'Hara's dealings with individual students grew until they became an account of incredible
activity. Sometimes he challenged youngsters of good living who
were not doing all that he felt they should. Sometimes students
challenged him, either trying to ensnare him in his advice or at
times because they had been given other counsel by their professors. Some of the contacts were physical. On a given challenge he
would forcibly eject a student from his bed in the early morning
hours; sometimes when challenged, and sometimes unchallenged,
to force an admission of laziness. His spectacularly rapid answer to
all kinds of questions was part of his effort to impress the student
that the wise man preferred the good life. Sometimes he had to be
quick to meet the attack of the pseudo wise.

When Joe Breig was a student, in an unbelievable bit of forgetfulness at Notre Dame he forgot to go to Sunday Mass until it
was too late. When he went to confession to Father O'Hara, the
priest merely expressed amazement that such a thing was possible
at Notre Dame. Later remembering that Father O'Hara had promised twenty-five dollars to anyone who would confess to a sin he
had not yet heard, he approached Father O'Hara and claimed
that prize, only to be told without hesitation that there would
be no prize because there had been no sin.[29] Some other quick
answers had specious logic, but the speed with which they were
rendered made them purposely effective.

There were some questions that arose repeatedly. Father Raymond Murray, C.S.C, who had worked untiringly to make sociology a respected subject at Notre Dame, never ceased to urge

that Catholic sociology be also practiced at Notre Dame. He was probably the chief instigator on campus of the repeated request that Notre Dame seek out and admit some Negro students. Vincent McAloon at Father Murray's suggestion asked Father O'Hara for an answer to the request and was shown the form letter used by the University, which promised to accept Negroes at the opportune time. He then simply asked Vince: "Any other questions?"[30] One not so sharp asked him why girls usually had more than one boy on the string, and he in turn asked why an automobile driver carried a spare tire.[31] Much of Father O'Hara's time and many of his *Bulletins* were taken up with the problems of sex that bother the adolescent mind. His patience with those who were discouraged, his willingness to talk and to listen at all times, and his sympathetic remedies were taken for granted. The subjects of these conferences whether within or outside the confessional were not the topics of later stories, but they form the basis for the opinion that he was a great confessor and the universal friend of the student. One alumnus recalls that it was "his feeling for people and to a degree his delight in matching wits with them" that gave him his power in conference.

His office in Sorin Hall and later in Dillon was a scene of matchless disarray. When he was in Sorin Hall, the piles of unclaimed bulletins, newspapers, and other literature accumulated without order on his desk. There were also rolls of chains for scapular medals, boxes of medals, and numberless pamphlets. The more formal office of Dillon Hall soon developed the same characteristics. The typewriter usually had in it a *Bulletin* in process of composition since he did not have time for re-writing. No reporter ever had to write news under more distracting conditions, and his ready quip was as quick on the typewriter as on his lips. The *Religious Bulletin,* as the alumni of the nineteen-twenties recall it, was part of the personality of Father O'Hara, and has never been more than a shallow imitation since he gave up its composition.

The *Bulletin* did have a wider circulation in later years, and sometimes, when reprinted by observing editors, it brought off-campus reactions. Such was the notable *Bulletin* of February 3, 1933, on "The Lay Cardinals."

You will find them in every parish. They correspond to what Rockne used to call in football, his "Board of Strategy."

Like the Roman Cardinals, they are not of Divine origin. Unlike the Cardinals, they are self-appointed.

The Cardinals meet the Holy Father face to face and give him advice when they are asked for it. The lay cardinals give their advice to the parish priest on their own initiative, and usually behind his back.

The lay Cardinals attend the Children's Mass (which is fitting in a way) and when the priest orders them out they say that his spirit is not Christ-like.

They object to the way the pastor spends the money they don't contribute; they call him mercenary when he lays before them the parish needs that would not exist if they did their share.

They eat meat at a Friday banquet so as not to embarrass the Mason to the right and the left of them, but when the Pope dispenses the whole Church on a holyday of obligation they say that religion is going to the dogs.

They speak a good word for their pastor only when he has ceased to be their pastor and his name and fame are brought into the conversation to the disparagement of their present shepherd.

Out of the wealth of their ignorance and inexperience they broadcast their views on Gregorian chant, homiletics, hermeneutics, the Pauline privilege, and ecclesiastical art.

When they receive Holy Communion it is with the Young Ladies Sodality instead of the Holy Name Society, when they come to confession it is five minutes after closing time, when they take a notion for the Last Sacraments it is two o'clock in the morning. But they are a godsend at a wake: they keep your mind off the corpse.

Not only did this *Bulletin* arouse interest and comments from off the campus, it gave him a good chance for the rest of the year to nominate someone for the lay cardinal's hat whenever such a person distinguished himself by something contrary to good religious practice. To the reader of the Pittsburgh Catholic paper who objected strenuously to the idea of these lay Cardinals, Father O'Hara insisted that the man lacked a sense of humor.

That spring also the *Bulletin* Editor tried with varying success to get up signed protests from the separate halls against the offering of morally bad movies in the South Bend theatres. On April 26 he wrote an answer to an invitation to a meeting of the Religious Education Association in Cincinnati to be attended by Catholics, Protestants, and Jews. His title expressed his firm conviction about such gatherings: "Oil and Water Will Not Mix." In another *Bulletin* of May 27 he expressed his notion of the teaching of literature that was at the base of his strictness on reading. ". . . A class in English literature of today that is not at the same time a class in Moral Theology entails a responsibility which we would not care to face at the Last Judgment. Let the students gripe—they do that far better than they study. But guide and protect their reading or their accusations at the Last Judgment will make you wish you had not shirked this responsibility."

The *Bulletin* of April 7 had asked for prayers for Father O'Donnell, the president of the University, whose illness following a bad cold had taken a turn for the worse. Father Charles O'Donnell's health did not greatly improve. He was able to return to the campus in June for the commencement at which Father Charles Coughlin was the baccalaureate orator and Governor Paul McNutt was the commencement speaker, and to the celebration that evening of the Laetare Medal's golden jubilee, at which John McCormack received the medal and Al Smith and other medalists joined in the celebration. Yet anyone who shook the hand of the President that day knew that he was still a sick man. Father O'Hara was also well aware of this because as a member of the Provincial Council he was in on deliberations about a replacement for the sick man. The vice-president, Father Michael Mulcaire, was not deemed suitable for the task. Father Burns called upon his friend, Father O'Hara, in whom he had great confidence, and as an obedient religious Father O'Hara accepted the assignment as vice-president of the University. Probably he seriously thought he could continue as a counselor of students and did not realize fully the change that had come into his life.

FOUR

Entering Administration

DESPITE HIS TERM AS DEAN OF THE COLLEGE of Commerce Father O'Hara did not think of himself as an administrator. When the students appealed to him as to the pope for a dispensation from their delinquencies, there was an accepted tradition that the prefect of religion had little or nothing to do with the administration of the University. It was true that he was very well informed on all that went on on campus, but his knowledge was privileged, used only, like the knowledge of a father confessor, for the benefit of the penitent. During the summer of 1933, however, Father O'Hara had to participate in another kind of action because as a member of the Provincial Council he had to join with Father James Burns, the provincial, and other members of the council to consider the problems of the Congregation of Holy Cross, both as they affected Notre Dame and as they touched the other institutions of Holy Cross. Their major problem was the illness of the president and superior of Notre Dame, Father Charles O'Donnell; and complicating this fact was a certain dissatisfaction with the administration of Father Michael Mulcaire, the vice-president. The two problems became one when it was necessary for the vice-president to act in the name of the sick president. In the judgment of Father Burns that man had to be Father O'Hara, who seemed to accept this as a temporary solution. He became vice-president and functioned as acting president.

When the University completed its registration of students in September, 1933; the total of 2,545 was slightly less than the registration of students in the previous year. That was probably the least of the manifestations of the effects of the depression on the University. For all practical purposes the student body had come back on the campus, and there were even a few empty rooms. There were many financial arrangements made with the individual parent or guardian for paying the board and tuition; there were many new kinds of partial employment, especially on jobs set up with government aid. There were also some feelings of dissatisfaction among students who did not have the money to go off campus for additional pleasures. The faculty remained the same in number and salaries were not cut, but there was some uncertainty about the future of the university.

Father O'Hara insisted that he would remain prefect of religion despite his assumption of the title of vice-president and acting president. Bravely he announced that he would have nothing to do with the disciplinary work of the University. The supervision of the employment that had grown into large numbers through the depression and governmental aid was to be assigned to the comptroller of the University, Frank Lloyd. The more active side of the work as prefect of religion was to be handled by Father John F. Cavanaugh and Father Francis Phelan as assistants. It was still hoped that Father O'Donnell would recover his health sufficiently to assume his work as president, and even in his illness he intended to perform as many of the tasks of the presidency as he could. Shortly after the opening of the school year he returned to the campus and endeavored to direct the University from his sick room in the infirmary.

Father O'Hara never seriously wanted to enter into the administration of the University. Some friends have quoted him as having said in conversation that he would like to be the president of the University, but these words could mean little more than the usual expression of the desire to make certain changes in the University if the opportunity were offered. Certainly not only did he not want to be president but the assumption of the even temporary direction of the University was a very painful sacrifice. To the family he wrote on July 13, the day the new obedience was made public:

You have probably heard the news of my change of obedience, and I want to warn you in advance that it is a reason for prayer and not congratulations.

As I wrote the Bishop, it will not mean that I give up my religious work among students, but (and you needn't tell him this) it will mean that the work will be greatly curtailed. I am going to miss that—and

I'm going to have the worry of administrative work which I hate. However, I am counting on your prayers to supply the grace needed for the work.[1]

To a close alumni friend, Bob Cummins, who congratulated him but expressed the hope that the new task would not keep him from writing the *Bulletin,* he replied:

Thanks for your good wishes, add a few Hail Marys to them. I don't like the change any more than you do, and I need all the moral and spiritual support I can get.

I hope to continue the *Religious Bulletin,* but I cannot make any promises now. If things go as they are, there will not be time in the twenty-four hours that I can squeeze it in. Father John Cavanaugh, '23, is pinch-hitting for me in the mornings' work in the chapel, and I may have to make an editor of him.[2]

Father O'Hara's solicitude about what Bishop Chartrand would think expressed not only his feeling of indebtedness to the Bishop but also his inner feeling that he was departing from the kind of work he and the Bishop thought most important in the lives of the young whom they served. The Bishop had really commissioned him personally at ordination to work among young men and had followed very closely everything that Father O'Hara had done not only with good wishes and prayers but with financial help and especially by furnishing hundreds of his little "purple prayerbooks" that had been an important tool in getting the students to make a proper preparation and thanksgiving after Communion. There was, therefore, deep emotion in the Bishop's handwritten acknowledgment of the announcement of the change on July 27.

Dear Father:
I have been waiting to write you to congratulate you upon the new honors that have come to you, but I have been suffering from some tooth trouble, which is now abating.

I hope you will not give up your big work,—*the big work,* at Notre Dame. At every Mass I consecrate you to the Sacred Heart, *you and your* work. Pray for me, *Semper, tibi devotissime,*

✠ Joseph Chartrand
Bishop of Indianapolis

To his immediate superior, Father Charles O'Donnell, who was trying to recuperate from his illness at the summer home of one of the trustees in Michigan, Father O'Hara wrote on July 13 his first report of his activities as acting president.

The obediences will be given out Thursday evening. I enclose the list. I have added notes in some cases to make clear certain points. Mother Vincentia is hard put: the Bishop has given them the Hammond school, which we rejected, and they have to take Sisters from St. Mary's to teach there; we are giving them Father Cunningham for full time, Fathers McGinn and Fogarty for three hours a week, and Father Bolger for one hour. We can make changes in this if these appointments do not meet with your approval, but Father Burns had promised this amount of help.

My own change weighs upon me, but I am going to try to make it with as light a heart as possible. I appreciate your trust in me more than I can tell you, but my nerves slip a notch when I think of breaking the ties of sixteen years. With your approval I want to cast off from the office whatever might interfere with a continuation of spiritual guidance (limited, of course)—employment, for instance (I would like to turn this over to Mr. Lloyd, if you have no objection).

One matter of immediate concern is the tuition charge for South Bend students. Father Burns suggests that this remain at $250 for the present, since both Indiana and Purdue have opened extension courses in South Bend. I told him that I would let you know what the Registrar has to say of prospects for villager students and will inform you of the view of the council in the matter.

I haven't had a talk with Father Mulcaire as yet; Father Burns promised to inform him of the change this evening. I will take up with him whatever business he is leaving unfinished. Minor matters, I presume, are to be handled as they come up; anything of major importance will be deferred. I don't want to break in on your rest—which is one of the most important things in the community just now—so my best judgment will be marshalled to separate the minors from the majors.

. . . .

Please command me at any time. I expect to be here every day.[4]

A few days later he wrote to Father O'Donnell another note suggesting that the changes in the prefects and rectors be made immediately so that the men could move to their new places before starting on vacations at the end of summer school. He also suggested that Father Keller be given a temporary assignment to replace Father Mulcaire in Portland while Father Mulcaire visited his sick mother in Ireland.

Father O'Hara received many letters of congratulation from old students and from friends, but for most of them the full significance of the change was not understood. The South Benders were better informed on the underlying meaning of the change. The *South Bend Tribune* noted in an article: "All idolize O'Hara on Notre Dame Campus," and added an editorial the following week.

The appointment of Reverend John O'Hara, C.S.C., as vice president of the University of Notre Dame to fill the unexpired term of Reverend Michael Mulcaire, C.S.C., is greeted with the utmost satisfaction by alumni of the university. Father O'Hara, as teacher and prefect of religion at Notre Dame, has been for years one of the most popular educators among students, alumni, and visitors. Apparently possessed of unlimited energy he has devoted his efforts to improving the spiritual affairs of the students in his charge and the results have attracted national attention in Catholic educational circles. His daily bulletin, a page of comment on life at Notre Dame, and other topics, has been a source of inspiration to students and also to alumni receiving it by mail. . . . Father O'Hara assumes his new and difficult task as vice president with the warmest well wishes of all the friends of the university who feel certain he will assist most satisfactorily in carrying on the traditions and purposes of Notre Dame.[5]

On July 22 he appeared at the organizational meeting of a group of women graduates of the University in Washington Hall. He announced again his intention of turning over the direction of student employment to Mr. Lloyd and the using of Father John Cavanaugh as his assistant prefect of religion to take his place in the Dillon Hall chapel. He added: "I shall disassociate from the office of vice president anything which will interfere with my duties as Prefect of Religion. . . , I shall still write the Religious Bulletin."[6]

Father O'Hara's position was a bit anomalous. In fact the actual president was Father Charles O'Donnell, but he was at the University only a few days in the year, and then usually in the infirmary. His illness was a streptococcus infection of the inner ear that had begun when he was a chaplain in World War I, but recently had begun to spread.[7] In the early period of the infection an operation might have eliminated the disease but would have rendered him deaf, and he chose rather to endure the sickness. His mind was not affected by his illness, and he continued to make all the major decisions. As acting president, Father O'Hara continued to act in Father O'Donnell's name in all important decisions and in public appearances. As vice president in his own right, Father O'Hara handled the correspondence of both offices, represented the University on lesser public occasions, presided over the Board of Athletics, and made decisions in minor matters, except in the handling of employment and discipline. He did have to answer special pleas for employment coming from alumni and at least in appeals from the decisions of the Board of Discipline he had to appoint a board of appeal.

In his role as prefect of religion he tried to maintain an office for student counseling in Room 141, Sorin Hall, when he was on campus, and he occasionally wrote the *Religious Bulletin*. Most of the *Bulletins,* however, were not composed by him. They did not sparkle, and the acting editor, Father John J. Cavanaugh, admitted in time that they were dull. At this time it is difficult to say which ones Father O'Hara wrote, although he apparently composed the highly emotional one on the death of Bishop Chartrand. The *Bulletin* had become a dialogue between Father O'Hara and the students on spiritual matters, while they tended to become just a notice without his personality.

Father O'Hara's health continued remarkably good under these circumstances, and it was helped by his swimming twice a day when that was possible. Undoubtedly his sinuses must have given him additional trouble, although he never complained of them or admitted to having their usual co-tormentors, stomach ulcers. His own old mentor, Father James A. Burns, the provincial, was only a few steps away most of the time for consultation on matters of administration. Father Steiner was available for advice on matters of construction, and Father O'Hara brought to his new situation sixteen years of intimate conversations with students. Few items that the members of the administration brought to his attention were entirely new. His problem was to keep out of his administrative knowledge the information he had obtained in confidential conversation, although he made a strenuous effort to make a clear distinction between the two kinds of information, refusing to use in disciplinary or administrative actions what he knew from student confidences.

Whatever may have been the wishes of Father O'Hara, he was the actual center of all Notre Dame activities. Besides the correspondence and other normal duties there were a few unusual incidents, such as the visit of the noted army flier Wiley Post, whom he greeted in the University parlor for interviews and photographs. For Guglielmo Marconi, the inventor of the wireless telegraph, a Senator, and a papal count, there were more formalities. There was another growing problem when the football team was tied by a second rate Kansas team 0 to 0, and the subsequent exhibitions of the team aroused the wrath of the alumni accustomed to the coaching wizardry of the late Knute Rockne. Father O'Hara found it trying enough to have to attend the games and entertain the dignitaries from other colleges and friends of the University before and after, but he had also to listen to the com-

plaints about the team and the coach. On October 16 he went to
Chicago to address a joint meeting of the Holy Name Society and
the Catholic Youth Organization of Bishop Bernard Sheil, and
took the occasion to say that the Bishop "had come closer than
any of his contemporaries to the heart of the boy problem."[8] On
October 18 he made his first formal appearance in South Bend at
the meeting of the St. Joseph Valley Notre Dame Club. In a
rather chatty talk he expressed the hope that Notre Dame men
would be courteous, loyal, and Catholic and that the manifestations of the last would be in studying and applying the teachings
of the papal encyclicals.

As the only top executive available to represent Notre Dame
at public functions he only appeared at functions that would not
take him away for more than one day at a time. His first speech
on public affairs was a luncheon address to the South Bend Chamber of Commerce on November 20. It was a strong defense of the
National Recovery Administration, which had been attacked by
the Chamber of Commerce of the United States and by Silas
Strawn of Chicago.[9] Just how conversant with New Deal legislation he was at that time is not clear, but he had written to Father
O'Donnell on July 7: "The present industrial legislation in Washington is the most striking moral innovation since the Industrial
Revolution began and President Roosevelt has stated privately
that it was based on the Labor Encyclicals." Silas Strawn, however,
had called the N.R.A. a strait jacket and had claimed that there
was not enough money or manpower to place the country in such
a position. He had said: "We cannot go along with the apparent
tendency of the N.R.A. to attempt the compulsory enforcement of
the codes." Father O'Hara answered him by saying that there was
no necessity of inviting force in the general regulation of business.
He thought the conscience of both capital and labor would give
"recognition to certain fundamental principles of honesty and
fairness." His criticism of the position of the Chamber was quite
strong.

If the Chamber of Commerce of the United States has in mind the
continuance of the *laissez faire* policy, it is blindly working for a per-
petuation of the conditions that brought on and will continue the
depression. If on the other hand, it is working simply to prevent the
pendulum from swinging too far in the other direction—as the pendulum will swing if common sense does not rule—then more power to it.
May God strengthen its arm.

. . . Ruthless competition, the employment of child labor, starvation
wages, unsanitary working conditions, seasonal employment with no

offset for the forced vacation periods, these and other unjust conditions have deprived the producer of his markets. If business is unwilling to clean its own house, then government must do it in the name of public welfare.[9]

There was much of the old commerce teacher in his talk.

As the football season multiplied the defeats, the sad letters of alumni and friends poured in. To some correspondents the defeats were a disaster that would in time engulf all of Notre Dame's accomplishments. How much of this reached the ailing Father O'Donnell is not clear, but his visitors brought enough of the sad moments that he decided that there should be a new coach. In the meantime his health did not improve, and he went on November 5 to the Mayo Clinic in Rochester, Minnesota, where he underwent minor surgery for the removal of his tonsils and various tests to determine the cause of his illness. When the team won the Northwestern game 7 to 0 and there were reports of progress at Mayo's, Father O'Hara wrote to Father O'Donnell that some had said that all the sick priest needed was a touchdown. When Father O'Donnell wrote by hand a brief note to his secretary, Eddie O'Malley, Father O'Hara took this as a sign of recovery. But he continued to be unhappy in his estrangement from his counsellor's job. To alumnus John T. Balfe of New York he wrote on November 13:

I suppose I will have to attend the Army game, although I find crowds quite distressing. The duties of my new job are not at all to my liking, but I have to make the most of the situation.[10]

On November 14, Edward N. Hurley, the long-time friend and benefactor of Notre Dame and active member of the Board of Lay Trustees, died of leukemia. His latest benefaction had been the gift of $200,000 for the commerce building, and in his will there was a bequest for an additional $25,000 for scholarships. Father O'Hara, Dean McCarthy, representatives of the faculty, and teachers of the College of Commerce attended the funeral. Father O'Hara had been a close friend to Mr. Hurley and through him had come these benefactions. With Albert Erskine, the chairman of the Board of Trustees, Hurley had been one of the most active of the lay trustees in handling finances, getting friends, and in arranging the financing of the stadium. His loss together with that of Mr. Erskine, who had died of self-inflicted wounds during the summer, created new problems in the Board of Lay Trustees. This was a new worry for Father O'Hara since Father O'Donnell would not be able to attend the fall meeting of the trustees.

Acting in the name of Father O'Donnell and with his guidance, Father O'Hara asked Byron V. Kanaley, an alumnus very active in the interests of the University, to allow himself to be elected chairman of the Board of Lay Trustees. He also consulted with Mr. Frank Lloyd, the comptroller, about the preparation of a financial statement about the University. This Mr. Lloyd sent to the trustees before the meeting. In the meantime he also sought the advice of Father Matthew Walsh, the former president, in the preparation of the president's report on the condition of the University.

The annual meeting of the Board of Lay Trustees was held on Friday, November 24, and Mr. Kanaley was elected chairman. The president's report summed up in unstartling fashion the condition of the University. The total registration of the University was 2,547, and there were only 20 undergraduates living off campus. The faculty numbered 194, including 56 priests, 1 brother, and 137 laymen. The salaries of the lay professors had been increased and no one had been dismissed because of the depression. Father O'Hara itemized the progress of the scientific departments, including the recognition given Father Nieuwland, who had received the Morehead Medal for his achievements in chemistry, the progress of Father Wenninger in biology, the work of Professors Maurus and Mahin, and the election of Father Charles Miltner to the presidency of the American Catholic Philosophical Association. He announced also the setting up of the new Department of Metallurgy under Dr. Mahin, which would offer the doctor's degree, and a new program in Mediaeval philosophy under Father Philip Moore, C.S.C., who had recently returned from studies in Europe. He also announced that plans had been drawn up by the architects, Maginnis and Walsh of Boston, for a new students' infirmary and for a residence hall for the faculty.

This seemingly boasting air was not the inner feeling of Father O'Hara, for in the same week he wrote to Father George Sauvage, C.S.C., the procurator general of the Congregation.

I appreciate your good wishes. This new job is not at all to my liking, and I need all the help I can get. While I am still Prefect of Religion, I have little time for the work, and since I have to be away often in the evening, there is a break in the continuity of calls. When a student tries to find me in the evening and cannot, he is less likely to call another time. I realize the importance of my present position, and try to fulfill the duties conscientiously, but it does not carry with it the satisfaction that is born of spiritual work. You should understand very well what I mean, because you have certainly experienced it in your own life.[11]

As a final act in a rather weird football season the Notre Dame team defeated the Army team 13 to 12 in New York on December 2. Since the team had not been expected to win and yet came back after being behind in the first half, the followers of the Notre Dame team were quite delirious in their joy. For the moment their attention was distracted from their earlier demands for a change in coaches. But apparently the ailing President of the University had not forgotten. Just when he and Father O'Hara made their decision to replace Coach Hartley Anderson with Elmer Layden is not clear, but since the two priests had not met for nearly a month and Father O'Hara insisted that the decision was made by Father O'Donnell, the latter must have made it before November 5 when he went to the Mayo Clinic. On Thursday, December 7, before the annual dinner for the football team, Father O'Hara obtained the resignations of Director of Athletics Jesse Harper and Head Coach Hartley Anderson. In apologizing to Father O'Donnell for not meeting him on his return from Rochester, Father O'Hara simply said:

> I am sorry I can't be on hand to greet you either in Chicago or South Bend, but I think it advisable to go into hiding for a couple of days.
>
> Harper and Anderson resigned this afternoon, Anderson very gracefully. The banquet this evening was very harmonious.
>
> Layden wants a conference before signing, and I am for having this at home. Boland has accepted. Elward will, I think, for I believe we can come to terms next week.
>
> It has been a hectic week, but Father Walsh has been an angel, and it hasn't worn me down any.
>
> The release is set for Saturday evening at six o'clock.[12]

Two days later Father O'Hara and Elmer Layden, who was a distant cousin, met at the O'Hara home in Indianapolis, and Layden signed the contract in the presence of Mrs. O'Hara. The official announcement of the change was released at six o'clock Saturday evening at Notre Dame. There were a few smug comments in the press about Notre Dame sacrificing Anderson to win games, and some claims that Anderson had achieved the purposes of the game, but Anderson himself proved to be a very loyal alumnus. He secured another coaching position at the University of North Carolina. Layden had been a successful coach since his graduation from the University and had also achieved a reputation as a fine Christian gentleman.

On the evening of the feast of the Immaculate Conception, shortly after Father O'Hara arrived in Indianapolis to meet Lay-

den, he lost his close friend, Bishop Chartrand. The Bishop had
attempted his usual stint in the confessional that day but had
been forced to give up. However, he performed his ordinary services connected with the First Friday devotions, but about seven
o'clock he suffered a fatal attack of angina pectoris and lived only
a few minutes. Father O'Hara was deeply grieved, and while he
had to return to the University, he came back on December 13
for the funeral. Apparently the laudatory *Religious Bulletin* of
December 9 on the Bishop was the composition of Father O'Hara.

Twenty-five thousand confessions a year . . . *"ego te absolvo a pecca-
tis tuis"* 25,000 times a year on the average . . . and for forty-one years
in the priesthood . . . twenty-three of them as a Bishop who went into
the confessional before 5:00 every morning and remained there until
9:00 (with time out for his Mass) . . . what a record of zeal.

To a relative who sent him sympathy on the loss of his close friend
he wrote:

I appreciate your expression of sympathy on the death of my dear
friend, Bishop Chartrand. I haven't been able to feel bad over the
occurrence because I know how hard he worked for the reward he is
having. It was a relief to know that his sufferings were over. He kept
hard at work until the end, and for the past several years he was in
no condition to work. His life was certainly an inspiration.[13]

To Bishop Alphonse Smith of Nashville, also a follower of Chartrand, he wrote later:

I can certainly appreciate what a loss you feel in the death of Bishop
Chartrand because I know all that he meant to you. I feel that he was
also my father and best friend, and although I did not live on such
intimate terms with him as you did, I regard him as the inspiration of
any pastoral work that I have been able to accomplish.[14]

But Father O'Hara could not tarry in his grief at the loss of his
friend or read the voluminous correspondence on the change in
football coaches. On December 19 he participated in a symposium
on "Social Justice" before the National Catholic Alumni Federation in Chicago that was sponsored by the Notre Dame Club of
Chicago.[15] Participating from Notre Dame besides Father O'Hara
were Dean J. E. McCarthy, speaking on "Social Justice in Business," Dean Thomas Konop of the Law School speaking on "Social Justice from the Law Standpoint," and Father William
Bolger, C.S.C, speaking on "Social Justice."
Father O'Hara, speaking on "Religion and Social Justice,"
opened his speech with a story about a manufacturer who had

learned by experience of the activity of Catholicism in fighting bolshevism and then gave a brief survey of the papal encyclicals of Popes Leo XIII and Pius XI on social justice, adding that the coercive measures of the N.R.A. were necessary in the existing emergency because the necessary good will for the attainment of social justice was lacking. He insisted on a three-fold duty of individuals to work for social justice: (1) to know the principles of justice, (2) to observe these principles in their own lives, and (3) to have the courage required to observe the principles of social justice.

After Christmas Father O'Hara went to the annual meeting of the National Collegiate Athletic Association in Columbus, Ohio on December 29, where he spoke as the chairman of the Notre Dame Board of Athletics on the new evils of college athletics. He spoke of the factors that had brought about the expansion of athletic plants since the war and praised the development of intramural athletics such as had developed at Notre Dame. He gave credit to the expanded college sports for the insistence on clean sportsmanship and for greater respect for competitors.

That same day Father O'Hara received the sad news of the sudden death of Professor Charles Phillips of the English Department while visiting relatives in Minnesota. Phillips, a former newspaper editor, had been a fine influence on the student body as a teacher and advisor and had filled a traditional spot on the Notre Dame faculty of a literary layman with wide intellectual interests.

Father O'Hara continued his speedy pace without hesitation. On January 12 he announced the formation on campus of a Catholic Action Club under the direction of Father William Bolger, with the assistance of Father O'Hara and Father John J. Cavanaugh. In announcing the Club, Father O'Hara praised Father Bolger as the one best fitted to direct its activities. On January 15 he spoke at the annual St. Joseph Valley dinner for the football team, warning the new coach not to endanger his health like the late Bishop Chartrand and the ailing Father O'Donnell. "But teach these boys that the best thing they do on or off the football field, is what they do for others and the highest thing they do is for God."[16] On the same day he issued a *Bulletin* on the condition of Father O'Donnell, saying that the reports were favorable and "there is strong reason to hope that the present course of treatment will prove effective in checking the infection and repairing such damage as it has done." To others he admitted that there had also been some less optimistic reports. He himself was busy preparing speeches that he planned to give on a trip to the eastern states. As he wrote to a friend, he would give the same speech in Providence and in Boston.

The first speech was given at a Catholic Action dinner sponsored by the Waterbury, Connecticut, Council of the Knights of Columbus, to which Father O'Hara had been invited by John Robinson, an alumnus. Present also were Governor Cross of Connecticut, Bishop Maurice McAuliffe of Hartford, and many other prominent Catholics. Father O'Hara was not the polished orator or the poetic writer that Father Charles O'Donnell had been. Even when giving a formal speech, Father O'Hara seemed to drop naturally into the casual narrative manner of speaking that had been so noticeable in his *Religious Bulletin*.

In the Waterbury speech Father O'Hara took the theme that the reason the Holy Father had found it necessary to call for Catholic Action was "because through ignorance and timidity Catholics have, until now, been unmindful of their glorious birthright." Repeating from his speech on social justice in Chicago the story of the industrialist, he claimed that the industrialist had found Catholic principles of social justice to be valid. Since the greater number of Catholics are among the less favored, he proposed that Catholics should broaden the chance for their less-favored brethren for Catholic schooling, since fully one-half of the adult Catholic population had received its training in non-Catholic schools. He spoke also of a second group of Catholics who were always apologizing for Catholic ideas, who did not appreciate their Catholic heritage. He claimed that F. D. Roosevelt had used the encyclicals as the basis for the N.R.A., that Harvard had brought in DeWulf from Louvain to teach Catholics Catholic philosophy, and that the University of Chicago had allowed Adler to reintroduce Thomas Aquinas. He praised the leadership of such men as Chief Douglas White and called upon the Catholics of Connecticut to manifest a higher type of Catholic Action.[17]

The next day Father O'Hara spoke to the Notre Dame men of Providence at a luncheon, and the evening of the following day, January 20, 1934, he addressed the Notre Dame Club of Boston, giving the same speech on both occasions. The title of his speech was "Debunking Education."[18]

Father O'Hara first apologized for speaking of the depression and explained that the word "debunking" was coined during the "mad 20's to describe a process, partly in the field of history, by which legend was winnowed from fact by the flail, and fact was flailed so unmercifully that nothing much but ugly fact remained." Writers of that time, he said, had presented Washington "as a bar fly, Lincoln as a visionary bumpkin, Napoleon as a paranoiac, and St. Paul as a mad epileptic." But he noted now that in the past few years the debunkers themselves had been debunked, and he intended to speak of this debunking of the debunkers in the field of education. He pointed out that one of the great blessings of the depression was that the financial situation had made impossible the wild programs of certain educational experiments. Two experiments that he cited were a course in contemporary civilization at Columbia University in which free love had been required, and the experimental college formed at the University of Wisconsin. He quoted other examples of educational experiments that prospered before the stock crash. On the positive side he quoted Canon Bernard Iddings Bell, who criticized the American colleges for their neglect of religion. He said this criticism was just, and the resulting moral chaos of such a condition was deplorable. He asked that he be not understood as saying that secular education had not done solid intellectual work, but he did insist that there was great confusion arising from the use of false principles. The cure for the evils he regarded as Christian education as proposed in the social encyclicals of Pope Pius XI. He then praised the system of Catholic education that had cost American Catholics perhaps a billion dollars. Secular educators, too, would have to learn the value of this religious education.

These comments on secular education before the depression were the kind of remarks that Father O'Hara had been making for years in his *Religious Bulletin*. But just as he was distressed when excerpts from the *Bulletin* were published in Catholic newspapers, so he was startled to find that a newspaper writer for the Boston press had grasped at his statement about Columbia and made of it a glowing charge against that university. He had said:

> Lest you think this caricature is exaggerated, I present as an example the 1931 report to the Columbia University Board of Trustees by President Nicholas Murray Butler. He lamented the steady decline in good manners and blamed this condition on the anti-philosophies and pseudo-psychologists of our day. Less than two months later, Columbia announced a new course to be required of all sophomores in a "freer conception of the relation to the sexes, unhindered by law or religion." The head of the university deplored the decline in good manners and his faculty required of students a course in concubinage.[19]

Some Boston reporter caught the last sentence and made a sensational story out of it which was flashed from coast to coast. Colum-

bia University was embarrassed. Her Dean Hawkes claimed that
the story was "made up entirely of whole cloth." He said that no
such course in concubinage had ever been taught at Columbia.
The next day Dr. John Thompson of the First Methodist Church
in Chicago and The Reverend Dr. Frederick Shannon in Orchestra Hall, Chicago, attacked the teaching of such a course. Other
ministers throughout the country continued the attack the following week. Then Professor John J. Coss of the Columbia Summer
School admitted that the course had been taught one semester but
had been dropped. Further, it was announced that the author of
the text that had been the basis of the course, a Miss Ruth Reed,
had become a Catholic and had publicly repudiated the book.
Father O'Hara received letters of protest from Dean Hawkes,
Professor Carleton Hayes of Columbia, and Father George Ford,
the Newman Chaplain at Columbia. When he was asked to comment further, Father O'Hara said publicly: "I am deeply gratified
that there should be resentment on the part of the Columbia University faculty that such a course was ever considered as part of
the curriculum."

When Father O'Hara returned to Notre Dame, he was forced
to go to the infirmary because of a cold. On January 29 he wrote
a detailed account of the incident to Father O'Donnell, whom
he was representing on the trip. He added:

. . . The matter died down in the newspapers then until yesterday
when Rev. John Thompson at the Chicago Temple enlarged upon
the airing he had given it the previous Sunday.

I have had some interesting letters about it, some of them from cru-
saders. . . . A lot of people are urging me to continue to wield the
cudgel now that secular educators are beginning to disavow their
liberal ideas. I shall go very slow, however, on any such general campaign, although I won't mind taking a whack now and then. Monsignor Shannon told me just before I went east that at the University of
Chicago now they become frantic if you recall any of the fads and
frills, they publicized so freely a few years ago. . . .[20]

But what was more sensible, after the doctors permitted him to
leave the infirmary, he went to Arizona and California for a rest.

Back at Notre Dame on February 16, Father O'Hara wrote to
Father O'Donnell about commencement plans. He approved
Father O'Donnell's suggestion of Bishop John McNamara of
Washington as the baccalaureate speaker. Secretary of State Cor-
dell Hull had begged off being the commencement speaker, and
Father O'Hara suggested Frank Walker or Homer Cummings. A
few days later he wrote that he had written invitations to Bishop

McNamara and Frank Walker. He also asked Father O'Donnell for suggestions for a replacement for Professor Phillips. In a post-script he mentioned that the criticism of Notre Dame in the report of Henry S. Pritchett of the Carnegie Foundation for the Improvement of Teaching had aroused comment. He enclosed with his letter a copy of his own reply to Pritchett that he gave to the press.

Henry S. Pritchett had been president of the Carnegie Foundation for the Improvement of Teaching when it achieved some notability on publishing, in 1929, Howard J. Savage's report on collegiate athletics. Now Pritchett had given more than a passing mention to Notre Dame in his essay in *The Twenty-Eighth Annual Report* of the foundation for 1933. The scathing tone of the essay is indicated in the title, "A Slump in the Football Trade." Commenting on the Harvard guarantees to visiting teams, he wondered if the amounts guaranteed had any relationship to the academic standing of the institutions receiving them. "For example, would the Notre Dame teams demand and receive a larger guarantee than a team from Johns Hopkins or Columbia." Later he mentioned Notre Dame again:

It is interesting to note that the best advertised football teams have been able to retain a paying business. When the Notre Dame team travels to the Pacific Coast to play the University of Southern California and stops en route in Arizona for mysterious practice, the newspapers are full of speculations as to the significance of these maneuvers and as to the condition of each of the players. All this makes free and effective advertising and swells the gate receipts. Last spring these two football enterprises felt justified in signing a contract for three years in their football business, which in spite of the fact that they are more than two thousand miles apart and the expenses of travel are heavy, will no doubt yield a satisfactory profit. These two institutions are among the most thrifty of all those engaged in the football industry. Notre Dame is a Catholic college. The University of Southern California was started by the Methodists, but it is now under the direction of an undenominational board. It would be a real contribution to education in the United States if these two institutions would indicate how far the profits of their football business are used in supporting their educational activities and still more interesting and important if they would indicate the relation of the football victory to the intellectual life.

In the essay were two other references to Notre Dame:

. . . No one can foretell what civilizing influence Notre Dame and Southern California may exercise upon the backward universities of Europe!
. . . It is a far cry from the devotion of the fathers who founded Notre Dame and of the earnest men who labored to create a university in

Southern California to the three-year contract these colleges have signed to exploit their football teams for commercial purposes.[21]

In his answer Father O'Hara charged that Pritchett had begun with the false assumption "that highly publicized football is inimical to the intellectual interests of the university. We wish to reiterate that if we ever found it to be the case we would drop football without a moment's hesitation." Father O'Hara was particularly anxious to answer the question that Pritchett had raised about the use to which these funds had been used at Notre Dame. He pointed out with pride that the University was supporting twenty priests who were studying in notable American and foreign universities in preparation for their work at Notre Dame. He also said that the University had protected its lay professors during the depression even though the student enrollment had dropped 600. Finally he added: "It will interest the Carnegie Foundation to hear that of the $4,000,000 increase in the material plant at Notre Dame during the past twelve years, only twenty percent is devoted to athletic purposes."[22] Father O'Hara was especially proud of the use that Notre Dame had made of its football income and would later approach the foundation for some of their money for the same purposes.

The reaction of the press to the exchange was generally favorable to Notre Dame, although few offered any defense of Southern California. Father O'Hara wrote of this to Father O'Donnell.

I am glad that you are pleased with the rejoinder to Pritchett. I judge from your previous correspondence with him that he spends his winters in Santa Barbara. On my visit there two weeks ago, I was edified to see so many old men playing shuffleboard and checkers on the public links in front of the bathhouse. I didn't think to look for Pritchett in the group. What a tragedy it would have been had I found him playing for keeps! The matter may yet bear investigation.[23]

On Washington's birthday he represented Father O'Donnell in accepting the American flag presented annually by the senior class. He called the flag presentation "one of the most beautiful facets in the many-sided life of Notre Dame." The offering of the flag, he said, symbolized their offering of themselves to their country for the common good, not only in war but also in peace. He recalled those who had presented the flag in 1918 and then went on to war. The present seniors were asked not to do that but to face the problems of peace. In discussing these problems of peace he made a special plea to them to have a full grasp of the rights of labor as outlined in the papal encyclicals and to apply Catholic principles in every field of life.

Father O'Hara continued to keep Father O'Donnell informed of his activities, and on February 26 told him that the choice for the Laetare Medal had been limited to Frank Spearman, Mrs. Nicholas Brady, and James A. Farrell. On March 6 he told him that Mrs. Brady had been the final choice:

> I want to jot down a few notes of interest.
>
> Mrs. Brady received the final approval of the committee. I am preparing things for the announcement.
>
> The Layden banquet in Davenport Thursday night was quite a success. It was the largest affair of its kind ever held in the neighborhood. The first football team and the first baseball team at Notre Dame were represented. The Notre Dame coaches present gave a good account of themselves in their speeches, and the whole impression was very favorable.
>
> Bishop McNamara has accepted the invitation to deliver the Baccalaureate sermon. I am still waiting the final word from Frank Walker. I shall probably call him up tonight.
>
> Dr. Tom Keefe is campaigning for an LL.D. for George Ade. If you care to give an opinion on this, I shall be glad to have it. If you have any particular nominations for the LL.D., I shall be glad to know about them, too. My impression is that you do not care to multiply these honors.[24]

There was a mysterious postscript to this letter saying that "Jim Boylan called up at noon today with great news! That must be the answer to the novena prayers. Hold on—*Prospere et procede.*" Apparently Father O'Donnell had told Boylan that he was better.

Writing Father O'Donnell again on March 12, Father O'Hara said that Frank Walker had accepted the invitation to give the Commencement address and that the Laetare Medal award had been well received locally and that Cardinal Hayes, Archbishop Murray, Bishop O'Brien, and Mr. Maginnis had sent in their congratulations.

When Professor Charles Phillips died in December, there was a general lament throughout the country. Later in the March 2 *Commonweal* Adolphus King, Jr., of Washington, D.C., criticized the University for making Phillips do the menial task of handling freshmen while the coach had assistants to do his menial tasks. "Dr. Phillips should not have been allowed to correct schoolboys' themes. That laborious work should have been done by a reader and his time husbanded for creative work. Our universities are penny-wise and pound foolish. . . ." Answering the letter in the March 30 *Commonweal,* Father O'Hara called the statement "an unwarranted and ungracious slur on the university where Professor Phillips spent what he described as the happiest days of his life." He answered further the charge that Phillips had been forced to work with freshmen. "But you could not keep Professor Phillips from encouraging boys by correcting their themes any more than you could keep the late Bishop Chartrand from his self-imposed duty of hearing Confessions from five until nine every morning. . . ."

Father O'Hara took up in the letter another implied accusation about the administration of Catholic colleges.

I refer to the assumption that it is the duty of these institutions to pay substantial salaries to men who will teach an hour a day and do research the rest of the time. . . . I can find no justification for turning the tuition fees of undergraduates over to men who neither teach them nor minister to them in any way. Training men for research is certainly a proper function of a graduate school, and there is always an incidental research product from this, but it seems unjust to charge to the unendowed university the support of the research worker. Endowment for work of this sort may come in time to Catholic universities as it has to secular institutions but until it comes it should not be considered reactionary to hold that the chief function of a teacher is to teach.

On March 23 Father O'Hara wrote to Father O'Donnell another newsletter in which he added:

I am delighted that you feel well enough to come back to your own room. Father Burns told me of your desires in this matter, and the news was very heartening. I hope the weather will soon be sufficiently temperate to warrant your coming north. Until now it had been excessively raw in March. . . .

We are keeping up our prayers that God will not let your illness go past this first year. The anniversary is almost upon us.[25]

On Good Friday he wrote another newsletter and added: "Your letter just received. I shall be on hand to greet you in Chicago."

Whether Father O'Hara actually thought that Father O'Donnell was getting well is not clear. Writing to Father Sauvage in Rome on March 20 about the possibility of awarding the Laetare Medal to Mrs. Brady in Rome, he said that a new physician had offered the opinion that Father O'Donnell's "difficulty in walking" was purely "psychological,"[26] but when Father O'Donnell reached Notre Dame on April 5 one leg was paralyzed. His condition grew steadily worse, and on the advice of a physician he went to Watkins Glen, New York, for special treatment. On April 24, after bringing Father O'Donnell back from Watkins Glen, Father O'Hara wrote to Frank Walker: "Father O'Donnell made the trip well enough, but I am afraid his condition is very bad. He is paralyzed from the waist down and is pretty helpless. His paralysis has progressed rapidly in the past week. The trip to New York was a mistake, but a physician in New York recommended it, and Father O'Donnell would not be satisfied until he had made the experiment."[27] Father O'Donnell was removed to Saint Joseph Hospital in South Bend on May 1. The end was to be expected at any time.

Father O'Hara continued manfully at his tasks, speaking at Columbus, Ohio, on April 14 and at the Universal Notre Dame Night celebration in Chicago two days later. In his speech he said he liked the word "universal" for the celebration because universal meant Catholic, and Notre Dame was above all Catholic. He added, according to the *Chicago Tribune:* "I see no way out of this confusion except religion. And by religion I mean something we feel, not something we put on like a garment, and not something we put in a strong box like a trinket!"[28] All groups have their unifying principles such as evolutionism, humanitarianism, or utilitarianism. "The unifying principle of Catholic education is God. Since inquiry into causes is the proper pursuit of the scholar, only that education is complete that goes all the way back to its first cause, God."

As usual, most public functions at the University came to a halt during the final examinations and the preparations for commencement. The University was also awaiting the final summons of its president. On the eve of commencement, Father O'Hara gave the visiting alumni the annual message of the President in the place of Father O'Donnell. He paid a brief tribute to Father O'Donnell and to the Apostolic Delegate, who was in attendance, as well as to the two commencement speakers. He reviewed the events of the year, including the change in football coaches, the plans for the Rockne Memorial minor sports building, the recognition accorded Father Nieuwland for his researches in chemistry, the setting up of a course in mediaeval studies under Father Philip Moore and Professor Pollock, and the flourishing religious life of the student.

According to plans Bishop McNamara gave the baccalaureate sermon. He urged the graduates to learn from the depression to avoid greed and selfishness. Archbishop Amleto Cicognani, the Apostolic Delegate, sang the Mass. The commencement address was given by Frank Walker, who paused before giving his written discourse to pay tribute to the priest who lay dying in the nearby hospital. He also urged the graduates to learn from the depression and to plan properly for the future. Early the morning after commencement Father Charles O'Donnell died. He was buried from the University church on Wednesday, June 6. The Superior General, Father James W. Donahue, celebrated the Mass. Father O'Hara was deacon and Father Carrico was subdeacon. Bishops Noll of Fort Wayne and Edward Hoban of Rockford and many other clergymen attended. There was no sermon according to the current Community rule, and the casket was the simple black box of the ordinary religious of Holy Cross. The severe simplicity caused comment. There were glowing tributes in the newspapers and in other publications, but the simplicity best expressed the sorrow of the University and the Congregation, which had lost one of its most brilliant and active sons at the age of forty-nine.

On the same day, June 6, in the Holy Cross House in Rome the Laetare Medal was conferred on Mrs. Brady by Father Julius Nieuwland, who was in Rome to receive an honor from international science. At Notre Dame after the funeral there was a period of sad silence fittingly devoted to the community retreat. There is a legend that Father O'Hara got on his knees to beg the Provincial, Father Burns, not to appoint him President. Certainly in mind, if not in fact, he was begging that he would not have to accept the burden and that he be allowed to return to counselling students.

Time magazine for July 16, under the title "Our Lady's Man," reported the appointment of Father O'Hara:

When a lay university's president dies or resigns all the world knows that months of excursions and excitements, requests and refusals, acrimony and argument will probably elapse before a new president is chosen. Last month died Reverend Charles Leo O'Donnell, President of the University of Notre Dame since 1928. Last week in Notre Dame, Reverend James Aloysius Burns, U.S. Provincial Superior of the Congregation of Holy Cross, arose at evening prayer to announce that he and four colleagues had that day chosen Reverend John Francis O'Hara, 46, to be Notre Dame's President.

Father O'Hara did not want the job. Titular vice President and acting President of Notre Dame during President O'Donnell's year of illness, he had already announced that he would keep on being the University's Prefect of Religion. But the Roman Catholic authority which made the choice of a new president so smooth and peaceful rests on unhesitating obedience. Father O'Hara accepted his orders without protest.

Father O'Hara sent a note of thanks to the editors of *Time* for their sympathetic account but did not raise the ban on the sale of *Time* in the cafeteria that had been imposed by Father O'Donnell.[20] The scene described by *Time* had taken place in the basement chapel. On the same day, July 5, Father O'Hara and Father

Matthew Walsh had been released from the Provincial Council and replaced by Father Kerndt Healey and Father Thomas A. Steiner, who immediately elected Father O'Hara president. The other obediences of the Province were announced later, including that of Father Hugh O'Donnell, former president of St. Edward's University, Austin, Texas, as vice-president.

Probably no one in the Community was surprised by the election of Father O'Hara, and only he thought seriously of opposing the choice. Except for his desire to avoid the job, he could hardly have had a better preparation for it than his year as acting president and vice-president because in that time he came into contact with most of the personnel and fiscal problems that he would now have to face on his own authority. He had discussed some policies with his ailing predecessor. When Father O'Hara was asked by the newspaper reporters about any change in policies, he indicated that there would be none. Basically there could be no change in the policies announced in the *University Bulletin*. In his first public address, given at the centennial celebration of the Catholic Church in Indiana on August 7 over station WKBF, Indianapolis, he insisted that Notre Dame stood for basic principles. He took as an example of Notre Dame's insistence on these principles the University's commerce program with which he had been so closely associated:

Notre Dame insisted on a strong cultural background as the most important asset of the business ambassador—and has had the satisfaction of seeing the trend in business education veer that way in the intervening years.

Against the prevailing materialistic philosophy of change and instability, Notre Dame has held with unerring faith to a belief in unchanging fundamental principles by which all the problems of life can be met as they arise—and if we have a mission in the educational world of today I believe it is to call the higher institutions back to the same belief.[30]

In answer to countless letters of congratulations Father O'Hara asked for prayers that he would do a good job in his new role. To those who understood he reiterated his regret that he had to leave behind his work of counselling students in the confessional. To Archbishop Cicognani, the apostolic delegate, he wrote:

. . . My heart is still in the spiritual work I did for so many years, but with Your Excellency's blessing I believe that my sense of duty can be brought to give proper attention to the wider problems that are now mine. For this work I treasure the approval of the Holy Father's representative.[31]

This is about as close as Father O'Hara came to stating the problems that faced him. Probably he never became reconciled to his separation from the role of prefect of religion. Nevertheless, he put all his power into carrying on his new task. This was characteristic of everything he did in later life: a complete dedication and an overwhelming loyalty to the task assigned, whether it be an argument on economics or social problems, a problem of administration, or facing criticism. He could be hurt and was often hurt by the criticism that his determination aroused in those who disagreed with him, but so long as he felt that he was in the right, such pain did not bother him. Disagreements never stopped him.

On educational policies Father O'Hara had the advice and experience of Father James Burns, C.S.C., on which to draw. On the condition of the physical plant he could always rely on Father Thomas A. Steiner, C.S.C, an engineer become priest and a long-time devoted friend. Nevertheless his was the task to guide Notre Dame out of the depression into new accomplishments. He had to guide his religious subjects, lead his faculty, plan the development and use of the financial resources of the University. His year under Father O'Donnell had allowed him to see intimately what had to be done. He had had a taste of executive power shortly after ordination when he tried to create a Pan American institute, but he had been defeated then primarily by the lack of finances and of qualified teachers. It was not surprising that his first efforts were intended to obtain those same means for a greater Notre Dame.

One of the first acts of the new president was to appoint Father Hugh O'Donnell, the vice-president, to act as the assistant superior and arrange for him to handle the ordinary permissions, to assign priests to missions, and to lead the community prayers in the basement chapel. Later when at the insistence of the superior general a separate house of residence for priests was instituted in Corby Hall, the Vice President and Assistant Superior became the superior of the hall. This did not mean that Father O'Hara was not available, because he was ready to talk to anyone at any time; the only difficulty was that his rapid-fire manner of talking sometimes embarrassed the more timid members of the community. Father O'Hara had also a local council in accordance with canon law. In this instance it consisted of four men appointed by the provincial, usually the vice-president, the director of studies, the prefect of discipline, and the treasurer. In the tradition established nearly a hundred years before by Father Sorin the will of the president seldom lacked the assent of his council and then not for long.

Father O'Hara had never been a man for sitting long hours in community recreations, but he knew everyone who helped him in his religious program—almost everyone at Notre Dame—and his first interest was in seeing that capable members of the community received a chance for advanced study or to develop his special talents. Father Leo R. Ward was given an opportunity to study at Oxford and Louvain, Father Thomas Brennan was asked to develop the Dante collection that the University had inherited from Father John Zahm, Father Moore was told to develop his mediaeval studies, for which he had been prepared by long years in Paris. Another of Father O'Hara's proposals was the establishment of a University quarterly that would have for its focal points the economic and political implications of the social encyclicals of the recent popes. He asked Father William Bolger, C.S.C., to assume the editorship of this quarterly, which did not then come into being.[32] Father O'Hara also thought of his lay faculty, but he knew that for any expansion there must be new funds raised. He had already learned that the endowment that had been raised under the guidance of Father James Burns in the early 1920's had not increased, and with the depression had scarcely remained constant. The object of his earliest travels as president was to consult with the lay trustees and other financial advisors of the University. He also decided to approach the chief educational foundations.

There are few records of his thinking because most of his advisers lived with him at Notre Dame, but when Father Burns was absent in Washington on October 4, Father O'Hara wrote him of his efforts.

This is the first chance I have had to express my appreciation of your kindness in seeing Governor McLean. I am glad you formed such a fine impression of the man, I thought I would enjoy knowing him. I believe, as you do, that his help will be of great benefit to us.

I had a fine visit with Ben Smith Thursday night. I went out with him to Bedford Village, and at eleven o'clock I drove to Stanford to take the train for Boston. The interview Friday morning with Mr. Phelan was satisfactory from some points of view. I gathered from him that bears and bulls are not entirely at ease at the same table. He made several recommendations for the Board. I left Boston in the afternoon and arrived in South Bend Saturday afternoon.

On Monday morning I saw Fred Fisher in Detroit. He and Mr. Phelan are very much in agreement.

Monday evening I saw John Murphy in Cleveland. Through him
I expected to meet Newton D. Baker and invite that gentleman to see
our Art Gallery. John told me that Mr. Baker was in South Bend. I
immediately called Hugh O'Donnell, who succeeded in getting Mr.
Baker to promise to come to dinner tonight or tomorrow night.

Tuesday at Pittsburgh I had a very fine visit with both Colonel
Church and Dr. Arbuthnot. Both of these gentlemen expressed a willingness to see our Art Gallery, and Colonel Church expects to come
within the next two weeks. I also had an interview with Colonel
Church's neighbor and good friend, John L. Casey, and Mr. Casey
has promised to escort Colonel Church to Notre Dame. The Novena
of the Little Flower ended that day and I think we owe our friend a
novena in thanksgiving. I told Colonel Church that I asked no information on his attitude, but he volunteered the statement that the project we recommend is the sort of thing that would interest the Board.
As you promised, he was extremely cordial, and he went fifteen minutes past his lunch time in his enthusiasm about our collection. I was
told previously that he always closed interviews promptly at twelve
o'clock. Dr. Arbuthnot was nice enough to call on me at the Cathedral.

I thank you sincerely for your kind words about the radio speech.
Through a mistake in timing, I cheated Father Connerton out of two
minutes.

My efforts to see President Keppel were unsuccessful so I am writing
him today and sending him the revised statement of our needs. In the
letter I am asking him to grant me an interview at the earliest possible
moment. I presume that some of our friends have reached him in the
meantime, and that he will be in a good mood to grant this request.
Colonel Church informs me that Mr. Keppel's father was an art
dealer.[33]

The enthusiasm with which Father O'Hara approached the
Carnegie Foundation for the Advancement of Teaching was not
shared by the Foundation president. Father O'Hara felt that the
Foundation, which through Mr. Pritchett had criticized the University for paying so much attention to football to the exclusion
of the cultural aspects of collegiate work, should be willing under
the circumstances to help Notre Dame's other effort. President
Frederick P. Keppel of Carnegie gave Father O'Hara a frosty
reception, claiming that he had many other appointments and
demanding that Father O'Hara give some reasons why he should
receive preference over those who had applied before him. The
program Father O'Hara presented him included $1,000,000 for
an art museum, $400,000 for a fine arts building, $4,400 for a
laboratory for testing art objects, $10,625 for various needs of the
Department of Fine Arts, $19,500 for the needs of the Department
of Architecture, $33,750 for fellowships in American church his-

tory to exploit the Catholic manuscript collections in the possession of the University, and $30,050 for the Mediaeval Institute.[34]

While these projects were not essential to the University, for
that very reason they could not be handled from the ordinary University budget. Further Father O'Hara always maintained that
these artistic elements were necessary to fulfill the Catholic ideal
of balanced education.

When he met a total refusal, Father O'Hara wrote a letter to
Keppel that may not have been diplomatic but that did explain
why he sought the grant.

You asked during our interview what reasons we could allege for
having our claims considered in advance of those submitted previously
by other schools. I hesitated to state the most obvious reason, lest it be
misconstrued as a criticism. On further consideration, I believe that
in the interests of frankness it should be stated, and since I have found
you so cordial and understanding, I believe you will accept it as I give
it, namely a statement of fact and not as a criticism. It is simply this:
From my first letter, you will gather that we were urged to lay our
needs before the Carnegie Corporation because Dr. Pritchett suggested
that we make our cultural facilities better known, and we judged that
his suggestion could best be met by our permitting the Corporation to
aid us in some phase of our cultural work. Under the circumstances,
action this year seemed desirable.[35]

The letter was dated November 28, 1934. Negotiations with the
Carnegie Foundation continued for about two years, and in later
years Father O'Hara sought aid for the scientific departments of
the University, but his efforts were fruitless. Later he maintained
that the foundation was dominated by men who were hostile to
religion and that he had been warned by his predecessor, Father
Charles O'Donnell, that he would get nothing. While Father
O'Hara was very successful in increasing the endowment of the
University in his two administrations, none of the money came
from foundations and his criticism of foundations was constant:
they were forcing religion out of the American colleges in return
for their grants.

Returning to the campus, Father O'Hara began to walk the
treadmill of the college president. He spoke at a pep rally for the
team on October 4, and sat in the President's box at the game
the next day. On October 10 he gave a radio speech in honor of
General Pulaski, the next day attended a reception given to him by
the lay faculty, and a dinner in his honor by the South Bend Chamber of Commerce on April 15. The next day James J. Phelan, the
lay trustee, died in Boston, and he and Father Francis Boland

attended the funeral. On October 31 with Dean McCarthy he attended the National Trade Convention in Boston. When Warren A. Cartier, an alumnus and also a lay trustee, died in Ludington, Michigan, Father O'Hara, unable to attend the funeral, visited the family the day before the funeral. On Friday morning, November 11, he presided at the dedication of the new post office building. Assistant Postmaster General Ambrose O'Connell, a Notre Dame graduate, sold the first stamp to Frank Walker, which was placed on a letter of Father O'Hara to President Roosevelt. That weekend Father O'Hara welcomed the lay trustees for the first time as president. Father Burns presided as chairman at the meetings held in the Engineering building; Byron Kanaley was president of the Board of Lay Trustees, and William C. Porter and Peter C. Reilly were elected to the board. Porter was an alumnus, and Reilly was a friend of Father O'Hara's father and now a successful manufacturer in Indianapolis. The most important business was the report on the investments of the University. While the losses in these investments during the depression had been remarkably low, the endowment had remained little more than the one million dollars raised under Father Burns ten years before. The chief recommendation of the Board was first to work out some plan to restore the losses incurred during the depression.

Father O'Hara's report was really a bird's-eye view of the University as he began his administration. The total enrollment was 2,637 students, of whom only 15 resided off campus. Beginning with the 1935–1936 year, registration for rooms was to be made according to the scholastic averages of the students. The work in mediaeval studies was being advanced with the return of Father James McDonald from Oxford to teach mediaeval English, the offering by Father Thomas Brennan of a course in Dante. Father Hugh Hoever, O. Cist., lectured on St. Anselm, and Dr. E. M. Chapman lectured on mediaeval philosophy. Visiting lecturers included Francis Sheed, Maisie Ward, Shane Leslie, who would also teach the second semester, Jacques Maritain, and Etienne Gilson. Four new classes had been added in the Department of Physics, and a seminar begun in nuclear physics. He listed many additions to the equipment of the laboratories, the addition of the Alice Wickett art collection to the Art Gallery, and the reception of funds for scholarships.

He also outlined what he considered the immediate needs of the University: a social center to be built on the site of Badin Hall at a cost of $250,000; a residence hall for graduate students; a new chemistry building costing $400,000; and an astronomical laboratory costing $25,000. In addition he wanted funds for scholarships for graduate students, since few graduate students in American universities could pay their own way. Probably the part of the report that was most characteristic of the forward look of Father O'Hara was his insistence on the development of graduate work in chemistry, metallurgy, and in mediaeval studies and on the necessity of bringing in scholars from outside the University, particularly from Europe, to stimulate its intellectual growth. He understood that if Catholic education was to expand at Notre Dame, the leadership would have to come from without, possibly from Catholic scholars of Europe.[36]

On December 6 the *New York Times* reported an interview with Father O'Hara on the question of American relations with Mexico. To the surprise of some he voiced the idea, often expressed privately, that he was opposed to any American intervention in Mexico, even for religious reasons. He claimed from his knowledge of Latin American affairs that any intervention by the United States would only create resentment in Latin Americans and not accomplish the good intended. He urged Catholics who were worried about Mexico to double their prayers for the religious welfare of that country, especially in connection with the feast of Our Lady of Guadalupe, which would be celebrated within a few days.[37]

In New York Father O'Hara made the acquaintance of the mysterious chairman of the Allied Chemical Corporation, Orlando Weber, who had an office on Broadway. At the suggestion of Martin Gillen, economic theorist and benefactor of Notre Dame and through the intervention of Frank Walker, Father O'Hara visited Weber and later as a result of this visit Father O'Hara asked Father Edward Keller to undertake certain researches under the direction of Weber.

After Christmas, through the planning of J. T. McGovern, Father O'Hara received an invitation to address the New York Sportsman Brotherhood Dinner on December 27. On the program also was Howard Savage of the Carnegie Foundation, the author of the exposé of the evils of college athleticism. Savage merely reiterated his charges about the excess of college athletics. Father O'Hara's topic was "Sportsmanship in Education," obviously a chance to renew his answer to Pritchett and perhaps Savage.

Father O'Hara began his speech with a reference to McGovern and their boyhood days and continued that now the important thing to remember was that in a contest the game is the thing and that the child is more important than the rules in education. Further he noted that since the beginning of the depression educators and even the North Central Association of Colleges and Universities were beginning to question the validity of the rules under which they had been operating. Turning to college athletics, he said he felt it unnecessary to argue the legitimacy of the college program. He argued that it was just as legitimate to allow the public to watch the game: ". . . At Notre Dame we have almost as many candidates for the debating team as we have for football, and we foster both activities by the same interhall system. But for some reason or other, the public would rather watch twenty-two men play football than listen to six men debate. . . ." To the argument that the funds derived from football are used for other things, he answered that "if the public interest in football can be made to pay dividends that will supply for waning interest from endowment funds, its place in the educational setup is probably secure, or at least for the period of the depression."[38]

To strengthen further Notre Dame's position on college athletics, the University announced after the Christmas vacation a new constitution concerning intercollegiate athletics. Besides setting forth the requirements for earning a monogram in the various sports, the manner of electing captains of the teams and deciding the eligibility of players, the constitution added some rules that placed Notre Dame athletic policies on a higher plane than those of most of her competitors. According to the new rules no student could be eligible for intercollegiate athletics after his eighth semester in the University, and an academic average of 77 percent in classes was a prerequisite for participating in intercollegiate athletics.

Among Father O'Hara's other speeches after Christmas was one to the Carroll Club in New York at the behest of Mrs. Nicholas Brady and another to a symposium at the University on January 15 on the possibilities of air science at Notre Dame, to which Father O'Hara had invited Professor H. J. Burden of the University of Toronto, Colonel W. A. Bishop of Montreal, Commander H. B. Grow of the Navy, Merrill C. Meigs of Chicago, and Will Rogers. Al Williams, the flyer, was invited, but bad weather kept him from coming, and Albert Zahm, the pioneer in air science, was ill and could not attend. That evening at the annual dinner for the football team given by the St. Joseph Valley Alumni the star of the talks was Will Rogers, whose speech was carried by radio throughout the Midwest. Father O'Hara had promised President Elliott to speak at Purdue on Washington's birthday, but when Father O'Hara's plans had to be changed, he gave the chapel talk at Purdue on Sunday morning, February 17, on "The Divinity of Christ." In his speech he contrasted the Christian man with the pagan man, and after specifying the natural virtues respected by the pagan man and the supernatural virtues practiced by the Christian man, he argued that the dividing line was belief in divine revelation and in the divinity of Christ. The remainder of the sermon consisted of the traditional proofs of the divinity of Christ.[39] The audience numbered about two thousand.

Father O'Hara had agreed with Father Burns that he should go to Europe to seek faculty members, and the superior general, Father James W. Donahue, had insisted that he go with him. So on February 23 the two, with Father Casimir S. Sztuczko, C.S.C., a veteran of the Polish parishes in South Bend, sailed from New York for Europe on the *Champlain*. Interviewed on shipboard about the purposes of the trip, Father O'Hara indicated that he hoped to re-establish the old Notre Dame tradition of having lecturers from Europe visit the campus, a tradition that had not been renewed since the war. He also hoped to bring back documentary materials for the Mediaeval Institute. In his view the philosophers of the thirteenth century would have a solution for the problems of the day that would avoid the extremes of the day, Fascism and Communism. He praised the American system of government, but added that certain abuses of that system had led to the depression.

Father O'Hara kept no diary of his trip, but he did write occasionally to Father Burns and to his mother. He was accompanied by his sisters, Eva and Helen, and his expenses were paid by personal friends. Landing in England after a rough voyage, he set to work immediately on the object of his journey. His attention to art galleries would indicate that his interest in the Notre Dame art collection also had a personal element. He wrote from London to Father Burns shortly after his arrival.

Father General changed his mind about wanting me in Paris first, so I disembarked at Plymouth Saturday and came directly here. It is cold but generally pleasant.

Sunday I heard Father Martindale preach. I called on him afterwards and told him he answered in his sermon the question I came to England to ask—about the present state of apologetics in England. Yesterday I saw Father Ward, Ronald Knox and Jerry Cullinan. I asked Father Knox to lecture at the coming Summer School—he will give me an answer in a few days.

Sheed is due back from Paris this afternoon, and he will arrange my trip to Yorkshire to see Christopher Dawson and C. Hollis. I have an engagement with Chesterton Friday afternoon. Father Knox is also to ponder the proposal to recommend a young man for the classics. He is, by the way, a delightful personality.

. . . .

I have done a bit of incidental sightseeing, but I am not good at that sort of thing. I did enjoy the National Gallery, Sunday, however—with its magnificent collection of world masterpieces.[40]

He wrote from Paris on March 21 to Father Burns.

You will understand my delay in reporting to you, as you must have learned from my letters to Father Carrico and Father O'Donnell that I have been on the run most of the time. I wanted to do better by the pen, but when I come in at night I am tired out—or often am preparing to move.

The enclosed letter from Desmond Fitzgerald should go to Father O'Donnell for my files. I consider it a splendid statement of the problem—of the case of principle vs. cases in the approach to our modern difficulties. Fitzgerald tells me that at one meeting of the Cosgrave cabinet three different ministers quoted from Maritain. . . .

I presume you have learned that I have Christopher Hollis for all next year and Desmond Fitzgerald for six weeks, Chesterton promises to come again and Father Ronald Knox was inclined to favor summer school, 1936. I invited Father Hugh Pope, O.P. and have permission to speak to the Master General about it. I thought of him for a course in Modern Apologetics at Summer School.

Pere Lattin was not at Louvain when I called, but I have given Father Donahue the name of a priest who locates lodging for American priests. I think that there is a chance that Father Ward may get accommodations at the Benedictines—but it is a long way from the University. St. Edmond's House at Cambridge offers accommodations if you want to send a man there for history or science.[41]

Later Father O'Hara stopped at Le Mans, the city from which the Congregation of Holy Cross had come, and met again Bishop Grente, who had visited Notre Dame in 1926. In Paris he also called on Archbishop Baudrillart and Clovis Brunel, the director of the Ecole des Chartes, where Father Moore had studied. He also made stops at Lisieux and Lourdes before going into Italy, where he visited Milan, Pavia, Florence, and Rome. In Rome he had a private audience with the Holy Father, Pius XI, and showed him photographs of the University.

Father O'Hara returned to New York on April 24, too late to attend the conferring of the Nichols Medal on Father Nieuwland but in time to give the chief broadcast on Universal Notre Dame Night, April 29. In that broadcast he first announced the blessing of the Holy Father that he had been authorized to give. He expressed regret at the passing of Father Charles O'Donnell and of Father John W. Cavanaugh, who had died on March 22. He announced the honors that Father Nieuwland had received, including the establishment of the Julius A. Nieuwland Fund for Chemistry by a grant of $10,000 by the Chemical Foundation. He also said that an anonymous benefactor had given the University $25,000 for a study in economics. When he returned to the campus, he repeated these announcements together with the announcement of the lecturers he was bringing from Europe. They included Arnold Lunn, a popular lecturer; Christopher Hollis; Desmond Fitzgerald; and the two French philosophers who had previously spoken at Notre Dame, Jacques Maritain and Etienne Gilson. He also said that G. K. Chesterton would come again. When this word got abroad, other institutions began to invite Chesterton also, and he was forced to say that he had no definite plans for coming.

While preparing for the annual commencement, Father O'Hara held the spring meeting of the lay trustees, a routine session, and entertained the aviators Al Williams and Eddie Rickenbacker, discussing with them his plans for aerial science at Notre Dame. Both remained strong personal friends thereafter. For the commencement services Father O'Hara invited the auxiliary bishop of Boston, Francis Spellman, for the baccalaureate sermon, and Shane Leslie, who had been teaching at Notre Dame in the spring, for the commencement address. Bishop Spellman and Father O'Hara had become acquainted some months earlier, and Father O'Hara was quick to recognize in him a friend of the University. A third honorary degree was given to Martin J. Gillen, a lawyer and theorist of Land O'Lakes, Wisconsin, who had become a benefactor of Notre Dame. Father Burns and Father O'Hara had cultivated the friendship of Gillen, and he in turn convinced Father O'Hara of the validity of his economic theories, especially about the distribution of wealth. The commencement ceremonies passed without unusual incident. At the alumni banquet on the evening before the commencement Father O'Hara reviewed the accomplishments of the University and laid particular stress on the religious life at Notre Dame, for that remained his chief personal interest even though he now had many other problems to worry about.

Father O'Hara spent most of the summer of 1935 on the campus, although he and Father Burns made two short visits to the restful country of Martin Gillen's Land O'Lakes. He was studying the reports of departments and supervising to some extent the remodeling and building on the campus. Above all he was storing up in his memory the facts about Notre Dame, its possibilities and its needs, so that when he left the campus in search of benefactors, he could suit the need to the prospective benefactor. During the summer months at Notre Dame the Holy Cross Fathers visiting the campus from Oregon and Texas and from other places frequently of an evening would gather on the benches in front of Sorin Hall or Walsh Hall. Sometimes Father O'Hara joined them, and there he expressed among other things the desire to replace Sorin, Badin, and St. Edward's Halls with new buildings, not that he did not like their traditions, but maintenance costs were very heavy. The first year as president had been spent in sounding out possibilities and seeking new openings. His presidency was just beginning.

FIVE

President O'Hara of Notre Dame

AS FATHER O'HARA READ THROUGH THE reports of George Collins of the Department of Physics, or of Professor John M. Cooney of journalism, or listened to the plans of Arthur Reyniers for developing the germ-free production of animals, he became very conscious that most of the plans for a greater Notre Dame depended upon him. The same was more or less true of his support for Father Moore's Mediaeval Institute or for the development of aerial engineering. When he was prefect of religion, he had not been bothered too much by the suggestion that Notre Dame was a "football school," but the unpleasantness of the Pritchett report and the cold reception from Keppel of the Carnegie Foundation were ample reasons for trying to strengthen the intellectual side of Notre Dame. Further, all these plans called for an expenditure of money for buildings, for equipment and libraries, and for professors. But a smiling optimism that dares and accomplishes in the face of opposition seemed part of Father O'Hara.

Not only was he confident that he would get the funds for all these projects but he even had other plans in mind. One field in which he had been interested for several years was the perfection of Catholic apologetics, in which college training in the humanities could be combined with journalistic skills, perhaps somewhat in the manner of his *Religious Bulletin*. And in the social sciences, where Catholic colleges were trailing miserably, there were opportunities for Catholic young men trained in social work and

for Catholic economists. Under Father Raymond Murray social
workers were already being formed who could take their place
in handling the social problems of the new urban civilization.
Father O'Hara was not reconciled to the vagaries of modern sociology—most of which he regarded as naturalistic—but he did
recognize the need of Catholic social workers. Also, in the depression there had arisen a new demand for economists to fit the social
encyclicals of the recent pontiffs to the realities of the depression
and recovery. Most Catholics in this field had been trained by
Father John A. Ryan at The Catholic University or by his co-
worker, Father William Kerby, but both of these men were in
reality theologians. Father O'Hara had come under the influence
of Martin J. Gillen and Orlando Weber, who considered economics as a separate science from theology, one that could be worked
out from statistical studies of the existing situation. Gillen and
Weber were willing to supply funds for such economic studies,
and to work with them Father O'Hara assigned Father Edward
Keller, C.S.C.

In all these programs of graduate studies scholarships were
necessary. Chemistry at Notre Dame was already beginning to
attract the funds necessary for its growing operations; when the
Department of Physics failed to get foundation support, the young
men in the department built their own machines with the lesser
funds that Father O'Hara and they were able to gather. From his
friends, especially the William Corbetts of Chicago, he secured
funds to develop a much needed library in mediaeval studies.
Notre Dame as a university was coming into being rather rapidly
under the optimism of its president. He also began to plan his
new scholarships in apologetics and to appeal to the friends of the
University and alumni for the necessary money for them.

Father O'Hara, despite all these endeavors, could not step out
of his role as president of a college. He gave the opening sermon
on Sunday, September 22,[1] in which particular stress was placed
on the fact that there is no conflict between science and religion;
he went to Cleveland to participate in the Seventh National Eucharistic Congress and to speak on "The Eucharistic Priests and
Catholic Action among Young Men,"[2] perhaps more as a former
prefect of religion than as an executive. And he gave a talk on
citizenship to a group of 132 aliens being sworn in as new citizens
in Judge Dan Pyle's court in South Bend.[3] He attended football
games and entertained the guests of the University, while finding
time to look critically at the University library.

Shortly after assuming the presidency, he had asked Paul Byrne, the University librarian, for a masterkey to the library, and in his free time and especially in the hour after lunch he visited sections of the library to search out books that he thought did not belong on the shelves. He particularly eliminated many books on sociology, anthropology, and criminology for which Father Raymond Murray had spent some scarce funds. When he destroyed a book, he saved the title page so that the librarian could pull the cards from the catalogue. One package of titles, mostly from American and English literature, counted nearly twenty-five. He continued to object to several popular American novelists. Speaking of his interference in the University library later, Paul Byrne said: "Surely no one can say that Father O'Hara was anti-intellectual. And on the other hand I do not know what term you might apply to his actions regarding books. He was in my judgment a highly intelligent man—though he was no great scholar—with a quick mind. He often irritated me as I know he did many of the members of the Community by his snap judgments and the positive stand he so often took on questions of moment. . . . He could be very broad on some topics when you felt that he might not be, and very narrow on others when you felt he should not be. Anyway I am sure that whatever he did he felt it was the right thing to do. He did accomplish a lot of good. . . ."[4]

In the fall semester of 1935 the lecturers from Europe began to appear. Christopher Hollis, a history teacher from the Jesuit College at Stonyhurst in England, gave regular courses for the whole year, and Desmond Fitzgerald gave courses for six weeks. Both of these gentlemen and other visitors, including Arnold Lunn, also gave public lectures that were well attended. As if to add to the electrifying life on the campus the football team won repeatedly by coming from behind regularly each week.

The joy of all this, however, was dampened on October 7 when word reached the campus that John F. Cushing, one of Notre Dame's most exemplary alumni and the donor of the engineering building, had lost his life in an air crash near Cheyenne, Wyoming. Father O'Hara hastened to express the great sorrow of the University at the loss and also gave the funeral sermon in Evanston, Illinois, on October 12. In this sermon, besides stressing the Christian faith in the life to come as the reward for this life, he drew his theme from a sermon that Bishop John Lancaster Spalding had given at Notre Dame on "The Ideals of Youth" when John Cushing was a student. The Bishop had distinguished between the ideal of the multitude—the easy life—and the ideal of virtue. John Cushing, Father O'Hara said, had already learned

of this ideal of virtue in his own home and had carried it out in
his later life. He paid special tribute to Mr. Cushing's fulfillment
of the two commandments of love and also his devotion to the
Blessed Virgin and to his alma mater, Notre Dame.[5]

The success of the new coach of football, Elmer Layden, as his
team won five straight games reached a climax in a heroic victory
over Ohio State in the last minute of play by a score of 18 to 13 at
Columbus on November 2. In football affairs Father O'Hara
kept as much as possible out of sight, although he did make the
trip to Columbus by automobile with Bishop Noll in order to
talk over some special business. And he did bring to the lay trustees' meeting a clipping from the Chicago *American* praising
Notre Dame for sticking to fundamentals, not only in football but
in true education as well. But he also had many other things to
tell the trustees. As he had written to the alumni in the November *Alumnus,* his real plans for the University were academic.
While maintaining the number of undergraduate students, he
hoped to build a hall for graduate students. He planned a new
biology building, additional equipment for the physics professors
who had built the new generator of electricity at a very modest
cost, and additional laboratory space for chemistry. The Mediaeval Institute needed additional library facilities, and he hoped
to build a $400,000 fine arts building. He also needed $450,000
in the fund for the Rockne Memorial building. Along with
these needs he insisted that there must be new and additional
scholarships for graduate students.[6]

To Father Burns, who was making a visit to the missions in
Bengal, he wrote a newsletter on December 6. Among other events
he mentioned the death and funeral of Bishop Philip McDevitt,
a friend of Notre Dame.

. . . Looking at the Bishop as he lay in state, I was reminded constantly
of Father Hudson. As Bishop Boyle said, however, they were more alike
inside than out.

On my way to New York that afternoon, I had a fine visit with Monsignor McMahon, and we talked over our plans for a higher degree
in Apologetics. He was strongly in favor of it. In a four hour talk, we
went over a great many things, and I received some sound advice from
the Monsignor.

I saw another group of Bishops at the installation of Bishop Ryan.
I had a particularly gratifying talk with Bishop Kelley of Oklahoma,
and a nice visit with Archbishop Glennon. Archbishops Murray and
McNicholas have also shown a very keen interest in Notre Dame. I
talked with them in Washington and Fort Wayne.

You will be pleased to learn that just before my visit to Washington,

I spent a day in New York. This was the day I went to Washington to invite the President here. Martin Gillen told me how much he enjoyed his visit with you. Martin and I called on Orlando Weber, and Orlando told me he wanted to make some plans for an Economics Research Division, to begin operations the next semester. I am asking Father Steiner's permission to separate Father Keller from other duties for this work, and will associate two other men with him. We estimate that the total cost of this project will be $50,000. On the same day, Francis Garvan told me that he will finance ten current scholarships in Chemistry, five to begin next September and five the following year. He also expressed a desire to help prepare printed matter for a quiet campaign to increase the Julius A. Nieuwland Fund, for which he made an initial donation of $10,000.

I am not sure that you heard before you left that John Cushing provided in his will for payment of the balance due on his pledge. Mrs. Cushing is pushing matters on this so that the money can come to us soon. Bishop McDevitt, we are informed by Bishop Leech, also remembers us in his will. Bishop Gannon has told me that he intends to send us now two of the statues that he has in his private collection. I have seen both of them, and they are splendid pieces.

You have probably been picking up news of the President's visit here next Monday. This occasion has kept everyone busy. You heard the beginning of this occasion—it will probably be some time before we hear the end of it. After we were confidentially advised of the President's acceptance of our invitation, I went to Washington and had lunch with the President. We had an hour together, and it was a very interesting time for me. The demand for tickets is terrific. We have done our best to keep the occasion on a sane, academic level.

Cardinal Mundelein will preside at these exercises, and he has been most gracious about the whole matter. I have already had a few very nice visits with him. The Superior General will return from Montreal in time to act as host to His Eminence.[7]

Of these items the most significant was that about the visit of President Roosevelt.

On November 15, 1935, The Commonwealth of the Philippines planned to inaugurate its first President, Manuel L. Quezon. Catholics who were watching the developments in the Commonwealth were very anxious that the new democracy would not manifest the irreligious outbreaks that had been witnessed in Mexico and Spain. Notre Dame was also interested because many Filipinos had attended the University. Sometime in October a zealous Maryknoll missionary, Father James Drought, M.M., approached one of Notre Dame's most loyal and active alumni, Father Michael Shea, a professor at Dunwoodie Seminary in New York, suggesting that Notre Dame have some kind of celebration of this inauguration of President Quezon and that on that occasion the University confer on Carlos Romulo, a prominent Filipino, an honorary degree. Father Shea telephoned the suggestion to Father O'Hara and followed the call with a letter:

Dear John,

This is simply a restatement of our phone talk about the Philippines. The apathy of our Bishops here (some exceptions) you know. Bishop Noll is one exception by the way. Notre Dame (Our Cardinal once called U.N.D. the pulse of Catholicity) in this can give and gain. The name U.N.D. front paged (as it will be—guaranteed) on the Independence Day in all papers in the Islands will be a grand start for Catholic hopes. It is more important to get this through than to honor Mr. Romolo [sic]. The Catholic aim—and in this I am giving the attitude of the Archbishop of Manila who constantly consults Father Drought by cable (this is *sub sigillo*)—is to secure the presidency of the University of Manila for Mr. Romolo. Romolo was brought back to practical Catholicity by Father Drought. The anticatholic gang are pushing one of the most rabid of their group for the University leadership. That is why Romolo is in the picture. Now it is more important to insure a N.D. manifestation; Romolo can be a sideline. Bishop Hurth, the N.D. Philippine students, Notre Dame graduates (Barry of '02 who went to Manila to do educational work) and other tangent reasons can give logical excuse for the demonstration.

My one pet reason for backing the scheme is down deep in the hope that American Catholicity may evidence more frequently a desire to promote Catholic zeal by giving just such assistance to our fellow priests who are smothering due to the aimlessness of our American Hierarchy. All this is, of course, old stuff to you. From a cultural point of view it is right in line with N.D.'s publicity campaign. Carl Ackerman will be on the job when he reaches Manila.

That was a great game Saturday; the N.D. spirit has revived. Every wish to all at N.D.

Yours as always,
Mike[8]

Carlos Pena Romulo was the head of a large Philippine newspaper syndicate and the publisher of the *Philippine Herald* chain. He was in the United States at the time and was a practicing Catholic. Apparently in the telephone conversation Father Shea said that Father Drought suggested that there be a convocation on the occasion of the inauguration of President Quezon and that on the occasion Romulo be given an honorary degree as a kind of recognition of Philippine independence. Archbishop O'Doherty of Manila cabled on October 25 in support of Father Drought's suggestion that Romulo was "well informed, reliable, outstanding figure in Philippine journalism and public service, a stout defender of Catholic policy."[9] Frank Murphy, the Governor General of the Philippines, also cabled of Romulo that "no private citizen labored more intelligently for advancement, political emancipation of his people."[10] Father O'Hara learned that Romulo was in Chicago and went to see him, and invited him to come to Notre Dame. He and Mrs. Romulo came on October 25 and cooperated in the planning of a celebration that was to be held on November 15. Father Drought wrote letters to Father O'Hara on October 23, 24, and 25 outlining how the event should be handled and who should be invited. At times he seemed to think that the celebration was his and snorted like an angry bull when the plans took some forms he did not like.[11] What he soon realized was that this had become a Notre Dame celebration, and Father O'Hara was in charge. As a matter of fact, one reason Father O'Hara had driven to Columbus to the football game was to have leisure to talk over the celebration with the Bishop.

The next weekend Father Hugh O'Donnell, the vice-president, after attending the Pittsburgh game and the consecration of Bishop Leech of Harrisburg, went on to Philadelphia on October 23 to invite Cardinal Dennis Dougherty, formerly a bishop in the Philippines, to preside at the convocation. The Cardinal received Father O'Donnell very cordially and insisted on his devotion to Notre Dame, but he would not accept the invitation because he was convinced that the Philippines were not ready for independence, he did not care for the men in the new government, and he was sure that the government would follow the trend of the Mexican and Spanish governments and turn against the Church. As a matter of fact, the Cardinal was so strong in his dire predictions that Father O'Donnell wrote to Father O'Hara, expressing doubts about the wisdom of holding the convocation.[12]

A second blow to Father O'Hara's plans concerned the other speaker. He had chosen Theodore Roosevelt, Jr., who had been Governor General of the Philippines. Roosevelt was quite willing but could not obtain his release from a similar celebration at Columbia University the same day. Because Father Drought claimed that the planner of the Columbia celebration was unfriendly to the Church, no further effort was made to obtain Roosevelt's release. The next one approached was Governor Alfred E. Smith, whose platform had carried a plank for Philippine Independence in 1928, but Smith declined.[13]

Originally President Franklin D. Roosevelt was to be invited to send a message to be read at the convocation, but now Father

O'Hara decided to ask the President to come himself, since
that would really give the convocation the recognition desired.
Through Frank Walker,[14] President Roosevelt was approached
and word was received on November 5 that he would come to
Notre Dame on December 9 at about one o'clock after he had
spoken at a farmers' convention in Chicago, provided that no publicity would be given to the plans at this time. Father O'Hara
accepted the new date, telegraphed a formal invitation to the
President, and went to Washington as soon as he could get free to
arrange the details, arriving there Thursday morning, November
14. Apparently at the suggestion of President Roosevelt, Father
O'Hara also asked Cardinal Mundelein to accompany the President from Chicago and to participate in the celebration. Cardinal
Mundelein accepted the invitation to come to Notre Dame and
preside but insisted on going to Notre Dame on his own. Apparently the Cardinal did not care to be associated with someone in
the President's party. He said also that he had an engagement to
sing a Mass in Chicago that morning, suggesting that the President should go on ahead and see the Notre Dame campus.

The announcement that President Roosevelt would come to the
convocation and receive an honorary degree at the same time as
Romulo would receive his raised two particular problems. The
first was the fear that the President's presence might change the
character of the convocation and defeat its original purpose,
namely, the honoring of the Philippines and the giving of Catholic recognition to the freeing of a Catholic people. This was particularly noted by Father Drought when the first publicity release
from Notre Dame stressed the presence of the Chief Executive
instead of the purpose of the convocation. The second problem
involved the current discussion between the Knights of Columbus
and President Roosevelt over American intervention in the Mexican persecution of the Church. On October 23 Supreme Knight
Martin Carmody had sent to President Roosevelt a formal petition to intervene in Mexico for the protection of the religious liberties of American citizens.[15] President Roosevelt had answered on
November 12 that it was improper for the American government
to intervene in the domestic affairs of another nation. Actually
Ambassador Josephus Daniels was asking the Mexican government
to stop the persecution, but did not want to do so as a result of
Catholic pressure.[16] In answer to the President, Carmody released
a statement in which he maintained that he had asked only for
the protection of American citizens in Mexico and pointed out
that while President Franklin D. Roosevelt had quoted a state-

ment of Theodore Roosevelt in support of his own decision, he had omitted two other paragraphs of the same document which could be used to justify intervention. The Catholic press generally was bitter in its criticism of the President's reply. Thus, for Notre Dame to give Roosevelt a degree at this time was almost treason to the Catholic cause. The chief critics were *The Brooklyn Tablet, The Catholic Review* of Baltimore, and *America*. The last was the most important because it seemed to encourage lesser critics. At the end of its comment *America* said:

. . . A Washington syndicated column was emboldened to say the other day: "F.D.R.'s appearance on the campus at Notre Dame (on December 9) is in one sense an answer to the religious issue raised by Carmody." That "issue" was raised, of course, six months ago.

Is it possible to say it clearly enough? What we want is not intervention in Mexico, but the release of our Government from a foreign entanglement that is as certain as it is disastrous to religion.[17]

It was notable, however, that no one referred then to Father O'Hara's interview of the previous December published in the *New York Times,* in which he had opposed intervention in Mexico.

Father O'Hara was embarrassed by the criticisms because they tended to obscure the real reason for the convocation. The most embarrassing newspaper comment came from Monsignor Albert E. Smith, the editor of the Baltimore *Catholic Review,* who announced on November 29 that he had been to Notre Dame and had been assured that the giving of the degree was purely to honor the Philippines and in no way was "an endorsement by the University of Notre Dame of the President's policy in respect to Mexico." Because the Monsignor seemed to imply that he had authority from Notre Dame to make the statement, Father O'Hara sent a brief note to the Apostolic Delegate, dated December 4, 1935.

Your Excellency:

My attention has just been called to a first-page editorial in the last Friday's *Baltimore Catholic Review,* in which the Editor, Monsignor Smith, assumes to speak for the University of Notre Dame, and with this assumption, assures his readers that the University deplored the failure of the United States Government to voice its protest against the persecution in Mexico.

I need hardly assure Your Excellency that Monsignor Smith received no such commission to speak for us, but I believe that this disavowal should be on record.

In the belief that more harm than good can come of a prolonged argument on the point at issue, we are planning to give the press no official statement on the matter. It is our belief that it will work itself out.

With renewed expressions of esteem and devotion for Your Excellency, I remain,

Your obedient servant in Domino,[18]

All of the background of the presidential acceptance of the invitation is not clear. Some presidential advisers were a bit fearful of the storm the Knights of Columbus and the Catholic press were raising. Ambassador Daniels in his letters expressed the concern that some Catholics might desert Roosevelt in the 1936 election. But there is nothing to indicate that the acceptance of the invitation to Notre Dame was not primarily a favor of Roosevelt to his close friend, Frank Walker, through whom the original invitation was issued. When the invitation had been accepted, Raymond Moley was instructed to prepare a memorandum for the speech, stressing the right of peoples to religious freedom. Apparently under the impression that Notre Dame was a Jesuit University, Moley devoted some space in the original draft to the dedication of the Jesuits to liberty and science, but his error was corrected with some impish joy by the President's aide, Steve Early.[19] This emphasis in the speech on the right to religious liberty was generally overlooked in the accounts of the convocation.

The convocation was one of the most elaborate in the University's history, thanks to the cooperation of civic officials. From Chicago, the President was accompanied by Postmaster General Farley, and his assistant, Ambrose O'Connell, Governor Horner of Illinois, and Mayor Edward Kelly of Chicago. At the station they were joined by Governor Paul McNutt of Indiana. It was estimated that nearly 100,000 persons lined the streets from the railway station in South Bend to the campus as the President and Father O'Hara drove to the University. At the door of Sacred Heart Church the President met the hosts for the convocation: Bishop John F. Noll, Cardinal Mundelein, and the Superior General of the Congregation of Holy Cross, Father James W. Donahue. Five other bishops were also present on the platform at the convocation, held in the University gymnasium.[20]

Father O'Hara opened the convocation with a greeting to the President and to the Cardinal. He spoke of the old ties between Notre Dame and the Philippines, particularly through Archbishop Peter J. Hurth. He greeted Carlos Romulo and expressed the hope that the Philippines would adhere to the social encyclicals, to which the President had also given his support. Then the citations for the degrees were read and the degrees conferred by Father O'Hara. Dr. Romulo responded first, giving a touching and eloquent address under the title, "The Mind of a New Commonwealth."[21] While glorying in the new freedom of the Philippines, he said that freedom would be "fortified by that Faith which outlasts because it transcends Time. This great heritage of the vast majority of our people is given witness today by Notre Dame and the prelates of the Catholic Church." Catholicism, he said, was not the religion of the state, but of the Philippine people. He recognized the dangers of Communism and said that they rejected it. Neither would the Philippines become a fortress. If war came they were sure that they "would not have to face it alone." Romulo violated propriety by speaking longer than the President, but the President told Father O'Hara that this was the Philippines' day. Romulo was, by far, the most eloquent of the speakers.

Cardinal Mundelein in introducing the President first saluted the University, which he said he had not visited in recent years because the University, being so prosperous, did not need his aid. Then he gave a strong tribute to President Roosevelt, to his courage, and especially to his coming to the aid of the common man. He spoke of his long and intimate friendship with President Roosevelt and told the students of Notre Dame that they were fortunate in having a President "who has given us all an outstanding example in his life of indomitable persevering courage. . . ."[22]

The President, after thanking Father O'Hara, Cardinal Mundelein, and the University, outlined the forty years that had led to Philippine independence. Then he quoted George Mason on religious freedom and said he expected this great principle to be accepted by the new Commonwealth. In conclusion he added that "I was more touched than by anything else by that word of the President of Notre Dame when he said I will be in your prayers. I appreciate that and I trust that I may be in your prayers."[23] Cardinal Mundelein then gave the benediction and the convocation ended. Writing to President Roosevelt the next day, Father O'Hara told him that he and several priests of Notre Dame had said Masses for him that morning.[24]

From President Manuel Quezon of the Philippines came a message dated December 10:

On behalf of my people and myself I want to thank you and Notre Dame University for your Philippine Day celebration stop We are deeply grateful for this evidence of your interest in the success of the Commonwealth stop with highest regards I am thankfully yours,

Quezon[25]

The following Monday Father O'Hara called again on the President at the White House to thank him for coming to Notre Dame for the convocation. As he wrote to others, the irritation felt in some sections of the country soon died out. Later when President Roosevelt received the printed book on the convocation, he wrote: "That day shall always stand out as one of the greatest days of my life."

The comparative quiet of the Christmas vacation was welcome to Father O'Hara, although he devoted most of it to perfecting his plans for the new buildings. Since the superior general had insisted on a separate residence for the priest faculty, the administration decided to restore Corby Hall to its first function as a Community building with an additional wing for a dining hall and recreation room. The students' residence to replace this was to be a building on the site of the old Carroll Hall gymnasium and parallel to Zahm Hall. Further plans were made for a new biology building. Early in March he went to Miami, partly for his sinuses but also to encourage the lay trustee, George Anson, to help in his building program. Interviewed in the *Miami Herald*,[26] he defended the youth of the day, while explaining with pride the discipline at Notre Dame.

In the March *Alumnus*[27] Father O'Hara announced his program for a "Graduate Apologetics for Laymen." He said that there had been a persistent demand for a new approach to apologetics in this country, that catechism-trained laymen were not prepared to deal with the followers of a wide variety of philosophies that attempted to replace Christianity. To meet this demand Notre Dame would offer in the following September, if there was proper financial backing, a two-year experiment in the training of Catholic graduate students who have been thoroughly instructed in scholastic philosophy as undergraduates and who have demonstrated an ability to write. The fundamental courses in the program would be (1) advanced apologetics, (2) Holy Scripture, (3) patrology, (4) Church history, (5) ethics, and (6) the art of writing. Of the visiting lecturers Arnold Lunn, Shane Leslie, and Christopher Hollis would be of assistance in the program, together with Fathers Miltner and Ward, who were returning from Louvain, and others already on the campus. To finance the program Father O'Hara said that there would be set up ten scholarships each to cost $1,500 a year. One fellowship, to be named after Father Daniel Hudson, the late editor of Ave Maria, would be open to donors of smaller amounts, and was begun with a gift of $25 by an unnamed donor.

This apologetics program was typically O'Hara, both in its pur-

pose and in its optimism, and he was to spend most of the next
few months trying to secure financial support for it. His chief
interruption in this task was an appearance at the celebration of
the golden jubilee of the University of Chattanooga on April 19,
at which he spoke on "Religion in Education." In a speech calling for balanced education he stated as a principle that there is
no such thing as education without religion and laid stress on
religion as opposed to the excesses of Fascism and Communism.[28]
His brief appearance on the air on Universal Notre Dame Night,
April 20, was to push his new apologetics program.

Father O'Hara had now wandered some distance from the simple counsellor of students in his efforts to finance an expanding
university. In a letter to Father Burns, who was returning from
India, he mentioned some of his plans, besides mentioning that
he was expecting a visit from Mrs. Edward Doheny.

The Superior General has held up one important matter for your
consideration. We have studied plans all winter for a new Biology
Building, and the final drawings should be in our hands in another
week. Under separate cover, I am sending on photographs of the
sketches made by the architects of both the Biology Building and
the new freshman hall that is now under construction.
In view of the possibility of a cornerstone laying for the Biology
Building at Commencement, I have tentatively invited Francis Garvan
to speak and have announced him for an LL.D. which will be conferred whether or not the cornerstone is laid. I think it is important
to have him here without any further delay. I think I told you that
there is some prospect of securing a gift this summer for the Biology
Building. . . .
Last week in New York I made final arrangements for the financing
of our research in Economics. The donation, which must remain anonymous, was $15,000 a year for three years. Fathers Keller and Fogarty
are in New York now, getting definite instructions on the project.
. . . As long as I have broken my promise to make this letter short, I
might as well tell you that Father Moore reports wide interest in the
Apologetics course. The plan of studies is developing gradually, and
I think we will have a nice field of candidates for scholarships. We
have funds available for four of these, with two more under way. I
will have to hustle this summer to complete the ten.
In case you have not had the full commencement program, I should
say that Archbishop Mooney will give the Baccalaureate Sermon and
Dr. William J. Mayo, the Commencement Address. Dr. Charles Mayo
will also receive an LL.D.[29]

The meeting of the lay trustees on May 15 and 16 was mostly
routine, although the death on March 20 of Miles O'Brien, one

of the most loyal members, was commemorated, and C. Roy
McCanna was elected to take his place as treasurer of the Board.
John Moody of the Moody Investor's Service was also elected to
the Board. On Ascension Thursday, May 21, at the request of the
students Father O'Hara joined them in a celebration of Peace Day,
in which he expressed a plea for the peace described by Pope
Benedict XV in his *Pacem Dei* of 1920.

The laying of the cornerstone of the new biology building was
planned for commencement weekend. At the ceremony on Saturday morning Francis P. Garvan of the Allied Chemical Corporation spoke on "Culture and Science Intertwined." It was a science
commencement, and in his speech to the alumni on the evening
before commencement Father O'Hara outlined for them the
growth of science at Notre Dame from the beginnings under
Father Joseph Carrier in 1865 through Father John Zahm, Professors Albert Zahm and Jerome Greene, and Father Julius Nieuwland. He told of the remarkable achievements of the new physics
department under Dr. Arthur Haas, Edward Combes, and George
Collins; he described the germ-free experiments of Professor
Arthur Reyniers and plans for a new building. The arts and letters came in for mention in the new apologetics scholarships, and
the new infirmary was mentioned along with plans for a new dormitory.[30] The next day Archbishop Mooney's sermon was on
"Christianity Is Built on Christ," and Dr. William J. Mayo spoke
on "Educating the Young Makes Better Citizens" during a commencement program carried by the National Broadcasting System.
The commencement was scarcely forgotten when on the following
Thursday word was received that Father Nieuwland had died of
a heart attack at The Catholic University in Washington. Word
was also received at this time of the death of Gilbert K. Chesterton, ending hopes that he might return to the campus.

Father O'Hara had expressed very definitely his insistence on
religion in education at the Chattanooga convocation in April.
In June he went to Cleveland to give the commencement address
at the Sisters' College and was even more explicit in his concept
of the role of religion in education. He criticized overspecializa-
tion and the lack of unity he found in the secular education of
the day. Catholic education, he insisted, had a definite unity since
it regarded all things in relation to God and the service of God,
while secular education, lacking this unifying principle, was in
a constant state of flux. He said that for the secular educator
"What is right today may be wrong tomorrow; what is vice today
may be virtue tomorrow; we may come back—perhaps we have

come back—to the Spartan level of canonizing a thief who is clever." Because of the unity of Catholic education he said it is "correct to speak of Catholic art, Catholic literature, Catholic science, Catholic philosophy, Catholic economics, and Catholic sociology." Concluding he said:

Of the three powers which Christ gave to His apostles—to teach, to rule, and to administer—only the power to teach can the Bishop share with the laity. The work of teaching sisterhoods constitutes one of the most beautiful pages of the history of the kingdom of God. It is the work that only God can reward, and may the reward be abundant.[31]

The summer months, with the exception of a fishing trip to Land O' Lakes, were spent mostly working on the financial and administrative problems of the University with Byron Kanaley, the chairman of the Board of Trustees, and Frank Lloyd, the comptroller. But he also paid close attention to many other matters, reviewing with those in charge the problems of the library, the apologetics program, and particularly the growing science departments. He also continued his examination of the library shelves and occasionally extracted books that he thought did not belong there. He continued to manifest his hostility to such writers as Hemingway and Hervey Allen, and such journals as *The American Mercury*. Nor did he lift the ban on *Time* at the University newsstand.

The requirement of the superior general that there be a separate house of residence for the priests at the University had its significance in the life of the priests at Notre Dame. With the exception of those in administration the priests lived scattered throughout the campus, one priest as a prefect to each floor of a hall. Meditation and Mass took place in the halls, and with the exception of those in administration who had their own common prayers, the only exercise in common was held in the late afternoon, and consisted of spiritual reading and rosary or Benediction of the Blessed Sacrament. The life of the Holy Cross priest at Notre Dame was that of a religious without the usual conditions of community life. As a result the religious life of the priest was individual. With the reopening of Corby Hall the common exercises were held in Corby chapel, and there were community recreations in the newly built wing, and meals for those not prefecting in the dining halls. More than others in administration, Father O'Hara was away from the University very much in his efforts to get the funds needed for his programs. His interior life was hurried more than that of an ordinary Holy Cross priest. Certainly his spiritual life centered around his Mass and office and his strong devotion to the Eucharist and to Mary and Joseph. Of his health we know very little. His graying hair was getting scarcer, and the lines of fatigue were circling his eyes. He went swimming in the lake when the weather and his appointments permitted. He admitted to some heart trouble and to bad sinuses. His spare time was spent reading the reports of department heads, and occasionally a book on the subjects about which he sought funds.

In the fall of 1936 he gave five talks on the Catholic Hour[32] on the general subject "The Catholic Church and Youth." In his introduction he insisted that the only program for modern youth was the perennial one, although he admitted that family life was in decline. He maintained that the family life for ten percent of the people lasted only four years and for the next five percent only ten years. Beginning with the second broadcast on September 13, he treated the four cardinal virtues with special application to the problem of modern youth. To these cardinal virtues he said the Catholic added the theological virtues of faith, hope, and charity. On Sunday, September 20, he also gave the opening sermon for the year, addressing himself chiefly to the freshmen and contrasting the world of 1936 with that of 1921. The changes of the past fifteen years he attributed chiefly to the World War. He asked: "Did this war end all war? Since the treaty of Versailles, hatreds and mutual suspicions have grown and festered until it would seem that only a spark is needed to precipitate another world conflagration." This situation did not arise overnight. In their fountainhead, he said, these troubles arose from the liberalism and religious indifference that Newman wrote about. He claimed that Newman and the recent popes in their encyिlicals had predicted this present unrest but that they had gone unheeded.

In August Father O'Hara had suggested to Arthur Hughes of Chicago, the president of the Alumni Association, that he offer to the Holy Father the support of the alumni against communism. When Hughes sailed from New York on September 6, Father O'Hara stated the alumni program carefully.

Mr. Hughes will pledge our allegiance in the fight for conventional institutions of society without which no group can hope for existence as a social unit. I speak of the four necessities—the home, education, the rights of property, and the rights of the State.[33]

The message that Hughes carried was chiefly a pledge of loyalty in the Pope's opposition to communism, but as Father O'Hara pointed out in his Chattanooga speech, he was just as much against fascism. He encouraged the New York alumni in their efforts to form study clubs on the problem of meeting communism, and he attended the meeting of the National Federation of Catholic Alumni in Chicago on September 21 to speak of the support of the Notre Dame alumni for the National Federation. He did seem wary, however, lest the national organization try to use the fight against communism simply as a means of getting members, and he was also cautious about joining up with any other group, especially in an election year. In most of the letters that he wrote to the alumni he stressed that the first efforts should be to gather information about communism and the activities of communists in the country and suggested that James Armstrong, the alumni secretary, make his office a clearing house for such information.[34] When Hughes had his interview with the Holy Father in the company of Father Frederick E. Hillenbrand of Chicago, the *Chicago Tribune* and many other papers carried the story with emphasis on Hughes's pledge of alumni opposition to communism. Some alumni wrote to Father O'Hara to urge caution, especially in a year of a presidential election, and suggested that any program be delayed until after the election.

When Father O'Hara sent the Pope two albums of photographs of the University, the acknowledgments had come in the name of Eugenio Cardinal Pacelli, the papal secretary of state. Late in the summer word was given out that Cardinal Pacelli would visit the United States and be the guest of Mrs. Nicholas Brady at her home in Manhasset on Long Island. The Cardinal left Rome September 30 and went immediately to the Brady estate. On October 9 Father O'Hara wrote a welcome to the Cardinal through Cardinal Hayes, inviting him to come to Notre Dame for a visit. He also sent a telegram to Mrs. Brady, repeating the invitation. Cardinal Pacelli wired back "Shall be delighted if my short stay will possibly include a visit to your institution in such case shall not fail to notify you." Father O'Hara immediately sent a letter amplifying the invitation in the name of the University and the Congregation of Holy Cross. The Cardinal answered by letter on October 18, thanking Father O'Hara but stating that it did not seem possible for him to visit Notre Dame. On October 21 Father O'Hara wrote a letter expressing regret that the Cardinal would not come but elaborating on the ways of coming to Notre Dame should the Cardinal find it possible yet to come. He also suggested that if the Cardinal flew to Chicago, the plane might circle the University so the Cardinal would get a glimpse of it. Father O'Hara added:

I look forward with pleasure to visiting Your Eminence at Inisfada next Saturday evening. A good non-Catholic friend of mine, Mr. Orlando Weber, is invited to meet Your Eminence at dinner Friday evening. I hope that he will have an opportunity to discuss briefly some of the thoughts on economics that he has evolved from a study of thirty years. It was he who furnished the material I presented to Monsignor Hurley in Rome last year. I believe that the work of Mr. Weber offers a new and valid approach to overcome Communistic propaganda, at least in this country.[35]

On Friday, with encouragement from Bishop Spellman, Cardinal Pacelli sent the following message:

In response to your letter I have arranged to leave Mineola airport at ten o'clock Sunday morning planning arrival South Bend about one thirty for one hour stop thence proceeding by airplane to Chicago.

Father O'Hara immediately invited the neighboring bishops to be at the reception, and Bishops Noll, Ritter, and Albers came. Sunday afternoon the Cardinal's plane was an hour late but the students stood in the rain at the entrance of the University until he came. He went first to the Church where all the faculty was assembled, the laymen in cap and gown, and the Cardinal gave them the papal blessing. From the church the procession marched to Washington Hall, where the honorary degree was conferred. In his brief salutation to the Cardinal Father O'Hara mentioned the alumni program against communism and that that Sunday was dedicated in Catholic congregations throughout the nation to the promotion of peace. Quoting Newman to summarize the ideals of the University of bringing religion and science together in one place, he said:

It is our humble effort, Your Eminence, to have this union of science and religion exemplified in the students who come to us; they in turn manifesting their good will, have won for the school the title of "The City of the Blessed Sacrament."[36]

The Cardinal expressed his gratitude in English and repeated the papal benediction before leaving the hall. From Minneapolis he later sent his expression of gratitude. Father O'Hara also wrote to thank Bishop Spellman saying: "We are giving you full credit for arranging the schedule of His Eminence to include your Alma Mater." Father O'Hara had two albums of photographs like those made for the Pope sent to the Cardinal, and he in turn shipped to Father O'Hara "a candle blessed at Candlemas day . . . as a token of my grateful remembrance.[37]

Father O'Hara entertained the lay trustees on October 30 and gave them a thorough survey of the progress of the University. Besides listing all the advancements, he noted the visitation of the president of the North Central Association of Schools and Colleges, and the high praise this man gave for the University's handling of employment and its rules governing athletics. Whether he was worried about his health or just curious, he went to Indianapolis for a physical examination. His friends felt that he was traveling at too fast a rate. As Byron Kanaley told him:

I think you ought to pay a little attention to yourself in the way of relaxing a bit once in a while a day or so. You are going a pretty hard gait. All you have to do to know what it means to be President of Notre Dame is to walk over back of the Seminary and take a look at the ages of the eleven Presidents who preceded you.[38]

But he did not stop except for a few days with his mother in Indianapolis on his way to Atlanta, Georgia, where he presented the Laetare Medal to Richard Reid on November 8. In New York for the Army game he gave a sermon at St. Paul's Church on November 14 on "Communism and Catholicism," and on Thanksgiving Day he gave the sermon at the annual Pan-American Mass in which, after reviewing the history of the Latin countries, he begged them to submit to the common mother, "Our Lady of America." After his trip to California for the Southern California game and banquet he did stop briefly for a rest at Palm Springs and went home for Christmas. But he had to perform humdrum services.

On January 10 there was a memorial symposium in honor of Father Nieuwland, at which Bishop Joseph Schrembs celebrated the Mass, Father Wenninger preached the sermon, and many noted scientists participated. The next day J. Edgar Hoover visited the campus and spoke to the student body. That evening at the annual football banquet Father O'Hara took the occasion to oppose reformers in college athletics and to maintain that the colleges could take care of their own problems. On January 25 the national alumni drive against subversive activities was opened with a meeting in the University gymnasium presided over by Father O'Hara, at which the chief speakers were Arthur Hughes, Professor Daniel O'Grady, Sebastian Bonnet, a postgraduate student from Spain, and an undergraduate, James J. Nerney.

On February 12, 1937, Father O'Hara wrote a letter to Professor Etienne Gilson that was in answer to a memorandum prepared by Father Philip Moore and Gilson on October 30, 1935, asking that an autonomous mediaeval institute be established at Notre Dame.

Father O'Hara was not prepared to answer that letter when it was received. Now he admitted that the proposition of Gilson was ideal, but before the institute could be really autonomous it must be financially autonomous. Such a feat, requiring an endowment of at least one million dollars, was quite impossible at that time. He apologized for assuming that Gilson had become a consulting director of the Notre Dame Mediaeval Institute and said that despite the failure to set up an autonomous institute Notre Dame would continue to prepare teachers in mediaeval studies and continue to publish the series of books known as *Mediaeval Studies*.[39]

At about the same time through Frank Lloyd Father O'Hara joined other religiously founded colleges in warding off an attempt by the Indiana legislature to impose taxes on the earnings of the University. In rejecting the proposal, which would have cost Notre Dame about $35,000 a year, Father O'Hara wrote to the governor to point out the taxes already paid by Notre Dame, the business the University brought into the state, and the services given by Notre Dame to the community by her building program during the depression. The amended legislation that was passed on February 26, 1937, lacked the proposed tax. The publicity surrounding the proposed legislation centered chiefly on Notre Dame as the main religious institution involved, at least in the proposed tax, and Father O'Hara made some efforts by published statements to correct the misstatements made about the tax and Notre Dame in *Time* and some other publications.[40]

As a symbol of the new Notre Dame, the Mathematics Department conducted a symposium on "Calculus of Variations" on April 7 and 8, in which participated some of the more important mathematicians of the country, notably Princeton's Professor Solomon Lefschetz, the president of the American Mathematical Society, and Marston Marx of the Institute for Advanced Studies. Notre Dame was represented by Karl Menger and Arthur Haas. Father O'Hara attended the symposium as host and as one who provided the means for this development.[41] He also gave an address to the National Catholic Educational Association at Louisville on March 31, and a talk at the first Fort Wayne deanery meeting of the Catholic Youth Organization on April 18. The next evening he spoke over the air from Washington on Universal Notre Dame Night. He then returned to Notre Dame, where he followed his traditional role of superintendent of construction of the new buildings.

The commencement of 1937 was a commerce commencement with honorary degrees for an old friend, Joseph Grace, who could not come because of the serious illness of his wife, and Dr. William S. Calcott of DuPont. The Laetare Medal was conferred at commencement on Professor Jeremiah Ford of Harvard, who spent a week of consultation with the President on the campus before the event. Later Father O'Hara went to New York to confer the Grace honorary degree in person. But the most important event for the summer was his reappointment as President of Notre Dame for a second term. To all who congratulated him he insisted that he would have preferred to become again prefect of religion. The only change noticeable in him was a decision to allow Father O'Donnell, the vice-president, to represent him at all games away from home and his determination to avoid as much as possible his long list of speeches. Whether this change was on the instruction of physicians or the advice of friends, there was an apparent effort to slow down the rapid pace of the first three years.

The University Council under his direction decided to limit undergraduate students to three thousand. The expansion on which he now concentrated was in bringing to the campus world-renowned scholars as visiting lecturers and in acquiring for the permanent staff as many distinguished professors as Notre Dame's limited endowment could provide. Only the chemistry department had a long record of training capable teachers in its graduate program. Advancement in other fields would have to come from outside the University. There were but two sources for these qualified college teachers. The first was the existing graduate schools of the country. In most of the fields of the University there were few Catholics of top quality available in American universities. Providentially there opened about this time a second source of recognized scholars among the politically disturbed universities of Europe. Father O'Hara had shown an interest in European scholars from the first year of his administration, and had invited English Catholic scholars to come to Notre Dame, but in that dominantly Protestant country they were few. The Nazi persecutions in Germany and the poverty of Catholic institutions in southern Europe now made available some remarkable teachers. The arrival of Karl Menger in mathematics and Arthur Haas in physics, Yves Simon in philosophy, Waldemar Gurian and F. A. Hermens in political science, added to the talents of Fathers Charles Miltner, Leo R. Ward, and Philip Moore and Professors Theodore Just and Andrew Boyle, gave Notre Dame masters who could speak the language of America's best scholars. Professor

John Nef of the University of Chicago called this "a Notre Dame renaissance."

But these programs intensified Father O'Hara's financial problems. The expansion of the Holy Cross Congregation in other parts of the country under Superior General James W. Donahue had led to demands on the previously established houses, especially Notre Dame, for financial assistance. Notre Dame certainly could not expect aid from the community beyond the endowment of the services of religious persons. The great philanthropic foundations had not yielded an inch in the solid phalanx they regularly presented to the pleas of Notre Dame, and other Catholic institutions, for aid. Notre Dame's alumni had scarcely been able to overcome the personal handicaps of the depression, and were yet unable to render much help except the gifts of the late John F. Cushing and the bequests of William Breen and Frank Phillips. There were only a few other sources that Father O'Hara had been able to tap, yet Notre Dame was trying to take a place alongside institutions that had nearly twenty to a hundred times her endowment. There was also a moral handicap at home in the feeling among many religious of the Congregation of Holy Cross at Notre Dame and elsewhere that Notre Dame had no business engaging in these higher studies. These conservative men, probably a numerical majority at the University, were not themselves producers of scholarly works and did not understand the importance of scholars to the undergraduate life and studies at Notre Dame. Just to try to solve these problems was enough to keep Father O'Hara busy; he had little time for speeches or civic activities during the year 1937–1938.

He did open the year with a radio speech entitled "Objectives in Education" and gave the opening sermon of the school year at Notre Dame. When the *New York Times* published on October 4 a letter signed by 150 Protestant leaders in support of the Valencia government in the Spanish Civil War, Father O'Hara signed his name to an answering letter written on October 14 by Father Samuel Wilson, S.J., the president of Loyola of Chicago, charging misrepresentation of the fact by the Protestants. He did send a telegram to Father Wilson, however, suggesting that the latter had accepted too much the charge of atrocities against Franco. In a conflict over communism Father O'Hara saw only one choice. The issue was not so simple to the French and German scholars who had come to the University and to their friends who were fighting fascism in Germany, France, and Italy.

On November 5 ground was broken for the new Rockne Memorial building on the west end of the campus as part of the trustee sessions. Father O'Hara gave the trustees his usual summary of the developments of the University during the previous year. Among the new professors entering the faculty were Menger and Artin in mathematics, Guth, Anthony, and Abbé Lemaitre in physics, Charles Dubos in English, and Gurian in political science. The chief benefactions had been those of Breen and Phillips, and the newest residence was named after Father John A. Zahm.

Apparently his sinuses were troubling him severely, and while taking care of necessary problems after Christmas, he wrote on January 3, 1938, to Bishop Aloysius Willinger of Ponce, Puerto Rico, who was in New York:

Most Reverend Bishop:

I am putting up a gallant fight against a temptation to visit Puerto Rico this winter in quest of some sunshine. My superiors have given me their permission for the trip, but I have not decided that I want to go that far away from home.

Perhaps you can tell me whether I could find in the neighborhood of Ponce the sort of thing I want. I have a persistent sinus infection, and the long winter months here make it active. It does not interfere particularly with my work, but since I cannot take a vacation in the summer, I try to find a warm spot to favor the sinus when I go away during the winter. I find that sun-bathing is the best thing for it—with sea bathing if this can be found. I wonder if there is a possibility of finding a quiet spot on the south side of the island where I can get the sun-bathing without scandalizing the good people of your diocese. I can take a Mass kit along in case you know of a spot where the isolation includes separation from a church.

Spanish surroundings make no difference to me. I passed three years of my ill-spent youth in South America.

If you will only tell me that there is no such place available my mind will be set at rest, and I shall go back to Arizona or California. Florida is banned, because there is too much society there. I dislike Palm Springs for the same reason, and a Caribbean cruise presents the same difficulty. I want to find a quiet rest if I can. I find it is pretty hard to hide out in this country.[42]

When he received an encouraging word from the Bishop, he began to clear his desk before joining him in New York, where the Bishop was preparing to leave for his diocese. He dictated a letter to Father O'Donnell outlining the problems that might arise in his absence and giving solutions to those that might not wait for his return. Then he added:

Although I expect to be back before the 22nd of February, I may accept an invitation to speak before the Harvard Club of Cincinnati on that day, so if you do not mind receiving another flag, I will be glad to have you prepare for that. You have been wrapping yourself in Old Glory to the satisfaction of everyone.

I hate to load all this work on you when you are so busy with the Rockne Memorial, but I don't think you or anyone else will be satisfied until I get the Halifax out of here![43]

In Washington he called on his brother Bob before joining Bishop Willinger. There are few references to the week spent in Ponce with the Bishop except that it was one of relaxation and sunshine. After that week he went on a ship tour of the Bahamas and spent one day with John T. McCutcheon of the *Chicago Tribune*. The sea was so rough on the day he returned that Father O'Hara gave up his promised return visit to the Bishop at Ponce and went on to New York, landing there February 15, where he found a letter from Father O'Donnell telling him of University business during his absence. Canon Lemaitre had arrived, and another successful mathematical symposium had taken place on February 12 and 13.

Father O'Hara tried to avoid as many public appearances as he could, but the list of these included a Communion breakfast of the Chicago Club on April 3, a special convocation at Indiana University on the topic "How Religion Can Stop Moral Decay," and a Universal Notre Dame Night broadcast on April 25 on the subject "You Are the Salt of the Earth." The theme of this broadcast was one that he used constantly throughout the year:

At Notre Dame you learned that man was created by an all-wise, all-good, all-powerful God, and that in all relations between man and man, God the creator must have His share. Marriage is a relationship, not simply between a man and a woman, but between a man and a woman and God. Business is a relationship, not simply between buyer and seller, but between buyer and seller and God. Government is a relationship, not merely between ruler and citizen, but between ruler and citizen and God.

Take God out of the picture, and the whole scale of values is changed. The cheap rewards of this life, be they honor, glory, power, possessions, pleasures,—take on tremendous importance. The battle is to the strong, to the cruel, perhaps to the barbarous. The machine gun and poison gas are of infinite importance to the man whose sole hope lies in the few years he has this side of the grave. Ambition can be intense and vice can be furious when its hour is short. Take away all hope of eternity and you unleash the full savagery of selfishness.

The world suffers from philosophies that leave out God. When God has no place in the family, the basic unit of society crumbles. When God is ruled out of business, justice and charity between men suffer, and our economic structure is undermined. When God is ignored in government, the omnipotence of God is transferred to the state. . . .[44]

He urged them as Notre Dame men to do their part to restore God to his place in the home and in society.

On May 2 and 3 Father O'Hara was very proud to act as host for some of the outstanding scientists of the country for a symposium on "The Physics of the Universe and the Nature of Primordial Particles." Among the participants were Arthur N. Compton of Chicago, Harlow Shipley of Harvard, and Carl D. Anderson of California. Notre Dame members of the symposium were Canon Georges Lemaitre and Eugene Guth.

The commencement of 1938 was the occasion for the University to celebrate the centennial of the Congregation of Holy Cross. The Mass on the day before the commencement was sung by the apostolic delegate, Archbishop Amleto Cicognani, and the sermon was given by Father James W. Donahue, the superior general of the Congregation. The Delegate gave the baccalaureate sermon the next day, and Terrence B. Cosgrove, a Los Angeles lawyer and an alumnus, gave the commencement address. Shortly after the commencement a general chapter of the Congregation was held at Notre Dame, to which Father O'Hara was an elected delegate from the American Province. He tried to have his close friend, Father James Burns, elected general, but instead Father Albert Cousineau of the Canadian Province was so chosen, while Father Burns was elected assistant general. His other close friend, Father Thomas Steiner, was elected the provincial of the Indiana Province.

After the chapter Father O'Hara and Father Burns made another of their visits to Land O' Lakes, Wisconsin, to the estate of Martin Gillen. That either Father Burns or Father O'Hara were great fishermen no one would suspect, yet they were fishing for large material things. Martin Gillen apparently was attracted to Notre Dame and also had a liking for Father Burns. Eventually his property was to come to Notre Dame, although death prevented him from setting up the kind of foundation for the University that would have eluded inheritance taxes. Father O'Hara was aware that Martin Gillen was also a soul that needed saving, and in asking permission to say Mass privately on the estate he was quite frank about this to the diocesan chancery. The eventual landing of this catch in the spiritual sense was of supreme importance to Father O'Hara. Gillen was also a close friend of Orlando Weber, the mysterious benefactor of the Bureau of Economics, and of Erwin Uihlein of Milwaukee, who also became a benefactor of the University. Later another benefactor of Notre Dame, Peter C. Reilly of Indianapolis, was also a frequent visitor to Land O' Lakes.

The political troubles of Europe had already been brought home to the University in the plight of those brilliant scholars who sought haven from the persecutions of Europe, but it was impossible to keep echoes of the European wars from Notre Dame. Members of the Notre Dame community who had read in translation the philosophical writings of Jacques Maritain looked forward with pleasure to his visit in the fall, but there were some who did not. Father Patrick Carroll, the editor of *Ave Maria,* was disturbed when he heard that Maritain had been invited to lecture on the campus and asked that the invitation be withdrawn. Father O'Hara did write a letter to Maritain to suggest that he give his opinion on the atrocities committed against the Church by the Spanish Loyalists, but he did not intimate in any way that Maritain should not come to Notre Dame. Later he wrote to Byron Kanaley that just as he himself had refused to be forced into a public statement about the persecution of the Church in Mexico, Maritain would not be badgered into a statement on the Spanish Civil War. To William Montavon, an alumnus, he wrote on July 19, 1938:

I have extended an invitation to Jacques Maritain to lecture at Notre Dame for two weeks in the fall and to take part in a symposium on Social Philosophy which we are arranging. I anticipate some criticism on this and I must confess that I have never seen an original statement of Maritain on the Spanish situation. I am aware that he has been subjected to violent attack, and it seems to be on the ground that he will not give a blanket endorsement because he does not like the political philosophy of the two nations that have lent active cooperation to Franco's movement in Spain.

It is my impression that Maritain disapproved of anything stronger than passive resistance to religious persecution. I believe that an instruction to this effect was given to the Catholics of Mexico in 1926. It has always been my attitude. Aside from the religious persecution, I have always recognized the right of people to rebel against the destruction of their liberty and the undermining of their natural rights.

On August 6 he added in a note to Montavon:

I have discussed some of the points of your letter with Waldemar Gurian, and I am inclined to confirm our previous arrangement, with the understanding that the shoe-maker stick to his last.

It would be much better if he could make a specific declaration that his position on Spain is what Gurian says it is. However, I have taken many beatings for failure to talk out on Mexico, and I cannot deny him the privilege of doing the same thing with regard to his position on Spain.[45]

On October 5 Maritain wrote from shipboard in answer to Father O'Hara's letter. He said that it was idle to say that he had not deplored the crimes against priests, the destruction of churches, the atrocities of all kinds committed by the revolutionary Reds. He had spoken explicitly in his preface to the book by Professor Mendizabel. It was to avoid atrocities that he wished peace for Spain, a peace of conciliation and mediation. In all this he had spoken only in full agreement with the spiritual authorities on whom he depended. Father O'Hara seemed satisfied. Neither did he take sides in the public debates between Professor Gurian and Arnold Lunn about the policies of Chamberlain that fall. Gurian founded *The Review of Politics,* and the symposium in which Maritain participated was a kind of initiation of the publication.

On November 2, 1938, Father O'Hara received a telegram from Secretary of State Cordell Hull.

I am much gratified to let you know that the President desires to appoint you as delegate of the United States to the approaching Inter-American Conference which will convene at Lima, Peru on December 9. The Delegation will sail from New York on November 25. Please telegraph me if you are able as I hope you accept the appointment and whether it will be convenient for you to be in Washington two or three days before the delegation sails in order that we may confer regarding the plans of the delegation.

Cordell Hull, Secy of State[46]

Besides his telegram of acceptance to Hull, Father O'Hara also sent a message to the President.

The Secretary of State informed me of your gracious act in appointing me as a delegate to the Inter-American Conference in Lima. I am deeply grateful for this mark of trust, and honor to the University of Notre Dame, and I pledge my best efforts in behalf of the interests of our country and of the Western Hemisphere. Since the visit of Secretary Root to South America in 1906, I have followed with keen interest the proceedings of these conferences, and I have noted in particular a better relationship since the enunciation of the Good Neighbor policy. May God bless your efforts and those of the Conference.

Rev. John F. O'Hara, President[47]

The appointment to the delegation was not really news since Father O'Hara had been sounded out early in October. As a matter of fact he had been sounded out two years before as a possible delegate with President Roosevelt to the Buenos Aires Conference of 1936, but at that time the superior general had insisted that he decline the appointment. This time, however, he acted with

the advice of the new assistant general, Father James A. Burns,
who felt that it was important that Father O'Hara accept. Strate-
gically Father O'Hara's appointment was important not only
because of his knowledge of South America but also because he
combined with that a position of an important American priest.

The proposed trip to South America was a distraction from his
other plans for the University. Father O'Hara was trying to get
benefactors for the proposed graduate hall, for special laboratories for Professor Arthur Reynier's germ-free experiments, and
for a new chemistry building. Besides outlining these needs and
the advanced work in the various departments at the meeting of
the lay trustees, he also announced for the near future the first
publication of the newly founded Notre Dame Economic Research Bureau. In the four years that Father O'Hara had been
president graduate work, which had previously been confined
almost entirely to the field of organic chemistry, had been broad-
ened out to include mathematics and advanced research in nuclear
physics, along with gathering together one of the best staffs for
research in these fields in the country. Philosophical study at
Notre Dame had been intensified by the acquisition of Yves
Simon and John Fitzgerald. Biology had acquired a separate
building and had added to its renowned botanical work the new
developments in germ-free life. The Economic Research Bureau
with Father Keller as its chief worker, assisted by Father O'Hara
himself and Dean McCarthy, was in Father O'Hara's mind an
important addition. He saw in the studies proposed by the
bureau statistical answers to some of the wild claims made by
Communists about the ill-distribution of wealth in the capitalistic
system. Also, in his persisting desire to carry on the distinction
between naturalism and supernaturalism he expected aid from the
philosophical writings of Professor Simon and the political studies
of the dean of the Law School, Clarence Manion. Father O'Hara
no longer counted on a quarterly under the editorial guidance
of Father William Bolger and had given support to Waldemar
Gurian in establishing *The Review of Politics,* a review devoted
to the "historical and philosophical approach to political realities."

Life magazine, sensing the burgeoning of the University, approached Notre Dame through the president of the Board of Lay
Trustees, Byron Kanaley, but Father O'Hara rejected the suggestion of an article in his answer to Kanaley:

Confidentially, I don't like to see the Blessed Virgin's school appearing in a magazine that specializes in nudity. I have seen very few
numbers of the magazines during the past year, but the numbers I

have seen have convinced me that there is no change in the general policy. Bare legs and bare backs are spread over the pages for their sales appeal. . . . If he wants an additional release, there is a very strong one in the fact that *Life's* editors have been collecting money for communists in Spain.[48]

Father O'Hara went to Washington first to be instructed on the purposes of the conference. There was no secret that the United States was trying to shore up its defenses in the Western Hemisphere in the face of the approaching war in Europe. The conference in Buenos Aires in 1936 had been only moderately successful. The new conference was intended to try for a better alignment of the New World powers against interference from the Old World.

On Sunday, November 20, 1938, Father O'Hara participated in a radio salute to the head of the American delegation, Secretary Hull.[49] Taking as his theme the advances in Latin American culture even before English settlement of the New World, and the anterior formation of its universities and ecclesiastical organizations, he also emphasized the North American failure to appreciate the spiritual ideals of South America. He praised Hull as one of the first to promote a sound mutual appreciation between the United States and South America. The delegation sailed from New York on the *Santa Clara* on November 25. Father O'Hara said Mass each day for the Catholic members of the delegation, although many non-Catholics, including Governor Alfred Landon of New York, also attended. Of the Sunday service *Time* remarked: "Lanky ascetic Father John F. O'Hara, President of the Notre Dame University and chairman of the delegation committee on intellectual cooperation and moral disarmament, repeated his Sunday sermon in Spanish."[50]

Although the most important discussions took place between the foreign ministers of the various delegations, Father O'Hara did much to promote good will. On the feast of the Immaculate Conception at the invitation of Archbishop Peter F. Farfan of Lima, Father O'Hara gave a sermon in Spanish in the cathedral for the members of the delegations and the people of Lima. In the conference Father O'Hara was given chief credit for directing the Subcommittee on Moral Disarmament, which was part of the Committee on Intellectual Cooperation. The resolution of the subcommittee was drawn up under his direction. It said:

The Republics represented at the Eighth International Conference of American States declare:

I—That within the fundamental principle of equality before the law, all persecution for racial or religious motives which place a num-

ber of human beings in the impossibility of obtaining a decent liveli-
hood are contrary to all its political and juridical rules.

II—That the democratic conceptions of the State guarantee all
individuals the essential conditions for the development of their
legitimate activities on a dignified human basis, and

III—That the said principles of human solidarity will always apply.[51]

Throughout the conference Father O'Hara pressed for intellectual exchanges, and after the conference he visited other Latin
American countries to promote the exchange of students. On the
final day of the conference he flew with young Peter Grace to
Arequippa and then went into the Andes to the Indian village
of Puno. In the village he said his own three Masses and afterward
watched about thirty Indian children receive their First Communion. The Indian women were in bright skirts and the men in
heavy woolen suits and blankets. The Indians came to the sacristy
for blessings on their Christmas cribs, crosses, and other memen-
toes. According to Grace their eager faces shone as Father O'Hara
later spoke to them in Spanish. Returning to Lima, Father O'Hara
joined in the signing of the decrees of the conference.[52]

Peter Reilly of Indianapolis arrived, and together he and Father
O'Hara sailed from Lima to Valparaiso and Santiago in Chile
and crossed over to Buenos Aires, Montevideo, Santos, and Rio
De Janeiro before returning to New York. In New York a dinner
was held at the Center Club in his honor. Dan O'Neill, the president of the club, was deeply moved as the old prefect of religion
in greeting the alumni called most of the Notre Dame men by
their first name and talked to them of their pasts. In his speech he
ascribed the unpleasant features of Latin American Catholicism
to the fact that Latin America had had no Middle Ages but had
jumped from colonial conservatism to a dynamic religious men-
tality. He pointed out that priests were too few and that there was
a lack of intellectual life among Catholics, despite the fact that
there were some brilliant Catholic scholars. He had asked Catholic leaders in Peru, Chile, Uruguay, and Brazil to choose suitable
students to receive scholarships to Catholic universities and colleges in the United States, adding: "I am sure that on their return
to their home countries, they will bring something from the
Catholic life of Americans that will help their bishops and their
lay leaders in their struggle to form an intelligent and zealous
Catholic citizen."[53]

Shortly after his return occurred the death of Pope Pius XI. In
his tribute to him and to his encyclicals Father O'Hara called
him Pius "the Great." On March 2, 1939, Cardinal Pacelli was

elected pope, and there was some pride in the fact that an honorary alumnus of the University had been elected to this highest post in Christendom. On Laetare Sunday the medalist for 1939 was Miss Josephine Brownson—the granddaughter of Orestes A. Brownson—who had worked so hard for the Christian instruction of those not attending Catholic schools. Also shortly after his return the first publication of the Economic Bureau came from the press.

Father Keller's book was entitled *A Study of the Physical Assets, Sometimes Called Wealth, of the United States, 1922–33*.[54] In his preface to it Father O'Hara explained that this was a research into "the Management of the Household Budget of the People of the United States." Again he said: "The first results of the research published in this volume are in reality a 'Primer of Economics: an Essay in Adult Education.' " The book was printed in large type, a bit too suggestive of a primer. The book was chiefly a statistical study and had for its purpose a statement of "Ownership of the Physical Assets" of the country.

The false theories used and conclusions drawn as to the ownership of "Wealth," such as—1% of the people own 59% of the Wealth, and/or 13% of the people own 90% of the wealth—have been publicized on the basis of studies of probated estates.

Anyone who permits himself a little common sense observation will admit such a concentration cannot exist.

He sees the great mass of people in possession of homes, automobiles, radios, household furnishings, and other Comfort Goods in which concentration is physically impossible and which account for over 50% of total Physical Assets.

Thousands of copies of Father Keller's study were distributed, and it was reviewed in many newspapers. Father O'Hara had viewed the study as a check against the wild claims of communists against a capitalistic system. It was immediately attacked by those who thought it a wholesale defense of American capitalism. The actual proofs in the book were not new, since they were gathered from government publications, but the method of study and the proposed conclusions were the subject of controversy. One of the first critics was Father Raymond McGowan of the N.C.W.C. Department of Social Action. In his column of April 13, 1939, which came out quickly after the publication of the book, he claimed that the publicity on the book was "leading the people to think that the wealth of the United States is pretty well distributed and so, too, its income. Actually, there is in the report only the slimmest figures on who owns what, and none at all on who gets

how much." Father McGowan then attacked the years chosen
for the study and the division of goods, and he wound up with a
stated preference for the reports of the Brookings Institution.

Father O'Hara immediately wrote a long reply on April 15 and
sent a copy to Archbishop Edward Mooney of Detroit, the chairman of the Executive Committee of the N.C.W.C. Besides criticizing what he called misstatements by Father McGowan of what
Father Keller had said, he concluded:

> I am afraid that you have missed the whole point of Father Keller's
> present study. His expressed intention (see page 12) is "to discover
> and present in simple language the truth concerning the goods or
> things which are fundamentals of material well being." I may say fur-
> ther that the University's purpose in establishing the Bureau of Eco-
> nomic Research was to discover the complete facts we need for the
> application to the United States of the Papal Encyclicals on Social
> Justice. If the present study and the succeeding ones will accomplish
> this purpose, I am sure that you and all right-minded people will be
> grateful for this assistance.

Father McGowan answered that he had criticized not so much the
book as the publicity about the book, but he reiterated his contention that the method used in it was faulty and any succeeding
study using that method would be faulty and mislead the public.
His final paragraph set out his purpose in criticizing the book:

> Nor, of course, is my interest academic. The Encyclicals insist on
> certain standards. When Catholic books intimate or publicity based
> on them intimates that we already have these standards pretty well
> accepted then ground is cut from under the effort to try to get people
> to do right. To avert this impression is why I write: I know that we
> both agree, as does Father Keller, that no such impression can be
> allowed to pass.

It was observed by several of those who had received copies of the
book at Notre Dame that the sponsor of the book, Orlando Weber,
was not mentioned. Former students of Father John A. Ryan who
were now on the Notre Dame faculty were quite of the opinion
of Father McGowan, but so long as the President of the University took personal charge of the defense of the book, the opposition on campus was restrained to quiet talk. There were two
other men on the faculty who received the same kind of protection for their publications. Dean McCarthy had been appointed
to the Indiana State Study Commission and soon published under
the auspices of the Bureau of Economic Research and Father
O'Hara *The Physical Assets of the State of Indiana.* Dean Clar-

ence Manion of the Law School published what was probably a high-school text, *Lessons in Liberty,* in which the Dean enlarged on his summer school commencement address of 1938, "God and Government." Because Dean Manion seemed to support Father O'Hara's contention that modern American legislators had forgotten the essential truths of the Declaration of Independence, Father O'Hara advertised the book and gave it away to many of his friends.

The Universal Notre Dame Night celebration for 1939 centered in Cleveland, and Father O'Hara gave a brief talk on the development of graduate work at the University. He also presided at the meeting of the lay trustees on May 5. The next day Bishop Spellman was announced as the new archbishop of New York, and Notre Dame had acquired another friend in a strategic position. After acting as an official visitor at Annapolis, Father O'Hara attended the installation of the new Archbishop.

While Father O'Hara was returning from the Lima Conference, Father James Drought, M.M.,[55] the first mover in the Philippine convocation, wrote to Father O'Hara concerning another proposal of his fertile mind. He suggested that at the invitation of the government of Venezuela a social commission be sent to that country to study its social conditions. Father Drought had first broached the commission to Venezuelan Minister of Foreign Affairs Gil Borges. He held later discussions with President Lopez Contreras and the Venezuelan ambassador to the United States. He also explained the project to the apostolic delegate in Washington because it was quite evident that the commission would not be invited by the hierarchy of this South American country, since "The majority of the Churchmen of South America look with suspicion upon the faith of the American Catholics." However, he was sure that when they went to the country, the hierarchy would be won over. He explained to Father O'Hara the intellectual origin of his plan:

During a visit to the capital city, Caracas, I noticed that the government officials shared with many influential citizens a sharp concern for the social ameliorization of the poorer classes within the state. Their anxiety is prompted not less by an ideal of good government than by the desire to prevent an encroachment of Communistic leadership, which would find a fertile field in socially or economically maladjusted groups.

The present government is a Liberal Republic but the people, controlled by Dictatorship for thirty years, have not yet acquired skill in managing affairs according to democratic processes. Even among government civil employees one encounters an admitted lack of technical efficiency in, and concept of, social economy. The good will in high places is relatively superabundant, but it desires, commendably, the delineation, by others, of efficient methods of operation.

He further pointed out that charity was then considered a function of government, but there was confusion on the extent of government operation.

He proposed that Father O'Hara be appointed chairman of the commission that would be invited by the Venezuelan government. Father O'Hara was enthusiastic about the proposal, and as chairman of the commission he began to make a list of competent members for the commission. He included Father William Cunningham, C.S.C., a specialist in education, as well as Miss Josephine Brownson, and sought also the assistance of members of the faculty of Fordham University. The commission sailed from New York on June 9 and returned June 23. Telling about the commission in the July 22, 1939, *America,* Father Robert Gannon, S.J., outlined its activities:

> The North American Commission, made up of twenty-one members and five secretaries, met a Venezuelan Commission of equal size at an opening ceremony in the Santa Capilla on June 21. Here in the presence of the Nuncio, The Most Reverend Aloysius Centos, and The Most Reverend Miguel Mejia, Auxiliary Bishop of Caracas, Padre Vincent Pardo, S.J., preached a sermon of welcome in English and Spanish. Benediction was given and everyone proceeded to the Municipal Theatre, where there were more compliments from our hosts. The Reverend John F. O'Hara, C.S.C., President of the University of Notre Dame, who had been invited by Father Drought to preside as chairman of the Commission, replied in Spanish on behalf of the visitors.
>
> The next morning the real work began. The group was divided into committees for the consideration of such problems as these: child welfare, public hygiene, organization of a public-service school, education (especially rural schools, teacher training and general administration), housing, press, finances, and labor relations. Each morning these committees, averaging ten members with a Venezuelan chairman, would work for three hours, and in the afternoon the Commissioners would meet for the reading of formal papers and further discussion. Bishop Mejia attended the session which was devoted in part to the burning subject of teaching religion in the public schools. Free time was devoted to visiting the offices of various Cabinet Members and making excursions to all sorts of institutions in and around Caracas. On the last day, recommendations from all the Committees were submitted to the combined Commission and drafted for presentation to the Government.

Father O'Hara wrote to President Roosevelt and to several of his friends about his experiences on this commission. To Constantine McGuire he noted that at the suggestion of the minister of education he "broadcast an appeal for general cooperation and social action—and the President dictated one page of my speech." To President Roosevelt he conveyed a special message from a high official of the Venezuelan government about the appropriation of American oil rights in Mexico. The Venezuelan official said:

We do not want Communism in this country. Our fear is that if it ever comes, the entering wedge will be a demand for the expropriation of petroleum properties. The populace sees both oil and money go out of the country but the populace does not realize that the oil companies have made a heavy investment, and are doing our country a great deal of good. They contribute a great share of our governmental income, they are rendering an excellent service. We want to protect them, and it will be much easier for us to do this if the United States pursues an energetic course towards the settlement of claims involved in the Mexican expropriation of American petroleum properties.[56]

Father O'Hara added his own observation:

My own feeling in the past was that bearing down on Mexico would alienate Latin American sympathy. I was a bit startled when the other view was first presented. These experiences had a cumulative effect on me, and this last, very specific discussion leaves me no other course than to present the matter to you without delay.

President Roosevelt wrote on July 17, thanking Father O'Hara for presenting to him the opinions of the presidents of other republics on the nature of his policy towards Mexico. He added:

The expropriation of the properties of the major petroleum companies in Mexico unaccompanied as it has been thus far by any arrangement for compensation has, of course, created a very difficult problem. . . . I am sure that you will agree that a satisfactory arrangement arrived at in discussion will produce a far happier and more permanent solution and better relations with Mexico than any arrangement that might have resulted from the "more vigorous policy" advised by the persons with whom you talked.[57]

Replying to the President on July 21, Father O'Hara said that he was exceedingly grateful for the confidence reposed in him by this letter and that he hoped for a favorable outcome from the Mexican conversations. Then he added:

Continuing on the personal note, I want to refer ever so lightly to the deep admiration I have felt for you for preserving silence under most unjust accusations in another international matter in which I

chanced to be a messenger. Great good was accomplished by your
energetic use of good offices in that case—and I trust that some time in
the future that your generosity and patience in that case may be made
known to the world.[58]

Back on the campus he presided at the summer school commencement, at which Richard Reid was the speaker. On July 27
he took occasion to answer a letter of Father P. J. Schmid of the
Josephinum Seminary of Columbus, Ohio, asking for a change
in University policy on admitting Negro students. Father O'Hara
said that his congregation conducted two Negro parishes, but that
one-tenth of the present student body was from the South and that
he thought more good could be obtained by teaching them Catholic Doctrine than by taking a chance on their withdrawal. In
another letter to Byron Kanaley on August 24, 1939, Father
O'Hara took occasion to answer a document prepared by Dr.
C. E. Stepan, M.D., of Chicago on "Problems of Higher Education."[59] His answer represents some of his views at the peak of his
presidency:

Here is a vicious circle from which Catholic education suffers, Dr.
Stepan proposes higher salaries: higher salaries cannot be paid when
the schools operate at a deficit—as many of them do; the deficit cannot be overcome until the schools discontinue giving large reductions,
and until the patrons pay their bills; the better-paying patrons cannot
be attracted until the higher salaries are paid.

Here's another one: The foundations will not finance research projects until they are well under way; research cannot be undertaken
normally without a pretty heavy expense; schools are not justified in
undertaking this expense when they are operating at a deficit or on
a slim balance in undergraduate work.

"Athleticism" can be an evil in Catholic colleges, but my impression
is that it is generally a blessing and not an evil. Unless Catholic
schools are giving moral and religious training they have no reason
for their existence. Provision for leisure time is an important feature
in any program of moral training of normal boys, and sports constitute
an excellent feature of any well organized program. It is our experience that intercollegiate competition is a distinct help to the intramural program. The only way to test the validity of intercollegiate
athletics is to consider each institution by itself and determine by an
intensive study of the whole institution whether the sports program is
a help or a hindrance to the realization of the objective of the school.

To wipe out or combine the smaller schools by decree is an impossible procedure; if it were possible, it might be unwise and it might
be unjust. As a matter of fact, the best-knit universities, as a rule, are
those that have grown from small beginnings. The few schools in the

United States that have been launched as full bloom universities have generally had a terrific struggle to achieve the organic unity essential for a well-conducted university. I can go over cases in detail, but it might be invidious to attempt this. It is far better to let these schools make their own attempt to struggle through. Those that achieve greatness have an everlasting stimulus in the traditions of early struggle. It makes the latecomers ashamed of themselves if they fall down on the job.

What I regard as one of the best small schools in the country is Carroll College, in Helena, Montana. It has an excellent faculty and a fine spirit, and it has unity of purpose that is missing in many larger institutions. I suspect that Carroll College would be wiped out if Dr. Stepan's plan were carried through. There are many other institutions that I would cite, but Carroll College is outstanding.

I do not believe that there is necessarily the destructive competition that Dr. Stepan imagines. Many of the small colleges in the country were started by Bishops who wanted to encourage vocations of their dioceses. Some of these are conducted by secular priests, other by religious orders, although usually the impetus came from the Bishops. These institutions were started because of the dearth of vocations in the dioceses, due to the lack of Catholic life and thought in a new country. They usually date back close to the beginning of the diocese. Only a few of them have come into existence later, when Catholic life was developed to the point where the poorer groups of middle class Catholics demanded an institution of higher education close to home, in order to eliminate expensive travel and the high cost of laboratories. Some of the smaller institutions established in recent years are teachers' colleges, founded by the Bishops in order to give the sisters of the diocese an opportunity to get their required degrees.

It is easy to blame the Catholic laity for failure to support higher education, but I am not inclined to do this. When I see what the Catholic laity in this country has done already for Catholic Action, I am edified and amazed. Just count up the contributions that the Catholic laity has made for Catholic grammar and high schools, for orphanages and hospitals, for seminaries and foreign missions, for many other diversified charities, and you have a record that is hard to beat. Then consider that the vast majority of our Catholics in this country are only a third or fourth generation from European peasantry, with its poverty and its lack of culture. If there has been any failure on that part of the Catholic laity to appreciate the advantages of graduate work, I would say that this failure is due largely to circumstances beyond the control of this lay group.

I am quite an optimist on the whole question. I believe that the trend is constantly upward, and that, with the blessing of God, institutions will continue to grow in the right direction. I am perfectly willing to concede that we are only in the beginning. A hundred years is only a day in the life of a great university. There is much to be done, but I believe that it will be done.

If you take the time to read this essay over, probably you can find many more faults. To my mind, the big thing right now is not to find fault but to find backers for Catholic schools. At Notre Dame, we rejoice in every blessing of God that comes to one of our sister institutions, and we help them in every way we can. Our greatest regret is that when we have to turn down a thousand students in a year, most of them will go to secular institutions instead of contributing their tuition money to a Catholic school that needs it.

On October 14 Secretary of State Hull wrote to Father O'Hara to ask him to participate in a conference on inter-American relations in the field of education at Washington in November. In his letter of acceptance Father O'Hara indicated his own activities.

At the request of a considerable number of South Americans, and moved especially by the pleas of certain members of the Venezuelan Cabinet, I appealed recently to the Catholic boarding colleges and universities in the United States, to grant scholarship aid to Latin-American students. The result has been gratifying. Approximately thirty half-scholarships have been promised, and I have placed the authorities of these schools in communication with men in South America who are in a position to select the candidates most likely to succeed. In addition, another priest and I have sought scholarships in American seminaries for Latin-American candidates for the priesthood.[60]

In a New York newspaper interview Father O'Hara stressed the high cost for Latin Americans to come to the United States because of the decline in the value of their currencies.[61] He added that the increase in trade with these countries should be followed by an increase in cultural relations. He urged American students to go to South America. "That is beautiful country down there, and, while Spanish and Portuguese are spoken there for the most part, it has produced a culture in each land which is neither Spanish or Portuguese, but entirely its own."

At the conference Father O'Hara stressed two points in his speech of November 10.[62] He had talked with a president of a South American country two weeks before, and the president objected to students from his country coming to the United States because they would not return. Father O'Hara pointed out that to avoid this problem as well as to avoid making the students unfit for good work when they return to South America, proper guidance must be given Latin American students. His second point was that American students going to South America likewise needed guidance lest by imprudence they damage the good relations with those countries. In closing he warned: "We must avoid the rash of experimentation which may set us back fifty years."[62]

After returning to Notre Dame, Father O'Hara spoke on November 14 to the Third National Accounting Conference at the Edgewater Beach Hotel in Chicago, taking the occasion to advocate the new methods of accounting used in the Notre Dame Economic Research Bureau. That weekend he also entertained the lay trustees, giving them a very optimistic report on the developments at Notre Dame. The number of students had increased to pre-depression figures, and a new hall, Breen-Phillips, had been opened that fall. The number of graduate students had doubled. He praised particularly the improvements in the Department of Philosophy and announced a new dean of the Engineering College, Dugal C. Jackson.

Just when Father O'Hara was first approached by the Apostolic Delegate to become auxiliary bishop of the Military Ordinariate is not clear. Members of his family and at least one of his secretaries maintain that he had been approached on the question of accepting bishoprics in Latin America, and one letter suggested that he had been offered a see in the United States. Such invitations, being under the secrecy of the Holy Office, would have been destroyed, as was apparently the invitation to enter the Military Ordinariate. Archbishop Spellman of New York had been made the ordinary of the military and had asked for Father O'Hara as his auxiliary, under the presumption that Father O'Hara's term as president would soon end and because of his unusual experience in directing young men. Father O'Hara had sent the Apostolic Delegate a negative answer and was preparing to go to the west coast on University business when he was summoned to Washington by the Delegate by telegram. The Delegate told him that as a religious under obedience he could not decline the assignment. Father O'Hara accepted the command and went on to New York to tell Archbishop Spellman of his acceptance. He then left for California while awaiting the formal public announcement. On the evening of December 11 he was the guest of Archbishop John Cantwell of Los Angeles. When the Archbishop saw him looking repeatedly at his watch, he warned him that he would not serve dinner until the proper time. But at six o'clock Father O'Hara announced that he was free to tell them that he was now bishop-elect of the Military Ordinariate. Archbishop Cantwell then went upstairs for an old episcopal rabat among his souvenirs and insisted that Father O'Hara put it on.

The Military Ordinariate

BISHOP JOHN F. NOLL OF FORT WAYNE
was a very matter of fact person, and from him Bishop-elect John
O'Hara received a message containing a sound evaluation of the
changes that had come into the new Bishop's life:

Only three minutes ago I picked up the evening paper and read,
with the greatest satisfaction and delight, of your elevation to Episcopal
honors.

Somebody got ahead of me. I had fully intended, at the next meeting
of the Bishops of our Province, to recommend your name. I would
have done it earlier, but Father Burns told me a couple of years ago
that he should like to have you remain in the post you then held
another term.[1]

Most of the religious at Notre Dame, like Bishop Noll, took for
granted that Father O'Hara would remain as president for the
remainder of this term and that a special rescript would be sought
from Rome to have him remain as president through the centennial of the University in 1942.

Just whether Father O'Hara had any idea that Father Burns and
Father Steiner intended to keep him in the presidency for another
term is not clear. Father Steiner, believing that he had already
rejected one bishopric, did not expect this election to another.
Father O'Hara, of course, had expressed repeatedly the hope that
he could be relieved of his administrative duties and return to
his favorite work as prefect of religion because the nostalgia for
those golden days when he shared the hopes and sorrows of a

thousand young men pursued him throughout his later career. But at the moment it is quite evident that the administrative duties of the presidency occupied his whole mind. In a real sense he was living the life of the University. Joseph P. Grace later expressed this fact very perceptively:

It will be hard on you not to continue to have Notre Dame in the hollow of your hand. You have put it on such a solid foundation that it will go along meeting your expectations & someone else will be able to take your place. The whole college will droop with sorrow at losing their much beloved President.[2]

Notre Dame did not droop because Father O'Hara's friends saw in his new appointment the honoring of a friend and those who had not agreed with his plans felt some release from pressure. But for the man himself there was no joy in leaving Notre Dame, and no desire for higher honors. It was as if an angel had lifted him up bodily and placed him in another world, much in the manner that the angel had transported the worker Habacuc to the lion's den to feed the Prophet Daniel.

At the moment his whole thought was involved in planning how he could best make Notre Dame the finest Catholic university. In five years he had achieved much, and with another four years there were great possibilities. He had brought into being the strong faculties of the Departments of Physics and Mathematics. With outside help from Martin Gillen and Orlando Weber he was sustaining the activities of the Notre Dame Bureau of Economic Research. He was the chief reliance for the development of the germ-free experiments of Professor Arthur Reyniers. To support Father Philip Moore in medieval studies he had obtained the financial aid of Mr. and Mrs. William Corbett of Chicago and of Michael Grace. The Department of Philosophy had been strengthened by the writing and teaching of Yves Simon and Fathers Leo Ward and Charles Miltner and the visits of Jacques Maritain and Etienne Gilson. *The Review of Politics* had been begun under the editorial guidance of Waldemar Gurian and Frank O'Malley.

It is probable that his trip to the west coast with Father Steiner, planned before he was called to Washington, had for its purpose to collect funds for these ventures and particularly to get alumnus Terry Cosgrove to build a graduate student hall. He had changed several department heads during the previous summer and asked the new heads to increase the range of their departments. To all these plans Father O'Hara had suddenly to bid goodbye. He no longer had any authority within the University. He did continue

—so long as there was no conflict of interests—to foster benefactions to Notre Dame. Through him the benefactions of Martin Gillen, Orlando Weber, Mr. and Mrs. Corbett, and Michael Grace, and many others continued to accrue to the University he loved so well. For some years he did much to maintain the work of the Bureau of Economic Research, sought foundation and other aid for Professor Reyniers, and obtained a grant of $100,000 for research in American history from the Hearst Foundation through his friend Richard Berlin.

He was faced with a new task about which he knew little. His new superior, Archbishop Spellman, who had received his formal appointment to the Military Ordinariate the same day, desired Father O'Hara to assume his duties as soon as possible. Already on December 4, while on the Los Angeles Limited, Father O'Hara wrote to the Archbishop:

Until I see the Provincial I cannot settle definitely the place of consecration, but I wonder if January 15 will do for the date. It will give me an extra week to prepare—and it is my Mother's wedding anniversary—the 62nd or 63rd, I forget which. She cannot attend, but it would be nice to honor the date she chose.

It was grand of you to give me a choice of residence, and I have given the matter much thought. I should like a parish where I can hear confessions, morning and evening—every day that I can be at home. If there is a run-down parish near a commuter's transfer point —from Brooklyn or New Jersey—a contingent of Notre Dame alumni will start using it as a convenient place for daily Communion—and I'll be back at the work I love. With confession hours 6–9 a.m. and 4:30–5:30 p.m. I would have plenty of time for other duties.

"Ipsam sequens non devias" I have chosen as my motto (from the II Nocturne of September 12). It ties up with Notre Dame, and also with Bishop Chartrand (*ipsa duce non fatigaris* from the same lesson by St. Bernard.) I left with Fr. O'Donnell sealed instructions on the coat of arms and wardrobe.

My suggestion on residence is only a suggestion, and if you approve it may take some time to work out. That is immaterial. I can suit myself to any arrangement in the meantime.[3]

The difficulty of suddenly changing his whole viewpoint from Notre Dame to the vague concept of the Military Ordinariate is shown more clearly in a note he sent to Professor Francis Kervick on January 4. "My regret at leaving Notre Dame is so keen that I find it hard to visualize future opportunities for good. However the grace of God can accomplish everything." But once the news of his appointment was public there was little chance for rest. He returned to Notre Dame on December 21. After a short visit with his family in Indianapolis he went to St. Joseph Novitiate in Rolling Prairie, Indiana, for a retreat. On December 26 Archbishop Spellman wrote him that Monsignor Casey would serve as master of ceremonies for the consecration and that he would pay the costs of the ceremony. He also suggested that the new bishop reside with him at 452 Madison Avenue at first, "until we have established our bearings in this situation." Monsignor Casey also sent some notes on the consecration ceremony. On January 3 Bishop-elect O'Hara answered Monsignor Casey.

The notes on ceremonies came this morning. Many thanks. I am having them mimeographed, and will be glad to send you extra copies for future use.

I may not have told you that the Apostolic Delegation promised to take care of the necessary dispensations.

My retreat ended January 1st, and I am now back at work. Things seem pretty well in hand here. The invitations came yesterday, and the mailing will begin today. The envelopes were addressed in advance.

It looked for a moment that there would be a run on bugias. Bishop Ritter suggested that I distribute them among the Prothonotaries Apostolic, but someone here advised that they be held for the Northwestern game. We needed twenty-four this year.

The mail is piled high, we are attacking it bravely.[4]

The Bishop simply did not answer the deluge of congratulatory letters and telegrams. He dictated answers to those letters that he alone could answer. Those whose letters to him concerned personal problems were told that his future address would be New York; letters dealing with future plans of the University were either answered with a suggestion that the subjects be referred to his successor or were turned over to Father Hugh O'Donnell, who was to be his successor as acting president. Father O'Donnell also assumed the task of making the arrangements for the consecration. In New York Archbishop Spellman began to form the Bishop's new office. He called on Monsignor George J. Waring, the chancellor of the Diocese of the Army and Navy under Cardinal Hayes, at St. Ann's Rectory and took back with him to Madison Avenue the current records of the Ordinariate. Then he wrote to Bishop-elect O'Hara on January 11:

I have just returned from a visit with Monsignor Waring, and I shall tell you the details when I have the pleasure of meeting you.

The conclusions are that the Chancery Office of the Army and Navy Diocese is to be moved uptown to some location in the vicinity of the present Archdiocesan Buildings. I agreed to keep the two clerks that Monsignor Waring has; Miss McMahon, at a salary of $44 a week, and Miss Flynn, at a salary of $15 a week. Naturally I wish to keep them both, as I do not wish to start any activity by discharging people. I think I shall carry out that plan I discussed with you over the phone and which seemed to meet with your approval, to appoint Dr. McCormick as Chancellor. He can supervise the arranging of the office, the details of it for you. Until we can get permanent quarters, would you be satisfied to have a desk in the Chancery Office at 477 Madison Avenue?

I have come to an arrangement with Father Lennon and your quarters will be available for you at St. Cecelia's Church any time after the 21st, as Monsignor's appointment as pastor of Tuxedo Park goes into effect January 20. If you are not happy in any way, you know that I will do everything that I can to make you so.[5]

When he came for the consecration, the Archbishop brought with him on the stationery of his New York office a handwritten letter predated for the day of the consecration.

Most Rev. John F. O'Hara, C.S.C.
Dear Bishop O'Hara,

You are hereby appointed appointed [*sic*] vicar general of the Army and Navy diocese with all faculties.

You also enjoy all the faculties of the Archdiocese of New York.
Devotedly in Christ
F. J. Spellman
Archbishop of New York
Military Vicar of the Army and Navy
Vicariate[6]

On Saturday, January 9, the city of South Bend gave a testimonial banquet in honor of the new Bishop-elect, at which F. A. Miller, the editor of the *South Bend Tribune,* was chairman, and the toastmaster was Paul G. Hoffman, the president of the Studebaker Corporation. The invocation was given by Rabbi Albert M. Shulman. Mayor Jesse I. Pavey of South Bend spoke for the city, and Congressman Samuel B. Pettingill made the principal address in presenting the Bishop-elect with a platinum watch. The Bishop-elect responded, thanking his hosts and praising the close cooperation between Notre Dame and South Bend. The closing benediction was given by Reverend Charles Tupper Baillie of the First Presbyterian Church.[7]

The officials of the consecration were the choice of the Bishop-elect, the minor officials being chosen from those members of the Community who had been most closely associated with the Bishop-elect in the administration of the University. Archbishop Spellman, the consecrator, brought with him the chasuble in which he had been consecrated by Cardinal Pacelli, now Pope Pius XII. The co-consecrators were the two Indiana bishops, Ritter and Noll, and the deacons of honor were from their dioceses: Monsignor Raymond Noll of Indianapolis and Monsignor D. L. Monahan of Fort Wayne, formerly an assistant in Peru, Indiana. The preacher for the consecration was Monsignor Thomas Shannon of Chicago, a friend of the Bishop-elect for many years.

On a briskly cold January 12 the clergy assembled in the Main Building of Notre Dame and marched through snow-plowed paths along an aisle of students and friends to Sacred Heart Church. There were five archbishops and about thirty bishops, three abbots and many monsignors. The solemn consecration of Bishop O'Hara —some say this function is the most splendid liturgical ceremony of the Church—was carried out in full detail, with the additional glow of dazzling klieg lights to aid the movie cameras that recorded the scene. Bishop O'Hara's mother was unable to come to the ceremony, but his sisters and brothers and many other relatives and friends were in the congregation when at the conclusion of the ceremony he went down the main aisle to give his blessing.

Monsignor Shannon took as the text of his sermon the passage from the Apocalypse, "Behold I set before thee an open door, and no man can shut it," making the open door the opportunity of the new Bishop O'Hara to serve God as a bishop. Referring to his special assignment, he added: "Soldiers are to be assets of Bishop O'Hara; men, not churches, not schools, not orphanages. He would ask for nothing more congenial. . . . After all, it is no new task for Bishop O'Hara to lead men to the feet of Christ. To how many has he not stood in the shoes of God these twenty years past? And no one knows better than he does the significance of the words 'I have called you. I am with you always.' " Praising Bishop O'Hara's Pan American activities, he also indicated his leadership in opposing the forces now at work "banishing God." Notre Dame was doing its share of world leadership in providing this leader against the evil forces at large in the world.[8]

Classes at the University had been dismissed that day, and the regular meals were served earlier so that the consecration banquet could be served in the west dining hall. The toastmaster was Father Monahan. Archbishop Spellman in his talk announced that Bishop O'Hara was his vicar general, with Monsignor McCormick as chancellor, and that he would live at Saint Cecelia's parish in the Puerto Rican neighborhood of New York so that he could serve the Puerto Ricans of the neighborhood. He mentioned that Pope Pius XII, as Cardinal Pacelli, had visited the University three years before, and now in a sense the Pope was visiting the University again, and added:

It is not that Notre Dame loses Father O'Hara. It is not that Notre Dame gives up Bishop O'Hara forever. It is that Notre Dame, through the personality of Bishop O'Hara widens the university's scope, and brings the spirit of Notre Dame into the Army and Navy, brings the spirit of Notre Dame unto our country, and the spirit of Notre Dame is a spirit of patriotism, the spirit of devotion to our country, the spirit of love for the Church. I am sure that the chaplains of our Armed forces, men of peace serving peace, will, under the leadership of their own Bishop O'Hara, inspire their men to live lives of virtue, lives of men ready and willing to die for country and for Church, and for man, and to live for country and for Church, and for man, which is even harder than to die, under the glorious leadership inspired by his glorious example.

Archbishop Spellman added that while he was by law the ordinary of the military diocese, in this case the auxiliary would be the ordinary and he would be the auxiliary.

In reply Bishop O'Hara used the phrase that he was "bankrupt" of words to express his gratitude to Notre Dame, where he had worked for thirty-one years. He had watched so faithfully the building of Notre Dame that the local brick layers union had made him a member and sent a certificate of his membership on ahead of him to New York. But he also expressed his willingness to serve God wherever he was called. Then he turned to his close friend:

I could not close without a special word of thanks to Father Burns, here on my right. He is the last man who would ever want a word of thanks, but I feel that I should say at this particular time that all the beautiful things that have been said about me during the administration of the last six years should be said of Father Burns, because all I tried to do was to carry out the plans that Father Burns prepared during his administration, and he, in turn, carried out the plans of Father Zahm and other predecessors.

The next day Bishop O'Hara sang a pontifical Mass for the student body in Sacred Heart Church. To the students he wrote on January 13 a final *Religious Bulletin* under the title, "Goodbye, Boys—God Bless You." His final sentence echoed his desires for the Notre Dame student:

The one thing that can keep Notre Dame a holy place of goodness and clean fun, is the supernatural spirit of sacrifice. . . . Holy Communion is the food of sacrifice—never let its tradition weaken or fade. Daily Mass is the sacred core of sacrifice. Daily visits to Mary, the

Mother of God—at the Grotto, telling your beads in a goodnight smile to the Lady of the Dome, these means of grace keep you close to God.

Archbishop Spellman had notified his friend, President Roosevelt, of the appointment of Bishop O'Hara, and the President had acknowledged through his secretary an invitation to the consecration. After the consecration Bishop O'Hara sent the following night letter to the President.

In line of duty and with warm personal pleasure I report as Ordinary of the Catholic Chaplains to the Commander-in-Chief of the Army and Navy. Archbishop Spellman, who consecrated me today and who is my immediate superior, joins with me in deep appreciation of the warm personal message communicated through Frank Walker. I hope to present my respects in person Monday, January 22, if a moment can be spared. Please accept my first episcopal blessing with full-hearted prayers for a continuation of strength and guidance from Almighty God.[9]

The President replied the next day by telegram:

Delighted to see you next Monday and to welcome you to the Military and Naval service stop Sincerest Congratulations on your election to the Bishopry.[10]

The Bishop traveled to Indianapolis for a brief visit with his mother and then went to Washington, where he preached at the annual "Red Mass" on Sunday, January 21. The next day he had his brief visit with the President before going on to New York. In the glowing words of the consecration sermon and the speeches at the banquet there was little reference to the fact that from being an administrator of a multimillion-dollar institution Bishop O'Hara had suddenly become second in command in an organization of limited size, even though its personnel was scattered throughout the world. It is doubtful that the change in dignity meant much to Bishop O'Hara, at least not as much as his separation from Notre Dame. But with his usual optimism he plunged into his new task. Since Monsignor James Lennon, the pastor leaving St. Cecelia's, was ill and could not move, the Bishop took up his residence at first with the Archbishop at 452 Madison Avenue, where he came in direct contact with the chancellor of the Archdiocese of New York, Monsignor Francis McIntyre, a tall, thin man with plenty of black hair, whose rather severe face was usually smiling. He spent much time talking with the Monsignor at meals and in the chancery office on the shaping of his own chancery office.

As the Archbishop had written before the consecration, the

chancery office of the Military Ordinariate was to begin with a desk in the chancery office of Monsignor McIntyre for the Bishop, one for Father Robert McCormick, and another for a stenographer. When Bill Reilly was added to the staff later, his desk was placed in another room.

The "Army and Navy Diocese" had functioned previously from the office of Monsignor George Waring at St. Ann's Rectory, 112 East 12th Street. Waring was an Englishman and a veteran of World War I. There had been three other vicars general during World War I, but the other three had become inactive, and all administrative duties were performed by Monsignor Waring under the late Cardinal Hayes. Because he received some applications for chaplaincies as soon as his nomination had become public, the Bishop wired to Monsignor Waring for papers on the applicants but was told by the Monsignor that all his records had been removed to the New York Chancery Office.

The Catholic Directory for 1940 enumerated the various groups of the Army and Navy Diocese as commissioned chaplains in the Army numbering thirty-four; in the Navy, nineteen; chaplains in veteran hospitals, sixty-six; auxiliary chaplains, twenty-one; military reserve chaplains, one hundred sixty-four; chaplains in the National Guard, sixty-three; thus, a total of three hundred sixty-seven. The *Directory* estimated the number of Catholics in the service at about 50,000. The customary way of estimating Catholics in the service was to take one-third of the whole force. In general, only those commissioned in the Army and Navy were on active duty, and they were scattered through the states and territories or on ships. The book of faculties of the *Episcopus Castrensis* pointed out that a time of peace offered greater spiritual danger for the chaplains than times of war because it was difficult to live a priestly life in military idleness. Thus, the book added, not every priest should assume the chaplaincy in such times, but only those outstanding for integrity of life. Further the book stated that it was difficult to get men to apply for chaplaincies because bishops were unwilling to be deprived of their services and because priests did not care to be classed as military chaplains.[11]

The chaplains remained under the discipline of the Church and received their faculties from Monsignor Waring's office until the appointment of Bishop O'Hara. Their location, however, depended upon their military assignment. Because the Army and Navy were being enlarged by enlistment in the growing world tension, there was need of some additional chaplains, since the ordinary ratio of chaplains by regulation was one to every 12,000 men. On January 17, Father McCormick, the new chancellor, sent word to Bishop O'Hara that the next examination for chaplains was set for January 30 and that they had two applications registered for regular chaplaincies for the three vacancies that were available. Two other priests, Father John A. Dunn of Baltimore and Father Paul A. Potter, O.S.A., of Chicago, had written in, and Father McCormick asked that Bishop O'Hara sign their papers and send them in.[12]

Bishop O'Hara visited his new office on January 25 and that evening attended a dinner with the "Fighting 69th" at the preview of the picture of the same name. Writing the next day of this experience to Martin Gillen he said: "There were 1600 present, and it was a perfectly delightful bedlam tough-boy style, in very orderly disorder."[13] He soon learned to avoid that kind of disorder. That day he went to Fort Wayne to attend the funeral of Monsignor John Durham. He told Gillen in the same letter that while he could not hope to keep up in science in his new position, he thought he could keep up his economics.

Before the announcement of his election Bishop O'Hara had asked Archbishop Spellman for some run-down parish near a commuter station where he could continue his favorite work by being counselor and confessor to the New York Notre Dame alumni outside of his office hours. The Archbishop modified this a bit by asking the Bishop to take over a run-down parish in a neighborhood occupied by Puerto Ricans so that he could use his Spanish to advantage. Nevertheless the Bishop opened shop and sent word to his friends, as he told F. Granger Weil on February 27: "At 125 East 105th Street I have something like the old Tower Room in operation, and I am always glad to see the boys."[14] Neither did he neglect the neighbors. Among the activities of this troublesome neighborhood was the Casita Maria, a settlement house for Puerto Ricans at 78 East 110th Street, the director of which was Miss Elizabeth Sullivan, later Mrs. Charles Ridder.[15] He visited the Casita when an opportunity offered. Joseph Grace was already listed as one of the honorary directors of the Casita, and after one visit Bishop O'Hara told his secretary, Bill Reilly, to send them a check for $100. A few years later when Thomas Watson offered him a gift, he accepted it for his "favorite charity, Casita Maria in Harlem."[16]

Just as the President of Notre Dame found it impossible to be regularly present in the Sorin Hall Tower Room for student counseling, so the new Bishop soon found that his duties of look-

ing after affairs in Washington, visiting and getting acquainted
with his chaplains, and fulfilling some other duties incumbent on
a bishop would not allow him much time for counseling alumni
or even for work in his office at 477 Madison Avenue. He did tell
his lay secretary, Bill Reilly, that in reality he had returned to his
old job as prefect of religion, only this time his penitents were the
chaplains, not the students, except in the indirect way in which
he was also chaplain to the youths of the armed forces. He wanted
to carry out his work in the same way. As he wrote in his first
circular letter on January 30, 1940: "It is my hope to address each
of you personally within the next few weeks but for the moment
please take my good intention for the deed."

On February 5 he went to Fort Devens, Massachusetts, where he
celebrated a pontifical Mass at the dedication of the Fort's first
real chapel. The sermon was given by Bishop Richard Cushing of
Boston, and as many chaplains as could come were in attendance.
On February 17 he wrote to his friend Martin Gillen to tell him
when he would be available for consultation in New York and
gave some indication of the beginning of his travels:

I have been away a great deal; hence the delay in getting organized.
Last Friday I left for Indianapolis, where I sang a Pontifical Mass on
Sunday. Sunday evening I drove to Notre Dame, intending to get the
train from there Monday morning. The sudden death of Father Wenninger, Dean of Science, caused me to change my plans. I remained at
Notre Dame for the funeral, and left there Wednesday evening. I
found New York digging its way out of a blizzard.
. . . I have no out-of-town dates for the first week of March. Tuesday,
March 5, I expect to leave for Chicago for the installation of Archbishop Stritch. From there I go to Fort Benning, Georgia. I expect to
return here the following Tuesday for the conferring of the pallium
on Archbisop Spellman. For the next two weeks I shall be in New York.
There may be an occasional out-of-town visit during this time, but the
only thing I can foresee is a possible call to Washington for a few days
to examine candidates for chaplaincies. I have some letters out now,
awaiting reply.[17]

The visit to Indianapolis included a luncheon with the Indianapolis Notre Dame Club and a Sunday Mass at the Cathedral.
The rest of the letter dealt with the Bishop's economic theories
and the recent statement of the bishops of the N.C.W.C., "The
Church and the Social Order."

When you get the full text of the Bishops' Pastoral letter I think you
will find more consoling things in it. The summaries were not done
by the man who wrote the letter. I have not read the whole text yet,

but I have observed that they insist that higher wages must come out of profits instead of increased prices. This is a good observation. You are showing no profits—therefore, there can be no increased wages. I note also that it condemns monopoly of craft which raises the wages of that particular group of working men in such a fashion that it makes their work unavailable to those in the lower brackets.

I wish that the income study were available now. Taken in conjunction with the pastoral letter, it would present a perfect picture. . . .

On January 30 Bishop O'Hara received an invitation from Professor J. A. C. Fagginer Auer of Wadsworth House, Harvard, to participate in a conference with other religious leaders of the armed forces on the topic "Religious and Moral Principles in Their Bearing on the Contemporary National and International Crisis." Since the invitation came through Cardinal O'Connell, Bishop O'Hara did not feel free to decline the invitation without consulting the Apostolic Delegate. However, when the Delegate implied that Cardinal O'Connell's part in the invitation was purely accidental, the Bishop declined the invitation, asking Professor Auer to seek a Jesuit from Weston College to represent the Catholic viewpoint. In his letter to the Delegate Bishop O'Hara reiterated his constant rule in public conduct in religious matters: "As a matter of policy, I have always refrained from participation in public religious conferences with Protestants and Jews."[18] While he welcomed Jews and Protestants to his table and joined them readily in discussing matters of economics and business, he invariably refused to join them in matters of religious discussion or practice.

On February 26 the Bishop sent his first circular to the hierarchy asking for enlistments in the chaplaincies. He told the bishops:

The Army and Navy are both calling for Catholic chaplains. With the increased enlistment, there is present need for four additional chaplains on active duty in the Army, and two in the Navy. Legislation now pending before Congress may increase the need.

We have recently queried seventeen Reserve Chaplains in the Army on the possibility of their accepting active commissions, and have received only one favorable response. Most of the men on the reserve list are beyond the age limit for active service; others have ecclesiastical duties that will make it impossible for them to accept full time service. These considerations are making it difficult for us to secure our quota.

This office will be pleased to receive recommendations from Your Excellency of priests eligible for the service who might be interested. I need hardly say that a very special vocation is required for the lonesome life of a Chaplain in peace time. Naturally, not so many priests are adapted to it, but those who find the life an attractive field for zeal, can do a world of good.[19]

The Bishop began his long-range traveling and in the first weeks of March went to Chicago, Georgia, New York, Notre Dame, and the west coast. Then back to Milwaukee. Most of his technical correspondence was handled by Father McCormick while the Bishop was visiting the chaplains, confirming, and getting acquainted with the problems of the Ordinariate. He did broadcast a Pan American speech on April 14 and a Universal Notre Dame Night broadcast on November 16 at Detroit, but the next week he went to Indianapolis, St. Louis, Little Rock, Memphis, and back to Washington and Annapolis. When the National Convention of the Chaplains' Association met in New York on May 21 and 22, there was a special dinner for Catholic chaplains at which the Bishop spoke. Besides comparing the men in the Army and the men at Notre Dame, he made a special appeal to the priests to make an annual retreat.

Whether or not you wish to follow the practice of annual retreat, and whatever means you may adopt to prevent spiritual staleness, I want to suggest that you keep the question before you. It is this: Is my point of view supernatural?

Why this stress on the supernatural? Because the world stresses the natural to such a point that unless you resist you will be wholly swallowed up in the natural. Social service is attractive and many of its applications are entrusted to chaplains. And the chaplain can become so busy that he can forget that in special service *his* motive must be the love of God.[20]

The Bishop was carrying into his new task the old conflict he fought at Notre Dame against naturalism. He seemed to ignore the approaching war clouds. Writing to Commodore Grow on May 25, he said he was trying to avoid all war news. "I won't listen to the radio, and I usually read my office on the subway trains instead of looking at the newspapers. On Tuesday and Wednesday evening this week I talked to the Army Chaplains Association and didn't mention war once."

He was again on the move, giving a memorial address at Arlington on May 26 and at Selfridge Field near Detroit on May 30. In these sermons he advised charity particularly toward those of other sections of the country. And he also warned against the errors that were driving towards war:

What error shall we avoid. Every error. Every false philosophy of life. And the all-pervading false philosophy of life that has thrown Europe into chaos today is the philosophy of materialism. It is the philosophy of those who place all paradise here on earth. It is the philosophy of those who see only the material want of the moment which must be satisfied to the detriment of the soul. It is the philosophy of those who are depriving our nations of millions of babies each year, while the farmer is at the lowest point of the economic scale because there are not enough mouths to feed.[21]

On June 2 the Bishop returned to Notre Dame to celebrate the pontifical commencement Mass and to receive an honorary degree, and on June 9 he gave the baccalaureate address to the class at West Point. The cadets were commended for their strict life lived for a "lofty and beautiful motive." He told them that it was easier to love one's country if they first loved God, and quoted the instruction of St. Paul to keep them from trying to serve their country from false motives:

I direct your attention to these considerations, my dear young men, because you are going out into a world that tries to make hatred instead of love a motive for service to your country. Hatred is a vice, and can never engender virtue. It is a negative thing, and produces only negative results. Love is a virtue and love is positive. . . .

The Bishop went on to criticize many of the remedies offered for the ills of the day because they attacked only symptoms instead of the disease. There is only one universal remedy, and that is Christ's command to seek first the Kingdom of God and his justice.[22]

On June 1 there issued from his office in New York a second circular letter that contained essentially the same message he had given the chaplains in his talk about their need of an annual retreat. He also spoke of some things he had observed:

The apostolic zeal and natural ingenuity of the Chaplains I have met deserves special commendation. You labor under difficulties, often very serious difficulties, and not the least of which is the absence of fellow-priests.

Some of you, I observe, have been able to attract individuals, both officers and enlisted men, who are earnestly seeking a high spiritual development; these men deserve encouragement for their own sakes and for the spiritual atmosphere they bring to you. However, I hope that all of you will make use of every reasonable opportunity you can find for associations with other priests. . . .

One further consideration for your encouragement. At present you are overrun with recruits, and your nerves are strained with the problem of assisting these boys to adjust themselves to their environment. Your fellow officers are also under a severe strain. These considerations make it more than ever necessary for you to place your faith in prayer.

What God asks of us is a human effort, based on a supernatural motive. Results are in his hands. If we take credit to ourselves for good results, we are likely to yield to discouragement when the results are bad.

The letter concluded with a plea for prayers for peace, suggesting that the chaplains have holy hours with prayers for that intention during the month of the Sacred Heart. He added that the Ordinariate was no longer a diocese but a vicariate and that it no longer included the Civilian Conservation Corps. There were new forms for marriage dispensations, but the Ordinariate had no jurisdiction over marriage unless the Catholic party was under the Ordinariate. Also, baptisms, marriages, and confirmations had to be recorded on the forms supplied for that purpose.

On July 3 Bishop O'Hara preached at the first solemn Mass of Father Daniel Gleason, C.S.C., a former New York policeman. He suggested that the priest's earlier experiences would give him a better understanding of the sinner. On Sunday, July 7, the Bishop presided at a military Mass on Governor's Island.

Although the country was not at war, the tensions resulting from the European conflict were being felt. By July, 1940, the Regular Army had increased to 423,095 men with 14,000 officers. The National Guard consisted of 226,837 men and officers, and there were 104,228 reserve officers. Already the chief of chaplains, Father William Arnold, an old friend from Peru, Indiana, had asked the Military Ordinariate for more chaplains. The Bishop laid his needs before the superiors of religious communities in a letter of July 27:

Fifty-three priests, Reserve Chaplains, are needed now for a year of active duty. From various dioceses we have gathered twenty-three volunteers, and we are now appealing to the religious orders to assist us. The age limit for entering chaplains is thirty-five; in exceptional cases we may be able to obtain waivers of this qualification for priests who are under forty.

In addition to these priests needed for extended duty, we have been asked to enlist two hundred and fifty new candidates for the Reserve Corps. The maximum age limit for the Reserve Corps is forty-two; the candidate must have been ordained three years. Reserve chaplains are required to serve two weeks in summer encampments.

If we cannot provide enough priests for these chaplaincies they will be filled by Protestant clergymen. And be it said to the credit of the Protestant ministers that they are applying for chaplaincies at the rate of thirty or forty a day.

The effort to multiply the number of priests in the service entailed much correspondence, and the Bishop noted to a friend that he and Bill Reilly "are worn to the bone trying to assemble 250 chaplains in a week."[23]

The Bishop also continued his travels, giving the sermon to the New York National Guard on maneuvers at St. Lawrence University Stadium at Canton on August 18. The gospel of the day was on the Sermon on the Mount. He began with the beatitudes and the other sublime teachings given on that occasion. On the warning of Our Lord against trying to serve two masters, the Bishop resumed a favorite theme:

. . . Far from being two opposing masters, the service of God and the service of country are so intertwined that we may say in all truth that no one can serve the one perfectly without serving the other.

Is this a harsh, unreasonable, an unChristian criticism of those who try to serve country without serving God? I do not believe that it is. I grant that many men try in all conscience to serve country well, and yet give little or no thought to God and his service. But they do not serve their country perfectly.

Likewise he maintained that "no man can serve God perfectly who refuses to serve the state to the best of his ability." "Christ taught us," he said, "by word and example:"

God, I say is our final end, and we have not here a lasting city. We do have a temporal end here on earth; given life we have a duty to sustain life, to preserve our health, to provide for ourselves and for those whom God entrusts to our care. Conflict arises, the struggle between the flesh and the spirit, between God and mammon, when we become so engrossed in the affairs of the world that we make them our final end.

He urged the soldiers to make the love of God the supreme motive for their service. He concluded with the poem of Joyce Kilmer comparing the trudging soldier to Christ carrying His Cross.[24] Here as in many other camps the Bishop found many Notre Dame men and thrilled them by calling them by name. Here also his services were well attended by the Catholics who had been trained to attend Sunday Mass in private life.

To the religious superiors who had responded to his call for help he wrote on August 21:

Thanks to the generous cooperation of the hierarchy and the superiors of religious orders, some seventy-five priests have already volunteered for the two hundred and fifty places in the Chaplains Reserve Corps offered us by the War Department.

Forty-five of this number have indicated their willingness to accept a year or more of extended duty with the Army. Our present quota for

extended duty is fifty-three, but I am informed that it will soon be
raised to *one hundred and fifty,* and we shall continue to accept
applications to that number.

Should conscription become a fact, at least *ninety* additional Catholic chaplains will be needed for each 400,000 men drafted.

Some of the superiors who have no priests to spare at the present
time but who expect to ordain a goodly number next year, are giving
us candidates for the inactive Reserve Corps now, with the understanding that some of them will be released for extended duty as soon
as they can be spared from the work of the community.

On August 28 the National Guard was mustered into federal service, and on September 16 the Selective Service Act was passed and
provided for the induction of approximately 800,000 additional
young men into the armed forces.

Meanwhile the Bishop was in Wisconsin in August for maneuvers and was returning from Florida on September 11 when he
learned that his close friend, Father James Burns, had died. He
hastened to the funeral but could not preach because of a sore
throat. Among those at the funeral were Mr. and Mrs. Trevor
Arnett, and in the exchange of letters with them about Father
Burns, Mr. Arnett quoted Father Burns's statement at the consecration of Bishop O'Hara. "I need not say we shall miss him here
—and I more than anyone else. A perfectly charming personality;
a big man; a man whose heart overflows with kindness towards all
men; one who never thinks of self except secondarily, and necessarily, and whose whole life and work is for others."[25] To this
Bishop O'Hara replied:

> While I appreciate the kind word you transcribed from Father
> Burns's letter, I want to warn you that he was giving giving [sic] uncon-
> sciously a description of himself. He had a very kind heart, and in our
> close association of more than twenty-five years he very graciously
> overlooked my many faults and tried to see in me the virtues he failed
> to recognize in himself. At the consecration banquet I gave a rude
> shock to his modesty when I acknowledged publicly that any credit
> I had received for conducting the affairs of Notre Dame belonged
> properly to Father Burns because I simply tried in my own poor way
> to carry out his program for the development of the University.[26]

His next trip was to Panama, going by air but returning by steamer
to get some rest.

Bishop O'Hara wanted to keep the work of the chaplains priestly
and did not accept some aspects of the work of the chaplain in the
prewar Navy. Writing to Father Lawrence R. Schneider of Cin-

cinnati about his faculties, he expressed his views about the Navy chaplaincy:

There are no special instructions which I can give you at the present time. However, I would like you to remember always that your primary obligation is to the Church and your sole purpose is the administration of the spiritual needs of the sailors. We will expect you to be just as exact in these matters while you are in the Navy, as you were in your own parish. You should always be very tactful in dealing with the officers, and I am sure you will thereby get cooperation. You must avoid, in particular, any participation in union services of the ministers and their religious sects.

It would be advisable for you when you are in port to become acquainted with the local clergy for two reasons: 1) a chaplain in the Navy is very much alone and being in groups of mixed religions, will need the companionship of other priests and the consolation that will come from that association; 2) there may be times when you might have to call upon the local clergy to help you in your work, and an attitude of friendliness will always make them cooperative.[27]

In his third circular letter he welcomed the new chaplains and urged the older chaplains to give the new men encouragement by word and example. He sent new forms for their reports and asked the Navy chaplains to report monthly like the others instead of quarterly. He added a typical word about Holy Communion.

One point needs to be stressed again and again. The primary purpose of the chaplain is to place the souls of his men in touch with God. He needs auxiliaries in this work, and no more devoted missionaries for this can be found than at least a small band of daily communicants. Encouragement to daily Communion can be offered readily through the sacrament of Penance; facilities for its use require early rising on the part of the chaplain. Most priests will surmount any obstacle to bring the sacraments to the dying; let us hope that equal zeal will animate all of you to encourage your subjects to *live* in the state of grace.

For the benefit of the new chaplains I quote a paragraph from a letter of a retiring chaplain who made a great name for himself:

"I am a veteran and know the army well. I think young chaplains should be professedly total abstainers. They should have zeal. Be good mixers. Have a fine spiritual reaction and know the meaning of priestly dignity. I am sure you will agree. These things are easy for the right type of men. To rotters they are miracles."

The Bishop added five notes, the fifth being a requirement of an inventory of all church property to be given to his successor when he was transferred.

After his return from Panama the Bishop attended the consecration of Bishop Bernard Espelage, O.F.M., in Cincinnati on October 9 and, after visiting his mother in Indianapolis, went on to Los Angeles, where he had promised Archbishop Cantwell to address a public session of the Sixth Convention of the Catechetical Congress on October 14. His topic was "The Need of Our Times," but he said the needs were not new; they were the truths of Christianity. He told the story of the Hoosier who tried to irritate the son of an Irish immigrant by noting that the Irish farmer had a new plow but stuck to the old religion, and who received the answer, "God did not make the first plow."[28] From California he visited camps in Washington and other places in the Northwest and Middle West.

On November 6 he wrote to a friend about the purpose of these trips and visitations. He could not attain what he wanted by letter writing, for he wanted to see for himself what were the needs of the chaplains and to hear from them their own stories. He was also quite pleased when he himself could perform some sacramental function in these visits beyond confirming. The chance to hear confessions or to counsel the ordinary soldier was eagerly grasped. He was well prepared from these visits to report to the bishops of the country at their annual meeting in Washington, November 13 to 15. Beforehand he had had Father McCormick send the bishops information on the methods for applying for chaplaincies and to tell them that the greatest need was for the Reserve Corps. Father McCormick enclosed a copy of the Bishop's talk to the hierarchy, since not all the bishops attended the Washington meeting.

The magnitude of his problem was based on the fact that by June, 1941, the Army planned to have one million men under arms and in camps, while the Navy planned to expand to 485,000 men. The law providing for chaplains provided that there be one chaplain for each 1,200 men, and the practice in vogue was that one in four of these chaplains be a Catholic priest. The Military Ordinariate hoped to have 500 Catholic chaplains, including the National Guard chaplains. Both the Army and Navy were cooperating in freeing the chaplains from "extra-curricular duties." The chapel situation in the camps was bad, although some posts had excellent chapels for general use by all denominations. A few posts had Catholic chapels. Many posts lacked proper chapel facilities, and nothing had as yet been done to provide chapel facilities for some of the larger training centers which would soon have from 20,000 to 60,000 recruits.

The general Army policy where there was no Catholic chaplain was to invite a civilian priest to say Mass and take care of sick calls or to provide transportation to the nearest church for Mass. The bishops were urged by Bishop O'Hara to report any failure to provide chapel facilities on posts in their dioceses. Finally he expressed the hope that the bishops would visit the military establishments in their dioceses and especially that they would confirm since this task was too large for himself and Archbishop Spellman.

The Bishop added his approval to the suggestion of Archbishop Samuel Stritch that recreation be provided for the soldiers when they leave the military posts and seconded Archbishop Mitty's appeal for support of the Chaplains' Aid Association. He further noted that in wartime the Coast Guard and Maritime Service were under the jurisdiction of the Navy and asked that the local bishops attend to the needs of the men in those services. He added two general observations on his problems:

Our opportunity: The present emergency would seem to offer a splendid opportunity for the spiritual development of young men in the Armed Forces, many of whom have had little or no contact with priests. It is my observation that the enlisted men of both Army and Navy are exceedingly frank and very natural in their religious practices. There has been a remarkable change in the quality of the enlisted men in the past twenty-five years. There are many adept missionaries among them now and their influence is bringing a real harvest of souls.

We are asking the chaplains to hold missions for the men this winter and next spring; most of them now have some form of discussion group, study club, question box or similar device of instruction. Many of them are quite busy with instruction classes for converts. The Religious Census of 1936 reports fifty-six percent of the population of the United States professes no religious affiliation. In this vast group of churchless citizens there must be millions of young men who crave religious instruction. The experience of the service chaplain is that such men welcome the slightest encouragement to a knowledge of God. Ninety converts have been reported by chaplains for the first nine months of the year.

On Sunday, November 10, the Bishop gave the sermon at the annual memorial Mass of the Catholic War Veterans of the New York City counties and the neighboring states. Archbishop Spellman presided, and there were 900 veterans present. In his sermon Bishop O'Hara made a special attack on some magazine articles on patriotism, particularly one letter of a youth who denied the moral basis of patriotism. The Bishop said that there was no question but that in war American youths would willingly defend their country as much as did English and French youths; further, true patriotism founded on man's duty to God would condemn the attitudes expressed in these articles. The *New York Times* of November 11 quoted him as saying that "the greatest service you can do for your country and your God is to work and pray for the conversion of the enemy within—conversion to God and true Americanism." Speaking of the nature of true patriotism, he added:

> Our task is primarily a spiritual one. It matters not how many men we gather to repel an invader if your chief enemy is already within the gates. It matters not how well we train them to shoot if our enemy is a mental and moral attitude of selfishness. Men who believe in God and eternity should have a clear notion of the state and their duty to the state. . . .

During the presidential campaign of 1940 Bishop O'Hara's friend, Martin Gillen, was very active in his support of Wendell Wilkie. Despite his pro-Wilkie letters to the Bishop there is little evidence that he could elicit any enthusiasm for that cause from the Bishop. Probably, while the Bishop did not change his ideas about the economic and labor problems of the country, he felt that in his new role he had a certain obligation to support President Roosevelt. At least such would seem to be the idea in his letter to President Roosevelt after the election:

Dear Mr. President:
    Now that the first rush of congratulations is over I want to add my word of felicitation on the most glorious victory of your entire career, and to assure you of continued remembrance in my Masses and prayers.
    At the same time I want to thank you for the interest you have taken in my work as military Delegate. Archbishop Spellman has told me of his recent interview, and of your concern for the spiritual welfare of the enlisted men.
    For your encouragement I want to say that I have been deeply touched by the sense of personal loyalty the officers and enlisted men of the Army and Navy have for their Commander-in-Chief. This knowledge will, I hope, lighten the burdens of your office in this hour of trial.[29]

President Roosevelt replied:

My Dear Bishop O'Hara:
    I am most grateful for the generous message conveyed in your letter of November ninth. Please accept this assurance of my heartfelt appreciation.
    It is a source of great satisfaction to know that so large a responsibility in providing for the spiritual welfare of our young men in the

military service is in your capable hands. And it is indeed grand to know that we have such a fine and loyal body of men serving so valiantly in the defense of the country.[30]

After the November meeting of the bishops in Washington Bishop O'Hara resumed his visits to the camps and posts while his chancellor and secretaries tried to answer the business requests of the chaplains. Writing to Father George Sauvage, C.S.C., in Rome on November 27, he said that "applications for chaplaincies are coming in at a sufficiently rapid rate to assure us the five hundred we need by next June."[31] There are not too many accounts of the friction that occasionally developed between the chaplains and some officers who were not congenial to Catholic clergymen. One instance was reported by Bishop Toolen of Mobile on November 30, 1940, concerning Father Joseph T. Callaghan:

I wrote Fr. McCormick in regard to conditions at Pensacola Air Station. As you know the Commandant there has not been anxious for a priest and I am wondering just why. Father Callaghan, as you no doubt know, has arrived and was greeted with the knowledge that there is no room for him at the Post, that he would have to find quarters outside. He will not be much use to the Post if he has to live in Pensacola. He is now living with Father Cusick at St. Michael's Church, Pensacola. We are glad to have him and to extend to him every courtesy and kindness, as well as southern hospitality but I did not like this fellow at the Post getting away with this.[32]

When Bishop O'Hara went to Charleston to see the superior officer, he found that the offending officer had been changed. In the meantime Father Callaghan wrote the Bishop that he had merely received a routine answer for any commissioned officer on the crowded base and that no hostility was intended. He quickly made other arrangements.

As the Bishop traveled from camp to camp, he became more concerned about the lack of chapels, and he took up this matter with General George C. Marshall. Finally on December 18 he wrote to the President about the bill before Congress to provide chapels:

I would appreciate an opportunity to defend the bill should there be any question in the mind of the executive budget committee as to the necessity of so many buildings for Divine Worship. I have visited a great many posts, and I have been distressed by the lack of accommodations for the worship of God. I see in the present emergency an opportunity to intensify the loyalty to God and country of hundreds of thousands of young men. If this opportunity is missed through lack of facilities for Divine Worship I fear bad results.

He also wrote to the President's secretary, Marvin McIntyre, of
his fears of the budget committee, and the President sent word to
McIntyre to have the Bishop see him the next time he was in
Washington.[33]

The Bishop's Christmas letter to the chaplains expressed his
regret that he could not keep in constant touch with them, but on
Christmas noon he broadcast a message on the blue network of
N.B.C. to the men of the armed forces.

After Christmas, apparently at the request of several South
American prelates, he sent a letter on December 28 to fifty-seven
provincial superiors of men's communities in the United States to
ask them to establish schools in South America. The letter is interesting as a sidelight on the general respect for his knowledge of
the problems of the countries of South America.

From time to time I receive requests for religious orders in the
United States to establish schools for boys in South America. What
they have in mind chiefly are institutions that we would classify as
commercial high schools. The difference would be that these institutions would take boys from about our sixth grade and carry them
through four, five or six years' preparation for business.

There are four such requests on my desk now. There is also an
urgent plea for American priests to labor in a vast missionary district
of Central America.

As you are probably aware, American Protestant missionary societies
conduct many such schools in South America. The Bishops tell me
that the boys who attend these schools become indifferent to all religion. It is with the hope of counteracting such influence that the
Bishops plead for the establishment of American Catholic schools.
The boys want to study English to prepare for jobs with American
firms or with firms doing business with the United States.

If you and your council can see the possibility of undertaking such
work, I shall gladly place you in touch with the South American ecclesiastical authorities who have requested such assistance. I might say
in passing that a few of these requests have been made by Bishops and
Papal Nuncios through our American ambassadors in Latin America.
The Ambassadors themselves realize the importance of American Catholic schools fostering better relations among the respective countries.[34]

Some of the communities were already engaged in such activities,
and some could not do so for some years. He was called upon to
use his knowledge of Latin America in other capacities, in Bogota
particularly.

In Bogota, Colombia, the American ambassador, Spruille Braden, was faced with the anti-American and pro-Nazi activities of
a certain Spanish priest who had even influenced the Archbishop

Monsignor Perdomo to issue a pastoral that attacked the United States. When Braden was in the United States, he took up the matter with Archbishop Spellman to see if some ranking American prelate could come to visit him to clarify the situation. First Archbishop Spellman arranged a luncheon at which Bishop O'Hara talked over the problem with Ambassador and Mrs. Braden. After the visit Braden invited Bishop O'Hara to come to Bogota in September, 1940. Circumstances prevented the September trip, but the Bishop did reach Bogota in January, 1941, where he was the house guest of the Ambassador. The Ambassador summed up the story of the visit:

. . . Bishop O'Hara came to Bogota and made the most magnificent impression on everyone he met and on the public generally.

There were amusing incidents as, for instance, when I took him to call on the Foreign Minister who was very much of a philosopher but also a free thinker, Dr. Louis Lopes de Mesa. This gentleman took it upon himself to suggest to the Bishop a series of reforms which he thought should be put into effect. He was quite critical of the Church. The gentleness but the skill and wisdom with which the Bishop rebutted the Foreign Minister's arguments was a delight to listen to.

Finally, on his last morning in Bogota, Bishop O'Hara asked me to wait in the upstairs living room while he went to say Mass in a convent close to the Embassy. When he returned from Mass in all his robes he asked me to come downstairs where he introduced a Monsignor (whose name I now forget) who, Bishop explained, had written the unfortunate pastoral letter, and in my presence instructed the Monsignor never again to let anything go out about the United States until he had cleared it with me for accuracy. I subsequently invited this Monsignor and others to luncheons and dinners at the Embassy, and thanks to Bishop O'Hara, friendly relations were cemented.[35]

Although the Bishop was back in New York to act as a co-consecrator of Bishop McIntyre on January 8, he did not stay there long. He had his visit with President Roosevelt on January 28, and from there he went south to Georgia, Florida, Cuba, and Puerto Rico, and back to New York on February 17. During his absence a special chancery for the Military Ordinariate had been opened at 33 East 51st Street. Bill Reilly, his secretary, wrote a description of the work of the military delegate for the Notre Dame *Scholastic* of November 7:

As a matter of fact he's away most of the time; he's as absent from here as he was omni-present at Notre Dame while prefect of religion. His diary, if he kept one, would read like a timetable, a combined timetable of railroads, planes and steamers. But he doesn't seem to mind. Although he rarely gets a chance to spend three consecutive nights in his home at St. Cecelia's rectory here, he comes back from his rounds of pullmans, planes and staterooms fit as a fiddle and ready to go. He has to be. In less than 24 hours he'll probably be off again, and in the meantime, there is the ever-increasing correspondence to handle.

After listing the number of chaplains and citing their far-flung stations, he added:

And among those outposts—he hasn't gone into the Pacific yet but he will—travels the former president of Notre Dame, exhorting priests and people on devotion to Our Lady and her Son. He is still the zealous confessor, making only one request of chaplains whom he visits, that he be allowed to have Saturday evening free so that he can hear confessions.

As bishop he now administers confirmation to soldiers, sailors and marines in the armed forces, his first tour a year ago taking him into the Northwest to Bremerton, Washington and to Long Beach, California, where he presided over an assembly of several hundred sailors hearing Mass on the deck of an aircraft carrier. And the trip took him to Fort Benning in Georgia by way of Chicago where he attended the installation of Archbishop Stritch.

Bill Reilly pointed out the similarity between the circular letters to the chaplains and the *Religious Bulletins,* especially in their insistence on daily Communion. And he concluded the interview with this observation: "He'll be back in a few days to tell us about the Notre Dame men he seems to meet everywhere, and we'll have a list of callers who wanted to see Father O'Hara here in New York."

Of course the circular letters were not daily and were written to priests not penitents. But some of the best notes from Bishop O'Hara then and throughout the war were handwritten notes— seldom more than ten lines—in which he talked directly to the priest or layman. But unfortunately such messages were seldom saved, particularly when they arrived in foreign encampments or on the battle front, and there are no carbon copies. He would write dozens of these notes in any night. He had more formal letters to write to superiors and to bishops. Thus on April 19 he wrote that the War Department had informed the Military Ordinariate that "all army Reserve Chaplains will be called to duty between now and June." This meant that those who could not do active duty had to resign their commissions. Circular Letter No. 5 urged the new chaplains to be grateful for the service of the older men. He added his special deal against discouragement:

A word about discouragement, which comes to some chaplains more often than encouragement. Don't be disturbed if your efforts meet with failure more often than with success. Don't compare one day with another—or one group with another. Start each day from zero. If you have one hundred Holy Communions one day and two the next, read it as a gain of two, not a loss of ninety-eight. Be sure that your effort is there,—that you can face God with a clean conscience. Results come in God's own good time, and credit for them belongs to God. "Still say, 'we are unprofitable servants.'"

One of the major efforts of Bishop O'Hara had to do with the public attitude on sexual sins in the armed services. He brought into the service a definitely high ideal that had been predominant in his *Religious Bulletin*. His chief opponent, he held, was the officer who presumed that all his men were not continent. He told the chaplains:

At a recent meeting of the morale officers of the Ninth Corps area it was stated by one of the speakers, a man of long experience in both Army work and public health service, that approximately 15 percent of the soldiers will go wrong in spite of all the helps, that 15 percent will remain continent even in the worst environment and that 70 percent are more or less weak, but will respond to good environment and such assistance as may be offered. . . .

He urged the chaplains to try to prevent talks by medical officers who presumed that one hundred percent of the boys will be incontinent and to report to the Ordinariate the sale or recommendations of contraceptive devices. Shortly after this he appeared before a Congressional Committee investigating moral conditions in the camps. He quoted the figures he had used in his circular and said that he believed that ninety-five percent of the young men would be continent because of their high ideals.[36]

Education and environment have spoiled the outline for very many of them and they have sought advice because of confused notions which come to them from outside their own hearts. Among the sources of confusion I feel that I should mention the behavioristic philosophies to which many of them are subjected in our schools, the false tone of certain motion pictures and stage productions, and particularly the pornographic literature of today. For enlisted men in the Army and Navy, I should mention the personal hygiene lectures given by some of the doctors, and line officers in the Army and Navy who have stated openly or insinuated that young men are one hundred percent incontinent.[37]

The Bishop resumed his travels. It was typical of him to tell a private who had thanked him for his services at Fort Sam Houston:

I enjoyed the spiritual experiences of the Field Mass and especially the opportunity to hear confessions on the previous day.

For sixteen years I spent most of my waking hours hearing confessions of young men and I am always glad to place my experience at their disposal.[38]

In his Easter circular the Bishop spoke of the many examples of great zeal he had witnessed in his travels, and he also spoke of the unfriendly officers the chaplains sometimes had to handle.

Most of the chaplains are quite young—may God bless your youth and the zeal which has inspired you to offer it for such important work. If experience has not given you natural patience, let grace supply the supernatural virtue. From many of you has come the complaint that while your superior officers are almost universally kind and understanding in supporting your efforts, junior officers are sometimes intolerant and stiff-necked in their attitude. Get your practice in patience with them. Disarm them with a smile—not a patronizing smile, but a soul-filling reflection of the Christian charity that is a part of your nature. Keep in mind that if they are Reserve Officers, the chances are that they have only recently come from professors who have done their best to abolish in their minds all notion of God and all respect for the Ten Commandments; they have not yet had the experience of the world that leads men back to God and to morality. Their professors have been theorists who have lived remote from life, glib in the small world in which their minds range. Only by close control of his human emotions can the chaplain open the minds of young materialists to the world of grace—and even then will seldom have opportunity to see the effects of his efforts; others will reap the harvest.

The Bishop continued to insist that the chief obstacles to the chaplain's efforts were these young graduates of secular universities.

But the Bishop was hard put to get the necessary chaplains. In a letter to bishops he said there were camps of 20,000 Catholics without a chaplain and miles of hospital corridors without them. He wrote religious superiors that the War Department wanted reserve chaplains who had been allowed to serve one year to remain in the service, and the adjutant general had refused to accept the resignation of some thirty of them. To get these men free, those who were physically unable to serve were advised to ask for medical examinations and others were to ask for deferments. He wrote: "The Department is embarrassed by the abundance of requests from the field for Catholic chaplains; we, too, are embarrassed, but our sorrow is mingled with joy that the needs of our men are so generously recognized."

Despite his many duties the Bishop did not neglect his interest in Latin America. On April 12 he blessed the new ship *Rio de Janeiro* of the Moore-McCormick line at its launching. Nelson Rockefeller, the coordinator of Cultural and Commercial Relations with Latin America, gave the address, and the daughter of the president of Brazil, Benhara Peixto, did the christening.[39] On April 14 at the Dominican Church of St. Vincent Ferrer he held a special service for the armed forces. He told the men that they had been called by the President to defend the principles they held most dear. As this was Holy Week, he asked them to make their sacrifice with the remembrance of the supreme Sacrifice they commemorated that week.[40]

Bishop O'Hara in his public addresses and letters spoke only of the better side of the activities of the Military Ordinariate. There were bound to be other matters. Some of the older men in the service had become set in their ways and did not accept the new situations. Some of them had lived too long alone and were not used to having companions on their post or camp. On April 25 he had to write a warning letter to a chaplain who had been very critical of his companion:

While I have often had occasion to commend you for your zeal, I feel that I should call attention to the necessity of tact and of a wide interpretation of Christian Charity in your dealings with fellow officers in the Army and particularly with fellow-priests.

I do not want to go into any of the details of the controversy with Father _____, nor do I want to censure either of you. Father _____ seemed to me to be a good zealous priest. If he resented your actions, it was probably because he misinterpreted your own zeal for this, that, or the other thing. I suspect that you have a tendency to be too rigorous and such a tendency may easily be misinterpreted as officiousness, or of some other less desirable quality.

It is just possible that your own conscience is too tender for Army work. . . .

Tact is, of course, essentially an inborn quality, but all of us must learn from experience how best to win the good will of others. We must never yield on anything essential but when we find it necessary to refuse, we can try to do so in such a gracious way that no sting is left. On the other hand it is possible to insist on our point in such a fashion that the other person makes it a point of honor to maintain his point no matter how wrong he may be. We need to recognize this stubborn streak in people; we need to learn how to walk around, instead of barging through.

I know that you will accept these suggestions in the spirit in which they are given, that you will think them over, pray over them and reach a fruitful decision. If in conscience you find it too difficult to remain in the Army do not hesitate to say so.

To another chaplain about whom some disturbing reports had been made, he wrote:

> If you have officers' hours every evening for the enlisted men, you are not likely to spend too much time in social visiting with the officers; and you will never lose their respect by giving most of your time to the men.[41]

He continued to pay close attention to the attitude of the military on social hygiene and went frequently to Washington to confer with the general staff on matters of sex instruction to servicemen. The Signal Corps even invited his criticism of films they had made. To Commander Roger Nolan, a physician whose advice in these matters he respected, he wrote: "Just at present I am asking the War Department to change a film which I have found very objectionable and I have mentioned to the General Staff the fine discrimination you have shown in your picture."[42]

Circular Letter No. 7 mentioned that Archbishop Spellman would celebrate his silver jubilee as a priest on May 14 and asked for prayers for their superior. On the occasion of the celebration Bishop O'Hara at the suggestion of the Archbishop talked at the luncheon about the Military Ordinariate. He gave favorable accounts of the reactions of the men in the services to the ministrations of the chaplains. Circular Letter No. 8 reminded them of the season of Pentecost and suggested that they find time for their annual retreats. He added many suggestions. One that was characteristic of the old prefect of religion advised them to cooperate with chaplains of other faiths and added:

> But not *communicatio in sacris.* If a Protestant chaplain asks you to partake in a joint service (or a regimental commander orders you to do so) explain to him politely that this cannot be done. We have our own pattern of religious worship, which is determined for us by the Sacred Congregation of Rites. Those who reject the authority of this Congregation (and of the other Sacred Congregations and offices which rule the Catholic Church) cannot reasonably expect us to sanction their rejection. We recognize their right to worship God according to conscience, and we expect similar recognition—which is guaranteed by our Constitution.

At the end of the letter he wrote an appeal for volunteers for foreign service, saying that the men in foreign service also had souls to be saved.

Although the endless journeys continued, they were interrupted on June 2 for an interfaith program on N.B.C. in support of the U.S.O. Program. Bishop James Freeman, the Episcopal Bishop of

Washington spoke from that city, Bishop O'Hara spoke from New York, and Rabbi Israel spoke from Baltimore. In his portion Bishop O'Hara described the fine-looking servicemen walking the streets of camp towns, looking for recreation. He indicated that the U.S.O. was intended to supply this need. He added:

Give him the shelter of his service building, give him an easy chair and a book, give him a place to write letters, give him a counsellor who will listen to his troubles and help him smile through them, give him a place for games, a meeting place when he is away from the restraints of military discipline, an inexpensive club. He doesn't ask for sympathy,—in fact he resents it. He is doing a job for his country and trying to retain his normal outlook on life at the same time. He wants to return to normal living a better citizen and a better man.[43]

On June 8 he went to Notre Dame for his annual retreat and as much time as he could spare for recreation. Some persons did not know that tall, thin person in the black trousers wearing suspenders over his shirt on his way from Corby Hall to the Rockne Memorial Building for a swim and a rest under the sun lamp. But to those who knew and greeted him, he was, despite the garb, the same old prefect of religion. From Notre Dame he went to the Norfolk Navy Yard, and thence to Bridgeport, Connecticut, on June 19 to address the Convention of Catholic War Veterans. The burden of his speech there was the obligation of the veterans to help the young men now in the service. His threefold message was that they must manifest by their interest in the young servicemen that they want the Catholic men to be true to their religious principles and that they want them to resist any subversive forces that would undermine their faith in God or loyalty to Church and country.[44]

William Montavon, formerly of the N.C.W.C., was now in the State Department dealing with Latin American affairs. He wrote to the Bishop about a proposed visit by a prominent clergyman who was not welcome and of other proposals on Latin American affairs. Bishop O'Hara gave some sharp answers to Montavon. ". . . I had dinner last night with a South American diplomat who told me of the glowing accounts of the 'Goodness' of the American people. These have been published. Two different people have written to him to say that his judgment cannot be true, because any country that would send Douglas Fairbanks as ambassador cannot be sound either morally or intellectually." He added some other pointed observations:

The official benediction given by the administration to the Red cause in Spain still rankles. So does the sponsorship of Comacho over Almazan. The people of South America are much more aware of these things than the people of the United States. As you well know, they miss nothing, either in the news or in the implications.

If Cardinals Lome and Capello could be induced to visit the United States, and a sensible program worked out from here, good would result. I mention the sensible program because so many of the visitors who have come as official guests have been rushed off their feet. In that, as in everything else, we have been feverish.[45]

On July 1 Circular Letter No. 9 announced that in addition to Monsignor Francis Walsh, previously appointed, seven new vicar delegates were to be appointed to share the growing tasks of the Military Ordinariate. Each was to have the powers of vicar general. Father George O'Connor governed the six New England states; Monsignor Walsh, the Middle Atlantic States down to North Carolina; Father John Brady of New York, the offshore Atlantic bases and the Canal Zone; Father Martin J. Nealis of Chicago, most of the Midwestern states west of Ohio; Monsignor Edward Quinn of Cincinnati, Ohio and the eastern Southern states; Bishop Mariano Garriga, Texas and Louisiana; Bishop Thomas A. Connally of San Francisco, the Far Western states; and Bishop James Sweeney of Honolulu, the offshore Pacific bases. There was to be one chancery but the monthly reports were to go to both the chancery and the vicar delegate. The Bishop admitted that his visits under the new regime would not be as extensive as before. In Circular Letter No. 10 he discussed the desire of Catholics to have their own chapels. He warned them not to be selfish toward the chaplains of other faiths: "Sensible generosity in meeting as far as possible the wishes of commanding officers and non-Catholic chaplains is dictated by Christian charity." They were to choose times and circumstances accordingly.

The Bishop, continuing his pleadings with bishops and religious superiors for additional chaplains, mentioned that several chaplains had become seriously ill from overwork. His Circular Letter No. 11 warned the chaplains that after his complaints to the War Department about regulations in some camps where soldiers were required to carry contraceptives when they left the posts, the General Staff had answered that any such orders were not countenanced by them. Such regulations were to be reported, and the soldiers were to be told by the chaplains to refuse to comply with the regulations. On August 11 he wrote Circular Letter No. 12 to console the chaplains laboring in the maneuvers:

Days of special hardships may be days of special grace. Recent reports, especially those of May, June, and July teem with references to bivouacs, maneuvers, patrols, alerts, problems, and other technical necessities of army and navy procedure. Supper at eleven and breakfast at one, sleeping under trunks of trees, lost equipment, nature's own transportation, mosquitoes, red bugs, cattle, barbed wire fences, dust, rain, mud, heat and humidity, thunder and lightning, C.O.'s and M.P.'s all the contrivances of nature and human intervention combine to disturb routine, to upset schedules, to interfere with the orderly flow of grace from God to man through ordained channels of the Sacraments.

Happy the chaplain whose spiritual ingenuity can turn every one of those difficulties to good account, can convert them into eternal graces. Happy the men who serve under such chaplains.

To these problems the Bishop added a brief discussion of the problems that had shown up in the monthly reports and the increase in the number of Communions. To aid in solving the problems arising about marriages between non-Catholic servicemen and Catholic girls some bishops had made the chaplains assistant pastors. In the next circular he announced the dioceses that were willing to make this arrangement and suggested that the chaplains in those dioceses apply for appointments as assistant pastors. So thorough were these instructions that Archbishop Spellman wrote him a special note of commendation of August 30:

You have heard hundreds of times and from hundreds of persons about the wonderful work you have done starting from scratch, quietly and successfully, establishing, developing, administering a vast and difficult diocese. But let me express once again my admiration and gratitude for it all. This note is occasioned by the reading of your latest letters to the chaplains and to the bishops.[46]

Bishop O'Hara got along well with the army officers. First of all his relations with Captain D. Workmann, head of the Chaplains' Division of the Navy, were very pleasant. The correspondence between the Bishop and the leaders of the Army and Navy was usually very courteous. The letters of General George Marshall show him to have been the thoughtful gentleman who attracted the affection and respect of those who had to deal with him. When the Bishop apologized for writing to that General of certain problems, the General replied: "We consider that you have a special status in connection with the Army which makes it entirely appropriate for you to do this."[47] The Bishop was constantly attacking regulations demanding compulsory acceptance of preventive measures against venereal disease and that men going on leave had to take contraceptives with them. When he learned of such regulations, the Bishop went to the officers to get the regulations rescinded. Two such regulations were issued in mimeograph form in Puerto Rico and Trinidad. Soldiers sent copies of them to the Bishop in protest. The instructions left nothing to the imagination and were insulting to the personal dignity and virtue of the men. In some of the correspondence between bishops and administrators of the armed services the latter answered boldly that they were conducting a war, but when they found themselves charged by the bishops on their own terms of not being interested in the morals of their men, they made a quick change from their untenable position. Bishop O'Hara never ceased his watchful activity on these matters.

The travels of the Bishop had some differences. He gave tonsure and the diaconate to Holy Cross seminarians in Washington, celebrated the opening Mass at Notre Dame, celebrated the first Mass in the new chapel at Fort Sheridan, and went from there to Camp Croft in South Carolina and gradually west to San Diego. From San Diego he reached Salt Lake, where besides his military services he celebrated the diamond jubilee of the diocese and the centenary of the Sisters of Holy Cross. Interviewed at Salt Lake City about the spirit of the soldiers, he replied that the morale of the soldiers was quite good despite some stories in the press to the contrary. "There is some 'grousing' but that is to be expected. The boys are just letting off steam."[48] From Salt Lake City he went to New York and then to Detroit on October 28 to discuss problems with Archbishop Mooney.

At the request of the apostolic delegate, Archbishop Cicognani, he agreed to go the National Eucharistic Congress at Santiago on November 6 and 7 to promote inter-American good relations. As one of the best informed men on religion in Latin America, the Bishop's letter of November 27 to the Apostolic Delegate gives in brief the importance of the Congress and of his presence there:

His Excellency, The Minister of Foreign Affairs, Senor Rosetti, explained to me the purpose of his insistence that the hierarchy of the United States be represented at the Eucharistic Congress. He was distressed at the representation in the United States of the so called Popular Front Government as Communistic. Himself a Catholic, he was confident that the Catholic people of Chile would respond to the call of the Chilean Hierarchy with a great manifestation of faith and he wished to have present foreign observers who could carry back to their own people the story that Chile remains fundamentally and whole-heartedly Catholic.

His faith in the people was amply justified. The complete success of the Congress went beyond the most optimistic expectations of His Excellency, Archbishop Caro, and his brother Bishops of the Chilean hierarchy. Each day there was a magnificent demonstration of faith morning and afternoon at the Masses and general assemblies. While I have no official statistics on the actual number of Holy Communions received, I made my own estimates at the two Communion Masses I attended. I estimate that at the Children's Mass in the Stadium there were 120,000 people present and 75,000 Holy Communions of children. I celebrated the Military Mass in the Plaza Bulnes. The communicants there were mostly military and I estimate their number at 10,000, while the attendance at Mass was approximately 100,000.

The reports I have of attendance at the Midnight Mass indicate that 300,000 men were present and at least one-half of them received Holy Communion. As at the International Congress at Buenos Aires, men were confessing in the streets wherever they could find a priest. Confessors were on duty from noon Saturday until four o'clock Sunday morning. Two additional masses had to be said after the Midnight Mass to accommodate the men who arrived late at the Plaza Bulnes. The men marched in torchlight procession, three endless columns of ten men abreast. I did not attend this Mass since I was to leave by airplane at 6 o'clock Sunday morning in order to reach Washington in time for the Annual Meeting of the Bishops.

Since there were many official visits to be made I had opportunity to attend only three of the particular sessions of the Eucharistic Congress. The session at the Catholic University was brilliant. It was particularly inspiring to pass through long lines of 1,000 university students standing at attention in the uniforms selected to act as a guard of honor before the Blessed Sacrament exposed throughout the Congress. Speaking to another University group, the Association of Catholic Students (which includes representatives of the National University as well as the Catholic University) I mentioned the example of Mexico where the Confraternity of Christian Doctrine dedicated to Catholic Action had produced such a revival of faith in the country.

The third particular session I attended was the Session *de Obreros*. This was regarded by Archbishop Caro as the critical point of the whole Congress since it was felt that any effort by subversive elements to disturb the Congress would be directed against the workingman. The committee had engaged the Caupolican Theatre which had a capacity of 12,000 persons. When the session began Archbishop Caro and I were at the American Embassy at dinner together with His Excellency, the Apostolic Nuntio, His Excellency Archbishop Subercaseaux, many leaders of Chile and heads of the Army and Navy. The American ambassador was most indulgent. Although the dinner was given in his honor, he permitted me to leave the dinner early with Archbishop Caro to attend the session. The addresses were admirably Catholic; one by a workingman from Valparaiso was a fervent plea for the practical Catholic life as a basis for the application of the principles of the Encyclicals in the problems of labor and capital. While the formal program of this meeting concluded at 11:30, the workmen insisted on additional speeches and carried the meeting past midnight. His Excellency Archbishop Caro was overjoyed and received the congratulations of the thirty Bishops present.[49]

After attending the bishops' meeting in Washington, Bishop O'Hara went to Philadelphia for the Seventh National Catechetical Congress. His first speech at the congress on November 16 was rebroadcast in Spanish to South America and carried in English by C.B.S. Church of the Air. His second speech on November 18 was read for him by Bishop Leech as he hurried to Los Angeles to attend the funeral of Angus McDonald, who had died on November 15. McDonald, one of Notre Dame's more noted alumni, had been a close personal friend of the Bishop. The Bishop in his sermon praised McDonald's stewardship and addressed to him a parting salutation. "You, Angus, built a rainbow over the Golden Gate that brings the rays of the setting sun to the beautiful bay of St. Francis. May it ever remind us to be faithful and wise servants."[50]

The Military Ordinariate had become a complicated but functioning organization before the Japanese attack on Pearl Harbor, December 7, 1941. The attack had changed the position of those Catholics who had been opposed to the American entry into the war, although it did not fully change their opposition to an alliance with Soviet Russia. For Bishop O'Hara, who apparently considered himself already officially obliged to support the attitude of the President because of his close connections with the armed services, there were to be no important changes in his official messages. The declaration of war, however, did bring new demands and many new volunteers from among the priests who wanted to serve their country in time of trial.

To the bishops he sent a letter on December 11, repeating the news that he had received from Monsignor Arnold that all reserve chaplains were now to be called into active duty. He had received twenty-six applications in the previous ten days, but he needed two hundred immediately. Archbishop Spellman had offered to release all New York priests who applied, but the Bishop said that he could not take all he needed from that one diocese. In his Circular No. 17 of December 19 he wrote:

Peaceful Christmas greetings were extended in the most recent circular letter. Before it reached some of you, the fury of war struck. You were at your posts. Many of you under fire! We renew those peaceful Christmas greetings now with a prayer for a great blessing of God on you in the new responsibilities you must assume—and which you will assume in the spirit of the Good Samaritan.

The only true peace this side of heaven is the peace of a good conscience, and that we trust is yours. You can find peace in the midst of fury—in the joy of unselfishness. And who has a greater opportunity for unselfishness than the service chaplain. May God strengthen you for the sacrifice you will make for your men—and to encourage them to the sacrifices they must make for their country.

The entrance into the war had made one important change in the administration of the Military Ordinariate. All movements of troops, and that included chaplains, were enveloped in secrecy. On January 6, 1942, the Bishop wrote: "The sudden shifting of troops is causing more changes than we have ever had to handle at once, and it will be another month or so before we catch up."[51] On January 14 he wrote again: "It is difficult for us to locate these outfits since the War Department will not give us any information on the movement of troops."[52]

In one sense the outbreak of war might have given the Bishop some assurance that his work and that of the chaplains were more purposeful. Happily the organization for taking care of servicemen had been perfected before the imposition of wartime secrecy, but the vast movements of troops toward conflict changed the whole atmosphere. The Bishop did continue to travel to the camps to see the chaplains and conduct services. With the cooperation of local bishops, the work of military vicars, and an increased staff at the chancery office the vicariate took a form more like that of a regular diocese. There was this difference that was proper to Bishop O'Hara. Just like a prefect of religion he was directly open to contact by personal visit or by letter. He talked to every chaplain who could come to him or see him on his travels. There were hundreds of five or ten line handwritten letters that answered the chaplains' queries. His office hours were not regular. Any day that the Bishop was not traveling would become confirmation day at the chapel in the Military Ordinariate for a soldier or sailor who had missed out elsewhere. When time permitted, the Bishop listened not only to the chaplains but also to the ordinary soldier or sailor.

In response to the first reports from the front he said:

A feeling of spiritual obligation comes from observing your magnificent response to the intensified obligations that have been yours since the morning of December 7th. There is nothing new in the obligations: you are still priests, with the yoke of the servants of God, ordained to save souls; you are still chaplains, charged by your government with the duty of maintaining a right spirit in the men you serve. But there is a new spirit in those men, and you are directing it

to the glory of God, the good of your neighbor, and the salvation of
your own soul.

He listed the privileges of the chaplains if they were taken pris-
oner and explained that they could give general absolution "Just
as soon as the chaplain judges it necessary." On February 5 he
wrote to the bishops that the Navy had sent out a circular author-
izing seminarians to enlist as ensigns. The Military Ordinariate
had not been consulted and did not approve of this for Catholic
chaplains, since they still required three years of ordination as a
minimum for application. On March 12 he reported the number
of chaplains and applications as 928 with 79 auxiliary chaplains.
He anticipated a need of 350 additional chaplains in 1942, most
of them before July 1.

To a zealous soldier who complained that his officers required
soldiers leaving camp to take a contraceptive packet he wrote:

We have never been able to get an order on this disquieting matter
except the correction of any commanding officer's decree that the soldier going on pass *must* carry with them. On every occasion that such
an order has been issued it has been corrected at our request.[53]

To another youngster who wanted to know if he was against soldiers marrying, the Bishop replied, explaining his pleas against
such marriages:

The warning was sent out on general principles. We started it on
the enclosed pamphlet before the draft began. Every chancery office in
the country has had to handle marriage cases that grew out of precipitate marriage that occured when troops were leaving for the World
War. Many of them were the first years in an undeclared war.[54]

In a speech to the New York Knights of Columbus on Washington's Birthday he defended the character of these youngsters:

To me as I visit Army camps and Naval stations, as I talk with soldiers, sailors and marines, with the men who form the flesh and blood
and spirit of our armed forces, the really hopeful sign of future greatness, of just peace, of glorious victory is the eagerness of these young
men of rank and file to know about God and the things of God.[55]

On March 6 in Circular Letter No. 19 he greeted the men with
a plea for prayer for each other:

The Grace of God be with you, wherever you may be! The scattering
of the flock is evident from the missing reports for January. This is
a mute appeal for all of us to intensify our responses to the plea
"Oremus pro invicem." Lent suggests that we offer our sacrifices for

the same intention, accepting them cheerfully and purifying our intentions constantly lest any grain of selfishness mar them.

On March 23 at the annual Communion breakfast for New York policemen he spoke against the proposal to set up a woman's army corps. The speech was noticed in the newspapers, and a few days later officials in Washington asked Monsignor Arnold to have the Bishop get in touch with them. The Bishop did not change his opinion, although he did accept the woman's corps when it was established. The Bishop did not amplify his speech at the time and went for a needed rest to visit Bishop Garriga at Corpus Christi and later to visit his mother, who had become seriously ill. On April 18–20 he ordained in Indianapolis Father Harry Stegman to the three major orders. Father Stegman had been his secretary while a student at Notre Dame and was to resume that work as a close personal aide in the Military Ordinariate after his ordination.

In Circular No. 20 dated May 11 the Bishop reported on a hearty reaction among the chaplains on his plea for prayer for each other.

The call to mutual helpfulness through prayer has awakened a hearty response throughout the service. From letters and reports we sense a profound appreciation of this appeal. May the response grow and be ever more earnest.

All of us are distressed, of course, at the lack of information that is part of war, particularly a world wide war. However, the effectiveness of our prayer does not depend on information on the welfare of our friends and co-laborers. We are grieved that no word has come of the fate of Fr. John J. McGarrity of Philadelphia, chaplain of the Langley. However, we know that God received our prayers for their welfare, whether they are *"in via vel in patria."*

He reported the death of one Philippine chaplain and of two retired chaplains. Bishop O'Hara's period of rest in Texas had been at the request of Archbishop Spellman, but his former Superior General, Father Albert Cousineau, C.S.C., to whom the Bishop had written about establishing a house in South America, also added a warning to his answer:

. . . I am so afraid that in the end you will be exhausted. I would ask again, dear Monsignor, to be prudent, and to please forgive me for repeating this advice so often; it is because we wish so much to keep you with us, because we all need you.[56]

But there seemed no end to his obligations. When not in his office he had other tasks, such as greeting President Manuel

Prado of Peru at St. Patrick's Cathedral on May 18 or addressing
the Diocesan Council of Catholic Women in Cleveland on May
23. There he made great sport of society planners:

Suppose, then, that economic planners instead of business men and
inventors had handled the problem. The Farmers' Protective Association would have slaughtered the cows and burned the wheat to keep
up the price and the Planned Parenthood Association would have
begun its campaign to make New York a ghost town.

My dear ladies, your greatest contribution to society is your band-
ing together to stress the eternal principles that must prevail if civilization is to survive.[57]

The Bishop expressed unrestrained pleasure in announcing the
decree of the Sacred Congregation of the Sacraments of April 30,
1942, allowing afternoon Mass and limiting abstinence from food
to four hours and from liquids to one hour. He wrote in his circular of June 8: "It would be difficult to imagine a finer testimonial to the regard of the Holy See for the desire of our Catholic
Servicemen to live close to God." He added that the dispensation
had been sought by Archbishop Spellman in January by showing
the Congregation the number of Communions despite the usual
difficulties. The privilege was limited to those who could not
attend Mass in the morning, but Bishop O'Hara explained that
this impossibility could be moral or physical:

It is our earnest desire that the chaplains place this faculty in
operation at the earliest possible moment for the spiritual benefit of
the men for whom it was sought. The chaplain must exercise prudent
judgment in the application of the faculty. In cases where the work
day ends at 4 p.m. the chaplain should make full use of the recreation
hour to begin Mass at the time most convenient for the men who will
want to attend. He should also provide an opportunity for confessions
before Mass.

The real source of the privilege was clear. While he gave credit
to Archbishop Spellman for obtaining the privilege, he admitted
in a letter to Father Joseph O'Callaghan: "My intention in asking
the privilege was to provide for both Mass and Holy Communion
in the afternoon, not in the morning."[58]

In his Circular Letter No. 22 of June 12 he expressed concern
about a new problem, the port chaplains, an indication of the
large masses of troops that were beginning to move overseas. For
the convenience of the chaplains in transit, the Ordinariate set
up a port chaplain service, but at the request of the War Department they could not announce the ports of the chaplains, although

their identity could be learned from the local chancery office. The port chaplains were urged to be on the lookout for units of men who had no chaplains. On June 23 he sent another appeal to the bishops, saying that he had on his desk 73 unfilled requisitions for Catholic chaplains. At the present rate of inductions he needed 63 priests a month for the Army and 15 for the Navy.

Bishop O'Hara's Latin American background and knowledge of Spanish added to his burdens. On June 29 he was again at St. Patrick's Cathedral, this time to welcome President Manuel Quezon of the Philippines and his wife and two daughters.[59] Again when Cardinal Maglione sent a letter to the apostolic delegate, Archbishop Cicognani, asking about the possibilities of American communities sending missionaries to Central America, the Delegate asked Bishop O'Hara to investigate the problem. The Bishop sent out on May 25, 1942, a letter to the American religious communities, referring to his previous letter of December 28, 1940, to the provincials:

I have now been asked by ranking ecclesiastics in the United States and abroad to survey the possibilities of American missionaries for Central American countries.

In the present instance no specific missionary territories are pointed out, but it is indicated that the work contemplated is largely among Indians and poor people of Spanish extraction who are absolutely destitute of spiritual ministration because of lack of priests.

In one particular country there is a mission district the population of which is estimated at two millions. It is inhabited entirely by Indians who will allow no white man but a priest to enter their territory.[60]

The Bishop apologized for making the appeal after robbing religious communities as well as dioceses of their priests for the service chaplaincies.

Writing to Archbishop Spellman on June 30,[61] the Bishop summarized the results of his investigation. He had received fifteen replies. He summarized also his answer to Cardinal Maglione: 1) he considered the Latin American field a fertile one for American missionary effort; (2) listed were communities that already had missions in Latin America: twelve communities of men and several of nuns; there were also individual priests serving as missionaries; (3) Latin American laws against foreigners would probably not be invoked against priests; (4) American home needs were also great; (5) he suggested that only religious communities be sent and they should be set apart; (6) The American missions should be in the poorest sections to prevent any resentment; (7) American missionaries should follow the Redemptorist plan of living in communities; (8) American secular priests should be excluded because of the great differences in living standards; (9) financial support should come from the United States; (10) some American communities whose missions have been closed in the Far East might have returned missionaries for Latin America. Finally, he was convinced that only an order from Rome to the superior generals would bring about a proper allotment of missionaries to this field. He also thought that responsible men in the State Department would welcome the advent of American missionaries in these countries. In his own community the Bishop arranged for Father Albert Cousineau, the superior general of Holy Cross, and Father John Cavanaugh to go to Chile the next year to establish a community at St. George's College in Santiago. But Bishop O'Hara's main business was not Latin America but the American chaplains.

Chaplain John F. Woloch wrote on June 15 from Midway that he had sent the Bishop a full account of the Battle of Midway but that the censor had withheld the letter as giving too much information of use to the enemy.[63] Most of Bishop O'Hara's mail was necessarily rather commonplace under these circumstances, and his own circulars urged the standard practices of piety. To a private who had written about the obscene magazines in his camp the Bishop replied:

> It is up to the Catholic men in the armed forces to do what they can do to stop corrupting practices. If the Catholics in the service will receive Holy Communion frequently and will protest against what is wrong, they can help. Most of all, they can give good example and encourage to clean living, the boys who are well disposed but who lack instruction. The Army is full of such boys.[64]

In such a large group of men that constituted the Catholic chaplains' corps in wartime there were bound to be cases requiring discipline. Occasionally the Bishop was warned of them too late to save the erring clergyman. Sometimes the frictions between the chaplains were what one might expect when strangers had to work together, especially among the older chaplains who felt that they had suffered the heat of the day before the younger men were called. In serious cases the Bishop withdrew his approval of the erring clergyman, and the priest was permitted by the service to resign his commission and leave the Army or Navy. In most of these cases the records were turned over to his home chancery offices or to his superior. When the charges were false or undeserved, the Ordinariate was able to protect the innocent person.

There are not many severe letters in the files of the Military Ordinariate because the delinquent person was often handled by personal visit. Nevertheless, one such bit of correspondence in the files of the Military Ordinariate exposes the disciplinarian the Bishop sometimes had to become. He wrote to one misled chaplain:

I am afraid that you missed a very important line in the letter to which you replied July 4th. I quote it: "If I have been misinformed you have only to tell me so."

To acknowledge your note of July 17, 1942. Your reference was not missed, under the circumstances your letter was considered unnecessary and uncalled for.

Awaiting the courtesy of reply to my communication of July 4, 1942, and with best wishes I am.[65]

On July 25, however, the Bishop felt constrained to write a more severe letter to the man:

Dear Father:

Perhaps I have been remiss in my duty to ecclesiastical discipline by not warning you previously that your attitude toward your Bishop merited ecclesiastical censure. I have tried to explain patiently that I was calling your attention to complaints and suggesting remedies if there was a basis for those complaints. This is not Army procedure, perhaps, but I regard it as sound ecclesiastical procedure when a superior is so far removed from his subject. I had no desire to enter into debate, and in every case I have accepted your word without question.

The intemperate character of your replies and your impertinence I have accepted as an individual, but as a Bishop I can no longer tolerate such conduct. I hereby give you canonical warning that any continuance of your impertinence will force me to apply ecclesiastical penalties. I beg you not to put me in this position. As I told you before, I have held your priestly work and zealous spirit in the highest regard, and I would hate to apply a penalty that would in any way reflect on your priestly character.

These disciplinary actions were relatively few. The Bishop certainly felt better when he could write as he did a few weeks later to another priest:

I deeply appreciate your tribute to Chaplain O'Connor. If you had labored side by side you would have had an opportunity to judge his qualities. I know how difficult the work has been. It was my first visit to an outpost that caused me to request the authorities to send roving chaplains to serve these men who lead so strenuous a life.

To another priest who had been maliciously treated even to physical suffering for refusing to cooperate in common religious service he wrote:

. . . I told you that I reported your case to Msgr. Arnold who promised to take action. Several of your priests wrote to protest against the outrageous treatment you received, for following your conscience. In the next Circular Letter of the Chief of Chaplains you will find a general statement on forced attendance at religious services.

Most of his less official correspondence, however, dealt with the pressing problem of the growing services and the increasing need of priests.

With the expanding force in the office, the Military Ordinariate moved again, this time to the second floor of the building formerly occupied by Cathedral College, 462 Madison Avenue. The Bishop also took up his residence with Archbishop Spellman at 452 Madison Avenue.

In the chaplain's report the Bishop insisted on statistics as he had at Notre Dame. And as at Notre Dame he did not take them at face value. He wrote in Circular Letter No. 24:

Statistics tell strange tales sometimes. Just how far they may be trusted is a favorite topic of conversation when someone offers them as proof.

We are inclined to mistrust statisticians if not statistics, when 121 chaplains set down in their reports for the month of April some number of Holy Communions for the First Friday—which happened to be Good Friday.

We are willing to let the matter pass—and will not allow it to break our faith in the honesty of chaplains' reports. We can think of half a dozen plausible explanations.

In the same letter the Bishop praised the practice of First Fridays. To a chaplain who had said his men were not interested in the daily Mass he warned that the chaplain was premature because attendance at daily Mass was usually fifty percent greater than the reception of Communion.

One incident of the war that was magnified to a minor storm arose from an account in the column of the war correspondent Ernie Pyle about Protestant and Catholic chaplains taking care of Catholic soldiers. The Bishop took time out to write to Pyle:

As one Hoosier to another I feel privileged to call you Ernie—and offer a friendly tip. Catholics around the country are bombarding me with copies of the enclosed column wanting me to call out the Marines or something. No doubt you are hearing from them, too, but some of them have been a bit hysterical, so I want to make a simple explanation that while a Protestant chaplain may offer a Catholic consolation and help him make an act of contrition, he cannot perform the "last rites"—which to a Catholic mean the Sacraments of Penance, Holy Viaticum and Extreme Unction. These Sacraments can be administered only by an ordained priest and can be administered only to Catholics. Sometimes an over-zealous chaplain tries to do too much.

Your batting average must be high. This is the first time I have ever heard a complaint on one of your columns and I know hundreds of your fans all over America.

Sometime later Ernie wrote back to the Bishop:

Your nice letter has overtaken me today—I'm pleased you call me Ernie; I might in turn call you "Dear Jack" except my secretary in Washington who is a stickler for accuracy apparently went to the trouble to check up on the convention and informs me in her enclosing letter that you were to be addressed "Your Excellency" and so be it, for I wouldn't want to shock my secretary.

Our dear friend, Sister Margaret Jane of St. Joseph's Hospital, Albuquerque wrote me about the mistake. . . .

Thanks so much for writing so kindly to me about it. We Hoosiers certainly are ubiquitous. I don't think I've ever been anywhere, including practically every camp over here, that I didn't run into one.[66]

The Bishop's Circular No. 25 of September 14 spoke of Archbishop Spellman's first trip as military vicar, this time to Alaska and the Aleutians. He warned the chaplains to expect the Archbishop at any time and at any place. Bishop O'Hara, who shunned the public phases of his work as much as possible, was sincerely happy to have Archbishop Spellman engage in these arduous trips, carrying the good will as well as the supervision of the Ordinariate to all corners of the service world. Of the Archbishop's report he said it had one common theme: his "constant edification at the heroic work of the chaplains in the field, at their interest in one another and at their zeal for their men." During October Archbishop Spellman and Bishop O'Hara carried on their discussions with the government about the possibility of giving priests some special insignia such as RC to wear. General Marshall opposed the plan, and Archbishop Spellman withdrew the suggestion. The matter had been called to the attention of the President, who favored the letters RC but took no action in the matter. Lest this suggestion be misunderstood, the next Circular Letter especially urged fraternal charity toward non-Catholic chaplains, even when recognizing the limits of canon law:

Frequent tributes to the character of non-Catholic chaplains come

to us in letters and in conversations with Catholic chaplains. It is well
for "boots" in the service to realize that the friendly helping hand
they have received may possibly be prompted by gratitude for a similar
welcome to the service extended by some Catholic chaplains in the
past. If any Catholic chaplain is lacking in Christian charity and gentle-
manness he should manifest towards his fellow officers especially his
fellow chaplains, he may dry up the spring of friendliness that might
otherwise constitute so many external graces to assist in the spiritual
work of the armed forces.

One of the popular stories of the first months of the war was
connected with a popular song. Father William Maguire, a Navy
chaplain, was said to have aided in furnishing ammunition, if
not of firing a gun, in the battle of Pearl Harbor and of coining
the phrase "Praise the Lord and Pass the Ammunition." When the
story was repeated in the *New York Times Book Review,* Bishop
O'Hara wrote a protest to the Macmillan Company, the publishers
of Father Maguire's book.

I am wondering if the item was really authorized. Father Maguire
in the last chapter of "Rig for Church" accounts very well for his time
on the day of the attack on Pearl Harbor. The alleged remark and the
alleged manning of a gun he has disavowed. If the charge were true,
it would be my duty as his ecclesiastical superior to remove him from
the service. The allegation that Father Maguire violated the Geneva
Convention does grave damage not only to him but to the whole Chaplains's corps. What I fear most is that the enemy may use his apparent
boasting of a violation as ground for harsh treatment of the sixty
chaplains who are in captivity.

When a Macmillan representative defended the story, the Bishop
wrote again on October 27:

. . . I was unaware that March of Time had dramatized the fictitious
incident. Whoever did it must have a guilty conscience. Some time ago
we received a call from March of Time and I answered that there was
no truth in the story. I am still awaiting a reply from the Navy Public
Relations Department.[68]

To make the denial stronger, Bishop O'Hara with Father Maguire
held a press conference in the office of the Military Ordinariate
on October 31 in which Father Maguire denied that he had or
had used a gun the day of the attack. In his sermon the previous
Sunday he did warn the men to be prepared.

Bishop O'Hara was not a fervent liturgist even though he had
a legitimate zeal for lay participation. A well-meaning but fervent
liturgist had prepared a paper on liturgical services and the war,
and decided to submit it to the Bishop before exposing it to the

public. The Bishop gave it more than a passing criticism, especially on the priest's plan for furnishing servicemen with missals. When the priest objected to the criticism, the Bishop replied:

. . . Perhaps I was a bit blunt—but working till midnight every night one hasn't much time for anything but plain facts.

I applaud the liturgical movement but I hope that those behind it will ever bear in mind that great Saints were produced without daily missals, that saints are in the process of making today in the armed forces, that missals cost money.

At the annual bishops' meeting, November 11 and 12, the Bishop gave a statistical report on the activities of the Ordinariate, with the increase in chaplains from 62 in January, 1940, to 1867 on October 27, 1942. He outlined his whole organization, its income, and its expenses. At the end he asked for 1,200 additional chaplains and funds to support the Chaplains' Aid Association. On November 26 the Bishop again gave the sermon at the Pan American Mass in Washington. In it he quoted the famous words of Commander John Shea to his son: "Be a good Catholic and you cannot help being a good American." Later a serviceman accused him of faking the sentence. On December 3 the Bishop replied to the man:

The line was in the original letter of Commander Shea to his son, but was deleted in the version published by the Associated Press and the United Press. Fortunately for the truth, and in justice to Commander Shea INS published in the line. The deletion was brought to the attention of the AP and UP, and both services took what they felt to be appropriate action; AP ran the dispatch again, giving the letter in full; UP published an apology and quoted the missing line.

I have not seen *Time* but I understand that it published the original AP version. The matter, I hear, was brought to the attention of Mr. Luce and in *Life* he ran the original letter, which contains the line in question. I have seen this in the November 16 issue of *Life*.[67]

Bishop O'Hara was particularly proud of the conduct of Catholic lay leaders, especially of those from Catholic colleges. To Brother Damien of the Christian Brothers College, St. Louis, he wrote on November 17:

Catholic education never before had the justification it has today. The Catholic Action of men in the service is extraordinary. These young men are zealous in their religion, and are real apostles in bringing their friends to the Sacraments, to the devotions, to novenas, to study clubs. Now that evening Mass is available, the weekday Mass is possible, and the privilege is well used.

Young men solidly grounded in Catholic principles and practice need have no fear of spiritual loss in the Army. The weakling will fall but the strong characters will bring many others to the throne of God. Whoever wants to be a good Catholic in camp will find plenty of good example.

What I should like to do would be to give your boys a glance through my daily mail, which brings so many hundreds of illustrations of my thesis, and from all over the world. Perhaps we can sum it up in a photograph of evening Mass on Tulagi, which appeared in the daily papers recently. It was at the close of the first day's battle when Tulagi was wrested from the Japanese. The boys knelt on the beach—and there were at least two lines of communicants as the picture shows. The boy nearest the camera is in shorts, with not even a shirt. To me this is the most inspiring picture of the war.[68]

The Bishop asked a friend to prepare a story of these lay leaders, but the task was never accomplished. As he wrote to one lady: "God has His own ways of bringing these young men to a realization of their religious needs. Every chaplain has hundreds of stories of returns to the faith."[69] Chaplains in the Pacific War and chaplains in the fleet or going to Africa were already giving refreshing accounts of the fine behavior and religious fervor of Catholic servicemen. Circular Letter No. 27 spoke of the peace and poverty of Bethlehem and hoped that in their impoverished situation "in New Guinea, or Africa, in Iceland or New Caledonia, or on a lonely atoll or in a California desert" they would have internal peace. "If there is one thing above all that has satisfied the souls of the priests who serve the armed forces, it is the simplicity of heart that characterized most of their men. The armed forces make duplicity difficult, if not impossible for most enlisted men, no matter how harsh or how evil may have been their background."

The circular letters do not make exciting reading after the war, but to many a chaplain alone on a ship, or a post, or on the front they gave spiritual aid. Beginning with Circular No. 28 they were printed. In it the Bishop requested that the chaplain say Mass daily. He was a bit sharp:

. . . Some chaplains from the devotion of their men have learned greater love for the Holy Eucharist. Some others sad to relate, seem not to have learned from anyone. When we hear of chaplains lying in bed in the morning to the scandal of fellow-chaplains, Catholic and non-Catholic alike, we begin to wonder what the powers of the priesthood mean to them.

Probably the best of the personal letters of Bishop O'Hara were as usual those little notes of five or ten lines in handwriting that made their point quickly. To a complaining soldier he wrote: "Don't write foolish letters like that or you will get to thinking that you will have to go over the hill or do something equally foolish, just because you talked yourself into it."[70] To a priest who had written about the heroic work of Father Falter, the Bishop answered: "It is too bad we cannot say anything in public about his work, but it might start disunity—if I read right the temper of the Federal Council which castigated us a few days ago. It is God's secret and will come out in God's good time." The Federal Council had objected to the American bishops assuming that Latin Americans were Catholics.

On December 16 Bishop O'Hara wrote to General George Marshall complaining about a circular distributed from Camp Wallace, Texas. To his complaint he added:

On the happier side I am glad to report that the practice of religion on the part of Catholic men in the service is a source of inspiration to the Bishops and priests and the whole Catholic population of the United States. At the meeting of the Bishops in Washington a month ago there was an expression of universal gratification that the Army policy had made such splendid provision, first in the liberal quota of chaplains, second in the provision of chapels, and third, in the freedom allowed chaplains in the exercise of spiritual duties. Every Bishop in the United States has abundant evidence to show that his men are corresponding with the efforts of the chaplains.

General Marshall replied on December 13 to Bishop O'Hara:

Certainly no one can disagree with your opinion that the publication from Camp Wallace, Texas, that was enclosed with your letter is in very bad taste. Prompt corrective action has been taken. Thank you for bringing this to my attention.

The expressions continued in the remainder of your letter are most encouraging to me. We have tried very hard to give our chaplains the maximum support and to do everything we could to encourage the religious life of the soldier. It is heartening to know that we have attained appreciable results, and that these results are known and appreciated by you and your associates.[71]

Some historians have regarded the year 1943 as the high water mark of the war, since after that year the allied powers were definitely pushing towards victory. The beginning of 1943 in the history of the Military Ordinariate seemed to call for the final effort to fill the needs of the chaplains' corps. At this time, also, Bishop William McCarty, C.SS.R., the zealous provincial of the Redemptorists, who had been so cooperative with the Ordinariate, was made bishop of Anaea and assigned to the Ordinariate. Bishop O'Hara sent to the bishops a list of the chaplains but said that complaints he had received indicated that the shortage of chaplains was endangering the faith of hundreds of thousands of Catholics in the service. There was only one answer: the number of Catholic chaplains had to be increased. One thousand more were needed—five hundred immediately, the remainder during the next three months.

There was little glamor in the heavy work at the Military Ordinariate. To Ray Geiger, a Notre Dame alumnus who was trying to promote nocturnal adoration among the troops in the camps, he wrote on January 1:

Not much happens here—except steady work. However we are thrilled daily with the reports that come to us from all over the world. The old Basement Chapel has spread out, and the same system seems to have gone everywhere. The Holy Father topped it off with afternoon Mass—and multipled the fruits of the chaplain's labors.[72]

But he said among other comments in Circular No. 29:

. . . I notice that a number of the larger posts with several chaplains attached do not have regular afternoon or evening Masses.
Ans. Let's hold a mission for chaplains.

But to a friend he noted in a letter of February 13 that there had been 900 converts the previous month. To another friend he said that he could serve best by remaining in his office. There he was dictating answers and interviewing those who came to his office. His chief worry was to get more chaplains and to see that all the requests of the men in the field were answered. He spoke again to the Knights of Columbus at their Washington's Birthday Memorial Mass. A photograph, taken that spring, of the Bishop conversing with the superior general of Holy Cross, Father Cousineau, shows that the strenuous life was beginning to tell. The shoulders were a bit stooped, and there was a puffiness around the eyes that indicated fatigue.[73] But his efforts to keep on the move and his quickness of tongue belied any mental fatigue despite his constant sinus trouble and increasing arthritic aches.

On March 11 he wrote the bishops and religious superiors that the number of unfulfilled requisitions for Catholic Army chaplains was 400, against which he had only 180 applications. He needed 220 more because there were at least 50,000 Catholic men without the services of a Catholic chaplain. The quota of Catholic chaplains had been raised to 2,250, of which they had 1,264 commissioned, leaving a balance of 916 to be supplied. In another letter to them he said that one priest in every twelve was needed in the services. He corrected any impression that Catholics were lagging behind Protestants in supplying chaplains, but that was no consolation if the boys were missing Mass and the sacraments through lack of priests.

Richard Berlin of the Hearst organization asked the Bishop if it were true that Bishop Cassidy of Fall River had opposed the WACS. Writing on March 27, the Bishop admitted that Bishop Cassidy was not alone:

. . . I took a crack at the proposals myself when there were about a dozen bills before Congress, some of them quite iniquitous. The Army and Navy wives put me up to it. Their great complaint was that they were not allowed to live overseas with their husbands but the Government planned to draft women and send them overseas to distract their husbands.

Mary Norton wrote to tell me that her bill was an ideal one. The WAAC system seems to be working out well, although I have heard a few complaints. The other spectre is still lurking on the horizon, however—the universal draft of women. The elements I find behind it are those who love the Russian ideal of womanhood typified by the housewife turned plowhorse.[74]

Far from envying the Archbishop's activities on the battlefront, Bishop O'Hara had only admiration for him. Writing to Mrs. E. L. Doheny in acknowledgement of her monthly donation toward the repair of chalices by the Chaplains' Aid Association, he added:

I have just heard the broadcast of Archbishop Spellman's address from North Africa. The Archbishop's persistent pounding at the forgetfulness of God so common today, and his insistence on the fundamental truths of the catechism, is one of the most effective external graces now operating to bring the world back to Christ. His fearlessness in going wherever chaplains are is winning for him a world-wide sympathetic audience. It is surely an inspiration to be associated with such a modern St. Paul—'in journeyings often.'[75]

But he had much dull routine to face. On April 20 he wrote the superiors that twenty-five chaplains would be admitted who were over fifty if they had a perfect score on the minimum requirements and that the services would accept those only two years ordained. He noted that he needed 998 additional chaplains, for whom he had 246 applicants. Circular Letter No. 30 contained a word about his favorite devotion among the servicemen:

The growth of devotion to the Blessed Sacrament among the men of the armed forces is one of the most blessed signs we have that the future of the Church is in good hands. Of more than immediate concern is the spiritual condition of the men themselves; they are living well—they are making preparation for a good death, the secret of a good life.

The letters from the front gave the Bishop heartening news, particularly about the servicemen and their acts of Christian leadership. He was especially proud when they were graduates of Notre Dame. To Larry Groden, who had been startled to find the natives of the Southwest Pacific Catholics, he wrote on April 12:

I see you find human nature pretty much the same the world over. However, from some of the letters I received from the chaplains, I take it we have some real Christians in the Solomons. They were tough to handle when the missionaries first went there, but they have been showing up our best marines and soldiers, who write that they are learning religion pure and undefiled from the fuzzywuzzies.[76]

With Father Maurice Sheehy, who wrote some suggestions about expediting the commissioning of chaplains, he agreed that there were unnecessary delays:

It is true that we have been dealing with symptoms rather than the root factors. The symptom to which attention has been directed most frequently is the apparent lack of Catholic chaplains. The root factor is the few months of delay between the application and field service—three months in the process of induction and two months in chaplain schools. Loyalty to the government keeps us silent about this in the newspapers—at present we have 140 chaplains chafing under this delay.[77]

Again on May 27 he sent abbots and superiors of religious an appeal for fifty chaplains, half versed in German and half in Italian, to serve in the prison camps.

Circular Letter No. 32 of June 10, 1943, related some of the consolations he was reaping in his mail.

The Holy Hour at jungle positions, the field Mass in magnificent parade ground, Easter morning in an old Arab stable, Easter in the Coconut Bowl of Guadalcanal, shepherds and their flocks drifting by during Holy Week services in the fields of North Africa—a thousand letters from near and far tell the stories of the return of sinners to the life of grace, and of strengthening of grace in the hearts of the just.

But apparently some of the chaplains were still having trouble with commanding officers who were trying to require joint religious services. He warned those chaplains to quote the regulations of Military Ordinariate. The Bishop urged the chaplains to send additional information, particularly stories of religious activities, and especially of the "lay chaplains" whether officers or men "who, in the absence of a Catholic chaplain, lead their men in prayers on Sunday, conduct novenas, enlist the services of civilian priests to say Mass on their ships while in port, and in many other ways manifest a spiritual leadership that sets them apart as real apostles." These he wanted for the history, yet to be written, of the Catholic layman in the war. He added a glimpse of his own contact with these lay leaders. "Many of these men, particularly in the Navy, visit the Military Ordinariate or Chaplains' Aid while they are in the port of New York to renew their supply of religious articles." He included with this letter a list of bad magazines according to the March list of the National League of Decency and a card containing the names of the fourteen—two new—chaplains lost in action.

The letters from chaplains and soldiers were mostly words of praise of Catholic soldiers, occasionally complaints about the administration of the Ordinariate, and sometimes shock at unusual things, such as naked natives, and Catholics in Africa and Sicily who did not go to Church. Father Fabian Flynn from Sicily wrote:

. . . As usual the engine-hood of my jeep (St. Michael) served as altar. And, as usual, the great no. of Holy Communions most encouraging. The piety & faith of our Catholic soldiers continues to edify & inspire. They are a source of amazement to the Sicilian whose brand of Catholicism is anything but heartening. Fact is, the apathy & indifference of natives to their religious inheritance puzzles our boys. They frequently remark it. The same conditions & bad example existed in N. Africa. Our boys are great for visiting churches & shrines and really *praying*. Honestly, it almost makes one an anti-clerical to behold the depressing results of centuries of Catholicism that somehow somewhere became effete. . . .[78]

The stories varied. Some chaplains were good observers and writers; others with great experiences simply told very little.

The Bishop found some time to be the chaplain to the Cathedral Canteen, which celebrated its second anniversary on June 27. For the members of the canteen he had a Mass at St. Patrick's and a Communion breakfast at Hotel Park Lane.[79] When he was in New York, it was the custom of the Bishop to go each evening to the canteen after leaving his office and spend considerable time talking with servicemen. The canteen was conducted by young ladies from prominent Catholic families who provided ample opportunity for dancing and other entertainment. Bishop O'Hara made sure that there was also an opportunity for confession in the building. At the breakfast when he was honored he responded with messages from Bishop Jean Marie Aubin in the South Solomon Islands and a radiogram from Archbishop Spellman overseas visiting the camps.

The Bishop seldom spoke out in criticism of American policies, but he did not always approve. When the Americans bombed Rome, he expressed regret, quoted another ecclesiastic as saying that even Attila had "hung back."

Bishop O'Hara never had any real authority over the chaplains' schools to which all the chaplains were sent either at the beginning or later on in their service. Yet so far as possible he always tried to visit the schools, and at the end of each term he, together with Bishop McCarty, would meet the Catholic chaplains at dinner at a city near the school, such as Boston when the Army school was at Harvard. The Bishop would explain the new decrees and rescripts and allow the men to question him freely. This enabled the Bishop to get acquainted with the new chaplains, and the new men to get important information about their future duties.

But the drudgery incidental to begging for more priests from Bishops and superiors went on. On July 28 he told them that the new authorization would call for 310 in addition to the 2,250 already authorized. At that time there were 1,688 Catholic chaplains in the Army with 144 applicants, and 486 in the Navy with 90 applicants. With the auxiliary chaplains and supervisors there were 2,211 priests and bishops serving the armed forces. "No other government," he wrote, "and no other hierarchy has ever assembled such a force of chaplains for its fighting men."

Circular Letter No. 33 of August 14 expressed thanksgiving that Archbishop Spellman had returned safely from his visit to the front but added six names to the deceased priests of the services, making a total now of twenty. Among other items he was proud to say that Communions had increased 300 percent since the introduction of the afternoon Mass, on weekdays 360 percent. But while most of the letters to the Bishop from the front were full of good news, except for casualties, there were other topics that caused him to frown and sometimes to hurry to Washington to protest to military authorities. Occasionally the rough life of the chaplains caused them to act on the level of some of the less careful men, some did not fare well under fire, but there were some of these cases that needed special care. He wrote to Father Austin J. Henry in New Guinea on August 31, 1943:

For a long time I have been battling against the stupidity of keeping men under fire so long that they drop in their tracks. It finally was announced that a rotating policy had been established by which there could be a turnover after a year, but then I was told that all action had to come from abroad. I think I accomplished something this time, but I am not too sure. Unless orders come soon, you may bring your case to the attention of the office of Chaplains out that way.

There has been a more rapid turnover in New Guinea and its area. The Navy in general has been better about this except in the case of Father Gehring, which I have been pushing since April.

If no relief arrives write me again; if necessary I shall go to the highest authorities. God bless you.[80]

On September 22 Martin Gillen died at his home in Killarney Lakes, Wisconsin. The Bishop, who had helped the old man back into the good graces of the Church, went immediately to Notre Dame and on to the Gillen home. The death had been unexpected, although Gillen had been ill. He was still working on a will to give his property to Notre Dame and even according to the old will nearly everything went to the University. He had been an important influence on the Bishop in convincing him of the validity of his economic opinions, particularly about the distribution of wealth and of income. He had also been instrumental in bringing Orlando Weber into the study. Gillen's admiration for the Bishop was very deep, along with his earlier devotion to Father James Burns. But the Bishop had to hurry back to his office and the mammoth task of building up the membership of the chaplains' corps. He wrote to the bishops and superiors of the successes and failures of his efforts. He added:

We have lost 148 priests. Twenty-one died, nine of them through enemy action. Fifty-eight are in captivity, illness, age and other causes have brought the retirement of sixty-one chaplains. The ten percent allowance for retirement seems reasonable.

The Bishop continued his interest in the lay apostolate among the servicemen, particularly when he could keep in touch with some Notre Dame graduates whose zeal he already knew. He was pleased when the photographs of Catholic activities began to pour into the Ordinariate. There were plenty about the Catholic missions in the Southwest Pacific. To Ray Geiger, the promoter of nocturnal adoration, he wrote on October 6:

They may not specialize in nocturnal adoration in the jungles, but they do build chapels. Our collection of pictures is mounting and every letter that comes tells of the large attendance at Mass—whenever the men can get there. It constitutes a unique mission. Daily Communion should spread in the United States when these men get back —may God bring them back safe and sound![81]

Circular Letter No. 34 mentioned the death of two more chaplains. He asked the chaplains to be patient with his repeated requests for reports on the sacraments, especially on marriages. He added some accounts of the heroic chaplains Fathers Neil Doyle and Terrence Brady, who had given their lives. On November 4 he prepared another statistical report for the bishops' annual meeting. He added a chapter on "Catholic Action":

The notable forms of Catholic action have been mentioned frequently in the reports of the chaplains, apostolic work for the conversion of sinners, and support of Catholic chaplains both at home and abroad. Only God knows the full extent of the apostolic work done by the enlisted men for the conversion of sinners; and only God knows the full extent of the support given the missions especially by those abroad. We have records upwards of $100,000 contributed through collections for the foreign missionaries—most of them held on the spot in the South Seas or in Africa. After the death of Father Neil Doyle, he was killed in New Georgia, we learned that on two occasions he had sent back to Mississippi funds collected for a struggling priest whose mission was near a camp where Father Doyle was stationed.

The Bishop continued his visits to camps and his attendance at other ecclesiastical functions. He watched carefully the reports and occasionally dashed down to Washington to enforce the religious rights of the chaplains or the men. When Archbishop Spellman received reports that the Bishop looked ill, he insisted that the Bishop go to the Mayo Clinic for a check-up. But when he returned to Indianapolis on December 22, the Bishop insisted that the doctors had found him in excellent condition. He remained a tall, thin man. His lack of weight was chronic, but his fatigue did not seem to bring on any new trouble. Sinus trouble and arthritis had been his in some fashion for years.

The story of Bishop O'Hara in these final years of the war is fragmented into far more pieces than the sunlight coming through a mediaeval window. He never thought of keeping a diary, and unfortunately neither did his secretaries who worked around the clock with him. Most of his nonwritten work could be listed simply as the confidential conversation of a confessor and intimate counsellor. Likewise most of the business of his trips to Washington—whether to act as a member of the Board of Trustees of The Catholic University, as a member of the Executive Committee of the N.C.W.C., or the Delegatus Castrensis defending the rights of Catholic soldiers or sailors—was usually secret and unwritten. In the last category of work the Bishop kept watch to see that local commanders were not violating the Army rule on contraceptives or infringing on other moral rights. To one general who was persistent in his opposition he wrote in February, 1944: "I appreciate your statement of the War Department's position. I see the point clearly although I cannot accept it, since to my mind it compromised with the precepts that one must never do evil that good may come of it. In the War Department's procedure the end is used to justify the means."

Two notes indicate the intensity of his work; one was to his friend, Father Thomas Blackwell of Los Angeles, on November 20, 1942:

It's a long time since I have seen California (a year and a few days to be exact, and I had only a few hours that time at Angus McDonald's funeral) and it looks as though it would be another long time before I can get away long enough to go there. Multiplication is the only arithmetic we know here now, and I have to supervise the tables.[82]

Again apologizing to Bishop Joseph Burke, the auxiliary-elect of Buffalo, on June 25, 1943, he said:

I can only plead confusion as the reason. Archbishop Mooney said to me today, "You can have your job." It *is* something of a nightmare, so don't hold against me my delay in wishing you all the blessings of God in your new work.

Finally in February, 1944, he did combine business with a trip to California. But before he left, he noted to his friend Richard Berlin: "I was in and out of the city four times, but was absent a total of twenty-seven days. I leave again Wednesday night."[83]

On January 26 he greeted another Latin American president, Medina of Venezuela, in a session at the Waldorf Astoria and then proceeded by way of New Orleans to California. He explained the elapsed time between circulars in Letter No. 35 of January 31:

The long interval elapsed since the last Circular Letter (October 12, 1943) indicates serious preoccupation with your problems, rather than the reverse. With more than four thousand priests serving the armed forces in one capacity or another, individual correspondence has taken up the time of the staff in unprecedented fashion. We regret the absence of circular letters during the interval, but we have tried to render faithful service in the solution of individual problems.

At the end of the letter he added: "We have no desire to stir up scruples but we urge you to pray the official prayer of the Church whenever you can. We all need prayer—and the world needs the official prayer of the Church to cover its headlong tendency to suicide."

From time to time conflicts arose between some chaplains and local commanders over the orders of commanders that the chaplains hold joint services forbidden by the Bishop. In most cases the chaplains were able to convince the officers either that the joint service would give offense to non-Catholics or, using the information supplied from the Military Ordinariate, that this was a violation of religious freedom. The proper cooperation between chaplain and commander was particularly important when a member of the chaplains' corps failed seriously in his duties. It was obvious that the priest who had ceased to function as a priest should be relieved immediately of his commission. Sometimes there was a difference of opinion between the commanding officer and the Military Ordinariate about the propriety of a chaplain's conduct, and in this situation the military eventually had to give way. The way the Ordinariate functioned in this problem was all outlined by Bishop O'Hara in a letter of January, 1944, to a southern pastor:

The answers to the questions are very simple. First: Chaplains are expected to follow the rules of fraternal correction as given in our Rule Book. If the man does not respond to correction, the Military Ordinariate should be informed. Similarly, if scandal threatens, we should be notified as quickly as possible. Second: Often it is best to use the telephone in reporting a case for immediate action. Third: I wish that a man could be removed fast. Unfortunately, the Army has many delays, and it takes almost as long to get a man out of the Army as it takes to get him in. However, in the month or so that elapses, the man is usually on good behavior.

I should add a word about procedure. We revoke our endorsement in a formal letter that gives vague reasons only. In a personal letter to the Chief of Chaplains we give as much of the real reason as seems necessary to enable him to present the case to the board in Washington —which he does by word of mouth. Usually, I talk the case over with the Chief of Chaplains and follow his advice in the minimum statement I am to give him in the personal letter.[84]

In most cases the correspondence dealing with these cases was turned over to the superior or chancery that had the future supervision of the former chaplain. Before action in a doubtful case, Bishop O'Hara gave the accused a chance to defend himself. He wrote to one about whom he had received charges:

Word had reached me that you have not been fully mindful of your obligation to give good priestly example. I would not want a supervisor not of the fold to request your return home—and yet that may happen if the reports are correct.

I am reserving judgment on the reports, however, until I hear from you. Please be perfectly frank. I want to help if I can, whenever any priest needs help.[85]

His Easter Letter, Circular No. 36, included his greetings on the feast.

Easter, like Christmas, has a special significance for the man in the service, primarily for the service chaplains. Many of you noted that the nearer one comes to the bare walls and privations of Christmas, the greater is the joy of the feast. You may note equally that the nearer one comes to the Crucifixion, the more you can feel the joys of Easter.

The letter included an account of the death of Father John Callahan in the crash of an airplane and that of Father Dominic Gillespie in Alaska. The Bishop announced the granting of privileges to use camouflaged vestments and altar cloths, and the use of substitutes for linen or hemp except for corporals, palls, and purificators. He listed the chaplains he knew who had received the purple heart. There was a request again for reports, with a notation that some had not sent any. He discussed many other details of chaplains' lives, warning against vulgarity, and announcing four new subvicariates. A new Navy ruling prohibited "proselytizing," and the Bishop had asked for a clarification of the ruling and insisted on the rights for chaplains to take those who come for conversion. The Bishop liked to print some of the letters he had received from chaplains, and he gave excerpts of one from a chaplain on a ship who went looking for his men.

Last Saturday and Sunday there were three and one half hours of Confessions alone. Once squared off, what real men they are in God's sight. Last month I've been averaging over one hundred Communions a Sunday, where it used to be thirty or forty.

The Bishop also broadcast an Easter message to the servicemen through the facilities of the Mutual Broadcasting Company. Insisting that the message of Easter was a message of hope, he emphasized the paradox of giving up the pleasures of this world for the rewards of a better world:

A better world can be produced only when people cast aside all notion of a better world and begin to fix their gaze on eternity. Honesty, sobriety, justice, mercy, love of the poor, the afflicted, the suffering, zeal for truth, charity without distinction, self-denial, self-immolation, these are the component parts of a better world, and they spring only from forgetfulness of the world, from wholehearted love and service of God.

Shortly after Easter in one of his letters to the bishops and superiors he raised the question of postwar planning for the chaplains:

Plan and set up with some seminary a working agreement to provide
for the mental and perhaps spiritual revivification of Catholic chaplains after this is over. For periods of perhaps a month to one year they
should be allowed to go back and check up on themselves, their
rubrics, English, Canon Law, etc. even points of morals and dogma,
perhaps. I know I'll need it more than anyone else. The Church would
reap tremendous fruits. The chaplains would be free to follow the
seminary routine if they cared to, to attend lectures and classes, and
plug up the weak spots in their sacerdotal armor.

In Letter No. 37 the Bishop included a model letter prepared by
a soldier to be sent to his home in case of his death. The last paragraphs of the circular were words of inspiration from the former
prefect of religion.

We are very mindful of the perils under which so many of our chaplains are laboring at any given moment. Your constant assurances that
you are offering the Mass requested each month for the intention of
the Military Ordinariate (Masses often said under the most harrowing
conditions)—these assurances make us certain that the great blessings of
God are attending your work, and that a vast harvest of souls is in the
making. You are not simply bemoaning the fact that so many of our
men have strayed, so many have grown up without instruction; you are
recognizing these men as your own responsibility now, and you are
doing something to acquit yourself of that responsibility before God.
You should know that the lion's share of the benefit of those Masses
is applied to those who are in the greatest danger, whether spiritual
or corporal; to the intercessory power of those masses we may well
attribute many of the miracles of grace that are happening, every day.
More than 9,000,000 Holy Communions were reported last year (a
gain of almost 200% over the previous year), and Holy Communions
are mounting up again this year. If you have made of the war a campaign of devotion to the Holy Eucharist, you have lent your hand to
God's work of bringing great good out of great evil.

                                                    God bless you!

Although there are paragraphs in letters and speeches of Bishop
O'Hara that indicate he knew well some of the darker pages of
service life and the misconduct of members of the service, he seldom mentioned these factors. When pressed by a chaplain in New
Guinea about the optimistic reporting of religion in the services,
he answered in a letter of April 19, 1944:

Don't worry too much about the rosy picture of religion in the Army
published in the newspapers. After all the various items published are

true. When we avoid painting a pessimistic picture it is because we feel that more harm than good will come of it.

If the chaplains will send us the results of a survey along the lines suggested in the latest circular letter, we will have a realistic picture to present for the benefit of the priests of the United States who have the problem to handle—first to the chaplains and men, and then to the priests back home and their parishes.[86]

The suggested survey had very realistic points for investigation.

To a lady journalist who was trying to estimate the number of Catholics in the service he wrote on March 2, 1944:

I am sorry that Catholic papers are publishing wild guesses about the religious complexion of the armed forces. No facts are available. The stories are based on calculations made three years ago by an unreliable statistician in the Office of the Chief of Chaplains. I questioned the figures at the time and demonstrated that the method used was faulty.

The situation changes from day to day with the draft. The sources of the data should be available after the war, since the religion of the men is now entered on the service record in the Army and the medical record in the Navy. Perhaps the government will tabulate and publish the figures; I do not know.

I have found your own tabulations very interesting, and an indication of the trend of the times and the growth of the birth control movement.[87]

To another young lady who asked his advice about getting married before her fiance went into the Army he wrote on March 20, 1944:

These are not normal times, however. If both of you by prayer decide you can stand a better chance of saving one another's souls by marriage, there is a better chance of success than is usual when separation follows marriage. But make the decision, both of you, on the question of eternal salvation. God bless you.[88]

To Father Edward Stanford, O.S.A., who had written in opposition to the proposed bill to enable servicemen to go to college, the Bishop wrote his feelings about the secular education that would probably be provided:

I don't know much you can say about it in a speech but the war has certainly shown up the secular colleges. The paganism of many officers, especially in the lower ranks, has completely disgusted many of the G.I.'s. I am sure you must have heard some bitter comments from among your chaplains and graduates.[89]

To those who had occasions to talk with Bishop O'Hara he gave

the impression of one having in mind a grand plan. That plan
was apparently the maintenance of religious life among the Catholic men and women in the services. Actually his chaplains were
in the hands of the military, and often he had only an inkling of
their location. He had their reports and the occasional letters that
he tried so far as possible to answer. But there was also a growing problem in caring for the troops who had not yet been sent
overseas. This problem he reported to the bishops in a letter of
June 24:

The situation forecast in our Circular Letter of last March to the
Bishops and Religious Superiors has finally reached us. Requisitions
from overseas are daily stripping military installations in the United
States of *all* Catholic chaplains.

One Bishop who has several hundred thousands of troops in his
diocese has just written: "I wonder if it would do any good if someone
could approach the Bishops and tell them the 'inside story' of the
dearth of Catholic chaplains. The situation is desperate, *really desperate*. Why don't our Bishops make use of the faculty to have their
priests say three Masses on Sundays? They can easily obtain this from
the Apostolic Delegate. This would release two thousand priests at
once for military service, and God knows they are desperately needed."

The Bishop said he could use the 2,000, but he was asking for
only 400 now. The number of commissioned Catholic chaplains
was 2,820 with 29 applicants in process and 1,258 auxiliary chaplains. Replacements for those who had died or retired were 132,
309 auxiliary chaplains had been transferred, and 400 volunteers
had been rejected on medical grounds. He added that to the chaplains' honor roll he had to add the names of three more dead.

Much of the accomplishments of Bishop O'Hara could not be
measured. He was the executive officer of a far-flung organization
whose brilliance in memory and accuracy in detail caused the
organization to function. Essentially Bishop O'Hara's communications were spiritual and confidential, much like that of the
prefect of religion of earlier days. The travels by air, train, and
bus that he made within the country and the adjacent areas were
not spectacular in themselves, although some of the field Masses in
the first years where secrecy was not important were very dramatic.
Yet the traveling from one end of the country to the other at top
speed was deadly. The golden worth of the Bishop's services was
his tireless efforts to keep in close touch with the chaplains. One
word that the local commandant was interfering in the chaplain's
work would send the Bishop to Washington in the chaplain's
defense, by mail, telephone, or in person. His circular letters

helped the isolated chaplains, and when he could, he sent one of those handwritten notes dashed off at night by the dozens.

The Bishop watched the monthly reports, and was happy when the number of Holy Communions and attendance at other spiritual services multiplied. He was saddened by occasional failures. His comments then and during the first years after the war indicated that he felt that there was a general increase of Catholic religious life in the men in the services, particularly because the chaplains had come in contact with so many men who had never talked with a priest since childhood, if then. He expected a renewal of Catholicism in the United States to show itself after the war. Much of this hope was based on the monthly reports, but some also came from the thousands of letters he exchanged with the chaplains.

Only a few of these letters[90] can be quoted—sometimes the greatest experience went unrecorded because the chaplain lacked the gift of composition. One letter was from a fellow Holy Cross priest, Father Joseph Barry:

Now I'll tell you the last story and go to bed. The officer on the pool table just gave me a dirty look. As near as I can make out he wants to go to sleep. This afternoon I said Mass atop one of the snow-covered mountains over which our troops so ably fought. In my congregation were Italians (mule-packers), French lads, British officers and American cliff dwellers. Well, you should have heard my instruction on the privilege of going to Communion and receiving general absolution. Believe it or not I had no trouble with my English. OK. I even got by in French. But the sons of sunny Italy were hard to convince until I finally said Papa dice, papa dice. O.K. as long as Papa speaks it must be o.k. I'll bet they had quite a bull session when they returned to their duck holes. Fox holes are out during the rainy season.

. . . Thanks for your nice Christmas message. Note the Protestant influence—fine message. I'm sorry.

Father William Lundy wrote:

. . . It's quiet now, the calm before the storm. Occasionally you hear a burst of fire. The 4th of July has just set in, the American children at home are probably getting their fireworks lined up. The American boys over here have also their fireworks. Those are the real things, the ones that whistle over your head. They give you the creeps. They are starting to go off now. You are just wondering where they are going to land. Sleep is out of the question. I spent yesterday and today out at the front lines with the boys. I came back spiritually happy. Thank God for His wonderful graces. I carried the Blessed Sacrament with me. I was able to hear their confessions and give them Communion right in their fox-holes. I told my assistant and some of the first-aid men how to dispose of the B. Sacrament, just in case I did not return. The fact that the boys were able to receive at the front lines was deeply appreciated by the boys. Many of them cried with joy. Our Lord seemed to direct me to the lost sheep. The result was that lots of them came back and they are out there fortified with the sacraments of confession and Holy Communion.

A fellow priest, Father Gregory Kennedy, told of the death of Chaplain Joseph Gilmore:

Father was fearless in the performance of his duties. . . . The night before his death the medical installation was bombed and strafed about eleven o'clock. Father was with the patients in the admission tent, and no one was injured. Father's sleeping tent had been strafed and bullets had gone through his cot and pillow. Later Father Leo Crowley visited Father Gilmore. Father had just retired about One A.M. when he was called to see a wounded soldier. The German bombers came in again, dropped 500 lb. bombs and strafed. The bombs hit the tent in which Father was anointing a soldier. A number of the soldiers were killed and Father himself was killed instantly by concussion, the body unmarked except a slight bruise on one cheek of the face. The colonel tried to locate a priest but it was not until three hours later that I was able to get there. Father's Catholic soldiers whispered the act of contrition and ejaculations in his ear, and prayed by him for some time after his death. When I arrived I recited the prayers of the ritual over the body. . . .

One postscript from the front must have given pleasure to the Bishop:

P.S. Your circulars reach here, most of them do I think, they are delayed. They mean an awful lot to us & your helping hints are most appreciated. Your words of encouragement are certainly helpful—those inspirational notes a delight. Thanks for everything & I shall always do my best for the boys & the priesthood. Might I suggest the Air Mail service for your letter overseas, the regular service is desperately slow & most uncertain. God bless you S.W.K [ane].

The frankness of some of the letters, such as that from Father Thomas Gilden, C.SS.R., must have pleased the Bishop, who liked manly directness.

I have prayed in my young life—but certainly never more fervently & more often than since we hit the enemy lines.
The men have been wonderful. Anybody that could hear their remarks—such as I never thought I would pray like that—I never felt God's presence as now—or saw them with rosaries & medals around their necks—must believe that our boys are coming near to God. One Prot. fellow had a medal around his neck. A buddy gave it to him. All

Eva, Patrick, and John F. O'Hara as children in Peru, Indiana.

John F. O'Hara as an undergraduate student at Notre Dame.

Will Rogers and President John F. O'Hara, C.S.C., at the Football Banquet, January 15, 1935.

At the Notre Dame-Illinois football game at Champaign in 1937; left to right: Dr. A. C. Willard, president of the University of Illinois; Governor Henry Horner of Illinois; Rev. John A. O'Brien, head of the Illinois Newman Club; and Rev. John F. O'Hara, C.S.C., president of the University of Notre Dame.

*Bishop O'Hara and his mother after his appoint-
ment as bishop of the Military Ordinariate.*

Bishop O'Hara at his installation as bishop of Buffalo, May 8, 1945.

Cardinal-elect O'Hara being received by Pope John XXIII.

Cardinal O'Hara with Bishop J. Carroll McCormick and Cardinal Montini in the Misericordia Hospital in Philadelphia.

appreciated prayer at the battalion aid station—all had a thank you, Father.

One of the most prized aspects of the correspondence from the Southwest Pacific was the account of the contact of the troops with mission Catholicism. Father A. T. Dielkemper, active in American missions, reported:

Being a missionary, I was most anxious to meet the native Christians of these islands, the Admiralties (this is no longer considered a military secret). The first impression of their Catholicity will always remain with me. The Missionaries may rightfully be proud of their achievement. It is another jewel in the glorious missionary history of the Church, one that today is added to their crown of suffering. When the natives realized through my mixture of language that the man in the jungle fatigues was a Catholic priest, they beamed with joy. Everyone was called out of the huts to shake hands with the paters [*sic*]. A baptism preceded Mass. The recitation of their prayers, their simple devotion inspired my men to say it was the most beautiful and touching they had ever participated in. All of those who could received the Bread of the angels. Within the walls of a hut Christ had returned to his children. In my second Mass the whole congregation responded in Latin. On another island they sang a *missa cantata*. May their faith never change.

The Bishop received a copy of a letter of the 34th Engineers to their general about their chaplain. Among other compliments they said:

Captain Boggins is the only Catholic chaplain in the large area. He regularly visits us and Catholics and Protestants look forward to seeing him. His cheerful smile, utter disregard for personal safety, and his simple straight talks make us realize what this war means. To show you how he cares for our safety he always shows visitors where slit trenches are before he begins his services and he never forgets to stress the need of following all directions for health and discipline issued by the authorities. We don't think any Army officer has done more to help you leaders to build our Army. Well, for us a group of Protestants to sing the praises of a Catholic priest shows what we think of this cheerful, fearless man of God.

Another cheerful letter from Father Bernard A. Burns was typical of thousands, despite its strictly personal tone:

I exchanged a suite of rooms with a bathroom containing a private shower (always hot water) for dust and flies and a helmet bath with cold, hard water. But I haven't a single regret. I do very little here, God knows; but I wonder what these "boys" would do without us! Never in the twelve years I have been a priest have I experienced such consoling work. I do not mean to "brag." Life like this makes a priest humble. He becomes humble with the realization that, in spite of himself, he does good. There are many obstacles to doing my work as I could have done it back at Holy Name Cathedral in Chicago. There are times when I know that I am not reaching all I should. But I hope that because there are so many priests away from the comforts of their home dioceses, living without the privacy we all long for among the soldiers, that some good will come of this horrible war. I never knew that grown men could be such boys away from home and I never realized how proudly the priest should bear the title "Father" until I got in. There should be hundreds more priests in the army. If you could only see the men who have been in these places without a priest for some time when one of us comes into their camp!

One of the early deaths among the chaplains that the Bishop seemed to feel quite keenly was that of an auxiliary chaplain in Africa, Father Regis Barrett, O.S.B. In the files of the Bishop's mail is a letter of one soldier to another about this heroic man:

Father Barrett as I think I have previously told you in other letters was a great character, to him belongs the honor of establishing the first American Catholic Church in this dark continent—a fact of which he was justly proud. He served in the last war and held the rank of major, and during the last war he personally established a college for Catholic Army Chaplains. He also served as a chaplain several years ago in Leavenworth Penitentiary, and from his experiences in the pen and in the Army, what he doesn't know about human nature and its failings, isn't worth knowing. I think I sent you a picture recently showing him at the ground breaking services for his church over here, a task at which he exerted every ounce of his mind and body. He had a jeep assigned to him and every day you could see him around the camp, out in the hangars talking to the fellows at work, down in the hospitals visiting and cheering up the sick, and long into the night, the lights of his rectory would be burning as he soothed the troubled minds of the fellows who went down there to talk with him regarding their wives and their families back home. And no one left his little study without having been consoled and having instilled in them the spirit and intense desire to carry on. I know this personally because when I received the news from you about Mom passing on I was beside myself, distracted in mind, and grief laden until I didn't know whether I was coming or going. But the minutes I spent with him gave me that quietness of the mind and the spiritual consolation that I was so much in need of at the time, and as I left his study and walked down the dark road back to the barracks I felt instilled with such a quietness of spirit that I hadn't felt for some time.

The war was beginning to take its toll in battles. Circular Letter No. 38, August 1, 1944, opened with an account of the loss of five chaplains: Fathers Joseph Gilmore; Thomas J. Barrett; Ignatius Maternowski, a paratrooper who was shot when captured; Philip Edelen, from wounds; and Dominic Ternan, shot while attending wounded soldiers.

The letters from the front give brief glimpses of these stories. Father Joseph A. Nee wrote on June 27:

Father Philip B. Edelen, Diocese of Raleigh, North Carolina, one of the Catholic Chaplains of our division was killed in action in the vicinity of Trevieres, France on the night of June 9, 1944. A shell exploded very close to him. He never recovered consciousness. Death came within a few hours. One of our priests gave him Conditional Absolution and Extreme Unction.

Father John J. Gallagher wrote on July 5:

I made a short trip and located Father Delaura this week. He is in great spirits and excellent health and is doing a marvelous job. I also had the good fortune to be present, by sheer accident, at an impromptu ceremony at which Father Kelly of the Hartford Diocese was awarded the Silver Star. I happened to be visiting a hospital where he is recovering from some slight wounds and his Colonel came to make the award. Judging from the story of his 'gallantry in action,' he richly deserved the recognition.

Father Stephen P. Kenny wrote his sorrowful story:

Father Bonner met his death about two fifteen on the morning of July 29th, as a result of an enemy air attack. Enemy planes attacked the unit area with anti-personnel bombs and strafing machine gun fire. Hearing the wounded call for help, Father Bonner left the slit trench and had crawled only a short distance in the direction from which the voice sounded when he was struck by a machine gun bullet. The bullet struck him in the left side and passed thru his body. Death was instantaneous. . . . Father Bonner was in every respect a Christlike priest. He spent his time in the Replacement Battalion in unremitting care for souls. Troops are constantly passing through the Battalion and Father was always on hand to see the men as they arrived and as they left. If at all possible he contacted every Catholic man to make sure he had been to confession. . . .

Father Clarence Ford, O.F.M., spoke of his fellow chaplains:

. . . I was the first American chaplain to have a Mass in a great Galic [*sic*] shrine. On this particular day I ran into a fellow friar, Francis Sullivan, just as I was going up for Mass. We had not seen each other since we left Bona's. You can imagine the panning and the ribbing he gave me. While we were shaking hands we ran into a former student, Zabowski. Zaboo came up to Mass with me because Sully had to get back to his unit. Sully found Father Dominic Tiernan's [*sic*] grave

and had enuf time to celebrate Mass at the grave. I had just finished
my third Mass for the repose of his soul. Dominic was a grand person
and I know what he must have gone thru. Many a time I rode the
ambulance between my own Aid Station and the Collecting Station.
I usually find all my Catholics at the Collecting Station and those
whom I miss are picked up by Father Purcell who works out of the
clearing station. We have been able to anoint quite a few lads with
this team work. Frs. Mullens, Kieran, and Hennessy work this same
way with Fr. Prudell. All these peres are doing a grand job. . . .

The Bishop's burdens were not lightened, although he did not
travel as much as earlier in the war. On September 3 he was again
the host of a Latin American President at St. Patrick's Cathedral,
this time President-elect Ramon Grau Martin of Cuba. One of
his friends, Thomas E. Murray, felt worried about the Bishop's
health. He wrote on September 22:

As usual nothing seems difficult or burdensome to you and this is
just another example of your ability to come nearest to perpetual
motion than anyone I know. However, if I may be permitted to say
so, a little more interest and attention to your health is in order. You
owe it to the great cause you serve so well to take time out more
frequently, to catch your second wind.[91]

But the Bishop answered him: "As Father Burns used to say, 'One
worry pushes out another,' and few worries ever last long enough
to cost me any sleep." There are no medical reports to contradict
his claim, but certainly the sinuses and the arthritic limbs that
caused trouble at Notre Dame could hardly have benefited by the
constant action either in the office or in travel. There was sincerity in his praise for the travels of Archbishop Spellman in the
circular letter of October 1 and in his report to the annual meeting of the bishops and his subsequent letter to the bishops and
superiors. He was able to talk of the large number of Communions among the servicemen while asking for chaplains for units
that did not have them.

While expressing poignantly in his Christmas letter of 1944 the
meaning of Christmas in wartime, he listed the new losses in chaplains and answered some criticisms about the fewness of chaplains
at the front in the Normandy invasion:

A field hospital is composed of three units, which may operate as
three separate units or as a whole unit. Generally they operate as two
units, sometimes as three, with a mile or two between the units. To
have complete coverage, it would mean two or three priests with each
field hospital, and a field hospital is rated three hundred beds. Obviously, it is impossible to have so many chaplains for such small units.

In the beginning of hostilities, a few days after the landings, this headquarters sent four Catholic chaplains on detached service with the First Army to work with these hospitals and collecting companies on the beaches. Unfortunately when they arrived, they were sent to other places. . . .

While he tried to cheer the chaplains at Christmastime, the Bishop recognized the weariness of their toil:

Weariness in soul and body becomes more evident the longer the war drags on. The quickening tempo of war does away with the staleness of which so many chaplains complained when life in posts became monotonous; but the pace of war accelerates fatigue.

Those who are weary need retreats and paradoxically, this relaxation, spiritual, and physical, is least possible when most needed.

The Divine Office, the visits to the Blessed Sacrament, the companionship of fellow priests help to relieve fatigue. Again, even these may be impossible. When nothing else serves, you still have your Mass and Rosary. Cling to these as your best chance to close out the world for brief intervals. Most of our chaplains are now either in combat or on the verge of combat. We are deeply sensitive of their serious needs, and our intercession for them is quickened accordingly.

But the Bishop also had some personal worries. On December 14 the O'Hara family learned that James O'Hara, who was serving with General Patton in the Battle of the Bulge, had been wounded on November 28, and at the same time the Bishop was deeply concerned with the health of his mother. She had had another attack of pneumonia, and early in December fell and broke her hip. The Bishop hurried to her bedside, but the complications of these sicknesses and her age were too much. She died Thursday, December 14, and was buried Saturday, December 16. The Bishop said a pontifical Mass, Bishop Ritter preached the funeral sermon, and Archbishop Spellman was present in the sanctuary and conducted the final services at the grave in Holy Cross Cemetery. As the Bishop wrote in answer to the letters of condolence, his mother had simply "gone home to God." On December 19 he assisted at the installation of Archbishop Ritter as the first archbishop of Indianapolis and the next day attended the installation of Bishop Ready in Columbus.

When he returned to New York after the Christmas holidays, he had to face renewed demands from the military for more chaplains. In his letter to the bishops and superiors of January 15 he said that the Supreme Command in the European Theatre had sent a chaplain back to insist on the immediate fulfillment of the requisitions for chaplains:

This chaplain paints a black picture. Many of our fine young priests are exhausted by their long work at the front, but they cannot be relieved because there is no one to take their places. More than a hundred hospitals have been left without priests because there are none who are not already assigned. Evacuation hospitals are the ones most lacking in chaplains, and the death rate is highest in these.

To strengthen his appeal he quoted a letter from a lieutenant on a ship:

In these trying days we need the teachings of our priests more than ever. We need them to guide us; we need them to go to when our hearts are broken, because we've been amiss without God; because we've been away from our wives, from our families too long. Don't you see, Father, we are like babes in the wilderness. The other faiths have their devotions, but we Catholics are alone with ourselves. We are weak, my dear Bishop; but here anything amuses us. Morals? "Some relaxation is necessary," is their reply.

The Bishop suffered in spirit with his chaplains. There is a kind of grim humor in his letter of February 10, 1945, in which he told the chaplains that they could hardly do more penance than they were now doing:

What all of us can do is quicken our *spirit* of penance. War is always wasteful but its most cruel waste is the suffering and shedding of blood that is not supernaturalized. What a chalice of propitiation would be offered if all the men in the armies were to offer their sufferings and their wounds and their lives in union with the sacrifice of our Divine Redeemer! But the world is cold and hearts are of stone and the multitude knows not God.

Not all sacrifice is wasted, however. Your efforts to keep your men in the love of God are bearing fruit and among the victims every day there are very very many who have won the Beatific Vision by their steadfast adherence to God's law and their zeal to spread His kingdom on earth.

His final Circular, whether he knew or not is not clear, was the Easter greeting of March 15, 1945. Holy Thursday, he said, is the priests' special holiday, but only one of the newly ordained apostles was beneath the cross a few hours later on the first Good Friday. He mentioned that every day he heard of priests who had suffered because they stood for the rights of their men and the rights of religion. They should take joy in their persecution so long as their hearts were right with God:

"Qui se existimat stare videt ne cadat." Sixty of our chaplains died since the enlargement of our armed forces began. Their lives were given cheerfully for their men, for not one of them came to service except of his own free will. "Videat ne cadat," was St. Paul's warning. Our chaplains have undertaken stupendous sacrifices. What folly it would be for them to undermine such sacrifices with any seeking of worldly reward or pleasures. "Tentatio vos non apprehendat nisi humana."

A priest is priestly as long as he is a man of prayer. Let your Holy Thursday resolution be never to neglect prayer, never to set aside the Divine Office if it can be fulfilled. Let prayer be the first order of every day, the only immutable in the life of the priest. Then it will be said of you, "Cujus finem interitus."

On March 10, the Apostolic Delegate announced that Bishop O'Hara had been transferred to the see of Buffalo to succeed Bishop John Duffy, who had died September 27, 1944. Although his authority there began immediately, he did not take over the see officially until May 8. On April 2 he sent his last letter as delegate, thanking the bishops and superiors for their cooperation. "Our Catholic men in the service," he said, "have participated in the grandest mission the world has ever known, and they have been led by a magnificent force of chaplains." And he added from the words of the Vicar Apostolic of Sweden about the airmen there during the war his words of praise for the "practical Catholicity of the American Service Man."

His final Circular letter was a joint one with Bishop McCarty in which he told the chaplains it was hard "to leave the fascinating work of the Military Ordinariate." He added:

"Ipsam sequens non devias." What we can do in parting is share with you a motto which has meant much to you and your men. Can any chaplain say that the men who correspond with the graces he offered them have failed to grow in devotion to Our Lady? Is it possible that the millions of rosaries supplied the men have been fruitless of grace? The years will show how devotion to Our Lady on the part of the future head of a Catholic family will bear fruits of conjugal fidelity and filial devotion that will mean a more vigorous Catholic Church and a more sound and loyal America than we have had in the past. Your men are a reflection of your devotion: If you follow Our Blessed Lady, so will your men.

After speaking sorrowfully of the most recent deaths, he warned the men that they would soon meet the problems of peace. He said there would be no sudden exit from the services, and they should be ready for the temptations of peacetime for enlisted men. He added a special word of gratitude to the chaplains' assistants who had served during his episcopate. He must have been thinking of his own assistants in the Military Ordinariate—especially the Holy Cross men, Father Harry Stegman, C.S.C., Father Louis Thornton, C.S.C., and Father Thomas Brennan, C.S.C.—who would not follow him to Buffalo—when he thanked the superior general, Father Albert Cousineau, for his congratulations. He added:

It is not easy to leave Archbishop Spellman and the work of the Military Ordinariate. It is even difficult to be cut off entirely from the community, as I will be in the new situation. However, there is a job to be done, and I am grateful for the prayers that will assist me.[92]

On April 27 Bishop O'Hara spoke at a Mass for Poland in St. Patrick's Cathedral, and he was undoubtedly conscious that he would have many sons of Poland in his new diocese. He took for his text the story of Nathan's reproach to David for his sin and Nathan's comparing David to the rich man who had killed the sheep of his poor neighbor. The comparison to Russia and her neighbor, Poland, was obvious. "We plead," he said, "yes for restoration of Free, Christian, Poland, but always with complete resignation to the Holy Will of God. . . ."

On May 6 Bishop O'Hara said a pontifical Mass of farewell in St. Patrick's Cathedral in New York with Archbishop Spellman presiding and preaching. The Archbishop's tribute to the departing prelate was threefold, referring to the three important works of the Bishop in his adult life:

Bishop O'Hara—Priest and Scholar
Father O'Hara of Notre Dame

Truth and wisdom were co-stars in whose life you walked. You lived and taught the truth with courage, knowing that "like the sun truth is sometimes obscured, but like the sun only for a time." You formed men of character who would be the conscience of the society to which they belonged, citizens of the United States, men of Catholic life and action. You taught men knowledge of God and knowledge of God's most noble creature, man. You taught men to know his neighbor, to love him, to help him, and you taught men to know his handmaids, the arts and sciences.

Bishop O'Hara—Warrior of God

As Military Delegate of the Armed Forces of the United States you were the guide and inspiration of our priests in the Chaplains' Corps and of Catholic men and women in the various services. Your friendship with them, your personal association, your letters and above all, your example taught them that the sacrifice of self is the test of love and complete sacrifice is perfect love. The courage of Christ went forth to Chaplains through your inspiration and your share in their greatness and goodness.

Bishop O'Hara—Shepherd

Of Shepherds it can be said, "The bravest are the most tender, the loving are the most daring." You, Bishop O'Hara, are that kind of shepherd. You will rule by serving. To your flock you will give devotion. For your sheep, if necessary, you will lay down your life like the Master as in full heart and gallant soul you now offer it at the word of Christ's Vicar, Our Holy Father, to the flock of Buffalo.

In his brief reply Bishop O'Hara thanked everyone, and spoke feelingly of the men in the service. He feared the evils of the peace but voiced also his confidence in the men in the service.[93]

SEVEN

Bishop of Buffalo

WHEN BISHOP O'HARA WAS TRANSFERRED to Buffalo, the leave-taking at the Military Ordinariate included few of the pangs that had accompanied his separation from Notre Dame. In a sense the Bishop was returning to his position as a chief administrator, although by that very fact, as he told his superior general, he was really moving farther away from Notre Dame. But there is no diary or letters telling his actual feelings when he arrived at the Buffalo station on May 7.

He had tried to simplify his reception. When the clergy had proposed buying him a limousine, he wrote to Bishop Burke on March 26:

> With regard to the automobile, I want to repeat that it should not be a limousine. It is handy to have a glass partition since that gives you an opportunity to get some work done on a trip, but I could never feel comfortable in a limousine, and I wouldn't know how to act in one. The simpler the car the better; and if there isn't a small car with a partition, then let it be a small car without one.[1]

Bernie Bird, a Buffalo Notre Dame alumnus, and other Buffalo Catholics had called on him in New York after the announcement of his election to offer their services, but he had insisted that there be no public reception for him. Nevertheless there were hundreds at the railway terminal when he arrived, so much so that he quipped: "As I look around it makes me think of a Notre Dame-Army game."[2]

The next day the installation took place in the cold, marble cathedral—called the New Cathedral as distinguished from the Old Cathedral of St. Joseph—in the presence of twenty-eight bishops and eight archbishops, including Archbishop Spellman, who had accompanied him and was the installing prelate.[3] In the ceremony Archbishop Spellman repeated the thought from his farewell of the previous Sunday:

Fortunate indeed are you priests and people, for you will find him a merciful shepherd and a prudent prophet, a noble priest gifted by nature with keen intelligence, virile charity and a gracious personality. You will learn to love him as he leads and to revere him as he serves you.[4]

Father Luke F. Sharkey of Saint Vincent's Church spoke for the priests of the diocese and related how the diocese had been so grieved by the loss of Bishop Duffy, who had been such a capable pastor, and how they had feared that they would not get a comparable successor. Then he added: "God had sent us a Bishop who is genuinely stamped with the seal of greatness that our tender regrets over the loss of Bishop Duffy are happily merged with the joy that our good fortune brings us."[5]

In his reply Bishop O'Hara returned to his old dichotomy of the service or nonservice of God. He took for his text Our Lord's warning in the Sermon on the Mount that "No man can serve two masters."

If we can adopt God's point of view the task becomes simple. . . . No, material things are not condemned in the Sermon on the Mount— or anywhere. They are good gifts of God. What is condemned is solicitude that makes this world an end in itself instead of a means to heaven. It is "solicitude" for material things that disturbs the balance of justice and creates family dissensions, neighborhood quarrels, civic strife and wars between nations.

Afterwards he turned to his traditional interests, characteristic of his zeal:

God has blessed the Catholics of Buffalo with zeal for Catholic education and for frequent and daily Holy Communion. Therein you have the wellspring of Catholic life and the fountainhead of good citizenship. The great lesson the Catholic schools teach us is the total necessity of Sanctifying Grace; the schools succeed when the child— and later the man—feels uneasy in sin, feels lost when he is out of favor with God. Confession restores the soul to grace and peace; frequent Holy Communion nourishes and sustains Sanctifying Grace.[6]

The next day in an interview he added a tribute to his flock.

. . . the people of Buffalo are good people and their good, sound home training is reflected in the faces of the thousands of children I have seen. Buffalo is a good example of what it means to live in peace and harmony. . . .[7]

Bishop O'Hara had begun the administration of one of the largest and most important dioceses in the country. It included the New York counties of Erie, Niagara, Genesee, Orleans, Chatauqua, Wyoming, Cattaraugus, and Allegheny. Of its approximate population of 1,300,000, Catholics were estimated to number 500,000.[8] Bishop O'Hara's predecessors in the see had all been men of distinction. The first two had been members of the Congregation of the Mission, John Timon (1847–1867) and Stephen V. Ryan (1868–1896). Their successors were James E. Quigley (1897–1903), later Archbishop of Chicago; Charles H. Colton (1903–1915); Dennis Dougherty (1915–1918), later Cardinal Archbishop of Philadelphia; William Turner (1919–1936); and John A. Duffy (1937–1944).

Bishop O'Hara's immediate predecessor, who had also been Bishop of Syracuse from 1933–1937, had been suggested prominently as a successor to Cardinal Hayes in the Archdiocese of New York. He had been a teacher at Seton Hall College and Immaculate Conception Seminary in New Jersey before his election to the see of Syracuse. In the Diocese of Buffalo he had inherited great debts, such as were common in many similar dioceses that had engaged in extensive building in the years before the Depression. The editor of the diocesan weekly, the *Union and Echo,* said of Bishop Duffy on his arrival: "Many problems faced Buffalo's new Bishop as he began his duties. The nation was just emerging from the depression years and many parishes were in an unhealthy financial condition. With the cooperation of priests and people a start was made in reducing the indebtedness and in cutting down the interest rate. With the improvement in business in general some parishes have been able to pay as much as $100,000 of their debt in a single year."[9]

Bishop Burke, the auxiliary bishop, in his statement on the occasion of Bishop Duffy's death, September 28, 1944 paid a similar tribute to the executive ability of Bishop Duffy:

His brilliant, analytical mind, tempered by years of teaching, struck quickly and truly to the core of questions that often baffled the efforts of less gifted observers.

Experts eagerly acclaimed his masterly direction of the financial affairs of parishes, burdened with what seemed an impossible problem of indebtedness. In the few years of his episcopate the debts of the diocese have been reduced by more than $2,000,000. Comprehensive in his love for all the members of his flock, he instituted the Missionary Apostolate where young priests are initiated into the exacting work of the priesthood and bring the truths and consolations of religion to the most remote portions of the diocese. . . .[10]

The Bishop went on to speak of the other apostolic works of Bishop Duffy, but most of these had been waiting for the extinction of the debts and the end of the war to attain full growth.

The living conditions of the Catholics of Buffalo had improved greatly in the three decades before Bishop O'Hara's appointment. The congressional investigation of the condition of immigrants in cities in 1910 had recognized five groups of unfavorable housing situations among the immigrants in the Buffalo area: the South Italian, the Polish, the Russian Hebrew, the German, and the Syrian.[11] In the intervening years not only had these very bad areas been cleaned up but many of these peoples had moved to better surroundings and achieved better living conditions. Just prior to the arrival of Bishop O'Hara the industrial area centered around Buffalo had enjoyed unusual prosperity because of the concentration of defense industries near the lake port. These economic factors, plus the advantages of a whole generation in this country, particularly a generation of American education, had softened and nearly erased the lines that formerly existed between these foreign language communities. There were still foreign language churches in considerable number in which sermons were given and confessions heard in European languages, but the enclaves had begun to disappear, and Buffalo as a Catholic diocese could be said to have the unity and prosperity of a rising Catholic population. There were few Catholics of great wealth, chiefly a few families that had been for several generations in industry, such as brewing or transportation. The prosperity of the ordinary Catholic family of the area came from working in well-paying industries or in the stores and service operations that catered to this prosperous worker group. The people no longer looked back to any foreign nationalism that had raised barriers between Catholics in the nineteenth century but forward to full American citizenship in a prospering country.

To carry on the Catholic portion of this social advancement Bishop Turner had established the Annual Charities Appeal in 1924. Bishop Duffy added to the charitable works supported by this drive the Missionary Apostolate to the neglected areas of the diocese and had begun to lay aside money for the repair of churches that could not be refurbished in wartime. In 1942 Bishop

Duffy had also set up a Youth Council and had begun to promote school athletic associations to provide recreation for the
youths of the diocese. He had also established the Bishop's Committee for Christian Home and Family to promote Catholic
family life and to combat propaganda for birth control and other
un-Catholic social theories, and the Confraternity of Christian
Doctrine to look after the Christian training of the thousands of
Catholic children who were not attending Catholic schools. For
those attending non-Catholic colleges he had fostered Newman
Clubs. In 1938, besides holding the first diocesan synod, Bishop
Duffy had established a school of Catholic Action for the clergy
and a Catholic Labor College for the laity, and encouraged such
activities as a Catholic Evidence Guild, a Catholic Speakers'
Bureau, a Pamphlet Society, and a Press Bureau.[12] Bishop O'Hara
had studied the summaries of these activities in the *Catholic
Directory* and in all available sources before taking his train to
Buffalo.

In stepping from the Military Ordinariate into the see of Buffalo the Bishop had exchanged a far-flung irregular organization
for a well-organized and strongly Catholic diocesan community.
Bishop Burke, the administrator, turned over to him a functioning chancery office, with a vicar general, a chancellor and assistants, consultors, districts, parishes, schools, religious communities,
colleges, and convents. The diocesan newspaper claimed for the
diocese 442 secular and 282 religious priests, 237 parishes with
resident pastors, 26 stations or missions, and 166 chapels in religious institutions with 29 resident chaplains. In the diocese were
2,640 religious women and 44 religious brothers. There were 4
colleges, 1 university, 3 diocesan seminaries and other seminaries
of religious communities, and 40,000 students in parochial schools
and academies. The paper did not mention the other 50,000 Catholic children attending the public schools. The diocesan editor
gave his own estimate of Bishop O'Hara's prospects:

Buffalo is a city possessed of many features to make it one of the
outstanding dioceses in the country. It is well organized, the Catholic
people are thrifty and cooperative and their clubs and organizations
are teeming with life and friendly spirit. Then, too, Buffalo always
responds to appeals for charitable and mission prospects in a big way.

All things considered, the combination of a live progressive people
and an experienced and active Bishop, such as Bishop O'Hara is,
argues well for the happiness and well being of our Church and city.[13]

These hopes were augmented by the news from Europe that at
least the European phase of the great conflict had been concluded.

Bishop O'Hara was among strangers, since he did not bring with him a personal secretary from Holy Cross as he had at the Military Ordinariate. In the interim since his election to the see he had depended very much on Monsignor Leo Smith, the assistant chancellor, so much so that he suggested that Smith had lost patience with him by the time he arrived in Buffalo. But apparently the Monsignor had no such feelings, and in time the exchanges between these two men were very helpful to the Bishop as he began the organization of his staff. The Bishop announced that his vicar general was the genial and pastoral Bishop Joseph Burke, but the "grand old priest" of the diocese, Right Reverend John J. Nash, was made a second vicar general. Monsignor Edmund Britt, Bishop Duffy's chancellor, was reappointed, and Monsignor Smith was elevated to the vice chancellorship left vacant by the death of Father Raymond Curtin shortly before. Within a short time Monsignor Smith moved into the episcopal residence at 1035 Delaware Street, where he could be of greater assistance to the Bishop. The pastors, the deans, the other officials of the chancery and the heads of the various departments and diocesan organizations remained the same. The functions of most of these offices were decided by canon law. In the United States by custom the chancellor functions as a kind of secretary of state for the bishop, and most appointments and diocesan actions emanate from his office. Most of the other diocesan officials are the same in each diocese, and the day-by-day problems of finance, of repairs, of buildings, of marriage cases and dispensations, are carried on by them without any direct consultation with the bishop, unless there be some unusual circumstance. All these activities, however, come to bear the characteristics of a bishop's administration after he has been in office for a while and has chosen for each office the man who he thinks will best carry out his ideas.

Bishop O'Hara had announced his chief characteristics: he was interested chiefly in the promotion of Christian education and in the increase in the practice of frequent and daily Holy Communion. And as the former prefect of religion he was to manifest a constant interest in the care of youth. There was one other notable characteristic of the O'Hara regime in Buffalo, and that was informality. Any priest could call on him at any time he was home. Frequently he answered the door himself. His first letter to his family after they had gone home was that he was alone in the big house at 1035 Delaware, and to avoid that loneliness he occasionally went to visit the rector of the cathedral next door. Soon Monsignor Smith moved into the house with him. His infor-

mality was also noted in his meetings, whether it was the meeting
of the consultors, or the pastors of a district, or the members of
some board. When the meeting opened, the Bishop set them at
ease as quickly as possible, usually by passing around his favorite
cigarettes. Then he went directly to the subject at hand. Later
when he obtained a car and a chauffeur he went about the diocese
studying its physical problems, sometimes finding his pastors not
expecting a call. On one occasion the pastor was starting for the
golf course. He did not detain him except to point out a spot on
the roof of the church that needed immediate repair.

The first problem of the new Bishop was a pleasant one: the
celebration of the victory in Europe. Just before he died, Bishop
Duffy had announced a plan for celebrating the return of peace
by having all-day adoration of the Blessed Sacrament after the last
Mass on the day the peace was announced. Bishop O'Hara ordered
the same kind of thanksgiving service after the last Sunday Mass
on May 13, with prayers and Benediction in the evening. That
Sunday morning he attended the Mass for the city policemen at
the Old Cathedral and urged them to the practice of frequent
Communion. That evening he returned to New York to handle
some unfinished business at the Military Ordinariate on his way
to the consecration of Bishop Vincent Waters in Richmond on
May 15. He made the latter trip with Archbishop Spellman, with
whom he discussed the problems of his diocese as he then saw
them. On their way back Archbishop Spellman had arranged a
conference in Washington between Bishop O'Hara and Secretary
of the Navy Forrestal. The Bishop made no minutes of this
meeting, but he told his family of the conversation and indicated
that the topic was about peace and conscription and that the
Secretary had agreed with Bishop O'Hara in opposing peacetime
conscription.

On his return Bishop O'Hara sent a note of thanks to the Archbishop in which he acknowledged his indebtedness to him:

While I can never put on paper or express *viva voce* the gratitude
I feel for your countless acts of thoughtfulness, I do want to set down
for my own personal satisfaction, my thousand thanks for everything.

Although our first meeting came only a few years ago, spiritually
our tracks seem to have crossed many, many times in the past, and God
had often led us by widely divergent paths to the same ends. Since our
first meeting you have mounted favors on favors; I can never hope to
catch up, or to express the gratitude I feel.

My brothers and sisters have asked me to associate them with my
expression of thanks for all you did to give me a good introduction to

Buffalo, and I am most happy to carry out their wishes. They feel as I do, and their prayers are added to mine that God may bless and protect you, and may lighten the burdens you take on for the glory of God and the good of souls.

I was especially happy to have had such a good visit on the occasion of the Richmond-Washington trip. As I suspected, my return ticket was in my breviary; I enclose it now, as you may wish to give it to Bishop Ireton at the Washington meeting.

I plan to attend Bishop Connolly's Pontifical Mass on the way to Boston. I have had to cancel the trip to St. Paul, as Bishop Burke is not too well just now, and I am taking over all the appointments for the next two days.[14]

Bishop Burke was in the hospital and eventually went to the Mayo clinic for a check-up, and Bishop O'Hara took over his confirmations and other appointments. He also tried with the help of temporary secretaries to answer the deluge of mail, especially from the chaplains. He had insisted that all the chaplains receive an invitation to his installation in Buffalo, although obviously most of them could not attend. Many of the chaplains were touched by this thoughtfulness and sent in a letter of gratitude. Many of them were frank in expressing their regret at losing his guidance, but others merely expressed their pleasure at his promotion to a more important see. Lieutenant Commander John G. Larkin in his letter of May 21, 1945, summed up most of the letters when he said:

Because I have been one of the earlier chaplains to know you at the rise of the national emergency I have some small notion of the magnificent work you have accomplished. I am not too good at handing out blandishments, you know that, so I'll simply use the highest naval accolade and say, "Well done."[15]

He was also missed at the Military Ordinariate according to Bishop McCarty, who wrote on July 25:

I do not need to tell you that we miss you in this office and at the house. The vacuum created is still here, but everything is going along nicely, thank God. Father Thornton is doing excellent work on the reports and Father Miller has brought the baptismal and marriage records up to date, and is now working on the files of the chaplains from World War One.[16]

To answer the chaplains the Bishop was forced to draw up a form letter to be typed by his temporary secretaries, with an occasional personal note to be added with the signature. But he wrote other letters in his new position, an easy adaptation for the editor

of the *Religious Bulletin* and of the circular letters. Some of his
pastoral letters were intended to be read in the pulpit, but others
were directed to the priests themselves to tell them what he
desired and to recognize their accomplishments.[17] The letter of
May 15 announced the annual retreat for priests; that of May 18
urged their participation in the United Nations Clothing Drive
but insisted that Catholics keep an account of what they gave;
and that of May 23 discussed the problems of the insurance on
the church properties. He said that some "existing insurance
coverages on parish properties were not sufficient to meet the
present high replacement costs." In his letter of May 31 he urged
prayers during the month of June for vocations to the priesthood.
His argument about the dignity of the priest was based on a parallel between the parents' relations to the child and the priests'
relations with the supernatural life of the Christian:

> With Catholic parents, the priest shares the responsibilities of spirit-
> ual parenthood for every child born into a Catholic home. Through
> the ministry of the priest in Baptism, the child is born into super-
> natural life: the child is placed on a higher plane than the merely
> natural, on the plane that leads to heaven. . . .

The Bishop went on to insist that the priest brought Holy Communion as the food of the child and the sacrament of penance as
the curing of wounds in this supernatural life. His next pastoral
in the *Union and Echo* seemed to come from his experiences in
the Military Ordinariate. He said that the reports of the chaplains
had shown that there were too many nominal Catholics in civilian
life. Only the immediate danger of the battle front had caused
men to prepare themselves for the reception of the sacraments. On
the other hand the fidelity of those who had been trained in
Catholic schools justified the claim that "Catholic education had
justified itself in this war as never before."

On May 31 the Bishop presided at the D'Youville College commencement as chancellor of the college by reason of his office. On
June 1 he announced his first changes in diocesan officials, chiefly
the increasing of the consultors from six to twelve. He interrupted
his round of confirmations to attend the installation on June 7
of Bishop James J. Connolly as auxiliary of Fall River and the
consecration the next day of Bishop Louis L. Kelleher in Boston.
From there he went to Washington to ordain a class of priests for
the Congregation of Holy Cross.[18] His relatives in Washington
thought he looked tired, but that did not prevent him from carrying out on June 15 the tradition of blessing babies begun by

Bishop Duffy. The *Union and Echo* estimated that he had blessed 5,000 babies. On June 24 he presided at the graduation exercises at the Little Seminary of Saint Joseph and The Little Flower, a minor seminary, which were held in St. Joseph's Church. The following week he announced the first notable changes of the assignments of priests.

On July 1 he preached at the Naval Training Center at Sampson, New York, at the Mass said by Bishop Kearney of Rochester in the presence of about 12,000 trainees. His sermon was similar to the one he had given at the St. Lawrence Stadium in 1940. Taking his theme from the text "No man can serve two masters," he denied that such a text meant that a man could not serve both the flag and the cross. "Far from being two opposing masters, the service of God and the service of country are so intertwined that we may say in truth that no man may serve the one perfectly without serving the other." While congratulating the sailors on their spirit of sacrifice for their country, he said it would be a pity if they would lose the eternal merits of their sacrifices by not being in the state of grace and offering their thoughts and words to God. He concluded with the poem of Joyce Kilmer on the soldier and the suffering Christ.[19] The sermon was well received, and the commander of the base sent a special letter of thanks.[20]

Shortly after returning from the Sampson speech the Bishop and Archbishop Spellman made a vacation trip to Land O'Lakes, Wisconsin, but met cold, rainy weather. Bishop O'Hara went from there to Indianapolis for a short visit to his family, returning to Notre Dame on July 17 and to Buffalo on July 20. On July 27 he flew to Denver to participate in a commemoration at Fitzsimons General Hospital of the one hundred seventieth anniversary of the founding of the chaplains' corps. He took his text from the day's gospel on the pharisee and the publican and advised the chaplains not to boast of their good deeds but like the humble publican to be thankful for their opportunity to serve. Speaking of the 3,200 priests commissioned and the more than 1,600 auxiliary chaplains, 80 of whom had died and 70 of whom had endured capture in the war, he said he would leave the praise for their services to God. He would rather look to the saints connected with the military found in the calendar of the saints during July. He mentioned four. Two were officers, St. Ignatius Loyola and St. Jerome Emilian; one, St. Camillus of Lellis, was a private; and one, St. Vincent de Paul, was a chaplain general to the French galley slaves.[21]

This trip and sermon was typical of the close connections Bishop O'Hara continued to maintain with the Military Ordinariate. He was constantly consulted by Archbishop Spellman and Bishop McCarty and was appointed a military vicar by the Archbishop. He also showed his interest in the returned veterans and made them an important part of his youth program. When he announced the annual Catholic high-school retreat for October 2–5, he insisted that all Catholic youth not in Catholic high schools attend this retreat and that special attention be given to veterans.

As a former prefect of religion and President of Notre Dame, Bishop O'Hara needed no special inducement to become especially interested in the diocésan youth. But he found that Bishop Duffy, the head of the national youth program in the N.C.W.C, had already begun a strong youth program in the diocese under the direction of Monsignor Leo Smith as diocesan director of the Youth Council. This Youth Council attempted to direct all the youth of the diocese between the ages of 12 and 25. While the Monsignor had associated with him in the diocesan council men and women with experience in directing social activities, the most important council was that of the parish. This parish youth council consisted of representatives of each youth organization in the parish: the president of the organization, elected delegates, and others appointed at the discretion of the parish director. The officers consisted of a president, vice-president, secretary, treasurer, and five chairmen of youth activities: religious, cultural, athletic, hobby, and social. Each year in the summer there was a training course for the leaders of these parish councils, and usually the Bishop made it a point to attend the closing ceremonies to distribute the certificates of leadership training and to praise the activities of the youth councils. Although begun under Bishop Duffy, these councils achieved their best results under the direction of Bishop O'Hara and Monsignor Smith. With the absence of Catholic high schools and with a large group of children not in Catholic schools these councils had a very important role to play in the direction of the Catholic youth of the diocese. Except for the greatness of the actual problem this intricate council system might have seemed top heavy and the dedication of so many priests and laymen a waste of energy. Actually they were scarcely adequate to the task.

Unlike his bizarre existence at the Ordinariate the regime in Buffalo was comparatively quiet. On August 1 he presided at the funeral of Paul Dearing, a very devoted public relations officer of the N.C.W.C. who was killed when an airplane crashed into the Empire State Building in New York. The next day he celebrated a Mass in memory of Father Nelson H. Baker at the basilica of

Our Lady of Victory at Lackawanna, and on August 8 he visited Camp Turner, the vacation camp for boys. When the war ended in Japan on August 15 he repeated Bishop Duffy's plan by having the all-day exposition of the Blessed Sacrament after the last Mass on the next Sunday in all churches with Benediction in the evening. He also changed the *oratio imperata* from that *in tempore belli* to that for thanksgiving and ended the special ejaculation for peace that had been recited at the end of Mass and in its place added the public recitation of the Divine Praises as a public act of thanksgiving.

One of the first problems faced by the Bishop was the repair of the New Cathedral. Announcements of pontifical services usually distinguished this marble church from the "old" nineteenth-century German gothic church that had a warmth in its stained glass window behind the altar and its dark stone arches that make it yet a center of prayer for downtown churchgoers. The new cathedral was a cold, white marble gothic structure. The use of marble was based on a concept of splendor that did not know that marble could not stand the cold weather of the lake-side city. The marble was described as "Pittsford Valley" from New England. The decay of the marble was blamed by some on the fact that the slabs were too thin and that they were not laid properly, but that did not change the fact. First the marble towers had to be removed. Further, the interior produced a twenty second echo for the preacher, and the marble ceiling began to disintegrate, sending down pieces of marble on the congregation. The cathedral was ruled unsafe. The Bishop called in Egger and Higgins, architects from New York, and they decided that the marble ceilings would have to be removed, and that certain other changes could be made to remove the echo.

Apparently the Bishop knew that some thought the whole building should be removed because in his pastoral letter announcing the repairs the Bishop said that the total repairs would not exceed $650,000, which was less than 10 percent of the cost of replacing the cathedral. Moreover, the Bishop said that the repairs would be paid not by the Cathedral parish alone but by the whole diocese. This caused another alarm that the financial plans of Bishop Duffy for the diocese would be upset. The Bishop also allayed these fears in his pastoral of July 24 in the *Union and Echo*.

. . . It is far from our intention to balk or delay other Christian works that are contemplated at the present time—least of all works of education. We want to increase the number of Catholic schools, especially high schools. We plan to erect as soon as possible the home for the aged and the home for infants, the funds for which have been collected through Catholic Charities. The fund for the Faith will continue to support the Missionary Apostolate, the work of the Bishop's Committee for infants, the released time instruction, the vacation schools, the youth movement, and many other missionary enterprises which it has fostered so well. . . .

The closing of the New Cathedral merely stopped the public services that the Bishop would have conducted there. On August 16 he presided at the commencement at St. Bonaventure College at Olean and received an honorary degree. He was present at the reception of the habit at the Sisters of St. Francis of Penance and Christian Charity at Stella Niagara and at the burning of the mortgage of St. Joseph's Church at Niagara Falls. On Labor Day he presided at the annual Labor Day Mass at the parish of Monsignor John P. Boland, the noted labor priest, at which Monsignor Boland preached. A few weeks later when Monsignor Boland issued the first number of the *Catholic Labor Observer,* the Bishop wrote a brief letter approving the publication, although he did not always agree with the Monsignor on labor affairs. On September 10 he issued a pastoral signaling the opening of the school year, and at the priests' day of recollection he announced that five parish schools that had been closed during the depression were being reopened.

Bishop O'Hara was very faithful in attending ceremonies honoring other bishops; thus he attended the funeral of Bishop Desmond of Alexandria in Boston on September 17, and the next day spoke at the consecration of Bishop Apollinaris Baumgartner, O.F.M. Cap., as bishop of Guam. In this sermon he pointed to the efforts of the German bishops to rebuild their churches and added:

In the consecration of a missionary Bishop we see mirrored the perennial life of the Church. While great cathedrals in Europe lie in ruins, chapels are springing up through islands of the Pacific, built with the combined labors of natives and our own soldiers and marines.

But he also noted that the Marianas to which the Bishop was going was missionary country only in a sense because they had had their Catholicism for two and a half centuries.

Bishop O'Hara relied a great deal on his pastoral letters that appeared practically every week on the front page of the *Union and Echo,* although these were sometimes supplemented by letters sent privately to the priests themselves. Most of the pastoral letters were to be read from the pulpit. As is usually the case when a Bishop writes many letters to be read from the pulpit, there were some complaints from the clergy about their frequency.

The Bishop recognized the justice of their complaints but told the priests that he had no other real means of getting to the people. He certainly had the knack of explaining what he thought about a subject and of laying down a regulation. But his journalistic talents were limited by his inability to use the sarcasm and other tricks of the former prefect of religion or even of the Delegatus Castrensis.

Much of the Bishop's correspondence during these first months consisted of letters from chaplains who had received the announcement of his transfer to Buffalo some time after the event. He also continued his exchange with some of the servicemen themselves and continued the indirect supervision of the booklet about chaplains, *The Priest Goes to War,* published that fall by the Society of the Propagation of the Faith. This booklet, prepared under the supervision of Monsignor Thomas McDonnell, while illustrating all phases of the chaplains' wartime activities, developed incidentally the close relationships that had existed between the chaplains and the missions in the Southwest Pacific. When the publication was delayed by technical difficulties, Bishop O'Hara had the editors include some photographs of the latest visit of Archbishop Spellman to the Pacific stations.

The *Union and Echo* through his letters and by accounts of his activities pictured a very active prelate speaking on the radio for the missions on October 20, addressing the Ladies of Charity of Wyoming County, presiding at a Boy Scout rally, opening a teachers' institute, and beginning Catholic Book Week with a special pastoral. He prepared a sermon to be translated into Polish and broadcast from Corpus Christi Church on November 4 that contains an unusual clarification of his notion of the supernatural life. Probably the Bishop planned the sermon to add to the appeal then being made for financial aid to the struggling and persecuted Poles in Europe because he referred to their troubles:

. . . We know that before another spring comes in Europe, millions of innocent people, victims of war, victims of imperialism, victims of hatred and revenge and envy, will yield their souls to God. For them we pray that their spirit will not break, that their love of God may increase as they come closer to the poverty and desolation of Bethlehem; for them we pray that the love of God may increase in their hearts as the hatred of men grows against them, for them we pray that their spirit may be that of the martyrs who united their sufferings with those of our Blessed Lord in His Sacred Passion and Death, and who were snatched from death to life eternal with the Beatific Vision.

The Bishop then began to talk about the supernatural life. He reminded his hearers that many of their sons were returning from the wars with medals and other rewards of merit, but that not all merit would be so recognized. Only God recognized all merit, but the merit would be supernatural. To explain what makes human life supernatural he drew upon the words of Our Lord at the Last Supper in which He claimed that He was the vine and that unless they abode in Him their works would not bear fruit. Outwardly, he admitted, men doing good works seem the same, but he distinguished three kinds of persons doing good works such as giving alms. The first committed sin—his action is hypocritical, done to lead someone to believe that he is charitable when he is the opposite or done to obtain some favor from one who witnesses the action:

The second man, let us say, performs an act of natural virtue: there is pity in his heart for a fellow creature in distress, but the giver is not in the state of grace, and he does not in any way refer his action to God, even by an habitual intention. His act is worthless; it may gain him temporal reward, or it may lead him to an Act of Contrition or to Confession to restore grace in his soul. But as it stands it is a natural and not a supernatural act.

The third man, we will say, is a true branch, that has remained in the Vine. He is in the state of grace. He has made his morning offering of all his thoughts, words, and actions of the day to God, and for the love of God he helps his fellow creatures. His reward is the reward promised for a cup of cold water given in Christ's name: life everlasting.

The Bishop then turned to the nature of the supernatural life. "Religion is something we live, not something we feel, not something we put on as a garment, one day of the week, and leave off the other six days; not something we put away in a strong box like a treasure." He insisted that religion consisted in keeping the commandments and participating in the sacramental life of the Church; that it was not made up of a series of heroic acts but was "the practical worship of God . . . through the humdrum daily routine."[22]

On November 10 the Bishop went to Washington to the annual bishops' meeting, attending for the first time as an ordinary. He went early to take care of some business matters and in the session was elected assistant chairman of the Department of Catholic Action Study, of which Archbishop Mitty was the Chairman. After a brief visit with his brother Robert and other relatives in Washington, the Bishop went to Notre Dame to attend the silver jubilee of the founding of the lay trustees of the University. He and Father O'Donnell had talked over these and other matters early in September when they met at the funeral of John Neeson, and the Bishop had agreed to return for the trustees' meeting.[23]

In celebrating the silver jubilee of the Notre Dame lay trustees Father Hugh O'Donnell decided to have a solemn convocation in Washington Hall on the evening of November 16. Bishop O'Hara presided, and Father Fulton Sheen gave a special address on the problems of Catholic education and the need of Catholic education at the beginning of the peace. Father O'Donnell then gave a brief history of the board, paying special tribute to Father James Burns, the president at the time of its formation, to the many laymen, many of whom were dead, who had served so generously on the board since its foundation, and to Father Charles O'Donnell and the other presidents. As a mark of recognition he presented to each of the trustees a special plaque honoring his services to the University. The announcement was also made at the meeting that Peter C. Reilly would become the new chairman of the board to succeed Byron Kanaley, who had been chairman since the death of Albert Erskine.[24]

There were two announcements at this public meeting that were of special interest to Bishop O'Hara, since they were the results chiefly of his own efforts. The first was the announcement that his friend, Peter C. Reilly, was giving a million dollars to Notre Dame to foster research in chemistry.[25] This was the largest single gift in the history of the University, and Bishop O'Hara had arranged the details of the gift with Reilly that fall. It provided for lectures and scholarships and was planned so as to grow into a five-million-dollar endowment. The second gift was the settlement of the estate of Martin Gillen, which was valued in excess of one million dollars. While the gift involved property in Wisconsin and Michigan, the Notre Dame-Martin Gillen Foundation was set up generally for educational and scientific purposes.[26] Most of the income was to go to the Notre Dame Bureau of Economic Research and other educational and scientific projects.

More than anyone else, save perhaps Father Burns in the case of the Gillen Foundation, Bishop O'Hara could be considered the one who obtained these two benefactions for Notre Dame, and it was peculiarly fitting to have him return on the occasion that they were announced, even if the announcements were only incidental to the celebration of the silver jubilee of the Board of Lay Trustees. There were other members of the Board of Lay Trustees that evening who had become benefactors to Notre Dame through the efforts of the Bishop. Among them was William J. Corbett, who had been a consistent benefactor, especially towards the Mediaeval Institute. Father Hugh O'Donnell announced that besides these latest gifts the endowment of the University had increased from one million to four million. He could have added that most of this, except the million raised in 1920–1922, came from the Bishop's efforts.

On November 24, shortly after his return to Buffalo, the Bishop fell while making a visitation to Our Lady of Mt. Carmel parish and broke some bones in his left wrist. To his many friends who sent messages of sympathy he explained that he had been so boastful of the good weather of Buffalo that he had carelessly gone forth without his overshoes and slipped on the icy pavement.[27]

When the Bishop spoke to the Fourth Degree Knights of Columbus on November 7, he had made some criticism of the direction of American foreign policy, especially regarding France. He was watching world affairs very closely as his letter of December 18 to Archbishop Spellman showed:

My Dear Archbishop:

I am so grateful for your kindness in returning Secretary Patterson's letter, and for using it so judiciously in the meantime. I have half a mind to suggest to him that as evidence of his good faith in the conscription of boys for universal training, he act now to correct the Army's policies which we found so objectionable.

I am glad to hear that the Forrestal letter has gone to the Military Archives. The whole Navy seems to be busy right now on a larger problem—the defense of its individual existence. I have been following the feud closely. Now and then I find something amusing. I have also been interested in the Pearl Harbor testimony. I hope that someone will make a timetable of the various admissions, comparing them with official statements and attitudes made public in 1940 and 1941. For instance: first, while Government spokesmen were insisting that the Conscription Bill was peace time conscription the Administration was definitely preparing for war, and categorically denying the fact. Second, when General Marshall was having difficulty finding thirty-six planes in the United States to send to Hawaii thousands of planes were being shipped lend-lease to England and Russia. Third, although General Marshall could not believe that Pearl Harbor would be attacked, General Drumm had outlined the attack just as it occurred and Admiral Richardson had refused to berth the fleet in Pearl Harbor for fear of such an attack. Where were General Drumm and Admiral Richardson during the war?

There are countless other little sidelights that are interesting.[28]

In his Christmas letter to the faithful of the diocese the Bishop urged each one to try to get one additional penitent back into

the Church. This had been a theme he had urged on the chaplains in the war. The theme of the letter, however, was one of joy
and optimism typical of the Bishop:

When we see people trudging faithfully to Mass through the ice
and snow, when we see the altar rails crowded with communicants,
when we see charity exercised so widely for the relief of human misery,
we know that there are vast multitudes of good people in the world.
Further, we know by experience that most bad people have some good
in them, some spark of love of God and neighbor that good people
can fan to a flame.

In the *Evening News* for Christmas he had a Christmas message
in which he asked why people had no peace.

Let our examination of conscience begin with the glory of God. Are
we, the victor nations, rendering homage to God as the source of
authority, of truth, and of justice? Is our justice according to the law
of God, or is it expediency? Was it right for us to exclude the name of
God from our deliberations at San Francisco for the formation of the
United Nations Organization? Was it right for the world-wide Educational Organization which met recently in London, to reject the resolution of the Panama Delegate who asked to have the name of God
included in the constitution of that body?

To add to the pleasure of Christmas a cable from Rome announced
on December 23, that his friend, Archbishop Spellman, was to be
made a cardinal. Since the Bishop could not pontificate because
of his wrist, he went to his home in Indianapolis for Christmas
day. On his return the heavy cast was replaced by a lighter one,
and then the cast was removed December 28, 1945. The Bishop
also announced that he would hold an open house on New Year's
day. He wrote his family that about six hundred came, and he
considered it a success. There were many prominent persons
among those who called, such as United States Senator James
Meade and State Senator Walter J. Mahoney.[29]

The Bishop was now ready for his first important move. Shortly
after his arrival Bishop O'Hara had discussed the school situation
with Monsignor Sylvester Holbel, the diocesan superintendent of
education, and they had agreed that there were not enough Catholic high schools.[30] This opinion was concurred in also by Father
Eugene S. Loftus, the director of Catholic Charities; Bishop
Burke, the auxiliary bishop; and several laymen with whom the
bishops had talked. The incentive for the high-school program had
also come from another direction. Monsignor Peter J. Adamski,
whom the Bishop had appointed to the important Polish parish

of St. Stanislaus and also made a diocesan consultor, called the attention of the Bishop to the fact that there was no Catholic high school among the Polish people of Buffalo. He contrasted this situation unfavorably with the Polish areas of Chicago and Detroit. The Monsignor felt that the Polish people of Buffalo had the same means and were ready to have Catholic high schools for their youth. This suggestion coincided with the Bishop's plans.[31] As the time approached for the annual Catholic Charities Drive, the Bishop called in his consultors and laid before them his proposals. His meetings were very informal. When everyone was seated, he passed around the usual cigarettes and went directly to the point. He had all the facts at his finger tips about the need of schools, the costs, and the obstacles. Basically his proposal was that all Catholic children should be in Catholic schools. For the high schools he wanted the tuition to be low, about ten dollars per person. To get the schools started the diocese would have to assume one-half of the debt.

The Bishop now called for a public meeting of 250 representative laymen at the Statler Hotel for February 3. When the meeting opened he informed the chairman of the charities drive of the new objective of the drive. He proposed raising ten million dollars for high schools within the next ten years. The Bishop admitted that the program was ambitious but said that "It comes in response to a popular demand for the extension of the moral and religious training of the parochial school system."

The raising of the funds would be included in the Annual Charities Appeal, and after the budget of the charities was taken care of, eighty percent of what remained of the subscription would go into the central fund for education and twenty percent would take care of the ordinary diocesan projects that were already supported from Funds for the Faith. He assured the laymen that he did not intend to change the destination of the funds already collected in the previous charities appeals and set aside by Bishop Duffy for the repair and improvement of charitable institutions.

The proposal was a large one and caused much discussion. Some of the more conservative clergy and laymen of the diocese probably were never strong for the program, but in general this proposal met the desires of the Catholic people. Buffalo Catholicism, recovered from its indebtedness through the wages earned in the defense industry during the war, was ready to advance a new step in culture through the promotion of high schools. The Bishop called the proposal "Perhaps the most ambitious undertaking ever contemplated by the Diocese of Buffalo." At the heart of the plan was the establishment of a central fund that the Bishop expected to reach five million dollars in ten years and that would be matched by similar funds raised in the parishes.

In the new high schools the minimum attendance proposed for each would be 400 pupils and the maximum 1,000 to save expenses. The Bishop outlined certain parts of the program:

Maximum tuition charge would be $50 a year, and operating deficits (it would cost $60 to $80 to educate each of a minimum of 400 students) will be met by local parishes, with some assistance from central funds.

The ownership and control of the high schools will be vested in the diocese, except in cases where parish groups prefer to invite a religious community to own and operate the school. Existing private and parochial high schools will continue to operate as before, except in cases where the parishes request that their facilities be merged into the diocesan system.

The amount of subsidy to be granted by the central fund to an individual high school will not exceed 50% of the construction costs. It has been estimated that construction costs would be at least $1000 per pupil or a minimum of $400,000 for a 400-pupil high school.

The Bishop added:

There are several factors at the moment which can influence this program. First, the raising of the funds; secondly, the shortage of building materials; and, thirdly, the shortage of qualified teachers for the proposed high schools. We estimate a need of approximately 200 teachers for the program.

We do not plan on vocational facilities within the schools, nor do we envision extensive physical training programs as allied to swimming pools in each building. The costs, as well as the need of specialized teachers, are prohibitive. Otherwise, each school would offer educational programs equal to those of the public schools, plus answering the need of the more Catholic schooling for the young people in our diocese.[32]

He also told the people that the existing high schools would not suffer from the program.

There was a pleasant interlude in the Bishop's daily fare before he started for Rome to attend the reception of the cardinal's hat by Archbishop Spellman. The Notre Dame basketball team played Canisius College on February 7 on its way to New York to play New York University. After the players attended Mass, they were the guests of the Bishop in his residence for breakfast. The players were a bit taken aback when the Bishop insisted on serving them coffee himself. He still felt close to the students of Notre Dame.[33]

The Bishop left Buffalo February 8 and attended a dinner given by the Knights of Columbus for Archbishop Spellman in New York before joining the Cardinal-elect's party, which also included the Chinese Cardinal-elect Tien. They left New York for Shannon airport on February 11, thence going to Paris, where they were the guests of the American Ambassador, Jefferson Caffrey, and met the Apostolic Nuntio, Archbishop Angelo Roncalli, later Pope John XXIII.[34] They arrived in Rome, February 14, to be greeted with a near riot between the photographers of Rome and those from America.[35] The secret consistory was on February 18 and the public one on February 21. Besides attending the public consistory Bishop O'Hara wrote a brief account of the ceremonies for International News Service.[36] He did not describe the ceremonies but laid great stress on his favorite theme about the consistory: the fact that the Pope had recognized so many different countries in his choice of cardinals and also the timelessness of the ceremonies. In a letter he told his folks that he especially enjoyed the international character of the assemblage and his meeting with such men as Cardinals Faulhauber, Von Preysing, and Von Galen of Germany, and Cardinal Sapieha of Poland, to whom he gave the greetings of the Polish people of Buffalo. On February 24 the Bishop had his own private audience with Pope Pius XII, in which the Pope had imparted a special blessing for the people of the diocese, adding: "Please tell them that I love them for all their good qualities, add that I am especially grateful for their generosity in answering every plea for the relief of the distressed peoples of the world." The Pope gave him three rosaries for his sisters and accepted a copy of *The Priest Goes to War*.[37] The Bishop joined Cardinal Spellman in another special audience for the many service chaplains who had come to Rome for the ceremonies.

The personal friendship between Cardinal Spellman and the Pope gave rise to a crop of rumors, the most persistent being that Spellman would be made Papal Secretary of State and that Bishop O'Hara would then become Archbishop of New York. John A. Boccio, a reporter for the Buffalo *Courier-Express,* took advantage of radio telephone and interviewed the Bishop. The Bishop told him: "People like to speculate. In fact they have been speculating on this for some time. I know absolutely nothing about the report. I would be only too glad to tell you—if I knew. I don't think anybody knows what's in the mind of the Holy Father."[38] The next day the rumor was denied.

On March 20 Bishop O'Hara presided at the annual commencement at Canisius College and received another honorary degree. In his speech he referred again to international affairs and the United Nations. He protested against any peace that would allow a larger nation to swallow a smaller one. He seemed to be criticizing the American acceptance of Soviet imperialism.

It seems the only safety of a small nation today is to sit unnoticed or unwanted. If we are a nation of principles, we'll defend those principles. Therefore it might be well to ask for a return of the good old American way of standing up for the underdog and defending all the rights of all the nations.[39]

To the graduates he gave praise, while deploring the losses to the Church from those Catholics who were trying to go through life with only a "fourth, fifth, or sixth grade knowledge of religion."

As the day for the Annual Charities Appeal approached, the Bishop expressed more concern over his high-school plan. On Sunday, March 31, he arranged a rally for the 500 appeal workers at the Statler Hotel, at which he went over the financing of the high schools:

If ten parishes formed a high school association to serve 400 students the total cost would be $20,000 or $2,000 yearly spread over a ten year period. The remaining $200,000 would come out of the central fund which, naturally, is part of the Catholic Charities Appeal.

It is true that this would be too much of a burden for the very small parishes but not for the majority of the parishes of the diocese. My experience with the people of the Diocese of Buffalo convinces me that outside assistance would be forthcoming to help solve the problem of the very small parishes.[40]

The Bishop had already announced that an East Buffalo School Association would undertake two new high schools the following September: one for boys under the direction of the Franciscans, which would utilize the lyceum of St. John Kanty parish, and the other for girls under the direction of the Felician Sisters, which would be at St. Stanislaus parish. The starting of these high schools in the Polish area attained the purposes of both the Bishop and Monsignor Adamski.

For a half hour that Sunday afternoon the Bishop conducted a question-and-answer period over Station WBNY on the high-school problems and that night gave a more formal broadcast in which he asked a minimum donation of ten dollars. In his broadcast of April 12 he talked about the afflicted who would benefit from the appeal. "Herein lies the philosophy of Christian almsgiving. The works of God are made manifest in the afflicted. God

permits affliction, but He brings good out of it." In a radio broadcast on April 13 he stressed another value of the appeal:

The highest motive for sacrifice is the love of God. It can do more
than any earthly motive, any earthly love to bring about unity of
mind, unity of heart, unity of purpose, unity of action. The unity
manifested by the response to the appeal of Catholic charities is very
consoling for it points straight to a great love of God.

How many contributions there will be to Catholic charities this
year we do not know. We do know that the closing of war plants has
caused the dislocation of many parishioners, that strikes have reduced
the earnings of many others, that gifts made through the division of
commerce and industry, have been reduced by the closing of some
plants and the curtailment of activities in others. To compensate for
anticipated losses in one group or another, there has been added a
generosity manifested by other groups and other individuals.

The city radio stations carried a broadcast appeal every day during the drive, and the Bishop added an appeal in the *Union and
Echo* of April 12. On April 15, when it was evident that the drive
had been a success, the Bishop broadcast a word of gratitude.

This has been a colossal success. . . . There is only one reason, love
of God and love of neighbor for the love of God. . . .

The story is repeated a thousand times over in our beloved America
which has truly been a land of liberty and opportunity for hard working immigrants, so many of whom knew only poverty and oppression
in the land of their birth.

The Bishop repeated his expression of gratitude in his Easter
letter, noting that they had exceeded the million dollars by
$13,000. In the letter he also congratulated the diocese on increas-
ing its attendance at Holy Communion 35 percent over the
previous year.

But he continued to urge the diocese to show its traditional
generosity. In a letter read during the Masses of May 5 he made
an appeal for the collection for the War Relief Commission of
the N.C.W.C. to be taken up May 12–19, and on May 11 he asked
for aid in the drive for food for the starving children of Europe.
He had been in Buffalo a year, but he asked that there be no celebration of the anniversary. Interviewed, he said simply: "The
people of the diocese are grand and that goes for the priests and
religious, too. In fact they are the finest people in the world."[41]

In a letter of May 8 the Bishop announced his intention of con-
secrating the diocese to the Immaculate Heart of Mary on May
12. Just when the Bishop began to have this special devotion to
the Immaculate Heart of Mary is not clear, although it was a

prominent devotion of the community at Notre Dame. He seemed to have been deeply impressed with the story of Fatima and recalled those visions in his letter, particularly the vision of May 13, 1917. He also recalled that the Pope had consecrated the whole world to the Immaculate Heart of Mary on October 31, 1942.

The activities of the Bishop during the next few weeks were quite routine except for his attendance at the celebration of the centenary of Fordham's charter and the investment of the pastor of his old parish in Peru, Indiana, Father Paul Welsh, with Monsignor's robes, at which he gave the sermon. On May 29 he blessed the new offices of Catholic Charities. The *Union and Echo* of the next day announced that Monsignor Edmund J. Britt had resigned as chancellor and that the Bishop's close friend, Monsignor Leo Smith, had succeeded to the office, with Father Bernard McLaughlin as his assistant. The June 14 *Union and Echo* announced that four additional high schools would open in the fall, two in Buffalo and one each in Lockport and Winchester.

The Bishop and his advisors worked out a program for the erection of these district schools that consisted of ten points: (1) Any pastor in the diocese was authorized to call a meeting of priests in his district for the purpose of the formation of a high-school district, and the ordinary or his representative would accept an invitation to attend. (2) At the meeting they would form a diocesan high-school association, although the officers would serve only in an advisory capacity since the diocesan authorities were the final authority in all matters. (3) From this advisory group the Bishop would appoint an executive committee of three to act as a steering committee and to act for the Bishop. The chairman of the executive committee also would act as chairman of the association. (4) An account first would be set up in the diocesan chancery. This would be divided between two funds, a plant fund and an operating fund. The diocese would contribute to the plant fund an amount equal to the contribution of the parishes. The diocese would also contribute to the operating fund, at least at the start, up to twenty percent of the operating deficit. (5) The principal would have the powers usual to such officers, but the diocesan superintendent of schools would have jurisdiction over the high-school personnel and the program. (6) The principal would always be a member of the community operating the school. Points 7 and 8 provided that the executive committee would negotiate for the leases and the terms for the rentals with the signature of the Bishop and handle the funds for the erection and operation of the school. The committee must

keep proper accounts. In point 9 the actual powers of the principal in financial matters were set down, and point 10 provided that
the agreement between the diocese and the community operating
the high school should be contractual. Monsignor Holbel was in
charge of this program, although the financial matters were
handled by the financial officers of the chancery.[42]

On June 1 the Bishop had told his sisters that he was going to
Japan in July on a mission decided in Rome while he was there.
He was to be accompanied by Bishop Michael Ready. The trip
was planned for June, but difficulties about passports had delayed
the timing until July 1 from San Francisco. The Bishop left Buffalo on June 22 by train. The two Bishops went by way of Honolulu, Guam, Iwo Jima, and Kwajalein, names that had figured
much in Bishop O'Hara's correspondence during the war. They
reached Tokyo July 4 to be greeted by Archbishop Paul Marella,
the papal delegate, and several Japanese bishops and laymen. The
welcoming speech was given by Dr. Kataro Tanaka, a noted Japanese Catholic layman, a cabinet member, and later Supreme Court
Justice. He said the bishops came at the Japanese darkest hour:

. . . Greater than our spiritual hardship is our spiritual suffering:
greater than the starvation of the body is the hunger of the soul. The
story of the criminal militarism of the last decade is but one chapter
in the history of our mistaken education. For we too long have sought
only material strength and prosperity. We have never known, or have
repudiated the blessings of the teachings of Christ. . . . We have erected
our houses without God. And this nation stands here today, dazed and
bewildered. Only the Catholic Christian Faith can hope to solve the
antimonies that threaten to cleave the nation into hostile camps of
left and right. . . .

The bishops were entertained by General Eichelberger on
July 6 and by General MacArthur on July 8. They also had an
interview with Emperor Hirohito. The Emperor seemed much
impressed by the statements of the Pope on world order and
wished to have more complete texts of the papal statements. He
also complimented the work of the nuns in Japan and mentioned
that he was the first member of the Japanese royal family to visit
a pope. He had visited Pope Benedict XV in 1922 when he was a
prince.

The bishops then visited many cities on the islands. On July
20 at Nagasaki in the south they visited the scene of the second
atomic bombing. The bomb that had been aimed at the industrial
section of the city had been swept by the wind instead into the
Catholic village of Urakami and had killed 8,000 Catholics of

the village. One of the ceremonies of the trip was the laying of the cornerstone for the new Catholic Church in Urakami. Over 500 people led by Bishop Paul Yamaguchi of Nagasaki waited two hours for the belated train bringing the bishops. Two laymen spoke for the Catholic people. One said: "We regard our loss as a trial from God to make our faith firm. Now we are doing our best to rebuild our Church and also doing our best to gain converts to replace the 8,000 Catholics killed."[43]

One highlight of the trip was a visit to a monastery of Buddhist monks at the ancient temple of Kyoto. The abbot of the Buddhist temple, Abbot Hashumoto, told Bishop O'Hara:

We would like to have your advice on present conditions. We would be very glad to cooperate with the Catholic Church in the struggle against evil in the modern world.

In answer, Bishop O'Hara proclaimed a common front with them against materialism and immorality:

I have come as a Catholic. I have been sent here to bring to all you Japanese people a message of peace from the Pope, in the very words of Christ: "Peace I leave with you: not as the world do I give unto you. . . ." We appeal especially to you to stress the importance of respecting the rights of the family as the basic unit of society. Anti-human and immoral doctrines are now spreading all over the world in an effort to impose divorce and birth control on mankind. These two ideologies are against human nature and divine law.[44]

The Buddhist monks gave the Bishop a Buddhist rosary, which he brought back for his sisters. The Bishop was enthusiastic about the Japanese people and gave optimistic reports to the press when he arrived back in San Francisco on July 28:

Against the naturally depressing experience of viewing the devastation in Japan, you come away with the thought that the Japanese people realize they face new world situations and that they are now doing their part in the betterment of conditions.

He said that the loss of state Shintoism had made the people turn notably towards Christianity. Both he and Bishop Ready insisted that the prestige of the Catholic Church in Japan must not be measured by the number of Catholics. Despite a persecution of 300 years the Catholic Church had made great progress in the recent 80 years, especially through education and social service. He saw a second spring coming, in which the most hopeful sign was the evidence of democracy.[45]

Shortly after Bishop O'Hara started for Japan, Bishop Burke

announced the suppression of the Buffalo Negro parishes, St. Augustine and St. Peter Claver. The parishioners were directed to attend the neighborhood Catholic churches where they lived. The decision was forward-looking but aroused some criticism at the time. But no one doubted the Bishop's interest in the colored faithful in the diocese. He had been especially attentive to the Knights of St. Peter Claver and was frequently photographed with their officers.

In his letter of August 16 in the *Union and Echo* the Bishop called attention to the Missionary Apostolate carried on by the newly ordained priests in parishes where there were no resident pastors. On Sunday, August 25, there would be open house at the mission chapels in Chatauqua and Cattaraugus counties. Bishop O'Hara proudly pointed out that where there had been only one chapel in 1940, there were now six and one more under construction. Already some of these mission chapels were being prepared for resident pastors. Furthermore, this year of pastoral work was an important addition to the training of the newly ordained priests who conducted them.

Writing to his friend, Samuel Crothers, on August 22, the Bishop expressed some of his reactions to recent events.

I wonder if I can give you some comfort on the world picture. I am thinking lately of the strange paradox that seems to be in the making. Everyone who persecutes the Church comes to an evil end. The persecution is widening every day. There are hundreds of new martyrs, and some of them are in countries where the Faith has not been too strong, at least in practice. From a supernatural point of view, this will hasten the day for the restoration of order in the world. I do not know whether you are familiar with the revelations of Our Lady of Fatima. One of them is that with the consecration of Russia to the Immaculate Heart of Mary, Russia will be converted. We seem to be a long step from that now, but it may be the darkness before the dawn. Japan certainly changed overnight. The priests and religious there have been extremely generous to Catholic charitable enterprises. One of them founded a chair of scholastic philosophy at the Imperial University of Kyoto. A Canadian Dominican occupies the chair at the present time, another priest from Maryland leaves Buffalo in a few weeks to teach English at the same Imperial University. . . .[46]

In his pastoral of August 25 on Catholic education the Bishop naturally referred to his visit to Japan, where Catholics were begging for schools. He told the diocese that he could not hope now to provide schools for the 50,000 Catholics who were attending the public schools, but he did not want a single empty desk in the schools that existed.

On September 1, 1946, the Bishop announced a novena in honor of Our Lady of Sorrows for peace and instructed pastors to make arrangements for confessions and to give Communion outside of Mass for those who could not come to the scheduled Masses. When interviewed on the thirtieth anniversary of his ordination, September 9, he said he no longer celebrated anniversaries. He did say he thought that while there was more irreligion in the world, the practice of religion among believers was more intense as was shown by the attendance at this novena. He thought it too soon to evaluate the effect of the war on religion. "Despite the popular slogan there were a lot of atheists in foxholes. But if there was any one in a foxhole with latent religion, the war helped to bring it out."[47]

On September 15 he spoke at the commencement of the Mercy School of Nurses. Again he pointed to the attendance at the novena as a symbol of the belief of the people that peace can be attained by God's intervention. He also laid much of the blame for the lack of religion in the world on recent writers. But the Bishop, still thinking in terms of international trends, added another thought that attracted wide attention in the press. The Bishop called on Catholics to rise in indignant protest against the foreign policy advocated by Secretary of Commerce Henry A. Wallace in a Madison Square Garden speech on September 12. In advocating peace with Russia, Wallace had said that the United States had no more reason for interfering in eastern Europe than Russia had for interfering with Latin America. He actually suggested giving the control of eastern Europe to Russia. Wallace was eventually to lose his secretaryship as a result of this speech, and the Bishop's comment may have had something to do with the popular clamor against him because it received wide notice. The Bishop accused Wallace of wanting to scrap the Atlantic Charter. The important passage was:

True we have looked forward to the implementation of the safeguards of the religious and political liberty that were promised when our consent was given to the rule, but when one of the highest officers in our Government calls for the scrapping of our concern for these 80,000,000—and of 200,000,000 not Catholic, who live under the same rule—we must rise in indignant protest against the stultifying suggestion and support the efforts of one master whose sworn duty is to see justice done in Europe and Asia as well as in America.

The one "master" whom he would serve was apparently the President, but the Bishop also had other criticisms of the government's policies:

We read of the Government buying up potatoes to stack in order to maintain their price while in every war-ridden country that was bombed in the name of Christian civilization there are millions of people suffering from undernourishment and from disease while tens of thousands are actually dying of starvation. And why is it proposed to destroy crops or turn them from this first natural use as food? In the name of money.

Criticizing the many strikes, he continued:

I recognize and I shall defend the right of labor to proper compensation. I recognize and I defend the right of labor to strike to gain proper compensation and to correct improper working conditions. But I beg labor to consider that money is in itself nothing. . . .[48]

A few days later Richard McClellan, the Labor Party candidate for the New York state assembly, took issue with the Bishop in a published letter about Wallace. He said that he and some other people were "resentful of the fact that a supposedly religious leader should meddle and interfere in a political discussion on how to maintain the peace. . . ."[49]

The Bishop continued his active ways. His letter of September 26 to the clergy argued that Buffalo did not have a real convert movement and suggested that an effort be made first to convert the non-Catholic members of mixed marriages. With his consent Bishop Burke on October 9 sent a letter to the clergy suggesting that telegrams be sent to Dean Acheson, the secretary of state, and to Senators Meade and Wagner to plead for freedom for Archbishop Stepinac of Yugoslavia, who had been arrested on September 18. Bishop O'Hara later sent a letter urging the support of CARE and encouraging support for the efforts of the Polish Catholic League. On October 8 he attended the installation of Archbishop Ritter as Archbishop of St. Louis and later the installation of Archbishop Schulte in Indianapolis.

On November 8 he sent the clergy a letter announcing that the celebration of the centennial of the diocese the next year would be celebrated at a Provincial Eucharistic Congress, September 23–25. In an accompanying letter he urged the children to pray for the success of the congress, suggesting that they receive Communion every day in preparation for the celebration.

His letters were numerous both in the *Union and Echo* and otherwise, nor did he stop his other activities. He described these activities to Terry Cosgrove in a letter of December 23:

> . . . I am sorry I missed you on two occasions. I have been in New York for a couple of visits this fall, but not for the Smith Memorial Dinner. I was in Washington finishing up the business of the Bishops' Meeting and on the day of the Trustees' fall meeting at Notre Dame. I returned to Buffalo Saturday morning and left that evening for Indianapolis to spend a day or two at home before attending Cardinal Stritch's Jubilee Mass on Tuesday.
>
> It was a busy fall, but I have been in Buffalo most of the month of December. I plan to spend a few days at home now, leaving after midnight Mass on Christmas. Unless something unexpected happens, I shall not be away from Buffalo for the next couple of months.[50]

He prepared a Christmas message for the press as well as a sermon for the midnight Mass in the New Cathedral. Taking for his text the message of the Angels, "Glory to God in the highest and on earth peace to men of good will," he found in it an example of the twofold division of the world that he liked to talk about. He mentioned the paradox that while man was made to glorify God, in the Nativity God really glorified man:

> When our Lord condemned the world, as something distinct from mankind, He referred to the spirit of materialism that is in every way opposed to the things of God. . . . The world loves power and honor and pleasure. To rebuke the world the Son of God, in His Incarnation, chose poverty, obscurity, suffering.[51]

If the Christmas letter and sermon seemed to lack some of the joy and good will that one might expect at Christmastime, there was probably a physical reason. When he arrived in Indianapolis the next noon, his sister's diary noted that he looked tired and worn, and had a badly swollen hand, which the doctor said was suffering from rheumatism. She noted that he was probably just exhausted. This was perhaps the first time that his extremely fast pace and endless use of energy had begun to catch up with him. However, he returned to Buffalo December 28, looking better, his sister wrote, but not well. He held his open house on January 1, had the consultors to dinner, and went to New York on January 13 to the dinner of the Knights of Malta.

Bishop O'Hara continued his interest in public affairs, noting to one friend that he was following the New York papers very closely. He opposed the new proposals for universal military training. As he wrote to Armand F. Andale on April 5, 1946:

> For your information but not for publication I can tell you that some of the most effective work done in eliminating the proposal for universal military training came from private representation made by

the Bishops, both to Congressmen and to members of the War and
Navy Departments. There have been some public statements, but most
of the work has been done privately.[52]

Earlier on January 13 he wrote to State Senator Walter J. Mahoney in praise of the Senator's stand on a medical measure:

Please accept my hearty congratulations on your defense of the natural law in reply to the physicians who insulted you by asking you to
legalize murder.

We have gone far from our moorings when such an outrageous procedure can be proposed. However, the calm assumption by men of
God's power over life and death, evidenced in the birth control and
euthanasia movements is but the logical outcome of the philosophy of
education which we imported from Germany two or three generations
ago.

Not long ago, Edgar Hoover said that the time had come when those
who will defend Americanism must stand up and be counted. The bor-
ing from within is more dangerous than any enemy from without.[53]

His opposition to the spread of Communism was clear in a
letter to his former secretary, Bill Reilly, on February 25:

I haven't had a chance to read the Collier's article yet, but I can
say that the sub-head is correct. "Though their numbers are not great,
Communists are kicking a loud and anti-U.S. fuss in South America."
The principal difficulties are: 1. lack of priests; 2. lack of Catholic
educational institutions; 3. hard-headed conservatism on the part of
the old land holders.

Under the last heading, I should say that while some of the conservative party members have spread beautiful legislation on the books in
South America, they have not been too practical in their applications
of their laws. The demagogues, chief of whom are the Communists,
have used slogans rather than facts in attracting their popular following. In most countries there is too much poverty, too little intellect.
However, the people are not much aware of their poverty until
agitators stir them up to resent it.[54]

Among his many letters was one in January laying down the rules
about attendance of Catholic children at baccalaureate or commencement services in Protestant churches. His ideas on this
interdenominational service had not changed:

First of all, Catholics are not permitted to attend baccalaureate or
commencement services held in a non-Catholic church.

Secondly, Catholics are not permitted to attend a Protestant service
anywhere. . . .

The exception was the inclusion in a ceremony of an invocation, blessing, or patriotic hymns that did not make it a Protestant service.

The Bishop was devoting more and more thought to the coming Eucharistic Congress. To the friends who sent him notes on the seventh anniversary of his consecration he thanked them and invited them to the congress.[55] On February 7 he announced that Cardinal Spellman would be the honorary patron of the congress, and the other bishops of the province would be honorary presidents. Bishop Burke was named the local chairman, although Bishop O'Hara remained the president of the congress.

He went briefly to Indianapolis February 7 for a couple of days of rest and admitted to his family that he was suffering from rheumatism, but he was back in Buffalo on February 12 to greet Cardinal Von Preysing. He also made three radio addresses in support of the Annual Charities Appeal: the first was an explanatory one on the history of the appeals and the destination of the moneys, the second was chiefly on the high-school program, and the third was an outright appeal to those who had not done their share in other appeals.

On April 27 Bishop O'Hara went to New York to preach at the Mass in St. Patrick's Cathedral honoring the centennial of the St. Vincent de Paul Society in New York. After outlining the history of the society, the Bishop referred to an old theme of his about the futility of humanitarianism:

Following the denial of the Divinity of Christ, humanitarianism proposes that "Man's obligations are limited to and dependent alone on man and human relations." In other words, God is left out. The humanitarian knows too little about God to consider Him, but he loves his fellow-man, and the worship that some people give to God, the humanitarian gives to humanity.[56]

On May 7 with Archbishop Spellman he went to Rapid City, South Dakota, for the installation the next day of his co-worker in the Military Ordinariate, Bishop McCarty, as bishop of that see. Back in Buffalo he kept up his pace of meetings and visits. On May 13 he attended the celebration of the centenary of the Diocese of Albany, and on May 22 attended the funeral of Archbishop Curley in Baltimore. He even had to interrupt his retreat at Notre Dame to be host to Archbishop Duhig of Melbourne, Australia.

Of more importance to him was his invitation to speak at the International Marian Congress at Ottawa on June 20. Bishop O'Hara's sermon was mostly a history of devotion to the Blessed Virgin. He drew also on his knowledge of wartime experiences, especially of the troops in the South Pacific, and related the story of Fatima and the faith of the people of Nagasaki. When he returned, he praised the congress in a pastoral about their own coming Eucharistic congress and said that its success was an answer to prayer, which was urged for the success of the Buffalo congress.

While much of his free time had to be spent planning the coming congress, he was pleased to entertain some of the foreign visitors from the Marian Congress on their way home. One of the most important of these was Cardinal Mindszenty of Hungary, who came on July 10. At this time the Bishop's arthritis became so severe that he asked his personal physican for some medication. Yet despite this he attended the meeting of the Board of Trustees of The Catholic University on July 30 and went on from there to attend the consecration of Bishop John P. Cody in Saint Louis and the consecration of Bishop Joseph Marling, C.PP.S., in Cincinnati on August 6. From there he went to Notre Dame for a few days of rest.

With the opening of the school year the Bishop faced the practical problem of arranging a suspension of classes during the congress. He announced that sessions would be canceled from September 23 for the rest of that week. In the remainder of this letter of September 3 he stressed the savings the parochial schools gave the American government, totaling 81 million dollars annually plus another 600 millions in buildings. But he added that the economic argument did not compare to the religious one: "Catholic schools exist because God is our beginning and our last end."

In a letter read in the Masses of August 10 the Bishop urged an expression of thanksgiving on the feast of the Assumption, the anniversary of the surrender of Japan. He told how the Catholics in Japan connected the end of the war with the feast of the Assumption and the fact that their church in Urakami was dedicated to the Blessed Virgin. Veterans were urged to be sure to express their thanksgiving in the coming congress. On September 16 the Bishop presided at the first Red Mass of the diocese and gave a sermon on the theme of the need to recognize the natural law. He spoke of the natural law and the lawyer:

. . . Law is ordained to point out his path and direct him on his course and he must of necessity know where he is going if he is to be directed there.

The Natural Law, as we know it, is man's participation of the Eternal Law, and its authority comes from God. It is false to say that there is no absolute standard of morality, which is everywhere and constantly identical. Morality is not made by kings or Councils, nor does it depend on popular opinion or the custom or traditions of places.

It is true that not all positive law can be traced directly to the principles of natural law because many positive laws may be said to be morally indifferent. . . .[57]

To the inspired teacher of devotion to the Eucharist at Notre Dame the holding of a provincial Eucharistic congress was naturally the finest way to commemorate the centennial of his diocese. Almost from the day of his arrival he seemed to have planned to make it a grand demonstration of faith in the Eucharist, and at least from January 1 he kept reminding his friends in all parts of the country that he hoped they would join in the Buffalo celebration in September. Of course, as in all his activities, the Bishop endeavored to use the occasion to get as many persons as possible to receive the sacraments of penance and Holy Communion as often as possible. His first appeal was to the children in November, 1946, when he asked them to go to Mass and Holy Communion often, daily if possible, and to pray for the success of the congress.[58] In this he was already achieving one of his aims. His second aim was to have a restoration of Catholic ideas in all walks of life, especially as centered in the Eucharist. To attain this he tried to gather aid not only from his friends in the hierarchy but from his lay Catholic friends and the lay leaders of the diocese.

The opening ceremony of the Centennial Eucharistic Congress of September 22–25 was the reception on Monday afternoon for Cardinal Spellman, the patron of the congress, and his two cardinalatial companions, Cardinal Motta of Sao Paulo, Brazil, and Cardinal Guevara of Lima, Peru, both personal acquaintances of the friend of South America, Bishop O'Hara. The crowds that witnessed the informal reception of the visitors by Bishops O'Hara and Burke at the railway station were said to number about 70,000, among whom a procession walked guided by an avenue of Catholic War Veterans and Knights of Saint John, while a band played the Notre Dame "Victory March." The procession went to the New Cathedral for the ecclesiastical reception. That evening in Kleinhaus Hall about 4,500 persons attended the civic reception by Mayor Bernard J. Dowdy, Albert T. O'Neill, and other representatives of the city and state. Three other cardinals were on the platform: McGuigan of Toronto, Gilroy of Sydney, Australia, and Bernard Griffin of Westminster, England. Bishop O'Hara gave a brief speech of welcome to the congress and expressed the hope that God would once more preside at the councils of men and bring peace. Finally Cardinal Spellman

responded with "Peace in the Eucharist," in which he first gave
a brief account of the career of Bishop O'Hara and of his great
devotion to the Eucharist at Notre Dame, in the Military Ordinariate, and now as bishop of Buffalo. He compared the prayers
that would ascend from the congress, praising God and obtaining
from Him lasting peace, to the torrents of neighboring Niagara.
As part of the evening's program Miss Jessica Dragonette sang
three selections, and the Buffalo Philharmonic Orchestra played
several numbers.

Tuesday morning for the opening in Civic Stadium some
15,000 persons attended as the apostolic delegate, Archbishop
Cicognani, celebrated the Pontifical Mass in the presence of the
six cardinals. In his sermon, "The Wheat of Christ," Cardinal
Spellman said: "It is folly for us to deceive ourselves that we are
at peace for in truth we know that naught for which we fought
has come to fruit! The whole world and every human being in it
today faces the greatest crisis in the history of civilization." Later
he added: "The Holy Eucharist is the Sacrament of Peace, and
every Catholic should pledge his word to Christ that every week
—every day if possible—he will pay a visit to the Eucharistic
King, there to prepare himself for God's great gift of peace—the
Eucharist." After the sermon Monsignor Smith read the message
of the Holy Father to the congress, and at the end of the Mass
Cardinal Spellman gave the papal blessing. Tuesday afternoon
pontifical vespers, presided over by Cardinal Guevara, were sung
by more than 20,000 high and primary school children in the
Civic Stadium. That night approximately 20,000 gathered in
Memorial Auditorium for a general assembly addressed by Joseph
Scott of Los Angeles on "Memories," Monsignor Fulton Sheen on
"The Redemptive Way of the Eucharist," and Archbishop Rich-
ard Cushing on "Catholics and Their Bishops." Archbishop
McIntyre was chairman.

Wednesday morning approximately 40,000 children gathered
in Civic Stadium for a pontifical low Mass celebrated by Bishop
Edmund F. Gibbons of Albany with Cardinal Spellman presiding. This was one of the most impressive ceremonies of the congress because everyone seemed to go to Communion. There was
no sermon because Bishop O'Hara wanted the ceremony to be a
simple manifestation of the faith of the children in the Eucharist.
He also remembered that they were fasting, and after Mass each
was given a bottle of milk and two doughnuts for refreshments.
At the same time there was a pontifical Mass of the Slavonic Rite
in the Old Cathedral, with Bishop Senyshyn, O.S.B.M., singing

the Mass and Bishop Daniel Ivancho preaching the sermon on "Catholic Unity." Also at the same time at Hyde Park Stadium in Niagara Falls Cardinal Stritch of Chicago sang a pontifical Mass, at which Cardinal McGuigan presided and Cardinal Griffin of Westminster preached the sermon on "The Sacrament of Unity." The combined choir consisted of seminarians and priests from Niagara University, St. Bonaventure College, and the Little Seminary of Buffalo.

Besides these general meetings there were sectional meetings at which bishops, priests, and laymen spoke of their own particular problems in relation to the Church and to the Eucharist. The section meetings on Tuesday were for such groups as social workers, workers in the press and radio, the Missionary Union of the Clergy and the Society of the Propagation of the Faith, teachers, nurses, office workers, and public service personnel. On Wednesday the sectional meetings were held for farmers, lawyers, bankers and businessmen, college students, dentists, and physicians. There were also sectional meetings that were followed by holy hours before the Blessed Sacrament for the youth on Tuesday, for mothers, priests, and workingmen on Wednesday. To get speakers for this congress Bishop O'Hara drew on his wide circle of friends, generally securing a noted leader in each field as speaker. The holy hour for the workingmen was held in Civic Stadium and was attended by approximately 40,000. Bishop O'Hara had written to Archbishop Mooney of his plan for this meeting: "Since the ordinary workingmen made up ninety percent of the heads of families in the diocese of Buffalo, we wish to honor them with an outstanding program that will stress the dignity of labor and the beauties of Catholic home life." The speakers for this special meeting were Cardinals Spellman, McGuigan, Griffin, and Gilroy, and Joseph P. Kennedy and Charles S. Desmond. There was a public rosary led by Monsignor Leo J. Toomey, while out on the playing field the Knights of St. John formed a living rosary. At the holy hour that followed, Cardinal Guevara presided and Cardinal Stritch gave the sermon on "Christ the King." The holy hour for working women was held at Memorial Stadium Wednesday evening and was attended by about 12,000.

On Thursday there was a pontifical Mass for women in the morning in Memorial Auditorium, at which Cardinal Stritch sang the Mass, Cardinal Spellman presided, and Archbishop Vachon preached on "The Fountain of Living Waters," on the place of the Eucharist in the Catholic home. That afternoon was the crowning event of the congress, the outdoor procession with the Blessed Sacrament in Delaware Park. The attendance at this ceremony, at which Cardinal Spellman carried the Blessed Sacrament, was estimated at 200,000. After giving Benediction of the Blessed Sacrament, Cardinal Spellman closed the Congress with a prayer and a poem of his own composition.

The Congress was one of the happiest events in Bishop O'Hara's life. The weather was beautiful and everything seemed to take place in good order. He attributed the general success of the Congress, and the fine weather, to prayer. In the four days there had been seven cardinals, thirteen archbishops, and forty-three bishops in attendance along with some 557,000 clergy and laymen.

On October 3 the Bishop sent a letter to the pastors thanking them for their cooperation in making the congress a success. He included a letter to the children parallel to that of November 8 of the preceding year, in which he praised them for their cooperation but asked them to continue their prayers of thanksgiving for the graces received and to pray for all those who had come to the congress. He asked them to receive Holy Communion frequently, and if possible daily, during the next year for that intention. Talking to his sisters over the telephone about this, he admitted that he felt that if he could only get them to go to the sacraments for a few years, they would acquire a lifetime habit.

As the diocese returned to a more normal pace the Bishop faced the realities of his flock. In his letter of September 25 on the observance of September 29 as Confraternity of Christian Doctrine Day he made his feeling clear that Catholic children in public schools should be in Catholic schools. "Nevertheless due either to the failure to provide sufficient schools, or their ignorance, or negligence of parents there are more Catholic students in public schools than there are in the Catholic school system. . . ." He said that the danger to faith in such an environment came from three sources: from the teachers, from the texts used, and from their fellow students. Parents with children in the public schools must take precautions on these three points. This obligation extended not only to the grade schools and high schools but also to Catholic college students. He urged Catholic college students in non-Catholic colleges to get in touch with the Catholic chaplains before they selected their courses. He also announced the retreat for Catholics attending the public schools would be held on October 23–25. Later in his message on the feast of Christ the King he added a note about Catholics' relations with non-Catholics. "Be it said of the fair-mindedness of the vast majority of our fellow citizens, their hearts are right, and there would never be any question in their minds if it were not placed there by agitators who have some cause to serve. . . ."

In asking the faithful to take the pledge to support the Legion of Decency on Sunday, December 14, the Bishop took the occasion to criticize some of the books that were being distributed by national book clubs. "If a Catholic cannot correct a book club by protest, he cannot in conscience continue membership. If Catholics would fulfill their duty and cancel membership when a bad book is sent to them, the editorial policy of the Club would be changed quickly." Previously in opening the Catholic Book Week on November 14 at Canisius High, he had said: "A book in which God does not appear is against God."

The Bishop had dedicated the diocese to the Immaculate Heart of Mary and had shown great interest in the visions of Fatima. When he learned that a replica of the statue of Our Lady of Fatima was to tour the dioceses of the world, he decided that Buffalo should be the first American diocese it would visit and announced the visit on October 31. The statue was met at the International Bridge and, after a visit to St. Mary's Church in Niagara Falls, was carried to the New Cathedral, where its visit was opened with midnight Mass on December 8. The Bishop estimated that at the Mass 1,500 people received Communion, and the Cathedral was crowded. Faithful from other congregations joined in the veneration of the statue, and there was a constant procession of people. There was an increase in confessions and Communions not only in the Cathedral parish but generally in the city during the visit, which ended December 10.

On December 13 the Bishop went to Notre Dame to preside at the opening of the First Natural Law Institute under the direction of his friend Dean Clarence Manion. The Notre Dame *Alumnus* reported his opening address:

> The keynote of the Institute was sounded by Bishop O'Hara, when he warned that mankind, as a whole, must return to the Natural Law or lose all concept of the God-given rights of man. Such a catastrophe as loss of this concept, he added, would give rise to more dictators like Stalin and Hitler who would enslave and degrade the entire world.[59]

Somewhat along the same line he said in his Christmas sermon: "Submission to the will of God. Therein lies the whole secret of peace, just as in rebellion against God's will is the secret of all the woes of mankind." In the same sermon he praised the American tradition of freedom and spoke highly of the Declaration of Independence and the Constitution, which defended and guaranteed rights. And answering those who appealed to the courts against released time for religious education, he added:

It is not to the Declaration of Independence to which these false prophets appeal; it is to the new and nebulous theory of "Academic Freedom," the substance of which seems to be that "the right to affirm is the right to deny," the right to cure includes the right to kill.

After Christmas at home he had a visit with Secretary Forrestal in Washington, accompanied by Bishop McEntegart, and attended the consecration of Archbishop O'Boyle in New York. On January 6 the *Evening News* contained a photograph of the Bishop presenting a check for $100,000 to Sister Mary Melania of the German Orphan Asylum from the Centenary Fund. The Bishop also announced on January 7 the Annual Charities Appeal for the week of March 14–21 and named Walter J. Thompson of the Buffalo Electrical Company as chairman. He mentioned that the construction of a Catholic high school in Lockport would soon begin, as well as another in South Buffalo. The appeal would be called the Silver Jubilee Appeal since it was the twenty-fifth appeal. He announced the vice-chairman the next week and held a meeting with the leaders of the drive on January 25, at which he gave engraved rosaries to 34 outstanding men and women for their work in the charity drive. He continued his endless rounds of meetings and conferences, but as he told his sisters over the telephone on March 5, all was not labor. That, he said, had been his lucky day because the Bethlehem Steel Company had given $100,-000 unsolicited to the new infant home at Father Baker's orphanage, he had obtained a deed from the government covering some property at Niagara Falls for a high school, and a note against the diocese for $69,000 had been canceled and another loan of $1,000 that he had not hoped would be returned had been repaid.

Yet the Bishop had not lost his interest in national and international affairs. In a letter to Father John Cavanaugh he sent a message for Congressman Robert Grant:

If you are in touch with Bob Grant you might add a postscript to my letter to him. What I see in the administration's demand for both U.M.T. and Selective Service is a plea for U.M.T. in the face of Russian aggression. If the country wishes to support the President's firm stand on Russia, it can best do it by reviving the machinery of Selective Service immediately, but stipulating at the time that no one shall be selected under the act without further action by Congress. Meanwhile the Air Force and the Navy should be strengthened to the utmost, and the Army thrown open to genuine enlistment. Apparently, in an effort to put over U.M.T. the Army has done everything possible to discourage enlistments.

And he added an interesting request to Father Cavanaugh:

I wonder if you can help me solve a problem here in Buffalo. I have heard that at Notre Dame a Catholic list of great books has been drawn up. I should like to have such a list for our Catholic readers, who would be happy to substitute good Catholic books for the Index books recommended by Great Books Enterprise.[60]

Before the charity-appeal drive the Bishop made two broadcasts in its support. In the first he concentrated on the high-school program and stressed the impossibility of teaching religion in the public schools. He quoted George Sokolsky on the Supreme Court decisions that now a man could not be called a communist unless membership is proved and that a board of education cannot dismiss a teacher for membership in the Communist party. Sokolsky had added that a teacher could not be dismissed for teaching subversive doctrine. The Bishop agreed with Sokolsky that Marxism teaches a philosophy that eliminates "religion, morals, faith, charity." The Bishop said the columnist could have pointed out endless cases of Catholics, Jews, and Protestants who have lost their faith because "they entered the classes of teachers who have not hesitated to take advantage of the immaturity of their pupils." In his second speech the Bishop gave a history of the appeals during the past twenty-five years and their accomplishments.

During the appeal he called his family to say that in two days over $800,000 had been raised and in the end the appeal raised $132,000 over the allotted million. Before the week was over he flew to Los Angeles, where his friend Archbishop McIntyre was installed as Archbishop on March 19. In a letter dated March 16 the Bishop announced a special indulgence for those receiving the sacraments and praying for the Holy Father between Palm Sunday and Low Sunday. He also asked prayer at this time for the right outcome of the elections in Italy. Monsignor Montini wrote on April 21 to thank the people for their prayers for the Pope.

When he decided that he could not go to Melbourne to attend a centennial celebration, he wrote to Cardinal Spellman to present his respects to the Australian bishops and indicated why he could not go:

The contract for Bishop Timon School, which was the deciding factor in my determination to stay home, should be let within a week. Bricklaying should begin next week on DeSales High School, Lockport. We may have a third project this summer—a temporary structure to house Bishop Ryan High School for the Polish parishes. The priests of East Buffalo have counted on the purchase of a public school building. If they are disappointed in this, we may have to build a temporary structure—of steel buildings purchased from the War Assets Administration—to relieve the present overcrowded quarters.[61]

On July 6 there was a regional congress of the Confraternity of Christian Doctrine. The region included the ecclesiastical provinces of New York, New Jersey, and Toronto. On July 5, the eve of the congress, the Bishop gave a welcome to the delegates over station WBEN, saying that Pius X had originated both the Confraternity and the periodical congresses. He quoted that Pope's encyclical of April 5, 1905, *Acerbo nimis,* in which the Pope had called attention to the "secularization" of much of the world's education by the political and philosophical liberalism of the nineteenth century. The Pope had insisted on the instruction of the catechism every Sunday and feast day and on the erection of the Confraternity of Christian Doctrine in every parish. Later in the same speech Bishop O'Hara praised Pius X for undoing the work of the Jansenists.[62]

Along with his interest in national affairs the Bishop had not given up his interest in the activities of the Notre Dame Bureau of Economic Research or in the publications of Father Edward Keller, C.S.C. He had not taken kindly to the critics of Father Keller, one of whom was Father Raymond A. McGowan of the Social Action Department of the N.C.W.C. When the Bishop received his prepublication copy of the Labor Day Statement for 1948 of the Social Action Department written by Father McGowan, he sent a letter of protest to Archbishop McNicholas, O.P., chairman of the Executive Committee of the N.C.W.C., against some things in the statement. He insisted that the statement did not recognize the friendly critics of labor, had only one sentence friendly to the Taft-Hartley Bill, did not pay attention to the demands of the common good, recommended the "industry Council" without defining what it was, and in its discussion on laws on public housing was too scant. He added, "To these specific points I wish to add a request that 'Statements of the Social Action Department' be again placed on the agenda for the Bishops' meeting in November."[63] He sent copies of this letter to several other archbishops and bishops. He received a few replies, and some bishops thought that the criticism about the absence of a definition of what was meant by an industry council was valuable. He also wrote on October 25 to Cardinal Spellman:

The only unfinished business I recall is the matter of the Industrial Councils. I am preparing for your Eminence a copy of a document which demonstrates that the "Social Action Committee" is campaigning for the Council proposed by Philip Murray in 1940. I shall include a criticism of the scheme by Father Cronin who says that it will work only in a totalitarian state. Murray calls for a system that will have absolute control over quantity, quality, price, and all conditions of production. I expect to have this copy ready in a few days.[64]

Later when the Bishops met Bishop O'Hara had little success in seeking a condemnation of Father McGowan's proposals.

The approach of the 1948–1949 school year gave occasion for the Bishop to write a letter telling of the accomplishments in Catholic education in the diocese since his arrival. Eight new parochial schools had been opened, five parochial schools that had been closed during the depression had been reopened, and three schools had been enlarged. Nine new schools were planned for the next year. Of the new diocesan high schools seven new ones were in operation and two new high-school buildings were under construction. Not only were the existing colleges and universities filled but one new college, Rosary Hill, conducted by the Sisters of Saint Francis, would open that September. He urged parents who were unable to find room for their young men or women in the local Catholic colleges to explore the vacancies in other Catholic colleges. He admitted that unfortunately there were not yet enough parochial schools to take care of all the Catholic children of the diocese.

At the dedication of the new Canisius High School on August 29 he took occasion to talk on one of his favorite themes—the costs of Catholic education as a saving to the public. He thanked the Jesuits for the new contribution to their "worldwide" system of educational facilities. He said: "The Community appreciates having the benefit of the four centuries of experience that have gone into the manning of this magnificent educational system." He then stressed the economic saving this plant meant to the community, since the building cost $750,000 or $750 per pupil. The cost of a public high school was $2,500 a pupil and that of the diocese was $1,500 per pupil. He further said that the cost of the eight new schools of the diocese was $870,000, or $435 per pupil. He said he made these observations to assure the faithful that the operational costs of Catholic schools were "usually about one-fourth of that of public schools. . . . We have no objection to swimming pools, but we are willing to wait for them while we provide the essentials." He wanted Catholic citizens to understand this:

I want them to know that even with their generous contributions for the construction and operation of Catholic schools, they are paying less than they would have to pay if they forgot their Christian obligation and threw upon the state the entire burden of their children's schooling.

The Bishop wrote another letter on September 10 in which he spoke of Catholics attending non-Catholic colleges and universities. These students should explore the possibility of acceptance at a Catholic college. In advising them to affiliate with a Newman club—which, he said, was established in each secular college in the diocese—he laid down some strict rules:

They are reminded that the reading of books against faith and morals proscribed by the Index is a matter of serious sin and that those proscribed by the Holy Father are forbidden to be read under the pain of excommunication. They are reminded also that Catholics are not free to take courses that deal directly with religious subjects, such as ethics, philosophy of religion, comparative religion, etc. if they are of a non-Catholic nature. Catholics are not permitted to use Bible textbooks not approved by the Church. In some universities, courses in literature demand the reading of books of an immoral nature, which cannot be read under any circumstances.

Students should seek advice and direction from their chaplains in regard to these matters. They should also join study clubs that will provide them with positive Catholic philosophical and religious teaching, without which their lives will have a spiritual vacuum which may be filled with harmful philosophies.

This was the old prefect of religion speaking.

In answer to an invitation from John H. Cassidy to attend a dinner honoring Monsignor John P. Boland, the Buffalo labor priest, and the tenth anniversary of the labor college, the Bishop wrote on December 13:

Monsignor Boland has done great service to the working man of the Diocese of Buffalo, the State of New York and the United States. Since we of the diocese are most directly concerned with the benefits of his labors, it is right that we should give him this recognition on the tenth anniversary.[65]

At the dinner on December 29 the Bishop was present and paid tribute publicly to Monsignor Boland. While the two men may not have agreed in some matters, their relations were always very friendly.

Another interesting sidelight on the Bishop's principles of conduct was the answer he sent on January 5, 1949, to a friend who asked him to officiate at his wedding:

Dear Charles,

While I appreciate the kind thought that prompts you to ask me to officiate at your wedding I feel that I must decline the honor. In the first place, I have not performed any marriage ceremonies in Buffalo, and I have officiated only twice since I came here, both times outside the diocese for relatives.

In the second place, I have in the past refrained from officiating at mixed marriages, because I feel that if I were to officiate it might weaken in some degree the action I must take to the encouragement of Catholic people to marry Catholics.

With the Catholic Church, I recognize that there will always be mixed marriages, but also with the Church I want to discourage them. A pastor has the duty to perform them for his parishoners if they fulfill the requirements of the Church in the matter. I have never been a pastor, so I have never had the duty.[66]

Urging the collections for relief and for War Relief Services the Bishop took occasion at a Holy Name rally on January 9 to make a special defense of Cardinal Mindszenty and urged the Holy Name men to protest the Cardinal's arrest. He made light of the charges against the Cardinal, saying that he himself had been guilty of the same so-called "crimes," such as using the black market. He named February 6 as Mindszenty day.

The Bishop as the assistant chairman of Catholic Action study went to Havana to attend the Second Inter-American Week of Catholic Action February 7 to 15. On his return he went to the Mayo Clinic for a check-up. He wrote of this to Father Cousineau, C.S.C.:

Since my return from Cuba I spent a week at the Mayo clinic at Rochester, Minnesota. I was having a bit of trouble with my feet and I thought that it would be well to have a check-up, since I had not had one for five years.

The doctors told me that my physical condition was excellent. Further they corrected the difficulty by the simple device of adding a bit of leather to the arch of the shoe.[67]

Whether the Bishop asked the doctors about his sinuses or other discomforts is not certain. Even the simple remedy for his feet did not prevent him having trouble with his knees a short time later. He was now preparing his data for his *ad limina* visit to Rome. In addition there was the Annual Charities Appeal April 3 to 10, during which the million-dollar mark was reached on the fourth day, with a grand total of $1,178,481. His pleasure over this was expressed in his Easter message:

Easter is the festival of God's love. It is only in the incarnation and the death of the Son of God and his glorious Resurrection that we can know the depth of that love. God willed the redemption in the form it took so that we might know the malice of sin and the infinity of divine love.

He was also pleased that Communions had increased in the diocese.

The diocese is blessed when this happens. The love of God radiating from your life of prayer will bring others to the love of God and will help cure the world's ills—for there is nothing wrong with the world that prayer and love of God will not cure.

The Bishop managed to keep quite well informed on matters of general public interest, although he did not participate in politics proper. His strong protest against the imprisonment of Catholic leaders behind the Iron Curtain showed his interest in international affairs, and he showed his interest in Catholic problems of domestic importance by his actions. He continued to act as a member of the Board of Trustees of The Catholic University and did not make friends there by his close scrutiny of the budget. He noted to another Bishop: "We surely need to keep a close watch on the Social Action Department . . . ," although he could not get the other bishops to censure the department. To the same friend he noted that the Executive Committee of the trustees of The Catholic University had rejected the proposed budget because it was based on an increased student enrollment. As this was the period in which college enrollments, expanded by the returned veterans, had begun to shrink, he said that the trustees had demanded to be informed of the basis of the optimism about the next year's enrollment. At the request of Archbishop Cushing he had also agreed to preside at the opening session of the Second National Congress on Catholic Youth in Washington on April 26. April 29 the Bishop and Monsignor Smith started for Rome for the *ad limina* visit.

Of this trip much was routine, but there were some personal side lights that he related to his family. Writing on May 6 he told of his search for his ancestors.

The day in Ireland was magnificent, but it revealed the fact that father had no ancestors. I searched the records at Gort in vain for an O'Hara or a Hare—there was not even a Hehir registered for those days. Bishop Rogers, with whom I stayed, promised to look into the records at Tubbers, a neighboring parish. At Kilrush I found no end of Galvins, but none of our names appeared, and no Brody to fit the description of Nancy's husband. There were only four Brodys in the book. Bishop Rogers is half Brody, so he is going after that one for me, too. There is one O'Hara family—Protestant—Gort. The pastor hoped that he was no kin of ours, and so do we.

An observation of the pastors: Some of the names quite numerous a hundred years ago have disappeared from the countryside.[68]

His letter of May 12 to Cardinal Spellman gave some information about the business phase of the trip:

Although the documents were delivered in the requested order, beginning with Msgr. Tardini the morning after my midnight arrival, I have delayed writing until after my audience. That came yesterday, and it was most satisfactory. His Holiness asked many questions about your Eminence, especially about your working too hard, and I "confessed and did not deny"—but added that it was after the example of His Holiness.

I have told His Holiness, Galeazzi and Tardini about your desire for a prompt return of Msgr. McMahon to the Near East; and I agree with Cardinal Tisserant that it was well for the Monsignor to be on the scene. And before I go on I want to congratulate Your Eminence on the stand of the Latin American bloc. I mentioned the name of Belaunde to Galeazzi and His Holiness.

Father Heston is making a good translation of the address made to the industrialists on Sunday regarding "socialization" of production goods. I thanked the Holy Father for that address and told him of the temptation of some of our social actionists to emulate the English trend. He thanked me in turn for Father Keller's "most important studies" which Galeazzi had gone over with him the previous evening. I also presented Coyle's statement before the Senate Committee. I have found an extra copy here and am giving it to Galeazzi—who sees the picture thoroughly.[69]

Of his travels in Europe he wrote on May 16 to his family:

You will not have a chance to answer this as I'll be on my way from here Saturday. I have an army engagement in Austria and Trieste Saturday to Monday and will then leave with the Colkets for an auto trip through Switzerland. We will arrive in Paris on the 29th or 30th. We will leave for home on the 30th arriving in New York at 7:45 Tuesday morning. The address in Paris will be the Royal Monceau Hotel but I don't expect to be there long—a day at most, and possibly not at all. Checking the itinerary I find that we leave Venice on the 25th from Lugano, continue to Lucerne on the 26th, and to Geneva on the 27th. The Royal Daniella Hotel in Venice will be the address on Monday and Tuesday, care of Mr. G. H. Colket. I don't know where we will put up for the night the rest of the week. I have winter clothing which I hear is needed in Switzerland. We will have to go by train through the Simplon Tunnel, since the St. Gothard Pass is blocked by snow.

Tuesday I attended a canonization and the Pope's Mass. Monsignor Smith arrived back from Fatima Saturday night full of enthusiasm.

Archbishop Schulte arrived at 4 A.M. Sunday, but was not at the canonization at 8:00. Archbishop Ritter, Bishop Helmsing and ten other Americans were there.[70]

Interviewed in New York and Buffalo by the local newspapers, the Bishop gave brief accounts of his visit with the Pope and of his travels in Europe. To John Boccio of the *Evening News* he said on June 1:

> . . . the pontiff displayed keen interest in diocesan activities, particularly the high school program, which the bishop launched several years ago, and the work of the Bishop's Committee for Christian Home & Family, which begins education of the child from the cradle.

"The spirit of the Italian people is excellent," Bishop O'Hara said. "Economically, spiritually and socially, they appear to be much better off now. I think they have shaken off the threat of Communism. From what I could observe and judging by what I was told, Communism seems to be just a nuisance."

To a reporter of the *Courier-Express* he spoke about international affairs. Speaking of the end of the Berlin Blockade, he said: "Maybe we will see a more reasonable policy." But he added about the Russians: "You must weigh every move carefully," and he asserted that Russian tactics may be designed to trick observers.

As is usual when a prelate visits Rome, he brought back honors for the leaders of the diocese. Ten priests were made monsignors. Six laymen were made Knights of Saint Gregory: John C. Brady, M.D., the president of the Catholic Physicians' Guild; Joseph H. Wechter, a justice of the Supreme Court of the State of New York; Patrick J. Dwyer, a contractor; Thomas G. Burke, a prominent lawyer; Francis E. Fronczak, M.D., a former commissioner of public health and trustee of Catholic Charities; and Joseph G. Lichen, a prominent Catholic of Lakeview.

When the Bishop returned to this country, he found that the Catholic press was discussing with some energy the so-called Barden Bill, which would have excluded private schools from the proposed government aid to education. Until this time the general attitude of Catholics throughout the country had been one of opposition to all federal aid or control of education. Bishop O'Hara was a firm believer in that tradition, since he was opposed on principle to centralization in government. In his letter of June 15 to the faithful he urged them to send telegrams and letters to their congressmen in opposition to federal aid to education. He said:

> For the past thirty years I have followed with interest the various

attempts that have been made to secure federal aid for schools and to transfer the control of the nation's schools from local authorities to the Federal government. It is my conviction that of all the bills that have reached the voting stage in those years, the present bills, Senate Bill 246 and House Bill 4043, are the least qualified to attain sound objectives and the most dangerous to our American traditions of education.

A frenzied opposition to Catholic education has been heard in support of these two measures. . . .

The following Sunday, June 19, Cardinal Spellman attacked the Barden Bill and its author, Representative Graham Barden of North Carolina. The public reaction to his speech was very strong. On June 23 Bishop O'Hara sent out a circular on the same subject and published it in the *Union and Echo.* He referred also to the Thomas Bill, which had passed the Senate. His points were not the same as those raised by Cardinal Spellman in his speech:

. . . The measures are anti-Catholic; they count the parochial children in determining the amount of aid to the states, and then count them out in the distribution of the benefits. . . .

. . . This is discrimination against Southern Negroes. There is an abundance of evidence available to show that the poorest schools in the nation are those provided for the Southern Negroes.

. . . .

The Catholic Church in the United States, in her constant opposition to Federal aid to education, has always maintained that educational problems can best be solved at the local level. That is still the position of the Bishops. During the past few years the Bishops have yielded a point in that they have tolerated the idea of federal assistance in areas of great need, provided that it can be demonstrated that local resources are inadequate to supply the minimum needs and provided also that the control is local.

At the end of the letter the Bishop estimated the savings to communities by the operation of the Catholic parochial schools. Then he concluded: "With Cardinal Spellman we ask you to pray for the misguided individuals in public and private life who are working to destroy our American pattern of education and life."

The summer was passed in routine work with a two weeks' vacation at Notre Dame in July. On September 9 he found occasion in certain industrial disturbances to publish in the *Union and Echo* a pastoral condemnation of violence in strikes:

Please announce to your parishioners that while Holy Mother Church defends the right of workingmen to form unions and strike peacefully for the defense of their rights and the redress of just grievances, this right may be used only after all other means have failed, and in the exercise of this right the workingmen must not go beyond just means to obtain their end.

Holy Mother Church does not and cannot countenance personal violence or the destruction of property in strikes. She cannot approve such means because they are contrary to the natural law. In her defense of the rights of workingmen, the Church has through the Popes, condemned violence and bloodshed in strikes. . . .

Most of his letters that fall were just the usual announcements of special collections with exhortations to generosity. He presided at the closing exercises of the diocesan institutes and also at the dedication of the new Christ the King Seminary on October 16. In his speech on the blessing of the cornerstone of Bishop Timon High School, a $950,000 building, he spoke again of the savings to the community made by the building of parochial schools. He also recognized a complaint that was being made that the city was losing $3,490 in taxes when the diocese took over the Kirke R. Wilson estate for a chancery office. He noted:

This amount is less than enough to carry two children through the elementary schools of Buffalo, from kindergarten to eighth grade. And yet the Catholics of this city carry more than 25,000 children through their elementary schools and 6,500 through their high schools without one cent of subsidy from taxes.

He claimed that buildings alone to house these Catholic students would cost $50,000,000. He then turned to the spiritual advantages of Catholic education, such as obedience to parents and to lawful authority and the power of prayer which these schools gave.

As if to emphasize his evaluation of the value and services of the Catholic schools, he continued to acquire properties for other schools. Several valuable pieces of property were acquired either for schools or for residences of the religious who were to teach in the schools. There was a bit of verse current about these purchases of old mansions on Delaware Avenue that went something like this:

> Little Mansion don't you cry
> You will be a convent bye and bye.

There was always considerable interest in the relations between Monsignor John P. Boland and the Bishop, especially among those who knew that they differed considerably on economic theories. The Bishop continued his fostering of the work of Father Edward Keller, C.S.C, and was usually very quick to oppose any theory that implied a radically unjust distribution of wealth in this country, or any theory calling for governmental interference to produce a better distribution. A letter which he wrote to the Monsignor on January 9, 1950, not only illustrates the Bishop's opinions but also shows his dexterity with statistics:

The article to which I made reference Sunday is published in the Catholic observer [*sic*] for Thursday, December 27th. It is on the editorial page and is entitled "One Fourth of Families Earn under $2,000.00."

The article is based on a recent publication of the joint committee on the income report: "Low Income Families and Economic Stability." The entire report needs to be studied—and it will well pay study. In my difference of opinion with the Social Action Department in the N.C.W.C., I have been very largely concerned with the condition of the lowest income group in the United States. I have asked the Department to seek them out, study their real condition of life, and make recommendations for the improvement of their status.

The report gives us a great deal of information under these heads, and I believe, shows where we can start to improve conditions.

The report indicates that of the nine million six hundred thousand families receiving less than $2,000.00 a year in 1948, three million three hundred thousand live on farms, mostly in the South.

One million seven hundred thousand non-farm families are headed by persons sixty-five years of age or over.

Two million two hundred thousand unskilled or semi-skilled workers, mostly unorganized labor.

Eight hundred thousand Negroes.

One million five hundred thousand of these families have widows as family heads. These include divorced persons and those widowed by death.

More than four million of family heads have no high school education.

One million five hundred thousand of these cases require vocational rehabilitation.

One line of investigation that suggests itself is the substitution of a local activity of the Marshall Plan when it comes to an end. Washington is suggesting constantly that there may be a depression when we take away from American business the five billion dollars or so we are giving to Europe each year. We could make up that market if we could increase the income of these nine million six hundred thousand families about $500.00 a year. We could do this by the application of point four of the present economic program to the local picture. We could do a much better job at home than abroad because the tastes of the people in the lowest income groups are already educated sufficiently to make them customers for American goods, while abroad there is a great deal of resistance to novelty among people of the lowest income group. Rex Tugwell learned this when he tried to force the Puerto Ricans to eat breakfast food. They wanted rice, beans, and fish and when he sent them breakfast food instead they said they would starve sooner than eat it. I don't blame them. Without refrigerators in a hot climate you can't do much with milk, and breakfast food is not particularly attractive without milk.

This is only one line of possible investigation and action. A study of the report will suggest others. Suppose we put our heads together on it one of these times. . . .[71]

In a supplementary letter on this subject the Bishop added: "One thing I want to know is how many in the lowest income brackets are receiving the major portion of their income from interest, dividends, rents and royalties."

His interest in getting every Catholic child into a Catholic school never abated. On January 11 he wrote that while some children could not get into Catholic schools, there were some vacant seats in some of these schools. He had heard that some Catholic children had even been told to go to the public schools. He wanted to avoid this if possible: "Let it be the rule hereafter—then, that no Catholic child be refused admission to a parochial school, if there be an empty seat in the class to which he seeks admission, whether he belongs to the parish or not." He asked Monsignor Holbel to take a census of the schools to see where these empty seats were and where there were applicants for them. If the children came from another parish, the other parish would be billed at twenty-five dollars per student. Later he wrote a letter on the value of Catholic education while announcing that there would be 700 additional seats in Catholic high schools the next year. He added:

The Catholic Church has in the past lost much of her potential strength among her educated people by the fact that so many of them received a fine secular education without a corresponding spiritual development along religious lines. If a man or woman received a college degree and has only an eighth grade knowledge of religion, the Church is deprived of spiritual resources she needs for her work in the world today.

Take one striking example. Of the five justices of the Supreme Court who were Catholics only one, Chief Justice White, is known to have had the benefit of a thorough training in Catholic philosophy.

When Congressman Chester Gorski wrote to make sure of the Bishop's position on federal aid to education, the Bishop gave a clear answer in his letter of January 19:

Under the circumstances I would prefer to see the majority of Congressmen vote against all federal aid to education. Up to this point, all federal grants have been non-denominational. I believe it would be fatal to the American way of life to introduce a discrimination pattern.[72]

By this he meant discrimination against parochial schools.

To help publicize the collection for the Bishops' Relief Fund to be held on the last Sunday of January, the Bishop held a reception at his home for twenty-five children from refugee families. *The Courier-Express* said: "Children from a dozen European countries, some of whom did not know a word of English a few months ago, climbed up on the Bishop's knees and talked freely in their new tongue." And the Bishop, speaking of the threats they might have endured in their former countries, said: "Here you can't distinguish them from other American children."

The Bishop's strong feeling on the matter of sex education brought him into public controversy when the film "Human Growth" was proposed for showing to the children of the city. The film was produced by the State Board of Health to teach matters of life by a study of anatomy.[73] The Buffalo Board of Education had decided to show the film to the children in the seventh and eighth grades of a public school. When the Bishop learned of this, he wrote a letter to the pastors forbidding Catholic children to see the movie. He told them:

Since there is abundant evidence that the film violates certain principles set forth by the late Pope Pius XI in his encyclical on Christian education I have no choice but to forbid Catholic children to attend the showing of this film and to forbid Catholic parents to authorize such attendance on the part of their children.

This authorization of the parents was required by the school board in its ruling. Some Protestant clergymen accused the Bishop of interfering in the school department, and they were answered at the meeting of the Western New York Catholic Librarians' Conference by Bishop Burke and Monsignor Holbel. Bishop Burke said: "We do not give up our rights as citizens because of our Catholicity," and Monsignor Holbel called the ministers' statement "a vicious attack on a decision made by the ordinary of the diocese."

In the meantime the Bishop did not relent on the Social Action Department of the N.C.W.C. To Archbishop McIntyre he wrote on February 24:

Did you notice the latest appeal of the Catholic Action Notes for financial contributions? It was stated that they wanted to have more of their funds from their subscribers, and take less from the budget of the N.C.W.C. Social Action Department. It seems to me that zero instead of "less" was what they explained last fall as the contribution of the N.C.W.C. to the publication.[74]

To Archbishop O'Boyle he wrote on February 27: "I want to congratulate you on the patience and perseverance you have shown in keeping the Social Action Department within bounds. There has been a vast improvement." But his feelings on these matters were not necessarily against the Social Action Department. On February 14 he sent copies of Melchior Payli's *Socialized Medicine and the Welfare State* to Archbishop O'Boyle and Cardinal Spellman. To Cardinal Spellman he wrote:

Oscar Hewing [*sic*] is expected to release soon a new plan for socialized medicine based on his trip to Europe. I have heard that the report was prepared before he made the trip. Be that as it may, our Catholic health problem may be in danger from socialized medicine, so I think our priests ought to have a broad factual background such as provided in the Payli book!

Along similar lines he wrote to Father Leo Gerry on February 20, thanking him for preparing a study of low-income groups:

Thank you very kindly for the tremendous job you have done in gathering data on low income families and on the problem of using surplus food for distribution among the needy.

. . . .

Curiously enough, it is possible for a millionaire to be in that lowest tenth. While there is insufficient data given on the source of income it is indicated that a very large sector belongs to the age group sixty five and older. Among my acquaintances over the years I have known quite a few wealthy people who have withdrawn their capital from investments, to save headaches, and who have decided to live from their capital for the rest of their lives. These people would certainly show up in the lowest tenth of income group, but they are surely not in distress.

Also he wrote to Thomas W. Pangborn of Hagerstown a note along the same general direction:

I am always gratified by evidence of American ingenuity. For six years I have been particularly keen in protecting from socialistic encroachment the American system that has done so much to make living pretty comfortable for the great majority of our people. I do not know whether you are familiar with the work Father Keller is doing at Notre Dame to protect private enterprise. If you are not, I hope you will look him up the next time you go to Notre Dame and have him give you some of his material.

As usual the financial welfare of the diocese was involved in the Annual Charities Appeal. When he announced the annual drive on February 26, the Bishop said that the budget for charities for the next year would be $701,591.02. Later he listed the expenditures planned for high schools. The grounds formerly occupied by the Business Institute of the Christian Brothers was to be made over into Bishop Fallon High School, Bishop McMahon High School was to be moved to Delaware Avenue, Bishop Timon High School was to be enlarged, and a new high school to be named after Cardinal Mindszenty was planned for Dunkirk. He listed the present enrollments and other charitable works of the diocese and mentioned that the diocese had contributed $338,234.40 to the missions during the previous year.

One of the most important groups by nationality in the Buffalo diocese was the Polish. Bishop O'Hara was very happy to cooperate with the leaders of the Polish community in their efforts to foster the welfare of their people in Buffalo. As in American communities of Polish extraction, the sad political situation in Poland found expression. When Bishop James Cassidy asked Bishop O'Hara about the recent refugee priests he answered on March 6:

We find some reluctance on the part of Polish pastors to take displaced priests, because they are used to doing so much work in English among the young people that they find an exile from Poland less efficient than a native born Polish priest. However, most of those have caught on quickly and the ones we have accepted here have done excellent work.

At about the same time in answer to a query of Father Felix Seroczynski of the Fort Wayne diocese, who was preparing an encyclopedia article, Bishop O'Hara gave a brief statement of the condition of the Polish Catholics in his diocese:

Here are some of the statistics you asked for: Secular priests, 109; Religious priests 49 (44 O.F.M. Conv., 2 Scholae Piae, 3 Society of the Catholic Apostolate); Polish parishes 43; territorial parishes with large Polish minorities 17; Polish grammar schools 32 with 9853 pupils; Polish high schools 5, students 1100 (There are Polish students in other Catholic high schools.)

There are two motherhouses of Polish Sisters in the Diocese, and one other community serves here. The Felician Sisters have 541 members, the Franciscan Sisters of St. Joseph 127, and the Bernardine Sisters 16 (These represent only the Sisters working in the Diocese of Buffalo.) The Felician Sisters conduct an orphan home of 343 children, a home for spastics, with forty patients, a working girls' home with 24 girls in residence and two day nurseries with 95 children. The Franciscan Sisters of Saint Joseph have a home for the aged with 85 clients.

There are 20 Polish pastors employed in strictly Polish parishes, and there are 7 assistants similarly assigned. The Polish seminarians number 33 in the Major Seminary and 41 in the Minor. These are studying for the Diocese of Buffalo. In addition there are 26 boys and 57 girls in training for membership in religious institutes.

Thus far there are five Polish churches that have introduced at least one English sermon every week.

Thus far we have received five displaced priests, and three more are expected shortly.

With regard to the Polish National Church, we keep a discreet silence. The one church manifests a little activity, but not much. Its membership is calculated to be less than 3,000. We have many returns on the part of the young people when they move to a neighborhood of the Church. By silence we have avoided the antagonisms which could give light to the whole schism.

Buffalo has a Polish mayor for the first time. He seems to be an excellent man, and is a fine Catholic. We also have a Polish Congressman, who is a trustee of his own parish church. One Polish physican, Dr. Fronczak, is a Knight of St. Gregory. The Judge of the Juvenile Court is Polish, so is the chairman of the School Board, Dr. Maria Kazmiersczak.

On the day before the Annual Charities Appeal, March 26, the Bishop went on the air to urge support. The drive was again more than a success and the one-million-dollar goal was topped by more than $200,000.

On May 8 the Bishop observed quietly the fifth anniversary of his arrival in Buffalo. But the Buffalo *Evening News* of April 27 thought his accomplishments needed recording:

Future historians will probably cite above all else the tremendous impetus which Catholic secondary education received under Bishop O'Hara's leadership.

On May 5, 1945, when he was installed in century-old rites in St. Joseph Cathedral, the eight county diocese had no diocesan high schools.

Today it boasts seven schools, will add two more in the fall. Present registration of 2093 will leap to more than 3500 by September. The cost to date has been about $2,500,000. The Bishop initiated the high school program to bring Catholic education to more high school students at a minimum tuition.

Bishop O'Hara has greatly expanded the Missionary Apostolate which carries the church into rural regions. He added several missions, saw nine churches arise. During his episcopacy a men's retreat house was started at Darby, a women's retreat house will be started soon on Delaware Avenue and another men's retreat house will be opened.

He initiated the Catholic Information Center and the Marriage Counseling Department.

Bishop O'Hara who was ordained to the priesthood 33 years ago, will be 62 years old Monday.

When he was interviewed on the eighth, he gave praise to Bishop Burke, the priests, and the people of the diocese, adding:

The supernatural spirit so manifest in the family life of the Diocese of Buffalo speaks well for the past and finds hope for the future. When families are inspired by the Holy Family, the sacramental life of the community is strong and only education is needed to produce sturdy spiritual citizenship.

I am grateful for the past and present. The future is in God's hands.

On June 1 he made another proposal to the diocese for improving the educational progress of the Catholics of Buffalo. There were 7,500 students from the diocese in Catholic colleges, but there were also 4,000 in secular colleges. He made a special plea that those who could should establish grants-in-aid so that the poorer students with ability could attend Catholic colleges. He asked that 2,000 people grant a 1,000 dollars for such scholarships and that some who could not give that amount give a partial amount to be added to other funds by the chancery or the college in question.

Despite all the building the Bishop had to admit that he had not mastered the problem of giving Catholic education to all Catholic children. In a letter of June 13 to the clergy for their information, and not for publication, he admitted that they were giving Catholic education to a little more than half of the Catholic children of the diocese:

In the city of Buffalo there are twenty-nine parishes that have public school enrollments of 200 or more. There are thirty-two such parishes outside the city. Nineteen of these sixty-one parishes have new schools (either recently completed or in construction or planning stage) that will help reduce the large waiting list for Catholic elementary education. But there are many thousands for whose spiritual needs there is no immediate provision.

On June 22 the Bishop went to Notre Dame to dedicate the first germ-free laboratory unit of Professor Arthur Reyniers. The Bishop had sponsored Professor Reyniers' projects, beginning during the period of his presidency of Notre Dame. Next to the Bureau of Economic Research Professor Reyniers' plans had been one of his most persistent interests, although he had not been so successful in getting financial help for these plans as he had been for Father Keller's studies. Notre Dame was still close to him. Shortly after his visit he wrote to Father John J. Cavanaugh, the president of Notre Dame, expressing some fears about the continued expansion of the student body. "In my own concern for the financial security of the University, I venture to express the hope that there be some contraction in the size of the student enrollment. The heavy salary expense for lay teachers at the present time must be back-breaking."

Bishop O'Hara watched rather carefully over Father Edward Keller and was always ready to accept any challenge to Father Keller's work, although he usually asked Father Keller not to reply to his critics. In the July, 1949, issue of *The Priest*, J.F.C., under the title "The Social Problem Today," referred to a previous article by William Hurd that had accepted statements of Father Keller on the distribution of wealth in the United States. J.F.C. rejected Father Keller's contentions on seven problems of social life of the United States. On August 23 Bishop O'Hara wrote to Father John F. Cronin, S.S., apparently J.F.C., in Father Keller's defense.

My concern for an impartial hearing for Father Keller is based on much more than the fact that I first assigned Father to his research work in economics; as a priest I have long been alarmed at the *ex parte* pleadings of priests which have often been based on erroneous data, taken from sources which have been far from impartial. My purpose in setting up the Bureau of Economic Research at Notre Dame was to arrive at the facts of our economy, in an absolutely objective spirit.

I enclose two of Father Keller's studies and a recent government publication, *The Gift of Freedom*. Too many of Father's critics have not read him attentively. The government publication is evidently intended as a reply to Soviet misrepresentation of the life of the "American Slave Laborer." Being slanted in that direction, it contradicts many of the conclusions based on the same data it uses.

The Bishop enclosed another letter of detailed criticism of Father Cronin's article with approximately eighteen points of criticism. In conclusion he hoped that Father Cronin would realize that he had misrepresented Father Keller's studies, although Father Keller and Father Cronin were in agreement on some of Father Cronin's seven points. Father Cronin was not unknown to the Bishop because he was chairman of a committee studying the industrial councils for the bishops, and had already sent a preliminary account of the committee's study. Of this the Bishop wrote to Archbishop O'Boyle:

Father Cronin's report on the deliberation of the Industry Council Committee reached me early this month and I have just completed a study of it. Since I have been a critic of the past Industrial Council recommendations of the Social Action Department, I think I should send you a carbon copy of my letter to Father Cronin. I am very happy over the results achieved.

Nevertheless the criticism amounted to some four typewritten pages, and full approval of the publication of the committee's report was never given.

On June 13 the Bishop sent a letter to the pastors discussing the expanding enrollments of the Catholic schools and suggested the use of double sessions of one or two sections of each school and the training of a corps of lay teachers in a special program at D'Youville College. This letter along with Monsignor Holbel's outline of the D'Youville experiment in training teachers Bishop O'Hara sent to Cardinal Spellman, who submitted it in turn to his diocesan school officials. On July 13 Monsignor John J. Voight submitted a rather devastating criticism of the program— chiefly that it would add an unsupportable burden on existing facilities and teachers. Cardinal Spellman sent this report on to Bishop O'Hara on July 22. On August 9 the Bishop, after consulting his own officials, answered Monsignor Voight's eight points of criticism with eight answers, proposing in some cases corrective measures that would erase the criticisms. His conclusion, however, did not admit of failure:

It is true that "Our Catholic schools can accomplish only so much." However, we are trying to have them accomplish just a little bit more. In five years we have increased attendance at Catholic schools only six thousand, and we want to see if we can double that number in the next few years. Many of our new schools are not yet at full capacity, since they start with only two or three grades.

That ends my reply to Monsignor Voight's memorandum. However, I feel that I should add a note on our experience with lay teachers. Many of them have done very well, and some of them have become nuns. We are hoping that the apostolic note imparted to the preparation this summer at D'Youville will be carried to the classrooms by these devout ladies, and that some more of them will feel the stirrings of the grace of a vocation.

When the Cardinal wrote in agreement with the Bishop's answer, the Bishop wrote again on August 28:

I am greatly encouraged by the commendation contained in your letter of August 18, with reference to our experiment with lay teachers in the parochial schools. Monsignor Holbel informs me that all but three of the newly prepared cadet teachers have already been placed, and that he is certain of assignments of those three.

He adds, however, that very few of the pastors are accepting the invitation to hold double sessions. Our letters had the effect of turning them to a search for more rooms. Many new classrooms have been reported, through the reconversion to classrooms set aside for particular societies that meet once a week or less often. This campaign had a very stimulating effect.

Sometime when I am in New York I want to go over with Father Rigney the motion picture problem. I know that one of your priests in the office of schools is devoting a good bit of time to visual education, but I have not heard much about it myself.

The Bishop was a faithful attendant at episcopal consecrations, going to those of Bishops MacKenzie and Markham on September 14 in Boston and Bishop Leo Pursley's as auxiliary of Fort Wayne, Indiana, on September 19, where he preached. He praised the examples of bishops in enduring persecution, especially Cardinal Mindszenty. He spoke of the heavy duties of bishops and of the fine work of Archbishop Noll in defending Catholic education:

. . . Among the peoples of good will in the world who uphold God's honor and obey God's law, Catholics are finding themselves more and more alone, as secularism advances and makes new victims. Whatever be the political or economic or social progress of various forms of secularism, there is no solid hope for the future of our beloved America if for its defense we must depend on statesmen and jurists who repeal the Declaration of Independence and its recognition of God as the source of man's rights, who exclude God from government and even deny His very existence. It can happen here. Anything can happen when God is rejected and the State usurps His place and His power. Among the things that are happening now are attacks on the Natural Law, on the Christian family, on religious education. All honor to Bishop Noll and *Our Sunday Visitor* for their vigilance in detecting and their courage in exposing the dangers to Church and Nation in the encroachment of secularism.

The Bishop had raised a similar theme on September 13 when he spoke at the annual "Red Mass" of the Guild of Catholic Lawyers of New York City in St. Andrew's Church. He praised the law and urged lawyers to work for its preservation and to cut off the threats to American liberties. He also spoke of the attack on the United States brought to the country by television from the U.N. He urged the lawyers to be willing to suffer for the right. He said:

Not too many individuals are willing to mount the scaffold with St. Thomas More for placing God before the king. The individual who speaks out for justice must be prepared for a certain inglorious form of martyrdom: scented whitewash is always at hand for appeasers, but cauldrons of pitch await the patriots.

In another passage he added:

The New York longshoremen are not charged with making the foreign policy of the United States, it is true, but they have a duty in conscience to form their own policy in accordance with principle. They believe with Abraham Lincoln that "No nation can exist half slave and half free" and they rightly apply the principle to the world in this day of swift communications. They are protecting human rights the world over when they refuse to handle products of slave labor. Lawyers and judges can protect them adequately only when they regard personal dignity and human rights as a gift of God, not as privileges granted by human convention which is always susceptible to veto.

The reaction to the Bishop's speech at the "Red Mass" was varied. John Q. Adams, the Notre Dame alumnus who applied the papal encyclicals to his business, complimented the Bishop on his remarks about the longshoremen. In answer the Bishop explained to him: "For the past forty-five years I have been aware of their possibilities for good or evil, and I was glad to have an opportunity to underscore something good, particularly because of the control of Bridges of the situation on the west coast."

In the meantime the discussion of the report of Father Cronin's committee on the industry council had been entered by Father Keller and Father McGowan. Of Father McGowan's criticism the Bishop wrote to Father Cronin:

I cannot understand the memorandum submitted by Father McGowan. Apparently he wants to throw out everything that has been submitted thus far and start anew, but with interpretations that are far from the mind of scholars who have brought the discussion to a very interesting point. . . . It is not possible to submit a report to the Bishops at this time. I see no harm in delay. I believe that a great deal has been accomplished already and I would prefer to see further study rather than a hasty conclusion drawn to reach a deadline.

A further clue to the Bishop's economic thinking is contained in a note to Archbishop O'Boyle on November 24. "I am glad that we have no jurisdiction over Bishop Haas. His recent address in Covington hails back to the days of President Roosevelt, and is just as inaccurate now as it was then. . . ."

On December 4 the Bishop wrote to Father John B. Tennelly of the Indian and Negro Mission Bureau in Washington of the progress of Catholic Negroes in Buffalo. He had begun by eliminating segregation in churches:

The work of conversion of Negroes goes on steadily, and I am pleased with the number of colored children in our Catholic schools.

We will ordain one colored priest, the Reverend Peter Carter, next spring. He received diaconate last week.

After Christmas, 1950, the Bishop attended the regular meeting of the trustees of The Catholic University in Washington as well as the annual meeting of the Knights of Malta in New York. Of this he wrote to his friend, Archbishop McIntyre: "I had a nice visit with Cardinal Spellman after the Knights of Malta dinner. It was like old times. I seldom get to New York anymore, you know." Shortly after that he promised to be co-consecrator in Montreal on March 16 of Bishop-elect Albert Cousineau, C.S.C. As he had business in Washington on March 14, he planned to go to Washington and from there to Montreal. Illness, however, forced him to cancel both trips. The physician diagnosed the illness as an infection of the gall bladder and wanted to operate. The Bishop delayed the operation, and the physician did not insist, but put the Bishop on a diet from that time on. Whether the diagnosis was correct is not certain, but this illness was the first trouble besides the sinus inflammation and arthritis that the Bishop admitted.

At Christmastime the Bishop had sent copies of Dean Clarence Manion's *Key to Peace* to many of his friends in the hierarchy as Christmas presents. The Dean had written into the book much also that the Bishop had said about natural rights. But on February 19 a group of Holy Cross student priests at Holy Cross College in Washington sent a letter to the Dean criticizing the book. Copies of the letter were sent to the superior of Holy Cross College, the president of Notre Dame, and others. Apparently the Bishop received a copy of the letter and immediately sent a note of sympathy to the Dean.

Today I received a copy of a letter written to you by a group of student priests at Holy Cross College, Washington. Since the letter is critical of your excellent little book, *The Key to Peace*, I want to send you this renewal of my recommendation of the book.

After discussing the general criticisms of the book the Bishop added:

The priests whose criticism has prompted this letter have evidently mistaken your purpose, or have tried to give your book a purpose which it could not have if it were to accomplish what it has already effected. I have found in your book no defense of Europe's bankrupt Liberalism; quite the contrary. You dismiss it abruptly: " 'Laissez faire' which no one defends." Your frequent references to brotherhood under God, to mutual rights and duties, to man's social state, relieve you of the implication that you are unconscious of the existence of the social order. Perhaps you want to write a book on that some day; or perhaps, you prefer to have that vast field developed as it is being developed now, by the Natural Law Institute of the University of Notre Dame.

In a letter of February 28, published in the *Union and Echo* on March 3, the Bishop used his flair for statistics on the question of birth control. He noted in the census reports a decline in the number of persons between the ages of 20 and 24, and indicated a connection between this decrease and the decline in the birth rate at the corresponding time. He added:

Those who say that the depression made it impossible to bring children into the world must explain away the fact that in a period of great prosperity, from 1926 to 1930, the decline in the births was even more rapid than from 1931 to 1935, the worst period of the depression and the relief records of those latter days show the larger the family the smaller was the likelihood of being on relief.

He concluded his letter with feelings of gratitude for Catholic teaching:

Those who love God and country will thank God for the children that were born from 10 to 24 years ago; they are the hope of the country now. They will also thank God for the greatly increased birth rate since 1946. At the same time they will appreciate more than ever the Catholic Church and the Catholic schools that place first the law of God for the salvation of the individual and the safety of the state.

The Annual Charities Appeal took place on March 11–18, and the Bishop made his usual radio speech on March 10. He summarized the accomplishment of the diocese in schools and added a rationalization of his purpose:

We are often asked, sometimes by Catholics, more often by those not of our Faith, why we have a Catholic high school program. Some who are honestly skeptical regard it as a waste of money, some few call it a divisive influence in the community, an undemocratic, un-American system.

The first reason for Catholic schools is, of course, a supernatural one. Anyone who believes in an immortal soul and in an eternity of reward and punishment must conclude very quickly that the soul is more important than the body, that life after death is more important than life before death. . . .

He then turned to the patriotism of the Catholic children in the schools:

Catholics claim no monopoly on patriotism, God forbid! This would be a sorry nation were that the case.

The Catholic schools teach patriotism by realizing that all legitimately constituted authority comes from God. . . . That final responsibility before the judgment seat of God is the impelling motive for all the sacrifices that go into the making of the Catholic schools.

On March 27 Bishop O'Hara gave the principal address at the civic reception opening the Catholic Educational Association Convention in Cleveland. The general theme of the convention was "Human Rights and Education," and the Bishop's speech was on "Human Rights and the Future of Freedom." The Bishop opened with a quotation from Lincoln's Gettysburg address and then defined three great crises in the history of the country: that of 1776, that of 1863, symbolized by the Gettysburg address; and the present crisis. Lincoln, he said, in 1863 was not a learned man, but nothing in his hard-earned education had led him to give up his belief in Providence or made him ashamed of God. Lincoln had solved the second crisis by the same principles of human rights and belief in God that he had found in the Declaration of Independence and by which the first crisis had been solved. The Bishop then quoted Dean Manion's *Key to Peace,* where the Dean contrasted the materialistic French Declaration of Human Rights with the American Declaration of Independence with its belief in the spiritual. The Bishop then turned to the United Nations, which he said "had its tongue in its cheek" and which had given out recently the new Declaration of Human Rights, voted by the General Assembly of the United Nations on December 10, 1948. He added:

The Thirty Articles of this Declaration of Human Rights are a strange hodgepodge of compromises and appeasements. Some of the articles can mean little or nothing to some of the nations that approved them. The boy Lincoln brightening his fire with spice wood to read his Bible, would have had little patience with this document. In fact, he might have spared his spice wood and used the Declaration to light up his reading of the Sermon on the Mount. . . .

. . . Let me say this, rights that belong to man by virtue of his human nature will exist as long as man exists because they are the gift of God. Freedom in their exercise is assured only when the state recognizes those rights as coming from God. . . .

His conclusion was rather strong:

. . . Those of us who are old enough to remember this country as it was at the turn of the century have lived to see the decline of Godliness and the swift spread of secularism that has come from education without God, particularly higher education, which has had the greatest growth in this half century.

Find a David among your pupils, with a slingshot and confidence in God. Find a Lincoln if you can. Inspire the single hearted and the pure of spirit. Enlist recruits for Father Keller's Christophers as well as Father Peyton's Rosary bands. Set them on fire to restore the recognition of God. Teach them to say, with Abraham Lincoln: "If He had a place and work for me, and I think He has, I believe I am ready."[76]

Bishop O'Hara's correspondence at this time showed a wide interest in public affairs and included letters from a wide circle of friends. To Shane Leslie, who was visiting and lecturing in the United States, he wrote on April 19 in answer to a query about the character of General MacArthur. "I know MacArthur very well, and when you come here I hope we can have a good session about the whole situation. He has been the hope of the Catholic Church in Japan. I am looking forward to a nice visit." To Merrill Meigs he wrote about MacArthur on April 17: "Perhaps the sacrifice of MacArthur was needed to bring our country to its senses. The inept statements of the British Foreign Minister helped our people to see the truth. Britain has lost face completely. . . ."

One of several reviews of Dean Manion's *Key to Peace* was written in *America* by Father Wilfrid Parsons, S.J., and was in turn criticized by Father James Gillis, C.S.P., who sent a copy to the Bishop. On April 25 the Bishop wrote to Father Gillis: "Your reply to Father Parsons is beautifully tempered, and the dignity enhances its effective arguments. I am delighted and I thank you in the name of Notre Dame as well as for myself. I appreciate having an advance copy of the column."

On April 29 the Bishop dedicated the new St. John the Baptist Church in Tonawanda. In his speech he told the members of the parish to cherish the fact that the Venerable John N. Neumann, C.SS.R., was the first resident pastor there. The Bishop had become acquainted with the story of Bishop Neumann when still at Notre Dame while looking for an American inspiration for students. He knew that he had been friendly with the Fathers of Holy Cross and that there were relics of the Bishop in the museum at Notre Dame. When the pastor, Father Charles Klauder, decided to erect a church, the Bishop had helped him plan it.[77] In his interest in Neumann as a possible American saint, the Bishop had little thought that he would soon become the holy man's successor in Philadelphia.

The Bishop's activities seemed unending, despite the fact that his health was not the best. He presided at the blessing of the babies on May 6, and the number blessed was estimated at 8,000.

He laid the cornerstone for the new St. Benedict's Church in Eggertsville on May 13 and ordained 16 priests on May 16, but these were just some of the items that caught the public eye. His correspondence on various topics continued just the same. He was particularly opposed to the publication of the report of Father Cronin's committee on the industry council plan until it met his criticisms. On May 31 Dennis Cardinal Dougherty of Philadelphia died and the Bishop went to the funeral on June 7. There seems to have been no idea in his mind that he might succeed the Cardinal when he wrote to Archbishop McIntyre the next day. "There was a great gathering yesterday in Philadelphia; I had a few minutes with Archbishop O'Boyle and I gather that we are still far from the report on the Industry Council Plan. My own remarks on the report are going forward to him today. Archbishop Alter gave him five pages of criticisms and I am giving him four besides a long letter." Archbishop O'Boyle invited him to meet with himself and Archbishop Alter on June 22 at dinner to discuss the plan. Later on August 10 he wrote to Archbishop Alter after reading his criticism of the committee report: "My first reading of your report leaves me in admiration at its clarity, simplicity, and thoroughness. Thus far I have nothing to add or subtract. . . ." He wrote to Archbishop O'Boyle two days later: "I am grateful for your kindness in sending me a report on the revision of the Labor Day statement. I am sure it will be a strong and acceptable statement." The discussion of the industry council was omitted from the statement. The report of Father Cronin's committee was never published, and when Bishop O'Hara became Archbishop of Philadelphia, he became treasurer of the Administrative Committee of the N.C.W.C. and no longer had supervision of the Social Action Department.

On June 26 the Bishop wrote to Bishop Scully of Albany about the reappointment of Sister Eucharista to the Board of Examiners of Hospitals of the State of New York. Some opposition to the appointment had arisen on the grounds that the Sister was too critical. Bishop O'Hara investigated the matter and had this to say:

If the change is really on the march in the nursing profession we cannot afford to lag behind any more than we have to. If we try to strengthen Catholic schools of nursing in connection with the colleges in every city that we can, we will be prepared for higher standards, if they are demanded later. In the meantime we can keep up such training facilities as we have, always trying to strengthen them on the educational side. If we can do this in a sensible way we will have a strong body of nurses working in our favor instead of against us when the crisis arises.

The Bishop spent two short periods of rest at Indianapolis and Notre Dame, but there is no definite indication that he was feeling serious fatigue. He was contriving to follow the diet prescribed for a gall-bladder infection. He returned to Buffalo on the occasion of the visit of Cardinal Piazza on August 1, and when Monsignor Giovanni Battista Montini, the papal Substitute Secretary of State, came to Buffalo on August 22. The Monsignor pronounced the New Cathedral Florentine Gothic in architecture. The Bishop wrote to his sisters that Montini, the present Pope Paul VI, was polished and cultured, and a delightful companion.

On August 23 the Bishop wrote his annual letter on education. Besides stressing the obligation of Catholic parents to supply Catholic education for their children, he estimated the progress that had been made in the past five years. Five hundred additional classrooms had been provided—three hundred for elementary schools and two hundred for high schools—but fifteen hundred more classrooms were needed. He was also disturbed to report that there were still some empty desks in the Catholic high schools, while insisting that there were enough Catholic colleges available for Catholic students. Also a private letter to the pastors about the teacher-training program at D'Youville College said that in six years the number of teachers had been increased 410. Of these the religious teachers were 155 in elementary schools and 106 in high schools, and 149 were lay teachers—115 in elementary schools and 34 in high schools.

Bishop O'Hara, while professing some antagonism towards sociologists, was constantly seeking sociological information about his diocese. He noted the uneasiness manifested among Catholics about Father Joseph Fichter's *Sociology of a Southern Parish.* Writing about the book to Dan Herr of the Thomas More Book Club, he observed:

It would be a mistake to transfer the conclusions of Father Fichter to the United States generally or even to the South generally. To understand the religious conditions in the Archdiocese of New Orleans, it is necessary to know the historical background of present day conditions. Very considerable progress has been made of late, particularly during the past thirty years. As I see it the increased attendance at Catholic schools and the increased number of daily communicants give great hope for the future.

On the eve of Mission Sunday, October 13, the Bishop gave his annual broadcast. He took up the charge made by the Communists that each missionary is an agent for imperialism and said that the Holy Father had taken note of the charge in a recent ency-

clical. To the missionaries the Holy Father had warned that they
must not become attached even to the land they were trying to
evangelize. Consequently, Pope Pius XI, twenty-five years before,
had predicted the dire plight of these missionaries, and had tried
to raise up native priests and bishops in the missions. The Bishop
spoke particularly of the work of the missionaries in Japan, noting
the existence of a Catholic boys' town there and of labor unions
following the papal encyclicals. Of the American missionaries he
said: "This is our beloved country at its best."

In early November he went to Washington for the bishops'
meeting. He told his family later that Cardinal Spellman and
others expected him to say something about going to Philadelphia,
but at that time he had not been notified. If he thought of the
possibility of the appointment, he must have dismissed it. He was
content to continue the work he was doing in Buffalo, but his
appointment to Philadelphia was announced on November 28.
The Apostolic Delegate wanted him to move before Christmas,
but the Bishop asked for more time. He visited the Delegate and
then went to Indianapolis, where his friend Peter Reilly was very
ill. Reilly died January 4. The Bishop could not attend the
funeral on January 8, the day of his installation in Philadelphia,
but he went to Indianapolis and said a Mass for his friend in the
Blessed Sacrament Chapel of the Cathedral on January 7. Reilly
had been pleased at the Bishop's promotion to Philadelphia and
had hoped to attend the installation.

There was an announcement that the farewell ceremony for the
Bishop would take place in the Cathedral on January 6. There was
to be no banquet, but rather rosary and Benediction of the Blessed
Sacrament in the evening. The party would leave the Buffalo
station on the Lehigh railroad at 8:00 A.M., January 8, and arrive
in Philadelphia at 5:10 P.M. A large group of the Buffalo clergy
went with him.

EIGHT

Archbishop of Philadelphia

AS THE TRAIN LEFT FOR PHILADELPHIA
the Archbishop-elect stood on the rear platform[1] until it left the
city and then went inside and sat down, obviously a tired man. The
hurried trip to Indianapolis to the funeral of his friend, added
to the excitement of closing the books in Buffalo while already
supervising the administration of the Archdiocese of Philadelphia,
had taken its toll. He had made many friends in his six and a half
years in Buffalo and had become deeply interested in carrying out
his grand plan for raising the cultural and spiritual level of these
second- and third-generation immigrants who had prospered during the war years. He had accepted boldly the challenge offered by
this emerging community, but while he had accomplished much,
the full fruition of his plans must now be left to another. Nevertheless he had no time for regrets because he already had on his
shoulders the care of a larger task. The momentary feelings of
disappointment that may have crossed his mind as he bade farewell to Buffalo, to accept a third major change in his life, seemed
to make his resolutions about the new task a bit more calculated.
He was coming to Philadelphia an experienced bishop.

Archbishop O'Hara was not a young, ambitious cleric looking
forward to a new and golden opportunity, but an aging priest who
had begun to feel the effects of a strenuous earlier career. And he
was now moving towards a greater task, a more prominent position, and farther away from his old ideal of prefect of religion.
When his friend, Father John B. Delaunay, C.S.C., sent him con-

gratulations on his promotion to Philadelphia and offered the hopes that he would soon be a cardinal, the Archbishop answered on December 22: ". . . a thousand thanks for your good wishes but please keep them in the safe and sane category. I have very little private life left and what I have I want to keep."[2] There were some rumors that he went to see the Apostolic Delegate to see if he could avoid the promotion. He told the family that he had been notified only a short time before the public announcement on November 28. He did call on the Delegate, who wanted him to move immediately early in December, but there is no evidence that he tried to avoid the appointment. His stated desire to keep his private life was a key to much of his conduct in Philadelphia. He did not consider ostentatious public actions part of his duty and avoided them with skill, while other administrative policies he pursued with the same skill because he had concluded that they were wise and effective.

The train made a brief unscheduled stop at Lehighton, and the Archbishop stepped off the train to greet the faithful, especially the youngsters who had assembled to see him pass.[3] When the train stopped in Allentown, Monsignor Leo Funk had arranged an unofficial reception for the neighboring parishes, and for the Archbishop to be greeted by a band playing the Notre Dame Victory March. At Bethlehem the train was switched from the Lehigh tracks to those of the Reading and joined to the coaches of the welcoming group headed by Bishop McCormick. Another welcome awaited him in Philadelphia, where the governor and the mayor met him at the railway station. From the station he went for a visit to the cathedral and then to the chancery office at 225 18th Street, where he formally presented his credentials to the interim officers of the archdiocese. He then retired to the archiepiscopal residence with the visiting clergy and his brothers and sisters, who had joined his party at the Philadelphia station.

Cardinal Dennis Dougherty, his predecessor, had been physically active almost until the day of his death at eighty-five. He was a short, stocky clergyman with a large head and a full face. In contrast, Archbishop O'Hara was a tall, thin man of sixty-three, who walked with a quick step, slowed perhaps by the work of the recent twenty years and a touch of arthritis. His thin, gray hair had receded from his forehead to an almost perfect tonsure, but behind those gold rimmed glasses there was still a twinkle in his eyes. There were slight puffs beneath those eyes, and thin lips formed a firm but smiling mouth. His hands were steady, although the flesh on them had receded and become spotty. He wore a close-fitting black suit with its short coat. The evening *Bulletin* summed it up in a few lines: "A tall slender man who weighed 170 pounds, Archbishop O'Hara has pale blue eyes and thinning reddish hair. He is an expert swimmer."[4]

At the formal installation the next morning the presiding officer was the apostolic delegate, Archbishop Amleto Cicognani. In the temporarily enlarged sanctuary were fifteen visiting archbishops, seventy bishops, and nine abbots. The body of the church was filled to capacity with monsignors, other priests and religious, sisters, distinguished guests and the close relatives of the Archbishop. The Apostolic Delegate in his sermon, after some pleasant comparisons between Philadelphia in Asia Minor and Philadelphia in "America Major," praised the Archdiocese of Philadelphia for its generosity in works of charity and education, mentioned the notable archdiocesan seminary, and spoke of the fine work of Mother Drexel and the Sisters of the Blessed Sacrament for the Negro and Indian Missions. He also mentioned the sanctity of the Venerable Bishop John Neumann, one of the earlier bishops, and praised the clergy, secular and religious, of the diocese. Finally he praised the "great heart" of the new archbishop that had been manifested in his work at Notre Dame, in the Military Ordinariate, and in Buffalo.

In his response the Archbishop spoke of the great tasks and of the generosity of the Holy Father and of his representative, the Apostolic Delegate. He expressed his willingness to accept his share of the burdens of the Holy Father, particularly at a time when one cardinal was imprisoned and other bishops, priests, and nuns were suffering for the Faith. He added: "Even in our own beloved America, so generous, so humane, so responsive to every call of the afflicted, the Holy Father is not spared, for there go about, 'like roaring lions,' false teachers and false prophets. Those who would impugn the loyalty and reclassify the citizenship of American Catholics. . . ." But he added: "Thanks to the innate common sense and spirit of fair play of the American people, this campaign of hatred will come to naught. . . ." Concluding, he added:

I have no program to announce, no theme to preach but the love of God. Recognizing my utter unworthiness to follow in the footsteps of such magnificent leaders as Cardinal Dougherty and his eminent predecessors, I only ask leave to second and encourage your efforts. If you will kindly tell me your needs, I shall do my best to meet them. I know no other way to serve. Working together, with the assistance of God's grace, we can help one another save our souls.

This simple and direct conclusion attracted much attention and called forth praise even from the secular press and some suggestions from the people of the archdiocese.

After the Mass there was a dinner at the Bellevue-Stratford Hotel at which Monsignor Francis J. Furey presided. Bishop Burke spoke for the Diocese of Buffalo and gave the Archbishop a tremendous spiritual bouquet from the faithful. Monsignor McCormick spoke for the archdiocese. The Archbishop responded again. The next evening there was a civic reception in Convention Hall at which Judge Vincent Carroll was chairman. The invocation was given by Monsignor Cletus Benjamin, music was provided by the combined high-school bands and glee clubs, and appropriate songs were sung by Miss Jessica Dragonette. There were about three hundred prominent people on the stage. Speeches of welcome were given by Governor John S. Fine and Mayor-elect Joseph Clarke; James E. Gallagher gave the welcoming address for the laity of the archdiocese. Probably none realized then that this was to be the last public reception for the new archbishop, although he may have been planning matters that way even then.

Actually Archbishop O'Hara had been directing the archdiocese ever since the public announcement of his promotion. Bishop Hugh Lamb, the administrator, with Monsignors Cletus Benjamin, Joseph Corr, and Joseph McGlinn had gone to Buffalo on December 13[5] to confer with him, and there had been many telephone calls between Buffalo and Philadelphia about matters that could not wait and about changes involved in the departure of the administrator, Bishop Lamb, to his own new see at Greensburg and his surrender of the administration to the incoming archbishop. The column and a half of appointments and clerical transfers that were published in the *Standard and Times* the week of his arrival undoubtedly had been approved by Archbishop O'Hara from Buffalo.

There was a notable coincidence in that Cardinal Dougherty also 'had come from Buffalo to Philadelphia. Both of these dioceses had large prosperous parishes of middle-class American Catholics who were children and grandchildren of immigrants. Philadelphia, however, had an older Catholic tradition dating back to colonial times when Jesuit missionaries from Maryland came to attend it. Philadelphia proper had been the first urban center of Catholicism in the present United States and had, not far from the Liberty Bell Hall and Constitution Hall, the ancient churches of St. Joseph, Saint Mary, and Holy Trinity. But because the vast majority of the archdiocese's million Catholics were post-colonial arrivals in America, the problems of the archdiocese were more like those of Buffalo than one might expect. The earlier Catholic traditions of such persons as Robert Walsh and Thomas Fitzsimons had not been lost, but they had not prospered in any outstanding way. The dominant families of Philadelphia were for the most part of colonial origin and were of either Protestant or Quaker background. *The Saturday Evening Post* of that day with its conservative Protestant-Quaker philosophy and conservative tradition was much more representative of Philadelphia than the large Catholic Cathedral of Saints Peter and Paul in which the Archbishop was installed, even if one rejected the popular tradition that its sides, begun shortly after the Philadelphia riots, were windowless to prevent bigots from throwing stones through any stained glass windows.

Philadelphia Catholicism had absorbed some of the Quaker conservatism of the environment. The quiet of the advanced years of Cardinal Dougherty had perhaps added to this conservatism. The *Catholic Directory* for 1952 that was published shortly after the Archbishop was enthroned had many statistics about the archdiocese that gave some indications of the task facing the new chief pastor. The territory of the archdiocese included not only the city and county of Philadelphia but also the counties of Berks, Bucks, Carbon, Delaware, Lehigh, Montgomery, Northampton, and Schuylkill, in which were large communities such as Allentown, Bethlehem, Chester, Easton, Pottsville, and Reading. The Catholic population, roughly one in four, was estimated at 1,114,-122 attended by 1,920 priests, including 672 religious priests. There were 401 parishes, 9 chapels, and 62 missions. There were 200 brothers and 6,825 sisters, 1 diocesan seminary, and 7 seminaries for religious communities. There were 7 colleges, 35 high schools under diocesan or parochial supervision, and 21 high schools under private direction. There were 300 parochial elementary schools and 20 private elementary schools, 19 orphanages and asylums. The total of youths under Catholic instruction was estimated at 201,507. In the government of the archdiocese the Archbishop had two auxiliaries, Bishop Carroll McCormick, and, to replace Bishop Lamb, Bishop Joseph McShea, whose appointment was announced February 9. The vicar general was Monsignor Thomas McNally and the Archbishop soon appointed Monsignor Philip Donahue vicar for religious. The chancellor was Monsignor Cletus Benjamin, and the vice-chancellor was Monsignor John P. Connery. As in every diocese there were the usual chancery officials, men of special training in canon law and expe-

rienced in administration, who took care of the ordinary discipline of the diocese, maintained the marriage court, saw to the
maintenance of the Catholic cemeteries, supervised the works of
education and charity in the diocese, and directed the activities
of the youth. Archbishop O'Hara knew from his Buffalo experience that these administrators of the works of the diocese functioned almost independently of his personal guidance except in
unusual cases. Gradually he became acquainted with them all and
the activities of the "Archdiocesan Office" on Summit Street took
on the personal characteristics of the Archbishop.

One of the first effects of the arrival of Archbishop O'Hara was
a speeding up of decisions. Under the aged Cardinal a request for
permission might not be answered for some weeks, and decisions
that were not pressing might not be given. Now the answers came
promptly. There is a legend of a pastor who told his friends that
he had written in the first days of the O'Hara regime for permission to install new heating equipment in his church. The next
day when a voice over the telephone said that he, the Archbishop,
was granting the permission, the cautious pastor, sure that his
friends were playing a trick on him, refused to accept the permission, only to find that it was really the Archbishop speaking.
There were other prompt answers because the Archbishop used
the telephone to great advantage not only for local calls but for
immediate conversation with his episcopal and lay friends. He
also liked to have guests at lunch to promote the social contacts
which he missed by his avoidance of public dinners. Frequently
his guests were non-Catholics, or business people, or prominent
lay Catholics who might otherwise not have met him.

Archbishop O'Hara brought with him to Philadelphia an interest in the cause of the Venerable Bishop John Neumann, an interest that had been intensified by visiting the scene of the Bishop's
earlier labors in the Buffalo area. Those close to him felt that the
Archbishop seemed aware that he was following in the footsteps
of the saintly Bishop of Philadelphia, who had begun the building of the parochial school system of Philadelphia. Archbishop
Cicognani had mentioned the cause of the Bishop in the installation ceremony, and the Archbishop began immediately to study
the circumstances that had interrupted the beatification process.

The simplicity of the man manifested in Buffalo seemed more
striking in Philadelphia, and his disregard for public ceremony
became apparent very quickly, although this was not approved by
some pastors who liked ceremonies and ceremonial dinners. There
were no more civic receptions for him. The Archbishop did not

dine out, and even in religious ceremonies he quickly formed the custom of vesting in the sacristy when he could, of wearing only the necessary episcopal vestments, and of departing after the religious ceremony. In his home the caller would often be greeted at the door by the Archbishop himself, and usually the episcopal ring was not on his finger, except when he was on ceremony.

After his guests for the installation had departed, he began to make himself at home in the archiepiscopal residence, although a visitor some weeks later thought he seemed quite lonely. He had not brought with him any personal companion or secretary from either Holy Cross or Buffalo. The house itself had been purchased by Cardinal Dougherty. It was a comfortable structure of granite and limestone entered through a small portico with white columns of wood. To the right on the first floor, besides the anteroom and foyer, was a rather large parlor containing many pieces of overstuffed furniture and floor lamps, and decorated with portraits of some of his predecessors and other paintings. Beyond this room was a corridor leading to the Archbishop's chapel, a smaller sitting room, and a consultors' room, with its large table and accompanying chairs, that could also serve as a larger dining room. The ordinary dining room was to the left just off the entering corridor and was done in white. The sisters' quarters were beyond the kitchen and were under the direction of the Sisters of the Holy Family, a community founded in part by Holy Cross Fathers in Canada. They had been in charge of the archiepiscopal residence since 1927. The private rooms of the Archbishop and his secretary and guests were on the floor above, and, besides the stairs, there was a small elevator to them. The furnishings of the first floor were grand enough to suggest a home of one in authority, but the rooms above were less elegantly furnished.

Shortly after the Archbishop had arrived, his upstairs office began to acquire that pell-mell piling of papers and letters that had been his trade mark as prefect of religion. For dictating letters he ordinarily used a machine, and the letters were actually typed at his office on Eighteenth Street. When the telephone did not suffice and the business was not too formal, the Archbishop liked his business acquaintances to come for lunch to discuss the affairs at hand. The guest might be met at the door by the Archbishop and escorted into the parlor. The Archbishop would sit either on a chair near his guest or join him on one of the large divans, close enough that he could reach to him thè inevitable cigarette. The cigarette had been his conversation piece since the days of Sorin Hall. Later when his physicians tried to get him to give up smoking or to limit his use of cigarettes, he would jokingly say that that would be too hard on those with whom he lived. Smoking was a graceful way of removing nervous tension without disturbing his visitor. In most cases his male visitor also smoked and felt more at home. So long as he did not have to go up or down the stairs, his guests saw only a tall, thin, smiling prelate with sparkling eyes and quick wit who seemed restless.

The Tuesday following his arrival a special train was arranged for the Archbishop and the clergy of Philadelphia to take Bishop Lamb to Greensburg for his installation. After the train began to move the Archbishop walked through the cars, endeavoring to get acquainted with many of the clergy of Philadelphia, but there was little in common between the Archbishop and his clergy, and some thought the strangeness very apparent. The next day at the official ceremonies of installation Archbishop O'Hara handed the crosier to the new bishop and led him to his throne as he himself had been installed the previous week by Archbishop Cicognani. The Archbishop also spoke briefly at the banquet that followed and then returned to his own archdiocese. His first pastoral letter was one of thanksgiving to the priests of the diocese for their "exemplification of the order of hospitality."[6]

In this first letter he made a special plea for the mediatorial work of the priest and mentioned the response of the faithful to his request that they make their wants known.

As Christ is Mediator between God and man, so is the priest as another Christ. Some people may fail to understand this at times, but the influence of the zealous priest, his example even more than his words, will make the lesson ever more universal. Zeal for the confessional marks the mediator. The priest whose great joy is to extend God's mercy to the sinner who repents, will understand that once he places the soul in touch with God, the work of divine grace takes over and transforms the soul. Frequent and daily Communion can make great souls of little souls and the wise pastor encourages the formation of great souls in his parish.

As Christ is the Mediator, Mary His Mother is the Mediatrix. When Mary is the Queen of the home, family life is sound. Family Prayer, very specifically the family Rosary, keeps the Blessed Mother enthroned in the Christian Family. Encouragement of the Family Rosary relieves the pastor of many heartaches.

In response to the invitation to make wants known, many good people have sent in letters, beautiful letters, some of them, calling attention to this or that possibility of good. All of them will receive attention and study; many of them merit action—but not precipitate action, since first impressions may sometimes be erroneous. But I thank all for the good will they have shown, and I ask God to bless all who willingly cooperate for the good of souls in this portion of His vineyard.

His letter to the religious priests, brothers, and sisters thanking them for their welcome spoke clearly of their connection in his mind with the problem of Catholic education.

The Archdiocese of Philadelphia is singularly blessed in its Catholic schools. We admire and we thank God for all the works of charity so well exemplified by our communities whether at home or in the uttermost parts of the earth. Special mention is made of the school because of the overwhelming importance in forming the spirit of the young, instilling the Catholic point of view, developing the flower and fruit from the bud that is entrusted to our care by Christian parents. And since the school is so important, the spirit of Christian charity must be exemplified, sometimes in heroic degree by religious teachers. But unsung heroism must be expected in every form of religious endeavor, with or without the special aid of religious vows, and we must endlessly encourage one another to the practice.

On January 25 the Archbishop presided at the funeral of Father John Stanton, C.S.Sp. The Archbishop wrote to the priest's nephew on February 14 that he felt it was the duty of the bishop of the diocese to attend the funeral of all priests. During most of his years in Philadelphia he never failed to attend the funeral of a priest unless there was an unavoidable conflict of duties. This was quite a chore and one from which most of his priests were quite willing to excuse him because among the large number of priests in the archdiocese deaths were fairly frequent.

On January 29 the Archbishop appeared at the dinner for the lay retreatants of Malvern held in Convention Hall. The Archbishop's words after the dinner were apparently informal. There were about 4,000 men present, and among those on the rostrum was Frank Leahy, the football coach of Notre Dame, who also spoke. The Archbishop told the men, "I am very pleased to see that you put first things first." The *Standard and Times* reported further:

His Excellency went on to say that he enjoyed being with people who said prayers, morning, noon, and night and who recognized the truth that every good thing came from God while they admitted their dependence upon Him. Continuing he stressed the need of prayerful intercession to the Sacred Heart and the Blessed Mother for the help needed to combat the ills of the world.[7]

The absence of the Archbishop from dinners and luncheons, and his obvious efforts to avoid unnecessary ceremonies, soon gave

rise to rumors of ill health. While it was true that the Archbishop
was on a diet when he came and was never in robust health during his years in Philadelphia, the consistency with which he
avoided dinners and public ceremonies was based on more than
illness. After twelve years as a bishop he had concluded that these
externals were not a necessary part of his episcopal work. He did
not use alcoholic beverages and was a scanty eater. He also had the
experience of feeling ill the few exceptions he made to this avoidance of public dinners. Nevertheless he was very gracious in his
public appearances, and non-Catholics who met him were sincerely desirous of attracting him to their public ceremonies. Actually in other communities his absences might have been a serious
defect in administration, but in Philadelphia the general conservatism of the area, the dominance of Quakerism, and the previous example of his predecessor, Cardinal Dougherty, who also did
not go to such public functions, made the policy of the Archbishop seem proper except to those pastors and their assistants
who wanted him to grace their celebrations. None doubted that
he was deeply spiritual, and the lay people who came to know him
thought his avoidance of display a real virtue.

    In a sense the Archbishop faced the perennial dilemma of a
Catholic bishop in the United States. Legally an American Catholic bishop has no civic or legal function, and certainly no political power, but there has always been the temptation for him to
exert political power, even though it has generally been resisted.
In one example, the Archbishop's unyielding opposition to communism, it can be said that he kept away from all civic politics.
Neither did he attempt in any way to wield social influence.
Perhaps the Church in Philadelphia suffered from this perfect
abstinence, but he did not lose any veneration from the faithful
by this severity of life. This strictness, which seems to have been
more severe in Philadelphia than in Buffalo, took him away from
many parish celebrations that followed dedications and blessings
to enrich parish life and promote the layman's joy in serving
the Church. The personal element in this lack of display was
also manifest in the continued correspondence with Notre Dame
alumni who knew him as prefect of religion. To one he wrote on
February 5, 1952:

    You are right. It is quite a step from the tower office in Sorin Hall
    to the Cathedral in Philadelphia. I think that all the old boys know
    that my open preference was for the purple stole instead of the purple
    robes, and except for religious obedience I would still be wearing the
    purple stole only.[8]

He simply wanted all glorification to go to God and His Blessed Mother, or to the Church or the community. This simplicity was the key to those letters that came to him all through his later life from alumni who begged pardon for calling him just "Father O'Hara" and to whom he usually retorted that they would lose membership in the "club" if they used any other title.

Another way in which the Archbishop profited by his experiences in Buffalo was in his use of the Board of Diocesan Consultors.[9] American dioceses have generally never had diocesan chapters, but instead each diocese has a group of experienced priests chosen by the bishop with care with whom he must consult in important decisions. When he was bishop of Buffalo, Bishop O'Hara had increased the number of his consultors and had consulted them regularly. When he came to Philadelphia, he established the practice of meeting with his consultors every month, except during the summertime, and of bringing to their attention his proposals about parishes and about schools, and other important decisions. The first of these meetings was held on February 4, and the Archbishop presented to the group some plans for new high schools, including his proposals for district high schools, and appointed a committee of the consultors to report on these matters. It was his custom not only to present his proposals for building and purchases of properties but also expenditures that he had to make or allow in emergencies were brought before the next meeting of the consultors. Faced with his large plan for improving the Catholic educational facilities of the archdiocese, he was able to draw upon the experience and wisdom of these consultors in planning. On more than one occasion he permitted the members of the board to alter his own proposals; he recognized his vicar general, Monsignor Thomas McNally, as his alter ego in the meetings, even permitting him to preside in his absence.[10] As a result, the members of the board and those who were aware of this policy had increased respect for his ability to use the advice and help of these experienced pastors.

Another facet of the Archbishop's program was his support of the previous policies of the archdiocesan seminary. As the Apostolic Delegate had noted in his installation sermon, Saint Charles Borromeo Seminary was perhaps the outstanding institution of the archdiocese. The dedication of the massive seminary during Cardinal Dougherty's jubilee year of 1928 had been a major event in the history of the Archdiocese. The completeness of the institution, its massive stone buildings, and its strong spirit had much to do with the character of the clergy and, one might say, of the

ecclesiastical spirit of the archdiocese. The fact that most of the
faculty had been trained in Rome, even though they may have had
several years in Saint Charles, also added a distinctive quality to
the group. Although several of the faculty had written books and
contributed to ecclesiastical periodical literature, Saint Charles
was not a speculative theological institution. Probably the conservatism in religious matters for which the archdiocese was
known had its stronghold in this remarkable institution. At first
the Archbishop made only one notable change. On the occasion
of his first visit for ordination he allowed the students to smoke,
and he also improved another of his favorite recreations by building a new swimming pool for them a year later. He also made a
minor change in the student body by allowing those bishops who
had once attended the seminary to send students to Saint Charles
and then accorded the same privilege to the other bishops of the
province.

An important factor in the stateliness of the seminary and its
maintenance was the seminary fund, part of which was invested
and part of which was collected each year. Some years later he
told of this to Archbishop Brady of Saint Paul.

In 1835, three years after the foundation of the Seminary Bishop
Kenrick outlined his plan for a Seminary Fund Society. Each pastor
was requested to appoint one or more agents in his congregation to
solicit membership in the Society, the members to pay annual dues of
one dollar. An annual report, by parishes, was to be made to the priests
in an open meeting.

While there had been modifications in the plan from time to time,
and the addition of perpetual memberships for deceased as well as
living benefactors on the contribution of $25.00, the plan is still in
operation. I discontinued the annual meeting, but the report is published annually in the Catholic Standard and Times. The solicitors
appointed by the pastors are very conscious of their prerogative and
zealous in the fulfillment of their duties. An announcement of the
annual collection is made on the feast of St. Charles, and the returns
are made during the week following Low Sunday. Some of the pastors
have enough solicitors to conduct the entire solicitation on one Sunday
afternoon. Some raise the money by social events, usually these pastors
have discontinued the solicitors.[11]

The permanent foundation for the support of the seminary became
one of the financial foundation stones of the diocese, and rumors
that the Archbishop thought of dissolving it seem to be without
foundation.

There arose about this time another rumor that later became
quite widespread. Since the late Cardinal had undertaken only the

most essential building operations during his last years, the story arose that he had accumulated vast sums of money that were available to the new Archbishop. The sum of forty millions was the figure most commonly given, a sum that corresponded closely to a figure covering the value of educational properties at the time of the Cardinal's death. Although the Cardinal had left no debt, outside of trust funds that were untouchable the accumulated expendable funds were only a small percentage of the vast sums stated in the rumors. Later when the Archbishop began his extensive building of schools and parishes, the disappearance of this mythical capital was given as the source of the operations. Considering that the Archbishop was a very capable financier, the rumors tended to give a false picture of his very adroit operations.

As has been mentioned, in February Monsignor Joseph McShea, who had been a secretary at the apostolic delegation, was named bishop of Mina and auxiliary to the Archbishop; and Father Gerald I. McDevitt of St. Thomas More High School was sent to the Delegation in Washington as secretary. At the same time Bishop Burke was made the Bishop of Buffalo to succeed the Archbishop.

As was his custom in Buffalo the Archbishop began shortly to issue frequent pastoral letters. The first Lenten letter stressed the sacraments, especially attendance at Mass and Communion, as the best ways of observing Lent, together with charity towards the poor and the sick.

The archdiocesan paper, the *Standard and Times,* was definitely on the conservative side on quasi-political matters, the side to which the Archbishop himself leaned. There is evidence that he occasionally wrote editorials for the newspaper, besides the signed editorials and pastoral letters that were printed there. At the time of the installation the editor was Andrew Kemper Ryan, and he was succeeded by Father Anthony Ostheimer. The editorials of the paper were well written in this, one of the better Catholic diocesan weeklies, and they usually expressed a definite criticism of anything that seemed libertine. The very action of the Supreme Court in accepting the cases concerning the recitation of prayers in the public schools, and the suits against censorship of movies in New York, produced editorial alarms that foretold sadder editorials when the Supreme Court made its decisions against the prayer and censorship. When the Yale Committee reported to the president of that institution on the charges leveled by William Buckley, Jr. against the University in *God and Man at Yale,* the editorial writer was quite partisan, ending his editorial with the sentence: "All hail to Mr. Buckley. He's the winner and still champion."[12] The editorial was unsigned and was probably not written by the Archbishop, who, however, did not always sign his editorials.

On March 2 the Archbishop presided at the annual memorial of Bishop Neumann at St. John the Evangelist Church. In preparation for the approaching centennial of the consecration of Bishop Neumann the Catholic Philopatrian Literary Institute held an exhibition of several relics of the Bishop, whose cause was now to be pushed by the Archbishop. At the Mass were Father Michael Curley, C.SS.R., whose biography of the Bishop would be supported and distributed by Archbishop O'Hara, and Father Albert Waible, C.SS.R., the vice-postulator of the cause of the Venerable Bishop. The Archbishop soon expressed some dissatisfaction that little progress was being made towards the beatification of the Bishop.

Although the Archbishop was no longer in charge of Social Action Study in the N.C.W.C., he did not lose his interest in the problem of the distribution of wealth. When he heard that the Pope had made a speech touching the subject to the Italian Association of Business and Management (UCID) on January 31, 1952, he wrote to Count Galeazzi for a copy:

As you know, I am deeply interested in the august wishes of the Holy Father in the field of business and industry, and I am delighted with the strong paternal character of this allocution. I am hopeful that when I come to Rome in May or June this year I may possibly have an opportunity to meet some of these gentlemen who have been honored so signally by the warm approval of the Holy Father. What is possibly a similar association has been inaugurated in a small way in this country. I have been asked to help give direction to this group and I want to be sure that I am on safe ground in any advice that I may give.

His Eminence, Cardinal Stritch, and His Excellency Archbishop O'Boyle, as Chairman of the Social Action Department of the National Welfare Conference, are fully informed of the activities of this group, but no formal ecclesiastical approval has been sought for the present, since the men who are working towards the adoption of a constitution desire to have something positive to present before they seek formal approval.[13]

The Archbishop did not list the members of this informal group, and there is no evidence that they did draw up a constitution. Apparently after a few meetings the plans for the association were dropped.

On March 14 the Archbishop preached at the pontifical "Red"

Mass at the Cathedral to celebrate the one hundred fiftieth anniversary of the formation of the Philadelphia Bar Association. The celebration was held at the invitation of Judge John P. Boland, the president of the St. Thomas More Society, and its chaplain, Father Bartholomew Fair. The Archbishop traced the meaning of natural law, telling the lawyers: "Since man is destined for a world beyond, God has given him a law to arrive at that end . . ." and "This direction is called the Natural Law because it is inseparable from his very nature."[14] On Sunday, March 16, he presided at the annual St. Patrick's Day Mass at St. Patrick's Church, making his first official visitation of the parish at the same time. The story that he originated the St. Patrick's Day parade is inaccurately connected with this first visit. On March 19 the Archbishop preached at the consecration of Bishop McShea. In his sermon he made a reference to Bishop Neumann, whose centenary he celebrated on March 28 at the Cathedral.

On March 25 he attended the consecration of Bishop Lambert Hoch at Sioux Falls, South Dakota, and went from there to the Mayo Clinic for a physical examination. The doctors at the clinic apparently decided that he did not have a gall-bladder infection and took him off the diet, but what they really thought was not recorded. The Archbishop was supposed to pick a doctor in Philadelphia to receive the report of the Mayo doctors, but, pleased at the good news of the clinic, the Archbishop apparently decided not to bother any Philadelphia physician.[15]

The April 11 issue of the *Standard and Times* published the annual report of the Catholic schools of the archdiocese. While the figures were practically the same as those printed in the *Catholic Directory,* the report gave the editors of the newspaper an opportunity to view the progress of the schools of the archdiocese with rose-tinted glasses.

. . . It is safe to say that nowhere else in America has so much effort been expended in improving and expanding Catholic secondary schools, and nowhere else has so much success been attained. In the immediate Philadelphia area there are 12 diocesan high schools with a combined enrollment of 21,542 pupils. Large central high schools serve the Allentown, Reading, and Pottsville areas with 19 parish high schools in other areas.

. . . The 1950–1 enrollment in the Catholic diocesan schools (not including Catholic private schools and academies) was 108,367. The 1950–1 enrollment in the public schools of the city in full time day classes was 212,816. . . . One out of every three children going to schools in Philadelphia goes to a Catholic school.[16]

The paper contained the report of Monsignor Edward M. Reilly, the superintendent of schools, dated February 4, 1952. It listed the advancements under Cardinal Dougherty since 1918, from 174 schools and 87,857 pupils to 305 schools and 135,025 pupils. In that time 9 diocesan, 22 accredited high schools had been established, and the 100 teachers of 1918 for 2,371 pupils had become 1,034 teachers for 28,804 pupils by 1952.

While such praise could be expected from the local paper, especially since there were incipient criticisms of Catholic schools, one did not have to be too closely conversant with the conditions of the archdiocese to know that everything was not as fine as the editorial writer said, particularly in the matter of secondary schools. The late Cardinal had ceased in his last years to expand facilities at a time when there was an increased movement of population into the city, and the facilities were not capable of handling the increased attendance. Archbishop O'Hara, fresh from his campaign to improve similar conditions in Buffalo, was not to rest long before attempting to improve the situation in Philadelphia, as the minutes of the first consultors' meeting bear evidence. But in Philadelphia he faced a tradition of fine schools begun many years before, of the first free Catholic high school in Roman Catholic High School, and a more conservative attitude on the matter of parish finances than he had faced in Buffalo.

There was also a brief flurry about the financial policies of the new Archbishop. Shortly after his arrival he became aware that pastors of several well-to-do parishes had on deposit in local banks large cash amounts in reserve for emergencies that did not seem to come. The local banks were enabled to do a profitable business with these funds, which were practically never withdrawn. The Archbishop suggested, but did not demand, that if these pastors would loan this money to the archdiocese, they would receive their interest—perhaps more than they were receiving from the local banks—and the archdiocese would have these funds available for its various activities. This suggestion gave rise to the rumor that financial stringency caused by the Archbishop's spending had forced him to demand these funds from the pastors. Although the Archbishop had behind him the successful financial work at the University of Notre Dame and in Buffalo, unfounded rumors of financial errors persisted even after his death. Actually, the archdiocese had only a relatively small debt at the time of his death, with the means of payment already arranged. In his financial activities the Archbishop had the assistance of a devoted and capable Catholic layman, George V. Mitchell, who had inherited the tradition of having a wise lay financial adviser for the diocese begun by Mark A. Frenaye back in the time of Bishop Kenrick, and a corps of devoted clerical workers.[17]

On March 14 Doctor E. A. de Bordenhave of Christ Church on Second Street wrote to the Archbishop to suggest that he be permitted to hold a reception for the Archbishop, at which the Archbishop could get acquainted with the Protestant and Jewish clergymen of the city. The Archbishop replied on March 18, declining the invitation:

It is surely kind of you to suggest a reception for me, and I hope that at some time in the future it may be possible to plan for something of that sort. For the present, however, it seems impossible.

Strange as it may seem, I have not yet had an opportunity to meet my own priests.[18]

But to anyone who knew the feelings of the Archbishop on inter-denominational meetings there would be no surprise that as late as May 14, 1954, Dr. de Bordenhave on another occasion repeated his request for permission to hold the reception without a favorable reply. The Archbishop may have been aware that any Catholic trained under the strict German pastors of the Diocese of Fort Wayne at the turn of the century would feel obliged to be all things to all people in matters of social and cultural affairs but would likewise feel obliged to allow no compromise in matters of religion. The Archbishop was pleased to have non-Catholics at table and seemed at times to prefer to talk with non-Catholics about his theory of wealth distribution, but once the question of religion was involved there could be no exchange. He held a similar attitude towards professors of cultural subjects at non-Catholic universities.

To a lady Quaker of Philadelphia who had written to Cardinal Spellman and been referred back to the Archbishop, he called attention to the similarity between the Quaker meeting and religious meditation.

If you are not familiar with the monastic orders of the Catholic Church, you might be surprised to learn how much "Quaker Meeting" we have. Meditation forms part of the life of every priest and every religious and of many lay people.

While we adorn our churches for the glory of God, the chapter room of a monastery is usually as plain as a Quaker Meeting House. Further, to control the distractions which earthly goods place in the pursuit of God, the Church approves of the vow of poverty for religious communities after the example of our Divine Master, the Church emphasizes the spirit of poverty for all of us.

To the Cardinal he explained his answer by saying: "The evidences of Quaker opulence I find about me constitute too much of a temptation for me to keep silent on the spirit of poverty."[19]

Similarly he wrote with sympathetic understanding to James A. Walker of Malvern, Scotch Presbyterian, who had raised some question of interdenominationalism:

Your remarks on your early training are almost identical with the advice I gave the Federation of Catholic College Students at Rosemont a week ago Sunday. I told them of God's command to love all men not to "tolerate" anyone. The word toleration has been a source of great evil. It had been abused to the point where people tolerate even those who would destroy our country and our civilization. We must love all men but be intolerant of the errors that would destroy all that is good in the world.[20]

To Monsignor G. L. Smith of Aiken, South Carolina, who thanked the Archbishop for the courtesies he had shown some of his non-Catholic friends from the South, the Archbishop explained why he maintained friendship with non-Catholics. "I like to have a group of non-Catholics among my friends, since they can be very helpful through their understanding of our point of view." But to Robert Bertram, who wrote to ask permission to have a joint session of a Catholic priest, a Protestant minister, and a Jewish rabbi during the Convention of the Pennsylvania American Legion, the Archbishop gave a clear negative, adding: "I am sorry to disappoint you but the type of program you suggest is one in which we do not take part. This decision is based on the judgment that religion suffers a loss rather than a gain from that kind of program." Instead, he suggested that there be three distinct services to fulfill the same purpose. Positively he gave the same advice to Father Louis Dougherty of the Catholic War Veterans on July 28:

It seems to me that Catholic War Veterans can fulfill a very real spiritual office if they keep fresh in the minds of their members that they are Catholics first and veterans second.

Every Catholic organization must have in mind first of all the honor and glory of God, second the salvation of its members, and thirdly the good of souls.[21]

The question of his attitude towards professors at non-Catholic institutions arose shortly after his arrival in Philadelphia. As a young priest in the summer of 1917 he had attended classes at Wharton Institute of the University of Pennsylvania, and officials of the University thought it appropriate that they would confer on him an honorary degree. The University sent a committee to call on him to ask if he would accept the degree. The Archbishop received them most cordially but would not accept the degree. He explained that he had been insistent that Catholics in the archdiocese attend Catholic schools, and the acceptance of the honorary degree might be interpreted by some as a change of attitude. He said he could not recommend that Catholics study under certain professors at the University and would, if pressed, give the names of some professors he had in mind. However the interview was very friendly.[22]

As if to bolster his plans for building more schools in Philadelphia, the Archbishop took the occasion of the Notre Dame Universal Night celebrations in Tulsa and Oklahoma City on April 16 and 17 and in Philadelphia on April 24 to attack the statement attributed to President Conant of Harvard that Catholic schools were "divisive." He called the statement "a shocking performance."[23] Later President Conant claimed that he had been misinterpreted.

Early in the spring the Archbishop had promised Cardinal Spellman that he would join in the Cardinal's pilgrimage to the Barcelona Eucharistic Congress at the end of May. The Pilgrimage left New York on May 15 with six hundred pilgrims. At the request of the Cardinal, Archbishop O'Hara conducted services for the group at Fatima on May 23. On that day he dedicated the archdiocese to the Immaculate Heart of Mary and arranged that on that day there would be ceremonies of this dedication throughout the archdiocese.[24] On May 26 he preached in Spanish in the Cathedral of Seville and later the same day gave another Spanish sermon to the people of Cadiz before going on to Barcelona, where they arrived on May 27. Of the congress he wrote to his family on May 31:

This Congress is strictly Spanish, which means that it has tremendous crowds, great enthusiasm, profound devotion, and more impromptu oratory than prepared addresses. The "spontaneity of the improvisation" is a triumph. We have a wonderful spirit on board. The presence of the Blessed Sacrament has been a boon, and our pilgrims are asking for special devotions on board to give them some prayers in English. We will have adoration all night tonight, and a group of Spanish officers will take part in the adoration.[25]

While in Spain he had gone with Cardinal Spellman to call on Franco and to visit the shrine of Our Lady of Montserrat. He also was impressed by a group ordination, of which he noted: "The most warming events were the mass ordination of 842 priests (an

act of reparation for the priests murdered in the Civil War) and
Franco's dedication of Spain to the Sacred Heart which took
place at the Offertory of Sunday's Pontifical Mass in the presence
of more than a million people."

From Barcelona the pilgrimage went on to Rome, where, among
other events, he had a conference with Count Galeazzi about the
Pope's speech to the Italian Association of Business and Industry,
an address he arranged to have translated into English by Father
Edward Heston. He summed up his visit for his family in a
paragraph:

Rome has been wonderful and I have been taking it easy—not too
much any one day. I had a private audience yesterday and a special
one today with Cardinal Spellman's 600 pilgrims. Some day next week
I'll have the *real* private audience (the one yesterday was with the
Eucharistic Congress Committee) and then I'll be ready to come
home. In case I haven't told you, the date set for the arrival in New
York is June 16th—a week from Monday. I leave Rome Friday the
13th for Le Mans.

By June 16 the Archbishop was back in Philadelphia. A short
time later, on June 29, he issued a ruling on collections to which
the faithful of the archdiocese were to be subjected. It was called
"The Missionary Cooperative Plan" and was to go into effect on
July 1. The permission for a missionary society to appeal in parishes was limited to the parishes assigned to a society by the Propagation of the Faith office. On such occasions there was to be one
appeal, and the collection was to be taken up after the regular collection. If the parish was out of debt, another appeal might be
permitted with the approval of the chancery office. On June 27
the *Standard and Times* also carried the Archbishop's regulations
for vacation schools for children attending public schools. In the
previous summers there had been 14,000 in attendance, and the
Archbishop requested a better attendance, since there were 23,454
Catholic children in the public schools. The schools were under
the direction of the Confraternity of Christian Doctrine and used
volunteer teachers.

On July 13 the Archbishop went to Atlantic City to attend a
business conference on the two following days. It was a confidential conference, but one he favored highly because it had for its
purpose the mitigating, if not the elimination, of the conflict
between labor and industry. He described the make-up of the
conference to Monsignor Montini in a letter of August 2.

Permit me to call attention to the following points:

1. The participating agencies represent the following groups:

     Finance—American Bankers Association and the Investor Bankers Association;

     Business—the three leading associations plus the grocers and dry goods associations;

     Farming—the three leading national associations;

     Transportation—the leading organizations for air, water, rail, truck and bus transportation;

     Labor—The American Federation of Labor and the Congress of Industrial Organization;

     General Public—two veterans organizations, two service clubs and the National Educational Association.

2. The representatives of the associations are all officers on the policy-making level and they are high class men.

3. No meeting is ever asked to vote on any resolution or otherwise indicate a majority opinion.

. . . .

There were very few Catholic representatives at the meetings, but I was treated with great courtesy.[26]

While he did not name the conference, he gave other details to Count Galeazzi in a letter of July 31:

I find that it was the twenty sixth quarterly meeting of this conference, which means that it has been in existence six and one half years. The seventy five men who were present all represent high rank in their representative professions and our labor organizations, and they brought into their deliberations a careful consideration of the common good.

Back in Philadelphia the Archbishop received a letter that recalled both his days in the Military Ordinariate and his experiences as prefect of religion.

Philadelphia Navy Yard
July 15, 1952

Your Excellency:

Our ship the U.S.S. Currituck, which is now at the Philadelphia Navy Yard, is planning to hold a Communion Breakfast following the nine o'clock Mass at St. John's Church on the sixth of August, 1952. Father Marley and Father Ruhl of St. John's have kindly consented and cooperated in this.

The Currituck has just completed a long Caribbean tour and will operate in European waters in the near future. We do not have a Catholic chaplain serving on board but Father Kelly here at the Naval Base has been assisting us in these preparations.

Will you honor us by delivering the sermon at this Mass? Breakfast will be served immediately afterwards.

[signed]   Very Respectfully yours
                Tom Coleman for
                The Communion Breakfast
                Committee
                USS Currituck A V-7

The Archbishop answered on July 29:

. . . while I have an engagement in Cleveland on August 6th, I am asking to be excused from that so that I can accept your invitation to speak to your group at the Mass at St. John's on August 6th. I miss the pleasant contacts I had with servicemen during the war, and I welcome any opportunity to advance their spiritual interests.

In his speech to the sailors the Archbishop talked of "lay apostles," especially of those he had learned about during the war. The Philadelphia papers picked up the story, quoting the inspirational ideas of the Archbishop. The chief of chaplains, Admiral Salisbury, an old friend of the Archbishop, read of the sermon and wrote for a copy, but the Archbishop told him that he had spoken without a manuscript.

At the spring meeting of the Administrative Board of the N.C.W.C., Archbishop O'Hara had told Cardinal Stritch about the Pope's talk to the Italian businessmen. As if to question its importance, Cardinal Stritch had asked the Archbishop to find out who wrote the speech for the Holy Father. The Archbishop sought the answer to this in his trip to Rome and wrote with some pleasure to Cardinal Stritch on August 4:

Your Eminence:

When we discussed the Holy Father's address of January 31, 1952, on the occasion of our meeting in Washington, Your Eminence kindly suggested that I get in touch with the person who had prepared the address.

I am sure that Your Eminence will be delighted as I am to discover that it was written by the Holy Father himself. I enclose a photostat of the original manuscript, with the corrections. In our struggle to interpret the Social Encyclicals it is certainly reassuring to find the handwriting of the Holy Father as a guarantee of his personal interest.

I am sending photostatic copies also to Archbishop O'Boyle and Archbishop Alter who have worked so hard on the Industry Council Report.

Cardinal Stritch answered on August 11: "I thank you more than words can tell."

On August 9 the Archbishop gave the opening address at the First National Congress of Religious in the United States held at Notre Dame.[28] The Congress was attended by over one thousand religious superiors, men and women, and was addressed during the session by Archbishop Arcadio Larraona, the secretary and acting prefect of the Sacred Congregation of Religious, by the Apostolic Delegate, and by many others. The Archbishop acted in a sense as the welcoming host at the opening address given in the Drill Hall on the campus. As an answer to the plea of the Holy Father in this time of crisis, he especially urged the superiors to maintain a spirit of unity.

Before leaving South Bend he went to a small church at Terre Coupe, some twenty miles away, to give confirmation to some Mexicans who had been prepared for the sacrament by his friend, Father Peter Forrestal. The Archbishop had taught Father Forrestal Spanish while he was a young lay professor and had long been an admirer of his unselfish zeal for the neglected Mexican migrants.[29]

When the Archbishop returned to Philadelphia, he called for the formation meeting of the Archbishop's Committee for the Christian Home and Family on October 5 in the auditorium of West Catholic High School. Because of the exceptional good resulting from a similar Buffalo committee he invited Mrs. Edmund Kelley of Buffalo to attend the formation meeting and direct the formation of the committee.

The Archbishop's major interest at this time was Catholic education. On September 5 the new school year began with an increase of 5,000 students over the previous year and with three new elementary schools and one new district school, Immaculate Heart Academy in Schuylkill County. On September 20 the Archbishop met the combined faculties of Catholic high schools at West Philadelphia Catholic High School. He admitted to them: "This is a period in which everybody is overburdened. You have accepted it beautifully, and I hope you will protect yourselves by not taking your job too seriously."[30] What he advocated was a relaxed attendance to the work of the schools that would permit them to meet the extra burdens. Arguing from his own experience as a youngster, he told the teachers that some seemed to think they must catch every breaking of the rule. Instead, he said, they should instill the love of God in the students, pay attention to the more important things, and leave more matters to the Holy Spirit.

On September 26 he published in the *Standard and Times* a

letter on the subject of the religious instruction of Catholic children attending the public schools.

Towards the Catholic children in public schools we have a solemn duty of which we are reminded from time to time by the Holy Father. Blessed Pope Pius X early in the twentieth century, reorganized and revitalized the Confraternity of Christian Doctrine. His successors have all stressed the importance of catechetical instruction particularly for those who are not in Catholic schools.

The Archdiocesan Director of the Confraternity of Christian Doctrine, the Rev. John G. McFadden, has been freed from his parish duties to give full time to the Confraternity. . . .

All priests who have the care of souls are requested to follow the official program for the instruction of children. . . .

The official program called for two hours weekly of instruction from September 28 to December 14 for all elementary school children and one hour weekly for high-school children. For adults discussion groups of from ten to twelve members were to be formed, and instruction classes were to be organized for converts.

Besides his Committee for the Christian Home and Family the Archbishop urged other religious activities. Beginning August 22, the Feast of the Immaculate Heart of Mary, the rosary was broadcast each morning at 7:15.[31] The Archbishop first led the rosary and Monsignor Benjamin then gave the accompanying meditation.

On September 13 *America* editorialized about some riots in Los Angeles against UNESCO and scored Catholic participation against UNESCO. When his friend Archbishop McIntyre scolded *America,* Archbishop O'Hara supported him with the words: "I quit reading *America* many years ago under the circumstances similar to those which brought your present trouble." But this was an election year, and no matter what provocation may have arisen, the Archbishop himself made no statement that could be considered political, even against communists.

But the Archbishop was not idle. At the first fall meeting of the consultors he brought up the problem of financing new high schools and appointed a committee to study the problem. When the committee reported at the October 6 meeting, the consultors voted their approval of the report. In the meantime the Archbishop prepared his first announcement on the subject for the *Standard and Times* of November 4. He announced that the collection that had heretofore been used only for the support of the seminary would now also carry the additional burden of certain new needs.

What are these needs? A minimum of ten additional diocesan high schools—perhaps more. Operating costs have risen; last year the Archdiocese had to meet the operating deficit of more than $160,000. Further, more ample provision must be made for the handicapped children, especially those with defects of sight and hearing.

There are other needs to be met on a diocesan basis, but we save their announcement until another time. It is our hope that by our combined efforts we can relieve overcrowded conditions in our diocesan schools and can extend our facilities to give the benefits of Catholic secondary education to those now deprived of them through no fault of their own.

God's blessing is assured those "who instruct others unto justice," and I invoke that blessing on those who accept this invitation to share in the educational mission of the Catholic Church and who support by their sacrifices the work of our consecrated teachers.

There were two points that the Archbishop stressed. In the first place he himself had come from a community in Indiana where schools were built and maintained only by sacrifice. If the Catholic Church was to continue to grow and to provide Catholic education, further sacrifices were necessary. The Archdiocese of Philadelphia had a fine reputation, noted by the Apostolic Delegate at the Archbishop's installation, as a generous giver to religious and charitable enterprises. Much like the Diocese of Buffalo, Philadelphia had a large number of lower middle-class Catholic families who were generous from their meager resources. At this time the Archbishop estimated that he would have to spend twenty-one million dollars in his high-school campaign, and while the sum grew through various circumstances to about twenty-nine millions, the faithful of the Archdiocese responded generously to the Archbishop's call.

The second problem facing the Archbishop was the actual financing of the project. During the construction period that extended through most of his regime the Archbishop personally controlled the entire operation. As one observer had remarked about the Archbishop's health, it may not have been good, yet that did not keep him from doing as heavy a job as anyone in the archdiocese. He engaged architects, among whom he had wide personal contacts; he established budgets that contracting firms had to meet; he opened the bids and awarded the contracts himself. His proposal was in general to provide 25,000 high-school places for students. As his secretary, Monsignor Joseph McGlinn, who was close to him during these years had said: "The Archbishop was a hardheaded, realistic, exacting businessman who forced

architects and builders to meet specifications he had determined
upon in advance." This not only was true of his high-school program but also was the case for the building of elementary schools,
over which he exercised a watchful guidance. The annual expense
for those elementary schools was nearly sixty millions a year, and
yet it was all financed successfully.

In fact, while not disturbing the organization of the Archdiocese, the Archbishop was his own superintendent of schools. With
his flair for statistics the Archbishop gathered the number of baptisms in a given area six years before the current year and set his
plans for schools to take care of approximately ninety percent of
these children. If the pastor did not understand, he would receive
a phone call from the Archbishop in which future school needs
were explained and the pastor warned to prepare to meet the
problem. If the pastor was hard to convince, he received direct
instructions from the Archbishop to have his new plans in the
chancery office within a definite time or another pastor would be
assigned to the rectory. Sometimes this meant merely the enlargement of the school. There were parishes that did not have schools
that soon found under the Archbishop's guidance that a school
could be supplied, and in some cases district schools were built
by the joining of several parishes in the project. And some pastors
who honestly felt that they could not build a school were happy
to do so under the Archbishop's direction.[32] It is not surprising,
however, that when Cardinal Pizzardo wrote him about this time
for a contribution towards the provincial seminaries of Italy, the
Archbishop refused the request on the plea that his building
program would not permit it. He told the Cardinal:

Our local needs are far greater than I realized when I first came here.
To provide adequate space for the boys and girls of high school age
will require an expenditure of between twenty-five and thirty million
dollars. Several of the existing high schools are operating at 150% or
more capacity: one with a capacity of 1400 has 2900 enrolled, going
to school in three shifts. We must in conscience relieve this tense situation, and must provide schools for 15,000 boys and girls who are now
in public secondary schools.

The elementary schools have similarly overcrowded conditions in
many districts, and the shifts in population have made necessary a
great many entirely new schools and churches. We can anticipate an
annual increase in elementary school children of some five thousand.
Our present registration of 175,000 children in the Catholic schools
will grow to 200,000 in a very short time.

Others were aware of the Archbishop's financial wizardry. At the meeting of the bishops in Washington on November 10 to 14 he was elected the treasurer of the Administrative Committee of the N.C.W.C. and made a member of the Board of Catholic Missions. And he also repeated his performance at the annual Pan American Mass at St. Patrick's Church in Washington on November 27. He first greeted the assembled notables in Spanish before speaking to them in English on the theme of good neighborliness founded on a recognition of God. Two days later the Archbishop was pleased to hear that his close friend Archbishop McIntyre had been named one of the new cardinals proclaimed by Pope Pius XII.

While the change in his task in the N.C.W.C. Administrative Committee took him away from the work of the Social Action Department, the change did not disturb his interest in the problem of the relations between industry and labor. Early in December he went to Fort Wayne to arrange for the publication of some papal documents, the most important being that speech of the Pope to Italian businessmen that he had brought back from Rome. Also on December 30 he wrote to Archbishop Alter, the chairman of the Administrative Board, his high opinion of the work of Father Dennis Comey, S.J., of Saint Joseph's College as a mediator in industrial disputes. Father Comey had been insisting on the free negotiation of labor disputes with proper respect for the common good. The Archbishop added:

During the year 1952, after a short strike, Father Comey already acting as arbitrator, was given "unlimited authority," within the terms of the contract between management and labor, to settle disputes. As a result, the Port of Philadelphia has had a peaceful and productive year.

For the decade that Father Comey has conducted his Institute he has had representatives of both management and labor attending his classes, studying the Social Encyclicals together, and praying together. Both sides of the labor contract have been taught that the common good must always be kept in view.

Apparently the Archbishop's health improved after he gave up his gall-bladder diet. He did not, of course, recover from all his troubles, but when his former secretary, Edward Boyle, wrote him about how well he looked in some new photographs, he answered: "I don't know about pictures, but I've gained twenty-five pounds in Philadelphia. The doctor at Mayo Clinic told me to eat everything and lots of it and I am trying to carry out his prescription."

Father Maurice Sheehy, who had found much comfort in the circular letters the Archbishop wrote during the war urged him to write similar letters to his Philadelphia priests. The Archbishop replied that he would have to wait until he got the feel of the place. Apparently by the first of 1953 he decided that he could avail himself of this too, and used it frequently. The letter of January 1 announced a collection for War Relief Services and Emergency for January 25. A letter of January 2, to be read to the faithful, announced that January 11, the Feast of the Holy Family, would be a day for family Communion, and a letter of January 6 urged the observance of the Church Unity Octave from January 18 to 25. He wrote three letters on January 12, one announcing January 18 as Catechetical Sunday, one announcing that he was sending to the pastors a copy of Father Curley's life of Bishop Neumann and asking prayers for the Bishop's canonization, and a third letter to the children through their teachers, with a note to the pastors. With such an abundance of letters one pastor wryly said that the Archbishop wrote many letters, but fortunately one did not have to do anything about them.

The letter to the children was an unusual one, however, since he tried a favorite scheme to get the children to the sacraments:

Now here is a special project for you right now. During the month of March this year, Saint Joseph's Month, we will hold a Catholic Family Life Convention here in Philadelphia. It will be for the whole United States but we arrange the program. Suppose each one of you were to offer ten Holy Communions between now and the 16th of March for the success of the Convention, that would mean more than two million Holy Communions! The prayers of children are powerful and God loves to receive them. If you make this offering for the Family Life Convention you may be sure that it will bear abundant fruit in making family life better in the United States.

Here is another project you can undertake at the same time. Among your friends and neighbors there may be children whose parents have not had the same training as yours have had, perhaps have even failed to send their little ones to the Catholic schools or Christian Doctrine classes offered by the Confraternity for those not in Catholic schools. Look around: if you know any such children, take them with you to the Catholic school or the Christian Doctrine class. Don't be impatient about it; just be nice to them, keep after them, pray for them. See that they make their First Holy Communion and are confirmed. It is the best thing you can do for them and their families.

Finally, a third project, or one for your family. If you are not in the habit of saying the Rosary as a family group every day, see that the practice starts in your family. If your mother finds it hard to get the time for it, give her a little more help with her work so she can get the time. You have Jesus, Mary, and Joseph with you in a family prayer, and they make your family a holy family.

The interest of the Archbishop in current affairs probably was

as lively as ever, but after his coming to Philadelphia he gave no
public expression of it, except where it affected his religious
program. Undoubtedly he continued to read the newspapers
carefully, and to talk with his friends Cardinals Spellman and
McIntyre when counsel was desired. For the rest he lived simply
in the house on City Line Avenue, except for his attendance at
funerals, dedications, and other religious ceremonies. There was
one striking phase of his life that seemed accidental, yet must have
resulted from the quality of his work: that was his choice as
speaker at the consecrations of so many bishops. While some of
the invitations came from personal friendship, there has been
some suggestion that the idea of the bishop's life of which he
spoke was attractive to them. Some say he expressed in these sermons his own notion of an episcopal career.

. . . To be in any measure fitted for the work of the priesthood, a man
must have a deep sense of his own unworthiness and his complete
dependence on God. It is not enough that his strength for the harvest
be from God; he must know and recognize and meditate on this fact
in order to keep an even keel between the crests of elation and the
troughs of depression to which human nature is prone.

That priest is well grounded in humility who keeps in the forefront
of his mind the admonition of Saint Jerome to one of his disciples who
was called to ordination: "It is easier to be called to the priesthood
than it is to deserve to be called." Saint James helps us to understand
that even the branch that bears fruit must be purged.

. . . .

As teacher he must heed the admonition of St. Paul: "Stand fast and
hold the traditions which you have learned, whether by word or by
our epistle." (Thess. 2:14) Above all he must "hold to the sound form
of the words." He must not be "carried about by every wind of doctrine." (Eph. 4:14) He must be no "respecter of persons." He must
"search the scriptures."

. . . .

If as teacher it is essential for the bishop to remain a branch of the
true Vine, how much more important it is for him in his office of mediator, of minister, as dispenser of the mysteries of God! He is the Father
of the flock. . . .

As father of the flock it is the priest's office to give spiritual life to
his children through the Sacrament of Baptism, to nourish them with
the Bread of Life, to cure them of their infirmities through the absolution and Holy Anointing, to bless them and pray for them. The bishop
feeds the sheep as well as the lambs. He protects faith and morals, he
strengthens the faithful through Confirmation, he provides for works
of mercy and instruction, he sends forth laborers into the harvest.

As shepherd, he must admonish his spiritual family and protect it from danger. . . .

Fortunately for our weak human nature, the love and affection of our flock usually outweighs the criticisms. Our danger may lie in the opposite extreme, namely that we foolishly accept for ourselves the devotion directed by the flock through us to the Good Shepherd Who gave His life for His sheep. . . .[33]

The Archbishop tried to live up to his own estimate of the duty of the episcopate, and while his fellow bishops seemed ready to accept the mandate of a bishop's career from him, the greatest testimony for his spiritual life was usually expressed by the laymen with whom he dealt. They included businessmen, newspaper writers, lawyers, and doctors.

Of his personal interests the chief one outside the sacraments was Catholic education both locally and nationally. Of the interest in research that he had developed at Notre Dame he continued a special concern for the scientific hopes of Professor Arthur Reyniers and his germ-free biological laboratories, but this was a field in which he himself could not work. His interest in economic affairs, particularly in the question of the distribution of wealth and the relations between management and labor that had been kindled so warmly in his dealings with Martin Gillen and Orlando Weber and the work of Father Edward Keller, C.S.C., remained active so long as his health permitted him to write letters and to encourage Father Keller. Another of his intellectual interests resulted chiefly from his conviction that there could be no compromise in the acknowledgment by government of the existence of God and the natural law. He accepted several invitations to speak at "Red Masses," and he distributed the publications of Dean Manion of Notre Dame that stressed these doctrines of the existence of God and natural law as enunciated in the Declaration of Independence. This conviction about the need of God in government caused him to regard as enemies of the Church not only the communist governments of the world but anyone suspected of being agents of those governments, those who would try to keep religion out of education, and those who seemed to want to accept communist governments as legal.

His appointment as treasurer of the Administrative Board of the N.C.W.C. was simply a chore of soliciting donations from the hierarchy and religious communities, and drawing up a budget and a financial report for the annual meeting. In his work on the Board of Catholic Missions he manifested a deep interest not only in the betterment of Negroes and Indians but also in the work of his former confrere in the Military Ordinariate, Bishop William McCarty, C.SS.R., now in Rapid City, South Dakota, who was heroically trying with little means to care for the Indians of his frontier diocese.

One of his first letters in 1953 was to Bishop Matthew Brady of the Education Department of the N.C.W.C. He questioned the wisdom of churchmen talking too much about the amount of construction of new school buildings that were being planned by Catholics. He did not reprimand the Bishop for questioning the ability of Catholics to build enough schools, but he did say that these statistics might be misused:

For this reason I feel that it would be a mistake to present the public with an inventory of our construction. The system used by individual Bishops and by the Education Department in the past of making a calculation based on the application of public per capita expenses to Catholic enrollment statistics has served a very careful purpose, but it gives no direct statistical information for any tax study that might be made by the Government. It was public knowledge that the Masons were financing the fight against exempting the Catholic schools from taxation. We know that it is their intention to wipe out existing exemption in one state after another if they succeed in the present California fight. Part of the fight locally in California has been the attempt to base assessment on actual expenditures for construction.

Somewhat in the same vein and as a result of his studies about population he wrote to Bishop George W. Ahr on February 2 some observations about the relations between the defense of the family and the protection of society:

The defense of the family as the basic unit of society—and therefore the defense of society—is by default falling more and more to the Catholics of the country. The ratio of Catholic infant Baptisms in the United States gives a striking demonstration of our duty and our opportunity. In 1951 we baptized 27.1% of the babies born in the United States that year against 22% in 1938. The total number of baptisms in 1951 was approximately double that of 1938. To put it another way Catholic births in 1951 increased 100% over 1938, while non-Catholic births increased only 54.3%.

Truly, divorce and birth control are eating away at society—and our Catholic people are exposed to constant dangers from the atmosphere in which we live. We need every help God can give us to protect Catholic family life.

When he was well started on his plans for building high schools, his successful financing naturally attracted the attention of fellow bishops who wanted to know how he did it. He told them airily, "I am using buttons instead of cash." As to his own personal finances, no one ever doubted that he kept nothing for himself, except certain funds that he had inherited from his parents and that he kept according to the old rules of the Holy Cross Congregation. Gifts that were not designated for the archdiocese were usually assigned to some needy charity that he knew, sometimes in South America or some other mission area. The ordinary small gifts he gave to the archdiocese. His cathedraticum, which might be considered his personal income, he gave back to the archdiocese in great measure, supporting various collections such as the seminary collection, to which he gave two months' salary, or $1,000. He gave five months' salary, or $2,500, to the Charities Collection and $1,000 to the Bishops' War Relief Collection. At the end of the year he would turn over what remained to the diocesan office of the Society for the Propagation of the Faith with a list of those who had begged of him during the year and allowed the officers to apportion the money to the need of those petitioners. During the year he himself took care of the missionary beggars he knew personally. None left him without something. In one case the sum was $38,000 for the expenses of a consecration of a missionary bishop. At other times he assumed the funeral expenses of a poor priest or the hospital bills of a needy one. The simplicity of the Archbishop's personal life was most clearly manifested in this detachment from wealth that fitted his approachableness and humility and his tone of sincerity.

Sometimes his benefactions outside the diocese attracted some questions. He sent $20,000 to the Pope for the sufferers from a flood in Italy and explained that he merely replenished the funds the Holy Father had already given to the suffering. A gift to Mexicans suffering from a hurricane, he said, was in thanksgiving that Pennsylvania had been freed from such damage by the turning of the hurricane towards a southern destination.

The Archbishop had asked for the children's prayers in preparation for the National Family Life Conference held in Philadelphia on March 16 to 18. The Archbishop wrote a letter of welcome for the visitors in which he stressed the family as that which resists the modern trend to "depersonalize" man. He was present when the Apostolic Delegate presided at the opening Mass, and he himself presided at the closing Holy Hour. And pleased with the success of the meeting, he wrote a letter of thanks to the children who had prayed so generously for its success.

When my time comes I want to be able to say that the children of the Archdiocese of Philadelphia are good children, that they receive

Holy Communion frequently in order to have the grace to avoid sin and grow in virtue, that they love the Mother of God and encourage the Family Rosary, that they try to bring other children to religious instruction to the Catholic schools, and to Mass and Holy Communion.

If I were called tomorrow I could tell our Blessed Lord that thanks to the prayers of the children the Family Life Convention was a great success. Many of you did far more than you were asked to do. You offered Masses as well as Holy Communions; some of you offered two or three times as many as you were asked to offer; most of you managed in one or another way to promote the Family Rosary.

When he was in the Military Ordinariate, the Archbishop had been instrumental in obtaining the first general permission for evening Masses. He was pleased to see the privilege extended again after the war. On March 20 he gave permission for nineteen specified parishes to have an evening Mass on Sundays and on certain specified days. The number was increased to twenty-two the next week. He tried then to get permission for a daily evening Mass, but told Father Heston, his procurator, that he would accept the decision of Rome, and added:

... Whatever the answer is will be perfectly all right with me of course, but since some of the finest vocations in the Archdiocese of Philadelphia have come from families of miners and factory workers, I want to find an opportunity for them to receive Holy Communion if the extension of the privilege can be made to fit their cases. If the first Mass in a parish is at seven o'clock or the only Mass is at eight o'clock, there would be little chance of their ever being daily communicants under the ordinary rules of the Church.

Archbishop O'Hara had been named by the Pope as vice president of the Permanent Committee on Eucharistic Congresses. Undoubtedly the most dramatic achievement of his years in Buffalo had been the Provincial Eucharistic Congress, which had, in fact, been an international affair. The courtesy of those cardinals and bishops of other countries who came to make the celebration such a success was not forgotten by the Archbishop, and he made valiant efforts to repay them. One of the first to be repaid was Cardinal Gilroy at the Congress at Sydney. By coincidence he had to delay his trip to Sydney to attend the funeral in Ottawa of Archbishop Vachon, who was the president of the Permanent Committee. In Sydney he gave three speeches at the Congress: at the Women's Mass, at the Citizens' Mass on "Citizens' Night," and on the next day at the special meeting of the university students. At the speech on Citizens' Night he spoke of the persecution that their ancestors had endured and spoke of the two very notable

Irishmen Australia had sent to the United States, General Francis Thomas Meagher and John Boyle O'Reilly.[34]

True to his policy of avoiding public celebrations, the Archbishop told his family that he hoped to hold the conferring of the pallium on May 12 to a simple ceremony, but he could not control the program. The presiding official at the Mass in the cathedral was Cardinal Spellman, who took the occasion to pay his friendly tribute to the Archbishop, whom he called a "humble priest and steadfast friend." The Cardinal said that the pallium was a symbol of authority and, therefore, of a trust and of the obligation of a shepherd. He conferred it in the name of the Supreme Shepherd, the Holy Father, who was a great example of the true shepherd. He added:

And because I know well and greatly admire this zealous priest of the Congregation of the Holy Cross, this wise and patient student counsellor and President of a renowned University of which he was one of the great architects and builders, this consecrated personification of the famous Spirit of Notre Dame, this organizer and inspiring leader of the heroic self-sacrificing Chaplains of the far-flung-world-wide diocese of the Military Ordinariate of our United States, this quiet, dynamic Bishop of Buffalo, and now friendly, efficient, and effective Archbishop of Philadelphia, one of the greatest sees in our beloved and blessed country—because I know him well, I say I know too that he is truly worthy of the precious trust bestowed upon him this day and that he will be ever ready to counsel, protect, guide and defend you, yes if necessary even die for you, the faithful, God-revering sheep of his beloved and loving sheepfold.[35]

At the luncheon in Town Hall after the ceremony these ideas were repeated and the Archbishop responded with gratitude to those who had come to honor him.

Archbishop O'Hara and Cardinal McIntyre, as in the days they lived together on Madison Avenue, were in frequent consultation and kept each other informed of their activities. Cardinal McIntyre, who had been invited to give the baccalaureate address at the University of Notre Dame, sent to the Archbishop a copy of a booklet, *Forces Affecting American Education*,[36] suggesting that he, too, might find some information for the commencement address he was to deliver at Duquesne University on June 7. The Archbishop told the Cardinal: "Perhaps the book will yield what I want for a commencement address on the Diamond Jubilee of Duquesne University. I shall have to make some reparation for Notre Dame's inviting George Kennan who denounced anti-communists in his speech on the campus." Mr. Kennan had given the principal address at the dedication of the O'Shaughnessy building at Notre Dame that spring.

In his sermon at Duquesne the Archbishop took his text from the Book of Genesis, in which God sent Abraham out of his country and promised him blessings to his progeny as a reward and compared that exile to the sufferings and exile of the Fathers of the Holy Ghost, especially Father Joseph Strub and his companions, five other priests of the community, who founded the University. He saw in their lives a contradiction between the totalitarianism of the *Kulturkampf* that had driven them from Germany and the Catholic philosophy of education. He then proceeded to use the booklet, *Forces Affecting American Education,* as an example of the philosophy of the National Education Association. He quoted the booklet as finding a contrast between the "exercise of intelligence" and eternity, and said that in such statements he found only confusion. He suggested that by making all matters relative the authors of the booklet denied the validity of the ten commandments.

There is a great field for public education, but those who are claiming for themselves a monopoly of its defense are its worst enemies. They have failed to see that the secularism they defend so roundly plunged the world into two global wars in one generation. Further, I find in their frenzy for experimentation in the schools no sense of responsibility to the souls of the children who are the laboratory material of their experiments. . . .

He then asked how the children raised in these schools acted in the war, saying: "I ask the question in all seriousness because as the spiritual director of a Catholic University I had the God-given opportunity to mend some of the souls that had been damaged by the progressive schools of the nineteen-twenties." Turning to Duquesne University, he praised its loyalty to Catholic philosophy throughout its seventy-five years and mentioned some of the priests who had directed the college during those years. "These young men and women whose academic achievement received the accolade today from Duquesne University can thank the Holy Ghost for their sound principles on which their love of God and country are grounded. When asked to give an account of themselves they will not have to shield themselves behind the Fifth Amendment."

A child adoption law was being proposed in the Pennsylvania state legislature. Because of the extreme powers to be given the State by Bill 480 the Archbishop thought it well to state his position in the *Standard and Times* of June 26. He made it clear that the opposition to the bill was not because the Catholic institutions were inferior. "Our standards in this matter are far above those which are regarded in social work as acceptable minimum standards." He objected to the proposed bill because it took away the due processes of law in handling children in the Catholic institutions. "We do ask for ourselves and other groups which conduct children's institutions and agencies as private works of benevolence and charity that we be not exposed to arbitrary interference without due notice and an opportunity to be heard."

The watchfulness of the Archbishop was tested again on the question of movies. In a letter of July 1 in the diocesan paper he maintained that the movie "The Moon is Blue" was issued by United Artists as an act of defiance to the Legion of Decency, since it did not have even the seal of approval of the movie industry's code. He urged the faithful to find out if there was any intention to exhibit the movie in their neighborhood, and if there was, to protest to the owners of the theatre where it was to be shown.

A new bill on the adoption of children, House Bill 1132, he regarded as objectionable as the other one. In a letter to the pastors to be read in the Masses on July 19 he urged that letters and telegrams of protest be sent by the faithful to the legislators. He sent his own telegram to the senators from ten counties as follows:

The sweeping powers given to administrative units of the State government in House Bill No. 1132 threaten the rights of all children of the Commonwealth. Intensive study of implications and possible consequences is required to remove a totalitarian threat. Despite the good faith of proponents the danger is present. I suggest postponement of the action until the next session of legislature with thorough study and open hearings in the interval.

There are no accurate figures on the number of letters and telegrams sent, but it was estimated that there were 15,000 letters received on Monday, 40,000 on Tuesday, and 40,000 on Wednesday, and about 10,000 telegrams. Word was promptly sent out from the legislators that further consideration of the bill had been postponed. To Harrison W. Fry the Archbishop related the incident two years later:

While I disliked to issue a statement at that time, I found it necessary. On Thursday of the week preceding that Sunday we were informed that Senate Bill 1132 would be passed without debate. We offered amendments. On Friday noon we were informed that these amendments were rejected. On Sunday morning we called for a state-wide protest. We know that 187,000 letters and telegrams were delivered in Harrisburg. How many were delivered to the homes of the senators we did not learn. The protest was effective.

While he was Bishop of Buffalo the Archbishop had shown more than usual interest in retarded children. Significantly, when he asked the faithful to send in their requests on the occasion of his installation, he received many requests for aid for retarded children as well as an avalanche of visits from parents of these youngsters. They found a responsive heart in the Archbishop. In a circular letter of July 27, published in the diocesan paper, the Archbishop announced that the children then attending St. Barbara's School were to be tranferred to St. Matthias School, and St. Barbara's was to become the first day school for retarded children who could profit by classroom training. The Sisters of Mercy of Merion agreed to staff the school, and the opening was scheduled for October. In addition he announced that two sisters from the Missionary Servants of the Most Holy Trinity who had received special training for the work would visit the other retarded children in their homes. These other children would be brought to St. Barbara's for First Holy Communion and confirmation. For the present the two programs would be confined to the city of Philadelphia. This was but the beginning of an unusual program of special education in the archdiocese, to which the Archbishop paid personal attention. He reserved to himself the giving of confirmation to the retarded. Later he supervised special programs for the blind and the deaf.

The Archbishop went to Notre Dame again for the opening of the Institute of Spirituality on July 31 and gave the opening sermon, calling the institute a proper sequence of the Congress of Religious held the year before, since its purpose was to intensify and strengthen the religious life. In his sermon he objected to any proposal that would allow secular studies to interfere with the proper religious formation of novices.

Although the Archbishop was actually leaving behind the university research on economics and the industrial conflicts of both Buffalo and Philadelphia, he had under his direction practical participants in these industrial problems, and he had not lost any of his interest in them. This was especially noticeable in his arrangement to have papal documents on the subject printed at his expense by the *Sunday Visitor* Press. When Robert Quigley of the Association of Catholic Trade Unionists wrote to the Archbishop on August 23, 1952, asking him to speak at the annual Labor Day Mass, the Archbishop did not accept because of the shortness of the time to prepare a suitable speech, but he did say that he would give an address at the 1953 meeting. On September 4, 1953, he notified Quigley that he would have for distribution at the Mass some 400 copies of his own pamphlet, *Six Social Documents of Pope Pius XII*. He added:

I have no objection whatever to the distribution of the Labor Day Statement. In general, it is an excellent statement, although it has some glaring faults. I have just received a letter analyzing the statement which I am sending to Father Ostheimer for possible use in the *Standard and Times*. . . . Paul Tafel [the author of the letter] is a convert to the Church brought to it by the Social Encyclicals of the Popes.

I have protested against the use of the term "industry council" because as proposed and promoted by the C.I.O. it was a socialistic device completely alien to the mind of the Holy Father. . . .

I am sure that your members want to have a current understanding of the social doctrines of the Catholic Church, and want to adhere strictly to the teachings of the Popes, so from time to time I may point out errors that may occur in popular misrepresentation. Since the point with regard to Industry Councils is of such great importance when I went to Rome last year I sought information on who were the Holy Father's consultants in these matters. I was agreeably surprised when I was handed the manuscript in the Holy Father's own handwriting.

The full title of Archbishop O'Hara's pamphlet was *Six Social Documents of His Holiness Pope Pius XII and a letter of His Excellency Monsignor Montini*,[37] and its purpose was to support the Archbishop's opposition to the industry council that had been sponsored by the Social Action Department of the N.C.W.C. Just as the followers of Monsignor John A. Ryan had argued repeatedly that the social encyclicals of the recent popes were the basis for their program of social reform, so the Archbishop was determined to find papal support for his opposition to certain parts of their program. The chief document for this purpose was the Pope's address to the Italian Catholic Association of Owners-Managers (UCID) on January 31, 1952, which he had been shown in the Pope's own handwriting. The Pope spoke about the "talk nowadays about a reform in the structure of industry," and had said that certain changes were infiltrating these movements:

Nor could we disregard the changes which distorted the words of high wisdom of Our glorious predecessor, Pius XI. These distortions have come about by overemphasizing an observation of wholly secondary importance (regarding the eventual juridical modifications in the relations between the employees subject to the labor contract, and the other contracting party), and by giving to this observation the value and the importance of a modern social program of the Church.

Meanwhile, they pass over, more or less in silence, the principal parts of the Encyclical, "Quadragesimo Anno," which contains the Church's real program: viz., the idea of a corporate, occupational order of the entire economy. Whoever sets about to treat problems relative to the reform of the structure of industry, without taking into account that every single business is, by its very purpose, closely bound up with the whole of the national economy, runs the risk of positing erroneous and false premises, endangering the entire economic and social order. Therefore, in that same address of June 3, 1950, we tried to place in its proper light the thought and the doctrine of Our Predecessor to whom nothing was more alien than to give any encouragement whatsoever to follow the road which leads towards the forms of any anonymous, collective responsibility.

It was this charge that the industry council would set up this "anonymous collective responsibility" that the Archbishop wanted to bring home to its proponents.

The other papal documents in the pamphlet were "The Discourse of the Pope to Representatives of the International Union of Catholic Employers Associations" of May 7, 1939; his discourse to the International Congress of Social Studies, June 3, 1950; his letter addressed to the thirty-ninth "Social Week" at Dijon, France, July 7, 1952; the radio address of the Pope to the Austrian *Katholikentag* in Vienna, September 14, 1952; and the Christmas Message of the Pope, "Calling on Mankind to Aid the Poor and Showing the Road to True Salvation," December 24, 1952, which was apparently added after the pamphlet was originally planned as a "Five Documents" pamphlet. Added to these six documents was a letter of Archbishop G. B. Montini, the substitute secretary of state of the Pope, September 22, 1952, to Archbishop Giuseppe Siri of Genoa. In general these documents called for industry and the worker to cooperate for the common good and to avoid the evils of socialism.

The Labor Day sermon of the Archbishop at the Church of the Assumption on September 7 consisted in bringing out the passages of these social documents that he felt proved his notion of the status of the economic problems of the day. After expressing pleasure at the opportunity to assist in their workers' solemn act of thanksgiving, he plunged into the notions that he found in the writings of the Holy Father, especially in the letter to the assembly at the Vienna *Katholikentag*. There the Pope said that the first phase of the modern social problem had revolved about the labor question and now that problem at least in its essentials had been solved. The Pope had gone on to say that at least two tasks faced the world in the second phase. The first of these the Pope had described as the attempt to overcome the class struggle by an organic cooperation of employer and employee and the second was the protection of the individual and the family from absorption by the state. The Archbishop continued with quotations from the Holy Father to illustrate these points. The Archbishop then made his applications:

His Holiness states that at least in the essentials the first phase of the social problem has been solved. The inherent rights of labor are widely recognized. In our own country we have proceeded far beyond that; labor in general has achieved a family standard of living that is beyond the conception of the laborers in most other countries.

In the second phase of the social problem the Holy Father underscores two grave dangers. The first is the so-called *class struggle;* the second is the Leviathan State.

The class struggle is outlawed. It is not only unchristian; it is atheistic. It is part of the communistic doctrine of economic determinism. . . .

The Archbishop then proceeded again to quote the Pope's explanation of these problems. He insisted that there was much more to be learned from the Pope's proposals that owners and workers act for the common good. The Archbishop maintained that the danger of absorption of the individual and the family into the state was treated more extensively in the Christmas message of 1952. The Holy Father regarded the family, the state, and private property as essential social institutions, and these tend to form and develop man as a person. The Archbishop said that the tendency to take away private property tended to depersonalize man. He listed five elements in this attempt to depersonalize man that were cited by the Holy Father, such as the socializing of medicine, the limitations of migrations, and the like. His fifth element consisted in that "The right to work is unreasonably restricted." The Archbishop added that the re-election of Senator Taft in Ohio meant that the workingmen of Ohio appreciated the protection the Taft-Hartley Act gave them against subversive leadership. There is no record of the reaction of the trade unionists to the sermon, but certainly it was not like the reaction that had come from his reference to the longshoremen at the "Red Mass" in New York three years before.

On October 5 the Archbishop went to New York to attend the double consecration of Bishops Dargin and Kellenberg. Cardinal Spellman was to have been the consecrator but was ill, and Cardinal McIntyre acted both as consecrator and preacher of the sermon. At the dinner following the consecration Archbishop O'Hara gave a brief speech in which, while praising the solicitude of the Holy Father for the Archdiocese of New York, he spoke glowingly of the Cardinal for whom he felt deep admiration:

The mighty burdens laid on the shoulders of His Eminence he has accepted cheerfully as so many opportunities to do good and save souls. Not only in the Archdiocese of New York, not only among the mission lands of every continent, among the war sufferers of many lands, he has "gone about doing good." Hour after hour for days on end, he has visited our wounded in hospitals all over the world, he has encouraged the practice of religion among men at the front lines and in training camps, he has brought consolation to prisoners of war in their stockades, and alleviated their hard lot, the while he has counseled rulers to listen to the Holy Father's plea for justice and charity, the only basis of peace.

On October 10 the Archbishop was particularly pleased to dedicate the redecorated St. Barbara's Day School for retarded children. Already there were 217 children enrolled in the school. He had solicited private donations for the school, and at the time of the dedication these gifts had amounted to $36,498, but he announced that more money would be needed to maintain the school.

On October 11 the Archbishop participated in a mammoth Holy Name Rally in Benjamin Franklin Parkway. This was the largest religious demonstration in the history of the city. The number of the faithful present was estimated from 250,000 to 330,000 mostly members of the Holy Name Society. The *Standard and Times* in its special photo coverage of the event said: "Holy Name men lined the entire Parkway from the Washington monument in front of the Art Museum to Logan Circle, and across from the banks of the Schuykill to Spring Garden." The Mass was celebrated by Bishop McShea, and the Archbishop presided and gave the sermon. On October 30 the Archbishop went to Notre Dame again to bless the Nieuwland science building. Probably few who attended the blessing of the new building understood how much the Archbishop was responsible for the very existence of the building, for which he had begun collecting while he was president of the University.

When the Archbishop announced the usual seminary collection in his letter of November 4, he took a glance backward at his accomplishments and a forward look that promised greater deeds. He mentioned that the funds collected the previous year had helped in taking care of St. Barbara's School, and now 600 retarded children were being cared for in three institutions, that a science addition had been made to one high school, Archbishop Prendergast High School had been opened, and construction was in progress at St. James High School in Chester. He then announced his plans for the addition of six new high schools for the archdiocese: Bishop Neumann High School for 3,000 boys in south Philadelphia; Father Judge High School for 2,500 boys in the Torresdale section; two high schools in northwest Philadelphia, each for 2,500, one for boys and one for girls; a high school in Pottstown for both boys and girls; and the conversion of Archbishop Prendergast High to accommodate an additional 1,000 students. In financing these high schools one-half of the cost would be borne by the seminary collection fund and one-half would be borne by the parishes concerned. He also announced three gifts: one of $12,000 and two of $100,000 for the fund.

To one so dedicated to the service of the Blessed Virgin the encyclical letter of Pope Pius XII setting the year from December 8, 1953, to December 8, 1954, as a Marian Year with the request that during this time prayers be offered for the return of all men to Christ, the return of peace, charity, and justice, and the restoration of the liberty of the Church in countries where Catholics were now experiencing persecution was bound to have great importance. In his letter to priests on November 4 he changed the *imperata* to the *Oratio de Sancta Maria* for the year. In his letter of November 11 he repeated the suggestion of the Holy Father that all should try to model themselves after Our Lady during the Marian Year. He also noted that the bishops of the country had asked that there be a national commemoration of the Marian Year by a novena from November 30 to December 8, and that a collection be taken up at this time for the completion of the Shrine of the Immaculate Conception in Washington. For family devotions during the coming year he suggested the practice of the family Rosary and the family Holy Communion on Christmas, Holy Family Sunday, Mother's Day, and the Sunday nearest the feast of the Maternity of the Blessed Mother, and that the boys also be dedicated to Saint Joseph.

Because during the last weeks in October some youngsters thought they saw a figure in the trees above some bushes in Fairmount Park near 51st Street, crowds began to visit the place daily. The reported visions increased as did the number of visitors, until late in October as many as 50,000 persons visited the scene and votive offerings began to collect beneath the bushes. But when the leaves fell, the vision also disappeared.

On November 24, writing to Burke Walsh of the N.C.W.C.

about these supposed visions in Fairmount Park, the Archbishop told him:

The site of the park where the apparitions are supposed to have taken place is across the street from a Communist belt and the enter-prising people there are not averse to selling vigil lights and rosaries to the people who visit the meadow. The gypsies flocked there in num-bers for a while, and when it was announced that there would be a special vision on October 25th and a good miracle would take place they came from various parts of the country. The man selected for the miracle was one of the leaders, but he died right there in the meadow. That dampened the enthusiasm of the gypsies.

Most of the children who had the visions are non-Catholics, and their stories do not hold together.

This background is strictly confidential and I would not want it referred to in any way. Neither do I want the story mentioned in the Catholic papers because I have far more correspondence now than I can handle. It will die a natural death if it is kept out of the papers.[38]

On December 12 the Archbishop presided at a ceremony in which the members of the Alliance of Catholic Women and 47 other allied organizations were taken into the Ladies of Charity, the official organization of St. Vincent de Paul. The Archbishop explained that he did this:

1. To make all those engaged in personalized charity and those who in the future will interest themselves in this work, recipients of many plenary and partial indulgences granted to the Ladies of Charity.
2. To stress the idea and need of personalized charity.
3. To give to the dependent children of the Archdiocese of Philadel-phia and those directly responsible for their care a remembrance, one a month in the Mass and Holy Communion of all the members of the Organization.

On December 10 the Archbishop took occasion to rebuke a pastor who had announced a charge of fifty cents a week for high-school tuition:

If the revenues of your parish are insufficient to meet the tuition charge, you have only to ask assistance from the mission fund. We have granted this to others, and we will grant it to any parish that cannot meet this expense.

The tuition fees were abolished because we found that in some cases they were keeping children out of Catholic high school. Those with weak faith are the ones most likely to excuse their children from Catholic education if there is a tuition charge.

Please write and tell me what steps you are taking to correct this wrong impression you have given your people.

The Archbishop continued to be uncooperative with any inter-

denominational project, but he was willing to explain his stand.
To Mr. Melvin Rose of the Bucks County Council on Human
Relations he wrote on December 23:

December 23, 1953

My Dear Mr. Rose:

I appreciate your desire to be helpful and believe that I understand
your proposed approach to a problem that is new to you. I cannot
encourage Catholic participation in your plan because the plan is not
accommodated to Catholic principles.

If a Catholic begins to think in terms of minorities he is forgetting
his Catholic principles. A Catholic is taught from his earliest years
that all men are children of God and their brother. The parable of
the Pharisee and the Publican is drilled into us when we are little
children, and the voice of conscience arises to accuse us if we begin
to feel at any time that we are better than someone else. If we yield to
the temptation and give some manifestation of a feeling of superiority,
there is someone in our neighborhood to bring us back to earth—a
little helper for our conscience.

So far as citizenship is concerned, our teaching from the cradle is to
"reader to Caesar the things that are Caesar's and to God the things
that are God's." Commander Shea expressed our feeling perfectly when
he said in a letter to Jackie the night before he went to his death, "If
you are a good Catholic, you cannot help being a good American."
If we fulfill our duty to immigrants, we welcome them as brothers. If
they cannot speak our language, we provide them with a church of
their own and a priest who speaks the language. But we encourage
them to learn English, adopt American ways, and become good citizens. When our colored fellow citizens wanted churches of their own,
we provided them—but they were always welcome in the Church provided for other congregations. Now that most of them do not want
their own church, we have taken the designation "colored" from the
five churches that previously had it in the City of Philadelphia.

Since our approach is purely a spiritual one, we see no need for civic
committees to serve our needs. As a matter of fact, the good intention
of committee members has sometimes been mistaken by newcomers.
I am sure that you would not want to seem patronizing to some of the
newcomers whom you want to help, but your well meant interest may
easily be misinterpreted by some of the recipients of your kindness.

All of us realize that our Catholic system does not produce perfect
results. However, those of us who have been around long enough to
have observed the assimilation of the immigrants from European
nations, whose traditional hostility kept their people from natural
understanding and satisfaction, have seen that the intermarriage of
children in the second and third generation has wiped out age-old
animosities in a surprising degree.

Just how often the Archbishop wrote for the *Standard and*

Times without signing his name is not evident. He also occasionally wrote for the *Brooklyn Tablet.* In the December 19 *Tablet* he published an unsigned review of Father Keller's booklet *Christianity and American Capitalism.* The review praised the book particularly for its application of the statements of Pope Pius XII on co-management to the proposed Industry Council of the C.I.O., adding that this condemnation of the C.I.O. plan should also be applied to other plans for industry councils. He said also that Father Keller did not fear war between management and big labor because he saw collusion between the giants. In the last paragraph the Archbishop urged the reading of his own pamphlet of the *Six Documents.*

The Archbishop celebrated Christmas at the cathedral, praising in his sermon the increased birth rate as an answer to social planners. He also joined the other bishops of the country in setting December 27 as a day of prayer for those behind the Iron Curtain. He kept up his round of dedications, blessings, and funerals of the clergy despite some handicaps from arthritis. To an Indianapolis friend who had watched him climb a stairs and had written to him about it, he noted: "For the past twenty-five years or so my hinges have been creaky, sometimes more than others, and I have grown accustomed to it. When I was a boy, I used to smile at the old ladies who would drop a curtsy to Our Lord when they came into Church. I think they did better than I do now." Some time later when he took two walks with Cardinal Spellman in New York he remarked: "They almost wrecked me. He can still walk fast, and I did my best to keep up to him."

Although the Archbishop tried to keep out of political matters, he could not keep silent when the Supreme Court reversed the Ohio Censor Board's prohibition against the movies "La Ronde" and "M." He wrote a letter in the *Standard and Times* to be read in all the Masses on Sunday, January 24. In it he praised the people for their participation in the family Communion and said they would need the added grace to endure the new decisions of the Court:

In effect the Supreme Court has ruled that the States may label as poison only what affects the body, not that which can destroy the soul.

While we can hope that the majority of companies will continue to respect and welcome censorship, we cannot rest there. Rejoicing reported from Hollywood this week indicates that not all men in the industry are decent. Parents must now become more acutely aware of their responsibility to the children God has entrusted to them and of the fact that their responsibility is primary. This is an obligation of the natural law, and affects all parents, not Catholics only. The Church will continue to help as in the past. The lists of the Legion of Decency will be available for the motion picture classifications; so will the lists of the National Organization for Decency in Literature, for periodical publications.

Among the new churches to be dedicated to Our Lady during the Marian Year the Archbishop announced on February 2 that the Blessed Sacrament chapel at the cathedral would be replaced by a new and more handsome chapel to be dedicated to Our Lady of the Blessed Sacrament. It would cost $650,000, and he suggested that gifts for this expense could be sent to the cathedral rectory or to the archdiocesan office.

On February 10 the Archbishop wrote a letter prompted by the reading of the annual reports of the pastors. In it he expressed his own desires and his appreciation of the problems of his priests:

Reverend Dear Fathers:

So far as a circular letter can be personal, I want this one to be just that, for it is an extension of the individual comments made as a post-script to the acknowledgement of your spiritual reports for 1953.

These reports have given a good examination of conscience and have suggested ways in which I may serve you and your parishioners to better advantage. Your difficulties face me as they face you. Your various solutions offer suggestions that will benefit all of us.

Certainly the convert work is edifying. Although in only a few par-ishes does the number of converts exceed one hundred, the number of parishes with twenty or more converts is growing. The inquiry classes offer new opportunities to those who are spiritually starved, and they constitute an invitation to further study.

It is gratifying to note that many pastors of national parishes report converts. Others seem to feel that it would be an encroachment on ter-ritorial rights for them to offer instruction to non-Catholics. That fear is groundless. Seek converts, wherever they may be available. Even though they may not be eligible for membership in your parish, they are eligible for membership in the Catholic Church, and God may have chosen you as the instrument of their salvation. The Good Samaritan asked no questions.

Every marriage revalidation means one or more souls snatched from the Devil—and what occupation could be more appropriate for the Marian Year than helping Our Lady crush the head of the serpent? The report shows how tremendous is our task.

The reports on Holy Communion give a great insight into the spir-itual tone of the parish. Each year's growth in the number of daily communicants will be reflected in other items. It is noteworthy that the pastors who provide the opportunity for confession in connection with daily Mass have the greatest success with daily Communion. "Confession on request" does not give the encouragement needed for beginners in the practice of frequent Communion. Each priest who makes his preparation for and thanksgiving after Mass in the confessional is an active promoter of daily Communion. The Holy Ghost solves most of the problems of the pastor if the majority of his parishioners are frequent communicants.

The matter of catechetical instruction for the children in public schools is covered by two items. Under "delinquent parishioners" should be listed those not attending confraternity classes; under "catechetical instruction" should be listed the public school children who *are* attending the classes. If there is a notable gap between the sum of these two groups and the Catholic school enrollment on the one hand, and the number of children baptized during the years that should furnish your present pupils, some research is in order. Some of that research has already been reported in response to a previous request, but more is in order.

There seems to be considerable divergence of practice in the matter of visits to the sick. This point needs no elaboration.

Several pastors mention that they seldom see their Catholic high school students, or that these students are rarely seen at the altar rail. A friendly interest on the part of the pastor may be all that is needed to awaken parish loyalty. A pastor may appear very formidable to the children in the elementary school—and he may be quite unaware of this. If this condition prevails, the children may be afraid to approach him after they enter high school—and a "wall of separation" is built up. A friendly interest in the progress of the student may break down this wall if it exists.

Some parishes abound in vocations, others rarely present a candidate for religion. Although a great deal of research has been made on this problem, especially in recent years, no one seems to know all the answers. However, each pastor and each confessor may with profit continue to study his own possibilities in this regard, and pray that God will bless with vocations at least a few of those children who receive from him the Bread of Life.

One final word for those who have contact with our Negro brothers. If in the Providence of God the present migration from the South gives us an opportunity to bring the truth of our religion, and the graces of our sacramental life, to these good people who have never before in their lives had contact with Catholics, we must not be wanting in any particular. We can thank God that we have already received so many of them into the Church, and we must bless God for every chance we have to partake in this apostolate.

The Archbishop's Lenten pastoral achieved more than usual publicity because of his suggested practices of penance. As usual he urged the attendance at the sacraments as the best form of penance, and suggested that they try to see themselves as God saw them.

How can we get the help of God to do that? First by prayer and frequent Holy Communion, daily if possible. Secondly by curbing our appetites, not only by fast and abstinence, but by guarding our eyes, our ears, all our senses.

Take the matter of television and radio. As the Holy Father has well said, these inventions can be for the glory of God, but they may also be a means of destroying both our spiritual and our intellectual life. Disconnect your set for a week, and then take an honest appraisal. Have you missed anything worthwhile? What have you gained? The art of conversation is restored to the family, perhaps many duties are performed that might otherwise have been neglected. Your own judgments may be more sound because you have missed thousands of words of propaganda.

Probably the Archbishop had no idea how much attention would be given to his suggestion about cutting off television, but the item was flashed from coast to coast and printed in *Time*. It drew many comments. To Captain Halphen he wrote about it:

I have been amused at the protests against the suggestion that radio and television be disconnected for a week. One honest operator said that if people disconnected for a week, they would never connect again.

To General Craugh he also commented:

Your appraisal of the New York *Times* is my own. I understand that while I was in New York Saturday the phone was ringing all the time. People connected with TV and radio were taking the word of the New York *Times*. I am sorry that I missed the opportunity to ask the question, "Does anyone believe the New York *Times?*"

On that weekend the Archbishop was in New York to help celebrate the thirtieth anniversary of the establishment of the Casita Maria among the Puerto Ricans, at which he had assisted when he was first living in New York and in which he had retained a lively interest.

When St. Patrick's Day came the Archbishop gave further evidence that his arthritis was a problem, although he probably had other reasons for not joining in the St. Patrick's Day parade. He told the managers of the parade: "I am afraid I must plead age and infirmities against possible exposure to the weather. It has been my experience that St. Patrick often tries the faith of the Irish with a touch of real March weather and I have passed the point where I can meet the challenge with impunity."

Archbishop O'Hara had not yielded his opposition to liberalism in religious matters, and those whom he thought were spreading this liberalism were not to be encouraged. When the Catholic Renaissance Society announced its program for its spring meeting and sent a copy of the program to him, he sent it on to Monsignor Francis Furey, the rector of the seminary:

I enclose the program of the Spring Symposium of the Catholic Renaissance Society. I have checked a few items on which I should like to have a bit of background. Johns Hopkins University usually escaped the Red headlines that are bestowed so liberally on Harvard, but I feel that it is just as Red as Harvard. I don't know anything about the Guggenheim Museum, but I know the Guggenheim Foundation has sponsored the higher studies of many Reds. I don't know what "Expressionist Criticism" is but I do have a vague idea of Existentialism. I hope the man from Fordham is able to handle the man from Hopkins if he gets out of line.

To Father Sylvester Holbel, the supervisor of Catholic education in Buffalo, with whom he had worked on many matters and who had asked his aid in getting a Ford Foundation grant, he wrote in a similar vein:

I am sorry to diappoint you, but I think you are very fortunate in having your application to the Ford Foundation rejected. I am sorry to see the grant go to Notre Dame, and I am sorry to see Notre Dame undertake such a study in public. I have the results of the Notre Dame study, but I have not had enough time to do much reading. History justified itself—thank God—but I understand that there will be a coalescence of the other "Social Studies." This is cause for serious regret because the term "Social Studies" was put over by people who wanted to turn the United States into a Socialist's paradise without our noticing the change. To do this, history had to be submerged in. a haze of other things, because the lessons of history would tend to keep us out of secularism. . . . Why can't our people be encouraged to get more college training? There are lots of people outside the Church who would be glad to keep us confined to vocational courses. Let's fool them!

Apparently the Archbishop referred to the self-study grant made by the Ford Foundation to Notre Dame. Later he was to express some misgivings about the persons invited from outside to advise the University in this process of self study.

"McCarthyism" was a term given indiscriminately to anticommunist activity at this time. For Catholics the fact that the man after whom it was named was a Catholic proved unfortunate because a Catholic who recognized that communism was against the basic ideas of Christianity had no choice but to be opposed to it. Like many defenders of Catholicism in the postwar world, Archbishop O'Hara tended to support any sincere opponent of communism. Likewise, in their desire to condemn anything that looked like communism the more conservative Catholics tended to defend Senator Joseph McCarthy. In abstaining from political affairs the Archbishop did nothing publicly that would indicate that he supported the Senator from Wisconsin, although the archdiocesan paper did indicate support for the Senator's charges against some government officials. Writing to a friend on April 12, the Archbishop indicated his approval of Cardinal Spellman's support for Senator McCarthy expressed at the Communion breakfast of the New York City Policemen on April 4, 1954:

> Cardinal Spellman did a good job—in a few words—at the Communion breakfast for Monsignor McCaffrey. The tremendous applause for Senator McCarthy was so significant and Monsignor McCaffrey approved it. The Cardinal added, "Monsignor McCaffrey has said everything. I can only add I dislike Communists and I dislike their methods."

However, the *New York Times* in reporting the affair did not seem certain about the meaning of the Cardinal's words on this occasion.

During the next few months there seems to be a contradiction between the statements about the Archbishop's health and his activity. It is true that he did not attend civic ceremonies or public dinners, but he did celebrate the pontifical Masses on the great feasts such as Easter and preached the sermons. He went to Washington on April 27 for the spring meeting of the Administrative Committee of the bishops and preached at the Mass celebrating the bicentennial anniversary of the Church in Pittsburgh. On May 8 he ordained 26 priests, 25 for the archdiocese and one for the diocese of Atlanta, and attended the annual meeting in Philadelphia of the alumni of the North American College of Rome on May 11–13. The next day he went quietly to Rome for his *ad limina* visit. The trip was apparently uneventful, and he was back for the celebration of the feast of Pentecost.

On June 4 the *Standard and Times* seemed definitely to defend Senator McCarthy. Yet the editor, Monsignor Ostheimer, in his column claimed that Senator Flanders was in error when he said that McCarthy had divided Catholics because the Catholic opposition to communism was religious and not political. He maintained that there was no Catholic attitude on McCarthy because that was not a religious but a political problem. There is no indication whether he sought or obtained the approval of the Archbishop before preparing his column.

Just when the Archbishop's knees began to stiffen so that others were aware of his condition is not clear.[39] Among the clergy of Philadelphia who noticed it was a fellow sufferer from the disease, better known as a very zealous leader of the Catholic Total Abstinence Union, Monsignor Keogh. He sent a list of suggested remedies for the disease including a fruit diet and a joking suggestion of "an apple a day." The Archbishop responded to the suggestions in a jovial way. "Many thanks for the suggestions. Some of them have worked in my case, some have not. My arthritis seems to be tied up with sinus trouble, and the sinus trouble is tied up with purgatory—and of the three, purgatory is the only one I take seriously." There were many rumors about the extent of his affliction, but he never talked about this illness except to explain his absence from some ceremony. His medical history at this time is not complete, but apparently the arthritic pains were fairly continuous, and his only consolation was his acceptance of them as his purgatory.

The Archbishop had agreed to preside at one of the sessions of the annual meeting of Serra International in Grand Rapids on July 8–10. He intended to go from there to Notre Dame for a rest. At the convention the Archbishop presided over the third session on the topic "Catholic Education." He was much disturbed by the paper given by Monsignor William McManus of Chicago, which expressed a pessimistic outlook on the ability of Catholic educational institutions to catch up with their task. The Archbishop interposed his own ideas in the discussion at considerable length to indicate that the Monsignor was in error in his statistics. The Archbishop was disturbed again when the Monsignor's paper later appeared in the *Catholic Mind*. He wrote of the meeting to Bishop Matthew Brady on August 30 and at that time thought he had won the argument.

I concluded by saying that if the Holy Ghost sends these children to us, we must provide for them. I might add here that Bishop Neumann, after thirty months in the see of Philadelphia, wrote home to his father that the parochial school enrollment had increased from five hundred to nine thousand. If he could build and operate schools one hundred years ago, we can do it today, and he established the first Catholic school board in the United States, got the children out of the church basements and one room schools, and did more than any of his predecessors or contemporaries to perfect the Catholic school system.

On July 20 the Archbishop sent out a letter that outlined his plans for additional help for retarded children. He intended to open two new schools for them, one in Allentown and one in north Philadelphia, near the Little Flower School. In his letters he mentioned among the accomplishments in this field that two hundred of these youngsters had received confirmation and that one hundred had made their First Holy Communion. He wanted $100,000 for these schools plus $30,000 for operational expenses. He acknowledged that he had already received $57,181 for the schools in five hundred and fifty-five donations. To the school in north Philadelphia he gave the name Our Lady of Confidence and always maintained a special interest in it. The program for the blind at St. Lucy's was brought about by the mother of two blind boys who convinced the Archbishop that once such children had learned braille, it was best that they be integrated with sighted children. According to this plan the children learned braille at St. Lucy's and then went to their own parish school. The Archbishop also improved the facilities of the Archbishop Ryan Institute for the Deaf.

The Archbishop seemed to be disturbed by the victories of communism not only in this country but also abroad. He wrote to a friend that he feared that the discrediting of the McCarthy investigations would lead to the discrediting of all investigations of communist infiltration. He definitely approved of an editorial in the *Standard and Times* of August 20 entitled "This Carnival of Hypocrisy," which accused both the Senators and the press of hypocrisy in their accusations against McCarthy.

The Archbishop seemed to be much disturbed by the communists' victories in Viet Nam, the most Catholic country in Asia, and the loss of one-third of the former French colony, especially the Catholics who lived there, to the communists. He had first-hand information from the scene in the releases and letters of Monsignor Joseph J. Harnett, who was acting for the American bishops in Saigon. On August 5 he wrote a letter to the pastors in which he proposed that the vigil of the Assumption be observed as a day of fast and abstinence for these people and that a novena of Holy Communions be offered for them during the week of September 8 to 15. He asked that the invocation "Blessed be God" against blasphemy be offered for them after every Mass. In addition he suggested that the three feasts of the Blessed Virgin in September be observed as days of special prayer for the same intention.

The Archbishop occasionally told his correspondents that there were too many sociologists and not enough economists studying the country. The reason for his opposition to sociologists seemed to be his feeling that they were all positivists in their approach— all disciples of Comte. Just why he thought the economists were free of this taint is not apparent. Perhaps he thought the statistical studies he liked so much were economical studies rather than sociological, but they did treat of social problems. Among his papers were left large graphs and whole pages of figures especially about population, broken down into states, areas, and dioceses. He also had a complete sociological study of the archdiocese which he kept under lock and key. His friends were startled by his ability to quote statistics on many subjects, much as he also was well-informed on the values of stocks and bonds, and on the values of the properties of the archdiocese. He was interested in showing the growth of the Church, the effects of birth control on the non-Catholic population, and the physical problems facing Catholic education in the increasing number of Catholic births in the country.

A perennial problem for any student of American Catholic life is the attempt to estimate the actual Catholic population. The late Archbishop-Bishop Noll struggled with this problem for years and tried unsuccessfully to get a question on religious affiliation into the census questionnaire. After a discussion of the problem in the bishops' meeting in November, 1953, Archbishop O'Hara drew up a "Memorandum" on the question that he sent to his episcopal friends. It was based on a comparison of the number of Catholic births and deaths. He listed many varying factors and in general thought that there were more Catholics in the country than the 31,000,000 claimed by the *Catholic Directory*. Most bishops thanked him cautiously for his statistics and added a few additional exceptions, but no one really tried to evaluate them.

On September 1 the Archbishop accompanied by Monsignor McGlinn, his secretary, went to the Marian Congress at São Paulo, Brazil, to return the favor of Cardinal Motta, who had attended the Buffalo Eucharistic Congress. The Archbishop presided at the open-air Mass on September 4 for the Communion of the children and students and spoke at the meeting of the university students on September 7 under the title, *Sedes Sapientiae*. He gave the sermon in Portuguese from a translation prepared by his friend Father A. C. Branco of Fall River, Massachusetts.[40] Writing after his return to Cardinal Spellman, he said: "Everything went well. There were 35,000 Holy Communions on the men's night so they feel the Congress was a complete success. Cardinal Piazza seemed to enjoy everything, especially the Venetian dialect he found among the immigrants of the second and third generation in southern Brazil."

In August the Archbishop had promised his old friend Monsignor D. L. Monahan of St. Patrick's church at Fort Wayne that he would preach at the Fort Wayne Marian Year celebration on October 7. He kept his promise despite his ill health. There were 10,000 people there to hear the Archbishop combine a kind of homecoming sermon in honor of Our Lady with a defense of the parochial school system for which the Fort Wayne diocese had long been known.

Back in Philadelphia the Archbishop was host to another Marian celebration on October 22—a Marian Congress of the Oriental Church under the partonage of the Exarchate of the Byzantine Rite. Co-sponsors were Apostolic Exarch Constantine Bohachevsky of the Ukrainian Rite and Archbishop O'Hara. Part of the ceremonies were held in St. Peter and Paul Cathedral, and part in the Byzantine Immaculate Conception Cathedral. The more massive ceremonies were held in Convention Hall. The ceremonies were splendid and impressive. Three cardinals—Agagianian, the Armenian Patriarch; Tien of China; and Stritch of Chicago—were in attendance. It was estimated that 30,000 attended, and in the procession down Benjamin Franklin Parkway on Saturday to the Cathedral approximately 25,000 participated. The Archbishop spoke at the Friday evening Divine Liturgy. He welcomed the Oriental clergy to the cathedral and thanked them for permitting him to participate. The unity of West and East, he said, was an organic unity, since they were members of the mystical Body of Christ. They were particularly united in their devotion to the Blessed Virgin. In the centenary of the dogma of the Immaculate Conception they should witness a renewal of faith, hope, and charity through the mediation of Mary; but they must not look upon the slavery of the Eastern Church under communist persecution with despair. They must expect rewards from this persecution in the East and the sufferings in Spain. He listed some of the sufferings of the Church behind the Iron Curtain and thanked God for an opportunity to help these persecuted brethren.

But these labors of the Archbishop were taking their toll. When Father James A. Donnellon, O.S.A., asked that he be allowed to have a special convocation in which the Archbishop would give a special discourse on Catholic education, the Archbishop answered frankly: "The simple truth of the matter is that time is running out for me so far as the preparation of speeches is concerned. If you could have some one else give the formal address and allow me to say 'due parole,' I think I could be present, but looking ahead I see no possibility at all of time for preparing a formal address." He did send President Donnellon a contribution to Villanova but asked that it be kept anonymous.

Probably the Archbishop had already prepared the sermon that he was to give on October 28 at the dedication of the new seminary of St. Pius X at Loras College. The coincidence of the name of St. Pius X and the Marian Year would have been sufficient inspiration for him, but his paper showed that he had been concerned with the problem of Catholic education and the pessimism about it that he had been meeting. He noted that Pius had issued an encyclical on the Immaculate Conception in which he reproached those who had not understood all that had been accomplished in the fifty years since the apparition at Lourdes. There were still complaints about the lack of accomplishments. "But if we borrow the eyes of faith of Saint Pius X we stand witness to the revival of faith, hope, and charity that we should expect to receive through the mediation of the Mother of God." He spoke of the current persecutions and testimonies of the Church. He said that St. Pius had prepared Catholics for this persecution:

. . . His decrees on frequent and daily Communion, and on the early Communion of children did more than anything else to build up in our generation a solid phalanx of the laity willing to resist death. His Encyclical on Modernism and his Apostolic Constitution condemning 65 modernistic propositions brought into sharp focus the central heresy of this age which was to give to error equal standing with truth before the bar of reason. Saint Pius revised the organization of the Church and prepared it to meet modern onslaughts with great efficiency; similarly he began the codification of the Canon Law which was completed in 1918. He gave new organization to the teaching of catechism and revived the Confraternity of Christian Doctrine which has been so fruitful in relieving the ignorance of those who lack the advantages of Catholic education.

Pope Pius X taught us also to go through the Blessed Virgin for these things and through her there has been tremendous growth of Catholic education:

. . . Divorce and birth control have wrought great havoc, and have even carried away victims from within our fold, but a more virile faith has rewarded those who have remained true to Catholic teaching. While our population has doubled, the number of pupils in our Catholic schools has more than trebled. Last year 60% of the Catholic children of elementary school age in the United States were taught in

Catholic schools, as against 50% in 1945. Almost 35% of our Catholic high school students were in Catholic schools last year.

Somehow the pessimism that the Archbishop refused to accept about the future of the Catholic schools seems to have settled on his thoughts about much of the Catholic press. He sent some warning advice to Father John Reedy, the new editor of the *Ave Maria*. After criticizing an article by Edward Fisher in the *Ave,* he said:

I have read one issue of the *Reporter*. I have found that it plugged the party line in several instances. Since then I have read that it regularly does so. I have never followed *Commonweal* because the first two numbers convinced me that it was anti-clerical. A few months later it published a vicious attack on Notre Dame. . . .

A week later, November 9, he added a similar observation:

. . . I haven't read either *Commonweal* or *America* for years because they leaned over so far backwards that they were upside down. Their difficulty seems to be that they trust the wrong people. . . .

On December 8, the Archbishop wrote another of his letters to the children of the Archdiocese. While the letter began with a word of gratitude and praise for the children's fine efforts during the Marian Year, the main purpose of the letter was to tell the youngsters about Patricia Anne Kuntz and to urge them to pray hard for the reversal of the decision of the courts. While the Archbishop felt that he had a right to attack the decision of the court and he knew an appeal by his lawyers was being made according to law, he hoped to bring about a strong moral pressure by this letter against the arbitrary decision of the court. The letter was not published, but the Archbishop sent some copies to his episcopal friends. But the moral appeal did not win. That same day there was a solemn closing of the Marian Year at the cathedral at which he preached on Our Lady as the "Star of the Sea."

The Archbishop did not harbor much affection for the liturgical movement, and liturgists had not passed many opportunities to criticize his defending Communion outside of Mass at Notre Dame, the bare ceremonies he permitted in wartime services, and the like. But he felt that what he did was the mind of the Church and that he followed. His deep desire that the sacraments be made available to all was not really at variance with the true liturgical spirit manifest after his death in the Second Vatican Council, but he did not see that then. When someone wrote to ask that the children be allowed to read parts of the Mass, he did not agree:

We have a certain amount of that in the diocese and sometimes a bit more than that, namely the recitative Mass. The Church uses the latter form with caution, and does not permit unlimited use. The reason for the restriction is that there have been some very rash statements by certain advocates of the recitative Mass who have dreamed a false theological concept of the "priesthood of the laity." Three times during the past year the Holy Father had to speak out against this heretical tendency.

As a means of instructing children in the meaning of the Mass, the reading of the Epistle and Gospel and an occasional use of the recitative Mass are very helpful.

Apparently the Archbishop, when he had his argument with Monsignor William E. McManus of Chicago and the N.C.W.C. Education Department at the Serra meeting in Grand Rapids, did not expect the paper of the Monsignor to appear in print. However, the *Catholic Mind* for December, 1954, printed it without any essential emendations. The Archbishop obtained several copies of the publication and sent one with a letter of criticism to Monsignor McManus's superior, Cardinal Stritch. He also sent a copy with a copy of the letter to his friend Cardinal Spellman.

While Monsignor McManus was very optimistic about the increase in the Catholic population and the growth of Catholic schools, he felt that one would soon outrun the other. His statistics were chiefly based on the number of baptisms. He then set forth a ten-point program to guide the planning for Catholic elementary and secondary schools. In Archbishop O'Hara's letter to Cardinal Stritch on December 21, the Archbishop expressed his concern about some of the statements of the Monsignor, listing them in the order in which they had appeared in the printed text:

1. ". . . the ideal of having every Catholic child in a Catholic school seems utterly unattainable, and we might as well stop dreaming about it."

If the Fathers of the Baltimore Councils, both provincial and plenary, were not afraid in their time to *legislate* about the ideal, to say the least it seems unwise for the Assistant Director of the Department of Education of the National Catholic Welfare Conference to advise, for the Men of Serra and the entire reading public, to "stop dreaming about it." This is all the more true when we consider that in the nine years since the close of the War we have not only met the increase in births, but we have advanced the ratio of Catholic pupils in Catholic elementary schools from 50% to 60%.

2. ". . . starting new schools, particularly in the home mission areas of our nation."

The excellent statements made at the Bishops' Meeting by the Bishops of Mobile and Nashville have caused me to do a bit of research on the "home mission areas." The basis of my investigation is faulty in that it used the *Catholic Directory* estimate of population, and we know that this contains errors. However, this basis gives good indications of both strength and weakness, comparing the respective ratios of diocesan and state Catholic population, and of elementary school enrollment of the diocese or state to the total Catholic elementary enrollment, I find that most of the "Home Mission" areas are abundantly supplied with Catholic schools—far better supplied than areas with large Catholic populations.

Using this basis and testing the states to see which ones fail to reach the 60% enrollment which is the average for the nation, I find a total shortage of 276,000 pupils; this is distributed among twenty states, but more than eighty percent of the shortage is in four states—Massachusetts, Connecticut, Texas and California. Most of the territories which have shortages have made great strides in building and enlarging school facilities since the end of the war.

3. ". . . release a large number of the teaching Sisters . . . so that they may go out to the frontiers. . . ."

While the comment above covers this suggestion to a great extent, it should be pointed out that the great increase in school enrollments in the home mission areas since the War indicates that *such release is going on all the time*. Incidentally, excellent lay teachers are supplying for the religious.

4. a. "Crowding fifty, sixty, and seventy pupils into a classroom may seem like zeal for Catholic education, but in many cases, it actually is a serious violation of the pupils' right to satisfactory and efficient education."

As a permanent condition, overcrowding is not justified; as a temporary measure, while additional facilities are under planning and construction, we can ask the Holy Ghost to help us, *lest the children be exposed to danger* in schools from which the Catholic religion is excluded.

Just what constitutes overcrowding is a matter of opinion. The National Education Association takes a strictly labor-union attitude in its constant protests. I have followed its annual pronouncements since the War, and it has never failed to stress "overcrowding" and "overburdened" teachers, even when enrollment was much lower than in 1934, which was the peak year prior to 1952, and the number of teachers was more than twenty per cent higher in 1934. From these statements I gather that N.E.A. is agitating for an average teacher-load of 20, a minimum beginner's salary of $4,000 (It was $3600 a few years ago).

In a public school where behaviorism is the philosophy of education, I can understand that the lay teacher may be under a serious strain, even with twenty pupils. In a Catholic school, where the Love of God rules, one is struck by the relaxed attitude of both teachers and pupils. In a letter received yesterday from a Mother Superior who has almost 1800 teaching Sisters under her direction, casual mention was made of the fact that in assigning teachers for next September, six will be held in reserve as replacements. This speaks volumes.

4. b. ". . . hang out 'no more room signs.' "

God forbid! If any pastor attempts that, I hear from the injured parents immediately, and we shop around for a vacant desk in some nearby school, or we buy or rent a house to take care of the overflow.

4. c. "State school authorities are already watching what we are doing in this regard."

As against this I offer the following: "Washington, December 5— The National Education Association reported that upwards of 700,000 children were being short-changed educationally this year because of a shortage of qualified public school teachers and buildings. The organization estimated that a number were on half-day or similar part-time arrangements, and said many thousands of others were in overcrowded classrooms." The state school authorities have their hands full with public school problems. On results we can meet them at any time.

5. To the Men of Serra, Monsignor McManus poses this question: Would you mind sending your child to a public school so that I may have space for a youngster who comes from a home where there is a mixed marriage or where home conditions are very bad and constitute a real danger to the child's faith?

The Men of Serra are promoting vocations. While the public schools of our nation have produced some notable vocations (among them Their Eminences the Archbishops of New York and Los Angeles, who have done so much to provide Catholic schools in their respective jurisdictions), it is commonplace that the great bulk of the vocations will come from the Catholic schools.

Further, what pastor can say with assurance that the parents in a good home can save the souls of their youngsters even if they go to a public school? The pitiful stories we receive from some parents who learn too late the dangers to their children, force us in conscience to make heroic efforts to provide schools for all. If in a particular place the Catholic population is too small for a school, and bus transportation cannot meet the needs, we may count on the grace of God to supply—but on the other hand we must avoid "tentatio Dei."

6. ". . . overhaul the whole administration so that we may deploy our resources. . . ."

What is suggested here is seemingly a plenary council, since it certainly crosses the lines of episcopal jurisdiction. Perhaps faulty statistics have led the Monsignor to the conclusion that the number of children without either Catholic schooling or Confraternity instruction is much larger than it actually is. As I showed at the Bishops' meeting the Confraternity of Christian Doctrine overestimated by one million the number of children without instruction—and we have no way of knowing whether those in classes this year have not had Catholic schooling or instruction in other years.

One source of such error is overstatement in the public school statistics. These may include adult education classes, discussion clubs,
and the like, and they may be as much as ten per cent.

7. "Collecting funds for Catholic schools should be put on a systematic business-like basis."

Personally, I prefer "widow's mite" and the generous heart of the
young people whose determination to have a school for the children
who are coming is one of the finest inspirations we meet in today's
expansion program. I was not aware that there is any difficulty gathering funds. I see Catholic newspapers from all over the country, and
there is seldom an issue without a story or two about the oversubscrip-
tion in this or that drive for a school. But aside from that, I question
the propriety of the Education Departments telling the Men of Serra
what the Bishops should do.

Your Eminence, I must apologize for burdening you with this letter,
which is entirely too long. But I am really disturbed in conscience,
and I do not know where else to turn for a possible correction of what
I believe is a dangerous attitude at *headquarters*. Both our NCWC
Department of Education and the National Catholic Educational
Association are involved.

If the Bishops one hundred years ago were not afraid of "the ideal
of every Catholic child in a Catholic school" we today should not give
way to pessimism. Had they been afraid, what would we have today?

. . . .

P.S. I enclose an extra copy of this letter which you may wish to send
to Monsignor McManus.

In a reply written a few days later, Cardinal Stritch showed no
inclination to reprimand Monsignor McManus. He told the Archbishop: "We must not give up an ideal. . . . Looking at the problem from the viewpoint of prudent administration even with the
building of more and more Catholic schools to take care of our
increased population I do think that in the present economic circumstances we shall not be able to provide, at least in our lifetime, Catholic schools for all our Catholic children." He noted:
"When we talk about mission areas, we are accustomed to lump
all areas into one whole" and that he had found from "experience
that this is a big mistake." On the question of releasing sisters he
maintained that "there was a point, however, beyond which we
can not go in replacing Sisters with lay teachers in our schools."
"As regards overcrowding in our schools, I have come in my experience to realize that in talking about Catholic schools we must
talk about them not only as educational institutions but also as
pastoral work."

Among the papers of Archbishop O'Hara there is a carbon copy of a *"Memorandum,* Thoughts suggested and questions prompted by the reading of Howard J. Savage's book 'Fruit of an Impulse— Forty-Five Years of the Carnegie Foundation.' " Since the book appeared in the spring of 1953, the five-and-a-half-page note probably was prepared late in 1953 or 1954. The Archbishop had not forgotten the cold reception he had received from Frederick Keppel, the president of the Carnegie Institute, in 1933–1934 and had always regretted the ability of this foundation and others to make religious schools give up their denominational character to get financial help. The *Memorandum* quoted several passages from the book that told of the exclusion of sectarian institutions from the benefits of the teachers' retirement program. He also noted the effects of the grants in standardization of educational methods and merely mentioned that the book told of the foundation's efforts to set up standards for college athletics. He suggested that the foundation was greatly responsible for the "flood of experimental projects" in education, quoting a statement that between 1915 and 1937 the foundation had spent $4,081,000 on such projects. The last half-page asked a series of questions. The first concerns the part played by the corporation in taking schools out of local control and in the training of administrators indoctrinated with a mechanistic philosophy. The other questions were:

To what extent was the Foundation responsible for dropping religion in the institutions of higher learning in the United States?

To what extent was the Foundation responsible for the elimination from curricula of higher studies of logic, metaphysics, and the other traditional branches of philosophy?

To what extent did the growth of secularism pave the way for Communism in the colleges?

It is not clear to whom he sent this memorandum.[41]

There is not much record of the benefactions of the Archbishop. He wished no thanks for himself, and wanted merely to make sure that he did not spend anything that properly belonged to the archdiocese. He would allow a friend to contribute to one of his private charities provided that the Archbishop's share in the gift remained anonymous. He explained to Peter Grace on January 3, 1955, the use of his Christmas gift:

I have sent Mr. McDevitt the receipt for the 56 shares in the Ingersoll-Rand Company. I shall preserve this for special needs which do not come under the usual categories of assistance which pertain to my office. Two-thirds of your gift of last year I spent on defense of the Church in several quarters where we were under attack. The other third went to pay the cost of a soup kitchen I gave anonymously to the St. Vincent de Paul Society in São Paolo. It struck me as pretty sad that with all the wild display of wealth in São Paolo, the St. Vincent de Paul Society locally was unable to obtain funds for a soup kitchen, an institution which is in itself an anomaly where there is so much wild spending on boulevards and skyscrapers. The answer, is of course, the absence of Catholic education. It seems the people simply don't know any better.

The Archbishop's pen was ever active. This is evident in a note he sent to his friend Bishop Leo Smith of Buffalo:

I have checked again on how much we will have to increase our facilities during the next six years in order to keep an even keel at 60% of our Catholic children in Catholic schools. I find that the average need is 195,000 desks a year in addition to what we have now. As a matter of fact, quite a few of those desks are already provided in schools which have not yet reached capacity in enrollment.

So far as our high school picture is concerned, we have no subscription for 95% of the total amount needed. Some thirty parishes are still to be heard from.

Just what brought about several bishops' interest in Bishop Navagh's work in the missionary apostolate at this time is not clear, but apparently other bishops felt free to ask the Archbishop about Bishop Navagh's work. He was very quick to cede any claim on the honor for the development. On February 6 he wrote to Father John W. Keogh:

The pastoral training is based on the system of Saint Joseph Cafasso. Bishop Navagh originated it in the Diocese of Buffalo, and directed the work for twelve years before he was claimed by Bishop Waters as his auxiliary.

The acute shortage of priests in Philadelphia makes it impossible to apply the system here, but this may be an opportunity when we have a more abundant supply of priests.

He later wrote to Bishop McGucken, then auxiliary at Los Angeles, on the same subject:

When Bishop Navagh began his work in the Diocese of Buffalo, he surveyed the most abandoned territory. Wherever he could find as many as seven families who acknowledged Catholic baptism, he set up a mission. By the end of the year, the number of families was likely to be twenty one. The other fourteen families had been hiding out, afraid to acknowledge their religion.

After a few years these early stations were able to stand on their own feet, either as parishes or with two united on parish and mission status. As the Faith became established in one section, the new priest moved to another. There is still virgin territory in the diocese of Buffalo and there will be for many years.

While Archbishop O'Hara had been in Buffalo, he had abolished the two segregated Negro churches and had been very cooperative with the Knights of St. Peter Claver, but he did not join in any agitation for the Negro. His policy in Philadelphia was practically the same. When Henry J. Tolan of Wayne County wrote to him to ask that the title of the Collection for the Indians and Negro Missions be changed as offensive, he was frank in his answer:

Usually I have one or two letters a year requesting the change you suggest. So far as I can recall none of them has come from colored people—although they do not hesitate to write the bishop if they have something else to talk about. The Indians themselves prefer segregation. I have often been told by them that they will go to their own church, but they don't like to go to white churches. Many Negroes felt the same way about it until the Communists started agitation and tried to make them unhappy. When they abolished the two Negro parishes in Buffalo, there was only one protest—and that was from a dear old lady who had gone to Mass at Saint Augustine's Church for thirty years and said she would never feel happy anywhere else.

To another person, Mrs. Joan W. Fisher, who had been disturbed because some relatives threatened to move into a mixed neighborhood, the Archbishop used skill in his answer:

You say that the Negroes are Protestants because the Protestants have been kinder to them than Catholics have been. To test that, I ask you to obtain a list of the Protestant churches in the city of Philadelphia in which white and non-white parishioners are mingled. You must be aware that there is no discrimination in any Catholic church or school in the city. You may not know that practically all of the non-Catholic students we have in our parochial schools and diocesan high schools are non-whites. We have a great many requests from non-Catholics for admission to our schools, but the only schools that have room for them are those in predominantly Protestant neighborhoods, where the Negro population is very heavy.

You ask us to imitate the National Council of Churches and issue a statement that discrimination is a sin. Actions speak louder than words. The non-whites are quite familiar with the fact that they are welcome in Catholic churches and Catholic schools, and they realize that the Catholics who run away from them are violating the commandment that we must love our neighbor as ourselves for the love of God. Public declarations have been used frequently by the Communists to make the Negroes unhappy, to create a spirit of unrest among them. We try on the other hand to make them forget their unhappiness. The fact that we have more than 2,000 converts among them every year in the city of Philadelphia is a good indication that they know they are welcome in the Catholic Church.

While the Archbishop was finding it more difficult to travel about physically, his facile pen seemed more active. He wrote occasionally for the Brooklyn *Tablet* and for the *Standard and Times,* but seldom under his own name. On February 11, however, he published the first of several notable editorials on education in the *Standard and Times* under his own name. These essays were usually reprinted in pamphlet form and sent by him to legislators, to other bishops, and to others interested in these problems. This first essay was entitled "A Critical Study of the New Proposals for Federal Aid to Schools." He admitted that he drew some of his information from two government documents: "Federal Aid to School Construction" by Charles A. Quattlebaum and "Hearings before the Special Subcommittee of the Committee on Education and Labor—House of Representatives."

The Archbishop began by attacking the figures on schoolroom needs, showing that far more important in this matter than actual increased births was the movement of population from farm to the city, and for a while in the Depression a countermove to the country. There were excellent school buildings that had to be abandoned because of the shift of population. Also discussed was the difference in valuation of property in various sections of the country that would nullify any general figure on needs. Next he attacked the notion of cooperation between the federal and state governments for new construction, indicating that the states were simply not doing their share. Then he raised a question about the schools built by the federal government in the Depression and asked how these buildings were being used, for it would be foolish to put up buildings that would be abandoned in ten years. An increase of the teaching load would take care of many local problems. Also questioned was the need to reduce one-room classrooms. He concluded that the members of Congress "should do all in their power to insure that precedence will prevail in the distribution" of aid to local communities in their problems of education.

Research into any congressional reaction to his editorial of February 11 and other editorials shows that while he received acknowledgements from some congressmen and requests for further information, no formal action was taken on them. To Representative Ralph W. Gwinn of the 37th District of New York, whose speeches the Archbishop occasionally quoted, he said he did not want to appear before Gwinn's congressional committee. "I feel that my physical presence before the Committee might constitute a distraction that would do more harm than good." It is also noticeable that Catholics who did not agree with the Archbishop did not attempt a printed refutation or disagreement. The Archbishop mentioned that he had once given some information to the *New York Times,* but "they had no room for it."

Acting as a member of the Board of Trustees of The Catholic University was quite a chore for the Archbishop, but apparently one that he took very seriously even when he could ill afford either the time or the energy. He was troubled in the spring of 1955 when he read certain announcements and wrote to the rector, Bishop Bryan J. McEntegart, about it on March 22:

In some announcements of workshops that reached me the other day I was startled to find the one I enclose herewith. I note that it is the Fifth Annual Workshop in Intergroup Education. I didn't hear about the other four. I have marked certain organizations that have a bad reputation and I am wondering if it is wise to give them a hearing on the Campus of the University. I can never remember whether it is the American Jewish Committee or the American Jewish Congress that was so often offensive in New York, but it was one or the other. I have never heard anything good of the Anti-Defamation League, and I do know that this league and the National Conference of Christians and Jews have lately issued some of the writings and records of Communist authors.

The Urban League has housed a good many fellow-travelers, so have some of these units of the Congress of Parents and Teachers.

Since I have never found any vestige of religious motivation in the activities of the groups mentioned, I wonder if it is prudent to bring them together on the campus of the Catholic University, where the supernatural law of charity determines our relations with our fellow men.

In the March 18 *Standard and Times* the Archbishop published his second study of the problems of federal aid to education under the title "Should Public Education Cost $19 Billions in 1965?" The subject of this editorial was a brochure of 62 pages published in December, 1954, by the National Citizens Commission for the Public Schools under the title "Financing Public Education in the Decade Ahead." The committee included many prominent names such as Beardsley Ruml, James F. Brownlee, Samuel C. Gale, and George Gallup. It had the financial backing of the most important of the large foundations and had for its purpose ". . . to arouse in each community the intelligence and will to improve our public schools." The Archbishop claimed that the commission had failed to accomplish its high purpose because "1) it has relied too much on assumptions, sometimes when the facts were available; and 2) it has picked up a figure from the right-hand column of a table and applied it to the left-hand column, where it has produced a variance of several billions of dollars."

Among the points of error in the brochure, he said, was the assumption that private education had reached the saturation point. It said that only "a small fraction of the child population is educated privately," but the Archbishop maintained that private education accounted for 13.9 percent of the white registration in elementary schools of the United States and 9.4 percent of the white registration in high schools, and 4.4 and 3.4 percent of the nonwhite registration respectively. He pointed out that in six years the growth in enrollment in private schools had increased 49 percent, whereas the enrollment in public schools increased only 20 percent. The Archbishop rejected the statement that the costs of the private and public schools are proportional, since so many of the teachers in the Catholic schools receive only a subsistence salary, and the construction costs of Catholic school buildings have been smaller. The *Statistical Abstract* was quoted to show that current costs were much below that estimated in the brochure. The editorial concluded with a table showing the projections of the brochure and indicating some of its errors.

The discouragement that the Archbishop continued to feel about international affairs seemed to be apparent in his Easter letter in the diocesan paper on the text "The Hour is Come for the Son of Man to be Glorified:"

These words of Our Blessed Lord, recorded in Saint John, were spoken only a few days before the crucifixion. We recall them for our Easter greeting because they can sustain us in the eclipse of civilization through which the world is passing.

If these words sound strange to your ears, it may well be that you are misled by material prosperity which abounds in our beloved America. They will not seem strange if you meditate on Yalta where three men sat around a table and divided a world that was not theirs. Justice and charity were absent from that conference of ten years ago. That is why the world today is an armed camp, that is why Cardinals languish in jail, why bishops and priests and nuns have been imprisoned or put to death or to work as slave laborers; why hundreds of millions of God's children have been delivered into the hands of God's enemies. . . .

And in his Easter sermon on the same text he spoke of the persecution of the Church, drawing attention to the sufferings in

Korea and in China. He noted that the attack was now against Catholic schools in England, the Belgian Congo, South America, and the Argentine Republic. He thanked God that in our country there was no government subsidy to be taken away. Some attacks were listed that were being made in this country, especially by the National Educational Association, on Catholic schools. The first step he predicted would be to undo the Oregon school-case decision, the second would be the proposal to license all schools, and the third to impoverish Catholic schools by taxes. He listed the proposal for federal aid to education as a form of this tax since Catholics would be taxed for schools they did not use.

The Archbishop was willing that Catholic schools accept aid that would not be considered as support of education. As he wrote to Bishop Dearden on April 26:

> While I have always objected to our schools accepting any kind of government subsidy I believe that parents are entitled to any sort of relief that is given to the parents of public school children. I like to think of this form of relief as "health and welfare service" and not as educational subsidy. More and more non-Catholics are beginning to see the fundamental injustice of school buses passing our children who are walking to Catholic schools.

On the same day he expressed to Cardinal Spellman some shock that other bishops did not share his views:

> At the meeting of the subcommittee on Education Thursday I proposed the elimination of the item on federal aid to education with its qualifying clause "proven need." I was startled to find that mine was a lone voice. Some of the men still think they can get federal aid; worse than that, they seem to want it. With our federal debt being the foremost item in the inflation that has us engulfed I should think that the Bishops would become a bit realistic. My own thought is to gather more and more facts on the waste of public funds that goes on in public school construction and operation, and then work through these to stop some of the stifling taxation that puts an extra burden on us Catholics. . . .

The Archbishop had compiled statistics on many social problems in his archdiocese, but he would not show them to outsiders. To Father Joseph P. McGeever of Saint Edmund's Rectory, who had made a special survey of a new housing area, the Archbishop was very grateful. He wrote him on April 11:

> I am most grateful for the very thorough survey of Wilson Parke Homes. As I suspected the percentage of invalid marriages is very high. Thank God 47 out of 66 are capable of validation.

Every low cost housing project I have seen surveyed has shown the
same tendency. Those who need low cost homes because they cannot
manage their finances are very often those who cannot manage their
lives. On the other hand, if 10% of the families have been evicted
since the beginning of the year, some of them must have been in hard
luck temporarily and were able very shortly to increase their earning
capacity.

It is a consolation to know that your new school will be able to
absorb the children in this project. May God bless the work and make
it fruitful.

To Father John W. Keogh, the zealous social worker and total
abstinence advocate, he wrote on April 1 that he would like to
lower the compulsory school age and make unions furnish compulsory apprenticeships to handle the youngsters of that lower age
who were problems.

I have a notion that the law would restore discipline to the secondary schools which badly need the sanction of dismissal for incorrigi-
ble pupils. So many children become delinquents only through
boredom in schools that the suggestion deserves good sound discussion.

The Augustinians of Villanova were planning to have a special
celebration of the four-hundredth anniversary of the martyrdom
of St. Thomas of Villanova on September 22 and asked the Archbishop to pontificate. Cardinal Spellman was to give the address.
The Archbishop asked if one of his auxiliaries might not take his
place:

What I have in mind is that with my arthritis I am a bit clumsy
going up and down the steps of the altar. I do a better job on the level
ground and I shall be very happy to accept your invitation to bless
Dougherty Hall. I would be present at the Mass of course with Cardinal Spellman presiding.

A few times a year I am required to pontificate in the Cathedral,
but I seldom do it otherwise.

It is of interest that while admitting the crippling nature of his
illness, the Archbishop never spoke of pain. When he was seen
without his ring, some opined that he did not wear it because
he was suffering from arthritis. He went up and down stairs by
strategy that lessened the bending of his knees.

About this time one of the priests of the archdiocese was
arrested on the complaints of persons who accused him of embez-
zling funds they had given him for the purchases of automobiles.
The priest was mentally ill and had already been suspended by
the Archbishop. One Philadelphia paper carried the story, and it

was then carried by the press throughout the country. Eventually the priest was committed to an institution through the efforts of Judge Vincent A. Carroll, who felt that the publicity not only was unnecessary but was a handicap in handling a case of mental illness.

The Archbishop's program for building high schools continued unabated. Of unusual interest was the announcement in the July 17 *Standard and Times* of the proposed Cardinal Dougherty High School in north Philadelphia, which would be the largest Catholic high school in the world. Originally there were to have been two schools, but when the plans were checked by zoning laws, a coinstitutional high school was proposed. The U-shaped building would have one wing for boys and one for girls with common facilities in the central wing. It was estimated to have 288,586 square feet of floor space and to provide 112 classrooms. The cost was estimated at $3,000,000.

Among his manifold interests the Archbishop had not forgotten his Puerto Ricans. On June 24 he went to New York to celebrate Mass at the Puerto Rican celebration of the feast of St. John the Baptist at St. Patrick's Cathedral. He returned immediately and presided that same afternoon at the Philadelphia celebration at the cathedral. Bishop McShea was celebrant of the Mass, but the Archbishop presided and spoke a few words in Spanish and English. It was estimated at the time that there were 540 Puerto Rican children in the Philadelphia Catholic schools. Bishop McShea was the official coordinator of Puerto Rican activities at the Casa del Carmen and St. Peter's parish.

In the July 29 *Standard and Times* the Archbishop published his third front-page editorial on the question of federal aid to education under the caption "Archbishop O'Hara Counts the Catholic Gift to the Public Schools." After referring to his other editorials, he said that the House Education and Labor Committee had reported a bill for federal aid to education. This bill called first for a four-year program of 400 million dollars for construction, the federal government to match state funds; secondly, for federal purchase of $758 million of school bonds in districts where they could not be sold at a reasonable rate of interest; and thirdly, for a pledge of federal credit matching state credit on bonds for education. The Archbishop then compared the cost in the various sections of the country for public school construction and Catholic school construction. In the northeast he found that Catholics by more modest construction and good management saved the public schools an average of fifty-two dollars per pupil.

The rate was less where there are fewer Catholics. On this basis
he maintained that the annual savings of Catholics to the public
schools throughout the country was $620,692,000, to which he
added $500,000,000 for the construction of buildings for these
Catholic children, making a total of $1,120,692,000[42] that Catho-
lics saved the public expense. To this he added savings in federal
and state taxes. In other words, the Archbishop said that the gift
of Catholics to the public schools was more than the federal government was being asked to give in the proposed bill. The second
half of the editorial turned to the Southern states and indicated
that since the South would expect a greater expenditure of federal
aid, they must also expect a greater degree of federal control. To
prevent federal control the South must reject federal aid.

Writing on August 29 to Mr. Francis A. Fink of *Our Sunday
Visitor,* who had reprinted the editorial of July 29, the Archbishop
explained the editorial further:

> I have made a distinction that is perhaps too subtle, since most of
> the Catholic commentators have missed it. My study has dealt only
> with the taxes actually collected—not with those which would be
> necessary if the Catholic children were all put over in the public
> schools. . . .
> When I say on my own that I don't want any part of tax money, I
> have in the back of my head that it would cost our Catholic people
> far more to finance their schools through tax money than it does now
> to finance them through voluntary contributions. We would really be
> in a mess if we had to accept tax money.

The Archbishop's objection to most liturgical reform seems to
have been based partly on the feeling that the liturgists were
breaking away from common practice and hindering the unity of
the Church. When a layman, Richard Maloney, wrote with pride
of efforts in Germany to increase lay participation, he was not
moved:

> I appreciate your telling me about the use of the vernacular in the
> High Mass in Germany. This is an abuse which it cost the American
> Bishops a great deal of effort to eliminate. As a matter of fact, I am
> not sure it is entirely eliminated in some of the national churches. In
> some of the earlier synods you will find a specific prohibition, which
> is in itself sufficient evidence that the abuse was fairly widespread.
> Recently the Apostolic Delegate gave an excellent address in which
> he called attention to the warnings of the Holy Father against the
> attempt to weaken the position of Latin as the universal language of
> the Church.

In the course of the letter the Archbishop told of the value of

Latin as a universal language and how soldiers in World War II found some South Sea islanders who said their prayers in Latin.

The Archbishop might be suffering from arthritis so that he could hardly go up and down stairs but that did not hinder him in his regular round of services. However, he did not stay for the dinners or breakfasts and avoided mounting steps when he could. His pen continued very active. His letter to Father John P. Green on October 22 on the appointment of a Catholic to the school board is a sample of his awareness to side effects of public action as well as an expression of his feelings on a delicate subject.

While I am deeply grateful to you for your wonderful tribute to Doctor Moss, I venture to suggest that the recommendation be made to one of the Catholic judges rather than to me. My own personal judgment is that it would be a mistake for the diocese to have an official representative on the Board of Education, since such a situation could curtail in some manner our freedom to speak out whenever the necessity for such action appears.

Judge Vincent Carroll might be in a position to place the matter before the judges who select the Board members. I mention his name because I hear that on occasions he has been influential in the selection of other Board members non-Catholic as well as Catholic.

There was much discussion in the Catholic press at this time over a paper read by Father John Tracy Ellis of The Catholic University at the meeting of the Committee on Catholic Intellectual and Cultural Affairs and later published in the fall issue of *Thought*. The Archbishop was never happy at that kind of criticism of Catholic educational effort. An editorial in the November 4 issue of the *Standard and Times* was captioned "Intellectualism at Low Tide?" and was not friendly to Father Ellis's conclusions. One paragraph said:

What is meant by an intellectual anyway? Is he one who uses sesquipedalian words? Is he the individual who is considered profound because no one understands what he is saying? Are we to sing the praises of the individual who isolates himself from the rest of the world, buries himself in his books, and becomes fogbound to everything about him, while we look down our noses at the individual who uses his God-given talents, is highly successful in his profession, but still retains the common touch? Are we to belittle the tremendous contribution of the great body of the good, sound citizens as we go about searching for a poet laureate?

The editorial indicated that there were intellectuals despite the means used by Father Ellis in his unsuccessful search for them.

December 5, 1955, was the golden jubilee of the papal decree of St. Pius X about frequent Communion, and the Archbishop was alert to such a momentous commemoration. On November 10 he wrote a letter to the children of the Archdiocese, sending the letter through the pastors and asking them to join in a celebration of this jubilee. In his letter he told the children that this decree together with that of 1910 had made every day Christmas. In thanksgiving for this gift he suggested that the children practice self-denial during the month before December 5 and that they join in a triduum of thanksgiving.

Receive Holy Communion more frequently during the month. Then on the first of December begin a triduum of Communions. On Thursday, the first, offer your Holy Communion for the Holy Father and all religious and priests, including your teachers. On the second, which is the first Friday, offer your Holy Communion to the Sacred Heart of Jesus in reparation for the sins of the world. On the third, ask our Lady of Fatima to intercede with her Divine Son to bring peace to the world.

These three Holy Communions make up your triduum, your three days' preparation. Then on Sunday, December 4, offer your Holy Communion in thanksgiving for the decree of Pope Pius X, and for the blessing of God on your family. Invite your father and mother, your brothers and sisters to receive with you on that day. Frequent Holy Communion helps to make your family a holy family, and that is what you want your family to be.

The response of the children to this letter according to the archdiocesan paper was very generous; some parishes reported thousands of additional Communions on these days.

In 1955 the Archbishop made the acquaintance of Roger A. Freeman, the special assistant to the governor of Washington, and also a man very much interested in the statistical approach to certain problems, especially education and finance. Writing to him on November 23, the Archbishop suggested that they compare notes:

If you are ever close enough to come for a visit I shall be delighted to have you. I see that we have many points of common interest. Archbishop Connolly is an old friend of mine. He took care of the military chaplains in the area of Northern California, when I was with Cardinal Spellman in New York in the Military Ordinariate. I saw him in Washington last week, but I did not know until my return to Philadelphia that you and he are friends.

Writing to to Bishop Dearden on December 16 on the same subject the Archbishop added:

I appreciate your letter and your comments on Roger Freeman's booklet. You have put your finger on the most crucial issue—federal control. It is the fear of this that has moved me to fight federal aid proposals, but I have tried to avoid any public questioning of the motives which actuate perennial promoters of federal aid.

I have learned that Mr. Freeman is a Catholic. I have invited him to visit me some time in Philadelphia and he has promised to make such a visit some time in February, on his next trip East. He seems to do quite a bit of analysis for the Federal Government.

Along the same line might be his comment to Bishop Jerome Hannon of Scranton on December 12:

Archbishop Cushing's forthright rejection of tax support to Catholic schools gave me a great lift. I hope it will be circulated widely.

A number of Catholic editors have caught the trick of the White House Conference. One day it was reported that the conferees knew only two or three possible states which could not finance their own educational needs; on the last day the prize representatives of N.E.A. who gave the chairmen reports announced that the Conference was overwhelmingly for Federal Aid. I am not sure yet the N.E.A. plan will succeed.

During the first part of December the Ford Foundation announced its grand gifts of millions of dollars to certain educational institutions and to hospitals. Of the $500 millions given away, over $100 millions went to Catholic institutions. Whatever objections the Archbishop had expressed to previous attempts of the foundations to dictate policies in Catholic institutions, they were not present against these gifts, which he called "magnificent contributions to our schools and hospitals."

One of the most interesting phases of the character of Archbishop O'Hara was his continued contacts with students of Notre Dame throughout his career. Some, such as Dan O'Neil, could share with him their spiritual and business experiences; others came to him to be told frankly the solution of their problems or to hear what they needed. Most of these contacts were in the Archbishop's home. His secretary was much impressed to see grandfathers kneeling in the archiepiscopal parlor to go to confession to the "Father O'Hara" they had known back at Notre Dame. One such student was Ted Dressen, who professed in a letter to have lost his religion and to be trying to recover it. He claimed that the prefect of religion had thrown him out of bed back in Lyons Hall. The Archbishop took the young man's challenge:

So far as devotion to the Blessed Virgin is concerned, keep it up with all confidence. The mistake we make with our prayers is that we try to tell God how exactly he should help us. God is infinitely wise, but we are foolish. If God takes some other way of answering our prayers, it is because the other way is better for us, even though we can't see it now.

I sent you a picture of Saint Pius X because he was the saint who gave us daily Communion. We Notre Dame men owe him a great debt of gratitude, because daily Communion transformed Notre Dame and gave the boys there a spiritual lift that strengthens them against the evils they will face in the future. Here in the Archdiocese in Philadelphia we have just had a triduum of thanksgiving for the decree on daily Communion which was published by Pope Pius X just fifty years ago.

In column one of the January 20 issue of the *Standard and Times* the Archbishop published another editorial on "Facts and Assumptions on Current Needs for Federal Aid to Schools." The Archbishop took as his point of departure the President's request in the previous year for 300,000 new classrooms plus 50,000 each succeeding year and his request for an appropriation of $7,000,000 within three years. This year the amount requested to be appropriated had been cut to $2,020,000 or less than a third of last year's request. He quoted the Pennsylvania Conference in preparation for the White House Conference on Education as stating that the most dangerous tendency is the "blind acceptance of the national trends as being valid in state and local situations." The Archbishop then proceeded to break down the figures offered by the United States Office of Education in preparation for the White House Conference into groups of states with varying needs. He showed that the needs varied greatly for the individual states. Further he quoted as an example a study made by the *Indianapolis Star* on Indiana needs showing that while some parts of the state needed thousands of additional classrooms, other parts had thousands of empty classrooms. The figures presented by the Office of Education did not allow for the shift in population from country to city and the like. The Archbishop felt that local authorities should be used first:

The most eloquent testimony to the ability of the local community to pay for suburban schools is furnished by the example of the Catholic parishioners. If there are Catholic citizens dwelling in these suburban communities, they will pay their taxes as good citizens, and they will erect their own schools with voluntary offerings. Furthermore, they may amortize the debt in ten years, as against the thirty-five customary if a bond issue is used in connection with a public school.

He concluded that there should be a close study of the facts to overcome the false impressions created by those offering propaganda for federal aid. In the same issue of the paper there was an editorial in a style that marked it as that of the Archbishop on the topic "Birth Control Hits Birth Controllers." Taking as its theme a complaint that not enough persons were taking courses in counseling, the writer indicated that the reason for the shortage of applications was the practice of birth control some twenty years ago. He noted that in 1950–1954 there were 19,410,000 infants recorded, but that twenty years before, when birth control made inroads into American life, there were only 10,640,000 infants. The difference of 8,775,000 that caused the lack of present-day students he called a "lost generation."

A news item that attracted the Archbishop's interest was the evaluation of the Catholic Church by the American Institute of Management. He called the audit friendly but with a feebleness. He thought the official grade of 88 quite good. On the criticism of the lack of depreciation reserve the Archbishop noted: "The history of the Church has many warnings that substantial reserves attract avaricious men, either from within or without the Church." He thought that American Catholics will find amusing that the Church should separate itself "from an air of intrigue and Latin thinking, yet not lose its tradition." He thought that the bishops were very happy about the contribution of its members. "However, the greatest wealth of the Church is the voluntary services of those who gave their lives to works of charity and zeal. . . ."

Another news item that amused him concerned the chief critics of the Church. When the Protestants and Other Americans United for the Separation of Church and State held their Eighth National Conference, the audience that came to hear Catholics attacked were startled when Dr. Willard E. Goslin of Peabody College of Teachers of Nashville accused Protestants of being the chief innovators of practices against separation of Church and State. Writing to Frank Hall of the N.C.W.C. News Service on February 3, the Archbishop noted: "The Goslin address to PAOU interests me strongly. Since it is so blunt I am wondering if the southern jurisdiction Masons have now decided that the organization is a liability instead of an asset to them. . . ."

Perhaps to say that the Archbishop left his heart in the confessional of the prefect of religion at Notre Dame is too strong, but his interest in what went on there never died. Consequently when the rector of Dillon Hall objected to the presence of the prefect of religion in his hall as an interference in hall discipline, Father Charles Carey, the prefect in 1956, appealed to the old prefect to

show that he had prior claim in planning for the hall. The Archbishop wrote to Father Carey on February 7:

You are doing a good job of putting your point over. However, I
want to give you a bit of historical background, which Father Steiner
can confirm for you.

When the dining hall was opened in 1927, which was four years
before Dillon Hall was constructed, Father Steiner and I, with the
approval in principle of the Provincial, designed a double chapel—the
front portion for daily Communion and the rear portion for daily
adoration—to be erected on the site of the west wing of Dillon Hall.
Father Steiner may have one of the old designs on hand.

When it was decided to erect Dillon and Alumni Halls in their present locations, it was agreed that the chapel of Dillon Hall should act
as the daily Communion chapel. As you say, the side altar, with a confessional adjoining, was set up for the convenience of off-campus students and any others who might come late to Holy Communion. The
proximity of the chapel to the dining hall was the principal factor
in this selection. The office of the Prefect of Religion was transferred
from Sorin Hall to Dillon; the two offices of the Prefect of Religion
and the adjoining pamphlet rack provided ample space for the usual
needs. It is only a step from the office to the chapel, and the bell at the
door could summon a priest instantaneously.

Dillon Hall is the interloper not the daily Communion chapel. If
daily Communion is to be made more difficult for the off-campus students, the Bishop of Steubenville should be consulted. He found the
Sorin Hall chapel not too much of an inconvenience—but that was
before Dillon Hall existed. Another man who might want to be consulted is the captain who led the paratroopers to Los Banos prison, to
rescue our Holy Cross members who were prisoners of the Japanese.
There are a few doctors and judges around over the country who might
also want to be consulted. And then there is Fred Snite, whose courage
in affliction gives a lesson to the whole world. When Fred would come
to Holy Communion in the Dillon Hall chapel at ten o'clock or so in
the morning, two or three days a week, he would smile very sweetly
and say: "I know I ought to get around in time to hear Mass, but it's
wonderful to be able to go to Holy Communion mornings I sleep over."

The whole campaign for Holy Communion at Notre Dame over a
long period has as its objective to demonstrate in a practical way to
individuals that the happiest days in one's life are those spent in the
state of grace. The fruits of daily Communion among the Notre Dame
students were attachment to the Mass, loyalty to Holy Mother Church,
fanatical devotion to Notre Dame. The attachment to Mass trailed
daily Communion by about a year, as a rule.

Another intervention in Notre Dame came when the Notre Dame
Scholastic printed an unsavory article, which was apparently

brought to his attention. He wrote to the President of the University:

What I am tempted to do is write a letter to the *Scholastic* editor, for publication, the letter to conclude with these words: If the sentiments expressed in this editorial are not resented by the student body at Notre Dame, then it is time to take the statue down from the Dome.

The Archbishop's brother Bob, living in Washington, had a cold when the Archbishop saw him when he went to consecrate Bishop Smith. The cold hung on, but the Archbishop was not prepared for Bob's death from a cerebral hemorrhage the night of February 8. The Archbishop sang the funeral Mass the following Monday, and Archbishop O'Boyle said the prayers at the grave. Cardinal Spellman was not notified and expressed regret at this oversight, since he had met Bob in England and liked him very much.

On March 16 the Archbishop went to Carroll High School in Washington to address the Eighth Annual Teachers' Institute of the Archdiocese of Washington. Some regarded this speech as the clearest statement of his desire that all Catholic children receive a Catholic education. He took for his topic "Catholic Education for All." He admitted that the topic was as broad as Our Lord's command to teach all nations. He said that the teacher should try to simplify his work. He continued:

And lest I be guilty of the vice of which I warn you, I will say simply that we must never lose sight of the fact that we are dealing with souls. The secularist who denies the existence of the soul, writes a thousand books to explain what makes Johnny tick. The Catholic teacher who follows the secularist up a dozen blind alleys, wastes precious time and risks failure. The good nun who spends as much time praying for Johnny as teaching him, takes Johnny as he is, soul and all, and never has to worry about his conditioned reflexes.

The Archbishop made light of the problem of the gifted child. In such problems the sister had solutions. And if sister runs out of ideas, all she has to do is to ask Our Blessed Lord at Holy Communion the following morning, and she will have her answer.

He referred to accomplishments since the war. "We had in our Catholic elementary schools in 1945, 50% of the children who had been baptized during the eight years which provided the normal enrollment for the eight grades at that time. In 1954–5, we were providing for $62\frac{1}{2}\%$ of the available children." It was estimated that Catholic elementary schools were educating 65 percent of the survivors of the Catholic children born in the years 1942–1949.

He noted, however, that comparative statistics between Catholic and public schools are not very useful because, for instance, of the large number of repeaters in the first grade.

He further talked about the problem of handicapped children. "Prudence" he said "must be our guide in these matters." He spoke of the wonders that medical science had been able to do for these retarded ones. These are very quick to learn a great deal about the love of God. Also he spoke favorably of those vocational classes that were being taught for those who were merely awaiting the legal age to quit school. These students he considered the source of more than their share of juvenile delinquents. Caustic references were made to courses listed under "Education for Democratic Living." He maintained that 45 percent of the work taken in night schools leads away instead of to college. He quoted from the *Chicago Tribune* on the finding of Professor Arthur Bestor of the University of Illinois on this tendency to vocational classes. He added:

I hope the time will soon dawn when Catholics will recognize the fact that in their own traditions they have not only the philosophy, but the methods and the record of achievement that makes them independent of the empirical systems of education that are falling apart all over the United States.

And he concluded:

We are doing all right—with the help of God. When we look at some of the educational palaces that are costing the state three times what we pay for comparable facilities, and when we realize that most of these are financed through bond issues that will add 50 or 60% to their cost, we thank God that we are building with the offerings of the poor and not with tax money. I am happy to echo the sentiments of Archbishop Cushing and Bishop Fletcher who have recently asserted that they would not accept one cent of tax money for the construction or operation of their schools.

Most of the letters that the Archbishop published in the *Standard and Times* or sent directly to the pastors dealt with the seasonal activities of the people or with the next collection. Sometimes, such as Easter, 1956, he looked abroad in his message. He spoke of the letter written by the Pope after his recovery from a dangerous illness two years before. Then the Holy Father had spoken of his dedication to peace and promised unremitting effort for a lasting peace. Yet the Archbishop noted:

Two years and many international conferences later peace seems just as remote as ever. All around the Mediterranean and in other places as well, the cold war threatens to break into a hot war. Justice had to be extorted rather than applied voluntarily, confidence is exacted rather than inspired.

What is lacking? The reform of the morals of mankind for which the Holy Father and his predecessors have appealed without ceasing. If those who have the full light of the Gospel will only lead the fullness of Christian life, the radiation of grace from their lives will touch the hearts of sinners and reform the morals of mankind.

In the April 20 issue of the *Standard and Times* there was an editorial entitled "The Professor's Wild Pitch," which seemed to be written in the style of the Archbishop. Professor John Meng of Hunter College, New York, at the Catholic Educational Convention had argued for the reduction of Catholic graduate schools to three, and a fifty percent reduction in the number of four-year Catholic colleges. The editorial answered that competition is good for graduate work and that the effort that enables more Catholic students to get a Catholic college education is good. The Meng recommendations were certainly unpalatable to the Archbishop whether he wrote the editorial or it was written by someone on the staff of the paper.

On May 1 the Archbishop preached at the consecration of Bishop Lawrence B. Schott as auxiliary bishop of Harrisburg. Some who heard this sermon felt that the Archbishop gave in it his notions of the episcopal office, backed by quotations from Saint Bernard and Saint John Chrysostom on the work of the teacher, the priest, and the shepherd. On May 22 he gave another consecration sermon at the consecration of Bishop Richard Ackermann, C.SS.R., at Pittsburgh.

In the *Standard and Times* of May 25 the Archbishop wrote but did not sign the first editorial under the title, "The Task is Not Impossible." Calling James M. O'Neill, the author of a newly published book, *The Catholic in Secular Education,* a well-intentioned pessimist, he blamed his pessimism on his lack of knowledge of theology and canon law. He implied that O'Neill had enlarged on the mistake of Monsignor McManus and had overstated the number of Catholic children to be educated by 26 percent, or 1,979,000. He forgot to include the infant mortality, the physically handicapped, and other factors affecting a total of almost two million children that O'Neill should have subtracted from his figures. The Archbishop noted that the percentage of Catholics in Catholic schools than was 56.6 percent instead of the 46.4 percent of Mr. O'Neill. He suggested a different way of calculating the percentage:

... the process is: total the infant baptisms for the eight years normally represented in the present eight grades of a diocese and make the normal allowance for death and disability; then compare the revised total with the present elementary enrollment in the Catholic schools of the diocese. Applying this rule of thumb, we find 28 dioceses in the United States that have 90% or more of their potential in the Catholic grammar schools; 10 more have between 80 and 90 percent.

The Archbishop seemed to be dealing constantly with the problem of higher education of Catholics in non-Catholic colleges. To a senator who asked him to name a candidate to a law scholarship which by its conditions excluded graduates of Catholic colleges, he wrote a refusal and asked in his answer of May 4 for a change of the law:

May I count on your assistance in correcting what I believe to be a serious wrong? I feel certain that the gentlemen who passed the legislation granting these scholarships had no intention of discriminating against citizens because of their religious belief. I believe it was their intention to help the recipients of the scholarships rather than the individual school. But the legislation does actually discriminate against the individual student who wants to keep God in the education process right through to his college degree. It tempts him to disregard his principles and accept a purely secular education rather than the one he would prefer.

To Brother Francis, F.S.C., of LaSalle High School he mentioned on May 24 the large number of applications he had received from those who wanted to go to secular colleges. "While I have not had a count this year, I am under the impression that I have had more than the 400 letters I received last year from those seeking admission to secular schools."

In May, 1958, the bishops of the United States received a letter from Rome concerning the public use of statistics about Catholicism in the United States. When a colleague wrote to the Archbishop about the meaning of the decree, the Archbishop expressed his opinion of some of the public statements being made at this time about the condition of the Church in the United States. Although he had plenty of statistics, he did not publish them:

The fundamental error of all sociologists is that they base their statistics on the assumption that there is no reason to assume that the Catholic birth rate is higher than the Protestant birth rate. I don't want to tell them that they can discover the white non-Catholic birth rate by subtracting the Catholic infant baptisms and the non-white births from the total. If they discover this they will rush into print with it and make hash of the good will that now exists between Catholics and non-Catholics, and at the same time they will put back the Catholic apostolate among the Negroes.

I have no doubt that Monsignor Ellis, Father Cavanaugh, and Father Weigel have helped precipitate the warning from Rome. Their blatherskite statements have embarrassed everyone.

The Archbishop continued his correspondence with the former Notre Dame student who professed to have lost his faith but was gradually regaining it. On June 4 the Archbishop told him of his own readings:

I have just read a good Notre Dame book, "Deliver us from Evil" by Doctor Thomas Dooley. It tells of his experiences with the refugees from North Viet Nam, most of them in order to practice their religion. The spirit of the book is magnificent, and the occasional references to Notre Dame make me regard it as about the best Notre Dame book I have ever read.

The author is quite young and just as much a squirrel as the boys with whom you traveled some twenty odd years ago. It has some very gruesome passages in it—description of the poor people who fled from the Communists, but it is truly inspiring.

On June 11 the Archbishop preached at the consecration of Bishop Edward Schlotterback in Wilmington. The Bishop was the new vicar apostolic of Keetmanshoop in Southwest Africa. This was the third consecration sermon in five weeks. Later the Archbishop was to give these efforts, along with his many other tasks, as the occasion of the collapse of his health.

The fact of the matter was that the dire predictions of his friends about the effects of his endless activity on his health which he had generally disregarded for more than twenty years had suddenly become so real that he could not deny them. Of all the aches and pains that can beset an active man none is quite so crippling as those generally called sciatica. The Archbishop had for years made light of his inability to go up and down stairs with any kind of ease, he had brushed off the nuisance of his continuous sinus trouble since his youth, and he had refused to undergo an operation either for suspected gall-bladder trouble or for a hernia. But now for the first time he could not do his work. There is no record that he called in a physician even then, but after a few days he did go to Indianapolis on June 28 for a rest. When his family saw that he could scarcely genuflect at Mass, they insisted that he call in a physician.[43] The medical treatments prescribed by the physician enabled him to move about with greater ease, but when the Archbishop returned to Philadelphia on July 14, the physician insisted that he return to Indianapolis on August

1 for a complete physical examination, since the deeper cause of
the disability lay elsewhere in his system. There was, however, one
puzzling note in this preliminary examination. The orthopedic
surgeon insisted that the Archbishop's bones were too soft for him
to have arthritis, although he would not say what the real trouble
was. To the friends of the prelate who had watched him fighting
bravely but without success against a crippling disease in his legs
and feet, this opinion was incredible. Although the Archbishop
repeated this diagnosis to his friends, there is some doubt that he
really believed it. At least he did agree to return to Indianapolis
on August 1 for the complete physical examination. While the
Archbishop had never enjoyed perfect health since youth, he had
been able to live and work zealously despite his physical handicaps until this series of incidents. This was a turning point in
his life.

NINE

Declining Health

THE ARCHBISHOP RETURNED TO PHILADELPHIA
to clear up his desk before undergoing the battery of tests that
the Indianapolis physicians had proposed. He already felt a bit
better, and his suffering did not prevent him from assuring Monsignor Francis J. Jansen in a letter of July 19 about his position
on federal aid to education.

Briefly the dangers I see are:

    (1) With state support goes state control;
    (2) What the state gives it can take away;
    (3) With the economies we effect both in construction and coop-
        eration, we pay less for our schools than we would pay if our
        payment were through taxation.[1]

Surely there was no weakening in that statement. On the same day
he wrote to Raymond Moley, who had manifested interest in the
editorials of the Archbishop on federal aid, explaining why other
bishops did not carry on the public fight. He told Moley:

A good bit of the reluctance of the Catholic bishops to speak out at
the present time against Federal Aid is based upon experience. Too
often in the past the N.E.A. frustrated in its repeated attempt to secure
federal aid, has used the Catholic Church as a whipping boy and has
refused to meet the real issues. There is now a growing awareness of
the real danger of federal aid, which is federal control, and the fight
during the past few years has been centered on the real issue. Indeed,
in my own independent action I have watched carefully the trend

towards a statement of the real issues, and it seems that the Governors by rejecting the White House Conference, did an exceptionally good public relations job on the eve of the House vote.

One other matter was on his desk and that was the proposal to make the possession of a master's degree a qualification for social workers. On July 30 he explained his proposition to Bishop Guilfoyle of Altoona:

The requirement of a Master's degree in social work can be a hindrance to effective work. The degree itself means nothing except success in examination. Unless a person has character and common sense to be a good social worker, the degree may be a hindrance. A poor worker may be kept because the agency needs one with a Master's degree. This requirement may wreck a good organization.

There is no record of the Archbishop's thoughts as he returned to Indianapolis on August 1 for an extended physical examination. In a letter written shortly afterwards he indicated that he had overtaxed himself in giving four public sermons a month (three for consecrations), but these sermons must be understood as additional burdens to an already heavy daily schedule.

The planned absence of the Archbishop from most public celebrations of a civic nature and his failure to attend banquets and luncheons had given rise to an accepted tradition that he suffered constant ill health. There was a factual basis for this belief because the Archbishop had had a chronic inflammation of his sinuses from his youth, and in the years since leaving Notre Dame the suffering from arthritis in his legs had increased. Nevertheless those close to him insist that no priest in the archdiocese was more active than he. His policy of avoiding public entertainment was one deliberately chosen after his years in the episcopate in the Military Ordinariate and in Buffalo, and while it did not always please those pastors who liked to have him grace their dinners and public services, it in no way kept him from fulfilling all other functions of his office. Another tradition that had grown up was that the common absence of the episcopal ring from his finger meant that he was suffering from arthritis that day. But no one thought of attributing to ill health the frequency with which he answered his own phone or opened the door of his home for the visitor.

This rejection of formalities was, indeed, part of his concept of his office. Once he had adopted the policy, there was perhaps more additional wilfullness in his telling those who invited him that having refused such invitations before he dared not now break his rule by accepting subsequent invitations. Nevertheless, Monsignor Joseph McGlinn, while insisting that the refusal to attend banquets was a matter of policy, also insisted that a steady round of such entertainments, especially public dinners, might have proved fateful for the Archbishop, who was indeed of delicate health despite his wiriness.

To those who had occasion to meet the Archbishop on business or even on social occasions his frankness and humility as well as his generous sense of hospitality excused any want of display. Laymen who dealt with him personally were charmed not only by his simplicity but by his spirituality. It was significant that those who had known him before his consecration, especially older Notre Dame alumni, persisted in calling him "Father O'Hara" and were encouraged to do so by the prelate himself. Perhaps in his personal life the Archbishop was showing his notion of the separation of Church and State. His sense of the spiritual could be said to sustain his arguments against federal aid to Catholic education. He firmly believed that religion was best served by concentration on spiritual affairs, despite the fact that his program of church and school construction was of the variety expected of a modern industrial corporation. Perhaps, also, his dependence on the spiritual may also explain why he allowed his health to be undermined until he virtually collapsed. Yet this same humility and simplicity led him to place himself entirely at the wishes of the physicians at St. Vincent's Hospital with one exception. He heard on his arrival in Indianapolis of the death of his friend Archbishop Noll at Fort Wayne. When he began his tests on August 1, he made an agreement with the physicians that he could interrupt the tests to attend the Archbishop's funeral.

The examinations and tests at Saint Vincent's Hospital were spread out over several days and occasionally called for his remaining in the hospital overnight. On August 8 the doctors decided that part of his trouble was diabetic and that he should go on a special diet. The final report was given by Dr. Hal Doran on August 13[2] and in its total aspect indicated that the Archbishop had suffered a general collapse. The report was technical but in effect it said that he had to some degree hardening of the liver, diabetes, chronic bronchitis, and hardening of the arteries about the heart with mild heart failure. The earlier pain in his legs they attributed to the hardening of the arteries of the lower extremities. Doctor Doran added: "Although the previous diagnoses sound rather foreboding, I sincerely believe that his present medication and good common sense and living habits can well

offer him a number of good years and active duties in the future."
The diagnoses were made without surgery and were not substantiated in everything when the Archbishop underwent surgery
some years later. The diet prescribed, along with certain medicines, was "high in carbohydrates and protein and low in fat."
The doctor added: "I have encouraged him to reduce his smoking to one half and to avoid alcohol, spicy and greasy food. In
addition, he is to wear elastic stockings while on his feet because
of varicosities." The doctor also advised against any trip lasting
more than three hours.

That the Archbishop faced this dire program with his usual
good humor and optimism was not unexpected by those who
knew him well. The physician was surprised:

. . . It was amazing to me all the times that I saw Cardinal O'Hara as
to how stoic he was. He always tended to extremely minimize his
symptoms and frequently made the statement that his own personal
health and feeling of well-being was actually secondary to his duties.
Usually, we had to drag symptoms out of him when we would find
some organic disease that should have been producing symptoms and
then when faced with direct questioning, he would usually admit to
having symptoms some times which were rather severe. I have always
felt that Cardinal O'Hara was extremely cooperative with us, that is
as far as he could be and still try to do a good job. He was obviously
not only an intelligent individual, but undoubtedly an extremely capable man as well. He was always very appreciative and gracious of our
medical care. . . .[3]

The Archbishop received the doctor's report on August 13 and
returned to Philadelphia the next day. Two days later he telephoned to the family that he already felt much better. On August
21 he made his first report to Dr. Doran:

The improvement noted while I was in your charge was continued.
I believe I have adhered faithfully to the diet and I manage to get
sufficient rest. There has been no gain in weight. It stands at 144 in
the morning before breakfast and 146 in the evening before retiring.
At St. Vincent's Hospital I weighed in at 150.5 pounds. I have ordered
the elastic stockings and they are promised for delivery Wednesday.
Meanwhile I use bandages. On most days I have managed to walk for
an hour or more with no ill effects. The legs are in better condition
than they have been for a long time.

While a diet that would cause his sparse figure to lose six
pounds in less than a month must have had a weakening effect
and induced fatigue, there is no indication of this in the correspondence of the Archbishop. Certainly his illness had no notice-

able effect on his school building program. The *Standard and Times* of August 16 gave a list of fifty-four new buildings or planned additions to the archdiocesan school system in connection with the announcements for the new year. Among these were seven high schools, twenty-one new elementary schools, and twenty-one other elementary schools enlarged or planned. The school issue of the paper also announced that there were 782 lay teachers in the Catholic schools of the archdiocese, and that in the archdiocesan high schools there was a tentative enrollment of 41,749, of which 27,806 were in the city of Philadelphia.

On the question of the proposal to demand a master's degree for persons employed in the adoption service, the Archbishop took up where he had left off before going to the hospital. In his letter of September 4 to Father James J. Marley he repeated his reasons for this policy:

Finally, I submit that since our Catholic philosophy of social work is totally different from the secularist philosophy that underlies courses in most of the Schools of Social Work in the country, only those who understand and appreciate our philosophy are competent to judge our procedures and our criteria for the selection of agency workers. We do not question the right of the State to judge us in matters affecting the physical and temporal welfare of our charges, but we claim full jurisdiction in the things of the spirit.

The Archbishop seemed to be trying to prove his good health. In early September he attended four funerals in five days besides entertaining Cardinal Ernesto Ruffini of Palermo on September 11 and 12. After that he spoke at the seminary, dedicated a church on September 16, and blessed a rectory on September 23. On September 26 he addressed the C.Y.O. Convention that had come to Philadelphia despite the local C.Y.O.'s refusal to affiliate with the national organization. But the Archbishop had a severe test of his cheer and optimism the second week in October. Since early in the spring the religious communities and the Society of the Propagation of the Faith had been planning a Vistarama of the Missions, a grand exhibition in Convention Hall during the week of October 7–14.

Despite his fatigue and crippled condition the Archbishop was much in evidence entertaining the visiting members of the hierarchy at the exhibition. The grand opening took place Sunday, October 7, with the Apostolic Delegate presiding at the opening Mass in the hall. Archbishop O'Hara was there and also visited the exhibition in street clothes with the Delegate. In published photographs taken at this time he looked thin and humped. On

Wednesday, October 10, the chief guest was Cardinal Spellman. Again the Archbishop was the host. Another important visitor was Archbishop Pietro Sigismondi, the secretary of the Sacred Congregation of Propaganda; and Cardinal Tien also came. The closing sermon was given by Bishop Fulton Sheen. In his letter to the priests on the Vistarama, the Archbishop insisted on the *oratio* in the Mass for October 14, the annual collection, and the renewal of memberships in the Society for the Propagation of the Faith.

There was no letup in the Archbishop's appointments. On October 18 he spoke to the convention of the Catholic Educational Association of Pennsylvania, on October 12 he presided at the dedication of Kenrick High School in Norristown, and on October 24 he consecrated Father Hubert Cartwright, the rector of the cathedral, as coadjutor bishop of Wilmington. In the meantime he published in the October 19 *Standard and Times* an appeal for a subscription drive for the paper. In the letter he said that Bishop Gerald O'Hara had complained to him that there was too little interest in this country in what the Catholics were suffering behind the Iron and Bamboo curtains. The Catholic press he insisted was the chief tool to overcome this indifference.

It is only through the medium of the Catholic press that our people can keep abreast of the far-flung activities of the Church both at home and abroad. A Catholic newspaper is not only helpful, it has become a practical necessity in every Catholic home—for information, for instruction and for inspiration.

On October 30 the Archbishop flew to Indianapolis for a check-up by his Indianapolis physicians. After the examination the next day the doctors told him that his trouble had cleared up, according to his sister's diary, but they suggested that he keep to his diet. Apparently the physicians referred to the temporary troubles. The Archbishop remained with the family until November 3 and had a pleasant visit. Elizabeth noted that he was much better but very thin, and that he said his three Masses All Souls Day without sitting down, where he had formerly been unable to say even one without sitting down.

Reporting to his close lay collaborator in Buffalo, Albert O'Neill, on November 5, he wrote:

I waited until my return from Indianapolis to give you the answer with the doctor's verdict. When the report of the tests was received the doctor said, "Perfect." I don't know what that means, but he told me to continue with the same diet and report again in a couple of months. He was not at all disturbed about the loss of weight because the system needs to lose it just where it was disappearing.

On November 2 the *Standard and Times* carried a special article on the educational advancements in the archdiocese since the coming of Archbishop O'Hara. This advancement had recently been noted by the dedication of Cardinal Dougherty High School, the largest Catholic high school in the world, on Sunday, October 27. On the same day the Archbishop had also dedicated St. Hubert's High School. There were now, since the Archbishop came, fifteen new high schools educating an additional 35,000 students.

Archbishop O'Hara had brought with him to Philadelphia a deep interest in the cause of his predecessor, Bishop John Neumann, whose process of beatification had been interrupted by some question about one of the cures attributed to his intercession. He saw a definite parallel between the efforts of Bishop Neumann to build a Catholic school system in times of depression and his own efforts to enlarge the school system of the archdiocese. He was also dissatisfied with the progress of the cause for the beatification of the Bishop. He regularly attended religious services at the tomb of the Bishop and encouraged Father Michael Curley, C.SS.R., in his preparation of a biography of the man. At his suggestion Father Nicholas Ferrante, C.SS.R.,[4] was named postulator of the cause, and an investigation was made into the circumstances which had delayed the process of beatification. Eventually Archbishop O'Hara succeeded in having a cardinal ponens appointed and in bringing a physician from Rome to examine into the circumstances of the miracle attributed to the intercession of the Bishop. Finally at the time of the bishops' meeting in Washington he obtained the signatures of the other bishops of the country to a petition for presenting the cause to Rome.

On November 19 the Archbishop wrote to Cardinal Spellman of another interest during his enforced stay at home. The lawyers of the archdiocese had won another victory in the case of Schade *vs* County Institutions. The Supreme Court had upheld the right of civil units of government to purchase care from private and religious child-rearing agencies. The original suit had been filed by Fred A. Schade against the Allegheny County Institution District to prevent the county from sending children for adoption to religious institutions. The case had been decided against Schade in the lower courts; he had appealed to the appeals court, where he won; the case was then carried to the Supreme Court of the State of Pennsylvania, where the appeals decision was reversed.

The Archbishop continued his heavy schedule of attendance at funerals, dedications, and jubilees, but he also found time to study the reports of government officials on internal security.

Although he never spoke of this in any official document, he occasionally talked to his sisters in Indianapolis about the activities of some persons mentioned in these reports, some of whom he had followed for some time. It was quite in keeping with this strictness on public affairs that he renewed his rule on the reading of forbidden books by college students. To Father J. Joseph Bluett, S.J., the president of St. Joseph's College, he explained his position in a letter of December 3:

My conscience on the matter of forbidden books was sharpened considerably by certain experiences at Notre Dame. A couple of popular professors fell through the ice when it was too thin; some of their students definitely left the Church.

In the case of the undergraduate, I want the assurance that a competent answer to the false philosophy or theology of an indexed book is bound up in the same volume with the offensive material.

When his friend Bishop Eustace of Camden died on December 11, he agreed to say the Children's Mass for the deceased on December 13 and to preach the funeral sermon on December 15. His words at the funeral were a bit sombre as he brought into his sermon the sufferings of the Catholics of Hungary in the Hungarian uprising of the previous weeks:

. . . The seeds of treason were being sown in our own country in the very hour when those words were spoken in the centenary year of the passion of Christ, 1933. Even now, we know all too little about what has been done to undermine the very foundations of our own beloved country, for every attempt to seek out the truth has met savage opposition. Perhaps the crucifixion of Hungary has done more than anything else to bring us to a realization of the bankruptcy of secular thought. On other occasions in the past, Hungary has thrown itself into the breach and saved Christian civilization. Perhaps that is what is happening now in the Providence of God. The symbolism of truth is in the release of Cardinal Mindszenty from his prison—although we know not what the future holds for him.[5]

The Archbishop recalled that Bishop Eustace had called for an hour of prayer for Hungary during the recent uprising and had wept to see the zeal of the people who came to the services that he himself was unable to attend. The Archbishop praised the Bishop for his humility. Bishop Eustace had no interest in public display and felt deeply the persecutions of the Church. Although the Archbishop did not say so, these two qualities were probably bonds of friendship between the two prelates.

Writing on December 18 to Harrison W. Fry, who wanted him to prepare a general Christmas message, he declined: ". . . I am

very sorry, but I am so busy now that I see no opportunity to prepare even a brief Christmas message." Not even the Christmas
season could lower his guard against interdenominationalism.

On December 18 the Archbishop held a reception at the Benjamin Franklin Hotel for the dependent children of the diocese.
Both the children and those who were expected to contribute to
the welfare of the children were there. Many came really to see
the Archbishop, who seemed to have fun with the children. But
those who knew him could not help noticing the thin, worn look,
the stooped shoulders, and the weakness of the fast-aging priest.
Since he could not pontificate in his cathedral while it was being
repaired, he went to Notre Dame to see his friends and then home
for the Christmas observances. He arrived in Indianapolis on
December 22 and went to the hospital for a check-up. Dr. Doran
increased the carbohydrates in his diet so that he could gain back
some of the weight he had lost. His brother Pat drove into Indianapolis from Topeka, Kansas, during his stay. The Archbishop said
his three Christmas Masses at the family home. Before he left for
the Midwest, he wrote a letter predated December 21 asking the
faithful to join in the annual day of prayer for persecuted people
on December 30. The uprising in eastern Europe made this plea
of special interest this year.

When the Archbishop returned to Philadelphia he issued his
annual appeal that the faithful celebrate January 13 as Family
Communion Sunday. This year he showed his preoccupation with
the persecution in eastern Europe, particularly Hungary. He
noted that efforts had been made there to turn the children against
their parents, against religion, and against God. He added:

> In our country we witness the onslaught of God's enemies in the
> attack on innocence waged by indecency in motion pictures and the
> other agencies of entertainment, in publications of many kinds, and
> the determined fight waged by organized atheism against any recogni-
> tion of God in public schools and in public assemblies. We see it also
> in the instability of marriage; disaster looms when a nation has 26
> divorces for every 100 marriages, as is the case in the United States
> today.
>
> On the Feast of the Holy Family, we call on our Catholic people to
> receive Holy Communion as family units. . . .

At this time the Congregation of Holy Cross, which he had
brought into the Diocese of Buffalo, had found it necessary to
withdraw from the high schools of that diocese. Bishop Burke
had written to him of the problems resulting from the change.
The Archbishop could not suggest another community to replace

them. Placing more students in the classrooms was one solution of the problem which he himself had supported both in Buffalo and in Philadelphia. He told Bishop Burke in his letter of January 4:

It strikes me it would be possible to manage the high school with a smaller number of teachers. Fifty is taken as a normal standard in Philadelphia and I don't hear anyone complaining about that. In the junior and senior year there may be smaller classes because of the number of drop-outs and the diversification of the curriculum, but we resisted any attempt to limit the class size to thirty or thirty-five. As a matter of fact, the city often runs classes of forty and forty-five. The state has no set limit.

There were other solutions for this problem that faced pastors throughout the country. Monsignor Francis J. Jansen of Hammond, Indiana, an old friend, wrote to him for an opinion of the proposals made in several Catholic publications that the earlier school grades be dropped in favor of the preservation of Catholic high schools. In private conversation the Archbishop insisted that the problem could be met without such actions and had expressed the opinion that the children would not enter a parochial school once they had developed associations in public schools. This was also what he wrote to Monsignor Jansen:

While I would like to think that we could provide a Catholic high school education for every Catholic boy and girl in the United States, I am afraid that we would lose far more than we would gain if we excluded the children from the Catholic schools for the first three years. Here in Philadelphia we have little luck getting children to transfer to a Catholic school after they have been a couple of years in a public school. If we start them off in the first grade, we are most likely to have them throughout the eight grades.

On another school question, that of free rides for parochial school children in public school buses and the decision of the Pennsylvania Supreme Court against allowing such rides, he wrote to R. H. Kelley about his attitude on governmental aid to Catholic schools:

It is quite unlikely that I would support any particular kind of relief. I prefer limiting my efforts to pointing out the inconsistencies and incongruities in these subsidies which must inevitably lead to control by the Federal Government of the local school system of the nation.

When John McDermott of the Philadelphia Catholic Housing Council asked permission of the Archbishop to make a survey of the housing problems of the city, he told him: "There is no necessity for the survey you wish to make. If the members of the council wish to have information for guidance in planning, the chancery can supply all the information that is needed." It was not surprising that a prelate so much given to statistics should gather them about every phase of his archdiocese. This information had been accumulated with the aid of a community of sisters who specialized in this kind of census and from the reports of the pastors. The Archbishop was quite pleased with his survey, but he refused to share his findings with sociologists and others not working in the chancery office.

His correspondence shows that while he was faithful to the physicians' limitation on traveling at this time, he maintained a wide variety of interests by correspondence and reading. To the President of Villanova he urged the abandonment of classes in remedial reading, noting that the University of Illinois had decided against them. To Monsignor Swanstrom of the N.C.W.C. Relief Commission he expressed doubt that the improved relations between Church and State in Poland following the Polish insurgency would last. To Bishop Jerome Hannon of Scranton he sent encouragement in that bishop's efforts to avoid cooperation with birth-control groups acting in the name of welfare:

It took some time for us to break Catholic affiliations with the local Health and Welfare Council. They kept coming back to our people under one new guise or another and always with a new batch of promises. The United Welfare appeals of one sort or another seek our cooperation and always assure us that there is a complete ban on the Planned Parenthood group. I always point out to them that among the recipients of funds are various family counseling services, all of which are basically Planned Parenthood groups. I do not find it necessary to point out to them another glaring obstacle to our participation—the sharing of their funds with proselytizing agencies set up in Catholic neighborhoods.

In his Lenten pastoral of March 1 the Archbishop called the purple of penance the purple of royalty, and asked that the faithful make their penance that year an act of thanksgiving for their faith. He called attention to the fact that there were more than two thousand non-Catholics attending the archdiocesan schools, although he did not say that these were mostly Negro children. He did observe that while he was happy to welcome these non-Catholic children, the vacant desks were available because the same number of Catholic children had gone to public schools. "When a Catholic rejects the faith there is always a well-intentioned non-Catholic ready to take his place and accept 'the pearl of great price.'"

In the March 8 *Standard and Times* the Archbishop renewed
his opposition to federal aid to education in an editorial entitled
"Federal Aid for School Construction—What Are the Facts?"
Calling on his flair for statistics and using the government documents that he had perused carefully, he called the statistics used
to demand federal aid for school construction a "jungle." His
figures showed that there were 67,098 classrooms built in 1955,
which at 30 pupils per room would provide classrooms for
2,012,940 pupils. Yet the number of "pupils in excess of normal
capacity of accessible public owned school plants in use" was
2,263,000. Besides indicating that there were errors in the statistics
used to arrive at these figures, he also showed that in the ten states
that provided most of the overcrowding, new houses had been
built and that other statistics indicated that they could take care
of their own problems. He claimed further that one reason for
the overcrowding was the practice in many public schools of making children repeat the first grade, with a result that in 1953 there
were 4,718,000 in the first grade and only 3,670,000 in the second
grade. His conclusion was that the real facts about the need for
federal aid to education were not known.

The next week the Archbishop treated another angle of the
problem of federal aid to education under the title "Does Federal
Aid Mean Federal Control?" He opened the editorial with a quotation from Secretary Folsom of the Health, Education, and Welfare Department that the idea of federal aid to education should
be dropped unless something was done immediately. He quoted an
answering editorial from the *Indianapolis Star* saying: "Okay, So
Drop It." In the first place he showed that there had been a tremendous building program since the war and this construction
was being continued without federal aid.

The Archbishop argued that the National School Board Association had gotten out of hand. Their proposal was that federal and
state aid be administered by the state education agency through
the local boards of education and "without restriction other than
simple accounting of receipts and disbursements." The Archbishop quoted Roger Freeman that the association wanted complete control without the acceptance or approval of the legislature
or governor. The Archbishop indicated that the purpose of that
action of the National School Board Association, an affiliate of the
National Educational Association, was to seize control of public
education. In other words, it was the objective of the association
to become "the only agency in the nation that has legal responsibility for the schools" with jurisdiction over the commissioner of

education, who would be appointed by the board. The Archbishop also showed that most of the members of this organization were graduates of fourteen institutions—that ten percent of the colleges furnish sixty percent of the leaders. In this he saw the skeletal organization that planned to take over control of the schools.

The Archbishop was gradually enlarging his activities again, but his friends noted that he had become unusually thin. At the suggestion of his sisters he made another appointment with the physicians in Indianapolis for March 15. The physicians insisted that he increase the quantity of the food he ate, except that he should not take salt. He wrote of this to Cardinal Spellman:

The doctor has put a stop order on my diet with the exception of salt. He wants me to restore ten of the lost pounds and then hold my weight at the new figure. I spent the last weekend in Indianapolis and he was quite pleased with the progress made.

His sister noted in her diary that when the Archbishop was in Indianapolis he spent most of his time working on his statistics, especially about aid to education. Later when President Truman made a speech on the need for such federal aid to education, he said that he was amused by the statistics used by the President. But he was not amused by the statistics that were appearing in the Catholic press indicating that Catholics could not hope to care for their own children with parochial schools.

To Father Joseph Fichter, S.J., a visiting professor at Notre Dame, he wrote on March 25, 1957, to ask for the data on which he had concluded that within ten years two-thirds of Catholic elementary school children "will be in public schools." Father Fichter answered him on March 29: "On the basis of reports around the country (I am thinking particularly of Monsignor McManus's article in *America*) I judge that we are about at the saturation point in elementary school facilities at this moment. We cannot keep up with the demand for teachers and classrooms." Such an answer was not satisfactory to the Archbishop, and he wrote again to Father Fichter on April 3, claiming that there were other statistics and that he thought the bishops were better informed on this topic. He admitted that in Philadelphia their potential was 1,900 in elementary and 1,200 in high schools without new buildings, but he added:

So far as I can determine in conversation with the Bishops the general feeling is that the Holy Ghost sends us these wonderful babies. He is going to provide the means of giving them a Catholic education of the best type possible. In a blind spirit of cooperation with the Holy Ghost we put up the schools, and we find that the teachers, both reli-

gious and lay, come from most unexpected places. So far as the children are concerned, they come in swarms. Our great regret is that we
cannot take the vast majority of non-Catholic pupils who apply to us.
About the only parishes that have them are the ones that have lost
a good bit of their Catholic population through movement to the
suburbs.

In the April 5 issue of the *Standard and Times* the Archbishop
published his third essay on federal aid to education under the
title "Federal Aid for School Construction—Additional Facts."
Taking for his target a statement by Secretary Folsom of the
Department of Health, Education, and Welfare that for the third
year in a row the estimated enrollments are "about 2,250,000
above capacity," he analyzed the statistics, showing that the worst
states were Southern states, while other states were building more
classrooms than they really needed. He then contrasted the statistics given out by the Department of Health, Education, and Welfare with those prepared for the White House Conference on
education. The variation in these figures amounted to 510 percent
in Montana, 470 percent in New Jersey, 466 percent in Oregon,
and 3,300 percent in Missouri. The statistics of Folsom were not
reliable at all. The Archbishop denied the Secretary's statement
that schoolrooms were not being built between 1933 and 1948,
maintaining that local governments had built in that time 18,000
schoolrooms and improved 51,000 schools. He concluded: "Confusion reigns. We see one possible good that may come of the
campaign for Federal Aid. The indifference to Arithmetic manifested by the educational leader of our country may arouse the
public to do something about it."

That the Archbishop was deeply convinced of the evils of federal aid is quite evident from his published editorials. But what
he hoped to achieve from the publication of these essays is not
too clear. The *Standard and Times* did not have national importance. Casual statements of the Archbishop show that he felt that
even most of the bishops did not share his opinion. He regarded
the granting of federal aid as an evil for the country, primarily as
giving improper power to the central government, and secondarily
as giving too much power to the National Educational Association and its lobby. So far as the Catholic Church was concerned,
he did not want the Church to receive federal aid because he felt
that the government would then dictate policies for Catholic
schools. Further he was doubtful that the aid would be given.
Since these editorials were reprinted as pamphlets and sent to
members of the hierarchy and to government officials, the Arch-

bishop certainly did not mean these editorials and his statistical
studies merely as an exercise in statistics. He definitely was out to
defeat federal aid. It is interesting in this connection to read a
note that he sent to Clarence Manion, the former dean of the Law
School at Notre Dame, who invited him to speak on the Manion
Forum. Writing to Manion on April 17, he declined the invitation: "After the bill was defeated two years ago I saw two different Masonic magazines that blamed me for presenting on the eve
of the vote secret orders of the Vatican for the bill to be killed."

There is no evidence that the Archbishop had any definite
effect on the legislators in Washington, even though he did send
copies of his editorials to them. He had explained to Representative Gwinn that he was afraid that he would embarrass the legislators if he appeared before their committee hearings. There is
no evidence that his editorials or pamphlets were ever discussed
in any of these hearings. There was also some divergence between
his point of view on federal aid to Catholic education and that of
the members of the Education Department of the N.C.W.C., but
there is no evidence of correspondence or discussion between him
and the directors of the Education Department of the N.C.W.C.

On March 28 there had appeared in the correspondence section
of the *New York Times* a letter signed by Joseph Duffy, assistant
professor of English at the University of Notre Dame, praising
Columbia, his alma mater, for permitting John Gates, the communist, to speak to its students and insisting on a "tradition of
free inquiry." A copy of the letter was sent to the Archbishop. To
Father Hesburgh the Archbishop wrote a letter of complaint on
April 8:

> Can you give me a lift with a difficult problem? Is there any conso-
> lation I can give to the friends of Notre Dame who are shocked at the
> letter of Joseph M. Duffy, Jr. to the *New York Times,* which he dated
> on the eve of the feast of the Annunciation?

On the same day he wrote to Cardinal Spellman:

> The Duffy letter left me speechless and I have wrestled with my con-
> science a week trying to determine what action to take. I enclose a
> copy of my letter to Father Hesburgh.
>
> The tragedy was intensified because the letter was written about
> the time George Shuster was received back at the University. The
> Duffy letter is only a little worse than Shuster's attack on Notre Dame
> in *Commonweal* after Father Burns[6] failed to show appreciation of
> George's talents.
>
> In the name of Notre Dame and the Congregation of Holy Cross I
> want to apologize to Your Eminence for the insult to the Catholic

Church which emanated from a misguided young man at the University. I'll feel better when I hear that he will not have his contract renewed. I would feel better still if I would hear from Father Hesburgh that he had been paid off and is no longer on the campus.

Apparently Father Hesburgh took neither action. Professor Duffy remained at Notre Dame. George Shuster continued to advise the administration at the University, received its Laetare Medal in 1960, and after his retirement from Hunter College became Assistant to the President of Notre Dame.

One of the effects of the increase in Catholic high schools in the archdiocese that soon manifested itself was the draining of any extra priests to fill out the faculties. This meant that there were also fewer opportunities to send these prospective teachers away for graduate work. To Father Herman Reith, C.S.C., of Notre Dame, who wrote to him asking him to send prospective student priests to Notre Dame to study philosophy, the Archbishop wrote on April 25:

Sad to say, our shortage of priests is such that we had to suspend for a time our program of sending priests on for advanced work. It may be shortsighted policy, but when we face a high school enrollment increase of 2,400 every year we must place in the classroom as many priests as we possibly can. When the ordination classes grow larger, we can return to our policy of graduate studies. . . .

The Archbishop kept active in all phases of his archdiocese, even though he did manage to avoid many public services. Under his direction Villanova University had opened a law school, and on April 25 the Archbishop said Mass at the dedication of the law school building. Also during the three days' celebration at the law school Chief Justice Warren spoke at the convocation of April 27.[7] On May 3 the *Standard and Times* had two consoling items for the Archbishop. The ruling of the zoning board by which he had been refused permission to build a high school in Wyncote had been reversed by the State Supreme Court on April 26. The property for this school had been purchased in 1954, but permission to build had been denied by the Board of Adjustment, and the archdiocese had carried the case to the Supreme Court. Another bit of good news in the paper announced that the seminary fund drive had collected $555,228.36 or $1,041.63 more than the previous year.

Although the name of Senator Joseph McCarthy had been in the Catholic press and on the lips of many Catholics during his career in the Senate, the Archbishop had carefully avoided any statement on the man, regarding that as a political question. However, the Archbishop had been friendly to anyone he considered opposed to the spread of communism, and the friendliness toward the Senator occasionally manifested in the *Standard and Times* received from him no word of disapproval. On May 2 the Senator died in a Bethesda, Maryland, hospital and was buried from St. Matthew's Cathedral in Washington. The *Standard and Times* of May 10 printed the eulogy of Monsignor John K. Cartwright and a long editorial in praise of the Senator. In the eyes of the editor of the *Standard and Times* the Senator was a devoted public servant who had been cut off prematurely in his work. He had suffered because of his exposure of the infiltration of communism into the government. The last lines of the editorial said:

Few Americans in our day deserve greater credit for alerting the country to the danger of Communist infiltration here. What a tragedy that a courageous "watchman of the citadel" should be so rewarded for his efforts!

To Mr. Henry FitzGibbon, who wrote about a memorial service for Senator McCarthy, the Archbishop wrote on May 15: "The *Standard and Times* has already mentioned a Mass for Senator McCarthy at St. John's Church. I have offered the Holy Sacrifice of the Mass for myself as I am sure many other Bishops and priests have."

On May 11 he wrote to Thomas Rowland of Holmes on the question of federal aid to education. His position was certainly clear in his editorials, yet he added to those explanations:

The question is a large one. Recently Archbishop Alter gave an excellent address in which he outlines the Catholic right to state aid for their schools. There can be no question in distributive justice about our right.

However, I hope that we will never accept any direct aid to Catholic schools. I have no objection to government paying tuition, as in the G.I. Bill of Rights, I have no objection to government bus transportation, lunches, health and recreation services. These are all services to the children and their parents.

I don't want the government to build our schools or pay the salaries of our teachers.

To Miss Geraldine Mazzeo of D'Youville college in Buffalo, who had written to him about her plans to attend Pembroke College, the women's college in North Carolina, to prepare for a career in the State Department, he gave some friendly advice. Since there was no Catholic Church within twenty miles of the college, he did not seem to think that attendance there would be the best preparation for a career in the State Department.

I hear you plan to enter the State Department. You should be well prepared in advance to recognize the errors that grow out of the pragmatism that rules there. Certainly, as a good Catholic, you don't want to add fuel to the fire by not recognizing error when it appears. The secularism that prevails in the secular colleges and universities—and in most Protestant institutions—has left us an easy prey to the wiles of Communism as practiced by the Soviet Union and its satellites.

That this very thin man was aware that his health was not too good was evident in some of his correspondence. To Monsignor Fink, who wanted him to preside at the National Convention of the Central Union and N.C.W.C. at Allentown on August 24–25, he said that he could not attend all the functions to which he had been invited and that Monsignor McGlinn would have to rule on the one he did attend. On June 3 he also turned down an invitation from Peter Grace to join a cruise that would offer useful rest and relaxation to a man not in the best of health.

However, age is no longer creeping up on me. It is galloping. I can always find an excuse for staying at home—an honest excuse. There is still much work to be done before I can feel that the spiritual needs of our Philadelphians are met reasonably well. While we are ahead of our needs in some parts of the diocese, we still face an annual increase of 15,000 people in the next six years. What the needs will be in the seventh year we will know at the end of 1957, when we count infant statistics. Thanks be to God, new babies seemed to be as welcome here as they are in the family of Peter and Margie.

About this time Cardinal Spellman sent him the manuscript of Father Robert Gannon's biography of the Cardinal. After reading the manuscript, he sent to the Cardinal a criticism and indicated that he had some objections to its publication that he would tell the Cardinal in person. Of the manuscript he wrote on June 10, 1957:

It is truly a great book and I am glad that it is written. There are a few small questions about publication at this time, but these we can talk over at your convenience.

. . . .

I would not anticipate any demonstration of bigotry on the part of the professional bigot. I can see them gnashing their teeth. On the other hand, the clarification of the record on the whole series of controversies is very valuable.

. . . .

The book is excellent throughout. Reviving old controversies has a very telling effect, since it clarifies the issues and drives home the Catholic position in every instance.

One of the chief opponents of Catholic education in the mind of Father O'Hara and later the Bishop and Archbishop O'Hara was the Institute of International Education. Writing on June 12 to Bishop Matthew Brady, the chairman of the Education Department of the N.C.W.C., the Archbishop explained his view of the Institute. He claimed that the Institute's appeals to Catholic colleges were merely window dressing:

During the war I was invited to Washington for a meeting on one occasion. I learned at the meeting that they wanted me to suggest some Catholic schools in South America that might be eligible for funds from the State Department budget. I told them in reply that meant they wanted to cover up for giving money to Protestant schools located down there. I was a little surprised when they admitted the fact. I gave them no names. Whether they ever got a list from anyone else I do not know.

If we look back over the records of the Institute from the early days —long before the Fulbright and Mundt Acts brought so many students to the United States—we find students coming from American missionary high schools and colleges in foreign countries, and from foreign universities, in countries where the Ministry of Education was always in the hands of Masons.

Neither can we overlook the fact that when Richard Pattee was in line for appointment to the office of Cultural Relations with Latin America in the State Department, he was passed over in favor of Ben Cherrington, a Y.M.C.A. worker in Denver, Colorado, who knew absolutely nothing about South America and had not even a smattering of Spanish. Cherrington whom I met in several South American countries when he was making his first trip around that continent, remarked constantly that he could never understand why he was chosen for a job for which he had not the slightest background. Laurence Duggan, his chief, did not enlighten me—and I did not ask him, I had already made up my mind that he was at least a fellow traveler—and that was many years before Whittaker Chambers testified that he was a member of a Communist cell in the State Department during the early days of the New Deal.

Again on the subject of Catholic education the Archbishop wrote to his Holy Cross confrere and noted theorist on Catholic education, Father William Cunningham, C.S.C., on the subject of substituting Catholic high schools for elementary schools. As he had written to Monsignor Jansen, for the Archbishop there was no real choice; to Father Cunningham he was very explicit.

From the point of view of a Philadelphian it is remote from reality.

As you know Philadelphia has always placed the school first in the establishment of a new parish. In this, it is like the old diocese of Indianapolis and Fort Wayne with the exception that in Indiana it is a reserved sin to send your children to a non-Catholic school if there is a Catholic school available.

1.) "We are not free to scrap the parochial school system." It was ordered by the Plenary Councils of Baltimore, which have the force of canon law for our country. It was also imposed by Pius X in his encyclical on Christian Education.

2.) Most of the protagonists of released time instruction of public school students agree that it is a poor substitute for Catholic education. I am not sure that our people must "choose" between parochial and high school. The states that have lagged most in school construction are not in any sense poor states.

Gradually the Archbishop had resumed his practice of assisting at consecrations and installations. On June 25 he celebrated a Mass for the Convention of the Catholic Theological Association and spoke a few words of encouragement to the theologians. He called them representatives of deductive science and urged them to be bold in resisting the "empiricists in their endeavor to find a substitute for God and the individual soul." At this time it was also announced in Rome that Cardinal Gaetano Cicognani, the brother of the Apostolic Delegate, had been appointed the final postulator of the cause of the Venerable Bishop John Neumann. The efforts of the Archbishop were gradually clearing up the causes of delay in this process.

The Archbishop's bad health in no way interfered with his planning and working for the improvement of education in the archdiocese. On July 7 he announced that three new high schools would be opened in September. On August 23, in the educational issue of the *Standard and Times,* the Archbishop published a three-column editorial on "The Post-War Progress of Catholic Schools," in which he estimated the Catholic contribution to the state through the support of its school system. The increase in the number of children in the Catholic schools in Philadelphia was a nation-wide phenomenom. The total increase in attendance in Catholic schools including colleges and seminaries from 1944–1945 to 1956–1957 was 2,067,162. Broken down, the increases were 1,885,096 for elementary and secondary schools, 261,100 for colleges, and 7,156 seminarians, or 80 percent in elementary schools, 61 percent in high schools and 71 percent for seminarians.

The question of attendance of Catholics at Catholic colleges was discussed. He admitted that there were no reliable figures, since some non-Catholics attend Catholic colleges. He found, however, by comparing the registration in Catholic colleges with the total college enrollment that 13.18 percent of the enrollment was Catholic. Based on the baptismal and total birth rates for the years from which these collegiate classes would have come, the Catholic enrollment should have been 23 percent of the total. On that basis 57 percent of the Catholic college students were in Catholic colleges.

Taking as a basis the lowest estimate at $1,000 a student, although some figure it to be at least twice that, he claimed that Catholic schools saved the taxpayers of the nation $400,565,036 a year, and in the Philadelphia area $46,234,466. He continued:

Even the lay teacher, employed increasingly since the War, brings to Catholic education a similar spirit of sacrifice. Not every lay person who aspires to the vocation is free to accept a position in the Catholic schools at a reduced stipend; there may be family obligations that make this impossible. But those who accept the invitation to sacrifice for the love of God and instruct "others unto justice" are richly rewarded in peace of mind even in this life.

The same issue contained a progress report on the growth of the school system in the archdiocese, listing among the increased or expanded facilities five colleges—including the new Cabrini College, six high schools, and fifty-three elementary schools.

Along the same line he wrote to Bishop George Leech of Harrisburg that the latter should emphasize the savings brought about by Catholic schools. He maintained that the parochial schools of the Diocese of Harrisburg had saved the State of Pennsylvania $7,620,000 last year if the figure was placed at $300 per pupil. He added:

When I talk about these matters at a school dedication, I emphasize to the audience that the saving they make is tremendous. If they had to pay taxes and their costs equivalent to those of the public schools, their bill for the Catholic schools would be nine million dollars, for they would lose the contributed services of teachers and administrators and would have to pay for a top-heavy administrative unit, in addition to adding the cost of school construction by including in the plan all sorts of extra rooms for fads and hobbies.

On Labor Day, 1957, the Archbishop celebrated Mass for the Catholic Association of Trade Unionists at St. John the Evangelist Church. In his sermon he warned the laboring men not to allow themselves to be used by others who did not have their interests at heart. He also urged them to bless their work by prayer and the frequentation of the sacraments. In its report of the sermon the *Standard and Times* said:

Alluding to the criticism which is often leveled against the Church for her alleged failure to develop lay leaders and scholars, Archbishop O'Hara said such fault-finding is often exaggerated. It overlooks the great contribution being made by the 95 percent of the laity who, he said, by their lives and good example, are spreading the Kingdom of God on Earth.

On September 21 the Archbishop was in Scranton for the opening Mass for the regional meeting of the Confraternity of Christian Doctrine, at which he gave the sermon. Taking for his text the verses from St. Matthew in which Our Lord told the Apostles that they are the light of the world, he distinguished three kinds of apostolic work: first that of the apostles, then the seventy-two disciples, and thirdly the missionary vocation given to all Christians that is intensified in this kind of meeting of the Confraternity. He quoted the words of Our Lord about this activity, of the candle that shines before men and the alms given in secret:

In the world-wide assault which the devil is directing today against the Catholic Church, the vocation of the lay Catholic to spread the kingdom of God takes on a new importance. With the clear vision of a saint, the Supreme Pontiff given us by the Holy Ghost to rule the Church at the beginning of the twentieth century, Saint Pius, made provision for the instruction of the laity, especially the children in the truths of the Catholic religion.

He then quoted the instruction of Pius X about the Confraternity:

We Catholics in the United States of America can never give adequate expression to Almighty God of our gratitude for the unique favor we enjoy in our independent system of Catholic schools. True, it was bigotry that provided the impulse which built and staffed the schools. When John Hughes became Bishop of New York he determined to put an end to an intolerable situation which he found there. . . . Looking back over the years, especially in the light of what is happening today, when state subsidies for Catholic education are withdrawn in one vast country after another, we can thank God that our spiritual ancestors of a hundred years ago were thrown on their own resources.

The Archbishop then summarized the statistics he had printed in his editorial a short time before. He then turned to the question of the current criticism of the Catholic effort:

If I depart from the lament we hear so much today, the lament that we lack a Catholic elite, it is because I believe that God knows our needs and sends us the leadership we need for the particular moment of our short time on earth. If God sends us more than scholars these days, I believe it is because we need saints more than scholars. And God is sending us saints. In his short but providential pontificate, Saint Pius X gave us daily Communion and the early Communion of children to prepare this generation against the assaults of the devil. This particular provision wrought phenomenal prodigies of grace in the souls of hundreds of thousands of young men who served in our armed forces. . . .

Philadelphia did not have the tradition of some of the eastern seaboard communities of a public school system in which many of the teachers were Catholic. But there was not only a number of these teachers; they even had their own sodality. When Miss Katherine J. Skelton of the sodality invited him to a Communion breakfast, he wrote her a friendly letter on October 24, 1957:

The news that you are planning to engage in a more active apostolate is very welcome. Activity is essential to the true spirit of the Sodality as the Holy Father has pointed out, and as we know from the beginning of the Sodality Movement. The Catholic teachers in the public schools have abundant opportunities to strengthen the faith and practice of children entrusted to their care. The exchange of suggestions among teachers will provide many avenues of approach to this problem that will not in any way intrude on legal restrictions. The Casita Maria in New York, the settlement house that has done so much to lead the way in the assimilation of Puerto Ricans into the Catholic life of the city was the direct result of the zeal of the Catholic teachers who visited the homes of children who were falling behind with their work. This was in the worst days of the depression. What the teachers found was appalling; but they did something about it.

The lay teachers in the Catholic schools have a wider field of action, and I commend them for their zeal and their spirit of sacrifice. In these days of expanding enrollments they have saved the structure of Catholic education and enabled the Bishops to overcome crippling obstacles.

On November 4 the Archbishop combined the celebration of the one hundred twenty-fifth anniversary of the founding of St. Charles Seminary with the opening of the refurbished cathedral. Since it was such a noted anniversay of the seminary, the ceremony was attended by most of the bishops of the province and by many bishops who had formerly been priests in the archdiocese. The improvement of the cathedral had centered mostly about the sanctuary, which had been lengthened 32 feet and was surrounded with an ambulatory. In the extended circular apse there were three stained-glass windows. The marble altar was surmounted by a massive baldachino supported by four massive columns of marble, and the baldachino was surmounted by two towering angels. Between the three windows were two pastel mosaics, and the windows and mosaics were separated by six massive pillars. The interior of the dome had been covered with a mosaic of brilliant colors with a representation of a huge dove. The lighting system had been improved, and a new amplyfying system installed. In the rear of the church a vestibule had been created, and nine outside doors of bronze added. A new and enlarged baptistry also had a stained glass window. Although there were some suggestions that there be windows in the side walls of the church they were not installed, leaving the church ordinarily dark—a strange reminder of the days when the lower windows were omitted because they might be broken by unfriendly non-Catholics, as had happened in the nativistic riots.

Of the Archbishop's activities during the bishops' meeting in Washington there is little evidence in his correspondence, except his signature on the annual letter of the bishops—this year on the question of censorship. However, to Father Francis Litz, C.SS.R., of Saint Peter's he wrote on November 20 after his return from the meeting:

> At the meeting of the Bishops in Washington I obtained the signatures of the four Cardinals and almost all of the Archbishops and Bishops present to a petition to the Holy Father for the beatification of Venerable John Nepomucene Neumann.

The devotion of the Archbishop to the cause of Bishop Neumann had been constant. His recognition of Bishop Neumann as an American saint while he was prefect of religion at Notre Dame had been enlarged when he crossed the footsteps of the young priest in the Diocese of Buffalo. Coming to Philadelphia the Archbishop seemed impatient with those who were not pushing the process of beatification, and this effort of getting the signatures of the bishops was a near culmination of his attempts to see his predecessor raised to the altar. There are some close to the Archbishop who think that he regarded the saintly Neumann as a model in his work for the Archdiocese, especially in his zeal for the erection of Catholic schools.

Beginning November 20 Philadelphia was the host for a Conference on Catholic Youth Work, the Diocesan Conference on Catholic Youth Work, and the National Catholic Youth Council. The Archbishop presided at the opening session, having welcomed the youth leaders to the city in a letter dated November 11. He stressed that their motto must be *sentire cum ecclesia,* and this unity with authority must be the essential of Catholic Action. He observed:

The Bishops, priests, religious men and women, and the Catholics of the Archdiocese of Philadelphia are of like mind with their guests this week. Like their guests they have been trained from their youth to place God first in all their actions. May the Holy Spirit strengthen all of you in your unity and give good fruit to your deliberations. . . .

Before going to the bishops' meeting in Washington the Archbishop had gone to New York for a meeting of the Board of American Missions on November 11. The bishops' meeting, however, kept him in Washington the next week and he felt that the trips were wearying him. He was becoming conscious of failing health. He confided to his friend Father Thomas Steiner in a letter of November 18 that he felt the travels that he had to make:

I didn't mind the wait at the airport one bit. I got my office said and then had a nap or two on the plane. That helped.

Cardinal Spellman called me up Friday night to say that I was elected to the job of assistant treasurer of the Administrative Board. I had looked forward to being off the Board this year, since my five years of membership were up. I had been on as an assistant since the beginning of the war and that meant two extra trips to Washington every year. My term as a member of the Executive Committee of the Catholic University also expired this year. The last time that happened I missed one meeting and then was brought back as consultant. I hope the thing works this time, because that required four trips to Washington every year.

Writing to Father Joseph McGrath, C.S.C., on November 27 he told him that he felt that he had to decline an invitation to the next commencement at Portland University by reasons of health. He told Father McGrath:

After keeping away from doctors most of my life, last year I caught a chain of circumstances that resulted in a rigid diet and a serious curtailment of activities. Any travel beyond three hours, whether by train or plane, gives me a setback. While my general health has improved and the diet is less strict than it was, I can't take many chances.

To Miss Mary Haverty of Atlanta he told of his regret about his illness in a letter of November 27:

It was just my luck to be taken down with flu while the Youth Directors were here and before the youths arrived. As a result of this I was bedfast and saw none of the young people who edified Philadelphia so much during the three day session. Cardinal Spellman told the youngsters that they constituted the largest crowd that he had ever witnessed receiving Holy Communion under one roof.

Acknowledging a letter of thanks from Archbishop Binz for hospitality during the youth convention on December 16, he explained his disability:

Many thanks for your kind letter. All thanks are due to us [sic] for the attention you gave to the Youth Convention in spite of the fact that you had so many cross currents to disturb you at the same time. My own physical weakness was so very embarrassing. I broke my rule never to attend dinner when I accompanied Cardinal Stritch to the luncheon on Thursday. The air conditioning went to work on me and the resulting flu kept me out of circulation for ten days.

After his return from Indianapolis he wrote to Bishop Edward Reilly, who seemed to think that he looked better:

Thanks for the favorable approval of my physical appearance. I had just come back from my quarterly checkup and the doctor had advised me to put on another ten pounds. He had reduced me to one hundred and twenty and when he saw that I carried one hundred and thirty without too much sugar in the blood he became generous.

The photographs taken of the Archbishop during the annual Archbishop's Christmas Party for dependent children in the Benjamin Franklin Hotel show him relaxed and not so thin.[8] He celebrated the midnight Mass in the redecorated cathedral and preached the sermon. In the contrast between the penitential season of advent and the light of Christmas he saw a message of contradiction prefiguring the eventual victory of the Church:

. . . New seminaries, new novitiates, new training schools for religious, are springing up all over the world to meet the demand for the Gospel. The breakthrough in communications which modern war-fare has brought about has served God's purpose by spreading a knowledge of the Gospel, so that millions yet unreached cry out, "teach us Christ!" The candidates for the religious life are more numerous than ever before, and this in a day when the world of darkness seeks by every means to corrupt children almost from the cradle.[9]

Before he left for Indianapolis for a brief vacation, he wrote a couple of messages. One was to Peter J. Grace on December 26:

While you never want to know what becomes of these gifts, I can't help telling you how I spent the last thousand of last year's contribution. It bailed out a family that was badly in debt when the mother was going to the hospital for her eighth child. Even the milk supply had been cut off because there was eighty dollars overdue on the milk bill. The family called me up to say thanks on Christmas night. (You saved another family when it was evicted after a sheriff's sale, by making a down payment on a new home.)

To his old friend in Buffalo, Bishop Burke, he also wrote that day:

This year I was back in my Cathedral for Midnight Mass. It was nice to be home for Christmas a couple of years while the Cathedral was under renovation (I got away with it only once in Buffalo). The crowd was immense and it seemed that everyone in the church received Holy Communion. Happily, this included a few Puerto Ricans—entire families.

Shortly after the Archbishop returned to Philadelphia, an important change in the charity traditions of the archdiocese was made. Because of changes in the administration of St. Vincent's Children's Hospital and Maternity Home and differences of opinions, the Daughters of Charity of Saint Vincent de Paul, who had managed the institution since 1868, withdrew, and in their place the Medical Missionaries and the Daughters of the Heart of Mary took charge. The Medical Missionaries took charge of all prenatal care and of children up to the age of one year; the Daughters of Charity assumed control of Sacred Heart Home for children. The change was announced by the Archbishop.[10]

The hurried way in which the first charities drive was conducted in 1958 probably occasioned the rise of a story that gained wide belief. This legend said that when the Archbishop was refused loans by Philadelphia bankers, he told them he could raise the desired amount in one afternoon in his own archdiocese, and in the resulting charities drive raised even more than the amount he requested. Actually the Archbishop could have borrowed in Philadelphia as much money as the Pennsylvania law allowed, and the banks were willing to lend even more in the name of George V. Mitchell of the Archbishop's office if the Archbishop wanted the money. This appeal was merely a change in the manner of raising the funds for charity. The Archbishop's office had formerly raised the charity fund by direct requisitions on the parishes. In this new way the donors could allow for income tax deductions, and appeals to the people could be made for definite charities.

The Archbishop announced the charities appeal at a clerical conference, telling the priests that the suggestion that there be such a drive had originally come from lay people:

The Catholic charities, which will be inaugurated this year, has been authorized in response to numerous requests from the Catholic laity for a medium through which they could channel their tax deductible gifts to the many works of mercy conducted under the auspices of the Archdiocese of Philadelphia.

The requests have come from laymen not only as individuals but as representatives of business, industry, labor, and other groups representing enterprises that have Catholic customers, Catholic employees and Catholic stockholders.

He mentioned two particularly urgent needs for the drive: the replacement of overaged buildings used for charitable purposes and the need of additional funds to meet the costs of operation in these charitable institutions. He also promised that employees would not be solicited in their place of employment and that no assessment would be permitted by labor unions.

Although the Archbishop performed many works of charity both within and outside the archdiocese, he had a special interest in retarded children. He had shown this interest during his episcopate in Buffalo, but he had special opportunities to carry out this work of mercy after coming to Philadelphia. The erection of and improvement to the School of Our Lady of Confidence and the other institutions for the blind, the deaf, and those otherwise handicapped were a special tribute to his zeal. When Mother M. Patricia withdrew from St. Mary's Institute for the blind, he expressed his regret in a letter of January 21, 1958, in which he also told of his first efforts for the blind.

As you know one of my first visits when I came to Philadelphia was to Saint Mary's Institute. Lacking any knowledge of the other needs of the Archdiocese, I wanted to make sure that we were doing what we could for the blind. While I was tremendously edified by the work of the Sisters, I was sorely disappointed with the physical plant and the small attendance. It was my hope that we could proceed without delay to remedy the situation, I even proposed to the Consultors that a home be given to the blind, or a new establishment be built on the grounds here. The proposal was promptly vetoed by unanimous vote of the consultors.

On January 23 Archbishop O'Hara gave the sermon at the installation of Bishop Howard Carroll as the Bishop of Altoona-Johnstown. For his sermon he took his text from St. Paul's First Epistle to the Corinthians and said that Saint Paul emphasized here his power, summing up his mission as an apostle in the words "The Kingdom of God is not in speech but in power." This power is threefold—to rule, to teach, and to sanctify, and it is this threefold power that the Church communicates to the new bishop at his consecration. He said that the whole history of the

Church is indicated in that prayer, which means that many nations have flourished in their youth but have declined in their old age, but the Church has always been there to use her power to bind up wounds and to keep alive the truth. He quoted the encyclical of Pope Pius XI on the priesthood in which he compared the priesthood to a lighthouse warning by its shining light of the way of truth. It is needed today. "Even now, we know all too little about what has been done to undermine the very foundations of our own beloved country, for every attempt to seek out the truth has met savage opposition." He said that Our Lord had foretold these days of trial. "In this our day, which someone has called a century of magpies and oral thinkers, more than two hundred of the successors of the Apostles have been silenced whether by death or imprisonment or exile or cruel torture in slave labor camps." He then spoke of Bishop Carroll's twenty years in the N.C.W.C. "The problems he met daily might be local, national, or international, whatever they were he gave to them his zeal, his charity, and his loyal devotion."

The Archbishop had shared with the late Archbishop Noll a desire to get reliable statistics on the religious affiliations of the American people. In March, 1957, the Archbishop had approached Robert Burgess, the director of the Bureau of the Census, about including in the questionnaire for the decennial census one question on religious affiliation. Although there was some willingness on the part of the Bureau of the Census, there was opposition elsewhere. Actually a trial census had been made by the bureau. On February 14 in another of his front-page editorials in the *Standard and Times* entitled "How Many Catholics?" the Archbishop examined the results of that trial census. The census sample made by the bureau of 30,000 families drawn from 330 localities estimated the Catholic population over fourteen years of age as 30,669,000. To this the N.C.W.C. had added an estimate of those below fourteen years of age to total the Catholic population at 43,635,000. Yet, the Archbishop said, the *Catholic Directory* estimated the Catholic population for 1956 as 36,386,350. The Archbishop admitted that these were not necessarily reliable estimates. One factor he noted was the lower percentage of Catholic people in the older ages. The median age of Catholics was 28.7, for Protestants 40.8 for nonbelievers 42.0 and for Jews 44.5. There is also the factor of mobility, and the fact that one new house might involve as many as seven people moving. The Archbishop hinted at several factors that affect these statistics. One was the percentage of Catholics among nonwhites, and second was the implication that there is a great loss of Catholics based on death statistics. Comparing birth and death statistics the number of Catholic deaths is theoretically 1,570,860 less than they should be. He rejected this conclusion because it does not show the number of deathbed conversions or repentances, which he claimed are very large, particularly since so many die in hospitals where they have the attendance of Catholic chaplains. He claimed that ninety-six percent of the Catholics would receive Christian burial.

During the war as the bishop in the Military Ordinariate the Archbishop had predicted that there would be a glorious period for American Catholicism when the many soldiers and sailors who had been so faithful to the sacraments in service returned to civilian life. It is interesting to note that in his Lenten pastoral of 1958 the Archbishop seemed to give his evaluation of the mixed results of that wartime fervor.

The riotous living, the social madness, the contempt for authority, the stupidities pursued in the name of recreation—the marks of barbarism that have characterized the prosperous years since the war have not left our Catholic people unscarred. On the other hand, thanks be to God, we have been blessed with a more intense Catholic family life than ever before; we have been able to feed the hungry, clothe the naked and harbor the harborless all over the world as never before; since the War our Catholic school attendance and our vocations to the priesthood and the religious life have almost doubled—so have the attendance at Mass and the reception of the Sacraments.

The plans for the first charity drive were gradually taking shape. The Archbishop had announced on February 14 that Father John Sefton was to be the executive director of the Charities Appeal under Monsignor Furey as director. He also appointed the members of the Executive Board—the deans of the archdiocese—and the directors of the appeal for each district. On February 26 the Archbishop blessed the headquarters of the Charities Appeal at 1823 Race Street near the cathedral rectory. Monsignor Furey announced that the solicitation among businesses would begin on March 31 and continue until May 2. There were fifty-three charitable institutions to be aided by the appeal, twenty-three of which were institutions for children.

The Archbishop had never flagged in his interest in the Puerto Ricans. He had continued his interest in the New York activities and had had a special care for the Puerto Ricans in Philadelphia. To Father Frederick Hickey, who directed the Casa Del Carmen, he wrote on February 26:

When we have a few graduates of Catholic high schools I want you to keep your eye alert for one or another who may be able to use a Catholic college education. A few good demonstrations may electrify the whole colony.

Also the Archbishop had not lost any of his interest in certain economic problems. On February 28 he wrote to Hamilton A. Long, author of *Usurpers, Foes of Free Man:*

If it is agreeable to you I will be glad to have the publisher send me four hundred copies which I can mail to our pastors and Catholic high school principals. In this way the publishers can save on the postage to individual recipients.

In the February 28 *Standard and Times* the Archbishop published another editorial against federal aid entitled "U. S. Education Observed from the Top Down." He began with a note that since the United States had launched its own satellite, the criticism of American education that followed the launching of the Russian sputnik had quieted down. He noted, however, that classes in "life adjustment and coeducation home economics" had received a large share of the castigation of American schooling. Now that the Office of Education had published the list of the subjects for which doctors' degrees had been conferred in the past year, he suggested that they see in what field the degrees are given. The vast majority were in science, numbering about forty percent of the total. But of the others he was quite critical. Of the one-eighth given in cultural subjects, since social science is included, he would rather see how much of real history has been included. Of the 16.7 percent given in education there is some question, since 100 degrees were given in physical education and 141 in industrial arts. Less than one percent were given in philosophy, but the Archbishop was not surprised at this since philosophy had long since lost out in public education. The total conclusion suggested that before giving federal aid to public education some attention should be given to the kind of education that is to be supported.

To Bishop McManaman, the auxiliary of Erie, he wrote on March 14 to give an unorthodox solution to problems of religious personnel:

When six communities rejected the high school at Dunkirk I opened the *Catholic Directory* at random and my eye fell on the Fathers of St. Edmund. The Superior General had done graduate work at Notre Dame and I knew him well. When I telephoned him he said: 'This is an answer to prayer. We have just finished a novena seeking such an offer. . . .'

The Archbishop had resented a speech made by Father John Cavanaugh in which he scolded Catholics for not producing great scientists. To Archbishop Brady, who had taken exception to the speech, he had written a note of congratulations, and on March 24 he also sent a letter to Brother Augustine Philip, C.S.C., who had sent him a copy of a speech made by Father Robert Gannon, S.J.

I am grateful for your kindness in sending me the excellent address of Father Gannon. His infusion of common sense has been the best by-product of the silly and unwarranted criticism of Catholic scholarship.

The Archbishop seemed to be a friend in need to Catholic conservatives. When William Buckley, Jr., wrote him on April 5 about a rumor that Father Ginder of *Our Sunday Visitor* was to be suppressed, he answered:

If such a move is contemplated it is not likely that I will be consulted on it. However, I shall keep my ear to the ground.

By a judicious use of reprints I am trying to make you and your cause better known. Until that friendly basis is established, a plea for Father Ginder might do him more harm than good.

The cause in question would seem to have been the cause of conservatism in general.

Tuesday, April 8, marked the opening of the annual convention of the Catholic Educational Association meeting that year in Philadelphia. At the opening Mass in Convention Hall the Archbishop presided and gave the sermon. He took his text from St. John's Gospel, the promise by Our Lord of the coming of the Holy Ghost. On this the one hundred fiftieth anniversary of the archdiocese and centenary of Lourdes, he asked the faithful to keep in mind the rule of Bishop Neumann, that the school must come first in every parish. The Archbishop said that these were troublous times, with education under severe criticism. Catholic education has fared better under the criticism because it has remained faithful to a program of basic education. He warned them not to blush at the praise because it was their obligation to give light in the darkness: "Woe be to us if the light that is in us be darkness, if we turn away from God-given principles of education to follow the twists and turns of pragmatism in its search for substitutes for God and the Soul." He quoted the Holy Father on their need to be instructed before they teach, but he insisted that they must also have religious training in the novitiates and seminaries. The lay Catholic teacher must also receive training similar to that of the novitiate or seminary. He urged them to know the history of Catholic education so that they could avoid some of the past mistakes when the wrong type of training had been used. Stressed was the proper kind of counseling because a bill had just been introduced to provide counseling by law, and this he regarded as undesirable. No chance was seen that Catholic schools would be asked to lead the way back to a sound system of education. He quoted a statement that only public education was American education and insisted that Catholics must be on their guard to preserve their rights as announced in the Oregon School decision by the Supreme Court. "Our own duty is clear to us, and we pray for the faith, the hope, and the charity to continue our work. . . ."[11]

Of the events that spring which most affected the activities of the Church in Philadelphia the most important for the archdiocese was the first Charities Appeal. In recognition of its importance the Mayor, Richardson Dilworth, published a special plea and made the day for the rally, April 9, the Archbishop's Charities Appeal Day. The gathering in Convention Hall on that evening included about 5,000 persons and was devoted to speeches and entertainment. Prominent persons in the entertainment world, headed by Hildegarde, appeared. The Archbishop spoke briefly, expressing his gratitude for the many things the people had done for him since he came to Philadelphia six years before, and he gave them his blessing. The Archbishop's Committee on the Laity announced that they had already raised over $96,000.

On May 2 in the *Standard and Times* the Committee of the Laity announced that they had raised $116,000 and that the official collection in the parishes would take place on Sunday, May 4. The Archbishop sent out a brief letter to the workers, saying that what they were doing for the needy, in the words of Our Lord, they were doing for Christ. He urged them to make the effort and invoked on them a special blessing.

The work of the Appeal intensified as the final day approached, and on the final day the Archbishop was present in the headquarters that evening when the tabulations were being made. When the reports gave assurance about 11:00 P.M. that the drive had reached its objective, the Archbishop led a group of workers to the statue of Our Lady of Victory, to whom the drive had been dedicated, for a brief prayer of thanksgiving. The Archbishop's Committee of the Laity under John Connolly reported a total in excess of $250,000. By May 16 it was estimated that the drive had already netted $50,000 beyond the two million dollars toward which they had aimed.

The Archbishop took notice of an Associated Press dispatch

from Harrisburg on the question of college dropouts and the
necessity of guidance. This had been a touchy subject for him
since Notre Dame days. The gist of the dispatch, based on a report
of the Pennsylvania education commission, was that there was a
"dire need of more guidance counselors in Pennsylvania private
and parochial high schools." The Archbishop noted in a memorandum he sent to the Catholic representatives at the state capitol
in Harrisburg:

The implication seems to be that in some way employment of a
recommended maximum of guidance counselors would cut down or
possibly eliminate the entrance to colleges of students who lack the
necessary intellectual ability ever to graduate.

We suggest that this conclusion is not scientific, that it lies entirely
within the field of theory, and that it should not be acted upon without
further study.

In his study the Archbishop drew on Bulletin 1958, No. 1 of
the U.S. Department of Health, Education, and Welfare, "Retention and Withdrawal of College Students." The most important
conclusion drawn from interviews with students was that the students had little use for "guidance counselors" and high respect for
religious opportunities. The Archbishop noted that the guidance
counselor was supposed to keep "confidential files" and that students could hardly resist the temptation to "goof" the files and
render the guidance a rating of zero. He insisted: "It is the College Board and Admissions not the guidance counsel of either
high school or college that admits students or turns them away."
Sending a copy of the memorandum to Father Martin N. L. Löhmuller in Harrisburg on April 20, he noted:

Of the greatest importance is the assumption that the counselors
are in some way responsible for the admission to college of high
school graduates who are not college material. This is a completely
false assumption. As I point out in the memorandum, the Board of
Admissions at the college itself bears the sole responsibility for admission. If a particular institution insists on accepting every applicant
who has a high school diploma, the Board is to blame.

So long as the Archbishop retained any portion of his good
health, he retained also his sense of humor. When Professor William Ball of Villanova wrote him about his debate with Sal
Robken and Leo Peiffer about Christmas displays on public
grounds, he answered Professor Ball on May 26:

While I like to give every one credit for good faith, I find it a bit
difficult at times. Often indirect action is more effective than direct. In

a recent interview with three dry goods merchants I mentioned that the attack on the Nativity scene might easily result in the end of Christmas business since not many people would be moved to present gifts in honor of a yule log.

The Archbishop never welcomed publicity on racial problems in the Archdiocese. He considered publicity on these sorrowful matters a trick of the communists to keep the less fortunate unhappy. Consequently when Father Leo R. Ward, C.S.C., of the University of Notre Dame wrote for permission to observe the racial problem in Philadelphia, he had only one answer in his letter of May 19:

> While I would be glad to have you as a visitor at any time, I would not want any publicity on any of the work here. Not many people want their parishes marked out as problems, and the colored people more than any other seem particularly sensitive on this point.
>
> So far as I can observe, color lines are for politicians not for priests. The Communists love to keep raw the wounds of discrimination. Here we do not discriminate and we do not even mention the word. I don't like to see it discussed in Catholic newspapers and magazines, because it grates on the nerves of the honest colored people. The honest ones don't have to be told who their friends are. They make their own observations and reach their own conclusions.

The Archbishop was a generous host, and Philadelphia was a convenient city for meetings, but it was quite clear that the Archbishop did not disagree with the decision of the consultors to check the number of conventions of which they had to take care. Writing to Father Gabriel Stapleton, S.D.S., about the National Theological Convention on May 21, he said:

> The Consultors have declared a moratorium on conventions for the time being, simply because we are having too many of them. We have a smaller number of priests than some of the dioceses of comparative size, and almost one fourth of our priests are teaching full time. We also have the largest number of parishes in the country. Three additional requests for conventions were considered at the May meetings and none of them approved. We need some time to catch our breath.

While the Archbishop was so very active in his own educational problems, he did not modify his ideas on the general policy that Catholics should hold towards federal aid to Catholic schools. He was quite disturbed when he noticed a change in the Education Department of the N.C.W.C. from an attitude of opposition to all federal aid to one of willingness to accept the federal aid that was offered to Catholics as well as to other schools. To his friend

Cardinal McIntyre he wrote on June 11: "The more I see of the
Education bill, the more I am convinced that its purpose is purely
political. They have tried hard to get us to take the blame for kill-
ing the bill. . . ." He was also interested in the cases coming before
the Supreme Court on the problem of the separation of Church
and State. When Porter Chandler wrote him in reference to the
suit in Abdington Township about reading the Scriptures in the
schools, he wrote to him on June 16:

Our relations with the vast majority of our non-Catholic fellow-
citizens are excellent. We want to keep them that way. If on occasion
we have to vindicate our rights, we try to do it quietly, without benefit of the press. The professional bigot thus has a difficult time in his
efforts to stir up dissension. This is hard on the fellow travelers who
try to carry out the Moscow mandate to "set brother against brother."

The Archbishop never ceased to think about his first personal
work as prefect of religion. As prefect of religion, as delegatus
castrensis, and later at Buffalo and Philadelphia the Archbishop
had been a strong advocate of the practice of frequent and daily
Communion and was always sensitive to the criticism of his practice of giving Communion outside of Mass when the one seeking
the sacrament was properly disposed. A seminarian, William A.
Toohey, C.S.C., had asked him for an explanation of his position.
He answered on June 30:

My dear Mr. Toohey:
Since I am not a speculative moral theologian I do not presume to
reply to the theoretical questions you propose in your letter.
Since my practice as Prefect of Religion at Notre Dame was sometimes at variance with the conclusions of speculative moralists, you
may reasonably conclude that I satisfied my conscience before acting.
The point at issue in your inquiry is the distribution of Holy Communion outside of Mass—for a reasonable cause.
If you have no objection, I will avoid the term "Communion of
Devotion." To me the term smacks of Jansenism in many of its conno-
tations not the least of which is the implied exclusion of the effects
"ex opere operato."
To me, the man who came fasting to receive Holy Communion was
seeking an increase of sanctifying grace. I can suggest a few of the
possibilities for this desire:
  (1) to overcome habits of sin;
  (2) to gain the grace of perseverance—missing a day might set him
      back;
  (3) to continue a novena for a very urgent intention;
  (4) to employ [implore] help in determining his vocation;
  (5) to bring about the reunion of his father and mother;

(6) to restore a friend to the state of grace;

(7) to obtain the grace to be a fearless Catholic.

You can take over from there and draw up a list of seven hundred reasons. The priest does not have to ask the recipient what the reason is. Such a question might bring the frank answer that the recipient felt that he could not keep out of mortal sin without daily Communion. If the priest received that answer he would be pretty slow about putting the question the next time.

Long before the broadening of the law on the Eucharistic fast, I gave Holy Communion to students at four, five, six and even seven o'clock at night, to students who were fasting from midnight—on the train returning to Notre Dame. I recall one instance that involved the refusal of a priest to hear confessions on Sunday morning. This boy fulfilled his Sunday Mass obligation at home then took the train to Notre Dame.

On one occasion an alumnus told me that he got a bit tough with an assistant at his own parish. He came to the sacristy asking for Holy Communion when the priest was unvesting after Mass. The priest told him to come on time if he wanted to go to Holy Communion. He replied: "If I go out of here and am killed by a truck crossing the street five minutes from now you'll feel like heck won't you?"[12]

Nevertheless the Archbishop did not approve of judging a Catholic layman by the one standard of attendance at frequent and daily Communion. Above all he insisted in a letter to John J. O'Connor III on July 7 that attendance at Communion must not be used as a criterion by which to judge a person's knowledge of his faith. He added:

Many low income individuals and their families suffer not from lack of faith as much a lack of management ability. Out of such low income families we have had some brilliant leaders of the Church and we have many authentic saints who will never be canonized. However, there will be many individuals who will drift with the tide and lose many battles with temptations.

The correspondence of the Archbishop during the summer months indicated that he had not yielded on any of his favorite themes. To Miss Jane Raffert, who had asked permission to read prohibited books on a list supplied for class, he gave a reply on July 7 that illustrates his objection to such readings:

Since some of the titles on the list you propose are forbidden, because of obscenity, and since obscene reading is forbidden by the natural law, not even the Pope can grant you a dispensation.

So far as Schopenhauer is concerned, I cannot in conscience grant you permission without knowing what priest you will have to guide your reading to make sure it holds no hidden danger for you. I don't know why anyone finds it attractive, but the world seems to crave pessimism these days.

The implication that you may be guilty of "anti-intellectualism" suggests to me you may have forgotten that the proper object of the intellect is truth. The truths revealed by God and taught by the Church are part of the deposit of faith which gives the Catholic a freedom of inquiry that the non-Catholic lacks. Lacking the great body of revealed truth, he can waste a tremendous amount of time looking for truth in places where we know it cannot be found. The present defense mechanism he has invented for himself is relativity and certainly no Catholic should fall for that.

Neither had the Archbishop yielded on the question of accepting federal aid for Catholic schools. Even when his friend, Archbishop-Bishop Gannon urged the acceptance of the aid, he could reject the suggestion with good humor:

God has blessed you with an optimistic spirit and this has helped you to do a tremendous amount of good in the world. I try to be optimistic on the strength of Our Lord's promise that the gates of hell shall not prevail against the Catholic Church, but I still remember the days of the A.P.A., and I have watched one country after another take away the subsidies given to Catholic education and social work, always in the hope of destroying our activities.

I am at one with you in preferring the Negro to the Mason in matters of cooperation. The real difficulty I see in that is that the leadership which commands a great deal of Negro voting strength at the present time is definitely anti-religious. They tell me that even in radio broadcasts from colored churches in Philadelphia there is now a definite attack on the Blessed Trinity and on the Sacrament of Baptism. While this seems incredible, in view of the traditional enthusiasm of the Negro for religion, it may open the door for many of them to enter the Catholic Church. Previously the *privilegium fidei* was closed to them by virtue of their baptism.

When he sensed that a bill was about to be enacted by Congress to provide college and university scholarships for gifted high-school graduates, especially in mathematics and the physical sciences, he published another editorial in the August 1 *Standard and Times,* "Federal Scholarships? Guidance? Loans?" He expressed his fear that the federal lawmakers would pass the bill because they were ignorant of the real situation. The problem was discussed under three heads. In regard to scholarships he told of a study undertaken by the superintendent of public instruction in Indiana. The investigation found that out of 2,000 seniors 703 took tests for the scholarships. Of the 53 eligible 37 already had scholarships, leaving only 17 scholarships fully needed. On the question of guidance he repeated what he had said in his essay on dropouts: Bulletin No. 1 of the United States Office of Education entitled "Retention and Withdrawal of Students" had shown that guidance was very little respected among students in the 147 institutions investigated. On the question of loans he suggested that Congress give loans only on a matching basis with the states and that for eligibility the students be limited by registration in an institution with certain qualifications.

One day a friend of the Archbishop along with a confrere of Holy Cross called and were invited to have lunch. During the meal his secretary, Monsignor McGlinn, pushed the conversation, making the guests manifest various opinions and prejudices to the enjoyment of the Archbishop. The conversation was sprightly, although the Archbishop ate little. After the luncheon the Archbishop delayed and probably went to his room to take some medicine, but he returned and led an interesting conversation about the religious and sociological facts of the archdiocese. As usual the Archbishop quoted many statistics without showing any document. As the guests were leaving, the Holy Cross priest congratulated the Archbishop on looking so well, meaning that he had his sparkle. The Archbishop beamed, as if this was the most welcome news he could have heard. As a matter of fact the priest thought the Archbishop had come to look small and thin, very much like his mother in the picture taken with him just after his consecration as bishop, and as he left the archiepiscopal residence he said he did not think he, the Archbishop, would ever live to be a Cardinal.

Certainly the Archbishop himself was not thinking about becoming a Cardinal. He was as devoted as ever to the problems of his archdiocese. His figure had become a little more bent and his thin frame cast a smaller shadow, but his spiritual energy seemed as great as ever. His ideas were remarkably the same. Thus, when William Kelley, a prominent banker and lay leader, asked about a closer participation in the work of the National Conference of Christians and Jews he explained to him why priests in the archdiocese could not participate:

I am very sorry to disappoint you, but in the Archdiocese of Philadelphia (and in most other Dioceses throughout the country), participation of Catholics in the National Conference of Christians and Jews is limited to lay people.

Years ago I explained to Dr. Clinchey, the Founder of the Conference, why this is so. In the Catholic Church the Sacrament of Holy Orders creates an essential difference between the priest and the lay-

man. Outside the Catholic Church this Sacrament is almost universally repudiated, and no essential difference between clergyman and
layman is recognized.

Also to Mrs. Anna Brackenridge, who sent him a letter making
odious comparisons between the staffs of Catholic and public
schools, he resorted to his traditional call for sacrifice to make up
for the deficiencies of Catholic institutions, but added a few statistics on the Catholic effort:

Eight years ago we had a few hundred lay teachers in our schools;
now we have eighteen thousand. We cannot make a Sister overnight.
While the number of vocations is increasing very rapidly, we still have
to wait a few years before we can have the service of girls who are
entering our convents.

The sacrifice is heroic. God is blessing us with a great number of
girls who are willing to make heroic sacrifices.

Relatively speaking, the sacrifices of the parents who send their
children to Catholic schools are very small. You mention the public
school in your vicinity has a limit of thirty to a class in the first grade.
This would require three and one third teachers for the one hundred
pupils you say are in the Catholic first grade in one room. To pay the
salaries of three and one third teachers in the public schools, an
amount in the vicinity of $13,333.00 would be required. Compare that
with the small stipend given to the community for the living expenses
of the Sisters teaching in the first grade and you will understand what
I mean. Your tax bill would be out of this world if the Catholic school
in your parish were closed.

On October 3 he sent a confidential letter to Bishop Dwyer of
Reno, who published a syndicated column in western Catholic
papers, about the increase in the Catholic birth rate since the war.
He insisted that he did not publish these figures because he was
afraid they might be misused by the sociologists who were down-
grading the future of Catholicism in the United States. He maintained that the Catholic baptismal rate compared to the total
birth rate had increased from 24.2 percent in 1946 to 43.6 percent in 1956. Writing again to Bishop Dwyer on October 15, he
offered the Bishop some explanations for the neglect of religion
by some Catholics:

1) The low rent housing project which gathers in the people who can't
   manage either their lives or their money. Invalid marriages abound
   in these places.
2) The neighborhood where immigrants, in sort of self contained enclaves, follow the customs of the old country including the custom
   of missing Mass on Sunday, and sending their children to the public

schools. (In these neighborhoods there is usually much improvement in the second generation and a splendid outlook for the third generation.)

3) "Society" neighborhoods, where Catholics sometimes suppress their religion or their religious practices, while they send their children to dangerous schools.

4) The areas where Catholics are few and far between.

On October 9 Pope Pius XII died at the summer residence at Castel Gandolfo. The Archbishop published a letter in praise of the dead Pontiff, in which he noted that despite the number of people who came to see him during World War II or afterwards the Pontiff never seemed to spare himself but tried to attend to all. The Archbishop seemed to have a deep affection for Pope Pius XII. He wrote: "The phenomenal range of his personal interests staggered the imagination of men of science." Giving a brief sketch of his life, the Archbishop noted that many already called him a saint and that he would be honored even by his enemies.[13]

When the new Pope, John XXIII, was elected, the Archbishop sent his congratulations to Rome and received in return a message of gratitude from the new Pontiff. Since the date set for the coronation was November 4, the Archbishop suggested that that date be observed by special Masses in the parishes of the archdiocese. He decided, also, to combine the Mass for the Pope with the annual Mass for the success of the seminary, since the date of the coronation was also the feast of Saint Charles Borromeo, the patron of the seminary. In his letter of October 22 the Archbishop announced the annual collection for the seminary and said that the Mass for the feast would be offered in thanksgiving for the blessings of the archdiocese, which were many. He also reminded the priests that this seminary collection had in recent years been used to take care of the deficits in the building of the new high schools.

To his friend, Father Thomas Steiner, who had asked about his health, he wrote an assuring message on November 5:

There was nothing to worry about, but I am grateful for your solicitude. The doctor asked me to set aside a week sometime in the fall when he could have a check on the tests he made two years ago. In his final report he said I had made progress in the most lines and had shown no deterioration in any respect. This was all to the good. He told me to continue the low salt and low fat diet. I am accustomed to this and it is in no sense a hardship.

Then he added a note about recent happenings in Philadelphia:

The last weekend gave me a strenuous Saturday. The Apostolic Delegate arrived from Detroit at six in the morning and departed at six in the evening. Most of the time we gave to the erection of the Metropolitan Province in the Byzantine Rite. We left the house at nine thirty in the morning and returned at five. However, it was an inspiring event. They used Convention Hall for the Installation of the New Metropolitan, and they had twelve thousand people present. There were hundreds of buses from all over the country.

The Saturday was November 1. Apparently the Archbishop was just a witness to the ceremony. The next week the Archbishop attended the annual meeting of the bishops in Washington, where he heard from Cardinals Spellman and McIntyre of the incidents of the papal election.

On Sunday, November 16, he presided at the centenary celebration of St. Lawrence Parish in North Catasauqua. That evening the message was received in Philadelphia that he had been named a cardinal. He was reading in his study Sunday evening about seven o'clock when he had a phone call from Chicago. A voice with a strong Italian accent, that of the Apostolic Delegate, told him that he was being named a cardinal and that the announcement would be made in Rome at eight the next morning.

The Cardinalate

THERE IS NO INDICATION THAT THE ARCH-
bishop knew before the telephone call from the Apostolic Delegate that he was being elevated to the College of Cardinals. There
is only a slight basis for the story that Cardinal Spellman had told
Monsignor McGlinn that the Archbishop would be named but
that the fact must be kept from the Archbishop lest he take steps
to prevent the nomination. At best, when Monsignor McGlinn
bade goodbye to Cardinals Spellman and McIntyre at the Rome
airport after the coronation of Pope John XXIII, Cardinal Spellman said smilingly he would convey the Monsignor's message to
"Cardinal O'Hara," but he made no positive statement of an
impending nomination. Although the Archbishop seemed to be
making progress in the restoration of his health, he had talked
with the superior general of the Congregation of Holy Cross,
Father Christopher O'Toole, C.S.C., about his desire to retire to
Notre Dame in case Rome released him from his office. As he was
to repeat several times in the next few weeks after his appointment
as cardinal, he had never desired episcopal or archiepiscopal honors and certainly not the cardinalate. His secretary, Monsignor
Joseph McGlinn, was in Rome when the news came, but he said
later that the nomination was a serious blow to the Archbishop
and that in the excitement or depression that followed the Cardinal-elect lost about ten pounds of weight that he could not afford
to lose.

When the Archbishop had finished his Mass on Monday morn-

459

ing, November 17, he consented to see reporters.[1] As a matter of
fact, he asked them why they had not come to the Mass. He told
them that the news "made me numb and I'm still numb. I just
can't get over it." Asked about his health, he said: "I feel fine,
only the doctor is trying to make a mummy out of me. He has me
holding my weight down." Asked about his age he said he was 70,
which placed him in the Holy Father's bracket. The Holy Father
was 77. To another reporter who asked if his family had expected
him to be made a cardinal, he said that they did not because they
were sensible people.

To the Holy Father he sent his formal thanks:

Profoundly moved by the condescension of Your Holiness I kneel to
offer humble thanks for the extraordinary recognition Your Holiness
has given the sound Catholic life of the good people of the Archdiocese
of Philadelphia. I dare not give thought to my own unworthiness.
Taking heart from the courage of Your Holiness in accepting God's
Holy Will I beg our Blessed Lady to obtain from God the graces I
need for the intensified pastoral work that will now be mine. As one
of the Bishops deeply moved by the pastoral message of your Holiness
to our meeting last week in Washington, I pledge anew my sentiments
of loyalty and devotion and humbly beg the Apostolic Benediction.[2]

The Governor of Pennsylvania sent a message of congratulations
on November 18, saying: "Your great record of distinguished
service to the Commonwealth of Pennsylvania and to your Church
has richly fitted you for the new responsibilities you will assume."[3]
The editor of the *Empire Star,* a Negro paper published in Buffalo, on November 22 commented about the Cardinal-elect:

In our opinion, one of the greatest acts of his administration of the
Buffalo Diocese was the edict abolishing separation of races in all
churches of the diocese. It came as a shock to many people, and there
were some objections but he had the courage of his convictions and
the determination to follow the course of right.

On December 2 he wrote to Bishop Mussio of Steubenville:

If I didn't know you so well I would lay your enthusiasm to that old
Notre Dame bigotry which refuses to allow an inch when Notre Dame
is compared to any other institution in the world.
Thanks for your wonderful pep talk and keep up the prayers. I
need them now more than ever, and I place special value on Notre
Dame prayers.[4]

Monsignor McGlinn was in Rome and remained there to make
the arrangements for the Cardinal-elect. To him the Cardinal
sent several bits of information and instructions. One letter,

December 3, dealt with the trouble he feared he would have with his feet.

Your friend, Doctor Hurd, has fixed me up with new shoes which are more comfortable than the old ones. I will do my best to last it out. The longest walk in the world is the one up the aisle of Saint Peter's to reach the throne. I don't want to have to ask for a chair to sit down in the process. I shall count on the Holy Ghost to take care of me.

To his friend Father Steiner, who had declined an invitation to go to the ceremony in Rome, he wrote on December 4:

In declining the invitation to go to Rome I believe you acted wisely and I feel better about it because it gives me assurance that you are taking proper care of yourself.

As much as possible the Cardinal-elect continued the regular services of the archdiocese. On Thanksgiving Day he presided at the Miraculous Medal celebration at the Church of the Immaculate Conception in Germantown, and on Sunday, November 30, he presided at the dedication of the Convent of the Sisters of Christian Charity at Reading. He was in constant touch with his family, who were intent on their preparations to go to Rome with him. He had also to decide what members of the clergy would accompany him. An agreement was made with Cardinal-elect Cushing that they would travel together, leaving from the Boston airport for the overseas journey. The family planned to travel by train to Boston and join there in the air entourage. The Cardinal-elect's departure was set for Tuesday, December 9.

The first formal ceremonies for the Cardinal-elect on December 9 began with the blessing of a new 9,500-foot jet runway at the Philadelphia airport. Then his party took off for Boston, where they were greeted by Cardinal Spellman, who was in that city for special services. That evening a formal reception had been arranged for the Cardinals-elect Cushing, Cicognani, and O'Hara, but Cardinal O'Hara took dinner with his family, who had arrived in Boston. The next day the Cardinals-elect Cushing, Cicognani, and O'Hara with their close friends took off from Boston in bitterly cold weather for the twelve-hour trip to Rome. In Rome they were greeted by Archbishop Martin O'Connor, the rector of the North American College and Cardinal Gaetano Cicognani, the brother of the Apostolic Delegate. The Cardinals-elect O'Hara and Cicognani went to the Holy Cross Generalate just outside of Rome for the evening. As the family memoirs note, Archbishop O'Hara was not well and did not participate much in the festivities. On Saturday, December 13, the superior general gave a public reception in the afternoon at Holy Cross College for the two cardinals in residence there, to which superiors and dignitaries came to meet them. Cardinal-elect O'Hara received his guests seated. On December 14 the Cardinal-elect observed the anniversary of his mother's death by a Mass at which the members of his family and the Notre Dame group in Rome attended in the chapel of Holy Cross College.

On Monday, December 15, took place the secret consistory at which those nominated by the Pope were made cardinals. Cardinals O'Hara, Cushing, and Cicognani awaited their notifications of their election at the North American College with their friends and relatives. When the new cardinals received their letters telling them of their election, Cardinal Cicognani, as the senior of the three, spoke their gratitude to the Holy Father. On Wednesday morning, the seventeenth, Cardinals O'Hara and Cushing with their families and friends had a special audience with Pope John. That afternoon there was a semipublic consistory at which the new cardinals received from the Pope their red mozzettas and birettas.

On December 18 there was a public consistory before the full papal court at which the new cardinals made their obeisance. An incident occurred as Cardinal O'Hara started his walk to the papal throne. As he related to alumnus Joseph Tierney: "One of the reporters caught a chance remark as we were moving in procession from a side chapel in St. Peter's to the altar of the throne to greet the Holy Father. From one of the bystanders I caught a greeting that didn't sound right to me. Looking over a few heads I spotted the culprit with his Notre Dame grin and said 'Father O'Hara to you.' That's the only way I ever wanted it and I hope that at least all Notre Dame men will remember that." At the presentation to the Pope each new cardinal made three genuflections as he approached the throne. Cardinal O'Hara was fourteenth in line. Then each received the galero, or broad-brimmed red hat, from the Pope. After this they attended a secret consistory in which they made their promises and received their appointments to their cardinalatial churches.

When the time came for the papal messengers to deliver the large red hats, Cardinals Cicognani and O'Hara and their friends waited in the recreation and reception room of Holy Cross College. As they received the hat, each gave a brief speech to express his gratitude and his feelings on the occasion. The voice of Cardinal O'Hara was clear, and he spoke with deep emotion, looking more ascetical than regal in his new red vestments. He stated simply what those close to him already knew: that the only purple he had ever desired was that purple band that he had worn as the confessor to the students of Notre Dame.

There was one other ceremony for the new Cardinal, the taking possession of his titular Church of Saints Andrea and Gregorio on the afternoon of December 19. The church on Celian Hill not far from the Coliseum, called San Gregorio al Celio, had been the church of Cardinal Griffin and the site from which St. Augustine of Canterbury had set out for England. San Gregorio is a large basilica. It was decorated in a festive manner for the cardinalatial ceremony. A cardinal red carpet stretched from the bottom of the stair up to the church level, then through the outer courtyard to the church facade. Within the church the cardinal's throne on the Gospel side of the sanctuary was resplendent in its red velvet with gold border. Long, wide red pendants with gold border hung from the high pillars. At the reception Cardinal O'Hara spoke first in Spanish to the Camaldolese Benedictines who had charge of the Church and then in English to the congregation. He spoke of Pope Pius XII and of his work and then referred to St. Augustine and the good that came of his missionary work. Leaving San Gregorio, the O'Hara motorcade, under the direction of alumnus Vincent McAloon, stopped for a brief visit at Santa Susanna, where Cardinal Cushing was accepting that church as his titular.

On the next day the Cardinal's party left Rome for the return trip. The story of what happened on that was replete with unexpected dangers. Apparently the plane developed some kind of trouble in mid-ocean, and oil for the plane had to be pumped by hand. In New York a transfer was made to a new plane, but that plane also developed some trouble, and it was necessary to transfer to a third plane, which left the airport over three hours late. As that plane neared Philadelphia one engine ceased to function. At the airport all emergency equipment was brought out, but the plane made a safe landing.

Sometime later, February 13, 1959, writing to Sister Helena, a cousin, about the trip, he indicated what he had endured:

. . . The trip to Rome had many perils. The oil distribution system was not working, so they had to use a hand pump all night to get us to New York.

We lost four hours there before we found a plane that would venture to carry us to Philadelphia. After ten minutes one of the engines on this plane went dead and we finished the trip on three engines.

Thanks be to God we made it and except for a great fatigue we did not suffer by the experience.

Before his departure from Philadelphia the Cardinal-elect had forbidden any reception to be held for him on his return. In carrying out his wishes the chancery officials forgot about his arrival at the airport, and someone arranged for a reception there. At least two thousand children and adults had been waiting since the expected arrival at 9:19 A.M. in a biting cold wind with the temperature at twenty-one degrees. When the plane finally came to rest on the runway, the time was after one in the afternoon. As the new Cardinal, dressed in civilian clothes, descended slowly from the plane, he expressed his only greeting: "It's great to be home." There was undoubtedly disappointment at the brevity of the speech on the part of many, but the reporter was also correct when he said the majority probably agreed with him. After shaking hands with the official greeters, and accepting a rich spiritual bouquet from two children, the Cardinal gave his blessing to the crowd from a nearby platform and entered the limousine to go to the cathedral. Along the way the car was stopped occasionally to receive the spiritual bouquets of other children waiting in the cold and lining the streets with their parents to the Archbishop's office at 225 North 18th Street. The Cardinal went immediately through the office to the sacristy and prepared to celebrate Mass before going to the cardinalatial residence on City Line Avenue.

Those who complained of the brevity of the Cardinal's greeting to the throng were probably not fully cognizant of the ordeal that the Cardinal had sustained. The long ride on the plane added to the ordeal of long ceremonies and receptions in Rome must have almost crushed the man, far from well, who never wanted any of these glories. His secretary said the appointment broke the Cardinal's heart because what he really wanted was to retire to the Notre Dame campus. What was more remarkable was that outside of a few joking letters to old friends he never betrayed his feelings to the public. The spiritual bouquet presented to him at the airport listed 783,716 Masses heard, 582,031 Communions received, 717,714 rosaries said, 649,951 visits to the Blessed Sacrament made, and 249,356 Stations of the Cross made. The other bouquets were similarly rich. Undoubtedly the Cardinal was deeply appreciative of these prayers, but he was scarcely able to express joy under such trying circumstances. Yet he tried to keep right on.

The reception of the Cardinal's hat made no difference in the manners of the Archbishop or his attendance at scheduled functions. He actually enjoyed the amusing incidents that he met. To his old friend, Laura Corbett, he wrote on December 31 that the best story was about a boy who had lived next door to the Archbishop and played with his bowl of goldfish in Buffalo:

When the news came from Rome on November 17 his mother asked him if he remembered me. The boy thought for a minute and said: "I don't remember him but I remember his goldfish."

All I can say is that I have never felt so much like a goldfish in my life. I no longer have any privacy and I am all decked out with no place to go.

The Cardinal could not answer all the letters he received. To his close friends Mr. and Mrs. Colket he wrote on December 29 about the Holy Father:

Certainly the Holy Father has brought the friendliness of the Po Valley with him to Rome. He is so natural that he is the delight of the reporters. Certainly I can say that he has killed me with kindness.

On January 4 the Cardinal wrote his annual letter on family Communion. Since this was the first letter of the new year, he said:

I pray that the New Year may be for each of you a happy and blessed one, filled to overflowing with that peace which the world cannot give.

God made us creatures to love Him and our neighbors, and in that loving to find peace. When fallen man subjugates his passions to the rule of reason and directs his will to obey the command to love God and neighbor, charity produces tranquility in the individual and peace in society. This charity is sorely needed by the great family of nations and by individual families, and grows strong in those souls in which Love Incarnate is received in Holy Communion.

He received additional requests to appear and to endorse projects. To Mr. Edward J. Burrell, who asked him to suggest an intention for the alumni for the year, he wrote on January 5:

In response to your invitation to suggest an "intention" I propose for your consideration, "The Blessing of God on the Negroes of the United States."

I have in mind the stress laid by our late Holy Father, Pope Pius XII, on the fact that the fastest growing Church in the world today is the Church in Africa. Paralleling this in the United States is the exodus of the Negro from the southeast to the north and west, where many of them for the first time come in contact with Catholic lay people and entrust their children to the Sisters for their education. The good will engendered by this situation makes these people conscious of many opportunities for blessings which never before had come to their notice.

To Bishop Cousineau on January 6 he confided that he had intended to resign before being made cardinal:

Through all the years since I left Notre Dame I have cherished the idea that the Holy Father might permit me to resign and return to the work of Prefect of Religion. I suppose I must forget about that now. Although everyone has been most kind to me in the assignments since leaving Notre Dame, I always placed the priestly work of confessions and Holy Communion above the administrative duties of the Church committed to my care.

Of course, being named cardinal caused him to be known by persons who might not know of the Archbishop of Philadelphia, but just as there was no change in his manner of greeting everyone there was no change in his fundamental teachings and practices. To Walter B. Brannan, Jr., a Baptist who had written to him about his opposition to birth-control propaganda, the Cardinal wrote on January 12:

I am writing this to you in confidence, not for publication. I do not wish to make public declarations that may be misinterpreted or may hurt the feelings of Protestants, either fundamentalists or modernists who are good neighbors, wherever they may be. In your case I have departed from my customary silence just to give you encouragement in your fight for the truth. May you have many followers in your determined effort to know and conform to the will of God.

While not interested in interdenominational exchanges, the Cardinal had no racial or national prejudices. In his acceptance of all peoples and all nationalities he could always recall his own experience in rural Indiana, and especially under Father Meissner, as he told Father John G. Engler on January 14:

The finest Saint Patrick's Day sermon I ever heard in my early life was preached by our pastor at home, Father Meissner, who was half Jewish and half Lutheran but all Catholic. His Westphalian accent was a bit heavy but he certainly pleased his Irish parishioners that day.

The Cardinal received many stray bits of advice about taking care of his health. His correspondence indicates that he never fully understood what his troubles were and that even when operations were performed, they were made to explore rather than from information. His letter to W. M. Hallenbeck on January 21 expressed some bewilderment about his failing health:

. . . It happens, however, that my own affliction is not arthritis. For many years I had been under the impression that it was. A few years ago I had to have an examination by an orthopedic surgeon and he

told me that my joints were so supple that I never could have had
arthritis. When I asked him what the affliction was he replied, "It's
not in my line."

Whatever it is it doesn't cause me too much trouble and I have managed to live with it. Just now the feet and ankles are fine and I am
having a bout with lumbago instead. I guess this is all part of my
purgatory and I don't bother too much about it.

Among Cardinal O'Hara's party attending the ceremonies in
Rome was Bishop John F. Dearden of Pittsburgh. While in
Rome the Bishop was named archbishop of Detroit and received
his pallium from the Pope himself. On January 29 Cardinal
O'Hara went to Detroit to install him in his new see. He returned
immediately to Philadelphia to preside at one of his favorite ceremonies, the Candelaria for the Puerto Ricans. The Cardinal presided at the distribution of the candles, and the photograph of the
ceremony in the February 6 *Standard and Times* showed him
thin, but seemingly well. The same issue of the paper published
the annual Lenten pastoral of the Cardinal. This letter he opened
with an old theme of his—the futility of the French government's
attack on the Church:

Dearly Beloved in Christ:
The world is homesick for the voice of a common father.

The evidence that leads to this conclusion is mounting day by day.
During the nineteenth century, in the backwash of the French Revolution, one European nation after another made war on the Catholic
Church and centered attacks on the Holy Father. In the France of
1904, Premier Viviani boasted that he put out the lights of heaven
when he expelled the religious and closed the Catholic schools. True
the lights were out, but they were not the lights of heaven.

The Cardinal claimed that World War I had shown the futility
of such planning, and the bankruptcy of such ideologies was further shown in the events of World War II. He then spoke of the
new Pope:

When God took the late Supreme Pontiff to his heavenly reward
He sent as his successor the Pontiff who has won for himself in a few
short months the name, "Good Pope John." His daily practice of the
seven corporal and seven spiritual works of mercy has won for him
the affection of mankind—and he had added a fifteenth work of
mercy—"to listen with patience to long speeches and not to make
them himself."

In prompt obedience to a divine inspiration His Holiness has called
for an Ecumenical Council, the purpose of which will be to promote
Christian unity. How better can we promote this desire of his heart
than by making this Lent the best Lent of our lives? . . .

In conclusion he urged a determined fight against selfishness, and that the sacrifices include Mass and Communion.

The Cardinal had suffered from several ailments since his return from Rome, none of which were sufficient to keep him from the public. However, on February 2 he took a plane to Indianapolis for a rest and to see the physician there. He told his sisters that the examining physician had said that he must have more rest and cut down on smoking. They thought he seemed willing to take more rest, and seemed content to relax at home. On February 7 he returned to Philadelphia, but on February 16 he went to Misericordia Hospital for minor surgery, but he seemed to be in good condition afterwards. However, some complications were found in his heart and lungs, and the physicians kept him in the hospital for various treatments until March 25. That day for the first time the Cardinal was able to walk about his flower garden—the longest walk he had taken since going to the hospital. His convalescence prevented the Cardinal from presiding at the enthronement of Bishop Wright as bishop of Pittsburgh on March 7. Monsignor McGlinn took over the Cardinal's correspondence during this period of rest, and he wrote to Charles E. McGinley of California on March 5: "Cardinal O'Hara is still confined to the hospital. . . . The doctors have ordered the Cardinal to take a complete rest and he is very scrupulous in observing their orders. . . ."

Apparently the first public appearance of the Cardinal after his operation was the brief visit of President and Mrs. O'Kelly of Ireland. Bishop Yuen had taken the Cardinal's place at the Palm Sunday and Easter Masses in the cathedral, and Bishop McCormick at Holy Thursday services. The Irish president attended Mass at the cathedral on Sunday and later went to call on the Cardinal at the cardinalatial residence. The next day, March 30, the Cardinal wrote to Archbishop Brady of Saint Paul: "Thank you for releasing the President of Ireland in time for him to spend a few days with us. He has charmed everyone."

On April 2 Dr. Thomas J. Ryan, who had been attending the Cardinal and had performed the latest surgery on him, died suddenly. The Cardinal attended his funeral at St. Mathias Church. On April 14 the Cardinal attended the Universal Notre Dame Night celebration, where he received a script and a plaque honoring him as the Notre Dame Man, not only of the year but "of years," which also recalled his years of service as prefect of religion, as well as his service to Catholic education in Philadelphia.

The Cardinal remained at the dinner just long enough to receive the designation and to give his blessing to the gathering. He told the audience: "I'm a little old to be out during the day and a little too young to be out late at night." Father Hesburgh, the president of the University, was present to make the award and to give the main speech for the occasion.

The Cardinal began to perform some of the duties of his office. The task of blessing babies was left to the auxiliary bishops. But he announced that he would do the ordaining of priests on May 7 and preside at the Charities Appeal Rally on April 19. He wrote a letter to the faithful on April 15 in which he thanked the workers for the great effort they were making for the appeal but asked them to redouble their prayers and efforts. At the reception for the workers on Sunday afternoon at the Sheraton Hotel he told them:

This is a never ending work. The Lord has more for us to do each time. The hands that guide the infant and the aged, that point out the way of life to the children and youth, these we support with your generous donations.

During these days we are offered an opportunity to support—in free enterprise fashion—the alleviation of suffering, the overcoming of handicaps, the rehabilitation of those who have made their share of mistakes.

The Cardinal looked thin in the photographs taken at the reception. On April 20 he received word that his resignation from the Executive Committee of the Catholic University had been accepted. On April 30 he went to New York to attend the funeral of Bishop Joseph Donahue, and while there he visited some sick friends, including Frank Walker and Mrs. Colket.

Cardinal O'Hara had never reconciled himself to the notion that Catholics should seek federal aid for Catholic education. It is not surprising to have him repeat his position to Archbishop Meyer of Chicago on April 27:

While I welcome the proposed return to the official Catholic position on federal aid to education (opposition to whatever would weaken or destroy local control), I need more information before I can form an opinion on the wisdom of certain proposals in paragraphs c, d, e, and f of Monsignor Hochwalt's letter to you.

He seemed to feel that there had been a shift in the Catholic position for some recent years, and now he thought he saw a return to the Catholic position of earlier decades, which opposed federal aid to education.

On May 3, the day set for the general solicitation of individual

families for the Charities Appeal, the Cardinal went to the headquarters in the cathedral auditorium to witness the returns from
the drive. When, after three hours, the proposed amount of $1,900,-
000 was reached, he again led the prayers of thanksgiving at the
statue of Our Lady of Charity.

On May 7, Ascension Thursday, the Cardinal ordained twenty-
three men for the Archdiocese of Philadelphia in the cathedral.
The next day he went to New York where he and Cardinals
Spellman and Cushing greeted the new apostolic delegate, Archbishop Egidio Vagnozzi. To Robert B. Cummings on May 6 he
gave an account of his time:

... I spent five days at home toward the end of last month. I have spent
one night in New York since then. I went in early enough to call on
Frank Walker. They were a bit worried about him that night but I
have heard from him since and he seems better. . . .
My first visit to New York since last August when I had a couple
of hours in town.

Writing to his friends Mr. and Mrs. Carlos Cariola of Santiago, Chile, on May 18, 1959, he explained the condition of his
health:

I returned from Rome just before Christmas. In the succeeding weeks
I tried to take care of the normal activities of the diocese and at the
same time catch up on greetings.
The strain was too severe and the doctor put me in the hospital. I
was under treatment for about eight weeks. Since then I have had a
reduced schedule and I am now trying to pay debts long overdue.

He managed to keep up his interest in the Puerto Ricans, and in
a letter of May 8 he suggested to Father Corbe that he get the
better students to aid the slower ones, an idea he had used frequently. Despite his precarious health the Cardinal attended
other ceremonies, including the silver-jubilee celebration in the
cathedral for forty-four priests of the Archdiocese on May 26, at
which Bishop McDevitt celebrated the Mass. Again on June 2 he
presided at the annual concursus at the seminary, and on June 3
he received an honorary degree from LaSalle College. To Archbishop Gerald O'Hara, who complimented him on the Charities
Appeal, he wrote on June 5:

... the children prayed, their parents worked, and the priests directed
with admirable loyalty. The superhuman efforts of the Committee of
the Laity brought forth an abundance of good will on the part of the
non-Catholics and in the space of one year the gifts grew tremendously.

The city now knows that more than half of the whole population is Catholic.

On June 14 Cardinal O'Hara wrote to Monsignor Newton Miller to choose a committee to prepare an agenda for the coming Vatican Council. The committee was to submit a document by August 18, 1959. Yet a stone in a kidney forced the Cardinal back into the hospital on June 17 for a painful but not dangerous period. When the Cardinal was released from the hospital, he began to plan a vacation at home, where he finally arrived on June 30 and stayed until July 7.

The Cardinal in his later years reminisced frequently about his early life in central Indiana. When the Sisters of Providence celebrated their eighty-five years in the parish at Peru, he sent a message for the local paper:

Sorry I cannot be with you when St. Charles' Parish shows its appreciation of the lives and work of the Sisters of Providence in Peru for the past eighty-five years. Our debt to them is very real. From 1895 to 1902 they drilled me in the essentials of religion and the arts. We did not have to unlearn what they taught us. Many of the things we must apply daily we learned best from them. God bless them and the pastors and priests who have rendered to Peru the devoted service which love of God inspires.

But the Cardinal looked with pride on his other education, too. Writing to Father Louis Thornton on June 26, he mentioned a visit of Cardinal Ottaviani:

Cardinal Ottaviani told me several times that he was simply overwhelmed by Notre Dame. He never imagined that there existed any place in the world a Catholic University of that caliber. Look back sixty years to Fathers Zahm, Burns, Cavanaugh and you will see the pattern the Holy Ghost followed. The statue on the dome and the statue in the grotto have given a lot of inspiration to the world.

And of his experience in Peru High School he had other thoughts. Writing on July 1, 1959, to Porter R. Chandler, he recalled:

When I attended public high school myself upwards of sixty years ago, I made such a nuisance of myself at Protestant religious worship that they excused me from attending any further sessions. The few other Catholic students who made no fuss were permitted to remain.

To Father Martin Löhmuller he wrote on July 13 a bit of advice on Pennsylvania legislation, House Bill No. 2188:

If high school seniors as a class may be forced to submit to psychiatric examination so can parents and ministers, so can members of the

Legislature, so can all the judges in all the courts in the United States of America.

He did not say that he had the Supreme Court justices in mind, but he was undoubtedly irked by the recent decision of the Court on the admission of the book *Lady Chatterly's Lover* into the country as not obscene.

There are no public statements or letters by the Cardinal on the Supreme Court decision on the admission of *Lady Chatterly's Lover* or the action of the Pennsylvania Supreme Court ruling unconstitutional a Pennsylvania law prohibiting the showing of obscene movies. The editorial "Obscenity and Legal Semantics" in the July 10 *Standard and Times* probably contained some of his ideas, but there is no indication that he wrote it. The new bill then under consideration against obscene movies was claimed by its backers to avoid the vagueness that was the basis for the adverse court decisions.

The Cardinal's efforts to provide Catholic high schools received a setback on July 30 when fire broke out on the top floor of Roman Catholic High School at Broad and Vine Streets, and completely destroyed the top floor of the building. While the second and first floors were damaged, they could be restored to use after some repairs, although temporary quarters were sought for September. Roman Catholic was the first free Catholic high school in North America, as well as the first central Catholic high school in Philadelphia, having been founded in 1890. The Cardinal's program took the loss in stride.

To one so determined as was the Cardinal not to compromise on the question of communist aggression and infiltration the announcement by President Eisenhower that he had invited Soviet Chairman Nikita Khrushchev to visit the United States was deplorable on many counts. The Cardinal sent a letter of protest to the President on August 3:

Today's announcement leaves a deep wound. This morning I offered my Mass for you and America. Every day every Catholic priest the world over prays with the people for the salvation of Russia. But in the opinion of many of us the hour of salvation for Russians and their captives is not advanced by photographs which seem to indicate an official approval of barbaric conduct. In St. Stephen's Mass today we are reminded of St. Stephen's prayer for those who stoned him to death, "Lord lay this not to their charge."

The President answered on August 10, saying that he regretted having aroused such deep feelings. He insisted that he and his advisers had weighed all the facts now being presented.

Quite in line with these feelings was the sending by Cardinal O'Hara of a check for $300 to William F. Buckley, Jr., of the *National Review* for nine two-year subscriptions to the magazine. The Cardinal subscribed to several journals that professed to be fighting communism and encouraged several men of minor importance who were engaged in fighting communist influence.

The Cardinal had been disturbed by the Court decisions allowing the showing of questionable movies and permitting the sale of literature he considered harmful. In the August 14 *Standard and Times* the Cardinal published an editorial on the front page under the title "Label It Poison and Lock It Up." He related how in the past a president of a state university in the Midwest had turned down a lecture by Bertrand Russell "in the name of common decency." In the intervening thirty years "common decency," he said, had lost ground, but the trend now was in the other direction and must be encouraged:

A few common sense leaders like J. Edgar Hoover and Postmaster General Summerfield are rallying the forces of good to wipe out juvenile delinquency and stop its greatest breeding ground—pornographic literature, motion pictures and the like.

He proceeded to cite the bill then before the Pennsylvania House of Representatives, Senate Bill 373, which he claimed met the objections of the recent court decisions. He continued:

We still have protection against poison, and heavy penalties are laid on those who fail to label poison for what it is and/or who are remiss in their duty to guard it against unwarranted handling and use.

The issue involved is moral, not political. Furthermore, although this appeal is made in the name of natural law and its tenet of common decency, I add a word to Catholics to remind them of their obligations to conform their conduct to the Ten Commandments and to use the Sacraments and prayer as the most powerful aids to keep the Commandments.

Put the label on moral poison and lock it up!

On August 21 the Cardinal was host to Cardinal Giacomo Lercaro, Archbishop of Bologna, who was on his way to attend the National Liturgical Congress at Notre Dame. The Cardinal showed his guest around the city and arranged that he visit and be entertained at the seminary. While Cardinal O'Hara may have been quite fatigued to act as guide to the visitor, he found an opportunity to give him a message. As he wrote on August 25 to Cardinal McIntyre:

Cardinal Lercaro left here for Chicago Sunday afternoon. The heat has been down. Out of two days we gave him an hour and a half of sightseeing, and even this was too much. However, he was very cheerful. He wanted to see some churches. I told him that we were too busy building schools to bother about churches—that when we got through with the original school plant and three additions, and had these paid for we would let the pastors save up to get a church. The schools and hospitals have startled him and he seems willing to settle for anything now.

The Cardinal was very much aware of the burden he was imposing on the archdiocese in his program of new Catholic high schools and announced on August 20 an increase in the charge of the parish for each student. One afterthought on this he expressed to Mr. John Eagleson in a letter of August 25:

Sometimes I wonder whether we are doing the right thing in furnishing high school education on a purely gratuitous basis. I certainly do not want to add to the burdens of families, but when students make good earnings after hours and then do nothing to help either the parents or the school, we may be held accountable for some of the selfishness that becomes a dominant characteristic in some students in later life.

When the Cardinal was visiting his family in Indianapolis, Father Richard Sullivan, C.S.C., the president of Stonehill College in North Easton, Massachusetts, had written to the family that Cardinal Spellman had asked him to name the new dormitory of the college after Cardinal O'Hara. The family was pleased but the Cardinal was not, yet he apparently did not forbid the action. In a letter of August 31 to Cardinal O'Hara acknowledging the Philadelphia contributions to the Near East Collection Cardinal Spellman added: "Thanks for permitting the building at Stonehill to bear your name. I shall help it. F.S."[5]

In his correspondence of the late summer of 1959 and in his talks with his family the Archbishop seemed to be seriously concerned with his visit to Rome that fall. Permission had been given by the authorities in Rome for the bishops to combine their attendance at the celebration of the hundredth anniversary of the foundation of the North American College in Rome with the quinquennial *ad limina* visit. The Cardinal used his energy and spare time gathering the statistics for his report. His insistence on attending the North American College celebration was unusual, since he had never attended the Roman college. However, by the special permission to make the *ad limina* on this visit he could fulfill two public functions at once, something he tried to do as often as possible since coming to Philadelphia. Then, too, the Pope was to come to the North American College for the ceremony, and there was also to be observed at that time the second anniversary Mass for Pope Pius XII, to whom the Cardinal had been very devoted. It was obvious that the Roman trip was going to be a severe trial. His sister noted in her diary that he was not looking forward to the trip to Rome with pleasure and that this was evidence that he was not well.

The members of the hierarchy manifested in many ways their feelings about the invitation to Khrushchev to visit the United States. Cardinal Spellman had called for a holy hour for September 14, the evening of Khrushchev's arrival, and Cardinal Cushing had arranged a special prayer to coincide with the Russian's visit. Other bishops had similar periods of prayer. On September 10 Cardinal O'Hara simply called for a special day of prayer and reparation on September 15 dedicated to the needs of America without making reference to the foreign visitor. In his letter asking for the day of prayer he added:

It seems singularly appropriate this year to dedicate this feast to the needs of America. Our Mass, our Holy Communion, our Rosary and other Prayers should be offered for the intention that God save America. We need also to perform acts of penance that will help awaken in us a true sense of reparation.

The leading editorial in the *Standard and Times* was a list of the evil deeds of the visiting Soviet leader.

On September 13 the Cardinal presided in the cathedral at the funeral of Father Joseph Cox of St. John the Evangelist, one of the most respected priests of the archdiocese. On that day his friend and fellow Notre Dame alumnus, Frank C. Walker, died in New York. The Cardinal went to New York for the funeral and flew directly from New York to Indianapolis for a brief rest. However, he was not in Philadelphia on September 17 when the Soviet chairman passed through on his way to New York. He returned to Philadelphia on September 22.

In a letter to priests in the *Standard and Times* of October 2 he said that during the month of October their pleas for an increase in religious vocations were placed under the patronage of Our Blessed Mother. They owed their profound thanks for the increase in vocations that they had already experienced and that their prayers must be for the whole Church as well as for needs at home. A vocational holy hour would be held in connection with the Mission Sunday services at the cathedral on October 18. He mentioned the efforts of the Diocesan School Office and the Serra

Club to increase vocations and urged the pastors to cooperate in instructing the faithful on the meaning of religious vocations.

On October 6 he left for Rome, and the October 9 issue of the *Standard and Times* announced his arrival there. The Cardinal planned his arrival in Rome in time to attend the anniversary Mass for Pius XII. The *Standard and Times* of October 16 published a photograph of Cardinal O'Hara being greeted by Pope John XXIII when the Pope visited the North American College. It may be a bad photograph, but the lines on the face of the Cardinal were very tense. While in Rome he stayed at the Holy Cross Generalate on Via Aurelia Antica and besides visits to the Sacred Congregation had a private personal audience with the Holy Father. There is little else known about this trip except that as he boarded the bus that was to take him to the plane in Rome, he stumbled and fell, hitting his arm. However, since nothing seemed to be broken, the Cardinal continued his trip, arriving in Philadelphia on October 16. He said Mass despite the injured arm and then went to the hospital for X-rays. The X-rays showed no broken bones, but the pain was intense as a result of the arthritic condition of the arm. The doctor kept the Cardinal in the hospital. For a while the fingers stiffened so that he could not use them, but by therapy the attendants improved this situation.

Cardinal Spellman had written on October 13 from Rome, and on October 21 Monsignor McGlinn sent his information about Cardinal O'Hara:

> I am delighted to send word that Cardinal O'Hara's visit to the hospital has been most beneficial. As Your Eminence knows, the Cardinal has had no medication through the years for his arthritic condition. Since his entrance into the hospital he has had heavy daily doses of cortex. The results have been amazing. The pain has abated; his joints are supple; and the sedimentation count has dropped from 90 to 40. Thanks be to God.

The October 23 *Standard and Times* published another photograph of the Cardinal with the Pope. Again the Cardinal looked really haggard. The letter published over the Cardinal's signature to start the drive for subscriptions to the paper was not of his composition. The new Monsignors, however, were announced under his seal.

If the story of the Cardinal's illnesses had been strange up to this point, it must be remembered that there had been no real operation and that the opinion of the doctors had been based on the limited information the patient had been willing to give. He seemed to think that there was only spiritual reward for arthritis.

As Monsignor McGlinn told Cardinal Spellman, Cardinal O'Hara had received no real medication for arthritis. His diet seemed to have been basically that given him by the doctors in Indianapolis in 1956, with some changes made after later checkups. As the Cardinal jokingly expressed it, the cortex taken for arthritis "smoked out" the real illness from which he had suffered in silence, for how long no one will ever know. When on October 28 he complained of some stomach pain, it was decided that the gall bladder was causing trouble and surgery was planned to drain the bladder. The incision found a perforated ulcer in such condition that peritonitis should have developed. Because of some congestion in the lungs they performed the operation under local anesthetic. The next day, October 29, to prevent the lung congestion from developing into pneumonia they gave him antibiotics. For a while he seemed near death, but he rallied successfully. He was now on the road to recovery, but it was to be a long one. He talked to his family over the telephone regularly and on November 10 told them that the stitches had been removed from his wound and that he was allowed to sit up five or six hours a day. Monsignor McGlinn wrote an encouraging letter but said that the Cardinal was very weak. Cardinal O'Hara was scheduled to preside at one of the triduum of Masses at the dedication of the Shrine to the Immaculate Conception in Washington on November 22. Realizing that he could not be present, the Cardinal sent a message on November 7 to the assembled bishops through Cardinal Spellman:

Though present only in spirit on this beautiful day of dedication of the National Shrine of Our Lady I join with the Cardinals and our other Bishops in the dedication of our country as Mary's land. I ask to share with our brothers in the Hierarchy my expression of deep gratitude. May God bless all of us and Mary ever protect us.

On November 15 Cardinal Spellman came to see him on his way to the bishops' meeting in Washington. At that time he planned to say Mass again on November 20. On the twenty-third Cardinals Spellman and McIntyre visited him on their way back from the Washington meeting. On November 27 he was allowed to return to his home after being in the hospital almost six weeks.

Besides testifying to the patience and good humor of the Cardinal even when being operated on very painfully under local anesthetic, Dr. Ward Sullivan remarked about the general conduct of the Cardinal:

During the stages of convalescence, the Cardinal made no effort to recall his unhappy or painful experiences, but preferred to talk about present and the future and other things and made no point of stressing his great cooperativeness or willingness to suffer. This was never permitted to be brought up at conversation with me. The Cardinal was very casual in the manner of dress. It was characteristic to see him in his convalescence wearing flannel pajamas, the top and bottom being of different pairs. The bathrobe was old and well worn. He never flaunted his humility; it just seemed a natural part of him. He never wore his ring. He wore his skull cap only when his head was cold and certainly was extremely pleasant and unassuming when I brought my ten year old daughter in to see him one day. . . .

The business of the archdiocese rolled on. The auxiliaries and visiting bishops cared for episcopal ceremonies, the chancery functioned almost as usual, and some letters were published, composed in much of his own style, about the seminary collection, changes in interest charges within the archdiocese, the usual Thanksgiving Clothing Collection, and the plans for the dedication of the shrine in Washington and for the triduum of November 18–20, ending with an act of consecration to the Blessed Virgin.

To Father Bernard Ransing, C.S.C., who had written from Rome, the Monsignor wrote reassuringly on November 5:

There was fortuitously no serious results from the Cardinal's fall in Rome, except for the severe pain from the arthritic condition in the right arm. His Eminence was, however, hospitalized for X-rays on the arm and while there developed stomach pains. He was operated on one week ago today and it was discovered that he has a perforated duodenal ulcer, so far gone that there was real danger of peritonitis. The poor fellow has had everything in the books since January. . . .

At this time the Cardinal received a formal invitation to attend a meeting of the President's Committee in Traffic Safety at Atlantic City on November 11–12, 1959. He noted: "If you have a file for strange happenings this belongs in it with the envelope." The envelope was from the White House.

The Cardinal reopened his personal correspondence only just before leaving for Indianapolis for a more complete rest. Writing to Sister Helena, his cousin, on December 16, he told her:

Please forgive my long silence. My return from the hospital came two weeks ago but only now have I found the energy to attempt to dictate. The last trip took forty-two days—a total of eighty-two days spent in the hospital this year with many weeks of convalescence in between. There were two major operations. I have gained sufficient strength to travel tomorrow evening to Indianapolis.

To the Apostolic Delegate he wrote the same day: "Please pardon if I dictate a reply to your personal letter. The arthritis limits my use of the right hand to signatures."

The Cardinal's medicine and formulae arrived in Indianapolis on December 16, a few days before his arrival. The note in his sister Bess's diary tells the story best:

December 20th: Father John came in early this afternoon, and I was shocked to see how weak he is. Monsignor McGlinn had told us he looked so much better that our hopes were built up too much, I guess.

December 22nd: Father John seems better today. Helen took him to the hospital for a checkup.

December 25th: Father John was able to say two Masses this morning but he had to sit down for all but the Canon of the Mass. He looks weak and miserable.

December 29th: We hated to see Father John go back but he felt he should see the doctor. He had a hard time climbing the steps to the plane.

December 30th: Father John called this evening and Eve said his voice sounded fine.[6]

On January 4, 1960, he wrote to his friend Mrs. Colket, and indicated a very high quality of resignation:

. . . It was medicine for arthritis that smoked out the perforated ulcer that seemed to have been tucked away for years without causing too much inconvenience except loss of appetite.

We know so little about the designs of God! Yet we do know that God leads through suffering to perfection, and that he spared not His own Son who suffered and died for us. Our best prayer is one for resignation to the Will of God, that His purpose may be accomplished in us.

To understand the full significance of this statement one must remember that Mrs. Colket herself was a victim of serious physical sickness.

To Father Richard Sullivan, who planned to dedicate a new dormitory at Stonehill College to the Cardinal, Cardinal O'Hara wrote the same day:

I wish I could finance the chapel myself and have it named as a memorial to Cardinal Spellman. While this seems impossible under my present situation I might find ways to help. What comes to me from Philadelphia I reserve for charity and education here. What comes in from outside has in a great measure been channelled into charities and education here—largely through the children's Christmas party.

There is little else to indicate the actual feeling of the Cardinal during this period of convalescence, since he was in the habit of making light of his sicknesses. He had, however, to refuse appointments.

Cardinal Spellman wrote him to congratulate him on his twentieth anniversary as a bishop. Cardinal O'Hara wrote him on January 4:

Step by step since that day Your Eminence has watched over me and guided my steps now on the broad highway and again down the narrow paths between hospital beds—until I stand before the throne of good Pope John to receive the symbol of membership in his Senate.

To his cousin Marie O'Hara on the death of Marie's brother Tom—after expressing his sympathy—he wrote:

Thanks be to God my own health is improving—but slowly. They will begin to cut down on my five medicines about the fifteenth of January, but I will still have the baby food three times a day.

In the issue of January 15 the *Standard and Times* printed a photograph of the Cardinal in his cardinalatial robes, but he looked thin and drawn, although the photograph was probably taken before the current illness. The same issue announced a meeting at Holy Child Church of the forty-four present directors of the Charities Appeal for January 18. The aim of the drive for 1960 was to be two million three hundred thousand dollars. On January 21, as a result of the action of the bishops of the province, there was set up the Pennsylvania Catholic Welfare Committee with William Ball as General Counsel.

On February 5 the *Standard and Times* published an unsigned editorial on the front page entitled "Were There Four Chaplains or Nine?" The editorial was intended to answer the criticism that had arisen from the Catholic refusal to participate in the dedication of the chapel in Philadelphia to the four chaplains who were said to have given their life preservers to others and gone down together with the sinking of the *S.S. Dorchester*. The editorial challenged the statement in the *New York Times* about the participation of Dr. Shane McCarthy at the dedication. Dr. McCarthy had made it clear that he was not participating as a Catholic representative, but had insisted that there was no religious service, that no one wore any religious garb, and it was understood he was only there as a representative of the President's Council on Youth Fitness. The editorial doubted the story of the manner of the chaplains' deaths, maintaining that the priest, Father Washington, would not have been holding hands but giving absolution. Secondly, it asked why only four chaplains are honored since there were five others lost in the sinking of the *S. S. Henry Mallory* three nights later in the same engagement. There is nothing to indicate that the Cardinal entered into this argument, but his rule about interdenominational services was carried out.

In early February, 1960, the chancery office in Philadelphia became aware of a questionnaire being circulated to certain priests throughout the country by Father Joseph H. Fichter, S.J., of Loyola University in New Orleans. The questionnaire asked very blunt questions about the feeling of the priest for his vocation and about other matters. When the matter was brought to Cardinal O'Hara's attention, he forbade his priests to answer the questionnaire and protested to the superior general of the Jesuits against Father Fichter. Writing to Cardinal Spellman on February 11, he said:

The enclosed exchange of correspondence is self-explanatory. The questionnaire came to my attention through a priest of the diocese who consulted the chancery on how best to prevent the harm which he saw coming from use of the questionnaire.

When Francis M. McClarnon wrote to say that twenty percent of the students of Lehigh College were Catholic and needed supervision, the Cardinal, who had been told of this before, answered on February 18:

However, I ask you to be patient. We have established more than forty new parishes because of the shifting of the population from cities to suburbs and the influx of many families from outside the diocese. The Catholic population has increased some forty per cent since I came here in 1952. Our high schools have doubled in registration, the elementary registration has increased eighty per cent and the college students almost two hundred per cent. While laymen occupy many positions on the faculties of boys' high schools and women in the grammar schools we are still hoping for an increase of priests in this very important work.

One of the most distressing features of this situation is that we must use as active pastors many priests who have reached the time of life when the burden should be eased. Last week one pastor died at the age of eighty-nine. Still on duty are twenty priests who have reached their golden jubilee in the priesthood.

On February 29 the Cardinal wrote to Bishop Lawrence Sheehan to thank him for a visit in which they had talked about the problems of Catholic education. Bishop Sheehan had supported at first the elimination of some elementary grades in favor of high schools, a policy to which the Archbishop would not give approval. On March 21 the Cardinal wrote to Mrs. Mary Cisco, who had complained about the cancellation of the Sunday after-noon Masses. He was forced by bickering. He told her:

From your letter I take it that you understand I had strong reasons for cancelling the Masses on Sunday. My conscience required me to act. I did not announce the reasons because they affected my conscience, not the conscience of the people.

The efforts to enable the Cardinal to move about were not very successful. Monsignor McGlinn wrote on March 23 to Thomas Coggs:

The Cardinal is trying to give the new truss a fair trial, but I am convinced that the surgical belt was more comfortable for him.

Bess's diary said that the Cardinal seemed to think he would have to have a hernia operation. "He has been wearing a belt, but with the sore arm he hasn't been able to adjust it properly."

On March 24 he wrote Bishop Greco about changes in the ver-sions of the Scriptures. "It would be a major tragedy in my judg-ment to use any word but virgin in the English rendition of the text of Isaias. The brief note of scholars would not forestall the criticism you have mentioned."

Although the Cardinal had carefully planned his building cam-paign there were worries about continued expansion. He wrote to Monsignor John J. Haydt on April 25:

We cannot entertain for the present the thought of any more high school building without having the money on hand. If the pastors who use the school now can agree among themselves to raise the money needed and this meets with the approval of the Committee now working on it, I shall be glad to place it in the hands of the pastors for solution.

The Cardinal did not then know that this was the conclusion of his remarkable campaign to get all Catholic children of the Philadelphia archdiocese into Catholic schools. A detailed sum-mary of his building and expansion was drawn up shortly after his death at the request of Bishop McShea. The report listed the expanded capacity added to existing schools during the years 1952 to 1960 as 610 classrooms. In addition, there were 133 new parochial school buildings with a total of 1206 classrooms, 8 new schools for retarded children, 20 new high schools owned and operated by the archdiocese with 746 classrooms, 15 new high schools operated by religious communities with 213 classrooms. Further, during his regime in Philadelphia two new colleges for women, Holy Family and Cabrini, were opened, and to the existing colleges 18 new buildings had been added. The total added classrooms for colleges was 200. According to the *Catholic Directory* the total number of pupils under Catholic instruction had increased from 201,507 in 1952 to 330,294 in 1960. In his program for Catholic high schools the Cardinal had proposed to spend twenty-one millions, but because of inflation he had actually spent approximately twenty-nine millions. But it should be added that the indebtedness from this building program was just about a million dollars, with the means available to pay it if necessary. The rumors of great debt that were current at his death were false.

In the meantime the Cardinal submitted finally to what he hoped would be his last operation before a return to health. He entered the hospital on May 4. As Monsignor McGlinn wrote to Mrs. Corbett on May 17:

His Eminence underwent the operation for the correction of the hernia on Monday, May ninth. While he is recovering nicely, he is still quite weak, but I hope that you will continue to keep him in your prayers.

But the news that the family received from Monsignor McGlinn was not so pleasant. On the ninth the Monsignor told them that the Cardinal had come through the operation but that his condition was serious. On the tenth the hospital would not say how he was. Later the Monsignor said he was better, but he had been so worried about the Cardinal the night before that he had called the hospital every two hours. The Cardinal became irrational and almost gave up. But now he was better. By the fifteenth the Cardinal was able to call his family himself. On the fifteenth the Cardinal developed some congestion in his lungs that caused him some trouble. On May 19 Cardinal Agagianian called to see him and, when the doctor came, suggested that the doctor tell Agagianian of his condition so that he could tell the Pope. On June 9 Cardinal Montini came to see him and had his lunch at the Cardinal's house at City Line Avenue. He told Cardinal Montini he had been having trouble again with his ulcer, which had been affected by intravenous feeding. On June 14 he was able to return home. Apparently the Cardinal had come much closer to death than his family knew, and some of the effects of his relapse after the operation were never to leave him.

After his return from the hospital the Cardinal made some effort to make the priests' retreat during the week of June 19. He attended a few conferences during the day. As he told Walter

Cummings on June 20: "I was not released as had been expected in May, but I was released actually on June thirteenth." On June 20 the Monsignor wrote to Father Edward Keller: "The doctors are exercising extreme caution because he still has some fluid in the left lung."

On June 7 the Cardinal wrote to Cardinal Gilroy about his experiences with the Sunday afternoon Mass and his reasons for stopping it. He mentioned commercial rivalry; one-third of the congregation was school children who had missed the children's Mass; and the Mass had appealed to the lax and lukewarm Catholics.

The May operation and its side effects certainly depleted the strength of the Cardinal. Apparently, however, he did believe the physicians who told him that he would fully recover by September. Some letters show a consciousness of his weakened state; others seem to have been written by another person, since they talked of plans to be carried out after the complete recovery in September. The telephone conversations with his sisters were sometimes so optimistic they were not prepared for the shock of his actual condition when he arrived in Indianapolis late in July. Those seeing him daily point out that on some days he seemed quite well and on other days he seemed to suffer a severe relapse.

Father Steiner came for a visit the latter part of June and the first week of July. On July 13 the Cardinal wrote to John T. Brady: "Although my health is not yet back to normal, there has been a constant improvement since I left the hospital a month ago. I am most grateful for your prayers for me which I reciprocate." But to John P. Brooks he wrote rather sadly on July 18: "Even the few weeks of convalescence at home have been insufficient to supply the strength I need to keep my mind on my work." To Father Kerndt Healy, C.S.C., at Notre Dame he wrote a bit more optimistically the same day: "A thousand thanks for your prayers and good wishes! As Father Steiner can tell you, my improvement is now more rapid than it was and the doctor says that by the first of September I should get around pretty well by myself." To Monsignor Antonio Caretta, his Roman attendant, he wrote on August 1: "I should like to tell you that you are having a good effect, since the doctors have given me an excellent report and tell me that I shall be able to serve full duty by the time you reach these shores early in September." He wrote to Vincent Carroll on August 3, 1960: "I hope to be able to install Bishop McCormick in Altoona and to consecrate Bishop Mendez, a confrere of mine, who has been named a Bishop in Puerto

Rico." To Miss Grace M. Brown he wrote on August 10: "I am most gratified for the prayers you are offering in my behalf. While the state of my health has been very poor for some time, I am gaining my strength day by day and expect shortly to return to full duty. . . ."

Just how he sent these letters and seemed so optimistic is hard to understand, since the diary of his sister tells a different story:

July 21st: We met Father John's train at eight this morning and were shocked when we saw him—he is so weak and has so much difficulty walking. The station manager brought him down on the freight elevator, and after we got home he had a cup of coffee then waited until nine-thirty to say Mass. Monsignor McGlinn had sent out his medicines and diet list, so we hope to take good care of him.

July 25th: We have been going to Mass early and receiving Holy Communion so that Father John need not feel that he must get up early for us. He can sleep as late as he likes. He is so weak that he must sit down during a part of the Mass and it takes him a long time. . . .

July 30th: Father John seems to be improving but he is terribly weak.

August 1st: Bishop-elect Mendez, C.S.C., called to ask Father to consecrate him since the doctor said Father John would be able to resume his normal activities by September 1st, he agreed. Bishop Mendez will come down day after tomorrow, and Father John called Monsignor to come out and bring the ritual, etc.

August 3rd: Father John seems much better today. He enjoyed seeing Bishop and Monsignor, but had to go to the hospital while they were here. The doctor found his blood sugar high and asked him to come to the hospital to stay overnight.

August 5th: We went to the hospital to see Father John and he looked terrible. He looked so listless, as though he were under sedation, but I think he is just discouraged.

This period in the hospital was very painful in many ways. They discovered there was no diabetes, but are worried about other things. He is not allowed to say Mass which is a terrible blow to him and he just doesn't eat. The doctor finally released him on August 10th, but while he was glad to be home, he just doesn't come back to his normal state. He did eat a little better, but so much of the time his stomach was somewhat upset—because of poison, perhaps—that he probably never got enough to eat. Occasionally he was induced to eat his breakfast early and then say Mass around noon, but if he woke up around eight he insisted on saying Mass first.

On August 15 the Indianapolis physicians sent a written report to the Philadelphia physicians on their examination of the Cardinal. It said in part:

Cardinal O'Hara was admitted to St. Vincent's Hospital on August

4 and dismissed on August 10, 1960. We would like to have kept him longer but he wanted to go to the home of his sisters and he promised to rest there for another week before returning to Philadelphia.

We were struck by the marked change in his condition since we last saw him. No doubt much of this is due to collapse which occurred during the hernia operation. He was weak and showed considerable listlessness and mental lethargy. His appetite was very poor and he was eating only small amounts of food. Except for the apparent change in his condition the only new finding was probably carcinoma of the prostate. . . .

Writing a few years later of this final examination, the doctor observed:

. . . He developed arteriosclerosis and it was, indeed, appalling to see such an intellectual and intelligent individual graually losing his grasp on his surroundings and, gradually but certainly, start losing his memory both for recent and past events. The last time I saw him, he was extremely ill and we also felt that he probably had cancer of the prostate gland as well.

The diary continued:

August 18th: Monsignor Benjamin of Philadelphia called this morning from the Marott Hotel and a little later he and Monsignor Noone came to the house. They had come in answer to a phone call from Father John who wanted them to go back with him—he just wasn't able to travel alone. Monsignor Noone called later to say they had a good trip. John ate a little on the plane and again when he got home so we felt better.

There was some confusion about the arrival of Monsignors Noone and Benjamin. Monsignor Benjamin had been named auxiliary bishop and was already planning to go to see the Cardinal. Monsignor Noone had some business to discuss with the prelate and suggested that they go together, although Monsignor Noone did not know of the appointment of Monsignor Benjamin, which had not been announced publicly. Apparently the Cardinal decided that he would return with them since he obviously could not travel alone.

The morning after his return to Philadelphia the Sister who served his breakfast welcomed him home. He told her: "Sister, the only home I want to go to is Heaven, and I shall be going there shortly." On the following Saturday evening George V. Mitchell of the archdiocesan offices found the Cardinal much weakened by the ravages of his sicknesses. At the end of the visit the Cardinal told him: "Excuse me; I have to go say my prayers, and to say them well because I don't have much time left." Apparently he had been informed by the doctors or sensed that he had cancer and was faced with the same kind of death that had taken his close friend, Father Burns.

That evening, however, Elizabeth's diary notes:

August 20th: Father John called and he seemed cheerful. . . . Monsignor Noone is staying with him. . . .

August 21st: Father John called. He seems lonesome, but he says he feels well—but, of course, he always says that.

August 22nd: Father John called again this evening. Eva said his voice was weak and he had little pep.

Father Bartholomew Fair had called at the cardinalatial residence to deliver some books on Tuesday morning, August 23. A Sister opened the door and asked if he wished to see the Cardinal, who was up. The Sister said the Cardinal was not feeling well, and Father Fair said he would not bother him that day. His condition apparently worsened steadily, and that afternoon he was taken in an ambulance to Misericordia Hospital. Monsignor Noone continued the story:

Shortly after arriving at the hospital at about 4:30 p.m. it was decided that major surgery was necessary. It was not possible to use sedation but only local anesthetic. It was necessary to make incisions entirely across the waist of the Cardinal and from his chest to his lower abdomen. About two quarts of liquid were removed. The doctors had practically complete access to every organ that could be causing difficulty. During the operation, the Cardinal was in great pain but prayed continually.

Monsignor Noone stated that during the night after the operation the Cardinal pitched and tossed a great deal in his fight to recover his health.

In another statement shortly after death, Monsignor Noone recalled that the final operation was made under local anesthesia:

His Eminence prayed calmly and courageously while the surgeons explored the tremendous area exposed by the huge incision. After about an hour and a half he was brought back from the operating room. Though he must have suffered greatly, he managed to exchange brief remarks with those around him, like "Are you still here?"

Tuesday night and all through Wednesday and Thursday he showed remarkable fortitude in that by his own wish and to avoid complications he was given very little sedation. His progress was so good that it was planned to have him out of bed for a while on Friday; however, his whole condition weakened so that there was a definite change which never improved. He had received the sacraments while fully conscious.

The diary of Elizabeth O'Hara had the following entries:

August 23rd: Monsignor Noone called to say that they took more than a quart of fluid from Father John. They are not sure all of it comes from the perforated ulcer, but are not sure just what other organs may be affected.

August 25th: Monsignor Noone called this evening to say, "The news is good." Father John sat upon the side of the bed today and the doctor is encouraged. . . .

August 26th: Monsignor Noone called this evening to say Father John is unconscious and the doctor says there is no hope. . . .

August 27th: We arrived at the hospital before three and were taken directly to John's room. He was unconscious—had been since the evening before—they were giving him oxygen. Someone told us that shortly before he became unconscious he was asked if he wanted anything, and he said, "I want to go home and rest." The Sister said, "I think the doctor will let you go soon," and he said, "No, I want to go to Heaven." I don't think he spoke after that . . . he died a little after three in the morning.

The report of the operating physician was substantially the same:

His Eminence was admitted because of severe abdominal pain and had an emergency operation a few hours after admission at which was found peritonitis, but the site of the rupture could not be located. Following the surgery His Eminence appeared to improve until the 27th of August the lethargy which progressed to coma occurred and his condition deteriorated until death occurred. The coma was assumed to be due to failure of the liver.

Monsignor Noone's account added:

To the edification of everyone he displayed a beautiful detachment and courageous resignation throughout this severe ordeal which ended so serenely when his eyes closed of themselves with his last breath.[7]

Death came at 3:06 A.M., Sunday, August 28. At his bedside were sisters, Elizabeth, Eva, and Helen; the attending physician, Dr. Charles Horan; Father Thomas Kearney; Bishop McShea; Bishop-elect Benjamin; Monsignor McGlinn; Monsignor Noone; and Father Nelson Curran. Joining in the prayers for the dying were Monsignors John Connery, James R. Cummiskey, Thomas J. Rilley, and Thomas E. Simons, and some Sisters of Mercy from the hospital.

The body was brought to the cathedral to lie in state Thursday afternoon, September 1. The first Requiem Mass was sung by Bishop McCormick that evening. The eulogy was given by Bishop McShea, who dwelt at great length on the physical suffering and the great patience and resignation of the Cardinal. The Requiem Mass for the children was sung by Bishop McShea on Friday morning and the eulogy was given by Bishop-elect Benjamin. The Mass on Saturday morning for the religious was sung by Bishop Leech, and the sermon was given by Bishop-elect Furey. In his tribute Bishop Furey mentioned the Cardinal's dedication to his religious community:

... If I were to be allowed to look at one single entry of the Recording Angel in our Cardinal's Book of Life, I think I would like to see how many hours he spent in the confessional throughout his priestly religious existence. Cardinal O'Hara never signed his name without placing after it the initials "C.S.C." He was justly and properly proud to be known as a member of the Congregation of Holy Cross. And how well he lived up to the name as well as to the ideals of his Congregation when, like our Blessed Saviour, he was called to carry a heavy cross of suffering and sorrow. ....[8]

The final Requiem Mass was offered by Cardinal Spellman and attended by Cardinals Meyer and McIntyre and a host of archbishops, bishops, priests, and religious. The eulogy was delivered by his co-worker in so many tasks, Cardinal McIntyre. Taking as his text the words of Our Lord "If anyone love Me, he will keep My word and My Father will love him and We will come to him and make our abode with Him" from St. John's Gospel, the Cardinal indicated that the life of Cardinal O'Hara was a fulfillment of this promise. Speaking of the Cardinal's dedication to the Eucharistic sacrifice, he listed the great accomplishments of the Cardinal as if the Cardinal himself was making his thanksgiving after the mass of his life. He reviewed his career from prefect of religion to his cardinalate. Then the official *Rogatum,* or obituary, was read by Monsignor Antonio Caretta, his Roman master of ceremonies, who had come from Rome for a friendly visit with the Cardinal, only to be a sad witness to his burial.

The late Cardinal had asked to be buried in the community cemetery at Notre Dame, where he hoped to be with his close friends Father James Burns and—then still living—Father Steiner and the other members of Holy Cross. But at the instruction of the superior general he was to be laid to rest temporarily in the apsidal chapel of Sacred Heart Church at Notre Dame until a permanent resting place was built for him in the church.

That afternoon the body of the Cardinal, accompanied by the auxiliary bishops and other clergy of the archdiocese, the attending priests of Holy Cross, and his family, was flown to South Bend.

The body was brought to Sacred Heart Church, where it was exposed for the veneration of the faithful.

There were no great throngs to view the remains. After all, twenty years had passed since he had been consecrated in this same church, and a new generation had taken over even in the neighboring city. Perhaps he should have been kept in his cathedral crypt, where he would be remembered, but he knew where his heart had always been—in the chapels at Notre Dame—and it was fitting that his remains be returned there.

This was, indeed, a fitting climax to the career of Father O'Hara, the great priest, an unwilling but heroically devoted president of a university, bishop, archbishop, and cardinal.

On Wednesday morning Archbishop Schulte sang a final Requiem Mass, and Bishop Pursley gave a final tribute before the coffin was closed and enclosed in a bronze casket. Bishop Pursley dwelt chiefly on the character of the priest and how the Cardinal had fulfilled his lofty dignity.

He closed with a passage from the "Ecce Sacerdos Magnus," which is sung when a bishop enters a church:

It is a soaring, inspiring song, full of the majesty of the divine priesthood, full of the promise of a more glorious entrance into the kingdom of heaven, full of the hope that lives in our prayers today.

It opens with these words and they shall be our farewell, our final tribute to John Cardinal O'Hara: "Behold a great priest who in his day was pleasing to God."

The final tomb is of gold and marble, and there is not much to the inscriptions to remind one of Father O'Hara, but at the entrance is a statue of the return of the prodigal son by Ivan Mestrovic. This might seem a bit improper at the tomb of the first Cardinal Archbishop of the Congregation of Holy Cross, but then one is reminded that the statue was presented by one of his student penitents, a fitting memorial to the unwilling Cardinal who wanted always to be Father O'Hara, the priest confessor always waiting for his penitent sons.

In his will besides the direction that he be buried in the cemetery at Notre Dame and that his library and furniture and all property and effects vested in him should go to his successor as archbishop of Philadelphia there was a passage that exemplified the spiritual aspiration and material detachment of this great priest.

"I hereby declare I have no property or effects to be accounted for by my executors or to descend to my lawful heirs or next of kin and that this will is made in order to transmit all titles and property in me legally vested according to my duty and as I am authorized by law to do that all trusts, confidences, and powers in me reposed may be faithfully executed and performed in all respects as I am authorized and bound to execute and perform same."

Footnotes

CHAPTER ONE

[1] The best study of the population of Ireland is by T. W. Freeman, *Pre-Famine Ireland: A Study in Historical Geography* (Manchester, 1957); also K. H. Connell, *The Population of Ireland 1750–1845* (Oxford, 1950) is useful despite its attempts to draw sociological conclusions. For a census of 1841 there is the *Report of Commissions,* XXIV (1843). The matter is treated also by R. Dudley Edwards and T. Desmond Williams, *The Great Famine: Studies in Irish History 1845–1852* (Dublin, 1956), 4 ff. The essay in the contemporary *Edinburgh Review,* LXXXVII (1848), 229–320 is unfriendly to the Irish, but quite realistic.

[2] Most of the data about the grandparents and their children are from notes furnished by Cardinal O'Hara's sisters, Elizabeth and Eva O'Hara and Mrs. Helen Ford. Some of the family data was obtained from *History of Miami County, Indiana,* 2 vols. (Logansport, Indiana, 1898), II, 696–700.

[3] Copy of the marriage certificate belonging to the O'Hara family.

[4] The diary is among the papers in the O'Hara home in Indianapolis.

[5] *History of Miami County,* 747.

[6] *Ibid.,* 748.

[7] Unsent letter to Labens Hutchins, M.D., September 3, 1957, Philadelphia Archdiocesan Archives (Phil. A. A.).

[8] Copy of letter of Cardinal J. F. O'Hara to Becker, June 6, 1959, Phil. A. A.

[9] Copy of letter of Most Rev. J. F. O'Hara to Howard W. Bishop, May 6, 1950, Buffalo Diocesan Archives.

[10] Official transcripts from the Peru Public High School, in the papers of John F. Cardinal O'Hara, C.S.C., University of Notre Dame Archives (UNDA). No marks are recorded.

[11] Letter of Miguel Páez Vilaró to Cardinal Spellman on March 11, 1963, in the papers of John F. Cardinal O'Hara C.S.C., UNDA.

[12] Letter in O'Hara family papers.

[13] *Ibid.*

[14] Cardinal J. F. O'Hara, C.S.C., to Father Raymond Teller, September 9, 1959, in Phil. A.A.

[15] Letter in O'Hara family papers.

[16] *Ibid.*

[17] Papers of John W. Cavanaugh, C.S.C., UNDA.

[18] *Ibid.*

[19] *Ibid.*

[20] *Ibid.*

[21] *Ibid.*

[22] *Ibid.*

[23] *Ibid.*

[24] *Ibid.*

[25] Letter in the papers of John F. Cardinal O'Hara, C.S.C., UNDA.

[26] Letter in O'Hara family papers.

[27] The letters of Thomas Steiner to Father Cavanaugh and the carbon copies of Father Cavanaugh's answers during 1911 are preserved in the papers of John W. Cavanaugh, C.S.C., UNDA.

[28] Letter of John F. O'Hara to the family, April 9, 1912.

[29] Copy of novitiate records in papers of John F. Cardinal O'Hara, C.S.C., UNDA.

[30] Letters in O'Hara family papers.

[31] *South Bend Tribune,* June 3, 1913.

[32] O'Hara family letters now in the papers of John F. Cardinal O'Hara, C.S.C., UNDA.

[33] *Ibid.*

[34] *Ibid.*

[35] A letter in O'Hara family papers.

[36] O'Hara family papers.

[37] *Ibid.*

[38] *Ibid.*

[39] Papers of John W. Cavanaugh, C.S.C., UNDA.

[40] *Ibid.*

[41] The *Indiana Catholic and Record,* February 25, 1916. An obituary notice had appeared in that paper on February 18, 1916.

[42] Now among papers of John F. Cardinal O'Hara, C.S.C., UNDA.

[43] Letter of Father Cavanaugh to Mrs. O'Hara in papers of John F. Cardinal O'Hara, C.S.C., UNDA.

[44] Carbon copy of the letter in the papers of John W. Cavanaugh, C.S.C., UNDA.

[45] Papers of John W. Cavanaugh, C.S.C., UNDA.

[46] Papers of John F. Cardinal O'Hara, C.S.C., UNDA.

[47] Papers of John W. Cavanaugh, C.S.C., UNDA.

[48] Papers of John F. Cardinal O'Hara, C.S.C., UNDA.

[49] *Ibid.*

[50] *Ibid.* Typed copies of these clippings.

[51] Carbon copy in the papers of John W. Cavanaugh, C.S.C., UNDA.

CHAPTER TWO

[1] Letter in the papers of John W. Cavanaugh, C.S.C., University of Notre Dame Archives (UNDA).

[2] Carbon copy of a letter of July 10 in the papers of John W. Cavanaugh, C.S.C., UNDA.

[3] Letters in papers of John W. Cavanaugh, C.S.C., UNDA.

[4] *Idem.*

[5] In the O'Hara family papers.

[6] *Idem.*

[7] Papers of John W. Cavanaugh, C.S.C., UNDA.

[8] In the papers of John F. Cardinal O'Hara, C.S.C., UNDA.

[9] *Idem.*

[10] *Idem.*

[11] In the papers of John W. Cavanaugh, C.S.C., UNDA.

[12] In the O'Hara family papers.

[13] *Idem.*

[14] Letter of Captain Murray in the papers of John W. Cavanaugh, C.S.C., UNDA.

[15] Letter in O'Hara family papers.

[16] Papers of John W. Cavanaugh, C.S.C., UNDA.

[17] Provincial Archives, Indiana, Priests' Province.

[18] *Idem.*, Father James Burns, C.S.C., to Father Andrew Morrissey, C.S.C., March 21, 1917.

[19] Charles F. Thwing, *The American Colleges and Universities in the Great War—1916–1919: A History.* (New York, 1920), 42.

[20] *Hispanic American Historical Review,* II (1919), 397–449.

[21] Father John F. O'Hara, C.S.C., to Edward N. Hurley, November 15, 1919. Papers of Edward N. Hurley, UNDA.

[22] *Ibid.,* April 17, 1920.

[23] In the papers of James A. Burns, C.S.C., UNDA. The letters of the O'Hara family during the trip contain about the same information; see O'Hara family papers.

[24] John F. O'Hara, C.S.C., to James A. Burns, C.S.C., August 19, 1920. Papers of James A. Burns, C.S.C., UNDA.

[25] Letter of Father John F. O'Hara, C.S.C., to Edward N. Hurley, October 1, 1920. Papers of Edward N. Hurley, UNDA.

[26] Under "Religious Data" in the papers of James A. Burns, C.S.C., UNDA.

[27] Papers of James A. Burns, C.S.C., UNDA.

[28] Copy in the papers of Edward N. Hurley, UNDA.

[29] Among "Reports" in papers of Matthew Walsh, C.S.C., UNDA.

CHAPTER THREE

[1] *Religious Survey 1925–26, Official Bulletin of the University of Notre Dame,* XXI, No. 4, 3–4.

[2] Interview with Father Cornelius Hagerty, C.S.C., who helped form the Carroll Hall group.

[3] A bound set of the *Religious Bulletin* is in the Notre Dame Collection in the University Library. The surveys were published as University *Bulletins.*

[4] *Bulletin of the University of Notre Dame, Religious Survey,* Series XVII, Number 1 (July, 1921).

[5] Letter of Daniel O'Neil to the author, October 16, 1963.

[6] Letter of Roy Geiger to the author, April 13, 1964.

7 Letter of Paul R. Byrne to the author, September 19, 1962.

8 *Notre Dame Alumnus,* I, 103, 127–8.

9 Letter of Daniel O'Neil to the author, October 16, 1963.

10 Quoted in the *Religious Bulletin,* October 6, 1922.

11 "Reports" in the Presidential Papers of Father Matthew Walsh, C.S.C., UNDA.

12 *Religious Bulletin,* November 27, 1923.

13 *Religious Bulletin,* June 9, 1924.

14 *Ibid.,* October 14, 1924.

15 *Ibid.,* October 16, 1924.

16 *Ibid.,* January 31, 1925.

17 *Ibid.,* January 7, 1926.

18 *Ibid.,* November 15, 1926.

19 *Official Football Review of 1926 University of Notre Dame,* ed. by Joseph P. McNamara, Franklyn E. Doan, associate editor, p. 5–6, "A Laurel Sprig."

20 *Religious Bulletin,* February 19, 1927.

21 *Ibid.,* December 14, 1927.

22 Presidential papers of Charles L. O'Donnell, C.S.C., UNDA.

23 *Ibid.*

24 In the O'Hara family papers.

25 Presidential papers of Charles L. O'Donnell, C.S.C., UNDA.

26 Published in quarto as *Official Bulletin of the University of Notre Dame,* XXV, No. 1, (Notre Dame, January, 1930).

27 Rev. Dr. Charles L. O'Donnell, C.S.C., *The Philosophy of Catholic Education* (Huntington, Indiana, 1930), 11 (italics of the speaker).

28 *The Scholastic,* LXVI (September 23, 1932), 8–9.

29 Letter of Joseph A. Breig to the author, April 5, 1964.

30 Letter of Vincent G. McAloon to the author, April 28, 1963.

31 Letter of John T. Balfe to the author. April 28, 1964.

CHAPTER FOUR

1 O'Hara family papers.

2 Father John F. O'Hara to Robert Cummins, September 9, 1933; papers of John F. Cardinal O'Hara, C.S.C., as vice-president, UNDA.

3 Papers of the vice-president's office, 1933–34, UNDA.

4 Papers of Charles L. O'Donnell, C.S.C., UNDA.

5 Clipping files, Office of Public Information, Notre Dame.

6 *Ibid.*

7 Letter of Dr. James Flynn to Father John F. O'Hara, C.S.C., October 31, 1933.

8 *Scholastic,* LXVII (October 20, 1933), 6.

9 *South Bend Tribune* and *South Bend News-Times,* November 20, 1933.

10 Father John F. O'Hara to John T. Balfe, November 13, 1933; papers of John F. Cardinal O'Hara, C.S.C., as vice-president, UNDA.

11 Father John F. O'Hara to Father G. M. Sauvage, November 21, 1933; papers of John F. Cardinal O'Hara, C.S.C., as vice-president, UNDA.

12 Papers of Charles L. O'Donnell, C.S.C., UNDA.

13 Letters of John F. Cardinal O'Hara, C.S.C., as vice-president, UNDA, folder marked "Personal."

[14] Carbon copy of letter dated January 4, 1934. Papers of John F. Cardinal O'Hara, C.S.C., as vice-president, UNDA.

[15] *Alumnus,* XII (February, 1934), 145–6.

[16] *Ibid.,* 139.

[17] Copy of speech in files of Office of Public Information, Notre Dame.

[18] Papers of John F. Cardinal O'Hara, C.S.C., as vice-president, UNDA.

[19] Clippings in Office of Public Information, Notre Dame.

[20] Papers of Charles L. O'Donnell, C.S.C., UNDA.

[21] *The Carnegie Foundation for the Advancement of Teaching,* 28th Annual Report of the President and Treasurer (New York, 1933), 31–34.

[22] *Chicago Tribune,* February 20, 1934.

[23] Letter of February 26, 1934; Father John F. O'Hara, C.S.C., to Father O'Donnell, C.S.C., in papers of Charles L. O'Donnell, C.S.C., UNDA.

[24] Papers of Charles L. O'Donnell, C.S.C., UNDA.

[25] *Ibid.*

[26] Papers of John F. Cardinal O'Hara, C.S.C., as vice-president, UNDA.

[27] *Ibid.*

[28] *Alumnus,* XII (April, 1934), 234.

[29] Father John F. O'Hara, C.S.C., to T. Van Meter, July 18, 1934, UNDA.

[30] *Alumnus* (November, 1934), XII, 35, 3.

[31] Father John F. O'Hara, C.S.C., to Most Rev. Amleto Cicognani, July 14, 1934; papers of John F. Cardinal O'Hara, C.S.C., as vice-president, UNDA.

[32] The outline of the proposed quarterly is in the Provincial Archives, Society of Priests, Indiana Province.

[33] Carbon copy in papers of John F. Cardinal O'Hara, C.S.C., UNDA.

[34] Mimeograph description of needs, *ibid.*

[35] *Ibid.*

[36] Papers of John F. Cardinal O'Hara, C.S.C., UNDA.

[37] Manuscript of speech in files of Office of Public Information, Notre Dame.

[38] *Scholastic* (January 11, 1935), 5, 20.

[39] Copy on file in Office of Public Information, Notre Dame.

[40] Provincial Archives, Society of Priests, Indiana Province.

[41] *Ibid.*

CHAPTER FIVE

[1] *Scholastic* (September 27, 1935), 5, 22.

[2] Copy of speech in the files of the Office of Public Information, Notre Dame.

[3] *South Bend News-Times,* September 27, 1935.

[4] Paul R. Byrne to the author, September 19, 1962.

[5] *Alumnus,* XIV (November, 1935), 35–6, 45.

[6] Papers of John F. Cardinal O'Hara, C.S.C., UNDA.

[7] Carbon of letter, *ibid.*

[8] *Ibid.*

[9] *Ibid.*

[10] *Ibid.*

[11] *Ibid.*

[12] *Ibid.*

[13] *Ibid.*

[14] *Ibid.*

[15] Clippings, *ibid.*

[16] Correspondence of Josephus Daniels in the papers of F. D. Roosevelt, Hyde Park, New York.

[17] *America,* LIV (November 30, 1935), 170.

[18] Carbon copy, O'Hara papers, UNDA.

[19] F. D. Roosevelt papers, Hyde Park, New York.

[20] Clippings, O'Hara papers, UNDA.

[21] Separately printed at Notre Dame, *ibid.*

[22] *Ibid.*

[23] *Ibid.* The corrected copy of the speech as given is in the F. D. Roosevelt papers, Hyde Park, New York.

[24] *Ibid.*

[25] *Ibid.*

[26] *Miami Herald,* March 14, 1936.

[27] *Alumnus,* XIV (March, 1936), 153.

[28] *Alumnus,* XIV (May, 1936), 217, 224–5.

[29] Carbon copy, papers of John F. Cardinal O'Hara, C.S.C., UNDA.

[30] *Alumnus,* XIV (June, 1936), 259–60, 274.

[31] *Cleveland Catholic Universe Bulletin,* June 19, 1936.

[32] John F. O'Hara, C.S.C., *The Catholic Church and Youth* (Washington, National Council of Catholic Men, 1936).

[33] *Alumnus,* XV (October, 1936), 5.

[34] File "Communism. Visit to Rome of Arthur Hughes," John F. Cardinal O'Hara papers, UNDA.

[35] File "Eugenio Pacelli," *ibid.*

[36] *Ibid.*

[37] *Ibid.*

[38] Letter of Kanaley to O'Hara, November 10, 1936, in files "Byron Kanaley, 1936–7," O'Hara papers, UNDA.

[39] O'Hara papers, UNDA.

[40] Files "Indiana Tax Legislation," O'Hara papers, UNDA.

[41] File "Mathematics Symposium," April 6–7, 1937, UNDA.

[42] Carbon copy, January 3, 1938, *ibid.*

[43] Carbon copy of letter to Hugh O'Donnell, C.S.C., O'Hara papers, UNDA.

[44] O'Hara papers, UNDA.

[45] This correspondence is in the O'Hara papers, UNDA, except that the original of the Maritain letter and two of Cardinal O'Hara's letters to him are missing.

[46] O'Hara papers, UNDA.

[47] *Ibid.*

[48] Carbon copy of letter of O'Hara to Byron Kanaley, November 19, 1938, O'Hara papers, UNDA.

[49] *Scholastic,* November 25, 1938, pp. 7, 22.

[50] *Time,* December 2, 1938.

[51] O'Hara papers, UNDA.

[52] Jeanne Webber, "Peter Grace lives up to a legend" in *Catholic Digest* (May, 1958), from an original story by the same author in *The Sign* (March, 1958).

[53] *Alumnus,* XVI (March-April, 1939), 137–8, 153.

[54] The correspondence on this subject is in the files "Economic Research," O'Hara papers, UNDA.

[55] The letters here quoted and related correspondence are in the O'Hara papers, UNDA.

[56] Letters of Franklin D. Roosevelt to Father O'Hara, July 17, 1939, *ibid.*

[57] Carbon copy of letter in O'Hara papers, UNDA; original in Franklin D. Roosevelt papers, Hyde Park, New York.

[58] Carbon copy in O'Hara papers, UNDA; original F. D. Roosevelt papers in Hyde Park.

[59] The letter of Stepan was returned and the carbon copy of the criticism is in the O'Hara papers, UNDA.

[60] Letter of Cordell Hull to Father O'Hara, October 4, 1939; carbon of O'Hara to Hull, October 9, 1939, in O'Hara papers, UNDA.

[61] Syndicated interview by Ira Wolfert, *Indianapolis Star,* November 9, 1939.

[62] Memorandum, "Secretary of State's Conference on Inter-American Cultural Relations," O'Hara papers, UNDA.

CHAPTER SIX

[1] Personal correspondence of Most Rev. John F. O'Hara, C.S.C., UNDA. Hereafter referred to as Per. Cor. M.R.J.F.O., UNDA. This is personal correspondence he accumulated during his residence in New York and deposited at Notre Dame when he went to Buffalo. The letters by the Bishop himself in this collection are carbon copies and do not contain his corrections or anything he wrote in longhand on the original before sending it. Many of the details in this and subsequent chapters, especially the dates of his visits home, have been acquired from the diary of Miss Elizabeth O'Hara, the Cardinal's sister.

[2] Per. Cor. M.R.J.F.O., UNDA.

[3] File of letters from Bishop O'Hara to Cardinal Spellman, UNDA.

[4] *Ibid.*

[5] Per. Cor. M.R.J.F.O., UNDA.

[6] *Ibid.*

[7] *South Bend Tribune,* January 10, 1940.

[8] *The Consecration of His Excellency John Francis O'Hara, C.S.C., D.D., Titular Bishop of Milasa and Delegatus Castrensis.* January 15, 1949. Sacred Heart Church, University of Notre Dame. Contains the accounts of the South Bend dinner, the consecration ceremony and dinner, and some of the speeches on these occasions.

[9] Per. Cor. M.R.J.F.O., UNDA.

[10] *Ibid.*

[11] Collection of materials on lay activity in World War II from the files in the Military Ordinariate, UNDA. Included in this collection, besides an incomplete file of the circular letters to the bishops and religious superiors, is a file of the circular letters of the Bishop to the chaplains.

[12] Per. Cor. M.R.J.F.O., UNDA.

[13] *Ibid.*

[14] Per. Cor. M.R.J.F.O., UNDA.

[15] Letter of Mrs. Charles Ridder to the author, September 26, 1962, and files, Miss Elizabeth Sullivan, "Casita Maria," in Per. Cor. M.R.J.F.O., UNDA.

[16] Per. Cor. M.R.J.F.O., UNDA.

[17] *Ibid.*

[18] *Ibid.*

[19] Collection of materials on lay activities from the files of Per. Cor. M.R.J.F.O., M.O. (Military Ordinariate), UNDA.

[20] Per. Cor. M.R.J.F.O., M.O.

[21] Collection of sermons in personal correspondence of Cardinal O'Hara, Archbishop's Residence, Philadelphia.

[22] *Ibid.*

[23] Per. Cor. M.R.J.F.O., UNDA.

[24] Collections of sermons in personal correspondence of Cardinal O'Hara, Archbishop's Residence, Philadelphia.

[25] Per. Cor. M.R.J.F.O., UNDA.

[26] *Ibid.*

[27] File, M.R.J.F.O., M.O., UNDA.

[28] Collection of sermons of Cardinal O'Hara, Archbishop's Residence, Philadelphia.

[29] Papers of Franklin D. Roosevelt, Hyde Park, New York, copies in Per. Cor. M.R.J.F.O., UNDA.

[30] Copies in papers of Franklin D. Roosevelt, Hyde Park; original in Per. Cor. M.R.J.F.O., UNDA.

[31] File, M.R.J.F.O., M.O.

[32] *Ibid.*

[33] Memorandum, Franklin D. Roosevelt, Hyde Park, *ibid.*

[34] Copies of this letter and the answers are in the Per. Cor. M.R.J.F.O., UNDA.

[35] Letter of Ambassador Braden to the author.

[36] *Dubuque Witness,* March 20, 1941.

[37] *Catholic Action* XXIII, No. 4 (April, 1941), 9–10, 28–9.

[38] File, M.R.J.F.O., M.O.

[39] *New York Times,* April 6 and 13, 1941.

[40] Collection of sermons of Cardinal O'Hara, Archbishop's Residence. Philadelphia.

[41] File, M.R.J.F.O., M.O.

[42] *Ibid.*

[43] Collection of sermons of Cardinal O'Hara, Archbishop's Residence. Philadelphia.

[44] *Ibid.*

[45] *Ibid.*

[46] *Ibid.*

[47] Correspondence of Cardinal O'Hara in the Archbishop's Residence. Philadelphia.

[48] *Salt Lake City Tribune,* October 12, 1941.

[49] Per. Cor. M.R.J.F.O., UNDA.

[50] Collection of sermons of Cardinal O'Hara, Archbishop's Residence. Philadelphia.

[51] File, M.R.J.F.O., M.O.

[52] *Ibid.*

[53] File, M.R.J.F.O., M.O.

[54] *Ibid.*

[55] *Ibid.,* February 24, 1942.

[56] Per. Cor. M.R.J.F.O., UNDA.

[57] Collection of sermons of Cardinal O'Hara, Archbishop's Residence. Philadelphia.

[58] File, M.R.J.F.O., M.O.

[59] *New York Times,* June 29, 1942.

[60] Special File, Per. Cor. M.R.J.F.O., UNDA.

61 *Ibid.*

62 Per. Cor. M.R.J.F.O., UNDA.

63 Copies of letters from Military Ordinariate, UNDA.

64 File, M.R.J.F.O., M.O.

65 *Ibid.*

66 *Ibid.*

67 *Ibid.* Unless otherwise noted this correspondence is at the Military Ordinariate.

68 *Ibid.*

69 *Ibid.*

70 *Ibid.*

71 Personal correspondence of Cardinal O'Hara in Archbishop's Residence, Philadelphia.

72 Per. Cor. M.R.J.F.O., UNDA.

73 Photograph in Cousineau file, Per. Cor: M.R.J.F.O., UNDA.

74 Per. Cor. M.R.J.F.O., UNDA.

75 *Ibid.*

76 *Ibid.*

77 *Ibid.*

78 Copies of letters from M.O., UNDA.

79 *Ibid.,* June 28, 1943.

80 File, "Post and Stations," M.O.

81 Per. Cor. M.R.J.F.O., UNDA.

82 *Ibid.*

83 *Ibid.*

84 Letter to Rev. Leo Flood, C.S.C., Per. Cor. M.R.J.F.O., UNDA. The "Rule Book" was that of Holy Cross.

85 Special File, M.O., UNDA.

86 Files, "Post and Stations," M.O.

87 File, M.R.J.F.O., M.O., UNDA.

88 *Ibid.*

89 Per. Cor. M.R.J.F.O., UNDA.

90 Photostat copies of these letters are in UNDA.

91 Per. Cor. M.R.J.F.O., UNDA.

92 Per. Cor. M.R.J.F.O., UNDA.

93 From personal correspondence of O'Hara family, Indianapolis. Copy in UNDA.

CHAPTER SEVEN

1 Letter of March 26, (1945) in papers of Bishop John F. O'Hara, C.S.C., Diocesan Chancery Office, Buffalo.

2 *Brooklyn Tablet,* May 12, 1945.

3 *Ibid.*

4 Manuscript in miscellaneous papers of Bishop John F. O'Hara, C.S.C., Diocesan Chancery Office, Buffalo.

5 *Brooklyn Tablet,* May 12, 1945.

6 *Union and Echo,* May 11, 1945.

7 *Buffalo Evening News,* May 9, 1945.

8 *Buffalo Union and Echo,* May 11, 1945.

9 *Ibid.*

10 *Buffalo Evening News,* September 28, 1944.

[11] *Reports of the Immigration Commission.* 61st Congress, Senate Document No. 338, Vol. 27 and 28. *Immigrants in Cities,* I; 617.

[12] *Union and Echo,* May 11, 1945, 16.

[13] *Ibid.*

[14] Original from New York Archdiocesan Chancery Office now among papers of John F. Cardinal O'Hara, C.S.C., UNDA.

[15] Correspondence of Bishop John F. O'Hara, C.S.C., Diocesan Chancery Office, Buffalo.

[16] Correspondence of John F. Cardinal O'Hara, C.S.C., UNDA.

[17] There is a file of these pastorals in the Diocesan Chancery Office at Buffalo, but it is incomplete for the first pastorals. The pastorals quoted are from this collection unless otherwise noted.

[18] Many details of his travels were derived from the diary of the Cardinal's sister, Miss Elizabeth O'Hara. Many other minor details were derived from this source.

[19] A copy of this sermon is in the papers of John F. Cardinal O'Hara, C.S.C., UNDA.

[20] Correspondence, *ibid.*

[21] *Union and Echo,* August 3, 1945.

[22] Papers of John F. Cardinal O'Hara, C.S.C., UNDA.

[23] Carbon copy in papers of Father J. Hugh O'Donnell, C.S.C., UNDA.

[24] *Notre Dame Alumnus,* XXIII (December, 1945), 3–6.

[25] *Ibid.,* 7–8.

[26] *Ibid.,* 8. Also correspondence in papers of John F. Cardinal O'Hara, C.S.C., UNDA.

[27] These and other letters are in the papers of Bishop O'Hara in the Diocesan Chancery Office, Buffalo.

[28] Letters from the Archdiocesan Chancery of New York now in the papers of John F. Cardinal O'Hara, C.S.C., UNDA.

[29] *Buffalo Courier-Express,* January 2, 1946.

[30] This information is from a conversation of the author with Monsignor Holbel.

[31] Interview by the author with Monsignor Peter J. Adamski.

[32] *Buffalo Courier-Express,* February 4, 1946.

[33] Account given by Mr. Bernard Bird, a Buffalo alumnus.

[34] Details from the diary of Miss Elizabeth O'Hara.

[35] *Buffalo Evening News,* February 14, 1946.

[36] Published in the *Buffalo Courier-Express,* February 21, 1946.

[37] Bishop O'Hara to his family February 24, 1946. In the O'Hara family papers, UNDA. An account of the trip was published in the *Union and Echo,* March 15, 1946.

[38] *Buffalo Evening News,* February 24, 1946. Other accounts were published in the Buffalo newspapers of February 23, 24, and 25.

[39] *Buffalo Evening News,* March 6, 1946.

[40] *Ibid.,* April 1, 1946.

[41] *Buffalo Evening News,* May 8, 1946.

[42] Typewritten copy of regulations in the Diocesan Chancery Office, Buffalo, by courtesy of Monsignor Bernard McCarthy.

[43] *Brooklyn Tablet,* August 3, 1946.

[44] *Buffalo Evening News,* July 26, 1946.

[45] Papers concerning the trip in the personal papers of Cardinal O'Hara, Archbishop's Residence, Philadelphia.

[46] Carbon copy in Diocesan Chancery Office, Buffalo.

[47] *Buffalo Evening News,* September 9, 1946.

[48] Copy in the Chancery Office of the Archdiocese of New York; photostat in papers of John F. Cardinal O'Hara, C.S.C., UNDA; *Buffalo Evening News,* September 16, 1946.

[49] *Buffalo Evening News,* September 21, 1946.

[50] Carbon copy in Diocesan Chancery Office, Buffalo.

[51] Collection of sermons of Cardinal O'Hara, Archbishop's Residence, Philadelphia.

[52] Carbon copy in Diocesan Chancery Office, Buffalo.

[53] Carbon copy in Bishop O'Hara's papers in the Diocesan Chancery Office, Buffalo.

[54] *Ibid.*

[55] Papers of John F. Cardinal O'Hara, C.S.C., UNDA.

[56] Collection of sermons of Cardinal O'Hara, Archbishop's Residence, Philadelphia.

[57] In papers of Bishop O'Hara, Diocesan Chancery Office, Buffalo.

[58] The preliminary pastorals, the account of the congress, and the papers of the congress are given in a special commemorative volume, *Buffalo Centennial Eucharistic Congress, Province of New York, September 22, 23, 24, 25, 1947. Official Record and History,* (Buffalo, 1948).

[59] *Notre Dame Alumnus,* XXV (December, 1947), 22.

[60] In the Bishop O'Hara papers in the Diocesan Chancery Office, Buffalo.

[61] Letters from the Archdiocesan Chancery Office of New York now in the papers of John F. Cardinal O'Hara, C.S.C., UNDA.

[62] Carbon copy in papers of Bishop O'Hara, Diocesan Chancery Office, Buffalo.

[63] *Ibid.*

[64] Correspondence from the New York Archdiocesan Chancery Office now in the papers of John F. Cardinal O'Hara, C.S.C., UNDA.

[65] Correspondence of Bishop O'Hara in the Diocesan Chancery Office, Buffalo.

[66] Carbon copy in Diocesan Chancery Office, Buffalo.

[67] Correspondence of Bishop O'Hara in the Diocesan Chancery Office, Buffalo.

[68] O'Hara family papers.

[69] Letters from the New York Archdiocesan Chancery Office now in the papers of John F. Cardinal O'Hara, C.S.C., UNDA.

[70] O'Hara family papers.

[71] In the correspondence of Bishop O'Hara, Diocesan Chancery Office, Buffalo.

[72] *Ibid.*

[73] The public discussion was reported in the Buffalo *News,* February 10, 1950.

[74] Unless otherwise noted, these copies of Bishop O'Hara's correspondence are in the Diocesan Chancery Office, Buffalo.

[75] Speeches and statements of Bishop O'Hara in the Diocesan Chancery Office, Buffalo.

[76] *Bulletin of the National Catholic Educational Association,* XLVIII (August, 1951), 54–57.

[77] Correspondence of Monsignor Charles Klauder with the author.

CHAPTER EIGHT

[1] Buffalo *News,* January 8, 1952.

[2] Letter in the Philadelphia Archdiocesan Archives (Phil. A.A.).

[3] Philadelphia *Catholic Standard and Times* (hereafter *CS&T*), January 11, 1952. This issue had a full account of the receptions and the installation.

[4] Philadelphia *Evening Bulletin,* November 28, 1951.

[5] *Buffalo Evening News,* December 1, 1952.

[6] Collection of pastorals in Phil. Arch. Archives. Quotation and references from pastorals and circular letters are taken from this collection unless otherwise designated.

[7] *CS&T,* January 29, 1952.

[8] Personal correspondence of John F. Cardinal O'Hara, Phil. A.A.

[9] Notes furnished by Monsignor Joseph McGlinn.

[10] Interview with Rt. Rev. Thomas McNally, V.G.

[11] Personal correspondence of Cardinal O'Hara, Phila. A.A.

[12] *CS&T,* February 22, 1952.

[13] Personal correspondence of Cardinal O'Hara, Phil. A.A.

[14] Collection of sermons of Cardinal O'Hara in Archbishop's Residence, Philadelphia.

[15] The official report of the physician was to be sent to a Philadelphia physician designated by the Archbishop. It is doubtful that the official report was as optimistic as the oral opinion given by the Archbishop to his family.

[16] *CS&T,* April 11, 1952.

[17] Most of the information about the financial operations of the Archdiocese was supplied by Mr. George V. Mitchell.

[18] Personal correspondence of Cardinal O'Hara in Phil. A.A.

[19] *Ibid.*

[20] *Ibid.*

[21] *Ibid.*

[22] No written record of this invitation has been found. The account is based on the recollections of Monsignor Joseph T. McGlinn, the Cardinal's secretary.

[23] Philadelphia *Evening Bulletin,* April 25, 1952.

[24] Collection of sermons of Cardinal O'Hara in Archbishop's Residence, Philadelphia.

[25] Original letters in the O'Hara family correspondence, Indianapolis, and copies in the papers of M.R.J.F.O., UNDA.

[26] Unless otherwise designated, the letters of the Archbishop are quoted from the carbon copies in the personal correspondence of Cardinal O'Hara in the Phil. A.A.

[27] These details were supplied from the diary of Elizabeth O'Hara. See also *CS&T,* July 25, 1952.

[28] Manuscript copies of these sermons are in the collection of sermons of Cardinal O'Hara in the Archbishop's Residence, Philadelphia.

[29] Father Forrestal was professor of Spanish at Notre Dame until his recent retirement, but took care of the Mexican migrants of the South Bend area in his free time.

[30] *CS&T,* September 26, 1952.

[31] *CS&T,* August 22, 1952.

[32] Notes furnished by Monsignor Joseph McGlinn.

[33] Sermon at the consecration of Bishop Schott in collection at Philadelphia.

[34] These sermons are in the collection of sermons of Cardinal O'Hara in the Archbishop's Residence, Philadelphia.

[35] *CS&T,* May 15, 1953.

[36] This was the 1953 yearbook of the Association for Supervision and Curriculum Development (Washington, 1953).

[37] (Huntington, Indiana, 1953).

[38] Philadelphia *Bulletin,* November 1, 1953, has photographs taken before and after the leaves fell.

[39] The physician who examined the Archbishop in Indianapolis in 1956 found it necessary to question him directly to get him to admit certain painful symptoms.

[40] Letter to Cardinal Spellman now in papers of M.R.J.F.O., UNDA. The sermon and its Portuguese translation are in the collection of sermons of Cardinal O'Hara, Archbishop's Residence, Philadelphia.

[41] Monsignor McGlinn recalls that the original copy of this was sent to someone connected with the Carnegie Foundation, possibly to Howard J. Savage himself.

[42] This figure is the one that seems most controversial, and, as he later noted, his argument was misunderstood even by the Catholic press.

[43] Most of this information is derived from the diary of Elizabeth O'Hara and from statements obtained from St. Vincent's Hospital, Indianapolis. Some information was found in occasional statements of the Archbishop in his letters to his close friends.

CHAPTER NINE

[1] Letter in personal correspondence of John F. Cardinal O'Hara, C.S.C., Philadelphia Archdiocesan Archives. Letters of Archbishop O'Hara quoted in this chapter are carbon copies in the Philadelphia Archdiocesan Archives unless otherwise noted.

[2] Copy of letter furnished by William T. Finney of St. Vincent's Hospital now in papers of M.R.J.F.O., UNDA.

[3] Copy of letter to William T. Finney furnished to the author by Mr. Finney.

[4] Letter of Father Francis J. Litz, C.SS.R., to the author, June 24, 1964.

[5] Sermon from the collection of sermons of Cardinal O'Hara in the Archbishop's Residence, Philadelphia.

[6] Father Matthew Walsh, C.S.C., was president of Notre Dame when Professor Shuster wrote the article in *America,* August 15, 1925.

[7] *CS&T,* May 3, 1957.

[8] *Ibid.,* December 7, 1957.

[9] Sermon from the collection of sermons of Cardinal O'Hara in the Archbishop's Residence, Philadelphia.

[10] *CS&T,* January 3, 1958.

[11] Sermon from the collection of sermons of Cardinal O'Hara, in the Archbishop's Residence, Philadelphia.

[12] Letter now filed among papers of M.R.J.F.O., UNDA.

[13] *CS&T,* October 10, 1958.

Chapter Ten

[1] The Philadelphia *Bulletin,* November 17, 1958.

[2] *Catholic Standard and Times,* November 21, 1958.

[3] Letter in papers of John F. Cardinal O'Hara, C.S.C., Philadelphia Archdiocesan Archives (Phil. A.A.).

[4] Carbon copy in papers of John F. Cardinal O'Hara, C.S.C. Unless otherwise indicated, the letters of Cardinal O'Hara quoted in this chapter are from the carbon copies of his correspondence in the Phil. A.A. at the chancery office.

[5] Letters of Cardinal Spellman from the New York Archdiocesan Archives now in the papers of John F. Cardinal O'Hara, C.S.C., UNDA.

[6] The portions of the diary of Miss Elizabeth O'Hara dealing with her brother, the Cardinal, have been copied for the author by her sister Mrs. Michael Ford, and are with the papers of John F. Cardinal O'Hara, C.S.C., UNDA.

[7] Statement by Monsignor John J. Noone filed in the Provincial Archives of the Indiana Priests' Province of the Congregation of Holy Cross, South Bend, Indiana.

[8] The sermons are quoted from the *Catholic Standard and Times.* The correspondence with the physicians is among the papers of John F. Cardinal O'Hara, C.S.C., UNDA.

Index

Ball, George, writes to Archbishop O'Hara, 450; appointed general counsel for Pennsylvania Catholic Welfare Committee, 480

Boland, Monsignor John P., and Bishop O'Hara do not agree, but are friends, 310; letter to, from Bishop O'Hara, 317–8

Breig, Joseph, and Father John O'Hara, 120

Burns, Father James A., superior of Holy Cross College, Washington, becomes a friend of John F. O'Hara, 35–6; advises on studies program for Father John F. O'Hara, 55; becomes president of Notre Dame, 66; begins reforms at Notre Dame, 68; faces financial problems at Notre Dame in 1921, 69, 83–5; approaches foundations for aid, 86; gives up presidency, 100; returns to Notre Dame as provincial, 113; decides that Father O'Hara should become vice-president and acting president, 123; guided Father O'Hara, 146; letter from Father O'Hara to, 147–8, 160–1, 169; paid tribute by Bishop O'Hara, 202; death of, 212

Byrne, Paul, writes of Father O'Hara's attitude towards the University library, 158–9

Carnegie Foundation for the Advancement of Teaching, 148–9

Cavanaugh, Father John J., assistant prefect of religion with Father Francis Phelan and editor of the *Religious Bulletin*, 125

Cavanaugh, Father John W., president of Notre Dame, John F. O'Hara meets, 17–8; arranges for John F. O'Hara to come to Notre Dame, 18; as president in 1909, 21; has contact with the students, 22; invites Thomas Steiner to study and teach at Notre Dame, 31; congratulates John F. O'Hara on his religious profession, 39; takes John F. O'Hara to New York to see Dr. Francis Quinlan, 40; plans for John F. O'Hara at Notre Dame, 46; preaches at First Mass of John F. O'Hara, 50; plans Latin American program with Father John F. O'Hara, 53–4; at the Notre Dame Diamond Jubilee, 60; retires as president, 66

Chartrand, Bishop Joseph, meets John F. O'Hara, 19; mentioned in letter, 42; attends funeral of John

W. O'Hara, 44; decides details of ordination of John F. O'Hara, 49; Father O'Hara uses methods of, to promote Daily Communion, 79–80; writes to Father O'Hara on his appointment as vice-president, 126; dies, 134

Cicognani, Archbishop Amleto, apostolic delegate, warned of misleading editorial on Philippine convocation, 165–6; attends centenary celebration of Holy Cross, 181

Columbia University, resents references to it made by Father O'Hara in Boston speech, 137–8

Confrey, Burton, defends Father O'Hara's work as prefect of religion, 108

Cushing, John, gives engineering building, 119; death of, in airplane accident, 159

Doan, Franklin, writes of Father O'Hara in the *Football Review,* 111

Delaunay, Father John B., teaches canon law and liturgy at Holy Cross College, 36; congratulates Archbishop O'Hara, 335–6

Drought, Father James, M.M., suggests Philippine convocation, 161; proposes a social commission to Venezuela to Father O'Hara, 189

Geiger, Ray, tells of his first meeting with Father O'Hara, 96–7; writes of Notre Dame men in the war, 244

Gillen, Martin, a benefactor of Notre Dame, receives honorary degree, 155; visited by Fathers Burns and O'Hara, 158, 181; receives letter from Bishop O'Hara, 205; dies, 249

Grace, Joseph, approached by Father O'Hara to aid the Department of Commerce, 72–3; receives honorary degree, 177; writes of Father O'Hara's appointment as bishop, 197

Grace, Peter J., with Archbishop O'Hara in Puno, Peru, 186; benefaction of, given away, 395

Guilday, Father Peter K., directs work of Father O'Hara, 56–7

Hull, Cordell, acting for President Roosevelt, invites Father O'Hara to Lima conference, 183; invites Father O'Hara to Washington conference on inter-American relations, 194

Hurley, Edward N., Father O'Hara seeks aid of, in planning Department of Commerce, 70; Father O'Hara writes him about his trip to South America, 70–3; gives funds for Commerce Building, 118; dies, 131

Kanaley, Byron V., becomes chairman of the Board of Lay Trustees of the University, 132

Keller, Father Edward, is asked to do research under Orlando Weber, 161; publishes book on distribution of wealth, 187; defended by Bishop O'Hara, 324; book by, reviewed by Archbishop O'Hara, 379

Kelley, Father Louis, teaches at Holy Cross College, 36

Layden, Elmer, choice of Father O'Donnell to succeed Hartley Anderson as coach of the football team, 133

Luther, Father Joseph, invites Father O'Hara to a spiritual leadership convention, 115

McAloon, Vincent, aids Father O'Hara, 120–1

McCarthy, James A., joins the Department of Commerce, 78; replaces Father O'Hara as dean, 89

McCarty, Father William, C.SS.R., made auxiliary bishop of the Military Ordinariate, 243–4; named bishop of Rapid City, 299

McGovern, J. T., arranges for Father O'Hara to address the New York Sportsman Brotherhood Dinner, 151

McIntyre, Francis, chancellor of Archdiocese of New York, 203; consecrated, 219; archbishop of Los Angeles, 307; made cardinal, 361;

exchanges letters with Archbishop O'Hara, 368

McNally, Monsignor Thomas, vicar general, permitted to preside at consultors' meetings, 345

Maguire, Father William, reported to have fought at Pearl Harbor, denies this in interview, 240

Manion, Clarence, writes book *Lessons in Liberty,* 189; his *Key to Peace* defended against critics of book, 328; quoted by Archbishop O'Hara, 330

Maritain, Jacques, invited to speak at Notre Dame, 182; writes on his attitude towards the Spanish Civil War, 183

Marshall, General George, exchanges letters with Bishop O'Hara on moral problems in the service, 227; opposes proposal to give Catholic chaplains special insignia, 239; another exchange with Bishop O'Hara, 243

Mathew, Father Theobald, quoted on the Irish Famine, 2

Meissner, Father Henry, pastor in Peru, Indiana, 7, 10

Mexico, Father O'Hara gives interview to the *New York Times* on relations with, 151; intervention in, discussed in Catholic Press, 165–6; correspondence on, 191

Military Ordinariate, established in World War I, reorganized by Bishop O'Hara, 204 ff.

Montevideo, Uruguay, the O'Hara family moves to, 11

Morrissey, Father Andrew, provincial of Holy Cross at Notre Dame, 21; becomes coadjutor superior general, 67; approves plans of Father O'Hara, 58

Mundelein, Cardinal George, invited to preside at Philippine convocation, 164; speaks in praise of Roosevelt in introducing him, 167

Neumann, Venerable John, C.SS.R., Bishop O'Hara renews interest in his cause when he arrives in Buffalo, 331; continues interest in Philadelphia, 348; Cardinal Gaetano Cicognani named postulator of cause of, 436; Archbishop O'Hara secures signatures of bishops for beatification of, 440

Notre Dame, University of, in 1909, 21; expansion and jubilee in 1917, 52–3; in World War I, 63–5; seeks endowment funds when faced with financial problems in 1921, 80–6; receives grant from General Education Board of Rockefeller Foundation, 86; student body in the 1920's, 90–2; faculty leaders in 1920's, 101–2; in the Depression, 117; in 1933, 124–5; growth under Father O'Hara, 197

O'Connor, Father William, master of novices, 33

O'Donnell, Father Charles, 17; sings First Mass, 27; preaches at funeral of John W. O'Hara, 44; replaced by Father John F. O'Hara as prefect of religion, 63; becomes provincial, 67; becomes president, 115; describes Catholic education on the Catholic Hour in 1930, 117; becomes seriously ill, 123; remains president even though ill, 128; receives letters from Father O'Hara on controversy with Columbia University, 138; continued illness and treatments, 142–3; dies, 143

O'Donnell, Father Hugh, appointed vice-president, 145; invites Cardinal Dougherty to Philippine convocation but the Cardinal refuses, 163; celebrates jubilee of lay trustees at Notre Dame, 283

O'Hara, Catherine Galvin, from County Clare, came to Boston and married James O'Hara in Worcester, 2; moved to Cass County, Indiana, after death of husband, 3

O'Hara, Elizabeth, attends school in Montevideo, then returns to Peru, 12–3

O'Hara, Ellen Thornton, daughter of James Thornton, marries John W. O'Hara, 4; goes to Montevideo with him, 11; returns to the United

States, 16; witnesses signing of Elmer Layden as Notre Dame football coach, 133; last illness and death, 263

O'Hara, Eva, attends school in Montevideo, then returns to Peru, 12–3

O'Hara, James, born in County Clare, left Limerick and married Catherine Galvin in Worcester, 2; died in Connersville, Indiana, 3

O'Hara, John Francis, born at Ann Arbor, 6; childhood in Peru, Indiana, 7; quoted on his youthful training, 9; in Peru schools, 10–1; goes with his family to Montevideo, 11; attends Sagrado Corazon, 12–5; in Santos, Brazil, 15; returns to the United States, 16; visits Notre Dame, 17–8; seeks employment in Indianapolis, 18; invited to Notre Dame by Father John Cavanaugh, 18; meets Bishop Joseph Chartrand, 19; becomes a student at Notre Dame, 20; a freshman at Notre Dame, 23–5; joins the *Scholastic* staff, 25; active as a sophomore and junior, 26–7; writes to Alexander Schroeder in 1910, 28–9; contributes to the *Scholastic*, 29–30; returns to Notre Dame as a teacher, 31; enters St. Joseph's Novitiate, 32; enters Holy Cross College, Washington, 35; experiences as a student in Holy Cross College, 36–8; goes to Holy Cross College summer camp, 38–9; makes his religious profession, 39; undergoes nose operation, 41; assists at death and burial of his father, 42–4; discusses his future at Notre Dame with Father John W. Cavanaugh, 45; plans to be ordained early by Bishop Chartrand, 48–9; ordination and First Mass, 50–1

returns to Washington, 55; plans a Latin American program at Notre Dame, 55; publishes article in *Catholic Historical Review*, 57; prepares to teach at Notre Dame, 58; spends summer of 1917 in New York and Philadelphia, 59; becomes

prefect of religion at Notre Dame, 63; becomes head of the Department of Commerce, 68; published articles, 69; writes to Edward N. Hurley of his plans for the Department of Commerce, 70–3; tells of his approach to Joseph Grace, 72–3; attends Foreign Trade Conference in San Francisco, 73–4; goes to South America in search of exchanges and students, 74–7; as a teacher of business courses, 77–8; reports to Father Burns on his work as prefect of religion, 80–3; aids in endowment drive, 86–7; plans growth of commerce work, 88–9; reports to Father Burns on the needs of commerce at Notre Dame in 1921, 88

and daily Communion, 90; his activities as prefect of Religion, 92–3; publishes pamphlet *Frequent Communion for College Men,* 94; the *Religious Survey,* 94; his appeal, 95; resigns as dean of College of Commerce, 100; and champion football team of 1924, 107; his day as prefect of religion, 109; asks elimination of off-campus students, 115; prepares a special report in 1929, 116; becomes member of Provincial Council, 119; moves office to Dillon Hall, 119; and Joe Breig, 120; his quick answers to students, 121; and the "lay cardinals," 121–2; becomes vice-president and acting president, 123

writes to Father Charles O'Donnell about the changes in appointments, 126–7; defends the New Deal, 130; signs Elmer Layden as coach, 133; attends funeral of Bishop Chartrand, 134; activity as vice-president, 137 ff.; visits eastern alumni clubs, 135; in Boston, 136; reference to Columbia arouses controversy, 137–8; answers Henry S. Prichett's criticism of Notre Dame and Southern California football agreements, 140; defends Notre Dame's use of

Charles Phillips, 141–2; appointed president of Notre Dame, 144; writes to Father Burns about his problems, 147–8; speaks to Sportsman Brotherhood, 151; goes to Europe for teachers and materials, 153–5; invites Bishop Spellman to give the baccalaureate sermon, 155

plans a program of graduate studies at Notre Dame, 157–9; and the University library, 158–9; writes Father Burns of his plans, 160–1; plans Philippine convocation, 163; confers honorary degrees at Philippine convocation, 166; announces a program of graduate apologetics, 168; speaks on the Catholic Hour, 172; signs letter on Spanish Civil War, 178; goes to Puerto Rico for a vacation, 179–80; invited to Lima conference, 183; seeks foundation support for Arthur Reyniers, 184; sails for Lima conference, 185; makes tour of South America with Peter Reilly, 185; writes preface to Father Keller's book, 187; answers criticism of Father William McGowan, 188; joins Father James Drought in a social commission to Venezuela, 189; corresponds with President Roosevelt on Mexican problems, 191; discusses condition of Catholic higher education with C. A. Stepan, 192–4; attends conference on inter-American relations, 194; elected auxiliary bishop of the Military Ordinariate and discusses the problems of the appointment with Archbishop Spellman, 194

consecrated bishop, 200–1; pays tribute to Father Burns at consecration dinner, 202; telegraphs President Roosevelt after his consecration, 203; takes up residence in New York, 203; begins his travels as auxiliary bishop of the Military Ordinariate, 206; begins circular letters to the chaplains, 207; describes status of chaplains to superiors, 207–8; attends funeral of

Father Burns, 212; explains his problems at the Bishops' meeting, 214–5; congratulates Roosevelt on his re-election, 216; visits Bogota, Colombia, to aid Ambassador Braden, 219; his activities as bishop described by Bill Reilly, 219–20; his relations with the chaplains, 223–4; writes to William Montavon on Latin American relations, 225; corresponds with General George Marshall on moral problems, 227–8; attends Eucharistic Congress at Santiago, Chile, 228–30; activities complicated by Pearl Harbor, 230; seeks missionaries for Central America, 235–6; corresponds with Ernie Pyle, 238–9; denies that Father William Maguire fired guns at Pearl Harbor, 240; pleads with bishops and superiors for more chaplains, 241; corresponds with General George Marshall on various matters, 243; suggests postwar planning for the chaplains, 254; receives letters from front, 257–62; attends the death of his mother, 263; transferred to see of Buffalo, 265; praised by Archbishop Spellman at departure Mass, 266–7

takes over his new see, 268; the installation, 269; his informality, 273; thanks Archbishop Spellman, 274–5; his interest in diocesan youths, 278; repairs the New Cathedral, 279; writes pastorals, publishing most of the letters in the diocesan paper, 280; and the jubilee of the lay trustees at Notre Dame, 283; announces his plans for building high schools, 285 ff.; accompanies Cardinal-elect Spellman to Rome, 288; goes to Japan with Bishop Ready at the request of Pope Pius XII, 292–3; speaks against proposal of Secretary Wallace, 295–6; announces a Provincial Eucharistic Congress to celebrate centennial of diocese, 296; interested in public affairs, 297; presides over the Provincial Eucharistic Congress in Buffalo, 301 ff.;

continues his efforts to get all Catholic children in Catholic schools, 306; attacks Labor Day statement prepared by Father William McGowan, 308–9; makes *ad limina* visit, 312–4; attacks Barden Bill, 315; letter to Monsignor John P. Boland, 317–8; writes on Polish in diocese, 321–2; defends Father Keller against criticisms, 324; illness prevents attendance at consecration of Bishop Cousineau, 328; consoles Dean Manion about attacks on his book, 328–9; interested in work of Venerable John Neumann in Buffalo diocese, 331; appointed archbishop of Philadelphia, 334

his installation, 337–8; brings interest in the cause of Bishop John Neumann, 340; avoids dinners and receptions, 343; meets regularly with his consultors, 345; and the archdiocesan seminary, 345–6; rumors of accumulated wealth, 346; accompanies Cardinal Spellman to Barcelona Eucharistic Congress, 353–4; proposes to increase the number of Catholic schools, 358–9; begins his pastoral letters, 362; expresses his notion of the bishop's role, 363; his charities, 366; receives pallium, 368; activities as archbishop, 369 ff.; publishes *Social Documents of Pope Pius XII,* 372; pays tribute to Cardinal Spellman, 375; and the Fairmount Park "visions," 376–7; reviews Father Keller's book, 379; and McCarthyism, 383–4; controversy over Father McManus' statements, 385, 391–4; writes *Memorandum* on book of Howard J. Savage, 395; publishes articles on public education in *The Standard and Times,* 398, 399, 403, 413; and old Notre Dame students, 407; the Archbishop and Notre Dame, 410–1; suffers a physical collapse, 415

undergoes physical examination in Indianapolis, 419–20; renews his activities, 421; continues interest in Bishop Neumann, 423; opposes elimination of early grades in Catholic education, 426; continues writing on education, 428; criticizes Professor Duffy of Notre Dame, 431–2; reads manuscript of biography of Cardinal Spellman, 434; opens rebuilt Cathedral, 439; obtains signatures of the bishops for the beatification of Bishop Neumann, 440; asks to be relieved of trusteeship of Catholic University, 441; first charities drive, 443; discusses figures on Catholic population, 445–6; defends his practice of giving Communion outside of Mass, 452–3; named cardinal 458

his reaction to the announcement, 459–60; flies to Rome with Cardinals-elect Cicognani and Cushing, 461; and events in Rome, 461–3; the return trip, 463–4; Cardinal undergoes minor surgery, 468; reminisces about early life, 471; protests invitation to Khrushchev, 472; has hall at Stonehill College named after him, 474; makes *ad limina* visit to Rome, 475; is injured in fall in a bus, 476; in hospital and operated on, 476; visited by Cardinal Spellman, 477; thanks Cardinal Spellman, 480; his educational accomplishments in the archdiocese, 482–3; undergoes another operation, 483; visited by Father Steiner, 484; visits Indianapolis, 485; returns to Philadelphia, 486; becomes ill again, dies, 487–8; funeral ceremonies in Philadelphia for, 489; entombment at Notre Dame, 490

O'Hara, John Walter, born at Connersville, Indiana, 2; leaves school and begins work for James Thornton, 4; marries Ellen Thornton, 4; teaches school, 4; moves to Bunker Hill, 5; edits *Bunker Hill Press,* 5; attends University of Michigan, 6; practices law, 6; named consul to Montevideo, 10; transferred to Santos, Brazil, 15; injured on boat, 16; lectures at Notre Dame, 32; last illness and death, 42–4

O'Hara, Robert, announces program of his brother in Latin American studies, 61; death, 411

O'Neill, Daniel, and Father O'Hara, 95–6; tells of his experiences with Father O'Hara as prefect of religion, 101

Pacelli, Cardinal Eugenio, invited by Father O'Hara to visit Notre Dame, 173; arrives by plane, 174

Polman, Brother Joachim, assistant master of novices, 32

Phillips, Charles, dies, 135; death occasions controversy about his services to Notre Dame, 141–2

Prichett, Henry S., writes criticism of football agreements between Notre Dame and Southern California, 139–40

Pursley, Bishop Leo, Bishop O'Hara preaches at consecration of, 326; preaches at funeral of Cardinal O'Hara at Notre Dame, 490

Quinlan, Joseph, seminarian of Holy Cross College and friend of John O'Hara, who dies, 40

Reilly, Peter, benefactor of Notre Dame, 283; tours South America with Father O'Hara, 186; dies, 334; Bishop O'Hara says Mass for family, 334

Religious Bulletin, the first, 97; others, 98–99, 104–115, 118–123

Reyniers, Arthur, plans germ-free biological laboratories, 174; Father O'Hara tries to get foundation aid for, 184; Bishop O'Hara dedicates laboratory for, 323

Rockefeller Foundation, approached by Father Burns in 1917 and in 1921–2, 86

Rockne, Knute, coach of the football team, 113; death, 118

Romulo, Carlos, invited by Father O'Hara to Notre Dame, 163; gives address at Philippine convocation, 167

Roosevelt, Franklin D., President, invited to Philippine convocation, 164; attends convocation and makes speech, 166–7; corresponds with Father O'Hara about Mexican problems, 191; receives telegram from Bishop O'Hara, 203; congratulated by Bishop O'Hara on his re-election, 216

Ryan, Father John M., teaches history at Holy Cross College, 36

Sauvage, Father George, teaches dogmatic theology at Holy Cross College, 36

Schroeder, Alexander, John O'Hara writes to, 28–9

Shuster, George N., publishes article in *America:* "Have We Any Scholars?", 108; mentioned in letter of Archbishop O'Hara, 431

Smith, Father John Talbot, John F. O'Hara summarizes lectures of, 25; writes essays for *Scholastic* on, 27

Spellman, Bishop Francis, invited by Father O'Hara to give a baccalaureate sermon at Notre Dame, 155; arranges visit of Cardinal Pacelli to Notre Dame, 174; now Archbishop, asks that Father O'Hara be named to the Military Ordinariate with him, 195; discusses the problems of the appointment with Father O'Hara, 198–200; consecrates Bishop O'Hara, 200–1; Bishop O'Hara praises the zeal of, in visiting the fronts, 239; thanked by Bishop O'Hara after going to Buffalo, 274–5; named cardinal, 285; and the Buffalo Eucharistic Congress, 302–4; attacks Barden Bill, 315; gives the pallium to Archbishop O'Hara, 368; manuscript of biography of, read by Archbishop O'Hara, 434–5; visits the ill Cardinal O'Hara, 477; thanked by Cardinal O'Hara for his help, 480

Steiner, Thomas, lives in Old College with John F. O'Hara, 31; guides Father O'Hara in handling physical plant, 146; refuses invitation to go to Rome with Cardinal-elect O'Hara,

461; visits Cardinal O'Hara, 484

Stritch, Cardinal Samuel, questions source of papal documents, 356; Archbishop O'Hara writes to, about Monsignor McManus, 394–5

Thornton, James, born in County Louth, married Ellen Brown in 1847, set up store at Lewisburg, Indiana and bought farm at Galveston, 3

Thornton, Ellen Brown, married James Thornton, 3; lived in Kokomo, 17; died, 38

Walsh, Father Matthew, succeeds Father Burns as president, 100; receives report from Father O'Hara, 104

Weber, Orlando, visited by Father O'Hara, 151; sponsors book published by Father Edward Keller, 187–8

Zahm, Father John A., former provincial, was friendly to John F. O'Hara, 45; promises help to John F. O'Hara to establish a course in Latin American history at Notre Dame, 46